▶ The Field of Social Work

Arthur E. Fink

SCHOOL OF SOCIAL WORK
UNIVERSITY OF NORTH CAROLINA

Everett E. Wilson

SCHOOL OF SOCIAL WORK
UNIVERSITY OF NORTH CAROLINA

Merrill B. Conover

SCHOOL OF SOCIAL WORK
UNIVERSITY OF PITTSBURGH

HENRY HOLT AND COMPANY · NEW YORK

To Our Respective Universities

22827-0315
Printed in the United States of America

Preface to Third Edition

Another edition seems to be required by reason of the pace of developments within the social work field. Human needs continue to be expressed with infinite variety and at times with increasing insistence. Other helping professions, such as medicine and teaching, are mindful of these needs and are developing new approaches and services. Social workers, whether in casework, group work, or community organization continuously feel the impact of "problems people present" and like the other professions are developing new services, adapting old ones, and occasionally dropping an outmoded service. Through the field of practice, in professional journals, at professional meetings, and in schools of social work there is a never-resting pursuit of ways and ideas.

One evidence of the acceleration as well as of the range within the social work field is reflected in the triple authorship of this revision. In the opinion of the original author a volume that undertakes to deal with as extensive an area as social work now demands the thinking and the experience of other persons. Mr. Everett Wilson carries responsibility for the chapter on social casework and Dr. Merrill Conover for those on social group work and community organization. Each co-author has been helpful in the selection of illustrative material as well.

It will be noted that several chapters have been added: a beginning chapter that records some of the kinds of difficulties which people bring to social agencies; a chapter on social casework; and a chapter on social services to the aged. In view of the widespread awareness of aging, the necessity for this chapter may be more easily understood. However, it is the belief of the original author that until Mr. Wilson's chapter on social casework there had not been an adequate treatment of casework in the previous editions of this volume. The chapter on people's problems grows out of the experience of teaching the introductory course to undergraduates. In addition to the added chapters, there has been a new selection of illustrative material.

Bibliographies have been brought up to date. A number of volumes are not included in the present revision but may be found in the 1949 edition. A list of sources for films has been included in Chapter 16. Usable films produced for social work purposes or adaptable thereto are in such continuous process of production that no effort is made to list titles—references to sources should prove ample.

As with the previous editions, there has been help from many people and sources. Even though, in order to conserve space, the prefaces to the first and second editions are here omitted, nevertheless a continuing indebtedness is expressed for the help of the persons named in those editions. Each contributor of illustrative material to the present edition has made valuable suggestions for improving the volume as have also the following persons: Alan Keith-Lucas, Isabelle K. Carter, Joe Hoffer, Herbert Aptekar, Annie May Pemberton, C. Wilson Anderson, Ernest Witte, and Rebecca Randolph. Teachers of the introductory social work course in colleges and universities throughout the country have been unfailingly generous in sharing, with the authors and the publishers, their classroom experience with the previous editions and in offering suggestions for improvement. The secretarial staff at the School of Social Work, University of North Carolina—Mrs. Bruce Stephens, Mrs. Donald Fouse, and Mrs. Twila Stevens—has deciphered, decoded, typed, and proofread, earning our gratitude many times over.

A final word of appreciation is due the universities on whose staffs the three authors serve. The dedication of this volume to our respective universities is in acknowledgment of the support these institutions have given to social work education and of their encouragement of a sound and basic liberal arts education.

Chapel Hill, N. C.   A. E. F.

Chapel Hill, N. C.   E. E. W.

Pittsburgh, Pa.   M. B. C.
February 10, 1955

Contents

v

Elements of the Casework Process: Problems of Definition; A
Goal of Helpfulness; The Role of the Client; The Role of the
Agency; The Role of the Caseworker—Current Issues in Case-
work Practice: Casework and Other Helping Professions;
Casework in Authoritative Settings; Research in Social Case-
work—Conclusion—Bibliography

Early Emphases—Influences from Psychiatry—The Depression
of the 1930's—The Role of Culture—Family Social Work Today—How a Family Service Agency Works—Family Casework
and Agency Settings—Developments in the Family Service
Field—Conclusion—Bibliography

Contemporary Public Welfare—A Federal Department of Pub-
lic Welfare—The State and Public Welfare—The County and
Public Welfare—The Social Security Act: Public Assistance—
Maternal and Child Health and Welfare Services—General
Assistance—Vocational Rehabilitation—The Offer of Services
in County Welfare Departments—Social Casework as a Method
of Offering Public Welfare Services—Trends in Public Welfare
—Bibliography

The Child in His Family and Group—Apprenticeship and
Indenture—Public Institutional Care: The Almshouse—Private
Institutional Care: Orphan Homes—Public Subsidy of Private
Institutions—Foster Home Care: The Growth of Children's
Aid Societies: Public Sponsorship—Relief for Children in Their
Own Homes—The White House Conferences—Contemporary
Social Services for Children—Financial Services—Child Caring
Services: Knowing the Child's New Home; Service to the
Foster Home; Ending the Service—Institutional Care; The
Caseworker in the Institution; The Modern Role of the Institu-
tion: A Way of Living; As a Treatment Center—Group
Homes—Part-Time Care: Day Nursery and Foster Day Care—
Adoption—Other Casework Services: Protective Services; Pro-
bation and Correctional Institutional Services—Homemaker
Service—Other Services for Children—Bibliography

CONTENTS

chapter 1

Problems People Present

All people have troubles. This may seem a rather pessimistic note with which to open a book, but a few moments of reflection by the reader will recall to him some of his own difficulties, some that he was conscious of as he was growing up, some of which he is aware are still within his family, and some that beset his friends and even total strangers. The reader, if he will reflect further, will realize that most of us manage to do something about our difficulties; that in some cases we get help from our families and friends and from the representatives of organized institutions, such as the school or the church. One of the other institutions set up by the community to provide help is known, certainly within recent years, as the social agency—examples of which are a family service society, a children's home, a child guidance clinic, a medical social service department within a hospital, a probation department within a court, a county welfare department, to mention only a few. In the chapters that follow the effort is made to discuss and to illustrate something of the difficulties which people bring to welfare agencies and of the efforts of responsible workers to help.[1]

In the current chapter actual instances are drawn from experience of reputable agencies and are presented in order to furnish a setting for the discussion which follows of services and of the agencies within which they are provided. No attempt is made to dramatize these requests for agency services. They are reasonably representative although not neces-

[1] Lee Steiner's *Where Do People Take Their Troubles?* (Boston, Houghton Mifflin Company, 1945) gives some idea of the endless efforts of people with problems to seek "cures" and of the infinite variety of "resources" available to relieve people of their problems as well as their cash.

1

sarily all-inclusive of the situations that arise day by day throughout this country.

The Bennetts

Ethel Harris had grown up in poverty, and when she married Larry Bennett, while he was in the army, she thought she had found happiness. Prior to this, at 19 years of age, she had become pregnant, and her family had practically disowned her. Following Mr. Bennett's discharge from the army, they came to their present community, bringing her illegitimate son with them. Mr. Bennett's family did not approve of Ethel and overlooked no opportunity to criticize and humiliate her. Increasingly, Mr. Bennett has resented the boy, David, and when he is drinking, he is likely to be cruel to him. There have been frequent quarrels between Mr. and Mrs. Bennett over David. By now there are four children of their own ranging in age from 1 to 5 years. David, who is now 7 years old, has had trouble with the rules at school and has been removed twice. He has gotten beyond the ability of his mother to handle him, and is now in a foster home. Mrs. Bennett has mentioned her willingness to have David adopted, but Mr. Bennett objects.

Mrs. Bennett says their troubles have increased since Mr. Bennett has gone on his drinking sprees and does not provide enough for their support. She stood it as long as she could and then appealed to the Domestic Relations Court. Mr. Bennett was sentenced to one year for nonsupport. The family is now receiving an aid to dependent children grant from the county welfare department.

Lee Boone

Lee, 12 years old and in the fifth grade, had been placed on probation by the Juvenile Court for incorrigibility and running away. Three months later he was in Court again for stealing and running away. Because of the conditions in his own home, the Court believed his interests would be better served in a suitable foster home.

For several months things seemed to go well in the foster home of the Monroes. There had been another boy in foster care in the home, but just before Christmas George had returned to his own home, leaving Lee to room alone.

Lee visited his own home during the Christmas holidays and returned to the Monroes when school reopened. After one night he ran away and returned to his own home, saying he was lonely and missed his brothers. He was returned to the Monroe home.

Late in January the school principal telephoned to the Department of Public Welfare saying she was through with Lee. He had given so much trouble in school that she did not think he could be allowed to stay.

Mrs. Lena Brown

Mrs. Lena Brown applied for old-age assistance claiming she is 67 years of age. She has difficulty establishing her age. There is no birth certificate because at the time she was born birth certificates were not issued in her county. Nor does she have a marriage certificate. Her first husband has been dead a number of years, and besides she married when she was under 16 years of age and without her parents' consent. In addition, she knows her husband falsified her age. She was married six years ago, but she and her second husband only lived together a year. She thinks he died of a heart attack in another state. She does not have the family Bible; that is with her sister in another state. Mrs. Brown is disconcerted when the worker says the Bible must be produced; a photostatic copy of the birth page is not adequate. She has a life insurance policy, but it cannot be accepted as evidence because it is too recent, having been issued six years ago. Mrs. Brown has a twin sister who is getting old-age assistance. She asked the worker, "Isn't that sufficient proof?" "It isn't," replied the worker, "because each application must be investigated separately."

Residence of one year in the county is a part of eligibility. This too presents some difficulty since Mrs. Brown is not too sure about the four addresses at which she has lived during the past year.

Another matter relating to eligibility is income or resources. Mrs. Brown's only money comes from her son who is self-employed. He can contribute a little bit to his mother's support—maybe $5 per week—but his income is uncertain and expenses are high. Besides he has his own family to provide for.

Robert and Lois Call

Mr. and Mrs. Call, aged 33 years and 30 years, respectively, have four children, of whom two are in foster care. One girl, aged 6 years, has been in foster care since babyhood—this is the child whose paternity Mr. Call disclaims. Another girl, Nan, aged 12 years, has been in foster care for four years. The other two children are with their parents: a girl, 9 years old, has been discharged from foster care and returned to her parents. She is said to be upset, aggressive, negative, and unable to adjust to a foster home. Mrs. Call is determined to prove she can straighten out this child, but there is every indication that the child needs psychiatric care. The other child, a boy aged 2, is in his own home, but the mother has difficulty in managing him, and recently there have been complaints of neglect.

It is around the 12-year-old girl, Nan, that the mother is having so much trouble. Nan is making a good adjustment in her-foster home. She is quite dependent on her foster mother. She enjoys visits from her family, but she does not evidence much feeling for her mother. She is caught in a feud between her mother and foster mother.

The mother is continually quarreling with the agency, the foster mother and the worker. She complains that Nan is too thin; she feels sorry for Nan having to go to bed by 7:30 P.M.; she thinks Nan has too much school work and too much work to do around the house; she believes Nan is getting too much religious training because Nan speaks of wanting to be a missionary; she has been told that Nan goes to school in ugly clothes. Mrs. Call feels that Nan does not say much to her when she visits. She is sure the agency has placed Nan in this foster home just to spite her, the mother.

Mr. and Mrs. Call have had marital difficulties for a long time. Mrs. Call declares that her husband beats her, and shows body bruises to prove it. Her husband does not visit the children in their foster homes, and leaves all the responsibility for the children upon her. She is thinking of leaving her husband, "He hurts the people who love him." To cap it all, Mrs. Call feels she has failed as a wife and a mother.

Rita Clark

Rita is 13 years old. For the first nine years of her life she and six brothers and sisters lived with their parents in a two-room apartment. When Rita was 4 years of age, her father lost both legs in an automobile accident. Despite vocational rehabilitation training he has resorted to begging. Rita's mother has been charged, frequently, with immoral behavior and drunkenness, and on two occasions has served time at the State Farm. Although she has been released, her present whereabouts are unknown. Since the parents separated several years ago, the father has been seen begging in distant places. His present whereabouts are not known.

For three and one half years Rita has been under the care of the local welfare department, during which time she has been in eight foster homes. She is now in the local detention home, following her last runaway, pending a vacancy in the state training school.

Donald

Donald, 11 years old and in the fifth grade, was having trouble in school. Not only was he failing class work, but also he didn't seem to get along with any of the children in his class. He had had the same kind of trouble last year in the fourth grade. The psychological examination showed his native ability was above his performance in school, and he should be doing better than most of his classmates. Even in the neighborhood where he lived, he didn't seem to have any friends. Most of the time he was by himself.

He didn't seem to be happy at home either, although there are signs that he is devoted to his mother. Two years ago his mother had a mental breakdown and was away for six months. During this time he stayed with his father, who had come for him from a distant state. His father and mother had been separated for a number of years and then were divorced about five years ago, just as Donald was starting school. Donald was given into the custody of his mother with the understanding he could spend a month each summer with his father. Three years ago his father remarried. After Donald returned to his mother at the end of the month that he had spent with his father that year, things never seemed right again with Donald. In fact, they seemed worse when his mother returned from the hospital and when Donald came back after staying with his father while his mother was away.

The teacher and the principal think Donald is not a bad boy nor a stupid one. They are at their wit's end how to help him.

Mrs. Lena Ferguson

Mrs. Ferguson, 50 years old, has been brought to a state mental hospital by the sheriff. Throughout the admissions interview she was dejected. As she talked to herself, she gave evidence of not realizing where she was. After a while she said this was the poor house, and later on declared it was a jail. When the social worker tried to explain that she was here after being examined by two physicians she observed: "Well, if I have to stay even though I don't need help, maybe it is God's will." She insists the Lord will look after her while she is here. She added that the only thing that bothers her is that there are not enough hours in the day to get the work done the Lord has called upon her to do.

After considerable effort and time the worker was able to get over to the patient the useful part she could exercise on her own behalf by helping with the social history which the doctors will need. Thereafter she answered fully all the questions put to her by the worker.

After the physician had his interview with her she proceeds with the nurse and the social worker to the ward. As she left, she remarked to the worker that this is the end of everything. The worker answered that she could look upon this as perhaps a beginning of something new and different. Her parting words were: "I hope it can be something."

Mrs. Floyd and Jimmie Joe

Mrs. Floyd, now 54 years of age, has been receiving an aid to dependent children grant for eight years since her husband's death. When her spastic son reached 16, the ADC grant was discontinued, and she and Jimmie Joe have been subsisting on a small social security check. However, this will stop next year when Jimmie Joe is 18.

Jimmie Joe at 17 years of age is completely helpless, and his only communication is expressed through his feelings and gurgling noises. Mrs. Floyd has devoted her life to caring for him and finds it a full-time and absorbing occupation. Recently, before she had to go to the hospital for an operation she went with Jimmie Joe to the County Home to spend the weekend. One night was enough to convince her he could not be left there while she was in the hospital. A church group paid his expenses to stay with his mother while she underwent and recovered from her operation.

Mrs. Floyd is now at home, but faced with a second and more serious operation. Her worry is over what care can be had for Jimmie Joe. Should he be placed in a special school maintained by the state for such children; should she try to get him to the hospital with her again and would the church group pay for him; suppose she doesn't survive the operation; even after she returns home she will always think that he will outlive her, and if so, who will give him the care and devotion she has all these years?

The Forest Family

Mr. Forest, aged 34 years, had done farm work and more recently had worked in a cotton mill. Two years ago when their only child, a boy of 6 years, was about to begin school, Mr. Forest sustained a head injury at work which left him "with the mind of a child," a speech impediment, and difficulty in walking. The doctors said he would never get better.

His wife, Mrs. Forest, aged 39 years and with a third-grade education, went to work in the local cotton mill. She worked when she could but when Mr. Forest was not well she had to stay home and look after her husband and their 8-year-old son. Recently, the mills have been on half time.

Mrs. Forest applied to the county welfare department for help.

Franklin Gardner

Franklin, a 16-year-old boy, was admitted to the hospital with serious burns on his thigh, arm, neck, and face. His mother, aged 52 years, was also admitted with more serious burns. The original story was that the burns were sustained in an explosion of a can of powder into which his cigarette rolled as he and his mother were stripping tobacco in a tobacco barn. After two weeks in the hospital, during which his father (with a rheumatic heart), had visited him once, Franklin expressed guilt for not telling the true story. On the day of the explosion he had been working with his father. His father had asked him to come with him somewhere, but Franklin said he didn't feel like it, so his father told him to stay and help his mother. "I felt all right, and I lied to him," he told the social worker. He also told the worker that it was not a cigarette that had caused the explosion; instead "I poured some of the powder out on the floor and struck a match to it, and I didn't move the can back far enough, and . . . Oh God. . . . Mama. . . . She was screaming. . . . She told me not to mess with that powder, and I was just a stubborn fool. . . . Oh, if I had only gone with daddy that morning; oh, if only I had gone. . . ."

A week after her admission the mother died of the burns. Decisions had to be made: when should Franklin be told, how should he be told, who should tell him—the doctor, the nurse, the hospital chaplain, the social worker, the father or a member of the family?

Mr. Gold

Mr. Gold, 70 years old, is a widower, who for several years has been living with his married daughter, Mrs. Singer. Until a year ago he had worked at his profession as an accountant. He suffered a severe shock, from which he has not fully recovered, when his 41-year-old son died six months ago. For seven years he had been living congenially with a family that has moved to another state. For several months after that family moved he had lived in a furnished room, eating quite erratically. Then he went to live with Mrs. Singer. Increasingly she had been finding it difficult to have her father in the home and still do her part with her own growing family. She is aware that her father is unusually emotionally dependent upon her and yet she feels the greater part of her emotional energy must be expressed toward and for her husband and children. It really doesn't hinge on money—Mr. Gold has some part-time work, draws some social security, and has some savings. His health is fairly good for a man of his years. He had a gall bladder operation five or six years ago, and has a mild arteriosclerotic condition in the heart region, which the doctors consider to be natural for a person of his age.

Mrs. Singer has mixed feelings as she talks this over with the agency worker. Is it fair to herself and her own family to divide herself like this? On the other hand, doesn't she owe it to her father to look after him for what he has done all his life for her? If he shouldn't be living by himself, and if it causes so much trouble to be with her family, and if he insists he won't go to an old-folks home is there any way out? What of foster care?

Rita Haynes

Rita, 15 years old, had been sent to the state training school for habitual truancy and being away from home, whereabouts unknown, for a month. Her mother and father were separated, and Rita preferred living with her mother when leaving the training school.

Sometime after Rita went to live with her mother, an older married sister reported that the mother was drinking heavily, staying out all hours of the night, neglecting the children, and leaving them in Rita's care. Then Rita had a fuss with her mother and went to live with her grandmother. At 16 years of age Rita stopped school and secured a job. After living with an uncle and aunt for a while, she moved to the home of another married sister. A short time after this, the sister phoned that Rita had lost her job, and within a few days a telegram from a place about 400 miles distant was received announcing her marriage. Later it is discovered that she is not married. The worker makes arrangements with Rita for her to live in a Girls' Home and give up her apartment with a private family. Rita did not appear at the Home. She later phoned the worker making an appointment in the worker's office, but did not appear for the appointment. A warrant was sworn out for her arrest, commanding her to return to the court for disposition.

Jane Hilton

Jane is 15 years old, unmarried, and in the sixth month of pregnancy. She is unwilling to return to her home in a small town from which she had come to this city several months before when she discovered her condition. Her father claims he can assume no financial responsibility— he has four children by his first marriage (of which Jane is the youngest) and six by his second marriage. He readily signs the papers for Jane's admission to a maternity home.

An aunt in her home town has offered to take care of Jane, but Jane is unwilling to accept her offer. She had lived with this aunt and recalled how strict her aunt had been with her, not allowing her to go out with boys. Because of this, she went out secretly, and in this way met the putative father. The latter disclaims paternity and doesn't answer any of her letters.

Before the baby is born, Jane is uncertain about what she will do.

Soon after the baby is born—a difficult delivery—her father visits and insists he cannot afford to care for Jane and her baby; besides there would be difficulties bringing up her baby in the same neighborhood. Jane and her father agree that adoption is the best plan, although Jane believes that she loves the baby—a boy—and is not sure about giving him up.

A cousin from a near-by city, with whom Jane had once lived, came to the maternity home, demanding Jane and the baby to be released to her. Jane is not sure this is what she wants. She feels that the cousin only wants her to come for the cousin's children. Shortly after this, the cousin persuades the father to sign the appropriate release papers and under guise of departing to his home the father turns over Jane and her baby to the cousin.

The Howard Family

The Howard family consists of Mr. and Mrs. Harold Howard, in their early forties, and two sons, 19 and 7 years, and a daughter, aged 4 years. Mrs. Howard had read an article in the newspaper about homemaker service and telephoned Family Service.

Mrs. Howard was stricken with pleurisy and has entered the hospital where she will be for at least ten days. The family has a part-time maid two days a week. Mr. Howard feels the 19-year-old boy—a senior in high school—is not reliable enough to care for the children. Mrs. Howard's sister took Mary, the 4-year-old girl to her home, but Mr. Howard still does not know how he will manage. He will be glad to pay whatever the fees are for homemaker service. The doctor now says Mrs. Howard will need at least two weeks of convalescent care at home after she leaves the hospital.

Mrs. Ella Johnson

Mrs. Johnson, aged 54 years, had been receiving an aid to dependent children grant since the death of her husband several years ago. There are five daughters: one, 22 years old, is married, employed, and living away from the home, the others ranging from 14 to 24 years are at home with Mrs. Johnson. The oldest of them, Hazel, has been contributing to the support of the family out of her factory wages. The remaining three daughters aged 14, 16, and 18 years are in junior or senior high school. When Mary reached her eighteenth birthday, the contribution by Hazel was considered sufficient to require cancellation of the grant for the entire family. Mary still has two years in high school which she wants to finish. The termination of the grant has produced a real crisis in the family. Should there be a larger contribution by the employed daughter, Hazel; should Mary drop out of school and go to work; should Mrs. Johnson, who has had no employment experience, go to work; should they move into the city from the little town where they are now living; should Hazel at 24 years of age forego her marriage opportunities?

Mrs. Victoria Jones

A worker from the American Red Cross telephoned the family service agency about the counseling as well as the legal aid service which the agency offers. Upon referral Mrs. Jones came to the agency to talk over her difficulties.

When Mr. and Mrs. Jones were married five months ago, they lived with Mr. Jones' parents. A month later Mr. Jones entered the army. Mrs. Jones and her husband's family could not get along so Mrs. Jones returned to her parents' home in a distant city. Mr. Jones visited her there on a Christmas furlough, and was agreeable to her staying with her parents until he was discharged from the army. Recently she returned to Mr. Jones' home to pick up the allotment check, only to find that Mr. Jones had visited his family without letting her know and had cashed the allotment check. He informed Mrs. Jones she was to receive no more allotment from him. He had been drinking, they quarreled, and she left his home, going to stay with her brother in the same city.

Mrs. Jones' father said he would give her money for the divorce, and when it was granted, she should come home. When her husband learned of this, he became so angry that he told her he would give her the money for a divorce. So far she has not received any of his money.

In the office of the family service agency Mrs. Jones is not sure divorce is what she wants; if only she could talk it over with someone and get her feelings straightened out as to what she wants to do.

Mrs. John Lane

Mrs. Lane is being treated in an out-patient clinic for a skin condition affecting her hands. The doctors believe there is some connection between the skin condition and her marital situation. Mrs. Lane, too, agrees there may be some connection, as she expresses a long standing dissatisfaction with her husband. There has been one separation between them on an occasion when Mr. Lane stayed out all night, and there has been serious consideration of divorce on a number of occasions.

Mrs. Lane is 30 years of age; Mr. Lane is 35 years. They were married when she was 15 years old and he 20 years. They have a girl aged 13 years and a boy of 7 years. Mrs. Lane has had illnesses since she was 8 years old. At 24 years of age she went to a tuberculosis sanatorium for three years, during which time the girl lived with her mother's parents, the boy with his father's parents. According to Mrs. Lane, her husband does not understand what being ill is like. "He's never been sick but one day in his life."

Mr. Lane is said by his wife to drink to excess occasionally. He works on the 11 P.M. to 7 A.M. shift in a cotton mill. Mrs. Lane has tried to get her husband to come in and talk over their marriage situation with the social worker, but he has managed to stay away, saying that so far as he is concerned there is nothing wrong.

John Martin

John is 15 years old, and with six brothers and sisters, has been referred to the Department of Public Welfare. The father who had been an undependable source of support had finally deserted, and the mother had remarried. The stepfather had been bitter toward the children, and since the mother's death the household has been in charge of a housekeeper. John had visited, with the worker, a possible foster home for himself, and since he had had a fight with his stepfather (whom he had knocked out), he wanted to be away from him and to live in a foster home. The agency had located a prospective foster home for John, in which there were four younger children of the foster parents. It was agreed that the stepfather could visit at stipulated intervals, but John did not want to see him: "You know that man hates my guts." His brothers and sisters have been placed in other foster homes. John wants to continue in his same school, and his present part-time job as well, even though the foster home is in a distant section of the city. The point comes up about his contributing toward his own expenses, and it is agreed that John will pay for his own clothing and the remainder of the foster care payment will be taken care of by the Department of Public Welfare. Question: Are there other matters to be worked out between the foster parents, John, and the agency?

Joan Mims

Joan, aged 13 years, is in the Family Court on a charge of delinquency. Mr. Peterson, 24 years, is also in, charged with contributing to the delinquency of a minor, growing out of Joan's having spent the night with him. Mr. Mims, Joan's father, has brought the charge against Mr. Peterson and resents the Court worker talking with him, Mr. Mims, about help for his daughter. Mr. Mims insists he can handle his own daughter, and he doesn't need any of the help of the Court with his personal affairs. The worker answers that the Court will decide about Mr. Peterson, but it also has a concern about Joan's welfare.

Mr. Peterson is convicted and sentenced (it later turns out that part of the sentence is for his failure to pay support orders previously placed upon him). The testimony showed that Joan had "picked up" Mr. Peterson and had contended that she was 18 years of age.

Mrs. Mims says she has prayed many times for Joan and has worried a great deal about her. She is inclined to place most of the blame on her husband, claiming even the doctor told her so. Joan maintains that she is afraid of her father and can't talk things over with him, and also says her mother and father don't get along any too well.

The father is more concerned that Joan had to appear in Court than about what help she might require. He resists most of the worker's efforts to help him to understand Joan—and then belligerently demands that the worker tell him what to do. The worker realizes it is not as simple as just telling the father what to do.

Jack Myers

Jack Myers, aged 12 years, is the youngest child of Martha and Jessie Myers. Mrs. Myers had three children born out of wedlock prior to her marriage twenty years ago. A maternal aunt reared the oldest child, the next child was placed in an orphanage, and the third child was reared in her mother's home. There were three legitimate children of the present union. John, now married, is living in another state; Patricia, 18 years old, is also married.

Mrs. Myers was in a mental hospital, diagnosed as a dementia praecox patient. During one of her probations Jack was born. A year ago Mrs. Myers died in the mental hospital. A month later Mr. Myers died of a heart condition and a kidney ailment.

While his father was in his last illness, Jack lived with a paternal uncle. His uncle beat him and would not permit him any friends, thinking they were too rough for him. His aunt fussed at him most of the time. Jack's sister, Patricia, brought him into the quarters which she, her husband, and their two children shared with her husband's aunt. Jack slept on a pallet on the floor.

This overcrowding was persuasive with the Juvenile Court, and Jack was placed in a foster home. Jack made a superficial adjustment and arrangements were suggested for a boarding home of twenty-eight boys living together who also attended the near-by public school. At first Jack was unwilling to go to the suggested boarding home, insisting he wanted to live with his brother, John. It was necessary to explain to Jack, despite his brother's apparent willingness, that with a new baby coming soon to John's household there just wasn't room. It wasn't until Jack spent a weekend in residence at the group boarding home and found himself accepted that he could begin to feel that as the place for him to be.

Mrs. Patricia Nolan

Mrs. Nolan, aged 30 years, divorced her husband about three years ago because he did not contribute to the support of their two children, a boy of 10 and a girl of 7 years. She and the children have been living with her aged parents. Her father died recently, and Mrs. Nolan and her mother are worried about how the medical bills of her father's illness are going to be paid. The only money they have had has been her wages as a waitress and the old-age assistance money her parents have been receiving. She had to leave her job to help her parents during her father's last illness.

Mrs. Nolan does not know what to do. Her mother is preparing to move to the home of another daughter and take the furniture with her. The landlord wants the overdue rent. Besides he is planning to repaint and repair, and Mrs. Nolan will have to get out.

Mrs. Nolan comes to the family service agency. She is confused about what to do. Should she put the children in an institution or in a foster home, or should she keep them with her?

Carl Setzer

Carl is a 13-year-old boy whose parents are divorced. Carl lived with his mother, but when he got into a series of difficulties, the court placed him with his father because the father's remarriage appeared to be satisfactory. Carl and his stepmother didn't get along, among other reasons, because she would not permit him to visit his mother. Carl finally ran away and went to live with his mother, his father declaring he didn't want to see him again. Carl's mother had remarried and wanted Carl to stay with her. However, she had to work because her husband was in prison. Carl became involved in several stealing episodes, and the court sent him to a children's institution—rather than to the state training school.

Here Carl seemed to have few friends; everybody seemed to "pick" on him; the smaller boys were afraid of him; the larger boys beat him up. Carl says he misses his mother and loves her very much. He is allowed to visit her one day each week, but not to stay overnight because of conditions within the home. There has been no contact with his father for three years, but lately Carl has been dropping remarks of various kinds referring to his father—remarks that have come to the attention of the housemother, the superintendent, and the social worker. He finally tells the worker he would like to visit his father, but would also want to continue to visit his mother.

Mrs. Shaw and Children

Four years ago Mr. Shaw deserted to another state, leaving his wife with five children under 10 years of age. A year later all five were admitted to a children's institution. For the first two years Mrs. Shaw visited the children frequently, but since the institution has moved some eight miles into the country, she has seen very little of them. She is working in town at a cafeteria on a seven-day-a-week schedule. She lives in a four-room apartment with her brother and a friend of theirs named Jim.

The workers at the institution—the housemother, the superintendent, and the social worker—are concerned about her apparent lack of interest in her children. She has visited them twice in the seven-month period from the time the institution moved in August to the present. Formerly the children left the institution to stay with her, but these last two contacts—in November and January—have been at the institution. On one occasion one of the girls happened to see her as she was leaving the institution for a bus at the conclusion of a visit to one of the brothers. The mother seems to prefer Billy who is 14 years old and almost totally deaf, and whom she taught lip reading. Bobby, aged 13 years, seems to remind her too much of her husband.

Elaine Troy

Elaine is a 7-year-old girl who has been referred by a psychiatrist to a residential treatment center for children. She is a rather disturbed child, both in school and at home. The immediate incidents which brought her to the attention of the Center involved her younger brother. Elaine had given him an overdose of sleeping tablets, and had also pushed him downstairs, both acts being short of fatal.

Elaine is the middle child—her older brother is 10 years old, the younger is 4 years old. Before Elaine's birth, her mother had wanted a girl, her father a boy. The father shows preference for the youngest child, the boy whom Elaine had sought to injure. The family has been burdened with debt, despite the fact that the father carries two jobs, a clerkship, and, in his off hours, operating a taxi. There has been considerable illness in the family, especially of the wife. Frequently the husband has accused his wife of feigning illness. For years there have been marital difficulties between husband and wife—the latter being ten years younger than her husband.

Miss Edna Tyler

Miss Tyler, 43 years of age, was admitted to a mental hospital a year ago, and was paroled to her family two months later. This family consisted of her senile mother, a crippled brother, and the patient's daughter

12 years of age. Four months later she was returned to the hospital by her family.

At the end of five months her physician, head of the Women's Group at the hospital, recommended placement in a working situation in the community. Miss Tyler had lived most of her life on a farm in a rural, mountainous part of the state, and did not want to return to her family. She feels that her family does not want her at home or even close by. She preferred to work in a factory as she had once done and to live in the city in housekeeping rooms. The doctor and the social worker believed this would be inadvisable, but instead thought that she should live in the home of a "careholder" (foster family care) in the suburb of the city. Miss Tyler and the social worker together went to the state employment office, but there were no positions available to meet Miss Tyler's needs. Following this, the physician recommended work in an institution where she could live. There were a number of institutions available: tuberculosis sanatorium, children's convalescent home, private nursing home, home for the aged, private mental hospital. Miss Tyler insisted she had had enough of institutions and wouldn't take a job in one.

Mr. and Mrs. Walker

Mr. Walker is 60 years of age; Mrs. Walker, 58 years. There are three grown children, two daughters and a son, who live in three distant cities. All their lives Mr. and Mrs. Walker have saved until they now own a modest home, debt free. Three months ago Mr. Walker suffered an incapacitating heart attack (coronary occlusion). Recently the doctor discovered Mr. Walker had a peritoneal abscess. It is unlikely Mr. Walker will be able to work for at least a year. Even after that, if he is still living, he will not be able to resume construction work but will be able to do sedentary work only.

Mrs. Walker worked as a nurse's aid earning $25 a week until her husband became ill, but she has had to give that up to look after her husband. The three married children have a hard time meeting the expenses of their own growing families.

Mr. and Mrs. Walker have used up whatever resources they have had. They have no income at present. They have never had to ask for help before.

George Watts

George Watts was in the hospital, having had his left hand amputated below the wrist. He had sustained a crushed left hand in an automobile accident. He is 20 years old, single, and had been working with his father on the family farm that depended largely on five acres of tobacco. George had gone to the third grade in school, and had had no training for any other kind of work.

There were a number of problems facing him and his family. The family consisted of his father and mother and two older and four younger brothers and sisters. How is the hospital and surgical bill to be paid? Is George to have an artificial hand? If so, is it to be either the hook type or a device resembling a hand—the former being more useful? How is this to be paid for? Is there any likelihood of training—or retraining? Would the Office of Vocational Rehabilitation be of help?

The Harry White Family

Mrs. White, aged 34 years, was reluctant to apply to the local welfare department because she and her husband had always been able to manage. About three months previously Mr. White had to stop work because he had become completely disabled by tuberculosis. There are three children, ranging in age from 5 to 13 years. All of their funds are used up, and they are now waiting for a bed for Mr. White in the state sanatorium. An aid to dependent children grant is approved by the county welfare board. When Mr. White enters the sanatorium, the grant is reduced. Mrs. White considered employment, but found she couldn't earn enough to pay for competent help for her home and children.

A year later Mr. White returns home, but must rest for several months before resuming employment. There is not sufficient money in the budget so arrangements are made for the children to receive free lunch tickets at school. While Mr. White is at home, interviews are held with a representative of the Vocational Rehabilitation Office in preparation for Mr. White eventually working.

A year and a half after he was stricken Mr. White is working again—on a flexible schedule—and is supporting his family unaided.

Susan Wilde

Susan, between 15 and 16 years of age, has been placed in the foster home of Mr. and Mrs. Holmes (who have with them their own two daughters, aged 6 and 3 years). Susan's mother is out of the picture; her father drinks to excess and has very little contact with his family that once included Susan and six other brothers and sisters. The foster parents—the Holmes—feel they must be quite strict with Susan, particularly about keeping her in at nights. They fear she may follow the example of her two older sisters, each of whom had a child born out of wedlock. Susan is inclined to put one of her older sisters, Karen, on a pedestal. Karen had been active in high school activities. The foster mother seeks to counteract this worship, saying that Susan has many of Karen's mannerisms and ways. Mrs. Holmes, knowing that Susan previously had entertained men in her own home while her mother was working, is worried about Susan's friends at high school.

According to the guidance teacher at school, Susan is a girl of mediocre ability—about a "C" student. However, according to this teacher, as well as other teachers, Susan is working diligently and to the extent of her ability. The school has no concern about Susan's behavior this year.

By now the foster parents are sure they can no longer have Susan in their home. Mr. Holmes has had an automobile accident recently, and there are other expenses in the home. Besides they have to think of their own two children. Mr. and Mrs. Holmes frequently find that they start talking about Susan and wind up quarreling with each other. Finally the foster parents talk it over with Susan and the agency worker. When Mr. Holmes said he wanted to know from Susan how she felt about the situation, Susan sobbed, said she liked it a whole lot and wanted to stay. A week later Mr. Holmes telephoned saying that he and his wife had had a big quarrel over Susan, and they had decided they could not have Susan in their home any longer.

Problems Brought to Group Work Agencies

A mother comes to the settlement house asking help because her son is running around with a street-corner gang, and she is fearful that he will get into trouble. Can the settlement get the gang interested in some constructive activities rather than aimless loitering, fighting, or stealing?

. . .

A department of public welfare worker comes to the community center and tells of aged clients, living alone in rooming house quarters, lonely, with little to do, knowing few people, and with few opportunities to meet other people, or to meet people with similar interests and needs. Could the community center initiate a program for them? Could it help them locate others who would be interested, and help them regain normal social living? Would it be best to offer a special program for the aged alone or would it be better to have them participate in the regular activities of the center?

. . .

A gang of 9- to 11-year-olds comes to the Y. W. C. A. and asks to have a club. Can they have a leader and a meeting room? What type of activity is most appropriate for this particular group of girls? What are their major social, emotional, and educational needs? Is the Y. W. equipped to offer a program that can meet their specific needs and interests?

. . .

A business men's club from a new and expanding suburban community approached a Y. M. C. A. located in the established section of the area. The new community has no facilities or organized activities in leisure time and recreational programs. Can the Y. M. help them? Should the community be helped to organize and conduct its own activities, should the Y. M. acquire a building in that section, should they offer a decentralized program making use of the church, school, and other available facilities such as homes? What is the best solution and who should be a part of the deliberations leading to such a decision?

. . .

A Juvenile Court knows of youngsters who could profit from a summer camp experience. Could the Scout camp provide such an opportunity for them? How disturbed are these youngsters? Will they fit in with the rest of the campers or will they stand out as different? How will they be accepted by the rest of the camp and how will they accept the other campers? Should the counselors know they are wards of the Court or just the camp director? How should a situation like this be worked out?

. . .

An institution for children finds its residents faced with boredom and inadequate leisure-time activities. There are also both problems and potentialities inherent in the group living that is a part of all institutional life. The institution employs a group worker to develop a leisure-time program and to help analyze the group living relationships. What activities are most appropriate for this type of setting? How much can the residents themselves be used in this program development? What is the appropriate role of the group work and recreation program in relation to the total institution service? How can the most constructive use be made of the group living arrangements, the work groups, the educational groups, the formal and the informal groupings?

. . .

A mother's group in a settlement house felt there was need for many more opportunities for families to participate in activities together. What could the settlement offer to help them? How should the program be organized? By whom should it be initiated? What type of activities are most appropriate for this? Who should be invited? How could whole families be interested?

. . .

Practically all group work and recreation programs are faced with the problem of offering activities that will attract and hold teenagers. At a time when teenagers are simultaneously breaking away from adult control and needing its support badly, what balance of responsibility and guidance can be shared with them to help them keep their interest and challenge them with genuine responsibility but at the same time give them adequate adult support?

Problems Brought to Community Organization Agencies

A new community has sprung up very rapidly around a defense project. People have come in from all sections of the country. They are strangers, with different economic, social, religious, cultural, racial and educational backgrounds. They have been uprooted from their home communities and have not yet put down their roots in a new one. How can these divergent elements be helped to weld themselves into a community with which people can identify; that can provide social controls; that can offer job, religious, and recreational opportunities?

. . .

The Community Chest has raised a substantial sum of money, but there are still more requests than available funds. By what criteria can the board of the Chest through its various committees and professional staff determine the relative needs not only for casework, group work, community organization, health and other welfare services but of the relative need for one casework service over another, or one health program over another? How is the community to know which agencies are meeting, through both quality and quantity of services, most adequately the needs they are set up to meet? What needs are appropriate for private funds and which ones for tax support?

. . .

The Health and Welfare Federation is asked to provide a volunteers bureau to locate volunteers, to help train them, and to help them become connected with a hospital, a recreation agency, a casework program or other health or welfare service needing the help of the volunteer. Not only do these programs need the volunteer, but also the volunteer needs the opportunity to offer his services. What is the minimum amount of training necessary before a volunteer can adequately serve? How can the unsuitable be identified and the potential contributors encouraged?

. . .

Two different communities request staff service from a bureau of community councils which operates as a part of a wider welfare federation. One community is facing a growing problem of juvenile delinquency and needs help in focusing community efforts and interest in an appropriate approach. The other community is facing a growing tension between racial groups. By what criteria can the bureau determine which community is presenting the most urgent need? Which should have priority?

. . .

A community has become concerned and interested in the problem of mental health facilities and services available to it. The state department of mental health or a private agency representative may be delegated to help the community decide what, if any, facilities and services it needs, who will sponsor it, how it will be financed, and who will staff it. By what process are such decisions made in order to be most beneficial to all concerned?

. . .

A family and children's agency with an established program requests the Community Chest for funds to open a branch office in a neighborhood not served by them. How is the Chest to decide whether the community needs this service? Is this the most needed service at this time? Is this the best agency to meet that need? On what basis can such a decision be made?

. . .

A community has a reputation for being disorganized, with little civic pride, an undue percentage of health and welfare services, high disease and delinquency and crime rates. How can such a community be helped to help itself?

. . .

For years there has been a Community Chest that has raised funds annually for those agencies that belong to it. This includes most, but not all, of the voluntary health and welfare agencies of the community. Based on a process which it is believed represents the will of the majority of the community, the decision is made this year to have a United Fund drive. Suppose some agencies refuse to join and insist on operating their separate drives at a later time? The United Fund makes its goal. Suppose the United Fund offers these agencies the sums that have been set aside for them as their share of the total amount raised? Suppose these agencies refuse to accept these sums? How is it possible to know what is best for the community?

chapter 2

The Development of Social Services—European Background

Social Work in Modern Society

A country such as ours that spends billions of dollars annually for what are generally termed social welfare purposes affecting the lives of millions of persons must consider such an activity, to put it temperately, important. John J. Corson answers his own rhetorical question "Can We Afford Welfare?" by estimating that in 1954 there was spent in the United States of America about $11 billion for social welfare, and that by 1960 the figure will be $20 billion. Despite the disagreement as to how this money is to be spent, what services are to be offered and by whom, the qualifications of the workers through whom the services are offered, and the degree of control to be exercised over the recipients there is substantial agreement that in a democracy like ours social work is essential.[1]

A glance at our activities and interests will give support to this premise. Our economy is primarily an industrial and commercial one, and only secondarily agricultural. Within the framework of such an economy there are insufficiencies everywhere. In a deficit economy these would arouse no concern, or at best they would point out the need for a more adequate productive system, but in an economy of abundance these same insufficiencies indicate a faulty functioning of the system. When

[1] Corson, John J., "Can We Afford Welfare?" *Community*, XXIX, March 1954, pp. 131–132, 140; for a sobering and realistic corrective see: Burns, Eveline, M., "The Role of Government in Social Welfare." *Social Work Journal*, XXXV, July 1954, pp. 95–102, 120–125; also in *Proceedings of the National Conference of Social Work*, 1954, pp. 65–84.

the industrial and commercial machine slows down or breaks down, human needs must be met. Industry and commerce assume very little responsibility for the fate of 10 or 15 million workers and their dependents, or for the effect on people of inadequate wages, or concern for the cost in human values. As for the disabled and the aged, one feels that until recent times very little effort had been made to accept any share of the calamity entailed.

The community reflects all of this: poor housing, poor health, lack of recreation facilities, low tone in community spirit. Within the community children escape from the schools because no one has seen the need to individualize the child within a massed system. In the family, so strategically crucial in the formation of attitudes and patterns of behavior, we find strife, disharmony, frustration and despair. In hospitals we find the demented, in institutions the feeble-minded, in prisons the desperate and the unfortunate. What of the aged, the dependent child, the blind, and the crippled?

These deficiencies are not without their antecedent causes, nor are they removed from our industrial and commercial development of the last three hundred years. They seem part and parcel of a highly competitive system that places a huge premium on success, a system that prospered under an economic and social philosophy of *laissez faire*. At any rate there developed—perhaps inevitably—within such a system a profession which undertook to provide a "connection," as it were, in the form of services, tangible and intangible, which would make possible a more effective utilization of human potentialities. Indeed, one might declare that the purpose of this developing profession of social work was to effect such an organization of potentials within the community and the individual so that those without resources or with limited resources, as well as those ineffectively using what resources they have, might be helped to achieve a more adequate way of life.

Looking at the role which this profession occupies in contemporary society, we must clearly understand that its function is not to guarantee happiness to any individual or community. Rather, it works toward two ends: first, the creation of those conditions which help to make a more satisfying way of life possible, and, second, the development within the individual (and the community as well) of capacities to live that life more adequately, even creatively. No individual, no community is required to surrender a present way of life, nor give up independence, nor subscribe to a philosophy alien to his or its present convictions. Social work as a profession seeks to offer a service to the individual and to the community that may be accepted or rejected upon the basis of the needs that it meets or fails to meet.

Origin and Development

An analysis of human behavior and attitudes strengthens the conviction that man's living together is characterized by a spirit of mutual aid as well as by a spirit of aggression and possession. Were it otherwise it is doubtful that human societies would ever have taken their present form. It is not enough to show the acquisitive, competitive aspects of the human pattern without balancing over against it the helpful and co-operative. Long before the Russian, Kropotkin, elaborated the thesis of mutual aid, there was abundant evidence that man had climbed the upward way by principles other than the Darwinian survival of the fittest. No group of men could ever be held together to form the family, the tribe, the state or the modern society without mutual assistance.

Long before the religion of the Jews and the Christians, expressions of benevolence had found their way into the life and literature of older and earlier peoples. Judaism, and later Christianity, made mutual aid an article of faith. For nearly twenty centuries our expressions of fellow feeling took their tone within the bounds of Christian teachings. Monastic orders gave food, clothing, shelter and relief to the poor. No state stepped in to define these relations, although a feudalistic society had long since been molded in the pattern of a mutual dependency. In a static world, in a world that looked not to this one for solace and comfort but to the world beyond, these relations remained fixed.

Once the ferment of ideas which we called the Scientific Revolution and the Renaissance had set in, enlarging man's mental horizon and eventually his physical world, these relations of man and the Church, of lord and serf no longer prevailed. The *status quo* had changed, and in its place stood the emerging state. It is one of these states, the English, whose history of public aid we shall sketch briefly as a prelude to the experience in America and in our own day.

As is so common in dealing with unpleasant situations, the answer given to the increasing problem of distress was repression and still more repression. The breakup of feudalism had cut loose from their dependence thousands upon thousands of workers who wandered about aimlessly and in bewilderment in search of employment and a place to take root. The dissolution of the monasteries made apparent a tremendous amount of poverty and cast upon the wayside in open view multitudes of the poor who had heretofore found some relief within the walls of the Church.

England met this widespread misery by enacting laws to repress begging. In 1536 Parliament passed a law decreeing that alms were to be collected by the churches each Sunday and that local authorities were to help to relieve the impotent and sick poor. Begging and beggars were to be discouraged; valiant beggars were to be returned to their own settlements, hastened on the way if need be by flogging and even mutilation. Attempts were made to stop such generous impulses as the giving of individual alms by assessing a fine tenfold that of the amount given. Harsh though this system may have been it signalized the transition of poor relief from an unregulated dispensing of aid by the Church to the beginnings of regulation by the state.

It was not long before it was generally recognized that a system of voluntary collection under voluntary agents furnished neither the necessary funds nor the essential stability of personnel to ensure even a modicum of relief. By 1572 overseers of the poor were appointed as civil officers to direct the expenditure of tax funds levied upon the local community for the purpose of relieving the poor. Within four years the justices of each county were empowered to secure by purchase or lease the buildings to be used as houses of correction. Here materials for work were to be provided for the unemployed to the end that work habits might be instilled, and relief be administered on a *quid pro quo* basis.

Commenting on these early years, Karl de Schweinitz in the volume so aptly titled *England's Road to Social Security* wrote in 1943:

The statutes from Henry VIII to Elizabeth established a principle and a tradition of relief locally financed and locally administered for local residents, with the overseer of the poor as the responsible official, and a system of public assistance that included direct grants of aid to the unemployable and a policy of work for the able-bodied. After two centuries of attempts to control poverty by repressive measures, government slowly and reluctantly came to accept positive obligation for the help of people who could not provide for themselves. The experience of the years between 1349 and 1601 had convinced the rulers of England of the presence of a destitution among the poor that punishment could not abolish and that could be relieved only by the application of public resources to individual need.[2]

The Elizabethan Poor Law

It was during the latter days of the reign of Queen Elizabeth that the confused jumble of vagrancy and poverty laws came to be welded into the organic unity that we have since called the Elizabethan Poor Law. It is the 1601 revision of the act passed in 1598 which brought order out of chaos and established the basis of poor relief in England, and even America, for over three hundred years. The act of 1601, often referred to as 43 Elizabeth, established three categories of relief recipients: the able-bodied poor, the impotent poor (unemployables), and dependent children. For the able-bodied poor employment was to be provided under pain of a session in jail or in the stocks for refusal to work. The almshouse was to be the sanctuary of the second group, the unemployables; while children who could not be supported by their parents or grandparents were to be apprenticed, the boys until they were 24 years old and the girls until they were 21 or married. For the execution of these legal provisions a tax was to be levied in the parish upon lands, houses, and tithes, which was supplemented by private charitable bequests of land or money, and by the use of fines for the violation of certain laws.

Though there were some who regarded this law as the model for all time, it soon yielded to an addition here, a repair there, an alteration in some other place. Inevitably the poor moved from one place to another, from parishes where relief was lean to parishes where, if relief was not ample, at least it was comfortable. Several hundred years before, by the Statute of Labourers of 1349, Parliament had ordered laborers to stay in their own parishes; but so acute had the condition of laborers become that no man would root himself to a spot where he was doomed to slow starvation. By the Settlement Act of 1662 each

<hr/>

[2] de Schweinitz, Karl, *England's Road to Social Security*. Philadelphia, University of Pennsylvania Press, 1943, p. 29. This volume is invaluable as a record of England's efforts over six centuries to deal with the welfare of people as a governmental responsibility. Every student who would understand developments in America as well as England should familiarize himself with it.

parish became responsible only for those who had legal residence within its bounds, which usually meant residence by birth. Furthermore those without legal settlement were returnable to their proper parish, while newcomers could only be accepted upon posting surety against becoming public charges.

Another extension of the Poor Law was the development of the workhouse test. Despite the supposedly deterrent or therapeutic effects of a parish list of relief recipients and their grants, there seemed no let-up in the size of the list. If anything, the public list grew longer and longer until in desperation, it may be, the workhouse test was devised. Bristol's experience, after the enabling act of 1697, whereby expenses were reduced, gave impetus to this method of work relief. Parishes were permitted to join forces for the purpose of establishing workhouses in which the poor might be lodged and worked. To refuse to work, however, was to court dismissal and to be denied any relief. To make matters even worse, at least so far as the able-bodied poor were concerned, parishes were permitted to "farm out" the poor on contract. This amounted, in essence, to an invitation to the lowest private bidder to exploit human labor to the utmost. So criminal and so degrading had such practices become through the years that finally, in 1782, Parliament was obliged to abolish "farming out."

A system of allowances was later devised which added to the miseries of the unemployed as well as of those who were barely managing to eke out a living. It is not intimated here that there was any deliberate effort on any individual's part to demean the condition of English labor, but the fact, nevertheless, remains that the effect of legislation presumably designed to improve the lot of the worker actually achieved the opposite result. The able-bodied poor were to be provided with work by the overseers of the poor and to retain their own domiciles. However, when the overseer had collected the wage and found it insufficient to support the worker and his family, a supplementary grant from relief funds was to be made. Such a wage subsidy, as might have been foreseen, depressed wages throughout England and tended to pauperize the entire working population. What employer would not pay a low wage if he knew the government would supplement it? What incentive was there to pay a "living" wage when the "dying" wage was sure to be added to? Was it any consolation to the poor that the same Parliament that enacted the allowance system also rescinded the workhouse test? Surely here was first-hand material for the pen of the English cleric, Thomas Malthus, upon which to base his population theory and his dire predictions of the tendency of population to outrun the food supply.

The Poor Law Revision of 1834

For two centuries England had struggled with the problem of a changing social order: the feudal system had disintegrated, the control of the Church over the lives of communicants had been slackened, a commercial and industrial economy had gained a dominant position. All the while, however, the lot of the worker and his dependents had fallen to lower and lower estate. In 1834 a Parliamentary commission presented a report which aimed to revise the Elizabethan and post-Elizabethan Poor Laws. Upon the basis of the committee's report legislation was enacted enunciating the following principles: doctrine of least eligibility, re-establishment of the workhouse test, and centralization of control.

An analysis of these principles substantiates the penetrating description of them, by the Webbs, as the "framework of repression." The doctrine of least eligibility meant "that the condition of paupers shall in no case be so eligible as the condition of persons of the lowest class subsisting on the fruits of their own industry." It mattered not how low the standard might be of the lowest paid common workman in England, no person receiving aid was to be as well off. Then, as if this were not enough, the authorities could always hold out as a threat the ever impending workhouse. Able-bodied poor could apply for assistance in the public workhouse, but refusal to accept the lodging and fare of the workhouse disbarred them from qualifying for any aid. Outdoor relief, i.e., outside of an institution, was reduced to an absolute minimum. The third principle, centralized control, was the only one that could be said to look forward rather than backward. A central authority consisting of three Poor Law Commissioners had power to consolidate and co-ordinate poor law services throughout the land. Parishes were no longer to be the administrative units; in their stead were to be poor law districts or unions administered by an unpaid Board of Guardians. This was really the beginning of the recognition that the problem of relief was larger than any single local unit.

Between 1834 and 1909 there were numerous changes in poor law legislation, the cumulative effect of which was to veer the entire system away from the principles of 1834. The most important changes were those that began to develop specialized care for certain disadvantaged groups. For dependent children district schools and foster homes were provided; for the sick, hospitals, dispensaries and infirmaries; for the insane and feeble-minded, specialized institutions; for the blind and the deaf, special schools.

Yet even these developments did not alter the fundamental changes which were taking place in this three-quarters of a century. The effects of the industrial revolution penetrated to the depths of British life. Pauperization, bad housing, poor health and faulty sanitation—these and many more effects became progressively accumulative like a snowball rolling downhill. By 1909 England needed another revision, and, judging by the signs of the times, one far more fundamental than that of 1834.

The Poor Law Report of 1909

England, or rather England's working class, was fortunate in having the dissenting voices of the Webbs (Beatrice and Sidney) on the Royal Commission on Poor Laws and the Unemployed. Through the Webbs (Mrs. Webb was an official member of the Commission) was expressed much of the enlightened thought on the fundamental problems of the British social and industrial order. It was no accident that the report of 1909 and its subsequent adaptations gave strength to principles which stressed curative treatment and rehabilitation, universal provision, and what for lack of a better term may be called compulsion. Cure was to be substituted for repression, and provision for all in the place of the punishingly selective workhouse test. Furthermore it was recognized that the state on occasion would have to exercise compulsion in the best interests of both the community and the individual, specifically, in instances involving restraint of vagrants, isolation of mental cases, removal of children from unfit parents, compulsory vaccination, regulation of child labor, and compulsory schooling.

If the principles of 1834 provided a framework of repression, those of 1909 may be characterized in the Webbs' terms as the "framework of prevention." A positive approach was to be substituted for a negative, an approach that made possible the utilization of human potentialities. The philosophy of *laissez faire,* that had built and sanctioned eighteenth- and nineteenth-century industrial England, was giving way before a philosophy that recognized the interdependence of the individual and the state as well as their mutual obligations. As a measure of this shift we need only look at the translation into action of the majority and minority reports. The majority report advocated the widening, strengthening and humanizing of the Poor Law; the minority favored the breaking up of the Poor Law and the abolition of the poorhouse and in its place the establishment of a national minimum of services. In the generation that has followed the dissenting opinion, as so often happens, has become the majority opinion. England's present-day organization for social security, although by no means perfect, transcends the Elizabethan Poor Law as the modern airplane transcends the cart of 1601.

Developments Since 1909

The legislative enactments from 1909 to date substantiate this statement. In 1911 the National Insurance Act which provided compulsory insurance against sickness and unemployment was passed.[3] In 1925 the Widows', Orphans' and Old Age Contributory Pensions Act extended the insurance principle to cover old age and death. Cash payments provided for: (1) pensions for widows of insured men, with temporary allowances for dependent children; (2) allowances during childhood for the orphans of insured persons; and (3) old-age pensions for insured persons, and for insured men between 65 and 70 years of age.

The Local Government Act of 1929 moved closer to the breakup of the old Poor Law which the minority report advocated. The Boards of Guardians were abolished and their functions turned over to the county (rural) and county borough (urban) councils which had been established in the latter part of the nineteenth century as the largest unit of local administration. Administration of relief through public assistance committees was to follow the general pattern of administration in health, education, and other activities carried on by the councils.

[3] de Schweinitz remarks that this legislation "applied an innovation only to be compared in importance with the legislation that between 1536 and 1601 established the responsibility of the state for guaranteeing the individual a protection against starvation." *Op. cit.,* p. 208.

The Unemployment Act of June 28, 1934, created an Unemployment Assistance Board operating on a national scale throughout Great Britain. Under its provisions unemployment assistance was to be available to the unemployed who were not covered by insurance or whose term of benefits had expired. Supplementary pensions were also to be granted to any person "entitled to receive weekly payments on account of an old-age pension, or a person who has attained the age of sixty and is entitled to receive weekly payments on account of a widow's pension." Once more de Schweinitz's observation must be relayed:

The development of National Assistance affected the unemployed, the aged and widows, and the war sufferers. Outside these categories local relief as administered by the counties continued, but with a diminishing part in the program of social security. That program at the end of the fourth decade of the twentieth century consisted of three defenses against want: social insurance, the largest; then national assistance; and for those not protected by the first two provisions, public assistance.[4]

The Beveridge Report

On November 20, 1942, Sir William Beveridge (now Lord Beveridge), chairman of the Inter-Departmental Committee on Social Insurance and Allied Services, presented the Committee's Report to His Majesty's government. During the preceding eighteen months Sir William and his associates had been executing the charge to survey "existing national schemes of social insurance and allied services, including workmen's compensation, and to make recommendations." The report emphasized four major principles: (1) every citizen to be covered, (2) the major risks of loss of earning power—sickness, unemployment, accident, old age, widowhood, maternity—to be included in a single insurance, (3) a flat rate of contribution to be paid regardless of the contributor's income, and (4) a flat rate of benefit to be paid, also without regard to income, as a right to all who qualify.

At the same time the Beveridge report was being prepared, England was engaged in a war for its very existence as a free nation. A coalition government was in power, but before World War II was over the report already was receiving consideration in Parliament. In June 1945 legislation was enacted providing for the initiation—a year later—of a sys-

[4] *Op. cit.,* p. 226.

tem of family allowances, one of the recommendations of the Beveridge report. In July 1945 the Labor Party came into power, and then acted upon most of the other recommendations of the report. On July 5, 1948, the National Insurance program went into full operation.

Social Services in Contemporary Britain

The National Insurance program took the place of the pre-existing Unemployment Insurance, National Health and Contributory Pension, and the Workmen's Compensation Acts. For all practical purposes everyone in Great Britain over school-leaving age pays contributions according into which of the three categories he falls—(1) employed persons, (2) self-employed persons, (3) nonemployed persons; and everyone is likewise entitled to benefits. The benefits are: maternity, sickness, unemployment, industrial injury, retirement, widow's, guardianship, and death grant.

The related services are (1) Family Allowances, (2) National Health Services, and (3) National Assistance. The system of Family Allowances provides eight shillings a week for every child after the first. The National Health Service provides, without charge, medical, hospital, and dental service for every man, woman, and child in Great Britain—the cost of this service being provided for almost entirely out of general taxation. The National Assistance scheme provides for those who for one reason or another are not *fully* covered by National Insurance. National Assistance was intended to make provision, especially in the early days of the National Insurance program, for those who would not have paid enough contributions to be able to draw retirement benefits or other benefits, and for others with special needs that are not met by their insurance.

The simplest and clearest statement of the program which went into full operation July 5, 1948, is to be found in a pamphlet prepared by the British Information Services entitled *Britain's Charter of Social Security,* July 1948. Its concluding statement is:

July 5th, then, marks one more stage on the long road of British social development. No one claims that the new charter is perfect; it will certainly be added to, modified and improved upon as time goes on, and as experience shows where its shortcomings lie. But in spite of whatever shortcomings there may be, it puts Britain well in the forefront of progress toward complete social security. . . .

The charter as a whole is, in effect an expression of the duty of the community to the individual. By his work and his social conduct the individual helps the community, and in return the community helps him when he is in need of help—and in the long run it is the individual who counts for most. The retention of the principle of contributions means that these social benefits are not simply a form of charity which pauperizes the individual, but the fact that the individual does not have to pay the whole cost himself means that society is not blind to its duties.

In conception the scheme is a compromise between fully government-financed services and services completely paid for by contributions, just as in administration it is a compromise between centralism and devolution of responsibility. In each, the compromise can be adjusted in the light of changing needs, and the scheme retains the advantages of flexibility without losing the other advantages of uniformity.

This division of responsibility between the central government, the local authorities and the individual himself is perhaps the keynote of the whole, but it is the individual for whom the whole exists. In a democratic country such as Britain that is as it should be.[5]

To the British the provision of these services is not considered as a condescending charity of the state. They are the services which an enlightened and democratic state, through its elected and accountable representatives, deem to be the right of a responsible people. Furthermore, they are regarded as an investment in the lives of the people as their energies and wills are directed to the survival of their country in this highly competitive contemporary world. This emphasis upon constructiveness and prevention, upon a healthier, more productive, and happier people is in marked contrast to the repressive legislation of the Statute of Labourers of 1349. It is also some measure of the creative humanity of a democratically oriented people.[6]

[5] See *Britain's Charter of Social Security,* British Information Services, July, 1948 pp. 22, 23–24.

[6] For further information on the Beveridge Plan and subsequent developments the reader is referred to: Beveridge, William H., *Social Insurance and Allied Services.* New York, Macmillan, 1942; May, Geoffrey, "Social Security in Britain." *Public Welfare,* V, January 1947, pp. 13–16, 24; February, 1947, pp. 30–35; Ring, Martha D., "Social Security for Great Britain—A Review of the Beveridge Report." *Social Security Bulletin,* VI, January 1943, pp. 3–30. Perhaps the clearest, most recent, and most adequate account is to be found in Hall, M. Penelope, *The Social Services of Modern England.* London, Routledge & Kegan Paul, 1952.

Private and Voluntary Services—
European Background

Even before the rise of modern European states there were social services of a primitive sort provided through the agency of the Church. Individual and institutional benevolences in obedience to religious teachings were manifested through alms to the poor, shelter to the homeless, and care and comfort to the sick. Monasteries and hospitals, the latter being charitable foundations for the sick, the destitute, and the aged, were most prominently identified in the alms-giving and sheltering role. Throughout the Middle Ages the religious guilds and craft associations also undertook to provide shelter and alms.

Yet for all the good intentions of individuals or organizations, private charity persisted without order or co-ordination. Rather than reducing begging and vagrancy, the indiscriminate giving of alms only encouraged greater reliance thereon. The Elizabethan Poor Laws had attempted to bring order out of the chaos of public relief, but it remained for the German cities of Hamburg and Elberfeld in the eighteenth and nineteenth centuries to develop the beginnings of an organized system. In Hamburg the first steps consisted of the establishment of a central bureau followed by the apportionment of the city into districts. To each district an overseer or supervisor was assigned, and associated with him were others who served voluntarily. These visitors called upon the poor in their districts and sought to render assistance as well as to keep themselves informed of conditions producing distress and poverty. Each visitor was to maintain close and friendly relations with the poor within his district. This friendly visiting, together with the districting principle and the over-all direction and co-ordination of a central board for the entire city, were the unique features of the plan. The only paid and officially constituted person was the chairman of the central bureau. As the work expanded from its beginnings in Hamburg in 1788 to its elaboration in Elberfeld in 1852 greater stress was placed upon the relation of the visitor to the person in need, the enlargement of the power of the visitor actually to grant relief, and the emphasis upon removing the causes of pauperism. While the Hamburg-Elberfeld system began essentially as a private venture and while much of the leadership and support, including the use of volunteers, continued from private sources, it eventually received public funds and operated under municipal ordinances. Its significance lies in its early enunciation of principles which underlay the later charity organization movement in England and America.

The Charity Organization Society

The scene now shifts from Germany to England. Within two decades of the initiation of the Elberfeld system the world's first charity organization society was organized. Over the years numerous organizations had developed, many of them expressing pet philanthropies, with very little relation to each other. Each association went its own way, unmindful of duplication and indifferent to responsible share in the total of privately supported welfare services. The state of affairs had become so insufferable that steps were taken to deal with the situation. In 1869 an organization was formed in London known as "The Society for Organizing Charitable Relief and Repressing Mendicity." By the next year this had become "The Charity Organization Society."

As the name implies the Charity Organization Society aimed to effect a co-ordination among existing welfare services and agencies. The granting of relief was the function of the existing agencies as it had been heretofore. The purpose of the COS was to develop a machinery and a technique whereby relief could be expeditiously and economically administered without duplication and competition. A central committee was established to which district committees were answerable. The district committees served as clearing house and central registration bureau. They were also to relieve such as fell outside the Poor Law, but only after making a thorough investigation. Arrangements were worked out between the district committees and the Poor Law officials so that there would be no overlapping or duplication of services. This society, while important for what it did for organizing private initiative and philanthropy in a co-ordinated service for the poor of London, is equally famous as a pioneering model which other cities, principally those in the United States, were to follow.

This necessarily brief résumé of European experience with public and private social services helps to make it possible to understand the background of developments in America. The remainder of this volume will therefore concentrate on the three centuries of American experience.[7]

BIBLIOGRAPHY

Books and Pamphlets

Beveridge, Janet, *Beveridge and His Plan*. London, Hodder and Stoughton, 1954.

Beveridge, William H. (now Lord), *Social Insurance and the Allied Services*. New York, The Macmillan Company, 1942.

Bosanquet, Helen, *Social Work in London, 1869-1912*. London, John Murray, 1914.

de Schweinitz, Karl, *England's Road to Social Security*. Philadelphia, University of Pennsylvania Press, 1943.

Hall, M. Penelope, *The Social Services of Modern England*. London, Routledge and Kegan Paul, 1952.

Queen, Stuart Alfred, *Social Work in the Light of History*. Philadelphia, J. B. Lippincott Company, 1922.

Rowntree, B. Seebohm, *Poverty and Progress: A Second Social Survey of York*. New York, Longmans Green & Company, 1941.

Titmuss, Richard M., *Problems of Social Policy*. New York, Longmans Green & Company, 1950.

Webb, Beatrice and Sidney, *English Poor Law Policy*. London and New York, Longmans Green & Company, 1910.

[7] For a fuller presentation of the background and development of social services in Europe, see Walter Friedlander, *An Introduction to Social Welfare*, New York, Prentice-Hall, Inc., 1955, Chapters 1-3.

chapter 3

The Social Services in America— From the Almshouse to Social Security

American Experience with Poor Relief

The main outlines of the English Poor Law have been presented as the background for the development of American systems of relief. When colonists came to America, they were largely from England, and brought with them English ideas, English common law, English institutions, English customs. The almshouse is a case in point. Pauperism was not to be made respectable. Poverty was an individual matter, signifying some moral flaw. Relief was to be as unpalatable as possible. The catch-all institution in the local community was the almshouse into which were herded the old and the young, the sick and the well, the mentally normal and the mentally diseased, the epileptic, the blind, the feeble-minded, the alcoholic, and improvident. As in England, almshouse paupers could be farmed out and children apprenticed. Those who managed to avoid the poorhouse—to call it what it really was—received outdoor relief (i.e., in their own homes). We stressed repression, we centered responsibility in the local community, we permitted only a minimum of state supervision and control, and, lastly, a generation later than England we passed our first social security act.

Local Public Welfare

Public welfare is a relatively new term. In the Elizabethan law of 1601 and the revision of 1834 the term was unknown. Destitution was a local problem and even though a governmental unit may have granted relief the service was termed neither public nor welfare. We of today who speak so glibly of public welfare need some perspective on its development in order to realize the long way we have come and, incidentally, to appreciate the long way we still have to go.

The people and the situations (but not necessarily the problem) with which public welfare has dealt have been essentially local, and the governmental unit which has usually granted assistance has been either the smallest or the one traditionally associated with the relief of distress. In our own country as far back as colonial days it was the parish, the township, the town, or the county rather than the colony which furnished aid. Even with statehood the tradition continued for almost a century in most of the Eastern seaboard states. This chapter is the story of the transition from the local, to the state-local, and finally to the federal-state-local area of welfare services.

From Local to State Welfare

Ever since colonial days and the early days of statehood there has been some form or other of welfare service provided by the local community. This has usually been relief granted in the home or relief granted in an institution, commonly known as the almshouse or poorhouse. However, as time went on, it became apparent that there were some services which were too costly and some which required institutional care beyond the capacity of the local community to handle. One of the earliest instances of this was the establishment of a hospital for the insane in Virginia in 1773. Every town, county or parish had its insane members, most of whom were lodged either in jail or the almshouse, but no local unit had enough of these individuals to warrant a separate institution. What was more natural than to look to the state to furnish care for this class of afflicted persons wherever they were found. An added advantage from the point of view of the town, county, or parish was that a local burden was shared, in some instances assumed, by the state. Later (in Kentucky, 1822) another group, the deaf and dumb, became special objects of state institutional care; followed in 1837 (in Ohio) by the blind, in 1848 (in Massachusetts) by the juvenile delinquent and the feeble-minded. The list is by no means complete nor is it brought down to date. It merely indicates that public services for the needy, the delinquent, and the handicapped of all kinds began in the local community and expanded outward to state areas.

So long as all welfare services were provided by the local community, there was little need for or concern with welfare organization. The overseer of the poor dispensed personally all forms of aid whether of cash or produce and operated the poorhouse as well. The only other local service available was that of the jail or house of correction and that usually came under the direction of the sheriff's office. When, however, the state assumed responsibilities for certain classes of what used to be called the "dependent, the defective, and the delinquent," some definite form of organization was necessary. Massachusetts was the first state to establish a state-wide organization. Created in 1863, the Massachusetts Board of State Charities was charged with the investigation and supervision of the entire system of charitable and correctional institutions and empowered to recommend changes directed toward the economical and efficient operation of such institutions. Furthermore, the secretary was required to oversee and conduct the "outdoor business" of the state, i.e., relating to the unsettled poor who had residence in no county and hence were chargeable to the state. By the exercise of these powers the state was able to check on the reimbursements for the unsettled poor and to achieve some degree of control over pauper relief whether it was on a state or a local basis.

From Supervision to Administration

The limitations placed upon a state board that could only supervise, investigate, report, and recommend were corrected through the establishment of boards with powers of administration and control. The state boards of control of Rhode Island and Wisconsin may be cited as examples. Salaried and full-time members of such boards were charged with the maintenance and direction of the charitable agencies of the state. They hired and fired personnel, controlled financial operations, and established policies for the conduct of the agencies and institutions. Such direct forms of control naturally lent themselves more readily to the institutional phase of the welfare program, but services traditionally local were touched as well. Some boards of control sought by suggestions and pressures of various kinds to raise standards of local relief, to encourage additional services for those in need, and to improve already existent services, particularly in the case of the almshouse and other local institutions such as the jail and the house of correction.

A glance in retrospect reveals that by the second decade of the twentieth century a decided shift in emphasis had occurred. Originally, local communities whether in Elizabethan England or Colonial America were slow to acknowledge the presence of need. The next step was no more willingly taken, namely, to meet these needs. It followed as an inevitable corollary to these two propositions that relief should be made as distasteful as possible and that the recipient or would-be recipient be discouraged from seeking public funds. State boards of charity or control represented little if any change of belief concerning the unfitness of the poor and handicapped. Their aims were to apply business methods in the realm of "charities and corrections," to increase efficiency of administration, to eliminate waste and, if not to show a profit, at least to show low operating costs.

However, by 1917 a positive approach was beginning to replace the negativism of the past three centuries. Public welfare was coming to be regarded as a service with constructive possibilities. True, there were individuals who always would need some kind of help, other individuals who would rather live on the public treasury than by their own efforts; but on the other hand there were many others, perhaps the bulk of all the disadvantaged, who required efforts directed toward their rehabilitation and self-maintenance. Once this latter conviction began to prevail it became necessary to implement it with effective organization. Although Kansas City, Missouri, had anticipated this development as early as 1910 with the creation of a Board of Public Welfare, it was not until action by Illinois and North Carolina in 1917 that the movement of state-wide organization really got under way. In that year North Carolina established a State Board of Charities and Public Welfare consisting of seven unpaid members who appointed a commissioner as the executive officer of the Board. The Board and the commissioner were charged with certain duties of study, investigation, reporting, licensing, and direct service. The latter pertained particularly to providing for the placement and supervision of dependent and delinquent children. An unprecedented feature was the specific instruction to encourage counties to appoint county superintendents of public welfare by joint action of the board of county commissioners and the county board of education. The Illinois setup contrasted in many ways with that of North Carolina. A Board of Welfare Commissioners had advisory functions only, while the actual power lay with the State Department of Public Welfare and the director who was appointed by the governor. The Department was responsible for the administration of the state eleemosynary and penal institutions as well as for the granting of paroles and the supervision of parolees.

From 1917 to 1929 most of the states had joined in the movement toward consolidation and co-ordination of welfare services into a statewide system. Each state sought to work out its own problems according to the exigencies of the situation and of the time. Thus some states established welfare departments headed by an executive appointed by the governor, with a board solely advisory to the executive. Other states have an appointed board that selects the administrator to operate the welfare department, with certain responsibilities allocated to the executive and certain to the board. A third group of states still retain a salaried board of three or five members performing all the functions of an executive board. In some states all of the penal, correctional, relief, health, mental hygiene services are under the direction of one department or board, while in other states, largely for historical reasons, there are two or more boards, departments, or commissions dividing the field. Some states make an organizational division between the institutional and the noninstitutional services. However, regardless of how administrative responsibility was delegated or whether agencies were single or multiple, there was an unmistakable trend in the direction of co-ordinating administration and supervision in a state department or board as well as tying in the local communities with the state agency. Yet throughout all these developments pauper relief still remained in the local town, township, or county.

The Federal Government and Public Welfare

Social work usage conceives of public welfare as those tax-supported services which are directed to the alleviation of distress, the prevention and rehabilitation of disablement, and the self-maintenance of the individual and the group of which he is a part. While no two readers will accept this tentatively offered description in its entirety, they will agree that at least the source of the funds for the initiation and support of such services is from taxes. It may be disputed whether public welfare work is concerned with alleviation of distress, prevention and rehabilitation of disablement, or self-maintenance, but there is no denial of the fact that the essential core of public welfare services can be distinguished from other governmental services such as public health, public safety, public works, public education. While there is, inevitably, a certain amount of overlapping of these services, nevertheless the central focus of each is readily identifiable and establishes it as one of the commonly accepted public services.

The very nature of public welfare organization and organizations prior to 1929 reflected the limited role which public welfare played in the life of most communities throughout the United States. Of the three areas of government—national, state, local—the first named offered the least share of services. The national government, narrowly interpreting the welfare clause of the Constitution since President Pierce's precedent-making veto in 1854 of the bill to provide care for the insane, had restricted its public welfare activities to traditionally federal, non-controversial areas. Four departments carried on services that are classifiable as welfare: Treasury, Interior, Labor, and Justice. The oldest of these services was that of the United States Public Health Service in the Treasury Department, which as far back as 1798 administered a health insurance plan for seamen. In later years the Service has administered hospitals and relief stations for seamen, Coast Guard workers, government employees, and federal prisoners, in addition to promoting public health work through supervision, research, education and publication. The Office of Indian Affairs (and its predecessors) had been providing services for Indians, as wards of the government, long before there was the Department of the Interior with which more recently it has been affiliated. In the main the objective of these services was to assist the Indian to achieve and preserve his own self-maintenance and cultural integrity. A program looking toward rehabilitation of the physically handicapped, developed from experience in World War I, was started in 1920 under the direction of the Federal Board of Vocational Education. Begun primarily for the rehabilitation of disabled soldiers and sailors, it eventually included other disabled persons. In 1921 the Veterans' Bureau took over that part of the program which affected soldiers and sailors. Later (1933) the other functions of the Board were transferred to the Office of Education, Department of the Interior. The Department of Labor, through its Women's Bureau and Children's Bureau, has done more than any single agency to make welfare an understandable function of the federal government. The contributions through study and research, supervision and consultation, interpretation, and publication, have long since justified the hopes of those who projected the Children's Bureau in the first decade of the present century. A fourth department which has carried out welfare services has been the Department of Justice, through the Bureau of Prisons and the Board of Parole. Before 1930 these services were under the direction of a Superintendent of Prisons. Five penal institutions were used, three of them penitentiaries for men—McNeil Island, Washington (1890), Leavenworth, Kansas (1895), and Atlanta, Georgia (1902), a reformatory for men at Chillicothe, Ohio (1926), and an institution for women at Alderson, West Virginia (1927). Parole supervision as an adjunct to prison administration was authorized as early as 1911, and federal probation in 1925, but both services were limited in their operation prior to the fundamental reorganization which resulted in the United States Bureau of Prisons in 1930.

A review of the first century and a half of our national existence reveals that welfare activities have been circumscribed by narrowly defined unquestioned federal functions. The national government has hewed to the Constitution line throughout that period. Two early deviations, a grant of land to Connecticut in 1819 and a similar grant to Kentucky in 1826 for education of the deaf and dumb, were scored by President Pierce as being beyond the province of the federal government. Indians, offenders against the laws of the United States, seamen, war veterans, government employees—these were considered legitimate charges upon the federal government.

However, the establishment of the Children's Bureau in 1912 signalized an enlarging concept of federal welfare function. Although the charge of the law creating the Bureau to "investigate and report . . . upon all matters pertaining to the welfare of children and child life among all classes of our people" stressed information and research rather than the direct service aspects of child welfare, nevertheless it was a recognition for the first time that the federal government had a share in the promotion of the welfare of children of America.

Federal Subsidies and Grants-in-Aid

One very significant factor which profoundly affected federal public welfare programs was the extension of the federal subsidy and the grants to states principle. Grants of land to states, the proceeds from the sale of which were to be used by the states for certain federally designated purposes, was a practice reaching as far back in our national history as the Northwest Ordinance of 1787. Later the Morrill Act of 1862 provided grants for specific educational purposes, i.e., for the support of land-grant colleges. Other grants of land were made subsequently for allied services such as a girls' industrial school (Alabama, 1899), a school and asylum for deaf, dumb, and blind (Arizona, 1910, New Mexico, 1898), a deaf and dumb asylum (Montana, 1889), charitable penal and reformatory institutions (Arizona, 1910, Idaho, 1890), reform schools (Montana, 1889, New Mexico, 1898).

The shift from grants of land to grants of money was readily effected. As early as 1837 Congress distributed a Treasury surplus to the states in the form of loans without the expectation of repayment. By 1887 money grants were made to state agricultural stations, a year later for state veterans' homes, then in 1890 to provide instruction in land-grant colleges. Succeeding these grants came others for forest services (1911), agricultural extension work (1914), highways (1916), vocational education (1917), venereal disease control (1918), vocational rehabilitation (1920), and welfare and hygiene of maternity and infancy (1921). These early developments may seem to bear little relation to present-day public welfare until it is realized that many of the current federal-state welfare programs are financed on the grant (grant-in-aid, matched grant, or subsidy) principle, and have derived from these early anticipations. During the booming 1920's few additional welfare services were taken on or supported by the federal government. Before the depression 1930's were over, the federal government had been irrevocably committed not only to the principle of contribution, but also to the necessity and desirability of assuming a partnership role with the states and local communities. This practice has continued to the present day, with grants being made available in a number of postwar programs of which one of the largest is in the area of mental health.

Noninstitutional Services Before 1929

Early in the twentieth century certain noninstitutional services such as pension laws for the blind, the aged, and widowed mothers with dependent children began to make their appearance. Although restricted in their original application, these services assumed ever-increasing proportions until they were embodied in the Social Security Act of 1935 and became the predominant and characteristic form of public welfare in the century.

Aid to the Needy Blind. Before 1929 the care of the blind had been assumed in some places by private organizations, in other places by public ones. Sometimes it involved institutional care, at other times educational and vocational training or retraining. Because the blind are frequently at a disadvantage in the labor market and less likely to earn sufficient money for self-maintenance, the movement for allowances from public funds got under way, long before public aid to dependent children or the aged. As early as 1840 the state of Indiana passed a statute to provide for the support of the indigent blind. Later, in 1866, the Board of Aldermen and Board of Councilmen of New York City passed a resolution outlining a procedure for handling applications for assistance to the blind. Before the century was out, one state, Ohio, had enacted a law providing for the relief of the blind. This law of 1898 was declared unconstitutional as was that of 1904. However, in 1908 a further enactment stood the test of constitutionality. In the meantime two other states had acted affirmatively and established precedent for pensions for the blind. The Illinois legislature acted in 1903 and Wisconsin in 1907. Thus by 1910, before any state had made pension provision for its widowed mothers or aged, three states had granted public aid to the blind. In the next decade, beginning with Kansas in 1911 and ending with Nebraska in 1917, eight other states enacted assistance laws for the blind, and a like number legislated during the decade ending in 1929.

Aid to Widows and Children. A second departure from the Poor Law principles as well as from traditional institutional care was the provision of financial aid to widows and other mothers with dependent children. Several centuries of Poor Law "treatment" of dependent children had revealed the tragic waste to so many families and children of methods of care that pauperized or institutionalized the child. The foster home movement which originated under private auspices in 1853 was an early innovation in child care, but it remained for the White House Conference of 1909 to advocate a form of aid designed to keep mothers and children in their own homes. That Conference went on record as declaring that children should not be deprived of their homes except for urgent and compelling reasons. Poverty of itself was not deemed an urgent or compelling reason. When aid was necessary to keep the home together, the Conference declared, it "should be given by such methods and from such sources as may be determined by the general relief policy of each community, preferably in the form of private charity rather than of public relief." The recognition of the vital role of the mother in the lives of her children and of the importance of the early developmental years in the home had found expression in a new concept of child care.

The first mothers' aid law in the United States was enacted in April 1911 for one county in Missouri, Jackson County. Allowances were made to mothers who were in need, whose husbands were dead or prisoners, and whose children were under fourteen years of age. In June of the same year the first law on a state-wide basis was placed on the statute books of Illinois, known as the "Funds to Parents Act." The Juvenile Court of each county was empowered to determine the eligibility of parents and children for such assistance and to decide upon the money necessary to provide adequate care for the child. Colorado, in 1912, followed Illinois and adopted a Mothers' Compensation Act.

Once having started, the movement spread rapidly. By the end of 1919 thirty-nine states and two territories had passed laws of various titles—mothers' pensions, mothers' allowances, child welfare, mothers' assistance fund, widows' compensation, aid to dependent children, "an act to promote Home Life for Dependent Children"—all aimed to meet the same need. Within another decade, i.e., by the end of 1929, five states and the District of Columbia had followed suit so that at the time of the depression of the 1930's there were forty-four states, the District of Columbia and the territories of Alaska and Hawaii which had made provision for aid to children in their own homes.

Old-Age "Pensions." Chronologically, assistance to the blind and to mothers of dependent children preceded assistance to the aged. The first state law providing financial aid to the blind was enacted in 1840, the first (state-wide) widows' pension law in 1911. Actually it was not until 1923 that the first operable old-age pension was on the statute books of an American state (Arizona's 1914 law, although the first was later declared unconstitutional, while it was the territory of Alaska that may rightly claim the first law, 1915, to stay on the books).

Long before 1923 it had become clear that relief granted according to the methods and philosophy of the Poor Law was self-defeating. Not only did it demoralize the recipient, but because of the damage it did to the individual and the family of which he in most instances was a part, it actually proved to be a costly form of assistance. Even though the per capita relief grant was low, the perpetuation of pauperization swelled the grand total of relief to large figures. Almshouse conditions were being exposed to public airing and the resulting stench often reached the nostrils not only of the social worker or of the sensitive public-spirited citizen, but also the ordinary hardheaded businessman and the equally vociferous taxpayer. Private relief with its best of intentions was in no position to meet so great a need. Private institutions reached only a relatively few needy aged. Social insurance schemes had not yet taken hold in this country. In the face of such convincing reasons for some form of assistance to the needy aged the wonder is that state aid was delayed so long. Even when the movement for old-age pensions did begin to produce tangible results the effects were not as pronounced as in the case of the blind or dependent children. Excepting for the moment Arizona's 1914 unconstitutional law and the territory of Alaska's of the following year, the state of Montana stands out as the first American state to enact an old-age pension law that survived the constitutional onslaughts. In the same year, 1923, another state, Nevada, passed laws which withstood the courts (Pennsylvania's law did not). Wisconsin in 1925, Kentucky in 1926, Maryland in 1927, and four states—California, Minnesota, Utah, Wyoming—in 1929 complete the roll by the close of the pre-depression era. Nine states and one territory had made their break with the Poor Law principle of relief for the aged.

Although the Poor Law had not yet been scrapped, at least its preeminence as a philosophy of adequately meeting human needs had been seriously questioned. Looking back on the comparative record of assistance to the blind, to children and the aged, one is tempted to observe that there may be a connection between the feverish activity on behalf of children between 1911 and 1929 and the prior neglect of them for three centuries. It may be as much in order to observe that apparently a correlation exists between the tardiness of care of aged prior to 1929 and the extreme solicitude, not to say generosity, that was manifested toward them in subsequent legislation. A basic trend within recent decades toward an aging population cannot have been without its effect on old-age security legislation!

Public Welfare Following 1929

A new way of looking at the problems of people and new ways of dealing with those problems and people began to emerge once we realized that the debacle of 1929 spelled finis to the postwar philosophy of the twenties. Prosperity, despite reassurances from high places, was not around the corner. Depression had come. Translated into human terms, depression meant that millions of workers were unable to earn a living for their families; that people, plain ordinary people, went hungry and sick; that despair and frustration seized those who became dependent; that rebellion swelled inside people who saw threats of mass starvation in a land of plenty. The efforts to find a balance in such a topsy-turvy world, to meet the immediacy of countless needs, demanded not a return to the Poor Law principles but an abandonment of them, as the Webb Minority Report of 1909 in England had foreseen. True we fumbled through the time-precious years of 1929 to 1932 trying to hold on to the old while fearful of the new. Yet although the dates 1933 and 1935 mark the legislative expression of a new philosophy of public welfare, the era begins not with the stamp of legislative endorsement but with the days and events that culminated in that legislation.

From Private to Public Agency

Until 1929 the private social work agencies had dominated the field of social work. The profession had been built largely through the efforts of workers associated with privately supported agencies. These workers and these agencies had fought for and achieved standards. They had initiated and developed social work training largely under private auspices. They looked with distrust, not to say disdain, upon the caliber of the work, and often the workers, in the public field. Furthermore, the private agency, particularly the family societies, had come to carry more and more of the load of granting relief to clients. In that process certain skills and techniques of handling relief had developed and the workers had been able to see on every hand the values of such service to the profession as well as to the client.

In view of all this, and of the very real fact, in many instances, that the public welfare field was poorly manned by incompetent people who were politically subservient, it is quite understandable that the private agencies would look with misgivings upon proposals to use public funds through public agencies for relief purposes. The response was to assert the willingness and the fitness of the private agency to do the job. At first this meant the expansion of community fund drives and the allotment of the increased sums of the various private agencies to dispense wisely. But the demands of the unemployed and their dependents increased enormously and private funds were obviously insufficient for the task. Many influential persons and a large number of private agencies conceded that the funds might come from the public treasury but be distributed by private agencies. After several years of experimentation the decision was made that public funds were to be administered by public agencies.

In the spring of 1929 there were almost 3 million unemployed workers. Instead of an expected decrease during the spring, the number kept swelling until in January 1930 there were 4 million unemployed. Before the year was out the total had reached 7 million, and by the spring of 1933 there was an estimated unemployed population of 13 to 15 million. These figures should be related to a gainfully employed population that usually numbered around 48 million workers.

Private social work agencies, which had usually carried the bulk of the relief load, were alarmed at the size of the job to be done. Their philosophy committed them to a policy of continuing to carry the load. This meant whipping up unprecedented drives for private funds. Thus a community chest that formerly raised annually about $3 million found itself faced with the demand to raise $5 million in 1931, $7 million in 1932, and $10 million in 1933, only to realize that the unmet needs exceeded the help already given. Community Chests that had formerly conducted separate drives, i.e., the nonsectarian community fund and the Jewish Fund, were joined but still their combined drives raised only a fraction of the money needed.

Besides financial drives to raise funds to be administered by the private agencies, a movement got under way for private charity and individuals to provide work for the unemployed. "Share-the-work" and "give-a-job" plans were put forth everywhere, and finally yielded to the American genius for organization. The block-aid plan, whereby individuals living within a designated area made job provisions for all the unemployed contained therein, expressed unmistakably the emphasis upon local and private responsibility. Apple-selling on busy street corners did the same.

Private charity was finding the size of the task far too large. Public agencies already in existence seemed even more powerless to contend with the very magnitude of the situation. Not even the administration, in an already existing local department of public welfare, of funds jointly provided from public and private sources proved adequate. The problem and the approach to it was no more local than it had been private. The next step was inevitable, namely the assumption by the state of a share of the total responsibility. Accordingly state organizations were created outside the established departments to administer the "emergency" program. Significantly enough, the first of many such state agencies was titled "temporary emergency relief administration," and was entirely separate from the department of public welfare.

The First Temporary Emergency Relief Administration

On September 23, 1931, the New York Temporary Emergency Relief Administration was established by the legislature to provide state aid for the unemployed. Funds were appropriated to reimburse cities and counties up to 40 percent of their expenditures for unemployment relief. Furthermore the TERA, as it came to be called, was empowered to make and enforce rules for the proper and efficient administration of relief. In October Governor Franklin D. Roosevelt appointed Harry Hopkins, an experienced social worker, to be Executive Secretary of the TERA. New Jersey and Pennsylvania also set up emergency relief organizations before the end of 1931, and were followed within the next year by Wisconsin, Rhode Island, Illinois, and Ohio. The size of the appropriations was unprecedented. New York's initial $20 million proved to be only one-half the total appropriation for the year; Pennsylvania had to revise its figures upward before its first year was out, and other states did likewise. As important as the size of the appropriations was the principle that such legislation embodied—a responsibility shared by the state and the local community for the relief of distress resulting from unemployment.

Despite these early state measures, the situation throughout the country grew worse and worse. Many states were constitutionally barred from using public funds for unemployment purposes; other states, particularly the smaller and nonindustrial ones, were without resources. To darken the picture still further, many local communities were unable to raise funds from taxes to receive state reimbursement, and in some instances there were individuals and groups that refused to admit a depression had arrived and that starvation was on hand. The valiant, if misguided, efforts of high government officials as well as leading industrialists and managerial talent to deal with the problem on a private charity basis were proving more and more fruitless. Already the movement had begun toward federal participation.

Two senators, Costigan and La Follette, succeeded in presenting overwhelming evidence of the need for federal assistance to the states, but apparently the time was not yet ripe for federal assumption of the burden, or even part of the burden. Their efforts bore no immediate fruit, for the Congress that first heard their daring proposals rejected the bills, under administration direction, in February 1932. The common arguments occurred over and over again. The government's credit would be impaired; age-old principles of local responsibility and relief would be abandoned; states rights would be violated; a bureaucracy would result; and federal aid, after all, was only a dole.

The Federal Emergency Relief Act

But the matter would not die. Within six months Congress passed a bill entitled the Emergency Relief and Construction Act. It authorized the Reconstruction Finance Corporation to lend to the states $300 million of federal funds "to be used in furnishing relief and work relief to needy and distressed people and in relieving the hardships resulting from unemployment." Time soon proved this sum inadequate. Conditions throughout the country grew worse. An election turned out the administration. Two months later, in May 1933, a new Congress passed the Federal Emergency Relief Act whereby $500 million was appropriated for relief purposes. Grants were made to states either on a matching basis, if the state was able to match federal funds, or as an outright grant if it was unable to do so. Before a year was over $1 billion had been appropriated.

The Federal Emergency Relief Act shattered all precedent. It closed the door on three centuries of the Poor Law. It signalized the acceptance of federal responsibility for the welfare of over 100 million people. It provided for federal leadership and for federal co-operation with the states and local communities in helping them to meet the costs of unemployment relief.

On May 22, 1933, the first day after he assumed office, Administrator Harry Hopkins approved the first grants to seven states. By the end of June grants had been made to forty-five states. In November of the same year the experiment known as the Civil Works Administration was begun for the purpose of putting a large number of workers on civil works projects at current rates of pay. From then until its termination in March 1934, over 4 million workers, half from the unemployed not yet on relief rolls, were placed on work projects. The admitted purpose of the CWA was to give a "shot in the arm" to the economic system by putting men to work and money into circulation. But the expenditure of almost $1 billion in less than half a year proved too costly even for the federal government.

From the end of the CWA to the inauguration of the Works Progress Administration several other experiments and expedients were tried. These consisted of programs for the relief of distress in (1) "stranded areas" or with "stranded populations" (such as the cut-over lumber regions, or the worked-out coal areas, etc.), (2) rural areas (Resettlement Administration, subsequently Farm Security Administration), and (3) urban areas (Emergency Work Programs with federal funds supplementing local funds).

In January 1935 President Franklin D. Roosevelt declared that "the Federal Government must and shall quit this business of relief." Lest it be feared that this meant a return to the Elizabethan days of 1601, it must be explained immediately that what the President intended was that home relief should be carried on by the local community, but that two other services were to be available. The immediate service was to be a work relief program under federal direction, the contemplated service was to be the enactment of social security legislation. In theory, then, all needs were to be met: for the employable a work program, for the unemployed with adequate work records unemployment insurance and old-age insurance upon retirement, for the unemployable, i.e., the young, the aged, the blind, an assistance program, and finally, for those who fall into none of these categories, local relief.

The WPA

The largest governmental work program the world has ever known began to take form under the Works Progress Administration, beginning in May 1935 with an initial appropriation of almost $5 billion. Despite reshuffling, title-changing, and retrenchments the WPA (subsequently Work Projects Administration) continued to provide a work program with the federal government paying the wage bill largely, and the state or local community serving as sponsor and supplying a share of the materials.

The CCC and the NYA

Two other developments must be mentioned, the Civilian Conservation Corps and the National Youth Administration. The titles obviously indicate the accent on youth. These services were pointed not so much at relief as an end in itself but as a means of maintaining and developing the natural resources of the nation and at the same time of maintaining and developing its human resources. In the CCC camps young workers, largely from relief families, were to carry on conservation projects such as reforestation, prevention of forest fires, soil erosion control, flood control and like work. The NYA projects were also for the younger adult group and were directed toward (a) aiding needy high school and college students, (b) assisting other young people on constructive work projects, (c) providing job training, counseling, and placement services, and (d) the development of constructive leisure-time activities.

While no one would claim perfection for any of these programs since

1933, least of all the leaders of them, nevertheless one cannot contemplate the imagination, determination, and energy that went into them without realizing the profound changes that had taken place within the span of half a decade. President Pierce's doctrine of a static welfare had given way to a dynamic concept of human welfare. The government, federal, state, local, did exist to insure the well-being of the people who constituted that government. If the "welfare" of 1854 did not meet the needs of people in 1933, what was more realistic and human than to broaden the area of welfare?

The Social Security Act

The experience during the depression of the 1930's with emergency relief and work programs demonstrated the necessity for more stabilized programs for dealing with some of the critical problems of unemployment, aging, illness, and disability, and the welfare of mothers and children. Steps were directed toward legislation which eventuated in the Social Security Act.

The Social Security Act became law on August 14, 1935. There are three main aspects or divisions of the original Act and its subsequent amendments. One pertains to the social insurance features; another to the public assistance provisions; and a third to public health and welfare services, especially services for children. The social insurance sections adhere to principles of social insurance by providing for contributions by and in behalf of workers against the contingency of unemployment and the certainty of retirement or death. The unemployment insurance (or compensation) provisions are worked out on a federal-state basis, while the old-age and survivors insurance provisions are entirely federally administered.

The public assistance provisions are based upon federal-state cooperation in the financing and administration of aid to the aged, the blind, dependent children, and the permanently and totally disabled. The source of the funds is federal and state, and, in many instances, from local communities (usually counties) within the state.

The third portion of the Act as amended to date provides for (a) maternal and child health services, (b) services for crippled children, and (c) child welfare services. These funds are provided for by allotment according to appropriations authorized by the Congress, and with provision for matching of federal funds by the states. Administration, as with public assistance, is federal-state-local. Vocational rehabilitation and certain aspects of public health work which were included in the 1935 Social Security Act are now in the Vocational Rehabilitation Act Amendments of 1943, known as the Barden-LaFollette Act, and in the Public Health Service Act of 1944.

Unemployment Insurance. Further examination of the original Social Security Act as amended to date should be helpful in understanding the principles inherent in it, and to some degree, its operation. According to the unemployment insurance provisions, the federal government levies an excise tax of 3 percent of payroll of employers whose employees come within the definition of the Act. Employers pay their state taxes according to their state unemployment insurance law, and in computing their federal tax they may offset the amount of the state tax up to a total of 90 percent of the federal tax. The remaining 10 percent of the federal tax is paid directly to the federal government.

In accordance with the provisions of the Social Security Act the states have passed acceptable unemployment insurance laws so that employers could qualify for credit against the federal tax. Furthermore, in order for the Secretary of Labor to certify grants for administrative purposes to the states there must be other acceptable elements in the state law.[1] The effect of these two sets of requirements has been for the state laws to contain a number of provisions of which the most important are:

1. Establishment and maintenance of personnel upon a merit basis;
2. Opportunity for a fair hearing, before an impartial tribunal, for all individuals whose claims for unemployment compensation are denied;
3. The making of reports as required;
4. Payment of unemployment compensation solely through public employment offices;
5. The payment of all money received in the unemployment fund of the state to the Secretary of the Treasury to the credit of the Unemployment Trust Fund;
6. Moneys withdrawn by the states from the Unemployment Trust

[1] Funds to the States for administrative purposes are paid by the federal government; theoretically, but not necessarily actually, out of the 10 percent which goes to the federal government.

Fund to be used solely for the payment of unemployment benefits;

7. Compensation shall not be denied if an otherwise eligible individual refuses work because (a) the job offered him is vacant due to a strike, lockout, or other labor dispute, or because the wage, hours, or working conditions are substantially less favorable than those prevailing for similar work in the locality, or (b) if as a condition of employment the individual is required to sign a "yellow-dog" contract, i.e., to join a company union or resign from or refrain from joining any bona-fide labor organization.

Unemployment insurance is not available for all workers. The federal tax which governs contributions applies, generally speaking, to employers who employ four or more workers "on each of some twenty days during the taxable year, each day being in a different calendar week." [2] Other workers are not provided for because they are in certain employments excluded from the tax provisions. The most important of these excluded employments are:

1. Agricultural labor;
2. Domestic service in a private home, local college club, or local chapter of a college fraternity or sorority;
3. Casual labor not in the course of the employer's trade or business;
4. Service performed by an individual in the employ of his son, daughter, or spouse, and service performed by a child under 21 years of age in the employ of his father or mother;
5. Service performed in the employ of the United States;
6. Service performed in the employ of a state or any political subdivision thereof;
7. Service performed in the employ of a foreign government;
8. Service performed in the employ of a nonprofit agency organized exclusively for religious, charitable, scientific, literary, or educational purposes, or for the prevention of cruelty to children;
9. Certain specified miscellaneous services.

By the amendment of August 10, 1946, Public Law 719, 79th Congress, maritime workers, previously *not* included under unemployment insurance, were covered. Maritime workers were not included in the

[2] A number of states, however, extend unemployment insurance to workers in firms employing less than four workers.

1935 Act either for unemployment compensation or for old-age insurance. However, the 1939 amendment included them for old-age and survivors insurance but not for unemployment insurance.

The tax specified by the federal law is upon the employer, and applies to the first $3,000 of an employee's remuneration in the calendar year.

When the worker's employment ceases, he is required to notify the nearest public employment office of his situation, to register there for re-employment, and to indicate his fitness and willingness to work. His waiting period (usually one or two weeks, although Maryland and Nevada have no waiting period) must end before he can receive unemployment compensation. The compensation paid bears a definite relation to his average weekly earnings (roughly one half up to a salary of about $50 a week), and continues to be paid for a stated number of weeks or until a certain sum has been paid. In the majority of the states benefits are payable for a maximum of from 20 to 26 weeks. There are certain disqualifications which affect benefit payments, such as voluntarily leaving a job, refusal of a suitable job, discharge for misconduct, or unemployment due to a work stoppage existing because of a labor dispute in which the individual is participating. Because the laws of the states vary, there is no uniformity of provisions for dealing with such situations. In some states the benefit payments are postponed, in others the benefit payments may be reduced or canceled entirely.

Even though a worker may have been on the job for a number of years and then become unemployed because of illness, there is usually no unemployment benefit paid to him while he is out of work. Four states are exceptions. Three of these states have separate provisions to pay disability benefits when illness or disability prevents the worker from being on the job. However, the worker must be covered under the unemployment insurance laws of the state. A fourth state provides temporary disability benefits through its state workmen's compensation agency. Unemployment benefits and disability benefits are not intended as a substitute for a job. Such benefits aim to give workers some protection against loss of income during the interval between jobs or before restoration to a job.

Old-Age and Survivors Insurance. Another part of the social insurance program is old-age and survivors insurance, frequently abbreviated OASI, which provides for benefit payments upon retirement and to beneficiaries designated by the Act upon the death of the wage earner. Under the 1935 Act and subsequent amendments through 1949 the excluded employments were essentially those named in the unemployment insurance sections. Approximately 35 million workers were covered. This is practically unchanged so far as unemployment insurance is concerned, but with the 1950 amendments coverage was extended to between 7 and 8 million workers, and by the 1954 amendments an additional 10 million workers came within the OASI provisions.

By reason of the 1950 and 1954 amendments there is now compulsory old-age and survivors insurance for practically all workers in industry and commerce; for most farm workers—whether farm employees or farm operators; for many domestic workers; for many—but not all—self-employed persons (industrial, commercial, professional). In addition, there is provision for voluntary inclusion within the old-age and survivors insurance system of employees of state and local governments and nonprofit organizations. By now the overwhelming majority of workers in the United States participate in the OASI program—whether on a compulsory or a voluntary basis. It must be noted, also, that additional workers are covered under other public retirement systems such as federal civil service, some state and local retirement systems not yet integrated with the federal program, railroad retirement, and military.

Insured Status. Monthly retirement benefits are payable to the wage earner when he is 65 years or older and has retired from covered employment. Benefits are also payable to his wife if she is 65 years or older. If his wife is under 65 years, she is entitled to benefits if she, together with her retired worker husband, have a child or children within their care. In the event that the wife was the wage earner and is the retired worker of 65 years or older, her dependent husband is entitled to benefits as well. Dependent children of the retired worker, if under 18 years and attending school, are also eligible for benefits. The benefit payments for the wife and dependent children are computed on the basis of one half of the retired worker's (the primary beneficiary) benefits.

Designated survivors of a deceased worker are entitled to benefits; his widow when she reaches the age of 65 years; his widow (or dependent divorced wife) of any age who has a child or children who are eligible and in her care; his child or children under 18 years of age; his dependent parent or parents if he leaves neither widow nor children. In the event that the wife was the wage earner and has died, the dependent widower is entitled to benefits. Extra protection for the survivors of workers is assured through a provision which will permit payment of the lump sum on the death of every insured worker. Widows, widowers, and dependent children are eligible to receive three fourths of the deceased worker's benefit.

Insured workers are either fully insured or currently insured. The benefits one can claim or one's survivors can claim are related to the worker's status as either fully or currently insured. A person is *fully insured* if he has had one quarter of coverage (no matter when acquired) for each two calendar quarters elapsing after 1950 or after the quarter in which he became 21 years of age, with a minimum of six quarters of coverage. If the worker has 40 quarters of coverage (10 years) not only is he fully insured, but he is permanently fully insured. A *currently insured* person is one who has had at least six quarters of coverage within the three years immediately preceding his death or his retirement (entitlement to old-age insurance benefits). A "quarter of coverage" is a calendar quarter (three months) in which an employee is paid wages of $50 or more in covered employment. For the self-employed person a "quarter of coverage" is a calendar quarter in which has been credited with at least $100 of self-employment income. Four "quarters of coverage" are credited for each year in which self-employment income is $400 or more.

During retirement the worker may earn additional money in employments within the provision of the Social Security Act up to $1,200 per year. It is when he earns in excess of this amount that his monthly benefit payment is affected. After 72 years of age there is no restriction on the amount the retired worker may earn without his monthly benefit payment being affected.

The monthly benefit paid to the retired worker or to his (or her) survivors is based upon his earnings up to $4,200 per year. The minimum benefit to be paid to the retired worker is $30 per month. The maximum monthly benefit for a retired worker is $108.50; for a worker and his wife, $162.80; for a family, $200. These increases are based upon the 1954 Amendments and represent a substantial increase over the earlier benefit scales.

As of the 1954 Amendments the following tax schedule (percent of earnings) is to be in effect:

Calendar Year	Employee	Employer	Self-Employed
1954–1959	2	2	3
1960–1964	2½	2½	3¾
1965–1969	3	3	4½
1970–1974	3½	3½	5¼
1975 and after	4	4	6

These monies are paid into and benefits paid out of a fund known as the Federal Old-Age and Survivors Insurance Trust Fund. This Fund is managed by a Board of Trustees composed of the Secretary of the Treasury, the Secretary of Labor, and the Secretary of Health, Education, and Welfare. The Secretary of the Treasury serves as the Managing Trustee of this Board of Trustees.[3]

BIBLIOGRAPHY

Books and Pamphlets

Abbott, Edith, *Public Assistance: American Principles and Policies*. Chicago, University of Chicago Press, 1940.

Breckinridge, Sophonisba, *Public Welfare Administration in the United States,* rev. ed. Chicago, University of Chicago Press, 1938.

Brown, Josephine C., *Public Relief, 1929–1939*. New York, Henry Holt and Company, 1940.

Burns, Eveline M., *The American Social Security System*. Boston, Houghton Mifflin Company, 1949.

Friedlander, Walter A., *Introduction to Social Welfare*. New York, Prentice-Hall, Inc., 1955.

Gagliardo, Domenico, *American Social Insurance*. New York, Harper and Brothers, 1949.

Haber, William and Cohen, Wilbur J., *Readings in Social Security*. New York, Prentice-Hall, Inc., 1948.

Kelso, Robert W., *The History of Poor Relief in Massachusetts, 1620–1920*. Boston, Houghton Mifflin Company, 1922.

Lane, Marie D., and Steegmuller, Francis, *America on Relief*. New York, Harcourt, Brace & Company, 1938.

---

[3] It is deemed desirable to interrupt this discussion of the Social Security Act in order to continue the historical background of contemporary social services. The additional pertinent material on the Social Security Act will be resumed in Chapter 7 in connection with services in a local welfare department.

chapter 4

The Social Services in America— From the Church to the Charity Organization Society Movement

Development of Private Social Work in America

Among the earliest of the agencies that ministered to the inadequate or the unfortunate were the churches and church societies. To them charity was intended for the deserving, meaning those of the right religious faith. Later this was supplemented by various nationality societies, such as St. Andrews for the English (1756), the German Society (1784) for the Germans, and the French Benevolent Society (1807) for the French. A decade later came the first of the many societies devoted to the problem of pauperism, with the title of the New York Society for the Prevention of Pauperism. Its purpose was to study the causes of pauperism and to promote measures for its prevention and elimination.

The Association for Improving the Condition of the Poor

The most impressive, and by far the most far-reaching in influence of the early societies concerned with the immediate problems of the city poor, was the Association for Improving the Condition of the Poor, organized in 1843 in New York City. According to its first Constitution the Association's aim was ". . . the elevation of the moral and physical condition of the indigent; and so far as compatible with these objects, the relief of their necessities." Relief was granted to individuals, but studies were made of the conditions under which people lived as well as causes of their poverty. Measures were initiated to improve the conditions and to prevent them in the future.

When the Association began its work there were some 30 to 40 societies in operation in New York City, each undertaking to provide for a particular need. The Association was determined not to grant relief to those for whom the public authorities had responsibility nor to those who were known to the other relief societies. It was to select "from the mass, for our own care and relief, every individual whose condition we can morally and physically elevate and to reject all others." [1]

The city was divided into districts and then subdivided into sections. Each district had an advisory committee, and each section a visitor. The visitors, all of whom were men, were unpaid volunteers.

Besides the relief-giving function the Association aimed to do something about the conditions that beset the poor. Among its earliest efforts were those directed toward the improvement of housing and sanitation. It is said that the report made by a committee to the Board of the Association in 1853 was the first tenement house report made in America. In 1855 a model tenement, "The Workingmen's Home," was constructed largely through the efforts of the Association. Other efforts during its early period resulted in legislation to prevent adulteration of milk, the establishment of medical dispensaries for the indigent sick, the construction of a public bath and wash house, the creation of a special institution for the ruptured and crippled, and, in 1849, the incorporation of the New York Juvenile Asylum, "a reformatory and disciplinary institution, for the education and elevation of vicious children and their subsequent indenture."

During the next period of its history—up to the end of the nineteenth century—the Association actively promoted many causes, among them: fresh-air outings (later homes and camps) for mothers and children, vacation schools (later taken over by the public school system), and a settlement house, Hartley House, in 1897.

From the turn of the twentieth century until its merger with the New York Charity Organization Society in 1939, the Association furthered its

---

[1] Brandt, Lillian, *Growth and Development of AICP and COS.* New York, Community Service Society of New York, 1942, p. 19.

program of improving the conditions affecting people. Many of the enterprises it encouraged, sponsored, or initiated have since become a part of the readily accepted social services: tuberculosis hospitals, health services for school children, convalescent homes for mothers and babies, school lunches, dental clinics, work relief projects, legislation for widows' pensions, venereal disease clinics, health centers, vocational guidance bureaus, mental hygiene clinics, apartment housing for aged, homes for aged.

Other cities followed the example of the AICP with equal emphasis upon a personalized relief-giving service and the improvement and prevention of conditions adversely affecting people: Brooklyn AICP, 1853; Baltimore AICP, 1849; Boston Provident Association, 1851; Philadelphia Society for the Prevention of Pauperism and the Relief of the Deserving Poor, 1855; Chicago Relief and Aid Society, 1854; St. Louis Provident Association, 1860; St. Paul Society for the Relief of the Poor, 1876, the last society to be established before the onset of the charity organization movement.

The Charity Organization Society Movement in America

Watson, in his volume on the charity organization movement in the United States, takes note of these early relief societies and conjectures upon their demise or their eclipse by the COS movement. The gist of his observations is that the AICP's despite their good intentions when founded became just one more relief society, failing to keep moving with changed conditions.

Within four years of the organization of the London COS the United States encountered the serious depression of 1873 as an aftermath of the Civil War. For the first time in American history it was realized that the resulting problem of unemployment was more than a local matter. Despite the hundreds of local relief societies, or perhaps because of them, it was generally recognized that the existing methods of private charity were inefficient and inadequate. Private organizations in such cities as Philadelphia and Boston had made some use of the Hamburg-Elberfeld system of poor relief, but it was not until 1877 when Reverend S. H. Gurteen in Buffalo, New York, drew upon his prior experience with the London COS, that the first similar society took form in America.

Buffalo was divided into eight districts, each with a committee and a number of family visitors. No relief funds were administered. The COS let it be known that its sole purpose was to help to organize existing local charities, and that each society was to keep its own autonomy. The new society decided it would cut across religious, political and nationality lines. The early purpose to investigate cases and refer them to the proper existing agencies demonstrated the compelling necessity of effecting some reform in the prevailing system of municipal relief and secured at the same time the interest of a number of public-spirited citizens.

Within six years 25 cities had adopted the central principles of the charity organization movement: (1) investigation of every applicant, (2) central registration, (3) co-operation of all relief agencies within the community, and (4) the use, in the main, of volunteer friendly visitors. By 1883 societies had been initiated throughout the East and Midwest: New Haven, Philadelphia, Brooklyn, Syracuse, Newport (Rhode Island), Boston, Indianapolis, Detroit, Cincinnati, Baltimore, District of Columbia, New York, to mention some of the earlier organizations. In some instances the societies were known as COS; in others they were called Society for Organizing Charity (Philadelphia), Bureau of Charities (Brooklyn), Associated Charities (Boston). Regardless, however, of title their function was the same, namely to organize the relief resources of the community in order to meet effectively the needs of those who were without means or those who possessed meager resources of their own.

A movement that met such widespread acceptance must have had much to recommend it. In practically every sense the time was ripe for it, and it was ripe for the time. The niggardliness of the Elizabethan Poor Law survivals in this country had reduced, or rather maintained, public outdoor relief to the beggar's level. Private charity which had made a thousand beginnings in as many places had incorporated the individualism of industrialists who had grown wealthy in an expanding economy. Each prosperous donor had sought to impress his particular private philanthropy upon any relief society willing to accept his largess. As a result there was such an overlapping and waste of private charity funds that more needs were unmet than were met. Coincident with the creation of large cities and scores of factory towns, much of the neighborliness that characterized a simpler society was gone. Coupled with this was the strong conviction that pauperism indicated a character deficiency and required the maximum of personal influence of the donor or the donor's agent upon the recipient.

Yet all of these conditions might have been present and no charity organization movement would have eventuated had there not been leadership ready and able to assume an active and energizing role. That leadership was on hand both here and abroad. Indeed the whole history of humanitarianism reveals that the very forces that create the needs by an alternate reaction produce individuals to whom these needs become a concern. One only needs to study the reform movements in England from 1832 on, or the efforts of humanitarians in this country from the time of the early Quakers and prison reformers, to realize the compensating effects of any system which carries its own inherent excesses. In short, the COS movement in America was no fortuitous or haphazard occurrence. The effects of the Industrial Revolution were felt acutely. The efforts of social thinkers and even of social reformers, joined with the rising temper of humanitarianism, were substantiated by a comfortable financial surplus. To all of this came a leadership which pointed the way to a sounder use of human resources. This movement illustrated the dynamic growth principles of any movement: a perceived need, a growing body of knowledge and experience to deal with that need, the material means available or discoverable, and all these fused into a unity by a driving leadership directed toward certain socially desirable goals or ends.

Expansion of the COS Movement

As one surveys the whole field of social work today, three main groupings of interest and activities centered around them are readily apparent. First, the preoccupation with the individual per se; second, concentration upon the group of individuals as the working unit; and third, concern with developing resources to meet human needs. To these three we have given the terms social casework, social group work, and community organization. The division within the charity organization movement exemplifies the first and third of these, while the social settlement expresses the second. Consideration of group work will be left for a later chapter, but the developments within the COS with respect to the trends toward individualization and community organization must necessarily be dealt with here.

An attitude which regarded the needy as victims of their own vices and failings, tended to absolve the social order of any responsibility for the conditions which reduced individuals to destitution. So long as such an attitude prevailed, it was consistent to make relief as unattractive as possible. A maximum premium was placed upon gratuitous advice, the arts of persuasion and the rigors of exhortation. But an awakened social conscience coupled with some comprehension of the economic and social order gave pause to so easy and comfortable a proposition and compelled attention to some of the factors that lay outside the individual. This realization was based, understandably enough, upon a rather fragmentary knowledge of "causes," but it tended to shift some emphasis from an internal to an external causation. It may be more accurate to say that the approach became twofold: first, to continue to give an individualized service in the light of a growing insight into human character (the more technical term behavior was to appear later), and second, to seek for changes within the existing framework of society that would produce less devastating effects upon the individual.

Among the earliest of these concerns was housing. Long before the charity organization movement had taken form proposals had been made for improving housing conditions for the poor in order to reduce the incidence of pauperism. Under the Hamburg-Elberfeld system efforts had been made to better housing for the poor. In London, Octavia Hill and Edward Denison, leaders in reform movements, had agitated for years in the same cause. Years later in 1892 Buffalo, the pioneer COS city, had managed to secure certain inspection ordinances. Brooklyn, however, was one of the early American cities to secure the enactment of a tenement house law in 1879, and later, under the inspired leadership of Alfred T. White, to erect model tenements. Edward T. Devine, in his reminiscent volume, *When Social Work Was Young,* has recounted the work of the New York Society in making available to the city of New York the services of housing authorities through the organizational channels of COS. Other cities also gave attention to housing reform, among which must be mentioned Chicago, Washington, Youngstown, and Columbus, Ohio.

The prevention of tuberculosis was another crusade in which COS workers were enlisted. As in the case of housing reform, the initial body was a committee within the New York Society (in 1902) which was still under the leadership of Edward T. Devine. This committee on Prevention of Tuberculosis wisely utilized the services of capable physicians and lay persons in working out a program of research into the social and medical aspects of tuberculosis, education of the public, encouragement of sanitaria for the care of patients, and relief of indigent consumptives. Several years later, in 1904, at a meeting of the American Medical Association, the National Association for the Study and Prevention of Tuberculosis was organized. In other cities, Washington, Minneapolis, Boston, Buffalo, Pittsburgh, and Chicago, the Charity Organization Society or its equivalent was active in tuberculosis work, laying the groundwork for an effective nationalization of a preventive program.

Shortly after the establishment of the first and second juvenile courts in Chicago and Denver, workers within the charity organization movement had become active in the field of juvenile probation. In 1900 the Buffalo Society organized a committee on probation which was instrumental in the passage of a state law to amend Buffalo's city charter permitting the appointment of two probation officers. Later the New York Society placed a woman probation officer at the disposal of a magistrate's court to effect a closer relation between the legal aspect of the court and the social rehabilitation of the offender. Societies in other cities followed with close interest developments within the court structure, particularly within the juvenile court.

One aspect of this concern with the operation of the courts was the effort stimulated by charity organization societies to secure a fairer distribution of legal services to individuals with limited means. Too often clients who came to the attention of social workers were in need of legal services but lacked resources to take advantage of or even to secure the protection of their legal rights. Both Baltimore and Buffalo established legal aid bureaus within their own societies to make legal services available to clients either without cost or at minimum cost.

Other areas in which the societies came to operate were those of desertion and nonsupport cases. Especially was this true in Boston, Philadelphia, and Chicago. Problems within the family also called for action, such as the inadequacies and lack of facilities for dealing with dependent and neglected children. The Children's Aid Society of Pennsylvania was launched in 1882 largely through the efforts of those associated with the work of the Philadelphia Society for Organizing Charity. Beggars and vagrants, whether within or outside of a family group, were touched by COS efforts. For a time in New York all beggars and vagrants were turned over by the Police Department to the COS, where aid was administered by means of wayfarer's lodges; these lodges were also provided in Chicago, Philadelphia, and Boston.

Social Reform and Individual Service

At this stage in the development of the movement two well-defined divergent trends could be identified. First there were those who maintained that the major effort of the charity organization movement should be to correct the external factors in the social organization responsible for poverty—lack of opportunity and individual and family demoralization. Accordingly, this group devoted its energies to such activities as proper housing, suitable health and sanitary facilities, compulsory education, control of labor exploitation by industry, provision of play facilities in congested areas, adequate relief, and varied forms of social legislation. Second, there were those who restricted their labors to the individual client with the aim of effecting a change within the individual which would enable him to utilize to the full his own potentialities. Quite naturally this latter group developed a more intensive approach to the individual client and gave form to the specialization of social casework within the larger field of social work.

A Professional Journal and a Professional School

Two developments in the latter years of the nineteenth century and the early twentieth need to be mentioned here because of their continuing contribution to the field of social work. One of these was the establishment of a professional journal, the other the founding of a professional school for the training of social workers.

The *Survey* and *Survey Graphic* date back to the Charity Organization Society of New York. As long ago as 1891, the Society had published the *Charities Review* and for the next ten years it continued to speak for the social work of that day. In 1897 *Lend-A-Hand,* published in Boston, was merged with the *Charities Review*. At this same time the COS had begun a kind of house organ, called *Charities,* which aimed to promote directly the work of the organization. Before the merger of the *Charities Review* and *Charities* to be known as *Charities* in 1901, each journal had published material of outstanding merit. Mergers were not yet over, for in 1905 *Charities* was joined by Graham Taylor's *Chicago Commons,* and early in 1906 by *Jewish Charity* to become *Charities and Commons.* After four years *Charities and Commons* became the *Survey,* taking its name from the monumental study in six volumes of the city of Pittsburgh. During all these years these publications had been under the wing of the New York COS, but in 1912 the *Survey* was separately incorporated. From then until it ceased publication in 1952 it was unequaled in the field of social work publications for pithiness, timeliness, and sprightliness of style.

Just as the *Survey* sprang from the charity organization movement so also have professional schools of social work. Staff conferences and supervision for employed as well as volunteer workers soon proved inadequate to keep abreast of changing demands of the job. Then followed informal courses and lectures for workers in the various societies, of which perhaps the earliest was Brooklyn, in 1891. The first decisive step was taken when, in 1898, the New York Society offered its summer school of philanthropy, with Philip W. Ayers, assistant secretary of the society, as its director, and with an enrollment of 30 students. For three years this Summer School of Philanthropic Workers continued until it was reorganized upon an eight months' instruction basis. The next year, the director of the New York Society, Edward T. Devine, along with his other duties, assumed the directorship of the first school of social work in this country.[2]

Everything that has been written here of the charity organization movement is pertinent to family welfare, since it is from that movement that the family societies of today have developed. The immediate relation was the creation of the Field Department within the New York COS in 1905. Four years later this led directly to the Charity Organization Department of the Russell Sage Foundation with Mary Richmond as director. In 1911 the National Association of Societies for Organizing Charity was formed with Francis H. McLean, formerly secretary

---

[2] Meier, Elizabeth G., *A History of the New York School of Social Work.* New York, Columbia University Press, 1954.

of the Field Department of COS, as its first executive secretary. Name changes since then indicate the trend in thinking: American Association for Organizing Charity (to include Canadian Societies), American Association for Organizing Family Social Work, the Family Welfare Association of America, and in 1946 the Family Service Association of America. In 1919 the periodical *The Family* was established and since then has served as an organ of education and opinion of much of the best of casework practice in the family welfare field. In October 1946 it was named *The Journal of Social Casework,* and in 1950 *Social Casework.*

The Origins of the Social Settlements

At least one other movement must be mentioned in this retrospective survey of the development of social work. It began, understandingly enough, in an area which had suffered earliest and most acutely the effects of industrialization—London, England. By the 1880's social work in England had consisted largely of the meager grants of a poor relief authority, the unorganized philanthropies (church and private) of benevolent individuals, and the organized efforts of the Charity Organization Society. It will be observed that in practically every case relief was directed toward the individual. It remained for the social settlement to shift this focus from the individual as an individual to the individual within a group. The unit of service had become the group. What was more natural, too, than that such work should emanate from, be supported by, and engaged in by that class that had benefited most by the industrialization of England—the upper middle class. The social settlement emerged from Oxford University and centered largely in the slums of London. Toynbee Hall, the first social settlement in the world, expressed from the moment of its founding in 1884 the conviction that individuals more fortunately endowed with this world's goods could, by taking residence in poorer areas of the city, share their culture and advantages with those to whom opportunity had never come. This sharing process was the substance of the early efforts of the "settlers," a contribution of the more fortunate out of his experience as well as a learning from the poor out of their experience.

The example of Toynbee Hall was carried to America, and in 1886 the first settlement in the United States, Neighborhood Guild, was established in New York City. Industrialization in America had not only created tremendous wealth, but also the very conditions that made that wealth unattainable to all but a few. Social work, including the latest addition of the settlements, tried to understand the problems of the disadvantaged and to help them to realize opportunities for effective living in a social order that was none too tender with those who had failed to succeed.

Conclusion

It must be obvious from the foregoing account that the beginnings of social work have been inextricably bound up with the fundamental economic conditions and changes within the social order and with the concomitant philosophies expressed therein. From the breakup of the old feudal order through the successive changes of mercantilism, commercialism, and industrialism there has persisted the basic and unavoidable fact of human need. To meet these needs society established certain services early based on the premise of individual responsibility. The individual who was in want had brought that condition upon himself through his own shiftlessness, ignorance, or incapacity. The answer was to meet that need as sparingly as possible; relief was not to be attractive enough, for instance, to tempt the lowest paid workman in England away from his job nor was any individual to be allowed to feel that society approved of his need. This all sounds quite Elizabethan, but it must be remembered that such was the philosophy dominant throughout the two centuries that followed.

Several centuries of attempts at alleviation had clearly shown the limitations of any program that dealt only with the result instead of the cause. It was like trying to sweep back the ocean with a broom. Little insight was gained into the nature of social problems until our understanding took in more than merely the fault of the individual. Only after we began to realize that there were factors larger than and beyond any individual did we proceed to the next phase—prevention. Then the role played by the entire nation—its industry and trade, its philosophies and social institutions—became evident. An awakened understanding of these forces showed their relation to the fate of the individual. Only with such understanding could an ameliorative and preventive program that saw the connection between cause and effect take hold. Social work became a part of the economy of the nation. As the new profession developed, it became clear that social workers who were called in after the damage to the individual had been done might well be looked to for consultation, direction, and action before the fact. This early concern with social problems gradually expanded (some would say narrowed) to working with those capacities within the individual which enable him to adjust to and use effectively his environment of things and people.

Important and as far-reaching as public welfare is today, it is evident, from even this sketchy historical review, how essential a part social work under private and voluntary auspices has played in the over-all development of social work. Even though the bulk of financial assistance is now carried by the public welfare agencies, it was the private societies during the one hundred years before our social security program that developed the basis for the present individualized services in all welfare programs. It was the private individual, or incorporations of a number of individuals, that early provided institutional care for disadvantaged persons—children, the aged, the chronically ill, the mentally ill, the feeble-minded, the blind, the deaf, the juvenile offender, and then later experimented with noninstitutional services for many of these. It was the private agencies that developed the basis for much of what today passes for social action whether through private or public channels. It was the private agencies that developed the basis for current group work services, whether today as social settlements or community centers under public or private auspices. It was the private agencies whose labors furnished the groundwork for much of present-day community organization whether in the area of voluntary community chest financing or joint planning by private and public representatives through the medium of community planning councils.

With all their mistakes, inevitable in any pioneering, the private agencies have consistently and conscientiously pushed for standards that ultimately have been accepted into sound social work practice. Furthermore, the adoption through public financing of many of the services developed by the private agencies has enabled them to move into new areas of exploration. These words are added not by way of defense or justification of the private agencies—they will stand on their record— but by way of explanation of the complementary role of the private and public agencies. These words also undertake to give some measure of the as yet undefined tasks lying ahead and calling for the necessary experimentation preliminary to public adoption and tax support.

BIBLIOGRAPHY

Books and Pamphlets

Andrews, F. Emerson, *Attitudes Towards Giving*. New York, Russell Sage Foundation, 1953.

—— *Philanthropic Giving*. New York, Russell Sage Foundation, 1950.

Boylan, Marguerite, *Social Welfare in the Catholic Church*. New York, Columbia University Press, 1941.

Brandt, Lillian, *Growth and Development of the AICP and COS*. New York, Community Service Society, 1942.

Bruno, Frank J., *Trends in Social Work as Reflected in the Proceedings of the National Conference of Social Work, 1874–1946*. New York, Columbia University Press, 1948.

Devine, Edward T., *When Social Work Was Young*. New York, The Macmillan Company, 1939.

Frisch, Ephraim, *An Historical Survey of Jewish Philanthropy*. New York, The Macmillan Company, 1924.

Glenn, John M. and Brandt, Lillian, *Russell Sage Foundation, 1907–1946*. 2 vols. New York, Russell Sage Foundation, 1947.

Henderson, Charles R., *Modern Methods of Charity*. New York, The Macmillan Company, 1904.

Lowell, Josephine S., *Public Relief and Private Charity*. New York, G. P. Putnam Sons, 1884.

Matthews, William H., *Adventures in Giving*. New York, Dodd, Mead & Company, 1939.

Queen, Stuart Alfred, *Social Work in the Light of History*. Philadelphia, J. B. Lippincott Co., 1922.

Richmond, Mary, *The Long View*. New York, Russell Sage Foundation, 1930.

Warner, Amos G., *American Charities*. New York, Thomas Y. Crowell Company, 1894.

Watson, Frank D., *The Charity Organization Movement in the United States*. New York, The Macmillan Company, 1922.

chapter **5**

Social Casework

The Nature of Social Casework

As has already been indicated, while programs were developing to meet the needs of people on a nation-wide basis, those who were engaged in their operation were continually reminded of the fact that the ultimate consumers of their services were individual human beings. It is unquestionably true that common problems are to be found among large numbers of people. In a population as large as ours, for example, there will always be a sizable number of children who are deprived of adequate parental care. It is also true that common solutions can be devised to solve these problems. All children can be given care in institutions or foster homes. But it is finally true that both the problems and the solutions have peculiar meaning for each of the individuals who encounter them. For some children, institutional care may represent the epitome of comfort, while for others it is pure agony. In a society that draws strength from a respect for, and the consequent contributions of, individuality it should not be surprising that a regard for the peculiar meaning which experience has for the individual has led to the development of the unique process which has come to be known as social casework.

All of us live in association with other people and in relation to such institutions as the family, the school, the church, and the job. Many of us, at one time or another, need to call upon the services of such professional practitioners as lawyers, doctors, and psychiatrists. These associations and relationships and services bring us many satisfactions, but they also bring vexations. Social casework is a method by which one individual offers help to another in meeting some of the problems that arise out of the fact that our world is organized as it is. While not inimical to change and indeed placing a premium upon human growth and development, social casework is not primarily a method of manipulating society to serve people. Its goal is to help the individual whose needs and resources are in conflict with the vicissitudes and exigencies of life. The following pages present a general description and a consideration of some of the basic elements and current issues involved in this subject.

Social Agencies. Social agencies, within which casework practice is to be found, exist in this country in great variety. They may be large organizations, employing several hundreds of workers, or they may be so small as to have but a single caseworker. They may serve a very restricted clientele, perhaps in relation to a single highly specialized service, or they may offer services related to a great variety of problems to all the citizens of a large community, a state, or the nation. They are to be found in large cities, where they may be organized in district units serving neighborhood areas, and in rural territories where one small office may be expected to give service to a county or to several counties covering hundreds of square miles. They may be staffed entirely by highly trained members of the profession of social work, or by untrained people with perhaps a small admixture of those with professional training. Casework may be offered in agencies operating primarily to make such service available, as a family service agency, or in a social service division which is but a small part of a larger organization such as a hospital, a school system, or the mammoth Veterans Administration. Because of all these differences it is not possible to present a picture of truly typical casework practice in a truly representative agency. Nevertheless, the description which follows contains characteristics which are quite generally found in such agencies.

The physical setting itself is likely to present a variety of faces, but the odds are very great that it will not be pretentious. The agency may be housed in an ordinary office building or in an old residence that has been converted into office space. It may be on the dingy side, or it may possess the comforts of air conditioning and good furniture in a setting of almost antiseptic cleanliness. It is likely that magazines and toys, bright pictures, and perhaps even drapes or an aquarium will reveal an effort to make the setting somewhat more congenial for the human beings whose cares are the objects of its concern.

The atmosphere is likely to be coolly businesslike and calmly unhurried, but also warmly responsive to the client. Based on an unsurprised and uncondemning acceptance of the peculiarities and eccentricities of human behavior, it is permeated by a feeling of consideration and permissiveness. It reveals a depth of interest in the client which is quite different from idle or morbid curiosity, and it implies a guarantee against prying into matters which the client is not at the moment willing to share. Also implicit in it is an assumption that the problem that brings him, while it might seem shameful or frivolous to others, is of importance to the client and therefore of importance to the agency. Somehow the impression will be given that the primary interest of the agency is in helping its clients rather than in judging them. This atmosphere of concern and respect for the client, which also carries with it something of expectation of him, is a product of the behavior of all the staff members with whom the client is likely to have contact. In a sound agency, even clerical workers are expected to make their contribution to the maintenance of an atmosphere of this character.

The Application. The casework process begins, in the great majority of cases, when a client makes application to an agency for service in connection with a problem that troubles him. A good bit of significance attaches to this matter of the initiation of the contact, for there is one thing of which caseworkers are quite certain and that is that their efforts can only be successful when they are directed in general conformity with the interests and purposes of their clients and that they are foredoomed to failure when they move in a direction that is in essential contradiction to the client's will. If this suggests that casework is not a method for coercing or beguiling people into doing "what is right," the inference is correctly drawn. It would not be correct to assume further, however, that the caseworker would support his client in antisocial or illegal activities simply because the client's will ran in that direction.

Because casework can be successful only as the client himself is somehow engaged in grappling with his own problems, it is now quite general practice for agencies to wait for the client to make some move toward them in the way of requesting the service they may have to offer. This represents a kind of testing of the strength of the client's interest in achieving the sort of change which effective use of the casework process is likely to entail. Exceptions are to be found when the agency is a probation or parole department, a mental or correctional institution, or one to which come complaints about the care that is being given to children. In these instances it is likely to be the caseworker who will make the initial step toward the client. Special problems appear in these agencies, which themselves initiate the process, but these problems must and can be met in ways which do not disturb the essential validity of the principle that, from the beginning, the client must be actively engaged in the casework process. Casework is not something that is done to the client; it is a joint undertaking in which he can and must actively engage.

When the applicant first presents himself, he is given some idea of how long he will need to wait before he can be seen by an intake worker. If he cannot be seen for several days, he will be given an appointment for a specific hour and some assurance that at that time he will be seen without delay. Ultimately, and hopefully sooner rather than later, the client will find himself face to face with the caseworker who will help him as he completes his application. In the best of circumstances, this interview will take place in a private office. Less desirably, it may be in a kind of interviewing booth which provides some, but by no means complete, privacy. Or it may be held in an office shared by several workers. In special situations the interview may even be held in the client's home.

In the course of the application interview, which is likely to last for approximately an hour or longer, the caseworker will help the applicant to express the problem as it appears to him and also to give information about the situation which forms the background for his problem. In doing this, the caseworker may make use of an application form from the beginning or he may introduce it in the course of the interview. In any event, he will enter on the form certain information about the problem and about the surrounding situation. In many agencies the applicant will be asked to sign the form as evidence of his intent to pursue, with the agency, efforts to find a solution.

The application worker soon learns that applicants cannot always ask immediately for help with the problem that is their major concern. Qualities of shame and guilt may make it impossible for them to reveal at once to the intake worker that which is really disturbing them. Applicants make their requests for help against a background of feeling, and the varieties of feelings are almost as numerous as the number of applicants. Some, to be sure, may make their requests as matter-of-factly as though they were ordering eggs from the corner grocer, but it is not really characteristic for the person seeking help with a serious problem to be in quite such complete control of his feelings. He is more likely to come obsequiously—meek, fearful, imploring—or demandingly—bitter, angry, accusing—or with some other combination of rather intense feeling. Even though these feelings are aimed directly at him, the intake worker knows from his training and experience that they are primarily an expression of the concern the applicant has for the trouble he—the client—faces. Drawing upon this understanding, and the patience it makes possible, the worker attempts to help the client move, at a pace that will be possible for him, to a formulation and recognition of the basic problem and a readiness to make use of the services that the agency can make available. This is not to suggest that application workers are people who calmly and impassively accept vituperation and abuse, but it may suggest the reason why many agencies assign to their application desks a worker who is particularly well trained, experienced, and skillful.

At the same time the worker is securing from the applicant information about his problems and the attendant circumstances, the application interviewer will also be giving information about the way in which the agency may be able to help. This will include some statement of the services that the agency is prepared to offer, the circumstances under which these can be made available, and what effort the agency will expect the client to invest in making constructive use of those services. If the request has been for financial assistance, the applicant will be given some idea of the amount that may be available, the conditions under which it is given, and the extent to which he will be expected to be responsible to the agency in the way of supplying necessary information. If the request has to do with assistance in regard to family or social relationships, it is very probable that he will be given to understand that this is not something that he can leave with the agency, like a broken watch, to be returned to him later fully repaired and in operating order. On the contrary, it will be explained to him that, while this is the sort of problem with which the agency can give help, such help can only be given on the basis of a joint undertaking between the agency and himself. An almost certain probability is that the agency would expect him to return, at scheduled intervals, for further consultation on this problem. Also, if the case involves marital difficulties, the agency may request or require that the marriage partner participate to at least some degree in the casework process. In any event, unless the problem is one which can be adequately dealt with in the application interview, the caseworker and the applicant will arrive, at some point before its conclusion, at some mutually agreed upon understanding of what the next step will be. This may involve withdrawal of the application on the part of the applicant, consideration of the possibility of referral to what might seem to be a more appropriate agency, a visit on the part of an agency representative to the applicant's home or to some other person involved in the situation, or a plan for the applicant to have a series of interviews, probably with a different worker, for continuing exploration and treatment with regard to his problem.

Continuing Service. From this point onward the nature of the casework process can be expected to vary greatly in accordance with the nature of the problem and the particular agency to which the client has come for help. In many agencies a large portion of the balance of the contacts would be held in the home of the client. This would be particularly true in rural areas where problems of transportation are serious ones for the client. On the other hand, the trend in a great many agencies is toward office interviews at scheduled times. This practice is consistent with the principle, stated earlier, with regard to the expectation that the client come to the agency to make application. His willingness to come to the agency for further help is an indication of his continuing interest and concern in arriving at a solution. Home visits, on the other hand, may promote the feeling that it is the agency's need and urgency to arrive at a solution which is more important than the client's.

Many agencies in which the casework process is carried on through scheduled interviews of an agreed-upon length also limit the number of such interviews. The agreement may be for a series of four weekly interviews of an hour each, with the understanding that at the end of the series a reassessment will be made by the worker and the client as to the progress that has been made and the prospect for further progress if the interviews are continued. The belief supporting this practice is that human beings grow in relation to the limitations which they must overcome. Strength, it would be held, can only be present in relation to situations in which one's strength is taxed. Continuing dependency upon the agency is not to be promoted. Many other agencies, however, do not operate on the basis of such planful use of time. Continuing interviews in such agencies may be held at quite irregular intervals, frequently depending upon the way in which the situation moves the worker or the client, and each interview may go on for as long or as short a period of time as the worker or the client see fit. Likewise, some agencies are disinclined to set a maximum period for which they will carry a given case and consequently may have cases open for quite indefinite periods of time.

Except in unusual circumstances, the same caseworker will be responsible for all of the agency's activities in regard to a particular case. The total of all cases assigned to him constitutes the worker's "caseload," and all interviews, all telephone calls, and all correspondence will be handled by him. Only in emergency situations arising from such causes as illness or other unexpected absence would one worker undertake to substitute for another.

It is characteristic of nearly all casework agencies that they keep a complete and detailed record of all their activities in relation to each case. Variations will be found in the form and extensiveness of this record from agency to agency, but maintaining some form of case record is one of the regular duties of nearly every caseworker. In many agencies the record begins with the application form or a "face sheet" which contains a summary statement of all the pertinent factual information about the client and his situation. It continues with a chronological narrative which usually gives in detail the substance of what went on between client and worker in each interview. The record also contains all correspondence, reports of examinations, and any other pertinent material that may have come into the agency's possession. Since much of what passes between the client and the worker is of a highly personal nature, agencies commonly take precautions to protect the confidentiality of their records from idly prying eyes. They may be kept in locked files, sometimes located in a special "file room" which can be securely locked when the agency is not open for business. The records are available only to responsible members of the staff, and even clerical and maintenance workers may be given instruction in the need to protect the confidentiality of the agency's records.

These case records serve many useful purposes. When, in an emergency, one worker must take over for another, or when a worker leaves the staff and is replaced by another, the record provides an account of the course of treatment that has been pursued and frequently suggests the plan for future treatment. The case record is also of value to the worker as he attempts to increase his knowledge and skill in the practice of casework. As he reads the account of the interviews and studies the ways in which the client has responded to the things that have been said, he gains new insight into the workings of the client's personality and new ideas as to ways in which to be helpful. Indeed, caseworkers often find this sort of heightened awareness occurring at the very time they are organizing their thoughts and recollections in connection with the process of recording. The case record can also serve as a tool for professional education when the worker presents a problem case to his supervisor, to a case consultant, or to a staff meeting. It similarly serves an educational purpose when used as a basis for learning in a professional school of social work. Records can be a source of useful statistical information about an agency's operation and a source of basic data for research projects designed to increase knowledge and improve efficiency. They are frequently encountered in professional literature as illustrations of theoretical and technical points.

While recording is of demonstrable value, it is also an expensive and time-consuming procedure. Consequently, a good bit of experimentation has been undertaken in the way of substituting summarized recording for detailed recording of the complete casework process, limiting the so-called "process recording" to a few selected cases which seem to have special educational value, using forms and check-lists in place of the narrative record, and utilizing such modern devices as disc, tape, and wire recorders.[1]

---

[1] In connection with mechanical recording devices, it should perhaps be pointed out that reputable agencies and professional practitioners would hesitate to use such devices without the knowledge and consent of the client.

The End of the Process. As has already been suggested, the method of ending the casework process is likely to vary considerably from agency to agency and from worker to worker. In some instances the ending may be quite clear-cut and perhaps even arbitrary. This would be true when a family is no longer eligible for public assistance, or when a child's adoption has become final, or when a homemaker can be removed from a family because the mother, who has been in a hospital, has returned home and is prepared to resume her housewifely duties. In some instances the process may end arbitrarily because the agency has set a limit to the amount of time it is prepared to invest in a given case. In all such cases, however, it is likely that the client would understand that he would be free to return for additional service should circumstances change in such a way as to seem to again make him eligible for help. In many instances, however, the ending of the process is less perceptible. It may be that the client will gradually reduce his visits to the agency or the significance of the problems he brings may diminish so that there is in effect a gradual withdrawal from service. Such cases may sometimes be kept open for long periods of time with only sporadic and relatively insignificant contact with the agency. In the best casework practice, however, the ending is likely to be quite clear-cut, for the client will have indicated some readiness to resume a life that is independent of the help of the agency, the worker will have helped him to assess his capacities for such a life, and they will together have arrived at a mutually acceptable decision that it is now appropriate for the client to attempt this.

No description of the casework process can typify an activity which is so complex and varied as this. The description that has been given may, perhaps, serve as a basis for the somewhat more theoretical discussion which follows.

Basic Elements of the Casework Process

Problems of Definition. It may well be that the term "social casework" is as inefficient a device for the communication of meaning as any word or phrase in the English language. In themselves, the component parts do not represent any very clear meanings, and taken together they do not suggest anything with which most people have had direct experience. The titles of such professions as medicine, teaching, and the law, while they conceal great professional mysteries, still carry to us quite reasonably clear impressions of the kinds of activities in which their practitioners engage. Most people have a fairly accurate picture of what is likely to happen to them when they call upon their doctor. There are few whose preconceptions about a visit to a social caseworker would be at all realistic.

One reason for the difficulty in arriving at a definition is undoubtedly the fact that casework is an evolving and expanding sort of activity. As indicated at several points in this book, there have been occasions within the present century when social work has seen and seized upon the possibility of extending its service to new groups of people through casework offered in new situations. A definition based upon the practice of the beginning of the century would be quite inadequate to describe the casework of today, and any definition that fits today's practice is likely to be equally inadequate for the casework of tomorrow. Another obstacle to adequate definition arises from the great variety of activities carried on by people with the title of caseworker, the great variety of agencies in which these people are employed, and the great variety of people who are covered by this title. The activities range all the way from the distribution of baskets of food, gifts, and toys at holiday seasons, through the administration of a variety of tangible services such as financial assistance and provision of care for children and the aged when families are unable to do so, to a kind of interpersonal counseling that can only with great difficulty be distinguished from the psychotherapeutic practice of a psychiatrist or psychoanalyst. Mention has already been made of the variations in agencies and in the backgrounds of the people who are employed by them as caseworkers.

With this vast range of differences, it must be obvious that any definition broad enough to encompass all of them would of necessity be so broad as to set almost no practical limits or boundaries to the process of social casework. Still, the process *is* recognizable; it is distinguishable in general if not in every particular from other kinds of activities; and it includes certain elements about which there would be, in all likelihood, quite general agreement on the part of the profession of social work as a whole.

In the first place, there would be just about universal agreement that casework has to do with individual people who have problems with which they want and need and seek help, and that the goal of casework activity is to be helpful and not hurtful to these clients. Another consideration might be that this help is sought and given within the framework of a social agency; that the process of helping is carried on between a particular professional helping person, the caseworker, and individual clients; and that the helpfulness arises partially from the resources of the agency but also partially from the resources of the individual caseworker —from his strength and knowledge and feeling and his ability to make these available for the use of his clients. It seems unlikely that there would be much dispute over the statement that services may be offered, through casework, to the economically disadvantaged and also to those whose difficulties arise from the nature of their social relationships, whether these be the result of breakdowns such as the dependency of children because of death of parents, or of psychological conflict such as is likely to be found in situations of marital discord. It would probably be further agreed that these categories are not mutually exclusive and are ordinarily found to overlap, but that one or another is likely to provide the primary focus of attention.

It is unfortunate but true that these elements cannot be combined to form the perfect definition of social casework. There is just enough doubt about each of them to give us pause before we can with confidence include it in a general statement.

A Goal of Helpfulness. Perhaps the greatest difficulty arises with regard to the proposition that the purpose of casework is to be helpful rather than hurtful. This is without doubt a simple and universally accepted idea. However, its very simplicity and ready acceptance constitute a problem, for it is meant to stand for something that is not essentially simple. Difficult questions arise. What is the nature of helpfulness, and what determines whether an act is helpful or harmful? Where does—or should—helpfulness end? An examination of these questions will suggest, perhaps, that the proposition is not so much erroneous as it is inadequate.

The question as to what constitutes helpfulness may seem, at first glance and in most situations, to be a simple matter. It frequently evokes the classic story of the drowning man for whom the caseworker can do nothing until he utters a cry for help, the point being that helpfulness consists of those acts and services which are responsive to the felt needs and stated requests of the client. Complications arise, however, when, as is often the case, the client is uncertain about the nature of his needs or is vague in the way he presents them. No worker who has ever faced the distraught wife who wonders whether or not to leave her husband, or the confused mother who wonders whether or not to place her baby, or the fearful patient who wonders whether or not to submit to the serious operation, will have illusions that this question is a simple one. Additional complications arise when the needs and requests of the client are at variance with the objectives of the agency which the caseworker must represent. For example, the worker in a parole department has as his purpose helping men released from prison make the sort of adjustment to the world outside that will be acceptable to society. If a particular parolee sees his need to be the procurement of a gun with which to commit new holdups, the caseworker can scarcely be expected to be helpful to him in this matter. In the same way, the worker in a public assistance agency must adhere to the standards of eligibility and the methods of determining the amount of assistance which have been developed by his agency even though these may be quite inconsistent with an individual client's assessment of his own need.

The implication in all of this is that while helpfulness may come from the outside—from the resources of the agency and its tangible goods and from the resources of the caseworker in the intangible attributes of his personality—it must also come from within the client and express itself in some reorganization of his own resources. There is a good bit of agreement that caseworkers cannot know what will be "the right answer" or what will constitute helpfulness for their clients. This is a kind of judgment they can never properly make. The client alone can decide this, on the basis of his own needs and desires. The caseworker can only help the client to arrive at that answer which will be right for him. There is a good bit of agreement that even if they knew the right answer, caseworkers would not know how to incorporate that right answer into the lives of their clients and that they would not have a right to impose it upon them either by force or guile.

The question which has to do with the extent and limits of helpfulness suggests the need for some means of determining when caseworkers have helped enough and when too much and when too little. This implies that the purpose is not helping alone, but helping toward some goal. There is a timeworn phrase that is subscribed to by many social workers as well as by many other professional and lay people— "helping people to help themselves." This suggests that the caseworker's helpfulness should begin when the client cannot help himself and should end when he can live independently of help. Unfortunately for simplicity, no human being can live independently. All of us persistently need to take both tangible things and feeling from others; strangely and conversely, no human being can ever encounter a problem in life for which there is not an ultimate solution, which can be arrived at without help, in death. Somewhere within these broad extremes the area exists within which casework operates.

With the reservations implicit in the foregoing considerations, perhaps the simple purpose, for casework, of being helpful rather than hurtful, can now be accepted with more reality and conviction. In any event, it should be more acceptable than would be its opposite—that the aim of the caseworker is to be hurtful rather than helpful.

The Role of the Client. The other generally accepted elements of the casework process do not present quite such formidable difficulties as does this matter of helpfulness. That a client stands at the center of the casework process seems obvious. There may be question whether the process exists for him or because of him, whether it represents society's effort to serve him or to control him, but there can be no doubt that his is a central role. This is a plain, but not entirely simple, fact. There is one major and one minor consideration which needs to be weighed before this element can be comfortably accepted for purposes of definition or description. The major consideration has to do with the nature of the role the client plays in the casework process. It is one with regard to which there is a good bit of agreement in theory but perhaps a bit less consistency in practice.

It is only as the client has some recognition of a need to change and some readiness to engage in a process of change that significant change is likely to occur. Most of us have had the experience of being placed under pressure from someone else to acquire new knowledge or attain new skill. Under these conditions our efforts are seldom successful to any remarkable degree. The situation is different when our own concern to learn has been involved. It is true that many individuals present an apparent pliability of character which seems to respond easily to attempts to mold it, so much so that they sometimes seem to be asking others to assume virtually full responsibility for their decisions; it is equally true that even the sturdiest characters do at times yield to external pressures. Still, caseworkers are quite generally convinced that there is little substance or stability, and therefore little virtue, in change that is induced from the outside, whether by the force of authority or the subtlety of persuasion. They are inclined to a belief that even the weakest individual has a capacity to bear, and indeed an inability to evade, responsibility for the consequences of his own decisions. While recognizing that the demands of society represent different things to different people and while believing firmly that society's demands should not be exorbitant for any individual, still they believe that every individual must and can face these demands in his own person, that he can often do this more effectively—or less disastrously—with help from another person, and finally that it has been possible to develop a professional sort of helping that is cognizant of the interest both of the individual and of society. Casework in the administration of financial assistance and other tangible services, in counseling, and in authoritarian settings, despite technical variations, is more or less consistent in observance of this elementary consideration.

The minor consideration with regard to the central role of the client in the casework process has to do with the fact that occasionally the caseworker will work with more than one person at a time. It may be that he will see both parties to a marriage, or a parent and child, or brothers and sisters, or some other combination of people. Hence, it is not strictly accurate to say that casework is always a process of working with an individual. However, the focus of attention will always be on the individual, and the difference between this way of working and that which would be appropriate to a class or club activity should be obvious.

The Role of the Agency. That a social agency provides the framework within which the casework process takes place is perhaps as obvious as the fact that a client plays a central role. Agencies such as the court, the prison, the school, the institutions for children, aged, and handicapped, or the hospital, while not primarily established to offer social services are included within this discussion because their objectives are more effectively attained through the utilization of casework services and personnel. Here, again, we must take into account a major consideration as to the nature of the agency's role and a minor consideration as to whether casework can ever take place outside such an institutional framework.

To deal with the minor consideration first, it must be recognized as a fact that nearly all the activity carried on in the name of social casework does occur within an agency setting. The only bar to the automatic and unequivocal inclusion of agency as an essential element in the casework process is the fact that some few people who are trained as caseworkers do maintain private practices quite apart from any agency structure. Without regard to the quality and effectiveness of what they do, an unanswered question stands as to whether the activities they carry on fall within the range of social casework or whether they represent a kind of helping activity which is sufficiently distinctive as to require a new and different title.

Although most of the people who are known as social caseworkers do carry on their work within the framework of a social agency, there is a good bit of difference of opinion on their part as to the significance of this fact. Most of them would agree that the agency does establish the general area within which they operate. It tells them the kinds of needs they will be expected to serve, the kinds of services they will be able to offer, and in at least a general way the ways in which they will be expected to go about their duties. Similarly, the agency tells the community, and particularly prospective clients, something about the kinds of services they can expect to receive from it and from its workers.

However, agencies themselves differ in the importance they attach to the matter of defining their services and establishing the rules or policies under which those services shall be given. Some agencies restrict their services to certain groups of people or to those whose problem arises from a certain type of situation. An example of the former would be a sectarian agency set up to offer services to the members of a particular religious group; examples of the latter would be agencies which offer only financial assistance to certain categories of needy people, or those set up to offer services to men in conflict with the law, or those offering services related to the adoption of children or to unmarried mothers. Even within those agencies which have established a relatively restricted and clear-cut area of service, difficulties will be encountered, for there are some caseworkers who take the position that once a client has come to them for help in connection with the particular need their agency has been established to meet they then become responsible for any other problems that may emerge as they continue to work with the client. In support of this position they would say that the casework skill with which they offer their specific service is based on sound generic principles which can and must be applied in the offering of any help through the casework process. They would say, in further support of their position, that it is senselessly uneconomical, if not absurd, to ask or expect a client to go to a variety of agencies for help simply because he has more than one problem.

On the other hand, there are a good many other workers in this same sort of rather highly specialized agency who would be inclined to maintain that the area of their responsibility is rather narrowly restricted to the specific service their agency has been established to offer or to the particular need it has been established to meet. They would readily agree that they have a responsibility to be sensitively alert to the presence of other problems, which may relate to the one which brings the client to their attention or which might be quite separate from it, and they would further agree that they not only have a responsibility to provide him with information about available resources for meeting such problems but also to help him in whatever ways they can to make effective use of such resources. They, too, would say that the skill with which they offer their particular service is based on sound generic principles which are applicable to casework activities in any area, but they would further say that it is not possible for them to develop the highest standard of performance in a specialized area such as, let us say, child adoption, and at the same time maintain adequate standards in such disparate areas as child guidance, probation, marital counseling, and the administration of financial assistance. They would also be inclined to say that it is no more senseless for a client to go to several agencies, or to several workers within the same agency if it is departmentalized, for help with a variety of problems than it is for him to go to his doctor when his head hurts but to his dentist when a tooth aches, or that he should go to one lawyer when he is a party to a civil suit but a different one when he is involved in a criminal action. In general, workers of this persuasion will feel that if the caseworker's service is of genuine value and meaning to the client, he will be entirely satisfied to go to some trouble to attain it; workers of the other persuasion are inclined to the view that it is part of the caseworker's responsibility to do everything reasonably possible to make the agency's services available in the most attractive and convenient form.

In addition to the agencies which serve a rather restricted clientele or which operate in a rather highly specialized problem area, there are other agencies, sometimes called multiple-function agencies, which offer service to quite large groups of people and which cover quite a variety of problem areas. Some agencies achieve this status by expressing their responsibility in such broad terms as to include almost every variety of problem; others achieve the same end by proliferating the number of specific problems on which they are prepared to offer service. In these agencies the same considerations with regard to specialization are to be found. Should one worker carry all the cases coming from a given geographical area or should he carry only cases of a particular kind? Should the agency be organized on the basis of functional departments, or will this in effect make of it only a conglomerate of substantially independent agencies? These questions become particularly acute in rural areas where it is altogether likely that the public welfare agency will be providing the only worker, or at best only a few workers, who nevertheless must deal with a great variety of problems.

This question of specialization is, of course, a very important one not only for social work but for many other areas of modern life. An apparently increasing number of caseworkers seem to be expressing the view that only through specialization can they hope that their capacities and skills will achieve their highest development. Many others, looking to the experience of other fields and particularly of medicine, are inclined to the view that with specialization will come a decrease in that sensitivity to the individual client which has always been characteristic of good social casework. Perhaps it may be urged that insensitivity is not an inevitable concomitant of specialization, and that it may be found occasionally among those who make no claim to specialized skill.

In addition to setting these broad limits, the agency also enunciates a basic philosophy and establishes certain more specific rules and regulations under which it, and its caseworkers, will carry on their operations. This philosophy and the attendant policies and procedures are, in most cases, a product of the combined thinking of the executive staff, the governing board, and the operating personnel. Some agencies place considerable emphasis upon having this material reduced to the clearest possible writing in a manual or set of administrative bulletins, and they devote staff and committee meetings to the task of ensuring that the material is up to date with reference to the kinds of needs the workers are currently encountering. In other agencies, similar material may be stated in only the most general terms, with refinements and amendments promulgated and passed along only by word of mouth.

Although agencies vary in the extent to which they enjoy the wholehearted support of the community, the law or charter and the policies and procedures do constitute a sort of contract by which the community gives its sanction to the agency's method of operation. While policies and procedures sometimes serve to restrict the caseworker's freedom of operation, for they set limits for him as well as for the clients, they also serve him as a source of strength when they make it unnecessary for him to exercise personal judgment at times and in situations in which this might be unsound. In public assistance agencies, for example, it is essential that all applicants and recipients be accorded equal treatment. Uniform rules of eligibility, including a standard budget, are one means by which the agency can attempt to attain this equality of treatment. Without such rules the worker would need to decide every aspect of each case on the basis of his personal judgment and the client would thus be subject to the predilections and prejudices of his particular worker. Of course, no matter how meticulously the rules may be drawn, there will be times when it will be necessary for the worker to exercise his judgment, for human individuality seldom fits neatly and comfortably into the categories that are devised for it. It is to be hoped that when such judgment is necessary it will be based upon professional discipline rather than upon personal whim.

Despite the many variations in agency structure and the different ways in which this is used in different agencies perhaps it is reasonable now to conclude that in a great majority of instances the agency is an essential element of the casework process.

The Role of the Caseworker. Just as the client and the agency are obvious but far from uncomplicated elements of the casework process, so too is the presence of a caseworker obvious while the nature of his role

is complex. Just as, in order to understand the meaning of the client
and the agency we must attempt to understand their individual peculiarities and differences, so too will we need to recognize that the caseworker also brings something of his own unique personality to the
process. When we remember that the title of caseworker is given both
to people who have been professionally trained in social work and to
people who are quite without training, we shall have little reason to
be surprised to find that different caseworkers do different things in
what seem to be similar circumstances. It may be a matter of some surprise to learn that differences of quite considerable magnitude, however, exist even within the group of well-trained caseworkers. This
fact will perhaps be a bit less disconcerting if we remember that even
in the much older and more firmly established profession of medicine,
with its more secure base of rigorous scientific research, there nevertheless exist quite marked differences in the methods and procedures of
individual practitioners. Medical diagnosis is by no means infallibly
and precisely uniform, and different methods of treatment for what
seem to be similar ailments are preferred by individual doctors. Beyond this, there is reason to believe that the physician's success in a
given case is dependent not alone on the objective methods of treatment but also upon the quality of the relationship that exists between
himself and his patient. This is without any doubt whatever a similarly
important consideration in the casework process.

While it is not reasonable to expect that all caseworkers will fit
into a neatly simple pattern, it may nevertheless be possible to find
certain attributes which would be generally characteristic of caseworkers as a group or which would at least be the characteristics one would
hope to find in that group. As has already been suggested, they are
quite likely to be warmly interested in, concerned about, and respectful
of other people. This will find expression in a friendliness which is also
characterized by restraint. In their professional relationships they will
be under an unobtrusive but nonetheless real professional discipline.
They may talk too much or too little, but the chances are good that
they will have a rather keen awareness of their natural projective and
receptive tendencies, and they will be inclined to exercise control over
those tendencies in keeping with the needs and interests of their clients
and associates. The chances are also good that they will be relatively,

but certainly not completely, free from prejudice. There will be some tendency for them to be aware of the prejudices they do have and, again, some tendency for them to exercise a discipline in their responses which will, as best it may, counteract those prejudices. In general, however, caseworkers will be more inclined to be interested and intrigued, rather than repelled, by difference. They are likely to understand that different values are attached to human behavior in different cultures, and when a client presents some vagary to them, they will be likely to understand it as an expression of difference in background. They will understand that the same words can mean different things to different people and that the same idea can be expressed in a variety of ways. Consequently, they will make a special effort to be sure they grasp the import, and not just the surface meaning, of what their clients say to them. Similarly, they will make special efforts to ensure that what they say is expressed in a way that will be comprehensible to the particular client. While one of their goals is to help their clients adjust to and live comfortably within the demands of society, they will have little tendency to try to induce their clients to adopt the coloration of gray conformity. Finally, caseworkers are likely to combine humility and an awareness of human limitations with faith in the capacity of all people to be both creators as well as the creatures of their circumstances.

If all of this sounds as though caseworkers represent a paragon of all the virtues, nothing could be further from the truth. While they strive to achieve a knowledge and understanding of human behavior, drawing upon the findings of individual psychology and the social sciences, and while they attempt to increase their sensitivity and freedom from prejudice and ability to be useful, they never attain perfection in these efforts. For the very reason that caseworkers do fall short of their ideals of performance, social work has provided a rather unique process in the form of professional supervision which is designed to protect the interest of the agency in its clients and at the same time to help the caseworker improve and develop his own skills in serving the client.

In this process of supervision the supervisor and the worker regularly confer together and the supervisor regularly reads some portion of the records in the worker's caseload. To the conferences, which are usually held at weekly intervals, both worker and supervisor, but more frequently the former, bring for discussion problems that have become apparent in the worker's performance. Quite frequently, in the process of discussion the worker himself will arrive at new insights and new ideas as to possible ways of proceeding. Occasionally, such ideas will come from the supervisor. It is not impossible, of course, that there will be times when the worker and supervisor will be unable to agree. At periodic intervals, usually annually, the worker and the supervisor will together prepare an evaluatory statement of the worker's performance, including an analysis of his strengths and weaknesses on the job. Throughout the process of supervision, a principle will be found in operation which is similar to one which underlies casework practice: Growth can come, for the worker as well as for the client, only from the capacity of the individual for change and from his interest in changing; help can be given, but it is only as it is taken and used that it is meaningful.

From all of this it may be seen that the caseworker is an essential but highly complicated element in the casework process.

In the case illustrations which accompany various chapters of this book it will be possible to see in operation the elements of the casework process: the goal of helpfulness, the individuality of the client, the structure of the agency, and the professional discipline of the caseworker.

Current Issues in Casework Practice

Casework and Other Helping Professions. Because casework is, as has already been said, an evolving and expanding activity which has not reached the limits of its development, it is beset by many questions for which answers are today only imperfectly known. One of these has to do with the relationship between that form of casework which is concerned with the administration of concrete services and that which deals with the adjustment of interpersonal relationships. Related to this is the question of the relationship between both of these kinds of casework activity and the somewhat similar activities of the psychotherapist, be he psychiatrist, psychoanalyst, or clinical psychologist. There is a discernible tendency on the part of some caseworkers to limit the meaning of the word casework to the area of tangible services, and to refer to work in interpersonal adjustment as counseling. However, the title customarily given to practitioners in both these areas remains that of caseworker, possibly because the title of counselor has already been claimed by other professional disciplines, such as psychology, education, the ministry, and the law. Distinguishing between casework, and particularly the kind of activity that has just been referred to as counseling, and the various psychotherapies is often a difficult matter. All of these disciplines draw heavily upon knowledge of human behavior provided by modern analytical and dynamic psychology, and all of them operate very largely on the basis of the individualized professional relationship between the worker and the client (or the therapist and the patient). Distinguishing features are evident when the caseworker is concerned with tangible services or is utilizing the structural framework of the agency, since psychotherapists do not ordinarily concern themselves with considerations of this character. Some caseworkers, however, and particularly those working in psychiatric settings such as mental hospitals and mental hygiene clinics, have some inclination to view their practice as being substantially the same as that of the therapist, and some psychiatrists assert the view that all casework is, in fact, a kind of psychotherapy. Despite all of the confusion that is suggested by this state of affairs, and the undoubted desirability of achieving more clarity on all these points, experience has demonstrated that representatives of the various helping professions can practice cooperatively, and the team approach that has been developed in some settings may hold promise of increasingly effective service.

Casework in Authoritative Settings. Another issue that is not completely resolved at this time is the matter of the applicability of casework in such nonvoluntary settings as correctional institutions, courts, and parole departments. Because successful casework is dependent upon a voluntary association of the client with the casework agency and the caseworker, it is sometimes maintained, these agencies with their underlying authority do not provide an appropriate setting for casework practice. The fact of the matter is that while the client can usually be compelled to make his physical appearance before the caseworker (and even this is not always possible, as in the case of the parolee who refuses to report to the parole office), there is no power on earth which can force him to bring to the process his own vital participation. For this reason, even in these agencies the caseworker offers service on the basis of understanding and respect for the client as a human being, and the client is free to accept or reject the service as he wishes. If he rejects the service, it is then his own responsibility to work out his own salvation on the basis of his own resources, and one of the factors he will need to consider is the authority and the power the agency may have to impose serious restrictions upon him. This is an authority that is delegated by society and properly exercised by the agency. It is not inherent in the role of the caseworker, and neither is it a proper part of his role to attempt to exert a kind of extralegal sanction upon his client.

There are some who believe that the mere suggestion of this authority in the background destroys the opportunity for successful casework. Steadily increasing, however, is the number of those caseworkers who, having experimented in this area, have come to the conclusion that it is entirely possible to offer the casework relationship on such terms that it can be actively entered into and used by the client, and not merely endured by him. The facts of law are frequently as hard for the criminal to bear as are the facts of medicine for the dangerously ill patient. In neither case is it the responsibility of the caseworker to mitigate the hardship, but it is his responsibility to help the client come to some terms with those hard facts which will be right for him. In a surprising number of instances the terms that are reached are also right from the point of view of society.

Research in Social Casework. One of the greatest needs of social casework today is for a strengthening of the scientific base on which it rests. Caseworkers have seemed a bit reluctant to engage actively in the sort of research that might bring progress in this direction. This is not to suggest that modern casework practice is based on nothing more rigorous than good will and fine intuition. An outstanding characteristic of casework through the years has been the critical self-examination to which its practitioners have exposed themselves. Evidence of this is to be found in their use of case records, the supervisory process, periodic evaluations of the quality of their work, and the growing literature of the field. Nevertheless, there is some reason to believe that caseworkers have been fearful lest the pursuit of knowledge become an end in itself which might deter them from their primary goal, which remains steadfastly to render helpful service to fellow human beings.

Slowly in recent years, there has been growing recognition of the fact that competent research may bring them new tools and new skills to make their services more helpful, and there is now increasing evidence of attempts to subject their practice to more carefully controlled examination.

A number of other obstacles have stood in the way of more thorough research. One has been the fear lest clients lose their identity as human beings when they were submitted to scientific analysis. Interestingly enough, this fear has not always been substantiated in experience. Another obstacle arose from the fact that for something more than the past decade the field has been split by the emergence of two quite articulate, if not vehement, schools of thought with regard to casework practice. This development, which was not unlike developments occurring in other professional fields such as medicine, psychology, and even architecture, provided rich stimulation, but at times the proponents of the two schools seemed inclined to belabor their opponents more with assertions of their convictions than with evidence supporting their views. There was some tendency to examine practice more on the basis of its orthodoxy with regard to the tenets of one school or the other than on the basis of its effectiveness in terms of the results that could be demonstrably attributed to the efforts of the caseworker. There is at present some intimation that the field is moving on to a new synthesis of theory and an accompanying new effort, in new ways, to validate the results of casework practice. This is not an easy task. Since other disciplines concerned with the helping process to date have not been able to provide any really substantial body of reliable information on this subject, it is not to be expected that the field of social casework will, except on the basis of tremendous effort, make any greater contribution. It does seem significant that at this point in its history at least some effort is being made.

Conclusion

The elements of the casework process, while they may be stated with relative simplicity, are in reality matters of considerable complexity. Combined, they constitute a process designed to be helpful rather than hurtful which is carried on within the structure of a social agency between a caseworker, who is concerned for the welfare of his clients but is also ready to represent the will of the community as expressed in the agency's policies, and an individual client who has come to the agency for assistance in connection with a problem, which can be expressed in finite terms, that arises in the course of his efforts to achieve his own well-being in relation to his financial affairs, his feelings about himself, or his relationships with others. It is not a process designed to bring about broad social change but, when it is successful, it is likely to result, for the client, in renewed strength which may make it possible for him to participate more vigorously and more effectively in creative and meaningful life with his fellow men.

BIBLIOGRAPHY

Books and Pamphlets

Aptekar, Herbert H., *Basic Concepts in Social Case Work*. Chapel Hill, University of North Carolina Press, 1941.

de Schweinitz, Karl, *The Art of Helping People Out of Trouble*. Boston, Houghton Mifflin Company, 1924.

Faatz, Anita J., *The Nature of Choice in Casework Process*. Chapel Hill, University of North Carolina Press, 1953.

Fenlason, Anne F., *Essentials in Interviewing*. New York, Harper and Brothers, 1952.

Garrett, Annette, *Interviewing—Its Principles and Method*. New York, Family Service Association of America, 1942.

Hamilton, Gordon, *Principles of Social Case Recording*. New York, Columbia University Press, 1946.

——, *Theory and Practice of Social Casework*, rev. ed., New York, Columbia University Press, 1951.

Hollis, Florence, *Social Case Work in Practice—Six Case Studies*. New York, Family Welfare Association of America, 1939.

Kasius, Cora (editor), *A Comparison of Diagnostic and Functional Casework Concepts*. New York, Family Service Association of America, 1950.

——, *Principles and Techniques in Social Casework, Selected Articles 1940–1950*. New York, Family Service Association of America, 1950.

Lowry, Fern (editor), *Readings in Social Case Work, 1920–1938*. New York, Columbia University Press, 1939.

MacIver, Robert M., *Contribution of Sociology to Social Work*. New York, Columbia University Press, 1931.

Reynolds, Bertha C., *Learning and Teaching in the Practice of Social Work*. New York, Farrar and Rhinehart, 1942.

Richmond, Mary E., *Social Diagnosis*. New York, Russell Sage Foundation, 1917.

———, *What Is Social Case Work?* New York, Russell Sage Foundation, 1922.

Robinson, Virginia P., *A Changing Psychology in Social Case Work*. Chapel Hill, University of North Carolina Press, 1930.

Taft, Jessie (editor), *The Relation of Function to Process in Social Case Work*. Journal of Social Work Process, Volume I, Philadelphia, Pennsylvania School of Social Work, 1937.

Towle, Charlotte, *Common Human Needs*. Washington, D. C., Social Security Board, Federal Security Agency, U. S. Government Printing Office, 1945.

Significant Articles

Aptekar, Herbert H., "Casework, Counseling, and Psychotherapy—Their Likeness and Difference." *Jewish Social Service Quarterly*, XXVII, December 1950, pp. 163–171.

———, "Evolving Concepts in Casework and Counseling." *The Social Service Review*, XXVIII, March 1954, pp. 74–82.

Biestek, Felix P., S. J., "An Analysis of the Casework Relationship." *Social Casework*, XXXV, February 1954, pp. 57–61.

———, "The Non-Judgmental Attitude." *Social Casework*, XXXIV, June 1953, pp. 235–239.

———, "The Principle of Client Self-Determination." *Social Casework*, XXXII, November 1951, pp. 369–375.

Bowers, Swithun, O. M. I., "The Nature and Definition of Social Casework," Part I. *Journal of Social Casework*, XXX, October 1949, pp. 311–317; Part II, XXX, November 1949, pp. 369–375; Part III, December 1949, pp. 412–417.

Munro, Marguerite, "Modern Case Recording: Integrating Casework and Supervision." *Social Work Journal*, XXXII, October 1951, pp. 184–187 and 197; or *The Social Welfare Forum*, 1951, *Procedings of the National Conference of Social Work*, New York, Columbia University Press, 1951, pp. 206–214.

Peters, Mary Overholt, "Talks with Beginning Social Workers, Part I: Gaining Perspective." *Journal of Social Casework*, XXVIII, June 1947, pp. 223–227; Part II: "Understanding the Client," XXVIII, July 1947, pp. 254–260.

Pray, Kenneth L. M., "A Restatement of the Generic Principles of Social Casework Practice." *Journal of Social Casework*, XXVIII, October

1947, pp. 283–290; or *Social Work in a Revolutionary Age and Other Papers by Kenneth L. M. Pray*, Philadelphia, University of Pennsylvania Press, 1949, pp. 244–261; or under title of "Generic Principles of Casework Practice in 1947." *Proceedings of the National Conference of Social Work*, 1947, New York, Columbia University Press, 1947, pp. 227–239.

Rawley, Callman, "A Sampling of Expert Opinion on Some Principles of Casework." *Social Casework*, XXXV, April 1954, pp. 154–161.

chapter 6

Social Services in a Family Focused Agency

Early Emphases

The early agencies ministering to the manifold needs of family members naturally reflected the prevailing thought currents of the times. Throughout the nineteenth century, and particularly in the last half, a preoccupation with the social conditions external to the individual bounded the scope and determined very largely the methods of working with individuals applying for help. Manipulation of situations and people was the accepted mode. If a family was in distress because the principal wage earner had lost his job, what was more natural than to expend efforts toward securing work for him? If children were not in school, the obvious thing to do was to get them into school and keep them there. If a husband and father deserted there was always the force of the law to be invoked. If children were neglected or mistreated, it seemed a simple matter to remove them from their homes and place them in an institution. If they were delinquent, recourse could always be had to the court or, better perhaps, to some recreation center or settlement house, or even to the church. Everything had its "cause," and the "cause" so often lay in the environment. The ready answer was to change the environment or remove the individual from the environment. A part of this service consisted of a plan brought by the worker to which the applicant was expected to subscribe. It might or might not be the client's plan, but what was important was that it was a plan.

Several decades of environmental emphasis were followed by an era during which psychology and biology reigned supreme. Toward the close of the first decade of the present century, Dr. H. H. Goddard, director of research at the Vineland Training School for the feeble-minded, introduced into America the work of two French schoolmen, Binet and Simon. Under the stimulus of the many studies undertaken throughout the country it became more or less a part of the scientific folkways of the day to apply mental tests to every individual who in any way became a charge upon the community. Family caseworkers succumbed to this mental-testing mania and emerged from it little wiser. Biologists, too, had propounded their theories of the inheritance of defects, mental and physical, and for a while welfare workers found an easy explanation for all destitution, whether of the Jukes, the Kallikaks, the Tribe of Ishmael, the Pineys, or others in the community not so visibly affected.

Looking back upon those years of groping one can readily understand the stability which Mary Richmond's *Social Diagnosis* must have introduced in 1917. Here for the first time was a philosophy and a definite technique of casework which afforded caseworkers, to use a technical expression, "a framework of reference." Investigation was for the purpose of establishing facts of personality and the situation upon which a diagnosis was to be made. The end of diagnosis was treatment, which consisted of a plan that took into consideration the entire family, for to Miss Richmond the family in its social setting was the basic social unit of our society.

Influences from Psychiatry

Nor were influences from psychiatry and the early efforts of psychoanalysis lacking. From an examination of the mental capacity and hereditary structure of the individual, workers began to inquire into the functioning of the emotional life. The shift from an economic and sociological determinism to a psychological determinism was evidenced by the social worker's appreciation of the emotional factors as they affected the development of the individual from the time of birth. For family workers emotional elements took on new significance in the recognition of the basic importance of the family and of family relationships in molding the life of individuals, especially during the early formative years.

World War I and the years that followed brought new impressions into the field of social work. Insight into the nature of war neuroses, the deepening knowledge gained from the mental hygiene movement spearheaded by the work of Clifford Beers, the unfolding of many of the earlier theories from psychoanalysis, and the contributions from medical social service departments of hospitals all served to give direction to a newer emphasis in social casework.

This orientation was definitely around the personality of the individual in contrast to the emphasis upon environmental factors. The dynamic psychology that was energized by contributions from psychiatry and psychoanalysis—whether of Freud, Adler, Jung, or Rank—turned attention to the inner life of the client. What assumed significant importance were feelings, emotions, attitudes, as these reflected the repressions, the conflicts, and the struggles within the unconscious life of the individual. The influence of the detailed and searching case history persisted. Instead of the social history, however, bearing accounts of grandparents, parents, births, deaths, operations, schooling, work experience, delinquencies, etc., there developed the technique of permitting the client to reveal at length his feelings and attitudes toward these events—the case history carrying in full this recital. The worker helped the client to express his feelings, and to work with these as they were expressed. Much of the worker's effectiveness depended upon his capacity to introduce those elements into the relationship that enabled the client to assume responsibility for his feelings and for his way of life. Many of these feelings were expressions of conflicts deep within the client's personality which required help in bringing them to the surface, facing them, and then going on to alter their basis or to go on living with them more comfortably than before. It was realized very soon that no worker could take over the client's feelings or his way of life. What the worker did was to help the client—when in need and asking for help—to utilize his own resources in managing his life on a self-sustaining basis.

The Depression of the 1930's

The year 1929 is generally agreed upon as marking the inception of the depression, yet for social workers, particularly family welfare and settlement workers, the anticipations of a collapse were discernible and already tangible a year or more before. The community as a whole, however, did not become actively aroused until 1931–1932. Until it did become aroused, the burden of relief fell most heavily upon the family welfare societies. Case loads which normally had been 40 or 50 per month rose to 60, then 80, then 100. By this time private philanthropy had reached the end of its resources, and government aid was inescapable. Public agency case loads began at 100 and quickly climbed to 200, 250, and then to 300 and higher. What became now of all this specialized psychiatric knowledge and skill when fathers were unemployed, mothers overworked, youth despondent, and the whole family starving?

The immediate task was to meet material needs. Food, shelter and clothing had to be supplied. Efforts had to be made to help wage earners find work, to keep children in school, to provide recreational and leisure-time facilities to individuals dangerously near deterioration. In the public relief office with its staggering case loads workers soon found need for all the skills developed during the preceding decade. People in need were of all classes: many could hardly bring themselves to ask for public help; some fought, in devious ways, against taking relief in any form; others had no hesitation in demanding their "due." Each of these "cases" was an individual, each with his own needs requiring more than merely material gratification. Caseworkers had to be sensitive to these individual needs and to discriminate between those instances in which material assistance was the chief factor and those others in which destitution accentuated existing difficulties and called for a specialized service beyond relief.

The family welfare societies naturally were not unaffected by the events of these turbulent days. Workers literally were swamped with the volume of cases. As the governmental agencies took over more and more of the financial load, family societies were faced with definite decisions about their own functions. Somewhat against their wills they were catapulted into being out-and-out relief agencies in the early years of the depression. Once, however, government had assumed the bulk of relief cases, the family agency was enabled to consolidate its previous casework gains with the experience of mass relief and was better prepared to work out a surer philosophy of family casework than ever before.

The Role of Culture

Note must be made of one more development, which affected the whole field of social work. Anthropologists, and particularly the social anthropologists who had studied the life of contemporary primitive peoples, had been producing an enormous literature of the influence of custom, habit, and forms of social organization upon the behavior of human beings. Sociologists who studied modern society were equally impressed with the role of custom, habit and forms of social organization. Culture, which consists of ways of doing things, ideas, attitudes, habits, behavior, and the material objects attached to these, came to be regarded as the all important aspect of human existence and a determinant of all human behavior. Social workers in turn were affected by the discussion of these culture phenomena and incorporated much anthropological thinking into their own philosophy and practice of casework. Particularly was this true in the family field because the family was regarded as the most fundamental of social groupings and the one which affected the development of the human personality more than any other. The insights that had been gained into the structure and functioning of the personality were fused with the knowledge derived from cultural anthropology. From this came a greater appreciation of the reciprocal interaction of the personality and the culture.

It is not without significance that one of the widely read books in this period (written by a psychiatrist) was called *Personality and the Culture Pattern,* a title which came from Ruth Benedict's *Patterns of Culture.* Caseworkers were constantly called upon to distinguish between difficulties which derived from the seemingly external cultural factors and those imbedded within the emotional make-up of the individual. Caseworkers needed to know and understand that even though man is born into a culture, grows to accept it, fills his status and plays his role within it, he nevertheless also becomes a dynamic agent within it, changing it to meet his own needs more satisfyingly. The skill of the worker very often consisted of an ability to select, out of the many difficulties with which a client was concerned, those for which the client was willing and able to assume some responsibility. This obviously was a shift in emphasis from that day when all problems were to be solved within the self and without relation to the reality factors in the social situations. A further complication lay in the fact that very often individuals were caught between conflicting cultures, of nationality groups, of age groups, and even of behavior norms. What was needed here was an outside person who could understand such conflicting situations and introduce a casework skill by working with the client on the problems of his own confusion and his capacity for mobilizing his own resources toward self-help.

Family Social Work Today

Although public welfare services go back to Elizabethan days in Great Britain and to colonial days in America, it was not until the time of the Charity Organization Societies that the rudiments of a professionalized helping skill were developed. From those Charity Organization Societies have come the modern family service agencies, offering increasingly, an effective helping service to persons with a variety of difficulties affecting them as family members. The aim of these services is to preserve and strengthen family life. The focus is upon the family as a whole; the help is offered to family members for them to use in relation to their own difficulties as these difficulties affect their own lives and the lives of family members around them.

What are these troubles that beset families? Actually they constitute the range of human troubles because most of us live as family members—very few of us live unto ourselves alone, not even the lone person on "skid" row. The troubles may be between adults within the family, for example, husband and wife, with all of the variety of difficulties in which grown-ups can get themselves involved. The troubles may be between the adult (or adults) in the family and the child (or children). The difficulties may revolve around economic and financial distress with all of the accompanying strains, or they may revolve around emotional responses ranging from minor irritations and eccentricities to frank and open mental breakdown. The troubles may also affect family members because of absence rather than presence—a deserting father or husband, a runaway, unwed but pregnant daughter, a son in prison, or a boy in detention. Physical illness, acute or chronic, the dependencies of old age, also bring their share of troubles to family units.[1]

[1] For a more explicit account of some of the individual and community factors bearing on people's troubles the reader is referred to the pamphlet by the arresting title *The*

These generalized categories could be itemized in a thousand or ten thousand separate "cases," each unique, and yet all having a certain common denominator. The common denominator is the reaching out beyond the immediate family grouping for help. Not a family exists that does not have its troubles. Perhaps the great majority of families manage to handle their difficulties themselves. Others may reach out for help to relatives and friends. It is when help from those sources is not available or is not effective (and nearness to a person often militates against the effectiveness of help) that the approach may be made to something as impersonal as a social service agency. It may be that this very impersonalness, coupled with experience and skill as offered by a professional worker, is what renders the family service agency a useful resource.

Family service agencies are supported by voluntary contributions usually through local community chests. Since the funds are limited and since the public welfare department is responsible for meeting the inadequacies of basic maintenance, the family agency cannot, and should not try to, make any long-time indefinite financial commitments to applicants or clients. The public welfare department grants financial aid according to rules of eligibility that have been defined in the law or developed through administrative regulations consistent with the meaning and purpose of the law: old-age assistance, aid to the blind, aid to dependent children, aid to the permanently and totally disabled, and general assistance. Most family service agencies have a modicum of financial assistance available which is used as an emergency and short-term resource. It may be used to help the client to use the service of the agency, but in no wise should it be used as a bait or a trap. The problems which bring persons to family agencies and with which such agencies are qualified to help usually involve emotional and behavioral complications that go far beyond the matter of financial assistance. The role of the worker is to focus on the basic problem that brings the

---

High Cost of Unhappy Living, published by the Family Service Association of America (undated), and also Buell, Bradley, *Community Planning for Human Services.* New York, Columbia University Press, 1952. For example, in the latter study, reference is made to the 41,000 families of St. Paul, Minnesota, who were receiving some form of agency service during November 1948. A group of these families, 6,600 in number and constituting 6 percent of the city's families, "were suffering from such a compounding of serious problems that they were absorbing well over half of the combined services of the community's dependency, health, and adjustment agencies." *Ibid.,* p. 9.

client and to deal with it as such rather than to tease or coerce the client by a proffer of financial assistance. When, however, funds are granted on an emergency and facilitating basis, the accountability for their constructive use is just as great, even though voluntarily contributed, as is true of the accountability of public funds according to law and administrative interpretation. In the responsible family agency funds used with the client are not an end in themselves, they are a means to a constructive end, designed to contribute toward the integrity—the wholeness—of the family group.

The foregoing reference requires a word further about the use of funds in a public welfare department. The worker in such an agency is offering, essentially, a family casework service. The same quality of casework service may be expected of the worker as in other caseworking agencies. It is not one bit less professional service because financial assistance is requested or granted. Nor is it a matter of granting assistance on a coin-slot basis and then assuming that casework service will follow. The entire service should be casework in essence. This point will be elaborated in the succeeding chapter which discusses public assistance as casework.

In the search for a focus for family casework, there seems to be fairly general agreement upon the necessity of dealing with the problems which concern the family as a whole. In discussing this M. Robert Gomberg observes:

> It is accepted generally that the essential purpose of the family agency is to help preserve and enhance family life and coherence, wherever this represents a solution for the family and is within the facilities of the agency. It follows, then, that in carrying out the agency's purpose, the worker's perspective must necessarily embrace the relation of the client's application to the family as a whole, and the effect that the agency's service may have on it. True, the client must be individualized, but certainly he need not be isolated from his role as a family member.[2]

In addition to all of the skills discussed in the previous pages which apply in all casework settings, the family caseworker must be aware, eternally, of the roles of the respective members within the family group. In our culture the roles of father, mother, and children are fairly well

---

[2] Gomberg, M. Robert, "The Specific Nature of Family Case Work," in Taft, Jessie (editor), *A Functional Approach to Family Case Work*. Philadelphia, University of Pennsylvania Press, 1944, p. 114.

defined and service to the family as a whole must be related to this. On this point Gomberg, with insight, remarks:

No worker must be concerned as to whether meeting a particular request in the way it is presented, while serving a specific physical need of the family, may, on the other hand, only widen the breach in family unity. Neither the worker nor the agency can decide for the client what he is ready or willing or able to do in meeting his individual family problem. But the agency does have a responsibility for the role it assumes in the client's life in offering or withholding service. It has a responsibility for the way in which it offers service and the condition under which it offers them.[3]

In the chapters that follow it will be evident that the focus of the service differentiates the various areas of social casework practice. The boundaries cannot be defined clearly in all instances; in fact there may appear to be overlapping, but a recognition of the focus of the service makes possible a clarity that leads to increasingly useful service.[4]

How a Family Service Agency Works

Practically all, if not all, of the family societies in the United States are located in cities, although their service is available to residents in adjacent areas. At the present time there are over two hundred and fifty societies constituting the Family Service Association of America offering a "range of services, provided by government and voluntary agencies, that are designed to strengthen family life and to help family members with problems of social adjustment and intrafamily relation-

---

[3] *Op. cit.*, pp. 117–118.

[4] As in every field of human endeavor, so in family casework there are differences of approaches, points of view, emphases, procedures, and techniques. The earlier review of developments from the early Charity Organization movement, through the period heavily influenced by the diagnostic approach of Mary Richmond, then the varying emphases from psychiatry and psychoanalysis did not give, perhaps, enough sense of differences up to the depression period of the 1920's and 1930's. The differences were there, but it is not necessary here to be detained too long with their exposition. What is important for our present purpose is to recognize the existence of two fairly well-defined points of view within the family casework field—or the larger casework field as well. Recent usage has placed the label *diagnostic* on one and *functional* on the other. Each has drawn upon different psychological orientations—the diagnostic largely from Freudian (Sigmund Freud) psychoanalysis, the functional from the Rankian (Otto Rank) therapy. Each stoutly defends its particular approach, emphasis, and technique as fundamentally sound and effective—i.e., helpful to clients. A provocative, but hardly productive, effort to deal with these two conceptualizations is found in Kasius, Cora, *A Comparison of Diagnostic and Functional Casework Concepts.* New York, Family Service Association of America, 1950. For a recent statement of the functional approach see Faatz, Anita J., *The Nature of Choice in Casework Process.* Chapel Hill, University of North Carolina Press, 1953.

ships." [5] Most of these agencies are private family societies, but in a number of instances they are associated with and a part of the local county public welfare department.

Where the size of the community and funds permit it, a staff will consist of an executive secretary, a supervisor or supervisors, and a number of caseworkers. A laymen's board of men and women usually serves in an advisory capacity to the executive and acts in a liaison capacity between the agency and the community. In the larger cities much of the executive's time and skill is spent in working with the board, with the supervisory personnel, and with various agencies in the community. Where the size of the agency does not warrant such specialization the executive may often serve as a supervisor and in addition carry a case load. Funds are usually allocated on an annual basis and may be derived from individual contribution, or the local chest or financial federation, or income from endowments that have been placed with the society.

The agency offers to provide a service to the entire community, and unless there are sectarian or racial restrictions, all classes of applicants are eligible. Individual members of the family group may apply of their own initiative, having known about the agency or having been told by a friend or a past or present client. Others may come by referral from another social agency, such as a children's aid society, a probation department, a medical social service department, or a public welfare office. In still other instances various groups in the community, such as the school, a church, or a service club, may suggest to a possible applicant the nature of the family society services.

In the course of the application interview the applicant has the opportunity to tell his story, the reason for coming, how he sees the difficulty which brings him to the agency, and where and how he wants the agency to help. Some of the worker's activity may consist of listening as well as in helping the applicant to express himself. From time to time the worker may enter a question or make a simple remark which will do much to bring out the real situation that troubles the person asking for help. The worker needs to know enough of the applicant's

[5] Blackburn, Clark W., "Family Social Work." *Social Work Year Book.* New York, American Association of Social Workers, 1954, p. 203.

difficulty to be convinced that it is of such a nature that the family agency can help. The intake worker, or application secretary, realizes that most frequently the presenting symptom—what the applicant sees as the trouble—may not be the real difficulty, but the worker accepts the situation as the applicant brings it, simply because it concerns such apparent external factors as unemployment, dependency, desertion, legal action, etc. If the worker has helped the applicant to express his situation as he sees it, and to ask for the services of the agency, and if the worker feels the agency can be of assistance, the applicant becomes a client and another worker, or sometimes the same worker, called a caseworker, becomes active. Social work usage now calls the client's situation a case, the record of the client's relation to the agency a case history, and the worker who continues the service with the client a caseworker.

The caseworker begins by meeting the client's difficulties where the client places them. It may very well be that the distress which brings the client is that of unemployment, desertion, legal action or the hundred and one other situations that convince the client of the need for help; and if this proves to be true, it is in that area that the caseworker exercises his skill in endeavoring to help the client mobilize his own resources and also to make available those of the agency and the community.

Interviews may continue over a period of time depending upon the needs of the case. They may be held at regular intervals, say once a week or month, or irregularly according to the client's needs or the worker's understanding of the situation. The visits may be made by the client to the worker's office, or by the worker to the client's home. All of these details of client-worker-agency relationship are mutually agreed upon.

Service will continue until such time as the client feels he has received sufficient help not to need the worker any more, or until the worker raises the question about ending the visits. Occasionally visits will stop because the client cannot take help, and sometimes because the worker cannot give help. In some instances the trouble may be so deep-seated as to require an intensive service beyond the bounds of a family agency. Frequently the worker will mention the possibility of getting further help in another agency or with a psychiatrist, provided the client is ready to use such help.[6]

Family Casework and Agency Settings

Family casework is practiced in family service agencies. That seems like a fairly obvious and complete statement. However, an analysis shows that it is neither obvious nor complete. The latest Directory of Member Agencies of the Family Service Association of America shows that while every agency member provides family casework services and while the bulk of the agencies provide only that, nevertheless, a number of them also provide child placement and travelers aid services. The fact that family service agency houses the travelers aid service or provides the travelers aid service through staff members may be a sign that it is more economical to accomplish all that within one agency setting, or it may be that quite properly the travelers aid function is essentially a family casework function. For the time being a family member, as a lone person, may be in transit and in distress, but the service needed is generally related to his family situation. These remarks are not to be interpreted as intending that the family service agency is taking over the travelers aid function. Travelers aid agencies still carry the bulk of their services in the familiar settings of railroad stations, bus terminals, and even airport terminals in cities where there is considerable in and out traffic. In many smaller communities where the volume of traffic does not warrant a service at the terminals, it may be provided through existing agencies—such as family service. The important point here is that wherever it is offered, it demands essentially a family casework skill and service.

Another service, provided under different auspices but essentially a family casework service, is that offered by the Home Service offices of the American Red Cross. This service developed out of World War I and had been strengthened in the intervening years up to World War II. During and after World War II these services have been accelerated, not only because of the size of our army, but also because of the rush by which we sought to demobilize our armed forces. With Selective Serv-

---

[6] A more technical, but nevertheless clear, statement of the casework services in a family agency is developed in the excellent monograph published by the Family Service Association of America entitled *Scope and Methods of the Family Service Agency,* 1953, pp. 4–8.

ice now apparently a permanent part of our national life, there is every indication that the services performed by Red Cross Home Service offices will continue as a characteristic part of the community's service linking the soldier away from home with his home and vice versa.

The Home Service program provides a casework service in personal and family problems to members of the armed forces and their dependents. It offers assistance in applying for government benefits. It renders temporary financial assistance to wives and children during the period pending the first receipt of family allowance or allotment and during periods when such payments are delayed or interrupted. It assists veterans and their dependents in the development and preparation of applications for veterans' benefits. It also makes appropriate referral to other community agencies for whose services the applicants may appear to be eligible. Throughout all of the foregoing there is emphasis upon the essential family casework care of Home Service.[7]

Family casework services are being offered under religious auspice —Protestant, Catholic, Jewish. In some instances these services may be set up within a family agency supported entirely by a denomination within a particular city or by the central or national administrative body of the organization. In other instances the family service may be set up by a number of churches or denominations within a given area, i.e., Family Service of the Main Line Federation of Churches, Inc. In some communities while there may not be a denominationally supported family service agency, there may be well defined policies worked out between churches and the agency—particularly concerning referrals, etc. There are many signs of an increased awareness by both churches and social agencies of the relatedness of their services. Instead of, as formerly, a strict delineation between the two areas, there is increasingly a disposition to deal with the respective forms of interest and to appreciate their essential mutuality. As social workers become more comfortable and less defensive in dealing with the clergy, and as ministers receive more knowledge of social welfare during seminary training and later by service on social agency boards, a more workable relationship is established between the two helping professions.

[7] Home Service is one of the many services provided by the American Red Cross and is mentioned in this chapter because its focus is family social work. Other services are within the area of psychiatric social work, medical social work, hospital recreation work and will be considered in the appropriate chapters.

Developments in the Family Service Field

It has been said several times in this chapter that family service agencies have lent themselves to meeting a variety of human needs. Frequently this has been expressed by setting up on an experimental basis a service in response either to an insistent community demand or to the conviction of the family agency staff. These services are sometimes referred to as "outpost" services, implying a reaching out from agency to community in areas not previously cultivated. The family service agency is usually in a better position to do this than other agencies because of its greater flexibility and usually because no new agency needs to be created to initiate the service. An example of this is in counseling services for industrial workers. In many such instances the family agency assigned a staff member to an industrial plant for the purpose of counseling with workers on problems, chiefly personal, which interfered with their industrial productivity and adjustment. Sometimes the help provided took the form of counseling interviews in the plant, or, more frequently, in the offices of the family agency. At other times the help might come from other community agencies to which the industrial worker had been referred, according to the nature of the problem presented and the help needed. A recent trend has been to work out these arrangements and services with the unions resulting in fuller participation and utilization of community services by the larger union membership.

Another area of service that has been given increasing emphasis by family agencies involves marital problems. Family service agencies, basing their philosophy of usefulness upon the wholeness of the family and its useful function for all members, have offered husbands and wives an opportunity to discuss their difficulties with a person skilled in counseling. Not only may the discussion of attitudes, ideas, and feelings be helpful to the marriage partners who are in conflict, but the response of the partners to the participation of the worker may make for movement toward unity rather than separation. However, even though the interest of the family agency is directed toward the unity of the family, there are times when neither the disposition of partner (or partners) nor the skill of the worker can bring this about—no more in this area than in any other can success be guaranteed. In all honesty, it must be stated that other professional workers—psychologists, sociologists, social hygienists—are also offering services to those with marital problems, each worker seeking to help according to his particular professional orientation.

Homemaker service has been demonstrated within recent years by family service agencies. This is a service provided by an agency to a family on a temporary short-time basis for the purpose of keeping the family together in its home while the mother is absent or incapacitated. The homemaker person is employed by the agency and performs, under agency supervision, the essential services within a home that enable the family members to stay together until the mother resumes her usual role. In most instances such services are designed to meet the needs of families with children, especially small children. However, this same principle is being extended to families in which there are aged persons and in which the family can remain together during emergency and short duration crises.

The payment for service on a fee basis is another development that has found increasing acceptance. There was a time when the underprivileged or marginal family was of especial concern to the family service agency and when much of the funds of the agency were used for material relief. With the assumption of the income maintenance function by the public welfare department the voluntary agency has been freed to deal with some of the other hazards to family integrity. Clients not only were willing to pay on a fee basis—as for other services, such as medical—but were more inclined to put a good deal of themselves into the taking of help. Agency workers were quick to appreciate the efficacy of such participation and to realize the meaning which payment has for clients.

Another development within recent years that calls for mention is in the area of social services for the aging and the aged. Recognition of this fact is reflected in the addition of a chapter on the aged in the present revision of this volume. There, not only is to be found the substantiation of our population changes, but also some description of the additional services that have been provided. The case illustration which accompanies that chapter is an instance of services made available to an older person within the setting of a family service agency. In all likelihood there will be an increase rather than a diminution of those services.

The inclusion of services to children and the joining of children's and family services within the one agency has progressed within late years. Sometimes this takes the form of certain workers being assigned to children's work or the establishment of a division within the agency. Frequently these latter arrangements come about through the merger of previously existing children's and family agencies. For example, the Family and Children's Society of Baltimore is a consolidation of the Family Welfare Association, Henry Watson Children's Aid Society, Maryland Society to Protect Children from Cruelty and Immorality, together with several other societies serving family members. In other instances instead of a family society and a children's agency being established separately, it is becoming more common for one new agency to be established which aims to serve all members of the family group.

Conclusion

Perhaps no more fitting conclusion for this chapter can be found than the words of Linton Swift, the General Director of the Family Welfare Association of America for the last twenty-one years of his life. Before his death in 1946 Mr. Swift had enunciated his philosophy in what he termed a creed for social workers. This creed stands not only for the principles of social casework but for all of social work under whatever auspices and in whatever agencies it is practiced. Mr. Swift saw these principles as an ideal toward which all social workers might well strive.

I respect the dignity of the individual human personality as the basis for all social relationships.

I have faith in the ultimate capacity of the common man to advance toward higher goals.

I shall base my relations with others on their qualities as individual human beings, without distinction as to race or creed or color or economic or social status.

I stand ready to sacrifice my own immediate interests when they conflict with the ultimate good of all.

I recognize that my greatest gift to another person may be an opportunity for him to develop and exercise his own capacities.

I shall not invade the personal affairs of another individual without his consent, except when in an emergency I must act to prevent injury to him or to others.

I believe that an individual's greatest pride, as well as his greatest contribution to society, may lie in the ways in which he is different from me and from others, rather than in the ways in which he conforms to the crowd. I shall therefore accept these differences and endeavor to build a useful relationship upon them.

I shall always base my opinion of another person on a genuine attempt to understand him—to understand not merely his words, but the man himself and his whole situation and what it means to him.

As a first essential to the understanding of others, I shall constantly seek a deeper understanding and control of myself and of my own attitudes and prejudices which may affect my relationships.[8]

BIBLIOGRAPHY

Books and Pamphlets

Aptekar, Herbert H., *Basic Concepts in Social Case Work*. Chapel Hill, University of North Carolina Press, 1941.

Buell, Bradley, and Associates, *Community Planning for Human Services*. New York, Columbia University Press, 1952.

Faatz, Anita J., *The Nature of Choice in Casework Process*. Chapel Hill, University of North Carolina Press, 1953.

Fenlason, Anne F., *Essentials in Interviewing*. New York, Harper and Brothers, 1952.

Gomberg, M. Robert and Levinson, Frances T., *Diagnosis and Process in Family Counseling: Evolving Concepts Through Practice*. New York, Family Service Association of America, 1951.

Hamilton, Gordon, *Theory and Practice of Social Casework*. New York, Columbia University Press, revised edition, 1951.

Hollis, Florence, *Women in Marital Conflict: A Casework Study*. New York, Family Service Association of America, 1949.

Hush, Howard, *Eastwick, U.S.A.* New York, E. P. Dutton and Co., 1948.

Josselyn, Irene M., *The Adolescent and His World*. New York, Family Service Association of America, 1952.

Kasius, Cora (editor), *Principles and Techniques in Social Casework: Selected Articles, 1940–1950*. New York, Family Service Association of America, 1950.

Koos, Earl Lomon, *Families in Trouble*. New York, King's Crown Press, 1946.

Mudd, Emily Hartshorne, *The Practice of Marriage Counseling*. New York, Association Press, 1951.

Robinson, Virginia P., *A Changing Psychology in Social Case Work*. Chapel Hill, University of North Carolina Press, 1930.

[8] Swift, Linton B., *The Family*, XXVII, May 1946, pp. 117–118.

Scope and Methods of the Family Service Agency. New York, Family Service Association of America, 1953.

Taft, Jessie (editor), *Counseling and Protective Service as Family Case Work.* Philadelphia, Pennsylvania School of Social Work, 1946.

——, *Family Casework and Counseling: A Functional Approach.* Philadelphia, University of Pennsylvania Press, 1948.

——, *A Functional Approach to Family Case Work.* Philadelphia, University of Pennsylvania Press, 1944.

Significant Articles

Gomberg, M. Robert, "The Responsibilities and Contributions of Social Work in Strengthening Family Life," *Social Casework,* XXXIV, October 1953, pp. 330–335.

——, "Trends Toward Family-Oriented Treatment in Social Casework." *Jewish Social Service Quarterly,* XXX, Spring 1954, pp. 255–263.

Hanford, Jeannette, "The Place of the Family Agency in Marital Counseling." *Social Casework,* XXXIV, June 1953, pp. 247–258.

Josselyn, Irene M., "The Family as a Psychological Unit." *Social Casework,* XXXIV, October 1953, pp. 336–343.

Lerner, Samuel H., "Effects of Desertion on Family Life." *Social Casework,* XXXV, January 1954, pp. 3–8.

Mead, Margaret, "What Is Happening to the American Family?" *Proceedings of the National Conference of Social Work,* New York, Columbia University Press, 1947, pp. 61–74; also *Journal of Social Casework,* XXVIII, November 1947, pp. 323–330.

Neumann, Frederika, "Administrative and Community Implications of Fee Charging." *Social Casework,* XXXIII, July 1952, pp. 271–277.

Scherz, Frances H., "What's Family-Centered Casework?" *Social Casework,* XXXIV, October 1953, pp. 343–349.

Smalley, Ruth, "The Significance of the Family for the Development of Personality." *The Social Service Review,* XXIV, March 1950, pp. 59–66.

Taft, Jessie, "A Conception of the Growth Process Underlying Social Case Work Practice." *Social Casework,* XXXI, October 1950, pp. 311–318.

Townsend, Gladys E., "Short Term Contact With Clients Under Stress." *Social Casework,* XXXIV, November 1953, pp. 392–398.

The Bolton Family

EDITH MITROCSAK,
Casework Supervisor
The Family Society
Wilmington, Delaware

In present-day America, the family is still the recognized unit in which we grow, develop, and live. When the balance within this family unit is disturbed so that the members within it find little emotional satisfaction and security, families and individuals often look to the outside for help. The community has provided agencies as one of the means by which a family can be helped to re-establish this vital unit. The Family Society of Wilmington, Delaware, which was established in the 1880's, is one of the agencies set up in one community to meet this challenge. Its function as stated in the agency *Manual* is "to give help to people who are troubled by problems disturbing their family life. Services are available to families and individuals irrespective of social, racial, religious, or other personal characteristics. Help is offered through counseling, financial assistance, and referral service. The basis for eligibility is determined by the immediate or potential usefulness of the service to the client. The medium for giving agency service is social casework, based upon a relationship process voluntarily established between client and worker, and consciously defined in terms of content and time."

The Bolton case, which follows, represents a problem which often reaches a family agency, and in which a unique service is offered through casework help. Mrs. Bolton, who was referred by the Legal Aid Society, an organization in the community offering free legal counsel to those persons unable to pay for it, requested an appointment to discuss the family situation with a caseworker. She was offered an appointment for May 7th. The application interview gave Mrs. Bolton the opportunity to tell the caseworker the nature of her problem and to explore with the worker whether she felt she could use the help of the caseworker in this agency with its specific service as a means of finding a more satisfactory adjustment for herself and her children.

The application is the first important step in the helping process. The agency's *Manual* describes the purpose of this part of the process as follows: "The client is given an opportunity to discuss his problem and to ask for the kind of help he feels he needs. The caseworker has the responsibility for helping the client to clarify his problem, and to understand the kind of help which is available through the agency. Together, the client and the caseworker evaluate and ultimately decide whether or not the services of the agency will be useful in a constructive way. If a client with his need, and the agency with its services, come together, continued service is offered."

In this application interview, Mrs. Bolton informed the worker that she and Mr. Bolton had been married for almost twenty years and that they had two sons, Arthur, aged 16, and Michael, aged 8. Mr. Bolton had been employed for twelve years as a mail man and had no other specific skill aside from being "handy" as a mechanic. Mr. Bolton had been arrested on a charge of threatening bodily harm against Mrs. Bolton and Arthur. He had been drinking and was becoming increasingly lax in his support of the family, which created frequent arguments in the home. The situation came to a head with Mr. Bolton's arrest as a result of Arthur's calling the police when he was frightened by his father's threats. At the court hearing Mr. Bolton was committed to the County Workhouse for ten days, primarily because of his belligerent attitude toward the judge in the process of the hearing. Mrs. Bolton decided she could not continue with the marriage and came to the agency to request help in re-establishing a separate home for herself and her sons.

During the interview Mrs. Bolton also informed the caseworker that she and her husband had been separated for a short period two years previously, but they were reconciled after Mr. Bolton begged her to return to him. After the worker referred to the two separations, Mrs. Bolton said that this time she saw no hope for a change and had already given up their house because she could not keep up the high rental alone. She had moved the two children to her parents' home, where she planned to stay until she decided what steps she could take to resettle herself.

The worker saw Mrs. Bolton as a mild woman of 39, who was disorganized and confused by the events of the past few weeks. The family had been in serious debt, and Mrs. Bolton had no means of supporting her family. She was, therefore, requesting some financial help. She presented herself almost as a lost "little girl," despite her many years of marriage and the fact that she was the mother of two boys. She spoke of wanting to complete arrangements to store her furniture and then needed help to plan how she could go on without her husband. The application was accepted.

Mrs. Dean, an experienced worker with three years' service with the agency, was assigned to Mrs. Bolton. The agency had agreed to help Mrs. Bolton and the children with a food allowance since her elderly parents were in no position to provide this need for them. As noted in the description of the agency's function, limited financial assistance (as defined by an agency budget) is available when the need exists as a part of the total service in order to make it possible for the family or individual to live while planning with the caseworker. Mrs. Dean planned for her first interview with Mrs. Bolton. By the time of the interview, Mrs. Bolton had made arrangements for storing the furniture, and she was ready to start planning for her future. As noted before, Mr. and Mrs. Bolton were in debt. They had purchased some new furniture and had paid for only a small part of it. This was one of the things worrying Mrs. Bolton when she came to see Mrs. Dean for her first interview. She avoided discussion of the separation itself, holding on to the specifics and arrangements for moving and settling the matter of the furniture. Mrs. Bolton came in for her appointment full of her problem, and it was clear that the impact of the separation was being felt by her in this interview. Mrs. Dean's interview follows:

5/18. Mrs. B arrived a few minutes late for her appointment for which she apologized. She looked worried and upset. As I commented on this, Mrs. B immediately plunged into telling me that last week her mother, Mrs. Ralston, had a bad nose bleed, and was now in the hospital. She went into great detail about what she had tried to do for her, and I commented on this being an additional worry and concern, with everything else she had. Mrs. B responded to this immediately, saying it was upsetting, all this coming on top of her separation and moving. However, she thought her mother would be in the hospital for at least four days, until they brought her blood pressure down. Then, in a rapid voice, Mrs. B said her father said that Mrs. Ralston probably had too much excitement. She guessed he meant that the trouble with Mr. B and her moving in probably attributed to her mother's attack. I commented that Mrs. B seemed worried about that too. In a nervous way, Mrs. B went on to blame herself and to say she did not know what else she could do. I recognized that she had been going through a lot too, and it could not be pleasant for her under the circumstances.

Mrs. B then told me that her husband had been released from the workhouse on Thursday, and was upset at finding them gone from the apartment. She did not know whether he had returned to his job as a mail carrier yet, but felt she would need to take some steps toward support for the boys, and was planning to talk with the Legal Aid about her next step with the court. Mrs. B related this reluctantly and with very little conviction. When I wondered if she was not almost sorry she had left her husband, Mrs. B said she would not have if there had been any other hope that he would "do right." She went on to tell me that the boys did not want to go through all this again, and neither did she. I thought it was a hard decision to make, and though she is feeling it had to be, it is a difficult one to make final. Mrs. B heartily agreed, but went on to tell me of a neighbor of her mother's who thought she ought to consider such a decision very seriously. On the other hand, she contrasted this with her parents' feeling that she should remain separated now. I thought this was always part of the problem, the pressures from interested friends and relatives, and that she probably could see something in what both were saying. Mrs. B sighed, and said she certainly could. She went back a bit, as to how things might be if he were different, but quickly remembered that she did separate before and returned to him, only to find a year later that they were back to the old trouble. I guessed it was a difficult thing to ignore, a plea from a husband and a promise that things would be better. At this spot, I felt a real pull on Mrs. B's part toward the hope that the marriage was not completely over, and some expression that maybe the workhouse "taught him something." I asked Mrs. B whether she really believed that just holding Mr. B in prison for ten days was going to turn the trick. She guessed not. I could understand how she could grasp anything different. On the other hand, maybe Mr. B might be feeling bitter about this too. Mrs. B was not too ready for this, and went on saying how hard it was going to be to plan now. I, too, thought that this was difficult to do alone, and hoped she saw this agency's help as a way of going ahead differently. Mrs. B brightened considerably as she said she never knew there was such a place before, and it was so good to be able to have someone to discuss all this with.

In the remaining part of the interview, Mrs. Bolton was able to verbalize her feeling that she actually did not want to remain separated. As the worker helped Mrs. Bolton to examine this wish, in relation to her initial request to the agency, Mrs. Bolton could recognize that she wanted to see her husband to find out how he felt about all of this. She responded quickly to the suggestion on Mrs. Dean's part that the agency was ready to offer help to Mr. Bolton too, should he feel he wanted to request an appointment. When Mrs. Bolton came to the agency, she had felt strongly that she could not go on with this marriage; her husband was failing in his responsibilities to the family, and more than that, the hurt was deep because he had threatened her and the children. This was the feeling that pervaded the application interview. Though a caseworker accepts this, there is also the awareness that Mr. and Mrs. Bolton have been married for twenty years. Under the best circumstances, Mrs. Bolton will not give the relationship up without pain and real struggle. In this interview Mrs. Bolton gave the clue which made it possible for the caseworker to help Mrs. Bolton recognize the ambivalence within herself and that there was a side of her which still wanted this marriage. Though prior to this interview Mrs. Bolton had set about involving herself in the externals necessary to carry out the decision she had made originally, this interview showed sharply that the meaning of the separation itself and the discomfort accompanying that was beginning to be unfolded. Her quick response to Mrs. Dean's recognition of this side, revealed clearly that her wish to set up a home without her husband was indeed not as strong as her words indicated at the time of application. On the other hand, for the worker to accept this as meaning that Mr. and Mrs. Bolton were now ready to be reconciled would be just as false. They had tried it a year ago, and it had not worked. The worker then can only offer Mr. and Mrs. Bolton the opportunity to consider this present trouble and to help them, through her knowledge and skill, to decide whether they are ready to go on together, or separately.

On May 21 Mrs. Bolton called Mrs. Dean to let her know that she had seen her husband and that he was anxious to arrange an appointment with her. Later that same day, Mr. Bolton called and an appointment was set for him for May 25. When Mr. Bolton came to see Mrs. Dean, his uncomfortableness was apparent, and he immediately tried to take over the interview by discussing a number of less important external problems, such as his job, etc. Mrs. Dean went along with some of this, but eventually took responsibility for focusing the purpose of their meeting.

5/25. Mr. B was a few minutes early for his appointment. He is a spare, brusque, sharp-featured man, who holds his shoulders tightly, giving the impression of moving deliberately. He took me in rapidly, but looked away just as quickly and made an attempt to appear casual by occupying himself with his pipe during most of the interview. He would often glance at the window as though avoiding looking at me. After introducing myself, I said I gathered he was not feeling too happy about being here today. Mr. B tossed this off by raising his shoulders, but said neither yes nor no. However, he quickly began to talk about his job, wondering whether the Postmaster would press charges because he had been absent from work for several days last week. I acknowledged that he probably was concerned about many things today. After some further discussion about this, Mr. B concluded in a rather resigned voice he guessed he would have to wait to see what they did. We were silent for a moment, and I finally said I gathered he was here because he needed to talk about his marriage. Mr. B began by saying how good his twenty years of marriage had been, and that he was sure he wanted to go back to his wife and children. He had even spoken to his wife and his oldest son, Arthur, about this yesterday, and they all decided there should be a reconciliation. I accepted Mr. B's feeling of wanting so much to return to his family, but I said I knew this was the second time they had actually been separated. Mr. B quickly came back saying that he and his family were going to get together, and nobody was going to try to stop them. I gathered that Mr. B was feeling that the agency was trying to do that. This he ignored by repeating that nobody could. It seemed to me that Mr. B was certainly feeling like an awful lot of people were getting in his way, and I thought it must make him puzzled or even angry. Mr. B gave a rather bitter laugh, denying that it bothered him. He knew what was best for his family and himself and that was that. I agreed that he and his wife were indeed the only ones who could decide their own next move, and it would be presumptuous on my part to say what was right or wrong for them.

Mr. B almost spit out his words as he minimized the whole situation leading up to his arrest. He told me in some detail the policeman who took him to the magistrate, and even the magistrate, did not know why he was arrested, he was not drinking, he was only "talking loud" in his home and he felt justified under the circumstances. I said that I knew it could not have been a pleasant experience for him. I recognized his feeling that he was arrested without justification, and that might make it more difficult for him to get beyond what happened; yet, I thought whatever happened must have frightened his son, who I understood, called the police. Mr. B stopped for a moment and then, as though ignoring the thought, went on describing what a terrible place the workhouse was. I thought it must have been just as bad as he described. For a moment Mr. B dropped his defensive tone, and said rather pathetically he was the only person in his family who had ever spent time in the workhouse. I agreed that that was indeed hard to have to bear, and

I was sure he did not want to go through the same experience again. Mr. B regained his former tone, and then said in a steely voice he was not going to.

The remaining part of the interview showed some move on Mr. B's part to consider how he and his wife might get together. By the end he was ready to say he felt the agency might help them. This gave me the chance to affirm that the agency was ready to offer help to him, and with both of them saying they wanted to consider a reconciliation, I offered them the opportunity of an interview together. This Mr. B grasped almost pathetically. We agreed that I could talk with his wife about it, and we set a tentative time for June 16, since I was going to have to be out of town for a week in between. As Mr. B left, he seemed quite subdued.

A caseworker must necessarily be the third person in this relationship, and though this couple chose to come to the agency, their feelings about the caseworker are as ambivalent as they are about all their other feelings at this point. Here Mrs. Dean knew that Mr. Bolton saw her as a threat to what he wanted to accomplish. On the other hand, the worker also represents the positive goal and the means of achieving that. The worker needs to be able to recognize both sides of Mr. Bolton's feeling and to be able to stand by him in his confusion and fear, as well as stand by Mrs. Bolton if she is to help them to arrive together at the decision to continue the marriage or to separate. Although the Bolton case had been accepted and work on it started almost a month prior to June 25th, Mr. Bolton's interview actually seemed to be the real beginning with the agency, as it related to their really taking hold of the problem at hand. In this interview, Mr. Bolton expressed all the bitterness of the separation, and his feeling of the threat the worker represented to him. The whole expression of this interview was one of "the world is against me," and this included the worker. However, Mrs. Dean could accept this negative feeling for what it was, and could begin to help Mr. Bolton take some responsibility for his own behavior and there is no question but by the end of the interview, Mr. Bolton was more ready to accept the agency being in on his life. This interview gave Mrs. Dean a vivid picture of Mr. Bolton and a beginning discovery of his pattern of behavior. There was an air of the "bantam cock" about Mr. Bolton, and his approach to life was to put out his fists first. Yet, Mrs. Dean could recognize that here was a fearful, frightened man, who was losing what was most important to him in his life, his family. It takes a tremendous amount of acceptance and understanding on the part of a worker to help a man with this kind of feeling, to believe that the agency is not against him, and to hold for him the positive goal of a whole family.

The suggestion to have a joint interview seemed right to Mrs. Dean at this spot. The interview involving both of them can represent symbolically their wish to be together and can be the spring board from which the family can go on toward a more mature understanding of themselves and of each other, which can be the only basis for a more satisfying marriage.

Mrs. Bolton was seen on June 4 for her appointment, and part of her interview follows:

6/4. Mrs. B came in a few minutes late for her appointment. When we settled ourselves in my office, I noticed her face was flushed and she seemed out of breath. I said it looked as though she had had to do some rushing to get here and suggested that she rest a minute. She was sorry to be late, but the buses are unpredictable. Mrs. B seemed to hesitate and I said she knew that I had seen her husband. Mrs. B nodded, saying he had called her on the telephone, but she had not seen him. I wondered then whether she knew that he had expressed a willingness to use the agency to see if they could work toward getting together again. This started Mrs. B talking at some length about her wish to have the family together, but she was also expressing some ambivalence about her feeling in relation to her husband. I acknowledged with her the question she has about it working. Mrs. B told me she had talked with her son, Arthur, and he is not happy where they are, and though willing to have his father come back to them, he wants none of the trouble to start again. I thought Mrs. B was caught between what Mr. B wants and what Arthur wants, so that she is not too sure what it is she really ought to be doing. Mrs. B continued to look troubled, and said she guessed that was true. She feels she has to consider what all this trouble has done to the children, and whether it is fair to them. I said then she really feels that if they go back together again, it has to be on a different basis, and Mrs. B replied, "Oh, yes." Mrs. B went back over some of the trouble spots, a good bit of it revolving around her mother's continual interference. She gave numerous examples of this. I said I could see how this did not help at all, and yet was this not going to continue if they returned to each other. Mrs. B looked unhappy as she said she guessed so. We agreed that she probably has some basis for feeling anxious. Here they are apart a second time and she is back in her parents' home. They have many debts and there was a chance they may not be able to make a better job of it. Mrs. B then became more critical of her husband, saying he really could have done better too. I tried to pull some of this together by restating that there were things that they will have to think about and try to find a different way of working with these problems, if a reconciliation is to be accomplished at all. Mrs. B agreed to this whole-heartedly. Mrs. B finished by saying she thought it was good that they were going to be seeing me together next time. She understood I would be away next week, and felt all right about it being on the 16th. Her husband would be calling her again and she would remind him of the appointment.

On June 16 Mr. and Mrs. Bolton were in the office for their ap-pointment.

6/16. Mr. and Mrs. B were prompt for the appointment. It was interesting to note Mr. B's actions in relation to his wife. He sat next to her and would occasionally reach over and pat her hand, almost to assure me that they were together in everything, including being against me, if that was necessary. Mrs. B, on the other hand, appeared rather unconscious of all this, and just sat looking pleased that they were here.

Mr. B started off with a "the world is against me" tone, by saying, "Well, I've lost my job out of all this." I said I was indeed sorry to hear that, and rather lightly, added that it sounded as though Mr. B is holding me somewhat responsible for this too. He looked slightly taken back, and quickly said he did not mean that at all, and then moved into an angry dissertation of the unfair-ness of his treatment at the court and at the Post Office. I agreed that this action seemed awfully severe for one infraction, and Mrs. B looked slightly uncomfortable. Mr. B quickly said the rules call for such an action, and I added then that it did not come as a complete surprise. Mr. B did not answer this directly, but moved on to how that did not worry him because he has several opportunities for jobs. I let Mr. B know I was glad to hear that, and asked if the dismissal would effect his getting another job. He said that when he heard he was to be fired, he quickly sent in his resignation, beating them to the draw by one day, so it will appear that way on his records. When I asked if that made him feel better about it, he just shrugged his shoulders. Mrs. B moved in here, in her way, to try to smooth things over by saying that records are important.

Mr. B went on to say more positively that one good thing out of this will be his getting the retirement money in a lump sum, which should amount to about $2,000, and he has already filed for the benefits. I thought that if things had to go this way, this money was coming at a good time. Both agreed that it would give them the opportunity to straighten themselves out financially, and perhaps consider a down payment on a small house.

We moved into a discussion of their plans and both Mr. and Mrs. B were together on clearing up their debts and putting a down payment on a house. Mr. B brought in the matter of looking for another job and also a new place to live. However, he was not anticipating any difficulty with either one of those. When I asked if there were not many details involved in such a transaction, such as the amount of the down payment, carrying charges, etc., Mr. B again thought he could begin talking business as soon as he receives the money. Then, looking at me, as though to get my reaction, Mr. B said he wanted to take his family on a vacation after he finishes at the Post Office. I laughed as I said Mr. B seemed to feel I could stop him from doing this. He looked a little flustered, as he denied this, and went on to say that he and his family have never had a vacation, and this seemed like a good time, maybe for a week at the seashore, where they could be alone. I said it sounded fine to me; my only question would be whether they were ready to enjoy it, when they were apart and plans still are not very concrete. Mrs. B looked a bit tentative, but seemed unready to say anything different from her husband. It was at spots like this, that Mr. B would reach over playfully and pat his wife's hand. Although I gathered that Mrs. B's parents were now interested in seeing them reconciled, Mrs. B complained mildly about how she was constantly being questioned by her parents on plans. However, Mr. B was more openly negative about them. They agreed on a number of things that were wrong about her parents. I thought that Mr. and Mrs. B certainly did not like the way Mrs. B's parents were involved in this, but actually it looked as though they wanted to help, didn't it? Mr. B said, "Oh yes, they would like us to be right next door to them." I could agree that this would be unwise under the circumstances, and I wondered how they were going to handle this. Mr. and Mrs. B struggled between talking with them and just moving away from them and handling it in that way. They agreed that it was something to be considered if they were going to make their reconciliation work. We agreed that it would be best, for the time being, for each of them to come in separately, and appointments were arranged in that way. It was decided that Mr. B would use his pay for his own expenses and that the agency would continue the food allowance for Mrs. B and the children. Eventually we could talk with Mr. B about his financial planning. As I made out the receipt for his wife to sign, Mr. B looked quite uncomfortable. I talked about this briefly, asking Mr. B whether he would like to sign the receipt for his wife, and he laughed, saying that was all right, his wife always handled the purse strings anyway. We then reviewed the appointments and then Mr. and Mrs. B left together, saying good-bye and thank you.

The focus for this service was now firmly established. Mr. and Mrs. Bolton were both ready, in their own ways, to tackle this problem of re-establishing their home, but recognizing that their relationship needed to shift too, if they wanted to avoid the pitfall of separation again. Though some financial help was given, Mr. and Mrs. Bolton could recognize that this help in itself could not accomplish their goal of a better marriage, and that the way in which they considered each step toward their reconciliation was extremely important. Some of the specifics of job and housing would have to be a part of these discussions. Mr. Bolton typically moved into this area with his usual pattern of behaving; he could get a job and a house easily. However, in the ensuing interviews Mr. Bolton was able to express his concern that he was not connecting with either job or housing. The situation in Mrs. Bolton's parents' home was a tense one; overcrowded conditions, and the Ralstons' impatience with Mr. Bolton for not doing better. Mr. Bolton, however, was getting meals with his family, and I gathered eventually was moving into the parents' home too.

Mr. and Mrs. Bolton were able to bring their fear about not being able to make this wish real and gain some support from the worker as the months went on. Mr. Bolton eventually moved in with his wife and children at the Ralstons' home, and though there was some satisfaction, there was also an accompanying dissatisfaction over the way they were living together. When Mr. Bolton received his retirement fund on July 24, which amounted to about $1,500, he was elated and felt they were now definitely on their way. Mrs. Dean was going on vacation on August 1, for a month, and saw Mr. and Mrs. Bolton together on July 31 to plan for this period. A part of this interview follows:

7/31. Mr. B started the interview by saying he was disappointed that he did not have a job, however, he had several possibilities and was fairly encouraged. He felt hopeful that by the time I returned, they would be getting along better. Mr. and Mrs. B agreed they wanted to use part of this money to clear up all their debts so that they could start out fresh. They estimated that this might take about $1,000 of it. Since the house seemed to be out of the question, they planned to use some of this money for their own living expenses. The agency could not continue to meet this need when there were available resources. I told Mr. and Mrs. B that if they needed to see someone in the agency, they could call Mrs. Robertson, who would be ready to talk with them in my absence. They wished me a happy vacation and we arranged for an appointment on September 1 when I returned.

On September 1 Mrs. Bolton was in alone for her appointment. She was depressed and discouraged. They had cleared their debts and were living on the remaining part of the money, but beyond the fact that the debts were clear, she saw little progress. Mrs. Dean soon saw that Mr. and Mrs. Bolton had been unable to sustain the positive gains they had expressed on July 31. Mr. Bolton had been asked to leave her parents' home because he was drinking and not meeting his responsibilities for re-establishing them. Mrs. Bolton began to question whether they were ever going to get together. Mrs. Dean helped Mrs. Bolton to try to express some of her feeling of being deserted by her during this month, and that perhaps had she been there, things might not have gotten this bad. Mrs. Bolton could do very little with this. Before Mrs. Dean finished with Mrs. Bolton, the receptionist informed her that Mr. Bolton was in the office. Since the appointment hour was practically finished and Mrs. Dean was unable to see Mr. Bolton that day, she went out into the reception room where she met a breezy, but completely negative Mr. Bolton. An appointment was arranged for him the next day. Part of Mr. Bolton's interview follows:

9/2. All the hurt that he was feeling about his wife's asking him to leave came out against her. At first Mr. B said he did not blame her, but eventually much of his feeling came out when he said he did not know whether she wanted to live with him any more or not. I said then that he really did feel that she had not taken his side. From this point on, Mr. B was able to express all the disappointment and discouragement he was actually feeling, and eventually broke down and cried, as he said he really was beginning to be afraid that he was never going to get his family together. I said that perhaps he felt everybody was deserting him; I had been away for a whole month and now his wife actually was deserting him. Mr. B dried his eyes and said it was not easy for a man to be crying over himself, and I agreed that it was not, especially in front of a woman. However, I said perhaps he did have something to cry about, and maybe he just had to do it. He went on to say that he thought he was licked, and that there was nobody who was going to hire him for a job, and told me of the number of possibilities that he had and he had heard from none of them. This he attributed to the fact that he had a record, and he was beaten before he even got an application in.

When I felt Mr. B was a little better able to accept some of the things I had to say, I let him know that I thought if he was beaten, then I suspected he was not going to be able to get a job very soon. He shot back at me several times, saying he knew better than I did. I said I guessed he did, and if he was feeling this way, then I doubted that I was going to be able to help him very much. I said I was beginning to wonder whether he was afraid to even face some of the people to let them know he wanted a job. This stopped Mr. B just a little bit, and he looked at me and said he really wanted his family together. I said I thought that was fine, but in order to accomplish that, I thought he was going to have to feel a little differently than he did. Mr. B moved back and forth on this, and eventually we left it that though he wanted his family, he felt pretty beat about it. We arranged an appointment for tomorrow and I said I would be in touch with his wife to let her know the time we were going to get together. This, we felt, was necessary because things actually had shifted back to almost the same as the time they came in. Mr. B said he would be here, and he left in quite a huff.

Here Mr. Bolton was beaten, hurt, and discouraged. He could see nothing hopeful for himself. Though Mrs. Dean could accept Mr. Bolton's feeling of desertion, at the same time, some challenge needed to be given to Mr. Bolton. It would not be helpful at this point to be falsely reassuring, for Mrs. Dean could not know how much Mr. Bolton would be able to move out of his depression until she could feel some willingness on his part to rally himself, if only against her. When Mr. and Mrs. Bolton came in together, Mr. Bolton had been drinking and his whole attitude was negative and argumentative. Mrs. Dean recognized this with him, letting him know that it would be difficult to discuss such an important issue when he was not thinking too clearly. Mr. Bolton, in a dejected voice, said he did not think there was much to talk about any more anyway, he's licked. Though in this interview Mrs. Bolton was more supporting and verbalizing her wish to work toward getting together, it did not reach Mr. Bolton. Mrs. Dean accepted Mr. Bolton's statement that he was licked, and wondered also if there was any point to his continuing with the agency, since the agency did represent help only if he could use the service and it could lead to the bettering of the family situation. However, Mrs. Dean felt she ought to see Mr. Bolton when he was not drinking, so that they could finish up together. Mr. Bolton's response was immediate and he grasped this appointment. Mrs. Dean was clear that she needed to hold Mr. Bolton to being responsible about even leaving the agency. Whether he could rally or not, was indeed a question, but he needed to leave this experience at least putting some parts of the puzzle together. This actually was the turning point for Mr. Bolton. He returned to the agency on September 14th, apologizing to Mrs. Dean for his behavior, and for the first time, accepted some responsibility for his actions.

However, he was deeply depressed, saying he was a "jail bird" and feeling he should leave his family altogether. He was tearful again, saying he thought maybe they would be better off without him. When Mrs. Dean said he could solve it that way, Mr. Bolton was then able to say he did not see how he could go on living away from them. Mrs. Dean let him feel as sorry for himself as he needed to, but recalled what he and his wife had hoped for by coming here for help. His preoccupation with being a "jail bird" prompted Mrs. Dean to wonder if he considered himself handicapped then. Mr. Bolton became angry at this, and began to regain some of his fight, and at the end of the interview he was more alive and discovering once again the fact that the worker was still ready to help him.

In the next four weeks, Mr. and Mrs. Bolton were seen regularly each week, but in separate appointments. Mr. Bolton made concrete his choice of living, and that it would be with his family. He made a serious search for employment and Mrs. Dean encouraged him every step of the way. This period was not without its disappointments and anxieties, but Mrs. Bolton expressed her feeling to Mrs. Dean by saying that even with the disappointments, her husband did not try to "drown his sorrows" and was able to "bounce back," even when turned down. Mr. and Mrs. Bolton were, however, unhappy about living with Mrs. Bolton's parents, but were fearful about any move until he had a job in hand. Mrs. Dean tried to test out whether that uncertainty would be any worse than the unhappiness they were expressing about living with the Ralstons. They agreed that it could not be, but their money was dwindling, and they moved slowly and cautiously on this idea. Mrs. Dean understood that, and could accept what she knew Mr. and Mrs. Bolton were ready to do themselves.

By the first week in October, Mr. Bolton secured a job, and though it did not pay as much as his previous job did, he was able to see that he would have an opportunity to qualify for subsequent pay raises. Both Mr. and Mrs. Bolton were elated, and when Mr. Bolton came in, he was quietly proud of his accomplishment. This is a short excerpt from the interview:

10/5. Mr. B came in for his appointment and though his stride was cocky, he seemed to have an air of assurance as he greeted me. He joked a bit about whether I needed a haircut (this referred to one of the interviews I had with his wife recently where she told me her husband had given her a haircut). I said not today, but went on to comment how happy he seemed today. He said he was for he had secured a job with the John Allison Company. I expressed my pleasure at this, and told him how very glad I was for him and his family. He soon became serious, however, and told me it was not the job he had wanted. I knew he had hoped to get a job in the new plant opening in Stanton, which would pay more, but I realized there was considerable question as to whether they would actually be in operation by the first of the year. Mr. B affirmed this, saying he felt he could wait, and if that opened up, he would have to make a decision then. He assured me his interview there was a positive one and they wanted him if they opened after the first of the year. I said it must make him feel good to know that, however. In a very serious voice, Mr. B went on to say that his "record" did not stand in his way at all. I said maybe he, too, felt differently about it now, and he agreed it no longer seemed to be an excuse. He then joked a bit again, but again returned to their need to look for a house. We talked about this a bit, and agreed that that was something that he and Mrs. B could do. Mr. B expressed concern about their savings dwindling, and I gave some assurance the agency could consider some help at that time. In concluding, we reviewed what they had been able to accomplish, and that we would be ready to think about how much longer they would need the agency's help.

This interview shows Mr. Bolton more responsible and planful. He and Mrs. Bolton were able to sustain their wish to be a family even with the difficult living arrangements. When Mr. and Mrs. Bolton found their search for a house discouraging and often fruitless, they shared the disappointments, and never gave up hope. After the joint appointment, Mrs. Dean set up appointments at two-week intervals, with the idea that the middle of November would seem to be right for them to finish with her and the agency. They could accept this.

During the remaining weeks they continued their search for a house, finally compromising on an apartment, and by the middle of November, they had a real prospect. By Thanksgiving, Mr. and Mrs. Bolton and the two boys were in their own apartment. Mrs. Dean saw them after that, since they felt they wanted to tell her how things were. At that time, they contrasted how they came to the agency and what her help had meant to them. Mr. Bolton said his wife was a "new girl" and the children were so delighted to be in their own home again, they did not mind not having much for Thanksgiving. Mrs. Bolton told Mrs. Dean that when she asked Arthur what he wanted for Christmas, his only request was for them to spend it together in their own home.

As noted earlier, the Bolton case was described as a problem that often reaches the family agency. Not all families are able to use and sustain casework help as the Boltons did. The extent to which a client will use casework help depends largely on how intolerable the disturbed part of the life problem he is experiencing, seems to him. Only the client can tell the worker this, but the skilled caseworker must be sensitive enough to recognize the often unexpressed wish, on the part of this troubled individual, to find a way out of his unhappy situation. The offer of the agency's service as a means of fulfilling this wish for a better command of his situation, is tremendously supporting in this beginning process. The case illustration, however, brings out clearly how the Boltons struggle against some of the conditions of this offer, yet it is Mrs. Dean's faithfulness to her purpose which eventually helps the family crystallize their eventual goal.

Though Mrs. Dean must be sympathetic and understanding, this alone is not enough. She must be ready to take responsibility for establishing the kind of professional relationship which can provide the support through which help can be given. In this case, Mrs. Dean respects Mrs. Bolton's decision that the marriage is no longer possible and stands ready to help her to re-establish herself apart from her husband. Mrs. Bolton's discomfort with this choice soon shows itself and this too, the worker accepts as a natural part of the move toward a truer reorganization of herself. If a marriage is no longer tenable, separation is one answer, but for the client to leave the familiar, as represented by twenty long years, for an unknown, is not so simple. It is this part, Mrs. Dean explores with Mrs. Bolton in the early interviews.

This does not mean the caseworker determines for Mrs. Bolton which course she will take, but rather in allowing her the freedom to express her uncertainty, without criticism, Mrs. Bolton can begin to identify and verbalize her doubts in a way which can make possible her own choice of direction. The client by no means travels this road without stopping to question its validity, and maybe even repudiates the choice altogether. This is very clearly brought out by Mr. Bolton's actions. He wants his family, but when faced with what it requires of him to organize new strength to make concrete his wish, he falters and projects the blame onto everyone but himself.

Thus the second step in the process becomes clearer. When the client can no longer find comfort in clinging to the projections he has built around himself, he discovers and can admit that he does share some responsibility for his plight. The worker helps him to see that this is not a loss of strength, but if he has had a part in creating this situation, he likewise can have a part in making it better. This discovery is essential, for it is the realization that he has within himself a capacity which has been dormant, but is now ready for use. In any process this sets in motion the most productive part of the experience, for it is here that Mr. Bolton begins to see that he can get a job and eventually a place for his family to live; the wish now becomes a reality. Though these are the concrete gains, they do not come about without real inner-reorganization on the part of Mr. and Mrs. Bolton. What then remains, is for Mrs. Dean to help Mr. and Mrs. Bolton to acknowledge the changes they have brought about with her help and the support of an agency which has concern for the whole family. In a sense, it is returning to Mr. and Mrs. Bolton their belief in themselves and their ability to move on independently.

This is the service the family agency offers to the community to many families and in doing so, fulfills its responsibility and justifies its reason for being.

chapter **7**

||||||||||||||||||||||||||||||||||||||||||||||||||||||||||||||||||||||||||||||||||||||||||||||||||||||||||||||

Services in a Local Welfare Department

Contemporary Public Welfare

The depression of the late 1920's and early 1930's coming with full force, the emergence of the federal government into the welfare field, the development of federal-state co-operative relationships, all these combined to produce marked changes affecting both the organization and the administration of public welfare services. Public welfare departments were facing some fundamental questions respecting both structure and function. Should these newer services be incorporated into the old framework? Or should they be allocated to a separate organization? This was more than an academic question, for the attitudes toward the public welfare job determined to a large extent not only the form of organization but the nature and content of the services to be rendered.

A fact of no mean importance was the size of the job to be done. Financial assistance to large numbers of needy individuals or families increasingly became a public agency function with public funds. By 1939, with federal work relief and public assistance programs in effect, the money payments reached into the billions of dollars. For example, according to the fourth annual report of the Social Security Board for the fiscal year, July 1, 1938, to June 30, 1939 (p. 273), payments in excess of $3,750,000,000 were made. A further substantiation of the size of the public job is to be found in the record of the number of recipients. In the month of June 1939 according to the fourth annual report of the Social Security Board (p. 280) there were more than 8 million recipients of public assistance, general relief, and work relief.

On June 30, 1943, the WPA program came to an end. War production had lessened unemployment. The public social services task was taking form consisting of (1) the traditional institutional services and general relief, (2) public assistance (aid to the aged, aid to the blind, and aid to dependent children, including other specialized children's services), and (3) social insurance (old-age and survivors insurance and unemployment insurance). These services were sizable whether measured by sums expended or individuals served.

A Federal Department of Public Welfare

More than a decade before the FERA and the Social Security Act efforts had been directed toward the establishment of a federal department of welfare. In 1921 a bill was introduced into the Senate for the creation of a Department of Public Welfare, but the bill failed of passage. In 1937 the President's Committee on Administrative Management recommended a Department of Social Welfare. Bills were prepared by members of Congress, but no further action resulted. Two years later, July 1, 1939, through an executive order President Roosevelt brought together as the Federal Security Agency a number of the federal agencies whose functions concerned health, education, and welfare. One step further toward co-ordination and unification was taken when on July 16, 1946, President Truman brought still other services under the aegis of the Federal Security Agency. At that time the President observed that "Broadly stated, the basic purpose of the Federal Security Agency is the conservation and development of the human resources of the nation." The size and scope of the Federal Security Agency and the importance of its functions clearly called for departmental status and a permanent place in the President's Cabinet. In number of personnel and volume of expenditures the Agency exceeded several of the existing departments. Much more important, the fundamental character of its functions—education, health, welfare, social insurance—and their significance for the future of the country demanded for it the highest level of administrative leadership and a voice in the central councils of the Executive branch. In April 1953 President Eisenhower elevated the Federal Security Agency to Cabinet status as the Department of Health, Education, and Welfare.

Like local and state units, the federal government operates some welfare services directly for those persons who are within its jurisdiction. For example, the District of Columbia Public Welfare Department, through funds provided by Congressional appropriation, offers welfare services very much like those of any local county welfare department. Administrative relationships to the Social Security Administration, Department of Health, Education, and Welfare resemble those of a state department of public welfare to the federal organization.

There are other welfare services which are provided directly by the federal government, such as those to offenders of federal laws—in federal prisons or through federal probation and parole officers. The Veterans Administration, through its social service departments of veterans hospitals and regional offices, offers services. The Bureau of Indian Affairs in the Department of the Interior as an auxiliary function must offer welfare services to Indians who are under federal jurisdiction even though Indians qualify for public assistance payments in the counties and states in which they have residence.[1]

Aside from those welfare services under its immediate administrative jurisdiction, the contribution of the federal government is essentially an advisory and supervisory one. Many of the acts of Congress provide for grants to states upon certain conditions so that the task of the appropriate federal agency is to maintain relations to the state governments to see that these conditions are fulfilled. The provisions of the Social Security Act, the Barden-La Follette Act of 1943 (Vocational Rehabilitation), and the Public Health Service Act of 1944 are cases in point. It will be recalled that federally appropriated funds are available each year to states for public assistance, child welfare, maternal and child health, and vocational rehabilitation on condition that the state laws under

[1] While the old-age and survivors insurance program is essentially a retirement program, nevertheless there is sufficient relation to welfare by reason of its survivorship provisions to receive at least mention here. In not a few instances beneficiaries—widows and children, and sometimes the retired worker even—are obliged to apply for public assistance at the present time because their benefits are so low. For example, in February 1953 there were 425,000 persons receiving concurrently old-age and survivors benefits and old-age assistance grants. The services of the United States Public Health Service should be mentioned also. At core, these are services in the area of health; nevertheless, there are welfare aspects to be considered, as in mental health and in certain research grants.

which the services are provided are consistent with the requirements of the federal statute. Relations are established and maintained between the Department of Health, Education, and Welfare and the state welfare departments not only to see that legal requirements are being met but, just as importantly, to render help to the state agencies and to effect a useful interchange of experience and knowledge.

The State and Public Welfare

The pre-1929 machinery for handling welfare problems of considerable magnitude proved to be inadequate. A number of states that had provided some welfare services through commissions or bureaus in time, through the encouragement of federal authorities as well as according to the informed judgment of its own citizens, established departments of public welfare. "Temporary" and "emergency" relief no longer corresponded to reality once programs of substantial proportions got under way following the passage of the Social Security Act. By now, and for some years past, each of the forty-eight states (and the territories) function through state welfare organizations. While the majority of these are called departments of public welfare, there are various titles signifying the same thing: social welfare, social security, public aid commission. In a few instances a new department has been set up along side the earlier welfare department, the former concentrating upon public assistance and the latter upon the traditional welfare services, mainly institutional. In no two states are all the welfare functions integrated into a single department. This is true not only because of lack of agreement as to what public welfare includes, but also because certain services may already have been allocated to other departments before the welfare department was established. Then, too, there is also the belief that many services which could be considered welfare in nature should be administered in units separate from the welfare department.

There are many examples of this tendency to scatter welfare functions. In some states probation and parole may be in the welfare department; in others it may be in a separate department of probation and parole. In some states crippled children's services may be in the health department; in others in the welfare department; and in still others in the education department. In some states correctional institutions are under the direction of the department of corrections; in others they are directed by the department of state institutions; and in still others by the department of welfare. All of this points to the conclusion that while the range of services constituting welfare are found within most state governments, there is no consistent pattern of departmental allocation.

In the counties the welfare services are furnished directly to the applicant; i.e., there is no additional person or organization that stands between the eligible applicant (assuming funds are available) and the public welfare worker. This is not so true with services furnished by the state organization, except in those rare instances of a state-executed assistance or relief program. Usually the state supervises the local administration of services such as public assistance or serves in an auxiliary and facilitating capacity to local administrative units.

The functions of state welfare departments are concisely stated by Marietta Stevenson.[2] She groups these as:

1. Administration or supervision of state institutions;
2. Public assistance, child welfare, and other direct care;
3. Development and supervision of local public agencies;
4. Supervision of private institutions and agencies;
5. Research and educational programs.

No attempt is here made to amplify these points, a task already well executed by Miss Stevenson. It must be said, however, that current public welfare practice operates with the state department in the pivotal position in relation to local units on the one hand, and to federal units on the other. This is the unmistakable and compelling development of the first two decades of the Social Security Act, offering further promise of mutually productive operation in all three areas.

The County and Public Welfare

Today most of the 3,187 counties in the United States have a public welfare department. In some states, even though counties exist as political units, they are not necessarily the operating and administering unit for welfare purposes. Welfare services may be provided on a district or area basis, on a town or township basis, or directly out of the state welfare office. Despite these variations, however, it may be said safely that

[2] Stevenson, Marietta, *Public Welfare Administration*. New York, The Macmillan Company, 1938, pp. 79–84; see also Miles, Arthur P., *An Introduction to Public Welfare*. Boston, D. C. Heath & Company, 1949, pp. 267–295, 363–382.

the bulk of welfare services provided locally is through county public welfare organization.

Many of these were begun during the FERA days, and subsequent to the passage of the Social Security Act developed substantial programs. Some of these services, such as providing public assistance, are links in the local, state, federal chain. Others, such as foster home care or adoptions, are part of a local-state interrelationship. Still other services, such as general relief or aid to transients, may be entirely local.

The services performed by local welfare departments (counties, and cities within counties) vary considerably in different states and different areas. For example, the returns from a questionnaire sent out in 1937 to cities with populations over 100,000 revealed an amazing assortment of services. Marietta Stevenson, who reported this in 1938, classified them under the nine headings of: public assistance, social service and other special services for adults, child welfare services, licensing and regulatory functions, institutional responsibilities, work relief activities, public works responsibilities, health services, and other functions which included public recreation and administration of employment service. The actual count under these headings was fifty-five. Obviously, no one department provided all these services, but the assortment gives some idea of the spread and variety of services in local departments.[3] Fifteen years later the substance of these services still hold; if anything, the list is now greater since additional programs—homemaker service and foster care for the aged, for example—have come under public auspice. The history of public welfare is a history of expansion of services as communities express their needs and call upon their established governments for help in dealing with increasingly complex problems.

The Social Security Act—Public Assistance

In Chapter 3 reference was made to the Social Security Act of 1935 and subsequent amendments. The services made possible by the Act were itemized, and the two insurance programs—Unemployment Insurance, and Old-Age and Survivors Insurance—were reviewed in some detail. In the present chapter there will be not only elaboration of the public assistance and child welfare programs but also elaboration of other services offered through local county welfare departments.

[3] Stevenson, *op. cit.,* pp. 92–95.

Besides establishing a precedent for a system of old-age and survivors insurance and unemployment insurance, the Social Security Act of 1935 for the first time in history provided for financial aid to the states in a federal-state co-operative program of public assistance. Three groups were differentiated from others to receive these services: the aged, the blind, and dependent children. In 1950 a fourth category—aid to the permanently and totally disabled—was added. Heretofore the individuals composing these groups had received what institutional or noninstitutional care was made available by the state or the local community, but it was not until the crisis of the late 1920's and early 1930's settled on this country that a newer concept of care came into being. The FERA, the CWA, the NYA, the CCC, the WPA had turned more and more attention to the federal government as an agency to meet problems beyond the province of any one community. At the same time the tradition of local responsibility, the undue (though necessary) emphasis upon federal control during the emergency period, and finally, the very honest conviction that certain values inhered in local participation, all these pointed toward a rejection of complete federal assumption. Yet the way was open to utilizing federal funds and leadership while still retaining a degree of local administration and financial contribution.

Grants to states for old-age assistance, aid to the blind, aid to dependent children, and aid to the permanently and totally disabled are made subject to acceptable state plans submitted to the Social Security Administration. In every instance of an award by a state or county to a recipient, certain eligibility requirements must be met. Need is the eligibility factor common to the four programs. Depending upon the type of assistance applied for, certain other eligibility requirements must be met, such as age, blindness, and deprivation of parental support or care because of the death, continued absence, or incapacity of a parent, or disablement (for persons over 18 years of age).

The state plan for the four categories must each provide: (a) that it shall be in effect in all political subdivisions of the state, and if administered by them, be mandatory upon them; (b) for financial participation by the state; (c) for a single state agency either to administer the plan or to supervise the administration of the plan; (d) for granting an opportunity for a fair hearing before the state agency to any individual whose claim is denied or is not acted upon with reasonable promptness; (e) for proper and efficient administration, including the establishment and maintenance of personnel standards on a merit basis; (f) for regular and correct reports; (g) that the state agency shall, in determining need, take into consideration any other income and resources of individuals claiming assistance; (h) safeguards which restrict the use or disclosure of information concerning applicants and recipients to purposes directly connected with the administration of the public assistance programs; [4] (i) that all individuals wishing to make application for public assistance shall have an opportunity to do so, and that assistance shall be furnished with reasonable promptness to all eligible individuals.

Besides these requirements which apply to the four public assistances there are other provisions pertinent to each of them. The state plan for aid to dependent children must also provide (a) for prompt notice to appropriate law enforcement officials of the furnishing of aid to dependent children in respect to a child who has been deserted or abandoned by a parent, (b) that the money payment is to be made for the needs of one adult relative with whom the child is living in addition to the needs of each dependent child in the family unit.

The additional pertinent provisions for the state plan for aid to the blind (a) permit the state to disregard the first $50 per month of earned income of the blind person, (b) permit an examination, to determine blindness or degree of blindness, by a physician skilled in diseases of the eye or by an optometrist (whichever the individual may select).

No state plan for aid to dependent children can be approved by the Secretary of Health, Education, and Welfare if it imposes a residence requirement which renders ineligible any child residing within the state who has resided within the state for one year immediately preceding the application, or which renders ineligible any child who was born within one year immediately preceding the application if the parent or other relative with whom the child is living has resided in the state for one year immediately preceding the birth. Likewise, no state plan for

[4] A modification of this was effected by an amendment, in October 1951, to the Social Security Act. Under Public Law 183, 82d Congress, states were permitted to make available for public inspection records of the disbursement of public assistance funds or payments. To permit public inspection the state must enact a law specifically authorizing such public access to records of disbursements. Such a law must prescribe the conditions under which access may be had and, also, must establish and enforce safeguards to prevent the use of the information for political or commercial purposes.

old-age assistance can be approved if it (a) imposes a higher age limit than 65 years, or (b) imposes a residence requirement which excludes a resident who lived in the state during five years of the preceding nine and who lived in the state for one year immediately preceding application, or (c) makes any citizenship requirement which excludes any citizen of the United States.

Federal public assistance payments are not to be made to individuals in institutions. However, there is an exception to the prohibition in those instances when a needy individual is a patient in a public medical institution other than a mental or tuberculosis hospital. A recent amendment to the Social Security Act provides that, after July 1, 1953, if a state makes payments to an individual in a public medical institution or in a private institution offering medical or domiciliary care it—the state—must also designate the state authority which shall be responsible for establishing and maintaining standards for such institutions (other than mental or tuberculosis hospitals). Applicable to all four categories—aid to dependent children, aid to the blind, aid to the aged, and aid to the disabled—is the change made effective October 1, 1950, permitting federal participation in payments made by state public assistance agencies directly to medical practitioners and other suppliers of medical services and remedial care.

The foregoing requirements of the Social Security Act as amended are set up as a condition for receipt of federal grants to the states for public assistance purposes. There is a prohibition that underlies each of them to the effect that no person may receive payment from more than one of the four assistance programs. Administrative costs are shared up to 50 percent by the federal government. The Act as amended to date specified the extent to which the federal government will participate in payments to qualified persons, setting a limit with respect to each category. Within recent years the federal share in assistance payments has been over 50 percent, with states and counties being responsible for the remainder. However, even though the federal share is specified, each state may pay its recipients as high as it chooses beyond the federal matching.

Because the federal matching is related to the payment which each state (including its counties) makes and because states differ in their wealth and capacity to make such payments there is considerable variation between them. This is reflected in the following analysis for the month of May 1954.[5]

SELECTED PUBLIC ASSISTANCE PAYMENTS, MAY 1954

	Old-Age Assistance		Aid to the Blind	
	State	Per Recipient	State	Per Recipient
High	Conn.	$82.30	Conn.	$92.66
Low	Miss.	28.20	Miss.	26.21
Average	U. S. A.	51.39	U. S. A.	55.85

	Aid to Dependent Children			Aid to Permanently and Totally Disabled	
	State	Per Family	Per Recipient	State	Per Recipient
High	Conn.	$132.63	$40.33	Conn.	$101.04
Low	Miss.	27.97	7.39	Miss.	24.60
Average	U. S. A.	85.00	23.81	U. S. A.	53.56

Some idea of the number of people reached by these four public assistance programs as well as the amount of money expended thereon may be gained from the monthly reports of the Social Security Administration. During the month of May 1954 there were over 5 million persons receiving public assistance. Almost half of these persons were receiving old-age assistance; over 2 million were receiving aid to dependent children; over 100 thousand were receiving aid to the blind, while more than 200 thousand were receiving aid to the permanently and totally disabled. Funds expended for this month of May 1954 were over $200 million.[6] For the fiscal year ending June 30, 1952, the payments for the four public assistances were just about $2⅓ billion.[7]

---

[5] Adapted from *Social Security Bulletin*, XVII, August 1954, pp. 26–28.

[6] *Social Security Bulletin*, XVII, August 1954, Table 8, p. 23.

[7] *Social Security Bulletin*, XVI, September 1953, Table 3, p. 23.

Maternal and Child Health and Welfare Services

In addition to the social insurance and public assistance features of the Social Security Act, there is a third part providing for maternal and child health services, services for crippled children, and child welfare services. The appropriation of federal sums for maternal and child health services is for the purpose of enabling states to extend and improve services for promoting the health of mothers and children, especially in rural areas and in areas suffering from severe economic distress. Each state plan must provide for: (a) financial participation by the state; (b) administration of the plan or supervision of the adminis tration by the state health agency; (c) establishment and maintenance of personnel standards on a merit basis and proper and efficient administration; (d) reports; (e) extension and improvement of local maternal and child health services; (f) co-operation with medical, nursing, and welfare groups; (g) demonstration services in needy areas and among groups in special need. The state plans are subject to the approval of the United States Children's Bureau, and allotments are made upon the basis of a flat grant of $60,000 to each state, with provision for each state matching some of the additional funds. Consideration is taken of the proportion of live births in the state to the total number of live births in the United States, as well as the state's need for help in providing these services.

Another appropriation under the Social Security Act as amended to date is for the purpose of enabling each state "to extend and improve services for locating crippled children, and for providing medical, surgical, corrective, and other services and care, and facilities for diagnosis, hospitalization, and after care for children who are crippled or who are suffering from conditions which lead to crippling." The state plan must conform substantially to the same requirements as the maternal and child health plan, except that the administration or the supervision of the administration need not necessarily be under the state health agency; nor is there any requirement in the Act for local services or for demonstrations. As in the case of allotments for maternal and child health, there is a federal requirement for state matching of a portion of the federal funds. There is provision as well for a flat grant of $60,000 to each state. The federal government also takes into consideration the number of crippled children in each state in need of services and the cost of furnishing such services to them.

A third appropriation is for establishing, extending, and strengthening child welfare services, especially in predominantly rural areas, "for the protection and care of homeless, dependent, and neglected children, and children in danger of becoming delinquent." For states to receive federal allotments acceptable plans must be worked out jointly between the co-operating state public welfare agency and the United States Children's Bureau. A flat sum of $40,000 is authorized for each state, with the remainder allotted upon the basis of the relation which the rural population of the state under the age of 18 bears to the total rural population of the United States under such age. Allotments for child welfare services, unlike allotments for maternal and child health and crippled children services, are not on a prescribed federal-state matching basis, but there is the expectation that state and local funds also will be provided in order for such services to be available to children within the state. The sums are to be used for paying part of the cost of district, county, or other local child welfare services in predominantly rural areas; for developing state services for the encouragement and assistance of adequate methods of community child welfare organization in rural areas and other areas of special need; and for paying the cost of returning any runaway child who has not attained the age of 16 to his own community in another state in cases in which such return is in the interest of the child and the cost thereof cannot otherwise be met. In this section of the 1950 Amendments the Congress added these words: "provided, that in developing such services for children the facilities and experience of voluntary agencies shall be utilized in accordance with child-care programs and arrangements in the states and local communities as may be authorized by the state." [8]

---

[8] The foregoing description of the original Social Security Act as amended to date is designed to provide the beginning student with an over-all view of the Act as it stands today. Many details have been omitted, purposely, in this account. For additional material the reader is referred to the excellent simplified analyses prepared by and obtainable from the Social Security Administration, Department of Health, Education, and Welfare, Washington, D. C., or from its nearest regional or field office.

The monthly issue of the *Social Security Bulletin* contains a wealth of material, including statistics on the financial aspects of the state and federal programs.

The serious student will find careful examination of Eveline M. Burns' *The American Social Security System* to be a rewarding experience. Published in 1949 by Houghton Mifflin, it now (1954) has added to it an appendix containing an analysis of the 1950

General Assistance

The foregoing completes the analysis of the provisions of the Social Security Act, but it seems necessary here to mention another form of public assistance, that is, however, not included in the Act. This is known as general assistance, a modern euphemism for what used to be called poor relief, and consists of aid in cash or in kind (groceries, goods, etc.) for those persons who are in need and yet are not eligible for the four categories of assistance discussed above. Like these assistance programs, it is administered by the local department of public welfare. The funds may be provided by the local county (or city, town, township), or by the county and the state, or entirely by the state. There is no federal grant for general assistance.

An examination of the statistics on general assistance indicates the meagerness of the grants, as well as the variations in some of the grants among the states. In May 1954 there were 304,000 cases (meaning individuals as well as families—an approximation of the number of individuals involved would be 500,000) to whom cash payments of almost $16 million were made. The average for the country as a whole was $51.13 per recipient. The state with the highest payment per recipient was New York—$74.24; the state with the lowest payment was Tennessee—$12.37.[9]

Vocational Rehabilitation

In Title V of the original Social Security Act there was provision for appropriation to the states for vocational rehabilitation of the disabled which furthered the program initiated by the Federal Vocational Rehabilitation Act of 1920. The incorporation of these services in the Social Security Act in 1935 further stimulated federal-state co-operation so that by the middle of 1943 all forty-eight states, the District of Columbia, Hawaii, and Puerto Rico had legislated in this area. In July 1943 the substance of the social security provisions along with strengthening amendments were brought together into separate legislation known as the Barden-LaFollette Act (Public Law No. 13, 78th Congress).

Amendments. As it stands, it furnishes a substantial basis for an intelligent understanding of our social security system.

[9] *Social Security Bulletin,* XVII, August 1954, Table 15, p. 28.

As with the other appropriations that have been discussed, there must be acceptable state plans as a condition of receipt of federal monies by the states. The vocational rehabilitation state plans must:

1. Designate the state board of vocational education as the sole agency for the administration, supervision, and control of the state plan (exceptions relating to commissions for the blind or previously designated vocational rehabilitation commissions are noted in the Act);
2. Designate the state treasurer as custodian of funds;
3. Specify the policies and methods under which the plan is to be carried out;
4. Provide that the services shall be available only to employable individuals;
5. Provide for the establishment and maintenance of personnel standards;
6. Provide reports;
7. Provide that no federal sums be used for repair or rental of buildings;
8. Make rules governing on-the-job training, medical and hospitalization fees, and prosthetic devices;
9. Provide vocational rehabilitation to any civil employee of the United States disabled while in the performance of his duty and to any war-disabled civilian.

This legislation permits federal funds to be used by the states for all regular administrative costs as well as for matching of state funds on a dollar-for-dollar basis.

The vocational rehabilitation services made possible under the 1920 to 1943 Acts are for handicapped civilians and war-disabled civilians, including merchant seamen and former members of the armed forces whose disabilities are held to be nonservice connected. These services include corrective surgery, hospitalization, occupational tools, prosthetic devices essential to obtaining or retaining employment, subsistence maintenance during training or retraining, guidance and placement of disabled persons. The Office of Vocational Rehabilitation, like the Social Security Administration and the United States Children's Bureau, is in the Department of Health, Education, and Welfare. Rehabilitation of persons having service-connected disabilities is the responsibility of the Veterans Administration.[10]

This recital of provisions of the Social Security Act was necessary to bring the account of public welfare services up to date. The activities beginning with FERA and culminating in the Social Security Act have defined a new area and given a new tone to the public services. It now becomes imperative to take stock of where public welfare organization and administration are during the second half of the twentieth century.

The Offer of Services in County Welfare Departments

While it is difficult to generalize with respect to 3,000 counties and 48 states and the District of Columbia (Alaska, Hawaii, Puerto Rico, and Virgin Islands could be included), nevertheless there are enough consistencies running through their welfare operations to attempt a description of public welfare as people encounter it in their home communities. These services may be classified as follows: public assistance (financial), caring and placing, counseling, regulation, services performed for other agencies, and referral.

The bulk of the local county welfare job—in number of people reached and amount of money expended—is public assistance, i.e., old-age assistance, aid to the blind, aid to dependent children, aid to the permanently and totally disabled, and general assistance. The common denominator of each of these is need—financial need. The distinction between them is the qualifying factor of: age, blindness, childhood, disability, unemployability, according to the various categories.

Persons who apply for public assistance may file an application at a local welfare office—county, city, or district within city. Eligibility is based upon proof of need as well as of on the other qualifying factors just mentioned. Let it be assumed that a man and wife, each 65 years of age, feel they are in financial need and hence entitled to, as they call it, their "pension." Whether they are eligible or not will depend upon their being 65 years or older and with insufficient resources. The applicant carries the major responsibility for ascertaining proof of

---

[10] Some of the possibilities for co-operative effort on behalf of the physically handicapped (and the crippled child as well) are detailed in Elledge, Caroline H., *The Rehabilitation of the Patient*. Philadelphia, J. B. Lippincott Company, 1945. Reference at this point to Chapter 10, Medical Social Work, may prove useful.

his age, but the public assistance worker stands ready to be of help, particularly since birth records were not always recorded officially six or more decades ago. The other aspect of eligibility is the determination of need. Usually this is based on a calculation (a joint enterprise of applicant and worker) of resources and the computation of a budget based on minimal needs. Resources may consist of income of any kind, whether cash or its equivalent, with consideration given to ownership of real estate, as well as personal property, insurance policies, and other assets which could be considered of value. Over against this is placed a fairly standardized budget, usually prepared by the state department of public welfare. If the resources exceed the budget items, the applicant is ineligible. If the resources are less than the budget items, the applicant is eligible for a cash grant monthly, provided there are sufficient funds available and the authorization has been made by the appropriate person or persons (i.e., superintendent of public welfare and county welfare board). Not infrequently, only a percentage of this difference between resources and needs is granted, because of lack of funds. For example, there may be a budgetary deficit—as it is called—of $60 per month and yet only 75 percent of this or $45 may be granted. Appeals are permissible both from applicants who are found ineligible as well as from persons to whom grants have been made and who may question the size of the grant. This appeals procedure is required by the Social Security Act and is provided for by the state department of public welfare. It is the responsibility of the public assistance worker to keep in touch with the clients at reasonable intervals to make recommendations with respect to the grants if the original situation changes, and to be available for such help as the clients may request that is within the function of the welfare department. This applies with equal effect to all of the public assistances even though the provision for general assistance may be locally financed and locally controlled.

A second group of services offered in the local welfare department may be called caring and placing. Receiving a child into foster care, securing a foster family to meet his needs, helping the child and the foster parents with the difficulties which sometimes arise are instances of the caring function. Somewhat the same may be said for foster family care for the aged (or older) person. Perhaps even what is termed homemaker service, whether for children or for aged persons, may be included in this concept of care. On the other hand, the placing service is characterized by the role which the department carries in adoption—the receiving of the child, the search for an adoption couple, the services involved in effecting the adoption. Increasingly, public welfare departments are engaged in caring and placing—functions which until recently were performed by many agencies supported by voluntary contributions.[11]

A third group of services consist of helping persons with difficulties of a rather serious nature, such as the unmarried mother, or the parent who is abusing or neglecting his child, or the youngster who is placed on probation by the juvenile court. These various persons may need financial help or they may not; their essential difficulty is in the area of behavior and help offered to them must be directed toward assisting them to assume a greater responsibility for their behavior. In many parts of this country the only resource for helping, in any measure, such persons may have to come from the local welfare department—with all of its limitations as to number of staff, training of staff, size of caseloads, multiplicity of duties.

The regulatory services constitute a fourth area: for example, the licensing of foster homes (actually it may be the examination of them and recommendation to the state department of public welfare), the determination of permits to solicit, whether granted to persons or to organizations, or recommendations to the court regarding adoption petitions.

In addition to all of the foregoing, the local public welfare department performs services for other agencies. It has a considerable task of certification, of doing the necessary preliminary investigation, and screening for: admissions to tuberculosis sanatoriums, institutions for the feeble-minded, state mental hospitals, and institutions for the aged. It may be called upon to certify with respect to financial capacity prior to hospital admission or to other institutions which provide services related to ability to pay for them. It may conduct the intake interviews for institutions or agencies within or outside the immediate area of the county. It may also conduct the out-of-town inquiries for other public welfare departments as well as private agencies such as Travelers

[11] Also see Chapter 8—Welfare Services for Children.

Aid Societies. In addition to all of these, it may carry out co-operative arrangements with the appropriate state agencies by providing services to parolees from correctional institutions. The superintendent of public welfare may even perform the school attendance officer job for the school system.

A final grouping to services of the local public welfare departments are referrals—usually to agencies for such other services that are not within the public welfare function or which other agencies are better qualified to provide. Instances are referrals to child guidance clinic, to family service agency, to hospital social service, to Veterans Administration hospital or regional office, to vocational rehabilitation facilities and services, to specialized institutions (such as those for the blind, the cerebral palsied, etc.), to legal aid clinics.

Social Casework as a Method of Offering Public Welfare Services

From Elizabethan and colonial days onward very little attention was given to the individual needs of persons asking for public relief. The poor were poor because it was their own fault. If relief was to be given them, it was to be so unattractive that they would be deterred from asking again, and the example would discourage other would-be askers. An approach to persons in need upon another basis came with the development of private social work, particularly of family casework. So long, however, as public welfare in the state government concerned itself largely with institutional care and management, and so long as public welfare in the local community consisted largely of pauper relief, there seemed little occasion or opportunity to use casework services. So long as private agencies could select their clients, and so long as the public institutions and poor boards had to take the rest, there was little sharing of this newer point of view that was called social casework. Today, the situation is changed. The public agency is empowered to administer a service to all who are eligible and as long as the money lasts. Can this be done on a mass basis and still insure a high quality of service to individuals who can make use of it?

To the uninitiated person all this talk about social casework may sound like the lingo of an esoteric cult. Could not anyone who learned the language be a caseworker? What is there to casework that could not be done by, say, a board member, a pastor's assistant, the chairman of the welfare committee of the Woman's Club? Whoever has read this far must realize that the practice of social casework is based upon a skill in working with people in difficulty, and that that skill is related to one's native endowment, one's own personality development, training, and experience. It demands infinite skill.

The process of social casework and its usefulness rests upon a conviction of accepting people as they are, respecting their rights to live their own lives according to their best lights, and a willingness to work with them on their plans rather than to make the plans for them. The worker's effectiveness lies in *what* he does in helping people and *how* he does it. He does not take over their difficulties nor their own share of responsibility, rather he helps them to face their difficulties and to carry what is their part of the load. Casework is a skillful way of working with people in trouble. It is not the only way. It is one way that has proven its value by helping people to develop their own capacities for useful and satisfying living.

Does all of this have pertinence for the public assistance job as we engage ourselves in the administration of the Social Security Act? Do public assistance workers operate on the basis of what Mrs. Rosa Wessel terms public assistance *as* casework. Indeed, we answer immediately, can public assistance workers operate on any other basis? Do workers see themselves as granting public assistance to an applicant and then undertaking to provide "service," or do they see that *what* they do and *how* they do it in the process of determining eligibility, or reviewing grants, as the very essence of helping? [12]

The Social Security Act in both its insurance and public assistance features marked a break with a three-hundred-year past. No longer were workers and their family members to lose their respectability because they grew old or were temporarily out of work. Not only were many of them to be eligible to receive financial benefits which bore a relation to previous wage deductions, but others not so covered under the social insurances were entitled to assistance, as a right, when certain eligibility conditions were met. This newer concept of the dignity of the human

[12] Wessel, Rosa (ed.), *Method and Skill in Public Assistance.* Published as *Journal of Social Work Process,* II, December 1938, p. 6 (Pennsylvania School of Social Work).

being has provided a valid basis for casework in the public assistances as well as in the other public welfare services.[13]

The rules of eligibility for old-age assistance, aid to dependent children, aid to the blind, and aid to the permanently and totally disabled (referred to as OAA, ADC, AB, and APTD) are laid down by state statutes and federal enactment. Applicants who meet these eligibility requirements are entitled by right to assistance through money payments. The lack of public funds may mean an inadequacy of grant or no grant at all, but that lack in no wise invalidates the individual's right to application or his eligibility. Furthermore, the law guarantees the right of appeal of any applicant. This appeal may proceed through local welfare department, state welfare department, or courts according to the provisions of the various state laws.

Another instance of the respect for human personality embodied in this twentieth-century legislation is the legal provision that limits the use by the welfare agency of information about the applicant or recipient. Whatever information is developed in the course of establishing or maintaining eligibility is to be used for the service of the individual, remaining the joint concern and property of the client and the agency, and not to become public property.[14]

These requirements in the laws fortify sound principles of agency administration in the development of policy. Such policy expressed through practice provides assistance on a fair and considerate basis. The needs of individuals are seen as varying just as individuals themselves vary from each other. The capacity of individuals to use money according to their needs is respected. The ability of individuals to manage their own affairs according to their lights is acknowledged. The desire of most individuals to improve their situation and to quicken their incentives is recognized and strengthened wherever possible. The *way* of the worker in dealing with the client is the measure of the casework job.

Casework in a public agency is related to the service for which the

---

[13] For a useful exposition of the possibilities of casework practice in public assistance see Wiltse, Kermit, "Social Casework Services in the Aid to Dependent Children Program." *The Social Service Review*, XXVIII, June 1954, pp. 173–185.

[14] Even with the so-called Jenner Amendment of the Social Security Act, October 1951, permitting public inspection of disbursement records there still remains intact the confidentiality of the worker-client relationship.

agency exists. Service begins with application for assistance. At this point the worker meets the applicant with the conditions of eligibility as defined in the law and agency policy. These must be clearly presented, in language which the applicant understands and in a manner that reveals a willingness to be helpful. Establishing eligibility then becomes a joint enterprise with the applicant producing the data to which he has access and the worker relating that to the agency requirements. In some instances the worker may be called upon to assemble other pertinent data which is more accessible to the agency than to the applicant. All of this is a shared experience, not a tug of war or a game of matched wits.

Throughout this the worker must understand how vital money is in our lives. The "our" means all of us—applicants, social workers, teachers, lawyers, plumbers, farmers. Money may mean status and independence; it may mean holding up one's head and walking surely. It may mean courage and resolution to face new demands; it may mean security. The lack of money—no matter the reason—may mean the denial of all these. The establishment of eligibility and the continuing payment of assistance signifies not a gift or sweet charity, but the faith of the state in the capacity of the individual to manage his affairs and to do so responsibly. It betokens also a practical as well as a philosophical conviction that whatever serves the welfare of the individual serves the welfare of the community too.

All of this is relevant to another aspect of casework in public assistance, namely, the conditions of continued eligibility. The use of public money requires a knowledge on the part of the agency and the worker that the facts supporting original eligibility are sustained throughout the period of assistance. Changes in the client's condition will affect his assistance payments, and when eligibility is no longer valid, then payments are terminated. This in no way compels a recipient to conform his life to the dictates of a governmental agency, or permits an agency to use the assistance payment as either a lever or a threat. Throughout the period of eligibility the public assistance worker needs constantly to be sensitive to the dignity of the human personality, the wish of most people to manage their own affairs, as well as the capacity of people to improve their lot to become self-maintaining and self-determining.

Another area of usefulness calling for the worker's skill is that of bringing to recipients knowledge of the resources in other agencies of the community. These resources may be medical, educational, vocational, or recreational and readily known to the worker but not so to other persons. Here again, in the process of referral there is real skill involved. The understandable hesitations of people to expose themselves to other agencies or to unpredictable and possibly uncontrolled situations must be taken into account by the referring worker. Frequently more than information is needed. To information must be added understanding.

Trends in Public Welfare

In our time and in this our country we can see evidences of attitudes and practices that have prevailed throughout three centuries of public welfare. At the same time, even though we stand in the midst of contemporary operation and are inextricably a part of it we can still discern some of the more pronounced trends. Without any question the most outstanding is toward an expanding service. This may be measured by dollars, by staffs, or more importantly, by the range of services and the number of persons whom these services reach. Welfare still assists the individual or family of limited means of subsistence and that is a tremendously important service. But it also undertakes to provide many other services as instanced by social security developments, veterans' services, vocational rehabilitation, child welfare services, to mention only a few. This expansion of service has been associated with a changed concept of the public welfare services. Assistance of whatever kind is to be considered not as a palliative or a stopgap, but as an investment in human beings, a means whereby, with help, individuals may discover and develop their capacities for satisfying and useful living. This applies to services for the aged, for children, for offenders, for the mentally afflicted, for the otherwise handicapped, in short for all those who look for help beyond themselves and their family.

Within recent years more and more attention is being paid to services for the aged.[15] The enlarging proportion of the aged in the total population is, without question, a determining factor in this development. Money grants to eligible aged persons is on the increase, accom-

[15] Substantiation of this point is to be found in the fact that a chapter—Social Services for the Aged—has been added to the present edition of this volume.

panied by liberalization of eligibility requirements. Recreational and group work services related to the needs of the aged are on the increase. Counseling services for the aged are coming to the fore. Increased and improved institutional services—in public and private homes—are evident, together with specially adapted programs in them. Planning in the housing field, particularly low-cost housing, is beginning to take into account the needs of older persons. While not related exclusively to the aged, nevertheless the problem of chronic illness has been receiving increasing attention; developments in this area take the situation of the aged as a point of departure for expanded services for all chronically ill.

A third discernible trend is the increasing provision for more adequate medical services for all the people. With the extraordinary progress of medical science it becomes clear that efforts must be directed toward distributing medical services wherever they are needed, and that financial provision also must be made for any interruption of earnings during illness. Many foreign countries have demonstrated the possibility as well as the desirability of such expanded services. The proposals in the last several Congresses looking toward health insurance as an integral part of a social security program have not been enacted, but they are unmistakably affecting the former fixed positions of those favoring the preservation of the *status quo*. Even the efforts to head off health insurance compel the enactment of programs that will provide more extensive medical service than heretofore. Because of the delays in the provision of a more equitable distribution of medical services, state and local departments of public welfare have had to formulate medical care programs for assistance recipients. In some instances there may be inclusion in the recipient's budget of a sum for medical care; in other cases the services of a county physician may be made available, while in still other instances there may be what is called vendor payments by the state or local department to the provider of the medical services.

A fourth trend is in the direction of providing more welfare services to more people through the Veterans Administration. It has been estimated that some 55 million people are directly or indirectly affected by services of the Veterans Administration. The services for which veterans are eligible are due them as veterans, and in the case of medical and psychiatric services are related to disabilities connected with their military experience.

A fifth trend is reflected in the expansion of the social security program. The amendments of 1939 included survivors under the old-age provisions of the original 1935 Act, and in 1946 an amendment extended protection to the families of veterans who die within three years after discharge. Another amendment in 1946, as noted in the previous pages, included maritime workers under unemployment coverage, as it had previously—1939—included them under old-age and survivors insurance. The 1950 and 1954 Amendments brought within old-age and survivors coverage an additional number of workers—principally the self-employed, farm workers, and household workers.

A sixth trend, and one not unrelated to the foregoing, is the movement toward increasing the inclusions within the social insurances and decreasing the public assistances. True, the same Congress that added coverage for the self-employed and farm and domestic workers also placed disability with the public assistances. However, there is a solid opinion that favors disability being tied to either old-age and survivors insurance or to unemployment insurance (or both, depending upon whether it is permanent or temporary disability). There is likewise some conviction about provision for disability being based on a separate insurance program alongside of old-age and survivors insurance and unemployment insurance. It is held in many quarters that the more persons who are insured against wage loss by reason of old-age, death, unemployment, disability, and even illness the less call will there be upon the residual assistances.[16] Certainly, such a development would not be unlike that in other countries whose social security program antedated ours by many years.

Another trend, and for the purposes of this chapter the last, is in the direction of greater integration of welfare services, national, state, and local. This means a bringing into more effective co-ordination the various services that minister to the welfare needs of people, whether this be social security measures, rehabilitation, correctional, institutional, veterans, etc. No longer can we afford the questionable luxury of each welfare service being operated without relation to the other. Not only does sound administration demand this co-ordination, but more im-

---

[16] For interrelationship between OASI and OAA see Geddes, Anne E., "The Changing Role of Old-Age Assistance." *Proceedings of the National Conference of Social Work,* 1953, pp. 238–249.

portantly, the needs of the people for whom welfare services exist dictate it.

Finally, let it be said that the day of the Elizabethan Poor Law, if not entirely gone, is at least going, and is being replaced by a positively oriented welfare based on the conviction of the worth of the individual and of the value of constructive public services.

BIBLIOGRAPHY

Books and Pamphlets

Blackwell, Gordon W., and Gould, Raymond F., *Future Citizens All*. Chicago, American Public Welfare Association, 1952.

Chevigny, Hector, *The Adjustment of the Blind*. New Haven, Yale University Press, 1950.

de Schweinitz, Elizabeth and Karl, *The Content of the Public Assistance Job*. New York, American Association of Social Workers (no date).

de Schweinitz, Karl, *People and Process in Social Security*. Washington, D. C., American Council on Education, 1948.

Faatz, Anita, *The Nature of Policy in Administration of Public Assistance*. Philadelphia, Pennsylvania School of Social Work, 1943.

Kasman, Saul, *Selected Readings for the Public Assistance Worker*. Chicago and Springfield, Illinois Public Aid Commission, 1953.

Kessler, Henry H., *Rehabilitation of the Physically Handicapped,* rev. ed., New York, Columbia University Press, 1953.

Landis, Benson Y., *Rural Welfare Services*. New York, Columbia University Press, 1949.

Leyendecker, Hilary M., *Problems and Policy in Public Assistance*. New York, Harper and Brothers, 1955.

Marcus, Grace, *The Nature of Service in Public Assistance Administration*. Washington, D. C., Social Security Administration, Federal Security Agency, U. S. Government Printing Office, 1946.

Meriam, Lewis, *Relief and Social Security*. Washington, D. C., Brookings Institution, 1946.

Miles, Arthur P., *An Introduction to Public Welfare*. Boston, D. C. Heath & Company, 1949.

Rusk, Howard A., and Taylor, Eugene J., *New Hope for the Handicapped*. New York, Harper and Brothers, 1949.

Stevenson, Marietta, *Public Welfare Administration*. New York, The Macmillan Company, 1938.

Towle, Charlotte, *Common Human Needs*. Washington, D. C., Social

Security Board, Federal Security Agency, U. S. Government Printing Office, 1945.

White, R. Clyde, *Administration of Public Welfare,* rev. ed., New York, American Book Company, 1950.

Wickenden, Elizabeth, *The Needs of Older People and the Public Welfare Services to Meet Them.* Chicago, American Public Welfare Association, 1954.

Significant Articles

Ball, Robert M., "Social Insurance and the Right to Assistance." *The Social Service Review,* XXI, September 1947, pp. 331–344.

de Schweinitz, Karl and Elizabeth, "The Contribution of Social Work to the Administration of Public Assistance." *Social Work Journal,* XXIX, July 1948, pp. 108–113, 120; XXIX, October 1948, pp. 153–162, 177.

Hoey, Jane M., "The Content of Living as a Basis for a Standard of Assistance." *Journal of Social Casework,* XXVIII, January 1947, pp. 3–9.

Marcus, Grace, "Changes in the Theory of Relief Giving." *Proceedings of the National Conference of Social Work.* 1941, pp. 267–279.

Merriam, Ida C., "Social Welfare Programs in the United States." *Social Security Bulletin,* XVI, February 1953, pp. 3–12.

Perlman, Helen Harris, "Case Work Services in Public Welfare." *The Social Service Review,* XXI, June 1947, pp. 190–196.

Smith, A. Delafield, "Community Prerogative and the Legal Rights of the Individual." *Social Security Bulletin,* IX, August 1946, pp. 6–10.

"State Responsibility for Definiteness in Assistance Standards." *Social Security Bulletin,* X, March 1947, pp. 29–34.

Townsend, Roberta E., "Fact and Feeling in Eligibility." *Journal of Social Work Process,* II, December 1938, pp. 15–31.

Wiltse, Kermit T., "Social Casework Services in the Aid to Dependent Children Program." *The Social Service Review,* XXVIII, June 1954, pp. 173–185.

The Tigner Family

KERMIT T. WILTSE, D. S. W.,
Assistant Professor of Social Welfare
University of California
Berkeley, California

The statutes setting forth the general provisions that will apply to the administration of public assistance in California include the following lines: ". . . It is the legislative intent that assistance shall be administered promptly and humanely, with due regard for the preservation of family life, and without discrimination on account of race, religion, or political affiliation; and that assistance shall be so administered as to encourage self-respect, self-reliance and the desire to be a good citizen, useful to society." [1]

In these words the law requires those responsible for the administration of public assistance to implement the purpose of the program in such a way that its total effect on recipients of assistance is a positive and constructive one. It is to be noted that the law says "shall"—a mandatory, not a permissive term. The public assistance worker in his intimate contact with individuals and families—every office interview, every home call, telephone conversation, letter written, or budget reviewed—must perform each of the many facets of his job in such a way that this broad social purpose is furthered, by however so slight a degree, in the daily living of each individual person touched by the program. Administrative process must share and consciously reflect a constructive philosophy which enables such a program to attain these objectives. Specifically, the hierarchy of supervisors and administrators stemming up from the public assistance worker must create the kind of agency atmosphere, leadership, and concrete help to the individual worker that makes it possible for him to carry out the basic purpose in an increasingly effective way.

[1] Paragraph 19 of Chapter 369, Statutes of 1937, California.

There is perhaps little quarrel with this basic purpose, a purpose expressed in these or similar words in the statutes relating to public assistance in many other states along with California. If, for example, we analyze the welter of so-called "restrictive" legislative proposals with reference to the public assistance programs poured into the legislative mills during the last few sessions in California, we see that each expresses the public concern with how the goal is to be accomplished rather than with the goal itself. Most people would want (even insist) that the benefits of the public assistance laws be administered in a nondiscriminatory manner and in such a way that recipients will be made more independent rather than less so, more rather than less self-respecting and responsible. The problem turns on the question of how this goal is to be achieved.

Certainly the largest proportion of the American public still believes that only a limited measure of self-respect is possible or desirable for any young and able-bodied person who must receive public assistance, and that the way to preserve independence is to make the rules of eligibility both strict and restrictive and the investigations of eligibility stringent and unrestrained. Dimly aware of the impulse toward dependence and irresponsibility within ourselves, we as human beings project into the social scene our own inner fear that living dare not be made easy for us or for anyone else or the impulse toward independence and self-responsibility will die.

Running through the case material from a county welfare department that follows we see this question of how is the purpose of the law to be implemented illustrated by a way of working with people that does accomplish the basic goals. Since this material is illustrative of one particular phase of public assistance, the aid to dependent children's programs stemming from Title IV of the Social Security Act, it is necessary to restate the basic purpose of this program as the framework within which the role of the agency in this case becomes clearer. In brief, the purpose of aid to dependent children is to make it possible for parents, or relatives functioning in the parental role, to provide a home for children, meaning a home in which children can live and grow toward such physical and emotional maturity that they can take their place in our complex society. It follows, therefore, that all factors in the family situation that bear directly on the quality of parenting being provided the children involved are the concern of the public assistance worker. How much money the family receives and what they do with it is only one of the factors to be considered. If the public assistance agency's function with reference to ADC is conceived in this complete way, the following case material and discussion will take on real meaning.

The setting of this case is a county welfare department of a semi-urban community adjacent to a large city.

The Tigner family, consisting of Mrs. Lillie Tigner, age 46, her daughter Annabelle, age 15, and two grandchildren of Mrs. Tigner, Ella Mae, age 7, and Walter Abbott, 5, have been receiving Aid to Dependent Children's Assistance for the past five years. Mrs. Tigner is separated from her husband, Annabelle's father, but he is also incapacitated and unable to contribute to her support. Ella Mae and Walter Abbott are the children of Mrs. Tigner's daughter, Martha Abbott. Their mother had left them with Mrs. Tigner since she became ill after the birth of Walter and was hospitalized at Johnstown State Hospital with symptoms of post-partum psychosis. Shortly after being admitted to Johnstown, she was taken out of the hospital on a visit by her husband and never returned. According to Mrs. Tigner she has never heard from the Abbotts as to their address, but occasionally received letters without a return address on them. They apparently were crop-following in distant parts of the state and were fearful of revealing their whereabouts because of Mrs. Abbott's status at Johnstown State Hospital. At the time the case was transferred to this worker, Mrs. Tigner had not been seen for the past two months. There were references in the record to the unsatisfactory housekeeping standards in the home and dissatisfaction about the inability of Mrs. Tigner to furnish more certain information as to the whereabouts of her daughter and son-in-law, parents of Ella Mae and Walter Abbott. However, there seemed to be no way for Mrs. Tigner to obtain more definite information.

8/15. I wrote Mrs. Tigner a letter saying that I was now her worker and asking for an appointment for a home visit on 8/29/53.

It is well to pause here and examine the fact that this worker visited by appointment only. Visiting by oppointment only is part of a "way" of working with clients of the agency that creates ". . . self-respect, self-reliance and the desire to be a good citizen. . . ." Self-respect is always a reflection of other peoples' respect for us. Is it necessary to belabor the fact that self-respect cannot be developed in an atmosphere of "sneaking up on clients," making unannounced home visits, or on a more subtle level not expecting the client to keep appointments and therefore failing to communicate to the client the agency's conviction that he can be a responsible partner in a shared undertaking? The importance of this kind of beginning with this family is seen as we proceed with the case material.

8/29. I called at the Tigner home and found Annabelle home alone. She said her mother was visiting a neighbor and went to call her, and she came immediately.

The Tigner apartment was in a state of complete disarray. It was dirty, unkempt, and there was an odor of stale food and accumulated waste with an obvious reflection of neglect and filth of long standing. For example, there were old bread crusts on the floor which looked stale and rags and bits of clothing piled in the corners, which had obviously been there for some time. It was difficult to find a place to sit and it was necessary for Mrs. Tigner to remove some of the clutter before I could do so. Mrs. Tigner herself was dressed in a filthy dress and the children all looked dirty and disheveled. I observed that Annabelle is extremely obese and that she spent most of her time playing with youngsters half her age. Ella Mae and Walter looked healthy, although obviously they had not been bathed in a long time. Mrs. Tigner is a large, obese woman, appearing lethargic in both her thinking and her movements.

I first inquired about the children's health. Mrs. Tigner stated that the children are in good health, except that Annabelle should be watching her diet but has a difficult time following recommendations made by the doctor at County Hospital. Mrs. Tigner tended to dismiss this as something which all children found difficult to do when they were her age. She was not too responsive to my comments that the obesity might be of great detriment to Annabelle's total health now and later when she became an adult. Mrs. Tigner thought she would have Annabelle re-examined at the clinic some time in the future, possibly before school starts.

I asked if she had heard from Mr. and Mrs. Abbott, and she said she had, but they never give a return address. She says she feels her daughter is in much fear that if she were to reveal her whereabouts she might be returned to the mental hospital at Johnstown. Mrs. Tigner also expressed some guilt about this inasmuch as it was she who had her daughter committed in the first place. Mrs. Tigner asked if I had any suggestions as to what would be done about her daughter if she were to return to this area. I commented that I was certain that if her daughter had been able to manage fairly well out of the hospital she had nothing to fear about rehospitalization but that it would be up to the medical authorities as to what procedures needed to be followed. According to Mrs. Tigner, she last heard from Mr. and Mrs. Abbott in December and has not heard from them since that time. She states that they have not sent support for the children during any of this period.

As we discussed her daughter and Mr. Abbott, I received the impression that Mrs. Tigner was probably not telling all she knew about the Abbotts. For this reason I speculated with her regarding Mrs. Abbott's fears of re-entering Johnstown and possibly Mrs. Tigner's position in protecting any information she might have about the Abbotts. I suggested that sometime it might be possible to convey a message back to the Abbotts about Mrs. Abbott's status at Johnstown, and if she could do so, it would be important that she be urged to do everything possible to clear herself with the hospital. Mrs. Tigner was rather quiet in this discussion.

In view of the great disorder in the house, I asked Mrs. Tigner whether she found the children somewhat demanding and how she herself was re-acting to the responsibility for their care. I gave her lots of support in the demands made by small children, particularly in view of her obesity and accompanying difficulty in being physically active. Mrs. Tigner immediately responded by saying that she did not find the children's care too great and that they seemed very much like her own because she had had them for such a long time. She seemed quite possessive and somewhat defensive when she said this, although there was not actually the degree of feeling attached to her words that I would have expected. She seemed to have very little feeling actually about the disorder in the house, almost as though this were routine and therefore of no special concern to her. I then openly commented that the house seemed to be in much disarray, and I wondered whether Annabelle was able to carry any share of responsibility for helping to keep it in order. This was also a responsibility in which the younger children could share, and my comments were again directed toward Mrs. Tigner's possible need for some help in this regard. Mrs. Tigner then reacted by saying that she had been slow to get started with her work that day but that she had been plan-ning to do some cleaning. This was as near as she could come to recognizing my implied criticisms of her housekeeping. In view of Mrs. Tigner's proven ability to handle money, I commented that she seemed to be doing very well with her budget. She then talked at some length about her food planning and how she has managed short cuts in order to stretch the funds which she had.

We had some further discussion about Annabelle and her needs. Again Mrs. Tigner tended to overprotect the situation, showing some unwillingness to recognize that Annabelle was any different from other children and com-menting along with this that she was glad Annabelle played with younger children and as yet was not fond of boys. I suggested to Mrs. Tigner that it must be hard to raise Annabelle without help. At the same time I pointed out that it was important for a child to have knowledge of her father and that in a separation of parents like hers this knowledge had to be provided by the mother. I recognized the importance of a mother's own feelings about the other parent and this would affect what she could tell a child and how she interpreted information. I tied this up with the needs of the Abbott children noting that she had to carry the same responsibilities for these children. Mrs. Tigner had been referring to the Abbott children as "my babies" and said that they called her "mother." She said this with some satisfaction, and I sensed her expectancy that I would approve such evidence of their affection. I suggested that it must be hard for her to remember that she was not actually their mother when so many "mothering" responsibilities were required of her. Certainly, they too would be confused if she was. However, at the same time that they loved her they did have parents and it was important that they know about them. I wondered how much she had been able to explain about their parents' absence in view of the difficult circumstances of their departure.

Mrs. Tigner commented on these remarks reluctantly, struggling with her words. As she talked, she attempted and finally used the term, "my grandchildren." She told about her daughter's illness, her fears about her daughter's behavior, and the circumstances which led to commitment. She readily admitted the guilt she felt for accomplishing this and said she wondered whether her daughter could ever forgive her.

She said that she did talk to the children about their parents but volunteered very little as to what she was able to say. I recalled to her some of the things she had already said, and together we selected what might be explained about the separation at the level that the children might be able to understand. I suggested that Mrs. Tigner might fear alienation of the children from her if they developed any real closeness with their parents and that this might also make it hard for her to talk about them. I reviewed the quality of affection she had given them and suggested that the important part she had played in their lives could never be "taken away" or lost to them.

I encouraged Mrs. Tigner to discuss Annabelle's ideas about her father. Mrs. Tigner then said that Mr. Tigner and she corresponded intermittently and that Annabelle writes to him also. Mrs. Tigner told me about her exhusband's incapacity and his inability to support her and their child, which had been confirmed by a report received through the district attorney's office. This had been the keynote of her explanation to Annabelle. Mrs. Tigner ruminated about her marriage and early life with Mr. Tigner, stressing her economic struggle. It was as though Mrs. Tigner was explaining some of her past and present behavior to herself as she talked about it to me. She commented once that she wondered why she told me these things as she had not thought about them in years. I gave her assurance that talking things out was appropriate and sometimes it helped us to understand ourselves better. She seemed to accept this.

My general impression of Mrs. Tigner is that she has a real affection for the children but I have some question as to its quality. This, I feel, is related especially to her inability actually to perform some of the basic services for the children, i.e., to keep them clean within certain bounds as well as to provide the kind of training and general care which comply with ordinary standards of "mothering." I was unable, however, to help Mrs. Tigner to express anything other than a complete acceptance of her position with the children and a need to say that everything was going along fine. She did show some concern about her daughter's position in relation to Johnstown Hospital and particularly about her own role in having helped to commit her. I thought she showed more feeling in this discussion than at any other time in the interview. I plan to follow up on these contacts in order to learn to know Mrs. Tigner more intimately and to continue to direct my interest especially toward her and her problems in carrying out her responsibilities toward this family.

In this first interview the worker immediately makes a series of pertinent observations with reference to the quality of care the children are receiving and Mrs. Tigner's relationship to them. These observations are relevant only if we keep clearly in mind that the larger purpose of the aid to dependent children's program is to help parents and children to remain together and to preserve and develop mutually satisfying family relationships. Society's interests as well as those of the individual are to be served no other way. Here the worker must rely on his knowledge of human behavior if he is to know the meaning to both Annabelle and her mother of the things he sees here, such as the filth and disorder, Annabelle's obesity and her mother's resistance to being concerned about it, and her mother's over-protectiveness of Annabelle as evidenced by her inability to expect certain responsibilities of her in relation to helping with the housework. Without knowledge of the meaning of behavior, the worker would not know what to observe or the meaning of what he sees; without clarity as to the purpose of the aid to dependent children's program he would not be able to relate this knowledge in any meaningful way to what he is doing with Mrs. Tigner here and now; and without great skill he could not put these two aspects together into a process that really helps the client do something about a situation that is, as in this instance, unsatisfactory to both the family and to society.

Perhaps the assumption that the situation as we find it here is unsatisfactory to Mrs. Tigner needs some discussion. We do not know at this point how much dissatisfaction she feels—that is, the degree—but there is some evident dissatisfaction to her in the uncertain status of her daughter with reference to the hospital and also some evidence of anxiety which she carefully controlled when the worker asked if she knew the whereabouts of the Abbotts. Less evident is whatever dissatisfaction she may feel about her care of the children, her overprotectiveness of them, and particularly the poor physical care she is giving them. In giving attention to these matters the worker proceeds from the fundamental fact that all human beings want to be in some degree of harmony with their society. All social life is based upon this fact and a person's ability or inability to respond to the demands of his social group is the measure of his health or illness. Social work—and the social worker—always relates itself to the healthy part of the client's personality, strengthening him for more personally and socially acceptable participation in society. The improvement that we see occurring in this family situation during the few weeks included in the portion of their record reproduced here testifies to the inner strength and health of the people involved as much as to the skill of the worker. The activity of the worker as reflected in this record takes on new meaning when seen against the backdrop of these profound social and psychological facts.

As we look at how this worker involved Mrs. Tigner in examining these factors in the situation unsatisfactory to her and to the agency, we see a real respect for the client's desire to be a better mother to the children under her care. There is quiet assurance communicated by every comment and question of the worker that things can be changed for the better, that Mrs. Tigner has the strength to do it, and the right to do it in her own way and at her own pace. The disorder and filth are not ignored nor is Mrs. Tigner told to clean her house. The worker discusses it openly and in realistic terms, endeavoring to help Mrs. Tigner identify what could be the source of the problem and exploring various ways she might deal with it, and Mrs. Tigner is neither pushed into agreeing to clean nor allowed to excuse herself from responsibility. The problem is simply identified, discussed, and left with her, but she is supported by the worker's genuine concern for her in the face of her many problems.

In the rather brief discussion of Mrs. Tigner's daughter and son-in-law, the worker gives Mrs. Tigner a completely new perspective on how she might help her daughter clear herself with Johnstown Hospital and hence be able to take a renewed responsibility for their children. The worker gave concrete information from his knowledge of mental illness and of hospital procedures. Sensing Mrs. Tigner's fear of betraying her daughter, he respects Mrs. Tigner's desire to protect her but says "out loud" some of Mrs. Tigner's unspoken fears, thereby making it easier for her to face and deal with them. The worker goes on to state the value it would be to Mrs. Abbott to clear herself with the hospital, but again respects the pace at which Mrs. Tigner can move and does not push her into either a confession of having covered up for her daughter or into an agreement to get in touch with her. In view of what the worker does in this interview, it is interesting to see what occurs in the second.

9/12. I wrote Mrs. Tigner for another appointment and called at the home today. I noticed when I arrived that a real effort had been made to clean the apartment. I immediately commented on how much better the apartment looked and of the considerable effort it must have taken to clean it. Mrs. Tigner was responsive to this comment and quite pleased that I had recognized her effort. An attempt had also been made to clean up the children, although their hair and clothes were still in disarray.

Mrs. Tigner, soon after my arrival, commented that she wanted me to know that she had seen Mr. Abbott, that he was now back in town and had come to see her. She posed this as a recent occurrence and said that she wondered if I had found out anything about her daughter's status at Johnstown as she hoped to be able to convey any message to Mr. Abbott for transmittal to her daughter. I said directly to her that this must place her in an embarrassing position, but that at the same time I thought it was quite urgent that every effort be made to convey to the Abbotts their responsibility in connection with the children and that I was looking forward to an opportunity to talk with them if they would agree to an interview. I suggested that possibly we might begin by talking with Mr. Abbott at Mrs. Tigner's apartment, and she felt that this could be worked out. She said she would talk with him and attempt to make an arrangement for an interview during the following week. She said that it was her understanding that the Abbotts were working locally and plan to live in the near-by city at least for awhile. Mrs. Tigner said she was most anxious that I talk with Mr. Abbott directly about all these things and it was agreed that an appointment next week would include a conference with Mr. Abbott, Mrs. Tigner and myself and possibly Mrs. Abbott, if she could be convinced that there would be no danger of her return to Johnstown for hospitalization. I said that I would make inquiry about her status and would come with information as to what steps she should take to clear herself. Mrs. Tigner expressed satisfaction with Mr. Abbott's return but could offer little detail about the Abbotts and seemed hesitant actually to discuss the matter.

It was agreed that we would need to know full details as to their whereabouts and future plans when I next saw Mrs. Tigner and Mr. Abbott. Mrs. Tigner hesitated to give any information as to the Abbotts' present whereabouts, again feeling that she was not free to do so.

The worker arrives to find Mrs. Tigner making a real effort to clean the apartment. We might suspect she is doing it only to please the worker unless we remember that in his first visit the worker was skillful and sure in identifying with Mrs. Tigner's dissatisfaction with her own housekeeping. However, we can expect that at this stage Mrs. Tigner will need the support of the worker's responsiveness to the effort she is making, and he gives it in a simple and direct way, again identifying with her effort and her satisfaction in the results, rather than focusing on the results and their apparent limitations.

Remarkable also is the fact that Mrs. Tigner is able to say she has seen Mr. Abbott, her son-in-law. She is still fearful of betraying her daughter and being responsible for her return to the mental hospital and not quite able to say she has been in touch with her also, wanting additional assurance about the probable action of the hospital authorities. In the discussion that follows, the worker consistently respects Mrs. Tigner's need to protect her daughter and son-in-law and recognizes with her that she is put in a difficult position. However, the worker is clear and emphatic about the value and importance to them of clearing up the whole matter of their responsibility to their children and of Mrs. Abbott's relationship to the hospital. He consistently stays with Mrs. Tigner's, and indirectly with Mr. and Mrs. Abbott's, desire to have things straight with the agency and to be relieved of their fear of the hospital authorities. At no point does he "take over" by urging her to clear themselves out of the agency's—and therefore his—need to get things straight. On this point rests the difference between freeing people for responsible action or trapping them into a struggle against the agency, leading only to further covering-up, avoidance of responsibility, and frustration for both agency and client. It can be readily understood that if the client's energy is mobilized into fighting the agency rather than working with it, he will have little left over for constructive change in relation to his problems. The importance of this fact is illustrated as we proceed with the Tigner family and see how Mrs. Tigner is able to put increasing energy into caring for her home and children as she is relieved of the burden of maintaining her very difficult initial position with the agency.

9/14. Mr. Abbott called at the office quite unexpectedly and asked to see me. He said he felt it was time for him to "make a clean breast of things." He said Mrs. Tigner had come to him in quite a state of anxiety during the week, saying she felt "the walls are closing in" and that they must stick together in order to clear their standing with the agency.

He confirmed the fact that he and his wife had been moving about a great deal since the latter's departure from Johnstown and that much of this was motivated by her fear of return to the hospital. He said, however, that as of the past December he and his wife had returned to this area and had actually stayed with Mrs. Tigner at her present apartment. He said that at present he and Mrs. Abbott are living at 125 Linden Avenue, in the city. He is employed at Allied Steel Co. and showed me a check stub which showed a net income of $69.53 per week. Mrs. Abbott had recently secured a job at the Continental Can Co. in Stewartville and she earns approximately $50 a week.

Mr. Abbott said that since 1948 when they left this area he had contributed a total of approximately $150 to $200 to Mrs. Tigner for the children from time to time plus some clothes which they bought for them on different occasions. However, he admitted that this had been a very small amount over such a period of time and that there had been no real duplication of support during that time. He also said because they were "in flight" they had never remained anywhere long and had a very hard time managing financially through all of this time. It was only recently since their return to the city that they felt they were in a position to assume some responsibility for the children, but at this time they found Mrs. Tigner was most reluctant to release them to their parents. Mr. Abbott quoted Mrs. Tigner as saying that the children were a financial insurance to her both as to income and as to an apartment in the housing project. He added that he knew she loved the children but that he had become very unhappy about her possessive attitude toward them. He was dismayed at the fact that he and his wife had to ask permission for each move they made with the children and that many times Mrs. Tigner refused such permission. She explained this to them by saying she had accepted responsibility for the children's care and that she wanted them near her at all times in case there were any visits made by a social worker from this department. Mr. Abbott admitted to some feelings of guilt about the whole situation but said he had been very uncertain as to what it was possible for him to do about it. When Mrs. Tigner had come to him with the story of my contacts and apparently her reactions to my interest, he felt the time had come to make a complete confession of the whole story in the hope he could straighten it out and could "square away" any financial obligation he might have. He repeated over and over that he was very fearful about his mother-in-law's reaction if she knew he had come here in this way. It was her understanding he would meet with her when I saw them both at the Tigner home this next week and it was for this reason he had come to the office immediately after work in order to give me a previous report. He said he felt there were probably going to be some things he could not say in front of Mrs. Tigner and this was why he wanted to talk with me in advance. At the same time, he feels now that if I can give him a definite lead during my conversation with both Mrs. Tigner and him together, he will attempt to reiterate many of the statements he had made to me so as to clear the air and to make more realistic planning possible.

Mr. Abbott said he was quite upset about the way Mrs. Tigner provided care for the children, mentioning he felt they were quite undisciplined and not properly cared for. He particularly commented about what he considered to be Mrs. Tigner's lack of understanding as to how to teach the children the difference between right and wrong. I thought he showed much sensitivity and understanding in this regard inasmuch as he stressed most importantly those things which to him reflected enforced control and punishment of the children and no attempt to help them understand the reasons why their behavior was dangerous to themselves and others.

Actually, Mr. Abbott was not sure how much his wife would go along with what he desired, namely, to accept the children in their home and to begin to assume complete responsibility for their care. He commented that his wife was very close to her mother and he knew she was somewhat in awe and fear of her. For this reason, he was anxious that the family relationships be handled quite carefully so as not to alienate the various members. At the same time, he recognized that Mrs. Tigner had tried to carry out her responsibilities and that they, the Abbotts, had placed her in a difficult position when they first disappeared.

I said at this point that I thought it was terribly important that Mrs. Tigner be clear about my coming and that he explain as much about the visit as he could. He thought he would do this before next Wednesday.

We might be surprised at the sudden willingness of Mr. Abbott to come forward to admit his guilt and assert his responsibility for his children if we do not remember two things: first, the desire in every person, operating in varying degrees, to be in harmony with the world around him, to be free of gnawing uncertainty as to his position in relation to important people and forces in his life; and, second, the fact referred to earlier that this worker had communicated to Mrs. Tigner, and to the Abbotts through her, his genuine concern for the difficult position they were in and a realistic conviction that the problem could be resolved in a way conducive to the greater satisfaction of everyone concerned. In view of these two points, Mr. Abbott's action becomes understandable.

Most of Mr. Abbott's "story" which he pours out to the worker in this interview is self-explanatory. It is easy to be critical of Mr. Abbott's lack of strength to cope with his mother-in-law's possessiveness toward his children and her stringent form of discipline that disturbed him. The fact remains, however, that if the purpose is to help him carry his responsibilities more adequately, we cannot begin by criticizing him for his failures. Rather, he must be accepted as he is, with full recognition on the worker's part of his strengths and his limitations, and be given support in being as responsible as he can. That he could accept responsibility was shown when he voluntarily came in and asserted it. The subsequent record attests to his ability, with the worker's steady support, to maintain his responsibility to his children.

It is interesting to note in this interview the way Mrs. Tigner had reacted to her two visits with the worker as revealed by Mr. Abbott. There was nothing in the worker's attitude or in what he said to Mrs. Tigner that suggested suspicion or an effort to force her to reveal her knowledge of the whereabouts of the Abbotts. As was discussed earlier, the worker's effort was directed toward freeing Mrs. Tigner to take responsibility for the facts in her situation and no longer to deny or avoid them. Here is an excellent example of a common human experience. To Mrs. Tigner it felt like "the walls were closing in" as soon as she was helped to feel the true weight of the façade she was striving to maintain.

The crisis now past, the case material reveals a rapid sorting out by the family of their involved relationships to each other and to the agency, aided by the steady supportive concern of the worker and his consistent help in focusing on the real issues to be resolved.

9/19. I called at Mrs. Tigner's apartment for my interview with her and with Mr. Abbott. I noted that the apartment was cleaner than at any time I had seen it previously and that Mrs. Tigner herself was in a clean dress and the children were all scrubbed and looking neat. She was very responsive to my comments about her appearance and about the apartment, although she seemed rather ill at ease about the whole interview. Mr. Abbott was also there looking a bit shy and ill at ease and wondering, apparently, how the interview was to start. I began by bringing out certain comments regarding the Abbotts, asking again some of the same questions I had asked of Mr. Abbott recently, so that the same information could be covered once again. Mr. Abbott was able to go over all the information he had previously given me at the same time that he maintained a running commentary toward Mrs. Tigner which was to say over and over again, "You know I love you, Mama, but I got to say these things or these people will find out anyway." With this he went over the period of time he had spent in the Tigner apartment, talked again about employment for himself and his wife, and then said he wished to make whatever amends would be indicated according to what the agency felt was a proper adjustment. He said he had discussed his whole situation with his wife who in turn was willing to go along with any plan that was decided, but shared her wishes with him for regaining a closer contact with the children. Mrs. Tigner participated here by saying she hoped they would not take the children away as she had become extremely fond of them and was hoping to be able to go on caring for them. She stressed over and over that the Abbotts moved about so much that she was afraid the children would not have the proper opportunity to attend school. She seemed to feel this was of extreme importance, having projected all of her rationalizations upon this point which she hoped would be an acceptable one. As we talked, I recognized with both Mr. Abbott and Mrs. Tigner their own personal needs and wishes in this situation at the same time that I pointed out what appeared to be a realistic fact, i.e., that the children needed to know their parents so that they could sort out their relationship to Mrs. Tigner. Nonetheless, sometimes it was a practical arrangement that children live with relatives. This plan could work only if it was agreed to and understood by all of the important parties concerned, parents, grandparents, and children, with each person aware of his individual rights and responsibilities. I commented that as far as the department was concerned, it was obvious that ADC grant would be terminated immediately for the children as their parents were able to assume responsibility for their care. Whatever plan was worked out about their continuing care would need to be agreed upon between Mr. and Mrs. Abbott and Mrs. Tigner, recognizing that Mr. and Mrs. Abbott have legal custody and control of the children. Our department was interested in knowing final planning as it might relate to members of the household who would be listed as sharing household expenses inasmuch as eligibility apparently would continue for Annabelle and Mrs. Tigner.

It was possible during this interview for all of us to talk together about the pros and cons of various plans, and it was finally agreed that Mrs. Abbott needed to be brought in quite directly to any of the final arrangements agreed upon. It was suggested by me that we meet again together, including Mrs. Abbott, during the following week and that in the meantime the family would have a chance to discuss exactly what they wanted to do about Ella

Mae and Walter. I would bring back the department's decision regarding reimbursement which may be required of Mr. and Mrs. Abbott. I also promised to learn specifically what Mrs. Abbott's status would be at Johnstown Hospital as I had been unable to do this as yet. However, I had some preliminary information that it was very unlikely that she would be returned for observation at the hospital if she had been able to function as adequately as reported. I hoped to be able to interpret some of these things to her when I saw her this afternoon. Mr. Abbott said he had made arrangements for my coming and that Mrs. Abbott would be expecting me after she returned from work at about 4:30.

It is felt from my observations of this family that it would be well to consider applying the provisions of the manual of procedure with reference to avoiding excessive hardship to a client in viewing any reimbursement or collection requests made of the Abbotts. In view of their present attempts to resume responsibility for the children and their limited resources, I feel they should be given every break possible so that by eliminating extra tensions they can use all of their capacities to tackle their present responsibilities. It would appear from my review with Mrs. Tigner of her income and property that she and Annabelle remain eligible for ADC from the information available to us at this time. Final budgetary arrangements will be made after my interview with Mrs. Abbott and a final conference with the family next week.

Later: I called on Mrs. Abbott at the Linden Street address. Their small sparsely furnished apartment was neat and clean and Mrs. Abbott, herself, presented her problems in a clear-cut direct manner. She talked about her feelings regarding the hospital, her fears in relation to it, and her worry particularly that she might have to return there. Much of the same information was covered in this interview as had been covered with Mr. Abbott and Mrs. Tigner. I felt that Mrs. Abbott had been currently informed of all that had taken place and that she was cooperating with her husband's plans insofar as she was able. At the same time, I sensed that she was not as anxious to assume complete responsibility for the children, particularly in view of her present employment. I gave her an opportunity to express this by introducing the idea as a possibility without placing any personal judgment upon it. She said, however, that she wanted to do the thing that was proper and commented that she felt she did not know the children too well because of her long absence and it was important that she get better acquainted with them. At the same time she said she did not want to hurt her mother's feelings inasmuch as she felt she had done a great deal for the children in their parents' absence. Her ambivalence actually was a way of saying that she had mingled feelings about her planning but at the same time was most anxious that she be approved of in whatever plans she accepted and was also anxious to go along with her husband's wishes. I speculated with her at some length as to what problems the children might present, the demands children of this age might have and their ready response to love and affection which they very much need from their own parents. Mrs. Abbott related very directly to this, remembering some of her own childhood experiences and saying at the same time that she could see personality differences between children which meant that each needed some special things from each of their parents. I thought she identified pretty well with their feelings, although I had some question as to her actual capacity as well as real wish to assume this responsibility completely. Mrs. Abbott actually was more self-concerned at this point about her various own problems and we talked together primarily of the big step they had taken in coming to the agency and in trying to straighten out their difficulties. It was arranged then that our next meeting would be one that Mrs. Abbott would try to attend, wherein we would examine the results of their planning in the same terms I had already outlined to Mrs. Tigner and Mr. Abbott. This was agreeable to Mrs. Abbott and she also looked forward to a report from me regarding the steps she should take to clear her status at Johnstown Hospital.

The clarity and completeness of the worker's recording of these two interviews reveals his sure and steady process of helping each adult in this family to sort out his individual responsibilities and those that are to be shared. Mr. Abbott uses the support of the worker's presence in saying, "I got to say these things or these people will find out anyway," and in so doing achieves a renewed sense of his own value and of his right to play a responsible part in his children's lives. Mrs. Tigner tries to handle all her guilt about deceiving the agency and denying the Abbotts their rightful place with their own children by emphasizing how much they have moved around and their consequent inability to provide the children a consistent school experience. The worker cuts through this to give recognition to and acceptance of her love for the children and her need to keep them with her and at the same time points to the fact that the children need to know their relationship to their parents as well as to their grandmother. We see the worker requiring each of them to be clear about what they want to do and can sustain. He makes sure that each understands the alternatives and the consequences of each possible course of action.

9/25. I telephoned Johnstown State Hospital and learned that Mrs. Abbott was still being carried as Absent Without Leave and that she could clear her status by getting in touch with the Bureau of Mental Hygiene worker. The latter would interview her, make a report regarding her experiences since leaving the hospital and would follow this with a recommendation regarding discharge if it seems indicated. From what I had told her about Mrs. Abbott, it seemed apparent to the Johnstown Hospital social worker that there would be no question but that discharge would be recommended.

Later, I talked with Miss Lydia Parsons of the Bureau of Mental Hygiene and arranged an appointment for Mrs. Abbott tentatively for the following Friday. Again the same information was confirmed through Miss Parsons.

Conference with Supervisor. It was agreed with Mrs. Olson, Supervisor, that the hardship clause would be invoked in connection with the period of ineligibility of Ella Mae and Walter Abbott which was actually designated as having dated from about January 1 to the present time, or a total of nine months. $328 was the amount of overpayment. Our interpretation of the hardship clause is that every benefit should be given to the family to assume their responsibilities at this time and in view of the emotional as well as the economic pressures which they had been under, it is felt they should be given every support now which might mean a continuing capacity to assume their responsibilities for the future. This interpretation will also be made directly to Mr. and Mrs. Abbott, as well as to Mrs. Tigner. Certainly responsibility for withholding information regarding the parents' location and ability to support was shared between the Abbotts and Mrs. Tigner with various factors playing a part in confusing their judgment in the situation.

9/27. A conference was held on this date with Mr. and Mrs. Abbott and Mrs. Tigner. Again the house was in good order and the children as well as their parents were neatly groomed. Everyone participated in outlining the plans that they had discussed and agreed upon. It was this: Mr. and Mrs. Abbott felt that in view of their present employment it would be best to leave the children where they were. At the same time they wanted to make clear their rights as parents to see as much of the children as they could within reasonable limits. This difference of opinion was discussed aloud again with Mrs. Tigner saying that she went along with this idea and would do all that she could to cooperate. With reference to the amount of money the Abbotts should pay to cover the cost of the children's board and room, Mrs. Tigner said that she would need only enough money to cover their food and she saw no need for asking for any other amount at this time. I made out a specific budget and went over each item with all of the members present. Total cost for food and share of housing was $56. This was the amount agreed upon for the Abbotts to pay, with Mrs. Tigner accepting this amount and the Abbotts agreeing to pay for the children's clothes and incidental expenses.

Overpayment. I talked at length with Mr. and Mrs. Abbott and Mrs. Tigner about the agency's attitude regarding the overpayment and why this interpretation was being made. They were most responsive and grateful and all of them expressed great relief for having finally discussed this. Mrs. Tigner talked about it as feeling like a tremendous load had shifted off her shoulders and that she had just realized how much the guilt of her knowledge had weighed upon her. My own speculation was that this had had a great deal to do with her recent slovenliness although I do not know to what degree. At any rate, everyone felt this had been an extremely fair decision from the department and that their present plan seemed to have a good chance of working out. The Abbotts said they hoped eventually to take the children into their care, especially if and when Mrs. Abbott concluded her employment after her debts are paid.

I explained to Mrs. Abbott exactly what I had been told by Johnstown State Hospital and she went along with every point of the discussion. She and her husband were going to keep this appointment which had been made tentatively for this Friday and would let me know of its outcome. She seemed to have lost a great deal of her fears earlier expressed and no longer was avoiding the possibility of a contract with the representative from the hospital. Mrs. Abbott commented that she felt quite free with me and much reassured and thought now that she had seen how justly and understandingly their whole situation had been handled, she felt she could expect and trust the same would happen with regard to her Johnstown Hospital commitment. I helped her to recognize that she had become more "sure" of herself through this experience and felt she would be able to take more responsibility for the results of the interview with the social worker from the Bureau of Mental Hygiene.

Summary. I think the interview today was a good clearing point for many factors in this involved family situation. I think that all of the members have arrived at a plan which permits them to assume their appropriate responsibility. I think that the primary service given in this case has been to clarify eligibility factors as well as to help with some instructions in "parenting" and to clarify inter-family relationships as they involved the various children and adult members. This was accomplished and future relationships with the agency can be handled by direct discussion as the need may arise. I feel that Mrs. Tigner needs much help toward greater understanding of children's needs as well as how to discipline and control them.

9/28. Notice of change put through this date showing a decrease in ADC for Mrs. Tigner from $166 to $101 with discontinuance noted for Ella Mae and Water Abbott effective 9/31.

At the end of the recorded material we see each member of the family taking a very different kind of responsibility for the children in the home. The case record material reproduced here represents a piece of social casework process, not the whole of this agency's relationship with this family. Much has been accomplished although much remains to be done as the worker indicates in his summary.

Everything points to the probability that Mrs. Abbott's status with Johnstown Hospital will be easily resolved, although our record ends before this is definite. We must remain even less certain about whether the Abbott children will live indefinitely with their grandmother or whether they will eventually move to a new home with their own parents. It seems probable they will remain with Mrs. Tigner at least until their parents are established in a more satisfactory home. More important than which place they are to live is a clear understanding at all times of who is to be responsible for each of the various aspects of their upbringing. Then the worker's efforts can be directed toward helping each member of the family carry his particular responsibility as well as he possibly can.

Certainly much remains to be done, calling for continued skillful service from this public assistance agency through its worker. But if we think back to the filthy apartment and the anxious and unhappy person the worker found on his first home call six weeks earlier, we know that these children will hereafter receive a far better quality of parenting. Recalling that the basic purpose of the aid to dependent children's program is to make it possible for parents to provide a home in which children can live and grow, we see that this purpose has been served in every act and word of the worker in relation to this family. At no time did he lose sight of this basic purpose. The fraud implications in this situation might easily have caused the worker to lose this basic purpose. He might have become engrossed in determining whether or not there was intentional fraud and in exacting every penny of repayment. By keeping his focus on the real needs of the people involved, this worker implemented to a remarkable degree the overall intent and purpose of the public assistance program, ". . . assistance shall be so administered as to encourage self-respect, self-reliance and the desire to be a good citizen, useful to society."

chapter 8

Welfare Services for Children

The Child in His Family and Group

Anyone who gives thought to the welfare of a child or of children must realize, inevitably, that what affects the interests of children affects the well-being of the entire group of which the child is but one member. To give some substance to these observations, let us examine certain situations involving the welfare of children to see how interrelated the world of the child is with that of the adult in the total community in which they both live. A child is born. Simply from the aspect of physical health, many antecedent conditions must exist in order to insure the child a decent start at birth. How healthy his parents are, how healthy other people are, how much public health there is in the community, these and many other factors determine what the newborn's start will be. The child grows up and begins to acquire an awareness of the world around him. We impress him into a school system. The kind of education he receives is determined not so much upon his native endowment as it is by the amount and quality of education which people unrelated and unknown to him possess. He enters the labor market. The kind of job he gets depends to some extent upon his innate capacity, but more largely is related to the economic organization of his own or other communities. Nor are his opportunities unaffected by such things as the state of the labor market, depression, and prosperity. His prior health experience and vocational training, or lack of it, determine his present availability for a low-pay or a high-pay job, a dead-end job or one that offers a chance for advancement and personal development. What is stressed here is the fact that a child comes into a world already made by other people, that his chance of survival in it and the possibilities of his own effective participation in it are matters usually beyond his control. The immediate bearing of these remarks is to make clear that child welfare services are not services for the child alone, but are part and parcel of the organization of community resources for the well-being of the whole group. They reflect the value the community places upon the child.

Apprenticeship and Indenture

By the time Queen Elizabeth had come to the throne of England in 1558 feudalism had given way to the early stage of capitalism. It was Elizabeth's statute in the forty-third year of her reign that set the precedent for modern states in the definition of responsibility for certain disfavored groups within the community, among them certain classes of children. The system of indenture and apprenticeship by which a child was bound over (i.e. indentured—the legal instrument was called an indenture) to another person or family was a pronounced development following 1601. As was so characteristic of much of the Elizabethan experience, this system spread to America. Indenture and apprenticeship as a means of dealing with children without support seemed a natural transplantation to colonial soil on this side, and it was quickly adopted, for the earliest record indicates that in 1636 little Benjamin Eaton was indentured by the Governor of Plymouth Colony to Bridget Fuller, a widow. Widow Fuller was to keep him in school for at least two years and to employ him in work for which she saw he was fitted.

Tender age was no bar to apprenticeship, for there are instances of the binding over of children hardly out of the cradle. For example, the court records of New Castle on the Delaware River for the years 1678–1679 show that the widow of the late William Hodges put out her son Charles, aged 5 years, to Thomas Jacobs for a period of twelve years. Thomas Jacobs in turn agreed to provide the boy with sufficient fare, apparel, washing, and lodging, to instruct him in the trade of wheelwright and at the end of twelve years to give the boy a cow and a calf. Incidentally, it was further agreed that Mr. Jacobs' son shall "larn ye sd boy to Reede as much as hee can teach him."

Apprenticeship of children whose parents were unable to support them continued beyond colonial days and well into the nineteenth century, even though alternative forms of child care had been developed. Homer Folks, as far back as 1902, observed that "the old-fashioned indenture or apprentice system passed largely into disuse, if not into disrepute, by 1875."[1] On the other hand, Lundberg, citing the repeal of a law in Mississippi in 1946, remarked, "care of children in almshouses and by binding out or indenture belonged to an era long past, although vestiges of these archaic methods were still to be found in a few communities not so many years ago, and some may still be in existence."[2]

The conviction—or perhaps it is merely a rationalization—persisted that the children of the poor must early learn the lessons of work and develop the habits of thrift. This is all the more amazing when a common spectacle these children have witnessed seemed to demonstrate that those who have most appear to work least, while those who appear to work hardest have least to show for it. Changing philosophies have condemned practices which sacrifice the welfare of the child through a system of child labor. In our contemporary industrial and social order, no child is of economic advantage during his minority, and any attempt to use the child for pecuniary gain is at the expense of his health, his education, his recreation, his physical and social development, as well as his start in life. Furthermore, our current convictions affirm that every child, rich or poor, is entitled to the basic minimum of health, educational, and social opportunities. In our present culture the child comes to be regarded as an investment, yielding returns later in constructive citizenship and productive living.

Public Institutional Care—The Almshouse

Almshouse care for children had no great vogue in the early days of the colonies. Not until after the year 1700 did this method of child care appear, and for many years it was outranked by apprenticeship and indenture. The first almshouses developed, naturally enough, in the larger cities, and later the movement spread to the others. New York, Philadelphia, and Boston early had their almshouses into which were herded helpless children who were without means of support. These

[1] Folks, Homer, *The Care of Destitute, Neglected, and Delinquent Children.* New York, The Macmillan Company, 1902, p. 41.

[2] Lundberg, Emma O., *Unto the Least of These.* New York, D. Appleton–Century Co., 1947, p. 299; see also p. 50.

children received hardly more than what might be termed a residual care. Inadequate diet and lack of proper sanitation took their toll in high sickness and mortality rates. A minimum of educational facilities and instruction did much to render them ineffective when they reached the labor market upon their discharge. The deprivation of the normal developmental experiences of home life crippled their capacity to make subsequent adjustments to other individuals and to community life.

One of the early developments which had some effect in breaking up such devastating situations was the gradual withdrawal of various groups of handicapped children from the poorhouse and the provision for them in specialized institutions. With the opening of the Hartford Institution for the Deaf in 1817 there was available a specialized service for the child as well as the adult. For the blind this service began with the Massachusetts Institution for the Blind in 1831–1832, and for the feeble-minded the way was opened through the Massachusetts Institution for the Feeble-Minded in 1848. For another group, delinquent children, specialized institutional care was signalized by the opening of the New York House of Refuge in 1825, which received both boys and girls. Within a year a second institution for juvenile delinquents was opened. The significance of this was that it was the first such institution to be established under municipal auspice—the House of Reformation of the city of Boston, 1826. As years passed, there was a further growth of these specialized institutions, both publicly and privately supported.

A further break with the system of mixed almshouse care was the step taken by the state of Massachusetts to place children in an almshouse solely intended for children at Monson in 1864. Two years later this institution was designated as the State Primary School, and the children therein were no longer to be designated as paupers. Another institution that served to deflect children from the mixed almshouse—and hence provided a welcome alternative—was the soldiers' orphans' home established after the Civil War. These were supported by public funds. Most made provision for children of any soldier or sailor rather than restricting admission to those children whose fathers had lost their lives in active military service. Later, in some states, these homes were authorized to receive other dependent children. About the same time that Massachusetts was instituting its State Primary School, another state, Ohio, was working out a variation known as the County Children's Home, with emphasis upon county initiative and financing. A few other states permitted counties to develop separate children's institutions, but the trend was more along the line set by Massachusetts, i.e., state homes. In Michigan the State Public School (opened in 1874 with its legal enactment in 1867) was intended to serve as a temporary home and school until the children could be placed in family homes. Other states, such as Wisconsin, Minnesota, and Rhode Island, within a decade followed the Michigan pattern. Some of the county homes, lacking other than local supervision, tended to degenerate into local poorhouses, but many of the state homes approached a high standard of child care. They were aided in this development not only by the fact that they were on a state-wide basis, but also because they were in a position to profit by developments within the larger national area of child care. Especially toward the latter part of the nineteenth century increasing emphasis was being put upon placing children in private homes, and some state schools came to regard themselves as functioning solely for short-time institutional care. A number of states went so far as to require that no child was to be kept in the state home for as much as sixty days without adequate evidence that every effort had been made for placement in a private home. Such laws further stipulated that the retention of any child beyond the sixty-day period should call for a monthly report of reasons why there was such a delay. Both Massachusetts and Michigan who, in the 1870's, originated the state school plan, did much to extend the principle beyond their own borders.

Another movement that contributed to the reduction of the almshouse care for children was the introduction of the principles and practice of foster home placement during the last half of the nineteenth century. This work will be treated in another section of this chapter, but it is well to remind ourselves that even though all these factors tended to render the almshouse obsolete, nevertheless it continued to house children well into the twentieth century. By now it must be clear that the almshouse has been the most deeply rooted of all our American social welfare institutions.

Private Institutional Care—Orphan Homes

The earliest orphan asylum in America was attached to the Ursuline Convent in New Orleans for the care of children whose parents had been massacred by the Natchez Indians in 1729. By 1740 the second was opened in Savannah by George Whitefield, the celebrated English preacher, and is still known as Bethesda.[3] Several other children's institutions were initiated before 1800, but it remained for the nineteenth century to lay an unprecedented number of orphanage cornerstones. The number of orphanages supported by public funds remained surprisingly small, in part perhaps because the almshouse still received children and in part because of alternative methods of care, such as apprenticeship and indenture, outdoor relief, and toward the end of the century, foster home care. In addition, the fact that private funds had so largely pre-empted the institution field made it less imperative for the public orphanage to appear.

By far the greater number of orphan asylums, as they were not infrequently called, were denominational in origin and management. In 1929 it was estimated that some 1500 children's institutions had been established in this country, of which about 60 percent were denominational. Other orphan homes which were nondenominational in origin and control have been established for a variety of reasons. One consideration, particularly in the early days, was to avoid the mixed almshouse care so prevalent for destitute children. Another was the substantial satisfaction an individual or group of individuals derived when a memorial in brick and stone was raised. A third motive undoubtedly sprang from a sincere conviction at the time that institutional care was the best method of providing service for children. Furthermore, buildings and staff and children were tangible and gave concrete evidence of monies expended. These, and other motives as well, undoubtedly influenced the founders of orphan homes; but who is able to single out any motive and declare it to have been the dominant one? Who knows, for instance, what motivated Stephen Girard, over a hundred years ago, to bequeath one of America's largest fortunes for the founding of a school for "poor, white male orphans"? Certainly during the first

---

[3] Both of these institutions were under private auspices, but by 1790 Charleston, South Carolina, had established the first public orphanage in the New World.

half of the nineteenth century it was as much a part of the folkways and the mores as foster home care and aid to dependent children are today.

One further point needs to be noted here. Free public education as we know it today was hardly known a hundred years ago, nor well developed until within the past fifty years. Early orphanages that included schools in many cases actually excelled the schooling facilities of many communities from which their children came.

In addition to the denominational and nondenominational institutions, there were orphanages established for special groups such as infants, or Negro orphans, or orphans of soldiers and sailors (when not publicly provided). Few of these have survived to the present day. They have become extinct perhaps more quickly even than the usual run of orphan asylums.

Public Subsidy of Private Institutions

During the last century the abundance of privately supported institutions for children, church—fraternal and philanthropic (privately endowed)—coupled with the disinclination to use tax money to build children's homes, produced a public subsidy system which turned out to be anything but a blessing. New York early granted public funds, in lump sums, to private institutions and continued the practice until it was legally outlawed in 1874. Thereafter the subsidy appeared in a new guise. Instead of an outright grant, a per capita sum was paid for maintenance of state wards in private institutions. This appeared to be an economy to the state because it obviated the building of state institutions, but in the long run it meant an increasing annual drain on the public treasury. The situation was further aggravated by the fact that seldom did supervision and control by the state follow the grants. The inevitable result was that private institutions ran their establishments their own way largely with public funds. Such a system also made it difficult to get children out of the institution since maintenance ceased as soon as placement in a foster home resulted. When one realizes further how zealous denominational orphanages were to retain children in their own faith, it is understandable that the system of public subsidy was tenaciously defended, and managed to persist despite legal handicaps. Prevailing opinion in social work is definitely opposed to the subsidy system.

Foster Home Care

Until 1853 indenture, institutional care, and outdoor relief were the chief services available to children in need in this country. It was the pioneer work of Charles Loring Brace that initiated foster home care by means of which a child could be placed in another home when conditions in his own home were so inimical to his welfare as to make removal from the home or giving him up necessary.

It was during the period of his training for the ministry that the opportunity came to Charles Loring Brace to head a children's mission in New York City. The mission in 1853 was renamed the Children's Aid Society, and almost at once Brace began to carry out his idea of withdrawing vagrant and destitute children from the streets of the city and transplanting them into suitable homes in another environment. As originally conceived, the plan was based upon the assumption that the child was to carry a share of work in his foster home, that the foster parents would be relieved of some cares, and that the Society would bear the expense of getting the child to the home and returning him if that were necessary. This latter point was of considerable importance because eventually the Society transported children as far away as Michigan, Wisconsin, and Minnesota. In all likelihood, these mass emigrations consisting of hundreds of children were founded more upon a desire to remove the children from city streets than upon a certain knowledge of the intricacies of child care. For the leaders of the movement the chief problems were those of gathering children, transporting, housing and feeding them rather than the problems of separation of children from kin and friends and the readjustment to a different home and strange people.

Despite all the shortcomings of the scheme, which were due to ignorance rather than to design, the fact remained that thousands of children were removed from city streets (largely from the eastern seaboard) and given an opportunity to start life again elsewhere. What was equally important was the beginning of a movement that approached the needs of children from a more promising point of view than had ever characterized indenture or almshouse care.

The Growth of Children's Aid Societies. Other private societies followed the New York Children's Aid. In 1860 an agency was founded in

Baltimore for the purpose of finding homes for destitute children. Within three years two other organizations were formed, one in Philadelphia which sought to board Jewish orphans in the homes of relatives or some other worthy family, and the other in Boston which began, rather uncertainly, to place children in foster homes, in temporary homes, or in their farm school. Other societies were organized in Brooklyn in 1866, in Buffalo in 1872; a decade later the Pennsylvania Children's Aid Society was established, and in 1895 the one in Rochester, New York. These societies were for the most part privately financed, although in some instances, as in Pennsylvania where the society accepted children from local counties, payment for board was made from public funds.

Another group of societies which formed part of this expanding movement of foster home care for children calls for separate mention. According to the evidence the establishment of the first state children's home society in Illinois does not seem to have stemmed from the work of Brace with the New York Children's Aid Society, but to have had an independent origin in the work of Martin Van Buren Van Arsdale. Van Arsdale, like Brace, had left the ministry for work with children, making a vow to himself during his first years of preaching that he would deliver all children from the poorhouse. In execution of that vow, years later, he organized, in 1883, the American Educational Aid Society for the twofold purpose of placing children in family homes and helping girls to get an education. Later this organization was termed the State Children's Home Society, not because it was publicly financed or sponsored but because its coverage was state-wide. After the title was changed to the National Children's Home Society, it began to grant charters to agencies in other states. Iowa was the first of these, to be followed by Minnesota, Michigan, Missouri, Indiana, California, Wisconsin, Tennessee, North Dakota and South Dakota.

Public Sponsorship. While the pioneering work of developing foster home services for children was privately initiated and directed, it was only a decade or two before a number of states had recognized their responsibilities for the welfare of children and were looking toward other means of care than indenture and institutions. Massachusetts was the first state to make a beginning in that direction when in 1869 it provided a visiting service to all children released from state institutions. This supervision led the way to the state paying board for many of its children who had been placed in private homes. Ten years later the practice of depositing children in city and town almshouses was outlawed, and in 1882 provision was made for the payment of board for children under 10 years of age, and in place of retaining them in the State Primary School it was required that they be committed directly to the state board of charities itself. The most important step in this development of home placement service was the abolition of the State Primary School in 1895 and the further extension of the principle of caring for children in foster homes instead of in institutions.

In 1899 New Jersey followed the example of Massachusetts by the establishment of a state policy of foster home care for destitute children. The creation of a state board of children's guardians centralized the control and placement of children, and made possible the use of private homes as boarding homes until such time as free homes could be found for the children.

Pennsylvania's approach was a recognition of the principle of foster home care implemented by the services of a private agency. When a state law, passed in 1883, threw upon the local communities and counties the care of children, no provision was made for adequate service for these children. Fortunately, the Pennsylvania Children's Aid Society had been organized the year before as a private child-placing agency, and it immediately offered to assist local authorities by working with them on a program of boarding or free homes. Many of the larger counties availed themselves of the Society's services, and in such instances payment was made out of county funds for those boarding homes which the agency secured.

Mention has also been made of a number of states that followed the Michigan state school plan and of other states (Connecticut and Indiana) that patterned their programs after Ohio's county home plan. In these instances, whether state home or county home, there eventually developed systems of placement which at first supplemented and later supplanted the institution. Thus by 1935 Michigan had adopted a state-wide system of child placement, and had surrendered its institution at Coldwater to another agency of the state government as Massachusetts had done with its State Primary School forty years before. In Michigan the institution became a training school for mentally defective children, in Massachusetts a hospital for epileptics. In Ohio and Indiana the emphasis still remained upon the county functions in child care and placement, but in both instances a state-wide child-placing agency has been established to handle those cases that could not be provided for by the local authorities. Every effort was made by the state agency to have the local communities develop their own resources and facilities.

Relief for Children in Their Own Homes

The system of providing assistance in the home of the applicant has, since its origin in Elizabethan England, been known as outdoor relief. This assistance has generally been allocated to members of family groups and as such we are justified in speaking of outdoor relief for children. Homer Folks wrote many years ago that outdoor relief of pauper children as well as of adults was the predominant method of public care in early colonial days. Its constant rival was the almshouse; and as almshouse care increased, outdoor relief decreased. Indeed in 1823–1824 Mr. Yates, secretary of state for New York, upon the basis of his investigations into the care of the poor, was convinced that almshouse care for children was superior to relief in their own homes. In describing children receiving relief outside of almshouses he spoke of their education and morals being neglected, their health impaired, their living in filth and idleness and likely to become "early candidates for the prison or the grave." At his recommendation outdoor relief for children was curtailed considerably and houses of employment were built in every county, in which paupers were to be maintained and their children to be carefully instructed, later to be put out in trade or business.

Despite this experience in New York, most other states continued outdoor relief to children. Even New York, when years later it realized the vicious effects of the mixed almshouse, reconsidered outdoor relief and re-established it along with institutional and foster home care for children. These systems continued in operation up to within recent times with relatively little change.

The first separate recognition of the dependent child in the home as substantiated by payments out of public funds came with the adoption of widows' pension laws beginning in 1911. Even though the laws in different states were variously known as widows' pensions, mothers' pensions, mothers' assistance, they all held in common the conviction that it was a valid use of public money to invest it in homes in order to permit mothers to continue care of their children in their own homes. It was not until 1935 that the federal government participated in the financing as well as in the policy formulation of such programs. The Social Security Act contained provisions for federal contributions to states to assist them in what was termed Aid to Dependent Children. This money appropriation, as noted in Chapter 7, was contingent upon certain minimum specifications to be written into the states' public assistance, or welfare, laws.

The White House Conferences

Five outstanding White House Conferences have served to focus the attention not only of social workers, but of the whole nation upon problems of child welfare. The first of these was called by President Theodore Roosevelt in 1909 and expressed its keynote in the words: "Home life is the highest and finest product of civilization. Children should not be deprived of it except for urgent and compelling reasons." The principle that children should not be removed from their own homes for reasons of poverty alone was the modern expression of a conviction that had been gaining ground for some years. A second principle embodied the thought and enlightened practice since the days of Charles Loring Brace, namely, that in those instances in which for sufficient reasons normal children must be removed from their own homes or given up by their parents the carefully selected foster home is the best substitute for the natural home. In addition, the Conference recommended that institutions for children should be on the cottage plan, preferably; that child caring agencies should be incorporated with state approval and the state should inspect their work; and that the causes of children's dependency should be studied and so far as possible ameliorated or removed.

Two outgrowths of this Conference have made it outstanding in the history of child welfare in this country. Within two years of the date of the conference the first state law appeared, implementing the principle of keeping children in their own homes through financial aid, and within another year the Children's Bureau was established in the federal government. The first widows' pension law was written in Illinois in 1911. It accepted the principle of the White House Conference, but broke with the method advocated by the Conference, i.e., through private charity.

The endorsement of the Conference as well as that of other organizations and individuals, including President Taft, of the proposal to establish a federal children's bureau resulted in its creation in 1912. Congress directed the Children's Bureau "to investigate and report . . . upon all matters pertaining to the welfare of children and child life among all classes of our people." In pursuance of this instruction the Children's Bureau, the first public agency in the world whose function was to consider as a whole the conditions, problems, and welfare of childhood, has developed a staff and a service that has nation-wide coverage. It has extended its investigations into the field of child development, child labor, juvenile delinquency, and into the community's provisions for children in need of special care whether they be in institutions, foster homes, or their own homes. The reporting of these investigations has followed naturally so that the Bureau has made its findings accessible to a national audience. A third function has been added from time to time by Congress, namely, the administration of certain federal laws affecting child welfare, such as the first federal child labor law (1917–1918); The Federal Maternity and Infancy Act (1922–1929); and in 1935, the maternal and child health, the child welfare, and the crippled children's provisions of the Social Security Act, and, during World War II, the EMIC—Emergency Maternity and Infant Care program. In addition, consultation and advisory service is rendered to states, localities, and organized groups concerned with the health and welfare of children.[4]

The Children's Bureau, which in 1912 was the child of the first White House Conference, became the parent of the second. In 1919, at the request of President Wilson, the Bureau organized the second conference which directed its attention toward the advancement of minimum standards of child welfare. Included in such standards were those relating to children entering employment, protection of the health of children and mothers, and protection of children in need of special care. These latter standards reaffirmed the conclusions of 1909 in all essentials.

[4] Originally placed in the Department of Commerce and Labor, it was transferred in 1913 to the newly created Department of Labor. In 1946 it was transferred to the Federal Security Agency. Since April 1953 the Federal Security Agency has been the Department of Health, Education, and Welfare.

A number of striking developments followed this second conference. One year before, only eight states had established child hygiene or child welfare divisions, while within the year that ensued thirteen states had laws providing for such services. Another milestone in co-operative effort to reduce unnecessary loss of maternal and infant life was the passage in 1921 of the Sheppard-Towner Act for the "promotion of the welfare and hygiene of maternity and infancy." By 1929 forty-five states and the territory of Hawaii were co-operating under its provisions.

The third conference, known as the "White House Conference on Child Health and Protection," was also organized by the Children's Bureau in 1930. It brought together what was probably the largest group ever assembled in Washington up to that time to consider the needs of children. Enjoined by President Hoover "to study the present status of the health and well-being of the children of the United States and its possessions; to report what is being done; to recommend what ought to be done and how to do it," some twelve hundred committee members brought together the latest findings of science as they bore upon the welfare of the child. Since then thirty-two reports covering every conceivable phase of child care have been issued and have proved to be a monumental record of the Conference, surpassing the achievements of any other conference on children's problems ever held. The Conference also produced a document known as the Children's Charter, which enunciated so clearly and compellingly the needs of children as well as the responsibility of parents, schools, churches, the community, and governmental agencies to meet these needs.

The fourth White House Conference, with President Franklin D. Roosevelt as honorary chairman, held an initial session in April 1939. Between that time and the second and final sessions in January 1940 considerable study and research had been given to the fields of interests of the Conference. A general report upon which there was substantial agreement and which was adopted by the Conference stressed a number of topics. Among these were the following: the child in the family, religion in the lives of children, educational services in the community, protection against child labor, youth and their needs, conserving the health of children, children under special disadvantages, and public administration and financing.

In addition to study and discussion before and during the Conference, it was decided to take steps to carry out the findings of the Conference. Accordingly, a nongovernmental National Citizens Committee was formed to carry the responsibility for follow-up activities, and a Federal Inter-Agency Committee to co-ordinate the work of federal departments whose work touched on matters affecting children. The National Citizens Committee immediately began plans for developing a long-range program as well as one to meet present and emerging situations. Emphasis was placed on co-operation with federal agencies, on dissemination of information, on stimulation of state and private agency programs and "consideration of the special needs of children growing out of emergency conditions, and cooperation with other organizations engaged in conserving and advancing the health, education, home care, and social protection of children under such conditions."

Hardly was the Committee formed than America faced a tremendous defense program and state of national emergency. At once the health and welfare of a recruited army became a pressing concern. The large number of selective service rejections brought out, more forcefully than anything else could have, the damage, sometimes irreparable, done to a nation's manpower through neglect of children's health and welfare. Every man turned down by an Army doctor was once a child. It was too easy for a nation of businessmen interested in reducing taxes to scrimp on maternal and child health programs. Now that these war babies of World War I were needed for defense, the sedate *New York Times* could remark editorially, "If all that could have been done for them after 1918 had actually been done, they would now be in better physical shape, not merely for a year of soldiering but for the battle of life." The closing sentences of the same editorial must express not only the sentiments of the hundreds of White House Conference members but of people elsewhere who have a concern for child life: "We may pray fervently that today's children will not be in 1960's mass army, and just as fervently that more than 60 percent of them will be in sound physical condition. To make this certain more attention must be given now to the health of all our children. If the cost is equivalent to that of a few bombing planes or even that of a flotilla of destroyers it will still be worth while."

The fifth conference, with President Harry S. Truman as honorary chairman, met in December 1950, and was called, appropriately, The Midcentury White House Conference. While its chairman and secretary were governmental officials and it drew upon the thirty-seven departments of the federal government whose work touched the lives of children and young people, in a very real sense, the Conference was a citizens' movement. The preparations for the Conference, its execution, and the follow-up programs involved upwards of 100,000 persons, some 464 voluntary organizations, with the bulk of the financing being supplied from voluntary sources. For the first time in the history of the Conferences, young people were represented on the various working committees, and about 500 persons under 21 years of age served as delegates to the meetings.

The stated purpose of the Conference was "to consider how we can develop in children the mental, emotional, and spiritual qualities essential to individual happiness and to responsible citizenship, and what physical, economic, and social conditions are deemed necessary to this development." All of the work carried on by professional and lay persons before the Conference, joined to the deliberations during the days of the Conference, produced not only enunciations on behalf of children and youth but actual on-going programs through organizations and agencies following the close of the Conference. These programs are currently underway and are intended to be increasingly effective on behalf of children and youth in America in the troubled times ahead.

Just as the 1930 Conference produced the Children's Charter so the 1950 Conference produced an equally epochal Pledge to Children. This Pledge to Children is not only a reaffirmation of the principles of the 1930 Children's Charter but a dedication to the end of securing for children those essentials of growth due children everywhere.

As was the case with the fourth White House Conference, the Mid-century White House Conference on Children and Youth took steps to translate the recommendations into action. The extensive preparation and planning by hundreds of organizations and thousands of persons not only insured the success of the Conference, but gave impetus to the formation of the National Midcentury Committee for Children and Youth. National, state, and local committees, with participation of agencies and persons concerned with children and youth, are carrying on active programs to move the words of the Conference into the deeds that will insure better opportunities and services for the present as well as the future generations of young people.

Contemporary Social Services for Children

At least three aspects of children's services at the midpoint of the twentieth century must be underscored: the range and diversity of services, the considerable use of tax funds for many of the services, and the emphasis upon the desirability of the child remaining in his own home and with his own family. In the ensuing pages the effort will be made to examine some of these diverse services, to gain some notion of the public expenditure on behalf of children, and to deal with services to children in their own homes as well as to children whose homes for a variety of reasons are no longer available to them. Discussion will center upon the financial service, child caring services, child placing services, other casework services, and homemaker services.

Financial Services

It is well to recognize at the outset that even though we hold that a child's own home and family are the best place for him to be, there are clear and compelling reasons at times why other services need to be offered to help him with some of the difficulties he and his family are experiencing. These other services must be offered not in the spirit of extremity, as a last desperate resort, but rather as a vital contribution to his needs and as essential to his welfare. They are to be considered as services designed to keep him in his home, and the decision must turn upon usefulness in the child's present situation and his future development.

A review of the foregoing pages reveals, despite an early and continuous emphasis on institutional care, an equally early and continuous concern to provide such support to the child's home and family as to enable him to remain there. This took the form of pauper (outdoor) relief, supplanted later by mothers' pensions, mothers' aid, etc., and, with the passage of the Social Security Act in 1935, provision for aid to dependent children. As the Act was written (Section 406a), a dependent child was defined as "a child under sixteen who has been deprived of parental support or care by reason of the death, continued absence from the home, or physical or mental incapacity of a parent, and who is living with his father, mother, grandfather, grandmother, brother, sister, stepfather, stepmother, stepbrother, stepsister, uncle or aunt, in a place of residence maintained by one or more of such relatives as his or her own home."

Besides cash payments under the ADC program (federal, state, and in some instances local contributions), children may receive on their behalf payments under the old-age and survivors insurance program—or both.[5] Not infrequently children may be members of households in which the adult may be eligible for aid to the permanently and totally disabled, old-age assistance, or general assistance, and in which the budget calculations of resources and needs take into account the presence of the child or children in the family.

According to a recent study, it was found that 3 percent of all the children in the population were in families receiving ADC, and 1.9 percent of all children were in families receiving OASI. About one fifth of the ADC families (85,000 children), were receiving OASI as well as ADC payments by reason of the death of the father, while the other four fifths did not receive any insurance benefits.[6] The actual figures for April, 1953, show 883,331 children receiving $23,667,700, or an average of $26.85 each, under OASI; while 1,513,014 children, about double the number, are receiving $47,169,319, or an average of $23.45.[7] A ready calculation can give some idea of the approximate payments for each year.

Child Caring Services

The financial services just mentioned have made it possible for many children to remain in their own homes (or in "eligible" homes within the definition of the Social Security Act) and for the family to be kept together. There are other children for whom other forms of care must be provided. These services will be called child care services where the emphasis is upon care, as distinct from the placement services where the emphasis is upon placement.[8] Despite efforts to keep members of

[5] It should be understood that payments to children under OASI are related to the previous contributions by the employed parent or parents and are not on a "needs" basis, as with ADC.

[6] White, Ruth, "Concurrent Benefits of Old-Age and Survivors Insurance and Public Assistance." *Social Security Bulletin*, XVI, July 1953, pp. 12–15.

[7] "Current Operating Statistics." *Social Security Bulletin*, XVI, July 1953, pp. 19–28.

[8] The writer is indebted to Alan Keith-Lucas for suggesting the distinction between the child caring and the child placing services. Access to Mr. Keith-Lucas' manuscript has proven an enriching experience.

the family together there are situations in which the best plan calls for care of the child in a foster home. Some children are deprived of their parents through death, desertion, or separation. Others may be without suitable care in their homes because of the continued incapacity of both parents due to permanent illness or mental disability, or of the inability of a surviving parent to carry the burden alone. Some children may need specialized care, occasioned by their own serious health or behavior problems, which may be beyond the resources of their own homes to provide. The decision as to removal or receiving of a child from his home cannot be undertaken lightly. No matter how unfortunate the family situation may have been, it must be borne in mind that the child has already put down some roots. The family still has meaning to the child: the child is bound to it by birth, by blood, and by relationship. In all these instances, and in others as well, provision must be made for a foster family home with parents who can give to the child the love, the care, the understanding, the guidance so essential to developing within the child his own potentialities for useful living.

Before the child enters into the care of a foster family, certain data must be known so that there may be a mutual basis of understanding. The child's physical condition and his health history is vital. The foster family must know what to provide or what not to provide in reference to diet, clothing, exercise, medical care, for example. Likewise the foster family should know something about mental capacity so that it will know what to expect of the child and of what help it may be in school and vocational opportunities. Another item of particular importance is a knowledge of the emotional nature of the child, his background, his previous experience in family life, his relation to parents, brothers, sisters; his attitudes, habits, and behavior. This information about the child enables the agency to work with the child, his own family, and his prospective family toward living arrangements which will have usefulness for all concerned. This does not assure a perfect home for a perfect child (even if, as is unlikely, they each existed), but rather produces a situation in which foster family and foster child can live naturally and with mutual satisfactions.

Numerous child caring agencies use a temporary foster home prior to a more permanent placement. When a child leaves his own home for any of a number of reasons, it is a wrench for him emotionally. Since birth the child has been establishing roots. These have served to help him feel he belonged somewhere and to somebody. It gives him stability and security. Yet the child who runs away, is recalcitrant, is even delinquent, is showing by those very signs his need to belong to somebody, somewhere, and to be accepted and helped. Now, for reasons usually beyond his control, he is threatened with the loss of or is losing his home. Instead of needing less he needs more care, affection, and understanding. Frequently the experience is so upsetting that he is in no way able to take on another home immediately, particularly a long-time home. He needs an interim period and experience during which he can get over some of his fear, rebellion, and resistance to help. Most of all he needs help in dealing with his own feelings of being rejected by his parents. While this struggle is going on in him, he needs to be in a situation where he can work out many of his feelings and at the same time be accepted for what he is and where he is in his difficulties. The temporary foster home does not necessarily demand the return or response from him which a more permanent home would demand. He is freer to test out for himself the kind of relationship he can take on. He can even express his inability to find a satisfying kind of relationship. At the same time he must meet the ordinary requirements of any home and is often able to feel a stability that lets him move toward a new pattern of living. In a temporary home the child needs to feel he has time "to come to himself," to try to say or express what it is he really needs and wants. A temporary foster home with foster parents who understand him will usually help the child and the agency to find out the kind of home of which he can best become a part. When he is ready to leave his temporary home, there will be a more permanent foster home waiting for him.

Knowing the Child's New Home. The job has only begun with the study of the child. Another assignment calls for just as much skill—the finding of the foster home. Some of the things the agency must know are the financial status of the prospective foster family, housing and housekeeping standards, make-up of the family group, the background, intelligence, education, and interests of the prospective foster parents. Equally essential is the willingness of the prospective foster family to share with the agency in the responsibility and care of the child. Foster parents, like all other people, look for satisfactions in their way of living. They expect foster home care to be a mutually satisfying experience. They know, or should know, it will have disappointments, "tough going" at times, struggles, recriminations, and sometimes heartbreaks. But so does any home. Foster parents need to face all this, to realize their responsibilities and the many demands which the care of any child makes upon them. They also have a right to hope for the joy that comes of having a child or children in their home and for the solid satisfaction of having a part in the growth and unfolding of another's life. The most important consideration is: What does this home have to contribute to the normal, healthy development of a prospective foster child? What is there in the adjustment of these family members to each other, to people outside the home, and to a foster child that will make this a mutually satisfying arrangement?

Service to the Foster Home. In addition to its study of prospective foster child and prospective foster family, the agency fulfills a third essential function—a continuing service to the foster home, which means to foster child and foster parent. This, basically, is a helping function to both the child and the foster parents. While the agency still carries responsibility to the parent or to the court for the child, actually it delegates the daily care and many attendant decisions to the foster parents. After all, it is with the family that the child lives and grows and not with the agency. However, the agency stays in the picture with the foster family, owing a responsibility to the child to assure a stability in the home so essential to his development. The agency also has a duty to be on hand in the event the foster home sustains a disintegration damaging to the child. The agency may furnish some direct service to the child such as that related to medical needs on a long-time planning basis (not the ordinary medical care which any family normally handles without outside consultation), or involving contacts with the child's own family. In most instances, however, the worker's prime concern is helping the foster parents with their relationship to the child. This in no sense implies that the worker tells a foster parent how to raise the child, but it does mean that the agency stands back of or alongside of the parent to help the parent over difficult places. The aim of the agency is to provide as natural a home environment as a foster home permits and to interfere as little as possible—if at all—with the mode of life of this new family grouping. What so frequently happens is that the child brings all his fears, sullenness, resistance, obstreperousness and other symptoms of insecurity and that the foster parent needs help in dealing with the child. What just as frequently happens is that as the child finds in this new home love, security, and opportunity for fulfillment, many of his emotional difficulties give way before the normality of living.

In the course of this service every effort is made to keep alive the child's contacts with his own family and vice versa, since in the large majority of cases foster children need to feel that they still are a part of their original family, and for the further reason that they will return eventually to their own homes. This is consistent with the principle that the agency service is *to* the parent *for* the child. A good agency will arrange visits of parents to their children and children to the parents under such circumstances that the contacts will not disturb the relationships within the foster home. Workers need to be sensitive to the feelings and attitudes of members of each of these groups and to be guided always by the principle that the welfare of the child is the paramount good in foster family care.

Ending the Service. A final function of the agency is proper termination of service. This ending may come with the attainment of the legal age beyond which the committing court does not assume jurisdiction. It may come when the original home is ready to receive him. It may be when the child—now grown—is ready to leave of his own accord. In all these cases the underlying service which the agency still has to offer is the working out with all parties concerned of constructive plans for the future. Necessarily central in all these arrangements is the child himself. Plans may require adjustments within his own home, educational, and even job adjustments. There will need to be preparation for a person's standing on his own feet and making his own way alone. Nor is this an abrupt process, but one in which the foster family, child, own parents, and agency participate over a period of time. After the child returns to his own home, there may be difficulties of one kind or another. These may be the difficulties that arise in any home, or they may be so accentuated as to require outside help. As always, the agency stands by, with parents knowing where again to turn for help. In all cases of helping the agency deals with the parents as responsible people and people who can ask comfortably for help of an agency that has meant something to them before in a tight spot.

Institutional Care

As a reaction to the predominance of institutional care for children throughout the nineteenth century, and in response to other forms of child care, and especially due to the impact of the 1909 White House Conference, there was a swing away from institutional care in the second, third, and fourth decades of the twentieth century. In all honesty, it must be admitted that the earlier institutions did tend to become too self-contained, too detached from the findings of progressive child care, and furthermore resistive to change. The reaction was expressed through a skepticism about the value of all forms of institutional child care.

All of this was not without its effects upon the institutions. Many of the forward-looking ones had been demonstrating by their programs that institutional care had its contribution to make to child care. These and others participated increasingly in the newer knowledge and newer practices, and by the midcentury it had become clear that institutions did have a valid service to offer. This was a service in its own right and not solely something to become reconciled to or justified only when all other services were tried and exhausted. Rather, today we find institutions for children taking their places alongside other services: as valid a function as exercised through foster home care, adoption, and financial services in the home. To approach this present status, many institutional leaders have had to do some serious thinking and to have effected some substantial changes. To maintain it requires constant study, self-examination, and resourcefulness in improving existing institutional services based on increased insight and understanding into human behavior—especially behavior of children.

Before proceeding further it is important to examine the statistics on institutional care and foster family care within recent decades. Between 1933 and 1950 (based on the most recent decennial census) the institutional population of dependent and neglected children dropped from 140,000 to 95,000, a decline of 38 percent. In contrast to this, the number of children in foster family care increased from 102,000 in 1933 to 170,000 in 1950, an increase of 40 percent. Evidence of another significant trend is reflected in the 187 percent increase in foster family care under public auspice coincident with the 11 percent decline in foster family care under voluntary agency auspice. All of these changes in type of care must be placed against the basic population increase in this country from 122 million in 1930 to 150 million in 1950, an increase of 23 percent.[9]

The Caseworker in the Institution. One of the many evidences of these progressive developments has been the increasing use of qualified caseworkers on the staff of children's institutions. In such institutions the caseworker is a regular staff member offering services encompassing admission, the child's stay in the institution, and discharge. The caseworker is governed by the admissions policies of the institution, and it is within these limits that he works with the applicant—it may be the parent (or parents) or the court. He explores with the applicant the child's needs as well as the family needs. He also clarifies what the institution offers. In addition, he and the applicant together consider available resources within the community. The conclusion to which they each come, and come together, is that in the light of the needs presented and the resources available, the institution is the service best suited for the child under consideration. It will be noted that this marks a decided shift from an earlier emphasis of the institution as the only service or the institution as the last desperate resort. As mentioned in the preceding pages, the modern institution is recognized as offering a valid service in relation to others on behalf of children.

A second area in which the caseworker functions is with the child during his living experience in the institution. Upon admission, the caseworker helps the child in his movement toward the cottage and the cottage parent (or houseparent). Sharing material with the houseparent about the child and the family may be helpful, but in all instances must be subject to the administrative policies of the institution—as indeed must all the professional activity of the caseworker. Likewise, the caseworker is of use to the child by serving as a resource to the administration and to the houseparent as the child enters into and becomes a

---

[9] U. S. Bureau of the Census, *Children Under Institutional Care and in Foster Homes, 1933–1935:* also letter from Dr. Martha Eliot, Chief, U. S. Children's Bureau, to the writer, dated October 30, 1953; see also U. S. Bureau of the Census, *U. S. Census of Population: 1950.* Vol. IV, Special Reports Part 2, Chapter C, Institutional Population. Washington, D. C., U. S. Government Printing Office, 1953.

part of the living situation in which he finds himself. The caseworker can be helpful around some of the difficulties which the child is experiencing in everyday living with other children and with houseparents. Such helpfulness must have a base that is nondisciplinary, nonauthoritative, and nonadministrative. Throughout all of this, the child must be free to relate himself to other members of the staff, including the caseworker, but primarily his relationship should be with the houseparent. The caseworker carries responsibility for maintaining relationship between the child and his family. The child will need to feel that even though he is away from his family, they still stand back of him. This may be a decided factor in his own efforts to make the necessary adaptation to institutional life. The maintenance of family relations and the improvement of the environmental situation will prove a real influence in hastening the day of the child's return, an objective which is to be desired by the institution, the child, and the family.

A third aspect of the caseworker's services revolves around the return of the child to his family. This step on the part of the child requires help from the worker in preparing both the child and the family for the reunion. It means the joint consideration of educational and vocational plans as well as of the demands which the outside community will make upon the child. In many instances return to the child's own home may be impossible. Rather than keep the child in the institution, the worker will need to find a suitable foster home, or make a referral to a child placing agency. Following the preparation and the planning will come discharge from the institution and the necessary help of the caseworker in making adjustments to family, to community, and to a different kind of world. The service which the worker offers may extend for a long or a short period of time depending upon the capacity of the child to make the essential adjustments. Its intensity will be related to the nature of the child's problems as well as to his ability to develop his own resources within himself. It is as important for the worker to know when to withdraw from such service as it is to know when to offer help. To continue supervision beyond the point of the individual's real need may serve to perpetuate his dependence as much as if he were still in the institution.

A word remains to be said for the institutional setup and staff. By common agreement the children's institution that is composed of cottages where children live in small informal home-life groups under the care of cottage mothers (and fathers) is to be preferred to the old regimented barracks-like institution. Any institution involves deprivations of some individual expression and demands subordination of the individual to the group more than is true of life outside of an institution. What so frequently happens is that after a time much of his individual expression is surrendered and he yields what is more dear to him, his own unique personality—that personality that holds within itself his capacity for creative living. In the older institutions with their entire domestic arrangements and economy centered around conformity this was especially true. In the newer-minded institutions, especially in those with the cottage system, there is far more opportunity for individual expression. At the same time the child can assimilate many of the values that accrue from the experience of making adjustment to group situations. It is in this combination of individual and group expression that the institution can make its most valuable contribution to the development of the child, provided the staff is alive to the functions of such an institution. In order to assure competent staffs familiar with the way human behavior is motivated and expressed, it is desirable that staff members have some training in social work, or at least some acquaintance with the philosophy and practice of social casework. One does not demand that a cottage mother be a graduate of a school of social work (any more than one demands the same of parents!), but that she embody understanding, sensitivity of feeling, and spontaneity and naturalness in her relations with people. Likewise, the same is to be expected of other staff members who come into contact with the children. Especially is this so for the superintendent or head of an institution. In addition to all of these desired qualities, one can fairly expect nowadays that he have the professional competence to operate a children's institution so that it becomes a constructive chapter in the lives of the children who, much against their wishes, are obliged to live for a period within it.

The Modern Role of the Institution: As a Way of Living. Many, if not most, of the children's institutions of the last century were known and operated as orphanages with admissibility of the child turning on the death of one or both parents. In contrast to this procedure, today orphanhood is almost the last, rather than the first, criterion for admission, and should never be the sole determinant. Families today break up for many reasons other than death. Families are smaller and there are fewer relatives able, or for that matter inclined, to provide alternate care for the child. More and more children's institutions are providing care for children whose parents for one reason or another can no longer provide the rearing so necessary for wholesome development. The following are some of the more important purposes for which these services are offered.

Some children have had such disastrous emotional experiences in their own families that they are not ready to take on a new set of intimate relationships immediately, but instead can benefit by the less personal tone of the institution. They are not ready for foster home care, certainly not until some of the pain has gone out of their hurt. Oftentimes the combination of skilled staff and the socializing effects of group living has value for such children.

Other children not as emotionally damaged, but who are obliged to leave one foster home before another is ready may find the temporary security of the institution a real boon and a valuable preparation for a placement to follow later. Some of these children may have had several unsuccessful foster home experiences and may be needing the institution to get a sense of being able to relate to others but without the degree of commitment so essential to foster family living.

In the case of the child whose parents are recently divorced or separated the institution may afford a kind of breathing spell, allowing the child to get some perspective on his relation to one or both of these parents. It is hardly likely that such a child will be ready for a foster home so soon after his own has come tumbling down.

Sometimes families break up in which there are three, four, or five children. Seldom can arrangements be made quickly enough to place these children in the same foster family or even in contiguous foster families. To locate foster parents who can meet the needs of such children requires not only time but infinite ingenuity and persistence. An institutional placement can be made more readily which will come nearer to meeting the needs of these children temporarily.

As a Treatment Center. It must have been evident in the foregoing paragraphs that the emphasis was on the institution as a way of living. This was predicated upon a temporary stay and as approaching, insofar as practicable, the ordinary "livingness" to which the community feels every child is entitled. True, problems are bound to arise in such institution living, just as problems arise in living in foster homes or in one's own home, and it is expected that the institution will be so staffed as to help children with the difficulties incident to growing up. However, within recent years an increasing demand has arisen for a kind of institution for children that is treatment centered. The institution with a properly qualified staff may serve a valuable purpose for those children who are so emotionally disturbed as to require residential and sustained treatment in other than their own homes or their foster homes. For this, there is required not only competent casework service, but available psychiatric consultation (or full-time service, depending upon the size of institution) as well as psychological testing service. The entire staff (professional and administrative) must be oriented to the problems presented by the disturbed child, and the program must be designed to provide the maximum opportunity for study and treatment. Along with the focus upon individualization, there must be an opportunity for experiencing what group living has to offer.[10]

Group Homes

One further word needs to be said, and that is to refer to the occasional use of what are called "group homes." They have been in use in Great Britain for some years and in this country are beginning to claim attention. These homes provide care for six, eight, or ten (usually unrelated) children living under one roof with a couple who serve as the parent persons of the group. In Great Britain provision is made for such group homes in the architects' drawings as part of the public housing projects carried on by the Local Authorities (local governmental unit). In the United States a number of privately supported agencies have experimented with such homes, which have the advantage of offering a degree of group living—a development somewhere between the foster home and the congregate institution.

These listings by no means exhaust the varied uses to which the modern children's institution is put, but they do give some notion of the changed use of the institution within recent times. It must be notice-

[10] Reid, Joseph H., and Hogan, Helen R., *Residential Treatment of Emotionally Disturbed Children*. New York, Child Welfare League of America, 1952.

able, by omission, that no mention is made of the service to babies and pre-school children. Almost without a dissent anywhere child welfare workers will insist that the institution is no place for babies or pre-school children. The findings of psychiatrists substantiate the thesis that nothing can take the place of the one mother person during those early years. Physically, emotionally, educationally (in a broad and basic sense) the baby and young child need the warmth, the spontaneity, the devotion, and the "humanness" of the mother or the mother person. The institution, no matter how well intentioned its staff, cannot provide these indispensables or furnish an adequate substitute.

Part-time Care: Day Nursery and Foster Day Care

Another expression of the conviction that children should not be removed from their own homes solely because of poverty is the service of the day nursery. This service, first introduced into the United States in 1854, aims to provide care in a day nursery for children whose mothers are unable to look after them during the day. It is the usual practice for such mothers, generally working mothers, to leave their child or children, usually under 3 years of age, in the day nursery and to call for the child after the day's work. This care may be either free or at low cost, and is designed to allow the mother who is obliged to work to do so and at the same time to provide care for the child during her working hours. Other resources for care and for keeping the child in his home should be explored before day nursery care is granted. Once day nursery care is provided, then every step is taken to insure adequate care for the child. This service will include attention to the educational and recreational needs of the child, as well as his physical needs. Many day nurseries provide a casework service to the family with a view toward utilizing the family resources in the best interests of the child and the family. Such day nurseries have integrated their programs with other social service agencies in the community, particularly with child welfare and family welfare societies.

An experiment known as foster day care has given promise of some interesting developments. Instead of providing day care for children within the institutional nursery, the agency seeks to place, by the day, children needing care in carefully selected foster homes. The child returns to his home at night and stays with his family whenever his mother is home, but when she is working, he is part of another home or family. In this way it is felt that the home ties may be preserved and at the same time the child permitted the freedom of individual expression which, in the day nursery group, must, so often, be subordinated to the group. As with other forms of child care utilized by social agencies, it is essential to have available to foster day care parents the services of qualified caseworkers.

Adoption

Another area which focuses upon the needs of the child is adoption. Many of the children who are born of unwed mothers are brought to the attention of reputable agencies. These agencies undertake to plan with the mothers the services which will best meet the needs of the child. Other adoptions may be made of children born of a married mother, but in which case the father—the putative father—is other than her husband. In other instances the family may be broken—perhaps catastrophically—and adoption may be the most fortunate solution of a tragic situation. In other cases legitimate children may be adopted by relatives, or they may be placed for adoption by agencies.

By whatever means children become candidates for adoption, there are actually three basic considerations: the needs of the child, of the own parent (or parents), and of the adoptive parent. If it may be assumed that a child is a possible subject for adoption, it is tremendously important to ascertain all the information available about the child and his background. The purpose of such knowledge is to facilitate the location of a family that will as nearly as possible meet the particular child's needs. Usually agencies will utilize a temporary boarding home for a period of time to provide him affection and security and also to gain additional understanding of him. In such a temporary home the child must experience acceptance of others and be helped to be ready, when the time comes, to move into the adoptive family. By the same token, the parents in this temporary boarding home must not only provide the warmth of human relationship while the child is with them, but must be emotionally mature enough to enable the child to leave them at the proper time.

Just as something must be known about the child, it is equally essential to know about the persons who wish to become the adoptive parents. Agencies must satisfy themselves not only about their physical, financial, and intellectual resources—to whatever degree—but their emotional needs and motivations as well. Again, it must be stressed that the primary concern is the child and his needs. Persons, for example, who want to adopt a child in hope that such a step will solve their marital difficulties are hardly likely to contribute to what the child requires. Indeed, they are likely to use the child for their own ends to the disadvantage of the child. On the other hand, there are couples who can provide a normal, healthy, and emotionally satisfying living relationship in which a child can grow and in which he can realize whatever potentialities he has within him. Such a living experience will further the child's growth in all aspects: physical, intellectual, emotional, and spiritual.

After a child has been placed in an adoptive home, there is a period of time ranging (depending upon state laws) from six months to one year before the adoption is final. During this period the agency worker offers help to the adoptive parents as well as to the child to surmount the quite understandable difficulties in the situation. All of us are aware of the strains and stresses in the own-parent–child relationship and of the necessity, at times, for parents to turn outside of the family for help. If anything, the situation is accentuated in the case of an adoptive family for at least two reasons: (1) the effects upon the child of what he may have been through earlier and (2) the disadvantage of not having the experience of dealing gradually with the child's problems that emerge. As the child and the adoptive parents increasingly work out their ways of living together, the worker withdraws so that when the adoption becomes legally final, the worker and the agency are ready to conclude their service to the family. From then on they enter the home only upon the call of the family, as is the case with other families in the community. Once the adoption becomes final, the (new) parents and the child have the same rights, duties, and privileges toward each other as if the child had been born to them.[11]

[11] For a more detailed account of social work practice as well as of the legal aspects of adoption, the following pamphlets are suggested: *Adoption Practice,* New York, Child Welfare League of America, 1941; *Essentials in Good Adoption Practices.* New York, State Charities Aid Association, 1950; *Essentials of Adoption Law and Procedure.* Washington, D. C., U. S. Children's Bureau, Federal Security Agency, 1949; *How to Adopt*

Not every child born out of wedlock becomes a subject for adoption, nor is every adoption that of an illegitimate child. However, since so large a percentage of children born out of wedlock and who come to the attention of reputable public and private agencies are considered for adoption, it seems pertinent to carry forward at this point the discussion of services for unmarried mothers and their children.

Every situation of illegitimacy involves the welfare of at least two people, mother and child. Others undoubtedly are involved, either legally or as relatives of the mother, but the needs of the mother and the child are paramount when they come or are referred to an agency. The first questions that arise are: What are the needs of this child? What are the needs of this mother? And what does the agency have to offer either or both of them? If the prospective mother comes before confinement and delivery, the agency works with her and what plans she may have, if any. It has been found that an agency can be useful in many instances before birth has taken place by talking with the mother and helping her to arrive at what she thinks she really wants to do for herself and her child. Even though she may be facing a crisis, she is at least likely to be able to consider with some calmness and judgment what is the best thing to do. It is then that the agency can work out plans with her for keeping the child with her, placing the child with relatives or friends, or for adoption, or in an institution. At the same time the agency can help her to decide her own subsequent actions. There is always the possibility that plans made at this time may not always be carried out after the birth of the child because the birth itself may have changed the mother's entire feelings about her previous decision. Again, the casework skills are the same: to help the mother arrive at the decision she really wants to make.

If the mother does not come to the agency until after delivery, the same questions will need to be faced: What will serve the best interests of the child? What of the mother? It must be emphasized that there is no one absolute rule of what is best because every situation is unique and because every situation has a new and different constellation of personalities in it. In some instances it is well for mother and child to remain together, in others the child may be placed with relatives or

a Child in Louisiana. Baton Rouge, Louisiana Department of Public Welfare, no date (probably 1949).

friends while the mother seeks to earn her living. In still other cases it may be well to seek foster home care or adoption for the child.

An adequate understanding of the situation confronting an unmarried mother and a child born out of wedlock leads to the conviction that such a child needs affection and security just as does any other child. He needs it not because he is an illegitimate child, but because he is a human being. The accident of his birth merely places upon his mother and anyone to whom she goes for help the responsibility for seeing that he has the opportunity to secure that love and that feeling of belonging. Without that start the child is handicapped from the outset in his emotional development, which may be as crippling as any physical illness. Consistent with this attitude is the practice of children's agencies of first attempting to help mother and child to remain together whenever that is possible. It may be that interviews with the putative father will reveal what possibilities there are of marriage of the parents, but in no instance is a marriage to be forced when there is every indication that such a move is contrary to the basic wishes and feelings of cither or both parents. Many agencies have found that more is to be gained by a frank conference with both parties than by the use of force. Where, however, marriage is not agreed upon willingly, consideration must be given to support by the father, and in cases of extremity the mother may be obliged to seek court action. This is usually done upon her initiative rather than by the children's agency.

Even though it may be deemed advisable to separate mother and child, it is not necessarily desirable to break the relationship between them. Many children born out of wedlock eventually are adopted. But in those cases in which adoption does not occur and foster homes are sought, it is just as important to secure suitable foster homes as it is for any other child. There will need to be the same care used in selection of the home as well as the same quality of supervision and planning for the adjustments when the child leaves the foster home. A continuing relationship with the mother is essential, especially if the child will eventually return to his mother. All of these matters have been discussed as part of the process of foster home care. What needs to be emphasized is that the child born out of wedlock is not to be treated as any different from any other child or as being in a class apart. What he needs for an opportunity to grow and develop is what every child needs—love and security. That the problem of his parents is difficult, and one upon which society heaps its scorn and disapprobation, means his and her needs will be greater and will require more help.

Other Casework Services

Protective Services. Other services to children, particularly within recent years, have focused upon help to the parent on behalf of the child. A particular instance of these services is to be found in those cases in which action is initiated by someone other than the parents where the parents have been unwilling or unable to provide the care for the child which the community considers desirable and essential. The child (or children) may have suffered neglect or abuse, and someone has had to intervene in order to call a halt to such experiences for the child as well as to help the parent (parents) to use himself otherwise than in ways destructive to his child.

Traditionally, the origins of such a service go back to the period when England passed Dick Martin's Act (1822) for the prevention of cruelty to animals. A similar act was passed in America in 1866, when the American Society for the Prevention of Cruelty to Animals was chartered in New York, and for a while the Society (SPCA) was called upon to intervene on behalf of children as well as animals. Miss Emma Lundberg's remarks are sufficiently revealing to bear repeating: "The New York Society for the Prevention of Cruelty to Animals had been in existence for eight years when it was discovered that 'with all the law there was no legal way of protecting a child.' It is related that a mission worker had discovered a child called Mary Ellen who was being cruelly beaten and ill-treated by a man and woman who had taken her in infancy from a charitable institution. Unable to gather evidence necessary to obtain court removal of the child, the mission worker appealed to the society for the protection of animals. The society held that 'the child being an animal' it would act, and Mary Ellen was taken to court and complaint was made against the guardians. The child was removed from their custody, and those who had mistreated her were sent to the penitentiary for one year. When it became known that the animal society would interest itself in children who were ill-treated, numerous complaints were received, and it was decided that a separate society should be formed." [12] Similar societies were organized in other cities. In many places the humane societies created for the protection of animals added to their activities the prevention of cruelty to children. More recently through legislation the state has added this as one of its court or welfare services.

In earlier years the emphasis was largely upon apprehension, trial, conviction, and punishment of the person by whose actions the child suffered abuse or neglect. This frequently—almost always—resulted in the removal of the child from his home, to be followed by institutional care or foster home care. Today, we are more likely to see as the purpose of our services the protection of the child, and to regard as the object of our services the parent. This shift emphasizes the conviction that some, perhaps not all, persons can be helped with their difficulties—even those difficulties that find expression in undesirable actions toward their children. It also involves a recognition that even if all homes are not perfect, there may be a great deal of attachment between parents and children that should not be too peremptorily or too thoughtlessly broken by agents outside of that home. What such parents are showing so many times are their distress signals that they need help in managing with the many problems they have. Caseworkers approach such parents with the offer of help, and, despite the community's attitude of indignation and hopelessness, in many instances have enabled such parents to come to a greater sense of their responsibilities and capacities. Such workers operate on the expressed premise that change must come about. The actual steps and action leading toward change must be taken by the parent as the responsible person. In no case can the worker take over for the neglectful parent, nor alter the family pattern of parental rights and responsibilities. There has been enough evidence of success of this approach (for example, The Protective Services, Baltimore City Department of Public Welfare) to believe in its soundness of helping parents, rather than allowing children to grow up with warped and unhappy lives. It is also a far better investment of the taxpayer's dollar to provide the kind of help, through qualified personnel, that makes it possible for families to stay together and

---

[12] Lundberg, Emma O., *Unto the Least of These*. New York and London, D. Appleton–Century Company, 1947, p. 103.

for family members to learn to trust each other, experiencing the joys, sorrows, and satisfactions that are a part of everyday living.[13]

Probation and Correctional Institution Services. When youngsters get into serious enough difficulty to come to the attention of the juvenile court, probation service will be necessary for those cases in which the court believes the child warrants continued help in his own home. In those jurisdictions where the juvenile court is of sufficient size, the case-work services to the youngster will be provided by its own probation staff. This is to be preferred to other arrangements, but the reality must be faced that in so many parts of the country due to the small size of the court the county department of public welfare is called upon to furnish such casework service. This is usually accomplished through specialized child welfare workers who undertake to help the child, and his family, with the difficulties that have found expression in his unacceptable behavior. Regardless, the service (whether provided by the court's probation officer or the county child welfare worker) is nonpunitive and is focussed upon helping the child to face and to accept, increasingly, responsibility for what he is and does. The place of the other family members as they contribute to the child's difficulties must be taken into account, but the child himself must be the person to whom the service is offered and the one who must remain the essential and primary client.

In all fairness it must be admitted that the juvenile industrial school receives its charges only after all other agencies in the community have failed or given up the job. Furthermore, it may be questioned whether the job of preparing youngsters for participation in a free society can be done in an atmosphere so unlike a free society as is inevitable within an institution. Admitting these two limitations apparently inherent in an institutional framework, it may be well to examine the task which any correctional institution has in adapting itself to the needs of the individual child.

Acting on the premise that the institution exists for the child and not the child for the institution, it becomes imperative that the two

[13] de Schweinitz, Elizabeth and Karl, "The Place of Authority in the Protective Function of the Public Welfare Agency." *Bulletin of the Child Welfare League of America,* XXV, September 1946, pp. 1–6; Hancock, Claire, "Protective Service for Children." *Child Welfare,* XXVIII, March 1949, pp. 3–9; Smith, Barbara, "Helping Neglectful Parents to Become Responsible." *The Child,* XIV, September 1949, pp. 36–38, 45–46.

basic needs of the child must be met: the need for security and the need for growth. In many instances the denial or thwarting of one or both of these needs has driven the child to such a pass that commitment seemed, to the community, the only way out. So the child comes to the institution with not less but more need for security and growth. This places upon the institution personnel the responsibility for affording to the child the opportunities for obtaining these satisfactions. He must be allowed to feel that he belongs, that he finds stability in the group in which he is thrown, that, in turn, he means something to someone else, that his home ties are maintained, that he can look forward to a return to his family, that his present experience enables him to carry more and more of his own responsibility for himself, that he can retain enough of his individuality to be himself when he returns to the community. If these opportunities are denied him in the institution, he will either fight his way through, possibly doing damage to himself and others, or he will become resigned and submissive so that while he conforms he is in no wise equipped to act as a free personality in the world outside. Adequate trade training within the institution may help him to earn his living, which is mighty important, but unless the institution has made other conditions possible, he will leave severely limited in his capacity for successful adjustments or creative living.

Within recent years foster home care of delinquents has been tried and found to be successful. The practice of today is far removed from the early efforts of Charles Loring Brace, yet it bears a distinct relation to his dictum in 1859 that "the family is God's Reformatory." Many juvenile courts have sought to provide foster home care for children who have been adjudged delinquent. It is not uncommon for such care to be in the homes of relatives in order that family ties may be maintained, but the primary concern of the court and the agency is for the quality of the foster home. It has been learned from experience that successful care depends upon careful selection of foster home and child to be placed. It is generally recognized that any foster home is an exacting task for all parties concerned. When, however, the factor of delinquency is introduced, it is extremely important to be sure that the foster home fits the child, and the child the foster home. This requires first an understanding of the child, then a thorough knowledge of the prospective foster home selected. Once the care is undertaken there is need for continued supervision of a helpful nature so that over a period of time the child achieves security in his new home and the foster parents gain satisfaction in the feeling of doing a constructive job. By common agreement a child has a much greater chance of development under such circumstances than in any other short of his own home.

If the child returns from the correctional institution to his own home —as is to be preferred in most instances—continued casework service is essential to help him to deal responsibly with his own limitations as well as with his capacities. Here, again, if the institution does not have its casework (or parole) staff that can reach out to him in his community, it will have to look to the local county welfare department to provide the needed services.

Homemaker Service

Occasionally situations arise in families in which the mother (sometimes it may be a foster mother) is obliged to be out of the home temporarily and the children and the father are faced with decisions as to how to manage. This is a particularly critical problem where the children are of school age or younger and where the father must continue with his regular employment. There may be a number of such situations with varying degrees of urgency. The mother may be confronted with a serious operation that will require not only a period in the hospital but perhaps a carefully regulated recuperation afterward. Or the mother may be on the verge of another confinement; or of commitment to a mental hospital or to a tuberculosis sanatorium; or there may have been death, desertion, or divorce. These are emergencies in which family (and sometimes friends) may help temporarily, but there may not always be family members available and within reach, or in a position to leave their own children. Increasingly services are being set up by both public and private agencies to minister to such needs. These are called homemaker services because another person comes into the home—temporarily—and undertakes to provide many of the services which are customarily the mother's in order to permit the family to remain together. Such a person may work an eight- or a twenty-four-hour day. The father may take over at the close of a day when he returns from his work or the demands of the family may be such that even though the father is present there is need for the homemaker's skills and presence throughout the entire twenty-four-hour period. Such homemakers carry on the usual duties of the mother—cleaning, cooking, sewing, washing, and the care of the children. Someone has described this as a service that tides over without taking over.

The homemaker is employed by the agency (a public welfare department, a family agency, a family and children's agency), recruited by the agency, trained by the agency, and paid by the agency. A fee is paid by the family receiving the service, usually on a scale based on the earnings and the size of the family. In addition, there is available to the homemaker, and particularly to the family, a caseworker whose service is to help with the various problems and difficulties which may arise.

Most agencies offering this service do so for a limited period of time, since such a service is to help in an emergency in order to keep the family together. In those cases in which it appears, after a reasonable time, that the emergency will continue indefinitely it will be necessary for the agency and the family to work together toward a more lastingly realistic plan. The contribution of the agency to the lives of the family members has been to help them to live through a critical period and to develop the resources to reconstitute their lives with satisfaction.[14]

Other Services for Children

Several important services relating to child welfare have gone unmentioned. One of these—crippled children's work—is considered more appropriately as part of the chapter on public assistance and social security. The same may be said for aid to dependent children in their own homes, another service available under the Social Security Act. A consideration of the juvenile court and of probation will be presented in the chapter on probation and parole.

There are many other services which touch the lives of children which might have been treated in this chapter. Hardly any phase of

[14] Homemaker service is not restricted to families with children, although the priority may be granted in their favor. The service has been adapted to the aged—again, in order to enable them to remain within their own homes rather than to be institutionalized or shunted elsewhere. See Chapter 13 on Social Services for the Aged.

social work can be considered as an entity unto itself, and this is especially so of children's services. However, the selection in this chapter has been directed toward those services which, primarily, are designed to aid the child, either in or outside of his own home. There are many other services which incidentally benefit the child, but in this chapter the emphasis and discussion has been on those services where the child is the primary consideration.

BIBLIOGRAPHY

Books and Pamphlets

Allen, Winifred Y., and Campbell, Doris, *The Creative Nursery Center.* New York, Family Service Association of America, 1948.

Abbott, Grace, *The Child and the State.* 2 vols. Chicago, University of Chicago Press, 1938.

Bishopp, Grace I., *The Role of Case Work in Institutional Service for Adolescents.* New York, Child Welfare League of America, 1943.

Bowlby, John, *Maternal Care and Mental Health.* New York, Columbia University Press, 1951.

Brooks, Lee M. and Evelyn, *Adventuring in Adoption.* Chapel Hill, University of North Carolina Press, 1939.

Burmeister, Eva, *Forty-Five in the Family.* New York, Columbia University Press, 1949.

——, *Roofs for the Family.* New York, Columbia University Press, 1954.

Cady, Ernest, *We Adopted Three.* New York, William Sloane and Associates, 1952.

Despert, J. Louise, *Children of Divorce.* New York, Doubleday & Company, 1953.

Deutsch, Albert, *Our Rejected Children.* Boston, Little, Brown & Co., 1950.

Edlin, Sara B., *The Unmarried Mother in Our Society.* New York, Farrar, Straus, & Young, 1954.

Folks, Homer, *The Care of Destitute, Neglected, and Delinquent Children.* New York, The Macmillan Company, 1902.

Fraiberg, Selma H., *Psychoanalytic Principles in Casework with Children.* New York, Family Service Association of America, 1954.

Gallagher, Eleanor G., *The Adopted Child.* New York, Reynal and Hitchcock, 1936.

Hopkirk, Howard W., *Institutions Serving Children.* New York, Russell Sage Foundation, 1944.

Hutchinson, Dorothy, *In Quest of Foster Parents.* New York, Columbia University Press, 1943.

Konopka, Gisela, *Group Work in the Institution*. New York, Whiteside, Inc., 1954.

——, *Therapeutic Group Work with Children*. Minneapolis, University of Minnesota Press, 1949.

Lockridge, Francis, *Adopting a Child*. New York, Greenberg, 1947.

Lundberg, Emma O., *Unto the Least of These*. New York, D. Appleton–Century, 1947.

McGovern, Cecilia, *Services to Children in Institutions*. Washington, D. C., National Conference of Catholic Charities, 1948.

Meyer, Gladys, *Studies of Children*. New York, King's Crown Press, 1948.

Page, Norma Knoll, *Protective Service: A Case Illustrating Casework Service with Parents*. New York, Child Welfare League of America (no date, probably 1948).

Podolsky, Edward, *The Jealous Child*. New York, Philosophical Library, 1954.

Prentice, Carol S., *An Adopted Child Looks at Adoption*. New York, D. Appleton–Century, 1940.

Redl, Fritz, and Wineman, David, *Children Who Hate*. Glencoe, Ill., The Free Press, 1952.

Richards, Edward A. (editor), *Proceedings of the Midcentury White House Conference of Children and Youth*. Raleigh, N. C., Health Publications Institute, 1951.

Rondell, Florence and Michaels, Ruth, *The Adopted Family*. New York, Crown Publishers, Inc., 1951.

Rose, Anna Perrott, *Room for One More*. Boston, Houghton Mifflin Company, 1950.

Schulze, Susanne (editor), *Creative Group Living in a Children's Institution*. New York, Association Press, 1951.

Smith, William Carlson, *The Stepchild*. Chicago, University of Chicago Press, 1953.

Standards for Specialized Courts Dealing with Children. Children's Bureau Publication No. 346, Washington, D. C., U. S. Government Printing Office, 1954.

Stern, Edith M., and Castendyck, Elsa, *The Handicapped Child: A Guide for Parents*. New York, A. A. Wyn, Inc., 1950.

Taft, Jessie (editor), *Social Case Work With Children*. Philadelphia, Pennsylvania School of Social Work, 1940.

Thurston, Henry W., *The Dependent Child*, New York, Columbia University Press, 1930.

U. S. Bureau of the Census. *U. S. Census of Population 1950*. Vol. IV, Special Reports, Part 2, Chapter C, Institutional Population. Washington, D. C., U. S. Government Printing Office, 1953.

Wasson, Valentina P., *The Chosen Baby*. rev. ed., Philadelphia, J. B. Lippincott Company, 1950.

Witmer, Helen, and Kotinsky, Ruth, *Personality in the Making*. New York, Harper and Brothers, 1952.

Young, Leontine, *Out of Wedlock*. New York, McGraw-Hill Book Company, 1954.

Significant Articles

Baker, Inez M., "Uphold Rights of Parent and Child." *The Child*, XIII, August 1948, pp. 27–30.

Bender, Lauretta, "Infants Reared in Institutions Permanently Handicapped." *Bulletin of the Child Welfare League of America*, XXIV, September 1945, pp. 1–4.

Gennaria, Marion, "Helping the Very Young Child to Participate in Placement." *Journal of Social Work Process*, III, December 1939, pp. 29–59.

Hancock, Claire, "Protective Service for Children." *Child Welfare*, XXVIII, March 1949, pp. 3–9.

Harral, Elizabeth, "The Foster Parent and the Agency in the Adoption Process," *Proceedings of the National Conference of Social Work*, 1941, pp. 411–425.

Jolowicz, Almeda R., "A Foster Child Needs His Own Parents." *The Child*, XII, August 1947, pp. 18–21.

Keith-Lucas, Alan, "Status of Parent During Placement." *Child Welfare*, XXXII, June 1953, pp. 3–5.

Levine, David L., "Separation as an Element in Day Care Planning." *Jewish Social Service Quarterly*, XXVII, June 1951, pp. 436–441.

Rawley, Callman, "Why Differentiate Caseloads in the Multiple Agency." *Bulletin of the Child Welfare League of America*, XXVI, January 1947, pp. 1–7, 9.

Ziner, Florence, "Achieving Foster Parenthood." *Public Welfare*, III, November 1945, pp. 254–256.

The Masters Family and a Children's Agency

DOROTHEA GILBE~~RT~~   ~~Director,~~
Children's Service Bureau
Shreveport, La.[1]

Three years ago Mrs. Masters phoned. Her call was reserved and brief. She gave her name, asked for an appointment and added that she had a two-and-a-half-year-old little girl. Her pediatrician had recommended our foster care, but "the child was in perfect health." She accepted the first time offered, two days hence, but called back the same afternoon saying, "Something has come up that will make it impossible for me to keep the appointment." When a change of time was offered, she thanked us but said she would call back later.

Six weeks passed before she phoned again. In the same curt, business-like way she arranged another appointment, and came exactly on time.

The first impression of Mrs. Masters was of a fastidious, pretty little person, tense, anxious, and very weary. She opened the interview in a prerehearsed manner explaining that she is a private secretary in a law firm. Dr. Ellis, her pediatrician had recommended foster care for her little girl and had particularly advised our agency. I told her that we do board children and know that Dr. Ellis, who has taken care of some of our foster children, has been impressed. She must have been giving this much thought since her first call to us. We, too, feel that the decision for a child to live away from his own home is a serious one. There is a little relieved sigh from her as I say this. I tell her that one of the services we have is just the opportunity for parents to discuss problems they are having in planning care for their children. Sometimes parents can find a way to keep their children at home.

---

[1] This agency provides casework service in planning for children and operates group care, foster family care, and day care facilities of its own for children who need care away from home.

he said she had better tell me about the trouble. All of a sudden her reserve crumbled. She bowed her head over the desk giving herself over to uncontrolled sobbing for several minutes. As her fists unclench and her sobbing subsides she fumbled unsuccessfully for a handkerchief. I put a kleenex in her hand. After blowing her nose and drying her eyes she looked up and gave me a rueful little girl smile. She said that she was so ashamed. She thought she had herself under control or she wouldn't have come. She then gave a spontaneous description of her difficulties with Judy with only an occasional faltering.

In summary, she told me that Judy, who is not quite two, has been a hard baby from birth, crying almost constantly so that neither of them (and it is sometime after the interview starts that I realize that there is a Mr. Masters) has been able to have a full night of uninterrupted sleep. She and her husband work, and Judy has been in a large (and expensive) private nursery during the day. She was troubled that Judy did not talk although she seemed to understand. Her walk was unsteady, and yet she dashed at things, often falling and bumping herself. They could not toilet train her, and although she ate enormously, she stayed thin. She had fought any attempt to feed her, refused to use a spoon, and threw food on the floor. Sleeping has been their greatest problem. She fights it, and when she does drop off, exhausted from screaming or crying, she seldom sleeps more than a few minutes, rousing herself (and them) with terrified screams. When I wondered if this has been something new with Judy, she assured me that it has always been this way.

She went on to give me some background on her marriage. Mr. Masters and she had married shortly before Mr. Masters had gone to Korea. He had been discharged three years later with battle fatigue and was in a hospital several months before coming home. He is drawing partial disability compensation and only recently had been able to hold a light, part-time job. They are largely dependent upon her very excellent earnings. Her husband seemed like a changed person to her. He was subject to nightmares, to inexplicable moods of discouragement and irritation, and sometimes she has wondered whether he is sane.

Judy had been born a little over a year after his return home. During her pregnancy the situation became so strained that, at the urging of her family, she left him, but they were reconciled after a fashion shortly before Judy's birth. Although her family would probably have helped them financially, they were so opposed to her marriage that she forced herself to work two weeks after Judy was born. Mr. Masters was then not working and took almost exclusive and, she thinks, very good care of the baby. When Judy was seven months old, Mrs. Masters says she herself had a nervous breakdown. She slid over this quickly, but did say that she was hospitalized for several weeks, and the baby went to a residential nursery, where she stayed for a year.

The nursery asked the parents not to visit since seeing them upset the baby. The matron frequently told them that the baby was not developing normally, was crying and screaming almost constantly, sleeping in only brief cat naps and not showing the kind of physical and motor development normal for a child of her age.[2] (Later the nursery described Judy as a baby who always looked frightened—"the baby whose hair literally seemed to stand on end.") Although Mrs. Masters' physician advised against her trying to work and that she should take care of the baby at home, the concern of the nursery was so great that under their urging they finally took Judy home about six months ago to their small, pleasant, thin-walled apartment.

Mrs. Masters decided to come to the agency because the family has been asked to move unless they could keep Judy quiet. She then put her fear into words that Judy may be retarded.

Mr. Masters and she disagree in their handling of Judy. Sometimes her husband has been so much more patient than she; and then again, when he is in one of his moods, he is apt to lash out at Judy for doing nothing.

He had not wanted Mrs. Masters to come to us and does not know that she is here. He thinks that they can work this out by themselves and is opposed to Judy leaving home again. Sometimes she thinks she should take Judy and leave him. Yet how can she raise a child alone, and Judy seems so very fond of her daddy. Sometimes she thinks that what is wrong with Judy is in them and not in her. The nursery where Judy is now staying has said that she is good during the day, and she

---

[2] For a discussion of the effects of group placement on infants see Bowlby, John, *Maternal Care and Mental Health*. Geneva, World Health Organization, 2nd edition, 1952.

herself has seen her looking happy and contented there. Since Dr. Ellis thinks Judy needs to be away from them, she would like to know about our boarding care and if boarding Judy seems the best thing to do. She thinks she can make her husband see it her way. I said that any boarding plan would need to be made with both her and her husband and, of course, only if it seems best.

Mrs. Masters listened attentively as I told her about our foster family care and asked questions from time to time. She then went back to her concern about whether Judy is defective, thinking maybe that what they want is help in knowing what to expect of their little girl. I found that some of the things which worried her about Judy were a natural part of being just two. It is also evident that her expectations of what a child this young should do are much closer to what one would normally expect from a 3- or 4-year old.

Finally she asks me if we don't have a day nursery, too, and seems puzzled and interested about why we would not see this as appropriate for so young a child.[3] As it became increasingly evident that she wanted to keep Judy at home, I raised the question of using the Child Guidance Center. She had phoned them a few months ago, but they could not give her an appointment soon, and her husband had been so upset at the idea that she had not applied. She felt that she knew us now, would like to think this over, and come back here if she could. She also would like to bring her husband with her because "we could explain things to him better than she could."

She brought Mr. Masters with her the next time very much as a reluctant little boy would be dragged to the dentist by his mother. This shy and gentle young man emerged as a much more forceful and perceptive person than she had pictured him, even though he was excessively preoccupied with his health.

He gave a picture of the compensating sweetness that Judy sometimes shows. He also feared that Judy might not be normal, but after the second interview neither parent returned to considering foster care. (Details of our discussions with Dr. Ellis are omitted. He concurred and shared his negative findings with us.)

After the third interview, we decided that as part of understanding

---

[3] See *A Guide for the Development of Day Care Programs*. New York, Child Welfare League of America, Inc., 1951.

Judy's needs at this time we could offer a psychometric examination and our own impression of Judy as the parents brought her to the office for brief play periods.

Judy was a slender, well-built, pretty little girl with her mother's fine-boned, delicate features. Her face had the puckered look of an old woman marked by fearful wide-eyed anxiety. In moments of comparative ease this relaxed into a puzzled frown. From the safety of her father's lap, she would occasionally smile fleetingly then bury her head on his shoulder.

On her first visit she refused to leave her father's lap although she showed interest in the toys he handled. On the second, she was able to get to the floor as long as he stood near her. Then she took all the toys off the shelves and arranged them neatly in rows or symmetrical piles. She seemed to enjoy stacking blocks carefully and meticulously. Beyond handling and arranging, toys seemed to have little meaning for her. After her second visit, our psychologist joined the group. Very tentatively Judy let her play with her, handing things back and forth. She was willing to wave bye-bye to her from the sanctuary of her father's shoulder.

The psychological examination, given on her next visit, and from the safety of her mother's lap, found a mental age only a little over a month below her chronological age. In her summary, the psychologist said:

This cannot be regarded as an optimum rate for Judy as her lack of co-operation and general insecurity undoubtedly prevented her from putting forth her best effort. The fact that she successfully completed almost all the items at her own age level and met with two successes at the 2 years 6 months level indicates that she is a child of at least average ability. However, she is not a youngster who is able to enter into a satisfactory relationship with others and her behavior throughout the examination indicates general immaturity for her age. Further testing at a later date when she has outgrown her negative phase would yield a more adequate estimate of her abilities.

During this time the parents found a small house where their concern about their neighbor's complaints no longer bothered them. They found a neighbor who had only two other children with her during the day to take care of Judy for them. They seemed closer together and better able to work out together a more consistent kind of care, though they continued to press Judy for the kind of achievements to be expected of an older child.

After this series of visits there was a brief reconsideration of foster care and also of the possibility of Mrs. Masters not working. Neither of these seemed desirable or practicable. Mrs. Masters, as a matter of fact, in one interview said that she could never seriously consider stopping work and said that the hours she was in the office gave her the only relaxation that she had.

They were then able to accept a referral to the Child Guidance Center. Three months later the Center reported that Judy had so distorted a personality and so little capacity to form relationships that she would not at this stage benefit from direct treatment. On the basis of the detailed history from the family, and the observation of motor development, they felt there was some indication of a behavior disorder based on an organic condition due to brain cell injury at birth from oxygen starvation. They were continuing to see the parents—she on a regular basis, he occasionally. There was no significant change in Judy's behavior.

Seven months later Mrs. Masters phoned saying, "We would like to come and see you again." I suggested that afternoon and heard a breathless little gasp when I asked her if that seemed too soon, she laughed nervously commenting she supposed she had better come soon while she "still had her courage up."

The Masters arrived walking very close together, and their greeting was warm and friendly. Though Mrs. Masters had pre-empted the closest chair, Mr. Masters opened the interview. "We have to find something to do about Judy." Mrs. Masters' eyes filled with tears, and Mr. Masters said that unless they can get some rest neither of them can stand the strain any longer. Today they want to talk about our finding a foster home for Judy. Together they gave me a picture of her continuing belligerence. They are giving all their time and thought to her demands. They continuously give in just to have even some quiet. "That isn't right, not for us or Judy." Mrs. Masters again dissolves into uncontrolled sobbing, and again when the storm is passed, she straightens up saying "You know I thought I had all of this under control." I tell them that I know how many things they have tried and how much

I know they have wanted to find another solution. She then tells me that she fears a repetition of her breakdown. She is so tired she can't think; has fainted at work; and in addition, has had colds and flu recently.

What they have in mind is a trial period so they can get some rest. They think Judy should remain under foster care until she is older and maybe by then she will have learned how to get along better.

I wonder how much they remember about our foster care. Mrs. Masters quickly said that she remembered everything. Mr. Masters says he recalls very little. He reminds his wife that he hadn't talked to me directly. While I explained, he listened carefully and asked thoughtful and leading questions. I told him that our foster parents are people who work with us, taking children into their own homes. They know children will come and go as parents make plans for them. Foster parents discuss with the caseworker the experiences the child is having and his development while the child is in their home, and that the parents will be visiting weekly and will from time to time have the children home for holidays or vacation. We go on into a discussion of the details of medical care, clothing, allowances, etc.

Mrs. Masters' only concern centers on being sure they can have Judy back when they are ready and that they can see her. Mrs. Masters questions visiting at all. As I explained why we believe visiting is good even if the child is upset, she says maybe what she means is that *she* will be too upset but she will go if it is best for Judy.

I finally comment that it sounds as if we already have Judy in a foster home. First we need to find a home for her, and if it can be found, help her move into it. We then discuss how we may do this. The worker who is going to plan for Judy would need to know her before we could decide on which foster home would be best. She would want to talk to the Guidance Center and their doctor. She would need to talk to foster parents to see if they will work with Judy for us. Judy, too, will need to have some trust in the worker before she is moved. We will also want our doctor to see her. It is hard to know how long this will take.

I asked them how long they had been thinking Judy would be away. Mr. Masters thought three months and she six. I say that for something that is as uprooting as this it would be well to think of three months as minimum; that probably the best thing for us to do is to go along seeing what does happen and settle on three months as a time when we will review our impression of Judy's progress and consider whether she and they are ready for her to move back home.

As we fill out the application form together, they describe little change in Judy. She eats somewhat better but is still messy and gulps quantities of food. She continues to have a bottle on going to bed and will ask for two or three refills of either milk or orange juice before going to sleep. She showed so much fear when they tried to move her bed into another room that she still sleeps in the same room with them. She moves about constantly and cries out in her sleep, occasionally arousing with nightmares.

There are times now when she puts a number of words together and her speech is sometimes understandable. With the least excitement though she jabbers unintelligibly and stutters badly.

Her resistance to using the toilet for her bowel movements is greater than before, although she now seldom wets herself during the day. She makes no protest on being put on the toilet but after she has been sitting for a time she will get up, pull up her panties and have her bowel movement in them. She loves her tricycle, but is reckless and is apparently unaware of the danger of darting out into the street. She exhibits little interest in other playthings beyond the old orderly arranging of them. She often chews on her hands or masturbates.

Her father's eyes suddenly fill with tears, and he says he doesn't see how he is going to bear to have her away from home. Then he adds thoughtfully he doesn't see how they can go on with things as they are. He then asks about their financial agreement with us which had been discussed only briefly before. They see no difficulty in being able to meet the full cost of our board and are quite sharing about their financial circumstances. Miss Lee, who was to be Judy's worker, met them and planned for her first visit with Judy.

Miss Lee heard Judy screaming when she got out of the car. (She had been trying to get into a jacket to go outside even though it was raining and was fighting her father's gentle insistence that she stay indoors.) During the visit her parents tried to force her to talk, which only increased her withdrawal. At first Judy stood close to her family, but was finally lured to play with the worker's purse and edged to within arms reach of her, retreating to her father when a play visit to the office with the worker was mentioned.

On the second visit after the same kind of tentative approach, Judy did eventually go out happily with Miss Lee to ride on her tricycle and show her around the yard. The suggestion from her mother that she could have a ride with Miss Lee evoked such panic that Miss Lee had decided to return another time when Judy got into the automobile and began fiddling with the keys. When Miss Lee asked if Judy wanted to take a little ride and come back home soon, she nodded her head quickly. She was very quiet while they rode slowly around several blocks. She greeted her mother with exuberance, beating at her with her fists, clutching, and butting her.

On the next trip Judy came to the office to "play" with the toys, which meant taking them all off the shelf and putting them back neatly. The third trip Judy began to test Miss Lee out by threatening to run into the street from the playground, but when she was told she must not go past the sidewalk, she didn't, although she would persistently edge toward it and put her toe over the edge. On this trip the worker said that next time she would take Judy to see a doctor.

At the Clinic, Judy used the worker's lap much as she used the lap of her parents as a safe spot from which she observed the world. She cried during part of the examination but was compliant. Physical examination was negative, height average, weight normal. A thorough neurological check showed no evidence of abnormality.

After this Miss Lee and the parents began to talk with Judy about moving. There was careful discussion of the things she should take along, her own bed, many of her playthings and her clothes. She began to talk about living with Mr. and Mrs. Frank.

Mr. and Mrs. Frank were a couple in early middle age who, at this time, had no other children in their home. They had had a recent successful experience in taking a severely disturbed child from us who in addition had needed extensive medical care. After a careful discussion of Judy they felt willing and interested in trying to take care of her.

When Mr. and Mrs. Masters came to the office to discuss placement, they were very much together. Although they were interested in knowing about the foster home and why we had selected it, they used most of the time explaining why they felt this step was necessary. So much so, that I raised the question of whether it really did seem good to go on. They then reaffirmed that things really had not been any better between them and Judy and that they must have time to find some perspective. The whole feeling as the interview was completed, the financial arrangements made, the agreement signed and the details arranged for the move the next morning was that they had accomplished something good.

In the morning Miss Lee found everything packed and ready. Judy, crisp and proud in a new dress, looked tremulous as she helped carry things out to the car and then climbed in. Her good-byes were perfunctory, so much so that both of the parents, close to tears, said good-bye and quickly dashed into the house.

On the way to the foster home Judy stood on the seat pointing out trucks, trains, and landmarks she had seen on previous trips but at the foster home, when the foster mother came out to the car, Judy made no move to get out until Miss Lee opened the door and offered to help her out. She walked into the house clinging to Miss Lee's hand. She did not respond to Mrs. Frank's greeting except by frowning and edging closer to Miss Lee. She stood by as an interested observer while the car was unpacked but did carry her dolls into the house. She watched with interest while the foster mother and Miss Lee put up her bed. When the time came to say good-bye, she looked frightened and her eyes filled with tears, but she allowed her foster mother to hold her hand while they both waved good-bye from the front door.

The decision to place any child is a serious one. It was doubly so for a child who had had as little basic security as Judy, as little real continuous relationship with people, and as divided a life. Adding another change to this child's experience might shatter the precarious adjustment she was maintaining—negative as it was. On the other hand, even though Judy might have stayed with her parents, the atmosphere of doubts, questions, concerns, anxieties, and rivalry was blocking her development.

Judy's foster parents were prepared for difficulties. From the first day most of the behavior that had been troubling to the parents disappeared. At the end of a month, Miss Lee wrote the following summary:

Since Judy went to live in the Franks' home, she has made a dramatic adjustment for a child with so many problems. She has been eating well, sleeping through the night and after she is put to bed with a story and has a little before bed play, drops off into a quiet and uninterrupted sleep. She has continued to wear diapers at night but during the day has taken care of her toilet needs well. She likes to have the foster mother take her to the toilet and to stand by until she is through. She seeks little companionship or closeness with Mrs. Frank, but watches for Mr. Frank's return home every evening and loves to romp and play with him strenuously. Although a bottle had been offered at bed time during the first week, she refused it, and after the first week, Mrs. Frank put it away. Much of her play has continued to be a routine stacking of objects on top of one another. There are times now when this orderly and rather meaningless routine is being displaced by real play with the thing itself. Judy continues to lead her foster mother or father to what she wants, but it is with a little twinkle and increasingly she is using language instead of gestures. The Franks are finding her a delightful child with a charming sense of humor, satisfyingly responsive. She still keeps a timid distance from neighbors and visiting children but is not openly unfriendly. They had to be quite firm with her about not going into the street, but after the first ten days found that they could trust her outside alone. Her bowel movements seem to be established on an every other day to sometimes once in every three days.

This pattern of living continued until September, four months after Judy had gone into her new foster home. It seemed like a miracle and for the parents a most disconcerting one. It would have been easier for them if Judy could have continued to show some of the troubles she had at home. As it was, they began to fall back into deep self-doubt and some mutual recrimination. When Judy's mother phoned the first day after placement, for the customary report on how things had gone and she heard that Judy had refused a bottle, had gone to sleep and slept well, it was almost more than she could bear. She said in a little weak voice, "Well, it looks as if we were what was the matter with Judy all the time." Before the first of their very regular weekend visits, they came to the office together to discuss details of her past week. Judy's mother pulled back from seeing her, wondering if maybe it wasn't too soon and if it might not be upsetting. For the next four months, however, they did visit, and it was almost unbearably disturbing to them that Judy seemed able to both welcome them warmly and to let them go happily.

In the beginning there was a too complete "we are here to learn" outward acceptance of everything the foster parents did for Judy, and it was only after a month or two that a healthy questioning began to creep into their office interviews. Mr. Masters made one or two opportunities to see us independently, but it was almost entirely Mrs. Masters who used phone calls and appointments to discuss her concerns about the marriage, about whether they were the right family for Judy, and about whether they could go on together. Two months after Judy was placed Mr. Masters was promoted into better and full-time employment which placed him in the position of being, for the first time, the major wage-earner for the family.

Both of them commented that although their life had been hard with Judy at home, they missed the things they had had to do. Without the constant busyness both of them had doubts about whether they really had enough mutual interests to make a congenial marriage. Mrs. Masters said, "You know there are just times when Mr. Masters gets on my nerves." Two or three weeks after Judy went into the foster home, Mr. Masters began to talk about taking Judy home. If Mrs. Masters had not held very firmly to saying she couldn't face it yet, he would have insisted. At the end of three months to the day, he arranged an appointment for both of them. After an hour and a half of discussion reviewing the foster home experience and their own setup, we decided that three months really was not long enough to hold the gain for Judy. Nor were they ready for Judy's return. We decided to reconsider once a month.

The next week they applied for a G. I. Loan on a house having separate but connecting bedrooms, screened play porch space, and a large fenced yard.

About a month later the foster parents had the opportunity for a week's vacation trip. The Masters suggested trying Judy out at home during this time. Mr. Masters, whose vacation was past due, arranged for a leave so that he could take care of her during the day. Judy greeted the news with a beaming smile.

Two days after Judy had gone home, her mother phoned she had had diarrhea since the night of her return, was vomiting and had fever. Our doctor saw her and recommended a diet and medication. After three days of treatment, Mr. Masters phoned, diarrhea was continuing, he was extremely worried about Judy. Judy was petulant and wilful, cried a great deal, slept poorly and wanted constant attention.

Miss Lee went with them to the doctor. Judy seemed a very sick little girl. Mr. Masters held her tenderly, stroking her hair and trying to interest her in things around them. He looked frightened and kept trying to reassure the worker, and with it himself, that he had been giving good care to Judy. No diagnosis was established. Two days later the foster parents returned. When the Masters talked with us about a time for the move back, they looked more drawn, more discouraged than they had for many months. They had hoped that this return home would be good; that perhaps they would not need to leave Judy in the foster home any longer.

On her return to the foster home, diarrhea stopped, and within three days she was back on her normal diet. Constipation became a problem, and for two weeks enemas and mild laxatives were prescribed.

Two months later, Mr. Masters began to press for Judy's return. Mrs. Masters became more nervous, developed unusual menstrual difficulty, had flu, fainted at work, and was finally admitted to a hospital where she underwent a long postponed repair operation. During this time, except for his working hours, Mr. Masters was in almost constant attendance with her at the hospital, cooked the foods that she particularly liked and took them to her.

Several weeks later Mrs. Masters requested an individual appointment. At this time she revealed that she was thinking of a separation. There was nothing specific beyond her feeling that she knew it would not be right to have Judy at home, she doubted whether she and her husband could be truly congenial, and she was feeling alone anyway. Mr. Masters talked constantly about having Judy home. She said that sometimes it seemed to her that he thought a lot more of Judy than he did of her; however, he has done so much for her. He is so proud of his work and his talking about it gets on her nerves and then she feels so ashamed of herself. We talked about the years when she had really felt as if she had two children and how strange it must seem no longer to be taking care of a husband and a child and earning the living, too. She tells then of just how much he did through these years that was thoughtful and good. She was no cook and loathed housekeeping, and her husband is a wonderful cook. In this interview there were real swings of emotion—diffuse dissatisfaction, self-doubts, flashes of new awareness as she listened to what she was saying. On the whole, it was a kind of declaration to herself that she could choose not to have her life go on as it was if she wanted to, but imperfect as it might be there were compensations. She asked for another appointment a week later.

This time she toyed with the idea of quitting work. On the other hand, it was nice to have the extra money. Her husband had been pointing out that they could now afford to have Judy home and her, too, if they managed carefully. She recalled her feelings of the previous week with wonder. She, in this hour, did a kind of verbal preliving of what it might be like to be a housewife and said that if she could have time with Judy without her husband around during the day, she could handle her better and maybe even get close to her. She then added, after a thoughtful silence, "I guess I'm really jealous of Judy." After all though she has never had a chance to take care of her by herself and she says earnestly that she does think she could learn to be a good mother, and then with an oblique little smile—adds maybe. She leaves still playing with the idea of handing in her resignation "after Christmas," and that would mean that they would be wanting Judy home in about six weeks.

Shortly after this both Mr. and Mrs. Masters came to the office together, ostensibly to plan about Christmas. Mrs. Masters would take a few days of vacation, and they were thinking it would be good to have Judy home—"a trial run" before she decides about resigning.

Both for Judy and her family, the days at home were not so good and not so bad. She was still negative at times and irritable, but they both said that it was much better than they had feared it might be. "Anyway, she did not get sick," and there were times of genuine pleasure with her.

Two weeks later they arranged an appointment to plan for her return. They were very serious as they told me that they had talked about this a lot and they would like to talk to me together about day care for Judy. They have to buy a new car. Their old one had literally worn out, and until they can get it paid for, they are going to need Mrs. Masters' salary, too. Mrs. Masters had been watching me closely, and then with a sly and very cute little grin, she said, "I guess you know we really wouldn't have had to buy the car, but I *know* I'm a good secretary, but I would just go nuts with nothing to do but try to be a mother, alone all day long, and I believe Judy would, too. Better to be a good secretary than a poor mother."

They had decided that Friday—ten days hence—would be the best time for her to come home, "If we thought it was all right." Then they would have the weekend together before Judy went to the nursery. As I comment that it sounds to me as if they are feeling pretty sure today that this is a good plan, Mr. Masters laughs, saying that even if I said Judy wasn't "done enough yet" they would probably take her anyway, and then adds, that seriously it does seem to them that Judy is ready and they are, too.

Mrs. Masters had brought a detailed list of the things she would like us to find out about Judy's "schedule" from the foster mother. She says with great earnestness that she wants everything to be just as it is in the foster home for Judy when she comes home. I comment that it can't really be the same. She looks at me with a puzzled frown for a moment, and then gives her spontaneous little laugh as she says, "I see what you mean. Mrs. Frank and I are not really the same people." I nod, and say that Mr. and Mrs. Frank don't run their lives on the same schedule either. She responds thoughtfully with, "I guess I can't learn to be a mother just by trying to act like somebody else," and Mr. Masters says he guesses when they made their list of questions they were going back into having Judy run their lives instead of their taking care of Judy. I reply that I know it is helpful to know how a youngster's days have been planned, so that they can know what she is changing from, not that they will want to keep it that way, but so they can know the places where she may find it hard to change because it is different.

They have thought about having Judy go back to her former day care foster mother. She was fond of Judy and they think, Judy of her. On the other hand, there aren't many things for Judy to play with there, and with a baby and a 5-year-old, there isn't much time for Judy. Maybe she needs a good group of playmates her own age. I tell them that I think they will know better after they have watched a group at the nursery for a while and then think about Judy in both places.

In the week that followed Mr. and Mrs. Masters spent a morning at our Day Care Center and reached a decision to try it.

The foster parents greeted the news of Judy's leaving with the mixed emotions that all good foster parents share—a sense of bereavement in losing a little girl who had become very much a part of their lives and a sense of pride in what they had done for her.

Judy herself "lighted up like a Christmas tree" when Miss Lee told her she was going home and would be "going to school."

On her trip to see the doctor, the same happy, bouyant mood prevailed. In his closing report the doctor says, "Interestingly, this little girl shows no stigmata of emotional difficulty. She is quite relaxed, happy, intelligent and curious about examiner's various procedures, etc."

The morning of leaving the foster home Judy watched for the worker with shining eyes, and she looked so excited she could hardly contain herself. She insisted on "helping" her foster father carry the boxes to the car. In parting she spontaneously hugged her foster mother and planted a kiss on each of the foster father's cheeks and asked him to carry her to the car. As they started, Judy did not look back but settled herself, smiled up at the worker and said, "Now we are going to meet Daddy." A moment later she asked if Mamma and Daddy would both be there. As they drove up to the office, Mr. and Mrs. Masters were arriving from the other direction. Judy spotted them at a great distance and began calling excitedly, "Hello, Daddy, hello, Daddy." As Judy rushed to them shouting almost hysterically, Mrs. Masters was closest and caught her to her, but after a brief moment she wiggled away and rushed to her daddy. When the time came to leave, Mr. Masters picked her up and carried her on his shoulder to their car. Mrs. Masters caught my eye, smiled a little ruefully and still smiling shrugged a little and followed them out.

Mr. Masters brought Judy to the Day Care Center the first morning and left her until after lunch time. She cried for about three minutes and then settled down, exploring and seeming to make friends easily. She had several hard bumps in the course of the first week without showing any pain reaction, and she stuttered some. At first she showed fear of heights but after the first two or three weeks became an intrepid and careful climber, loving to sit on the highest solitary point attainable. She ate all foods and at first would come back for even fourth helpings. Toward the end of the first month this slacked off to a more normal intake. At nap time she dropped asleep slowly but once asleep her nap was long and undisturbed. In the second month the teacher noted that she continued to be an energetic child. She was able to cry when she got hurt or somebody hurt her feelings. She was abnormally startled by sudden sounds and movements. She showed wholehearted enjoyment of activities and "the rougher the better." She developed a passion for playing in water, and the teacher thought she could let water just run over her hand for hours just for fun. She wet herself on two occasions and was extremely disturbed by it until reassured.

When her parents arrived, she would become babyish, jump up and down, squeal and shout and would start to run out of the door too soon, often quite out of the parents' control. In the third month bad stuttering appeared, and both Mr. and Mrs. Masters came in together for an interview concerned that she was being more difficult at home. The trouble was not as severe as formerly but bad enough that they were fearful of building up to real trouble again.

In the fourth month they reported improvement at home, stuttering disappeared, and it was evident that Mr. and Mrs. Masters were probably closer than they had ever been in their pride in her obvious cuteness and charm. They continue to be rather "muscle bound" as parents, particularly Mrs. Masters, but they can laugh together about it when she becomes overconcerned and tense.

At the present time the Masters family seems to have found a livable and reasonably satisfactory kind of balance which is permitting Judy a period of uninterrupted healthy living. With this new security and continuing achievement, Judy and her parents are building, we believe, an inner core of self- and mutual confidence that may be strong enough to fortify them in future periods of stress.

As new problems occur, they will probably be better prepared to seek and use help before real crisis is reached.

As a family and as individuals, they will probably continue to be more vulnerable to stress than many families but in the meantime a little girl has her parents with her who are also growing in understanding and affection.

chapter 9

Psychiatric Social Work

The Extent of Mental Illness

While mental disorder was not unknown among primitives nor among earlier peoples of our Euro-American culture, there has never been evidence that it constituted anything like the problem that it does for us today. In more ways than one it is a problem of our contemporary complicated and fast-moving civilization. There are some who hold that next to the problem of building the peace the problem of mental health (the obverse of mental disease) is the most important task of our day. Many see an interrelatedness between the lack of emotional maturity and stability and our current nightmares of war, poverty, and crime.

It is well to look at what estimates as well as facts are available concerning mental disorders. In March 1946 the Surgeon-General of the United States Public Health Service, Dr. Thomas Parran, testified before the Senate Subcommittee on Health and Education that "Eight million persons, more than six percent of the population, are suffering from some form of mental illness." [1] Dr. Parran, who was appearing in behalf of a bill to provide federal financial support and leadership in the area of mental health, went on to state that half of all hospital beds in the United States, some 600,000, are occupied by mental patients. Observing that this figure included only the more seriously ill, Dr. Parran added that "actually it by no means indicates the full magnitude of the problem, or even of the number of patients totally disabled by mental illness, since the number of admissions in the hospitals of many

[1] *Hearings before a Subcommittee of the Committee on Education and Labor, United States Senate. Seventy-ninth Congress, Second Session, on S-1160.* U. S. Government Printing Office, Washington, 1946, p. 7.

states is determined by the number of available beds rather than by the need." [2] Each year 125,000 new cases of mental disease are admitted to institutions, and according to Dr. Parran 10 million persons of the current population will require hospitalization for mental illness at some time in their lives.

At the same hearings Major General Lewis B. Hershey, Director of the National Selective Service System, testified that of the 5 million men rejected for military service, 1 million were so rejected for mental disease. This constituted the largest single cause for rejection among all registrants. "Of this, 400,000 are under 26 years of age." [3]

Brigadier General William C. Menninger, Chief, Neuropsychiatric Division, United States Army, speaking before the American Psychiatric Association in 1946, elaborated the points he had made several months previously before the Senate Subcommittee. "During the period of January 1, 1943, through December 30, 1945, approximately 1,875,000 men were rejected for military service because of neuropsychiatric disorders. This represented 12% of all men examined and 37% of the men rejected for all causes." [4] Approximately 1 million patients with neuropsychiatric disorders were admitted to army hospitals during this same period. This constituted 6 percent of all admissions and a rate of 45 admissions per 1,000 troops per year. About 380,000 men were granted medical discharges from the Army because of neuropsychiatric disorders. This number added to the 137,000 administratively discharged for personality disorders brings the total discharges to over 500,000 men.

Placing alongside of this the Navy experience for the years 1942, 1943, 1944, and the first six months of 1945, Captain Braceland, Chief, Neuropsychiatric Division, United States Navy, showed that 76,721 persons were separated from naval service for neuropsychiatric disabilities. In addition to this, there were 91,565 recruits rejected at the training centers because of inaptitude and various neuropsychiatric disabilities.

Dr. Parran also stressed the economic cost, aside from distress to

[2] *Ibid.*, p. 7.

[3] *Hearings before a Subcommittee of the Committee on Education and Labor, op. cit.,* p. 47.

[4] Menninger, William C., "Psychiatric Experience in the War, 1941–1946." *The American Journal of Psychiatry,* CIII, March 1947, p. 578. General Menninger's testimony before the Senate Subcommittee is recorded in the Hearings referred to, pp. 58–63; see also Menninger, William C., "Facts and Statistics of Significance for Psychiatry." *Bulletin of the Menninger Clinic,* XII, January 1948, pp. 1–25.

patients and their families. He stated that in 1942 the total budgets of public psychopathic hospitals were $170 million and estimated that at the current rate of increase the cost in 1952 would be one quarter billion dollars. Counting loss of income to patients plus the cost of maintaining mental hospitals and health services Dr. Parran cited the 1936 estimate of $1 billion.[5]

Other studies before and since World War II support these assertions, especially those conducted in an urban center, Baltimore, and a rural county in Tennessee. After allowing for differences in the two areas, the estimate arrived at is 6 percent of the population suffer from some type of serious mental disorder. Applying this figure to the 1954 population of 160 million provided a valid basis for calculation of almost 10 million persons experiencing serious mental disorder.

Another measure of mental disorder may be the number of resident patients in long-term mental hospitals. According to Felix and Kramer of the United States Public Health Service patients in mental hospitals numbered 3.8 per 1,000 population in 1950. Again using the 1954 population of 160 million there is substantial basis for an estimate of over 700,000 persons in mental hospitals. (Felix and Kramer deal adequately with the various factors that need to be taken into account when the increase in hospital patients during the present century is considered.) A final figure on the extent of mental disorder is that of admission to mental hospitals each year. For the year 1949 there were over a quarter million admissions, a figure larger than the discharges from or deaths in mental hospitals.[6]

Earlier Notions of Mental Illness

Before there was ever a knowledge of mental hygiene or a mental hygiene movement there were centuries of misguided, or unguided, ignorance about the nature and causes of mental illness. Despite our contemporary concern over the unprecedented apparent increase of mental cases, a little reflection or, better yet, study will reveal that men-

---

[5] *Hearings before a Subcommittee of the Committee on Education and Labor, op. cit.,* pp. 8–9.

[6] Felix, R. H., and Kramer, Morton, "Extent of the Problem of Mental Disorders." *Annals of the American Academy of Political and Social Science,* CCLXXXVI, March 1953, pp. 5–14. This up-to-date review of available statistical information should be related not only to the Congressional hearings already mentioned but also should be used for reference to the several sources upon which it is based.

tal disorder was not uncommon among earlier peoples. Among pre-literate cultures and in the civilizations which followed, the person of disordered mind was variously conceived of as a madman, a fool, or one who had outraged the gods. Such a person may have been deemed to be possessed of a demon, or to be the victim of magic wrought upon him, or as one being punished for his sins. It has only been within relatively recent times that any light has been shed upon the origin of mental disease. It has required the scientific investigations within the larger field of medicine to prepare the way for inquiry into causation.[7]

The emerging concept of causation within modern times helped to effect a changing practice in the care and treatment of mental disease. When demons or spirits were believed to possess the body of a man, the common practice was to exorcise or drive them out by incantations, ceremonials, and other ingenious devices, thereby releasing the affected person from supernatural influences or freeing him from the power of magical spells. At another time prayer and sacrifice served as propitiation for the sins that had invited mental disorder. The fancied potency of herbs and drugs very often supplemented other propitiatory exercises. During the Middle Ages persons possessed of evil spirits were physically scourged and tortured, and in many instances were burned, hanged, or drowned because of the conviction that they practiced witchcraft and sorcery. Our own experience during colonial times, hardly more than two centuries ago, stands as a mute testimony to our nearness to such beliefs. Even within the nineteenth century when a limited knowledge of causation provided no answer to the eternal "why," we oscillated between punishment of the insane as criminals and in-

[7] It may be an open question whether today we know more about mental disorder than the primitive did. The difference may lie in the interpretation which a more scientific point of view has made possible. Understood within the terms and values of an earlier period, the savage drove to a logical conclusion—granting his premises. Likewise in an age whose total set of values is related to the struggle between the forces of good and evil, the deity of good, the devil of evil, and in which the life here was a preparation for the life hereafter, the notion of demoniacal possession was entirely logical and, what is more, satisfying. As far as "causation" is concerned, the very concept belongs to this age, and is a part of modern scientific folkways. Once more it is necessary to sober ourselves with the realization that we are not necessarily any "smarter" than primitive peoples. In this connection it is worth noting the startling parallel between present-day shock therapy and the primitive or religious practice of driving out evil spirits or the devil! See Boas, Franz, *The Mind of Primitive Man*. New York, The Macmillan Company, 1911; also Deutsch, Albert, *The Mentally Ill in America*. Garden City, Doubleday, Doran Company, 1937, revised 1949.

difference to them as baffling enigmas. When the answers were sought in physical disorders during that same century, our "treatment" emphasis was entirely custodial for all victims and restraint for violent cases. Not until the ferment that is psychoanalysis quickened our thinking and enriched our insight did we understand the psychogenic factors in mental disease. Then only could we supplement and, in many cases, replace custody with therapy. The organized efforts to translate this realization into action is the story of the mental hygiene movement.[8]

The Impetus from Psychiatry, Psychoanalysis, and Psychology

Throughout most of the nineteenth century emphasis had been placed upon improvements in custodial care of the insane. What study there was of mental disease concerned itself largely with descriptions, climaxed in the classification system of Kraepelin based upon symptoms rather than causes. At about this same time Sigmund Freud was beginning his studies of hysteria which were to eventuate in psychoanalysis and to provide a far more fruitful approach to the phenomena of mental illness. Freud's analysis of the unconscious opened up the possibilities of a wholly new orientation to the human mind and personality. A dynamic conception of personality appeared which was to modify forever, if not eventually to replace, the old static view. There were many American psychiatrists who, although not psychoanalysts in any sense of the term and certainly not Freudian, came to express the psychoanalytic point of view. These men—such as Adolph Meyer, August Hoch, C. Macfie Campbell, Thomas W. Salmon—affected the development of psychiatry immeasurably. William Alanson White and A. A. Brill were perhaps the only avowed Freudian psychoanalysts among this early influential group.

Developments within the field of psychology were also spreading into the field of human behavior. The many researches into the problems and processes of child growth produced increasing evidence of the vital importance of the early years of the child's life. It was becoming clear that early emotional experiences as well as their resultant attitudes had lasting effects upon the personality. Psychometric studies, i.e., of individual differences, showed the wide variations of human

[8] Deutsch, *op. cit.*, Chapter I.

intelligence and abilities. The growth of psychological clinics, of which Witmer's in Philadelphia in 1896 was the earliest, made possible the accumulation of considerable knowledge about the nature of these individual differences and their role in the development of the individual.

Thus by the first decade of the twentieth century there were signs upon the horizon that presaged a new departure in the study and treatment of mental disease. Psychiatry was turning from preoccupation with custody and classification to a concern with causes; psychoanalysis was introducing a dynamic approach; while psychology was tracing the growth of the child and stressing the nature of individual differences. The cumulative effect of these varied approaches was the emergence of an entirely new outlook upon mental (personality) mechanisms, health, and illness. Essentially it consisted of a recognition that the human personality is basically emotionally motivated, and that behavior can be understood better by taking into account the forces that lie beneath the threshold of consciousness.

Clifford Beers and the Mental Hygiene Movement

When it is remembered that the preventive ideal had already begun to find expression in medicine and public health, it is understandable and even predictable that a movement embodying this principle in the field of mental health would develop eventually. The mental hygiene movement is an illustration of this. There might be some honest difference of opinion as to when this would have taken place, but there can be none about Clifford Beers being the precipitating factor. Without Beers the movement might have been delayed for years, but that it would have been started eventually is beyond question.

What then was the contribution of Clifford Beers? To understand something of its uniqueness, it is necessary to bear in mind that it was hardly more than a hundred years ago that the French alienist Pinel struck the chains from the insane at the Salpêtrière. Throughout the succeeding century, abroad and in America, asylums had continued to emphasize custodial care with little insight into why patients were what they were. Despite increasing refinements in asylum care and despite some knowledge of classification of mental disease, practically all institutions, public and private, were still pervaded with the densest ignorance concerning proper care and treatment of patients. For those innocent and harmless inmates who created no disturbance there was such care as met the necessary standards of decency and fairness. However, obstreperous victims, whose disease expressed itself in disorderly and violent ways, were exposed to the degree of harshness and brutality that their disorder aroused in attendants. It was not unusual for patients to be beaten, choked, placed in isolation or in the strait jacket for days at a time.

It was into this situation that Clifford Beers (1876–1943) came as a patient. Beers had entered upon a business career during the three years following his graduation from college in 1897. For six years he had carried around with him a fear of epilepsy that by 1900 had become an obsession with him. His attempt at suicide was unsuccessful, and for the next three years he was a patient in three different institutions of the state of Connecticut. The first was a privately owned asylum run for profit, the second a private nonprofit-making institution, and the third a state hospital. In all three the treatment was equally harsh and brutal, consistent with an ignorance that shrouded the very origins and nature of mental disease. Beers' treatment was not unusual for the day; if it had been perhaps his life subsequently would not have been given over to the mental hygiene movement. It was just because it was so characteristic of institutions of the day that upon his recovery and release Beers wrote, at white heat, of his experiences while under institutional care. What spared the book from being just another "exposé" of asylum conditions was its sincere conviction and the author's foresight in having his manuscript examined and criticized by a number of outstanding psychiatrists and psychologists. A Mind That Found Itself appeared in 1908 with an introduction by William James, the outstanding American psychologist and philosopher of his generation. Within the same year the first state mental hygiene committee was formed in Connecticut, followed the next year by the National Committee for Mental Hygiene.

Mental Hygiene Emphases

The originating, driving force of the movement was Clifford Beers. In the face of repeated discouragements, financial and otherwise, he persisted, with the aid of his book and his organizing abilities, in his efforts to bring about improvement in the care and treatment of the mentally ill. The brutalities he had experienced in three institutions were not peculiar to him alone. They were recognized as the inevitable product of the almost universal ignorance of the very nature of mental disease. It was realized that even though individual instances of brutality might be dealt with by discharge and punishment of the offending attendant yet more than that had to be done to overcome the prevailing attitude of the entire personnel. This attitude in turn reflected the beliefs generally held throughout the country.

While this first approach, improvement of institutional care, held constant, the attack was proceeding along other lines. The nature of mental disease and the process by which it develops were being studied. This called for an understanding of mental disorders that went far beyond the traditional concepts of classification and etiology that had been in vogue for over a generation. An analysis of causative factors demanded a positive approach that went to the roots of the disorder rather than a mere exercise in classification based on certain well-defined symptoms. The study of mental disease had to pass out of the realm of categories into the dynamics of personality development and personality adjustment.

A third essential in the early aims of the mental hygiene program was the recognition of the importance of prevention. Desirable as it might be to have institutions more humane, and valuable as theories of causation were, nevertheless it seemed just as imperative to be able to prevent the addition of millions of new recruits or potential recruits to the already large army of mentally disabled. Prevention was obviously predicated upon a knowledge of causes and had to wait for developments in that field. Stress was placed upon the positive ideal of prevention, not merely upon its negative aspects. It was just as vital, perhaps more so, for a person to be helped to attain and maintain a healthy, functioning personality as it was to be reminded perpetually of what not to do in order to avoid commitment to an institution. This concept of prevention had taken its place in medicine, especially since the beginning of the twentieth century, and had furnished an example which the mental hygiene movement quickly made its own. This was consistent with the pattern of moving from cure of the patient after he is sick to assisting the well person to stay in health.

A fourth and indispensable emphasis of the mental hygiene movement was the dissemination of knowledge concerning causes, treatment, and prevention. It was not sufficient that psychiatrists alone be acquainted with the nature of mental disease; it was just as necessary to have the general public informed. The National Committee for Mental Hygiene, with Clifford Beers as its secretary and backed by most of the outstanding psychiatrists of the country, carried on a campaign of enlightenment through the medium of books, pamphlets, public meetings, and study groups. State committees for mental hygiene materially assisted in carrying on these labors with individuals and groups. That such efforts were not without their appreciable effects was reflected in the increasingly widespread acquaintance by large segments of the population of the general concepts of mental hygiene and of their utilization in everyday living. Perhaps for the first time in history a people had become conscious of what mental health meant and were implemented in some degree to attain it.

A final guiding principle of the mental hygiene movement has been the search for those ways and means by which people may be helped to live constructively and to realize their own capacities for living. Prevention may very well revolve around what should not be done to such an extent that mental health becomes a preoccupation with the negative. It may be very much like the man who is so careful not to get sick that he has no opportunity to enjoy health. While an original concern of the mental hygiene movement was a consideration of the psychoses and neuroses, attention has shifted more and more to all forms of maladjustment which the individual is experiencing within himself or with the larger groups of which he is a part. This has resulted in a renewed interest in helping to release individuals not only away from the disabling disorder but toward the direction of positive mental health. The ultimate goal is the enrichment of human experience so that individuals may live creatively and be free fully to develop their potentialities.

The Development of Psychiatric Social Work

The shift in emphasis, around the beginning of the present century, from custodial care to individualized study and treatment prepared the way for a new departure in the kind and quality of care accorded mental patients. This first found expression in the newly opened psychopathic hospitals, neurological clinics of hospitals, and hospital social service departments. Psychiatrists were becoming increasingly aware of the crucial importance of the effect of emotional experiences upon the personality development of the individual. They were at the same time taking into account that environmental pressures upon the individual were factors to be reckoned with in any form of mental disability. The early psychopathic hospitals, of which the first was established in Michigan in 1906, concentrated upon the study, diagnosis, and treatment of the earlier and more hopeful forms of mental disease. As part of this study and diagnosis, the psychiatrist gathered material on the life histories of patients. Gradually, however, this assignment was delegated to field workers who functioned under psychiatric direction.

The first instance of the actual employment of a social worker in a hospital occurred in 1905 in the neurological clinic of the Massachusetts General Hospital under the direction of Dr. James J. Putnam. In the following year a social worker was employed in the psychopathic wards of Bellevue Hospital, New York, for the purpose of assisting patients who were recovering from mental illness. The New York State Charities Aid Association, through its committee on mental hygiene, had in 1910 secured the appointment of an "after-care worker" to supervise patients discharged from two of the state hospitals of New York. It was not until the next year that the first social worker was placed upon the payroll of a state hospital for mental diseases, the Manhattan State Hospital. In 1913 two Massachusetts hospitals, Danvers State Hospital and Boston State Hospital, each placed a social worker upon the staff.

The real impetus to the development of this work came when, in 1913, the Boston Psychopathic Hospital began its social service department under the leadership of Dr. Ernest Southard and Miss Mary C. Jarrett. Hardly had this project started than World War I began. By the time the United States was drawn in, in 1917, it had become clear that the developing social service in civilian hospitals would be just as necessary, if not more so, for army hospitals. The practical difficulty that needed to be faced was that there were not enough specially trained social workers to meet emergency needs. Accordingly, plans were made to enlarge the training facilities at the Boston Psychopathic Hospital, and eventually an arrangement was effected whereby an emergency training course was given under the joint auspices of Smith College, the National Committee for Mental Hygiene, and the Boston Psycho-pathic Hospital, with Miss Jarrett in charge. It is generally believed that the term describing this new specialty, psychiatric social work, was coined by Dr. Southard and Miss Jarrett. In their book *The Kingdom of Evils,* they expressly state that this branch of social work was a new emphasis rather than a new function, having grown out of ideas and activities that already existed in scattered forms. In this respect its development is not unlike that of medical social work.

Out of these first training courses of eight weeks' duration in 1918 there came the establishment, within a year, of a permanent graduate school of social work training at Smith College. Other schools, already established, such as the New York School of Social Work, the Penn-sylvania School of Social and Health Work, and the Chicago School of Civics and Philanthropy, continued their interest in the field of psychiatric social work and added to its rapidly enlarging area which already was going beyond the bounds of the hospital. Within a decade there was not a school of social work that did not pay its respects to the psychiatric point of view, and for some it constituted the cornerstone of the curriculum. Nor was there a single agency or a phase of social work that escaped the impact of its principles or implications.

What Is Psychiatric Social Work?

Psychiatric social work is social casework practiced in hospitals and clinics in which the ultimate responsibility for the treatment of mental and emotional illness is carried by the psychiatrist. To some readers this may seem an oversimplified statement, to others it may seem so am-biguous as to be meaningless, while to others it may seem to emphasize settings rather than the worker. To all, the answer must be made that there will be no unanimity of definition among social workers, even among those called psychiatric social workers, but that for the purposes of this chapter and this treatise this definition will remain the basis for our discussion. It certainly is consistent with the study recently carried on by the American Association of Psychiatric Social Workers.[9] The

[9] Berkman, Tessie D., *Practice of Social Workers in Psychiatric Clinics and Hospitals.* New York, American Association of Psychiatric Social Workers, 1953; see also booklet prepared by the American Association of Psychiatric Social Workers "What is Psychiatric Social Work?" (no date, probably 1954).

emphasis will be upon the setting in which and through which the services are offered: the mental hospital, whether state, federal, military, or voluntary (for profit or nonprofit); the clinic, whether attached to hospital, or a community mental hygiene clinic, or child guidance clinic —regardless of method of financing. Included with this emphasis must be the team relationship of psychiatrist, clinical psychologist, and psychiatric social worker—a team relationship that is a genuine operational one rather than superficial and lip-serving.

Psychiatric Social Work in Hospitals for Mental Illness

When hospitals for the mentally ill moved beyond a preoccupation with custody and classification to a felt concern for treatment, it naturally followed that adjustment of the individual upon discharge assumed considerable importance. This "after-care" program Dr. Adolph Meyer traces back to the Switzerland and France of a century ago, and then to our institutions in America for the mentally ill.[10] By the end of the first decade of the twentieth century a number of "after-care agents" had been employed, and psychiatric social work in the hospital for mental disease was well underway.

This early interest in after care has continued with increasingly effective programs being developed in both parole and foster care. A working distinction is frequently made upon the basis of the patient returning to his own home in the case of parole while the arrangement whereby the patient goes to a home other than his own is referred to as foster care. Some workers are inclined to characterize the patient in foster care as one who is not well enough to take his place in his former environment or to earn his living, but this differentiation is by no means commonly accepted. To most workers the test is: Is the home from which the patient came able to receive him, and is there a reasonable prospect of a satisfying adjustment? If the original home is no longer available or would be seriously prejudicial to the welfare of the patient, then an alternative home should be found for him. This decision is an especially crucial one in all those instances where a liv-

[10] Meyer, Adolph, "Historical Sketch and Outlook of Psychiatric Social Work." *Hospital Social Service*, V, April 1922, p. 221.

ing experience outside the institution will assure not only what the institution has to offer but much more by way of satisfying usefulness.

Before amplifying these remarks about after care, it will be well to trace the points at which the social worker encounters the patient. Admission to a mental hospital is a medical decision usually based upon the sworn statements of two physicians. Occasionally, there may be descriptive material about the individual, his family, and his community which has been prepared by a county welfare worker in those states and counties where such arrangements have been established. Psychiatric social workers may see, at intake, relatives who have brought the patient to the hospital. Here there may be received material, or additional material, about the patient. The emphasis at this point, however, will be to assist the family with some of the problems arising from the fact of the patient's admission, to deal with some of their fears and anxieties, and to try to make understandable the hospital facilities and programs. This contact with the patient's family is important because it sets the tone and the nature of the continuing link between the hospital and the home. The quality of this early contact may have a great deal to do with whether the patient's family leaves thinking this is the end or thinking this is the beginning. Because of the usual stereotypes about mental illness and mental hospitals, there is a real service to be performed which will help the family to see the possibilities of treatment and restoration rather than to continue to regard commitment as an irrevocable doom.

When the patient is in the hospital, the psychiatric social worker continues contact with the patient, the family, and the community. The actual medical and psychiatric treatment is carried on by the physician and the staff associated with him, but there are many instances in which the social worker will be called upon to work with tangible as well as intangible matters as they affect the patient. In the realm of feeling, for example, there may be occasion to deal with the meaning of illness—with the patient as well as with family members; there may be matters to be handled affecting the marital partner. Or there may be very practical problems with which help must be given—legal matters, insurance, housing, clothing, etc. These services of the social worker are performed as a professional operation and as part of the treatment team whose existence is solely for the patient. The psychiatrist is necessarily working with the illness of the patient, with those aspects of illness that interfere with resolution of the patient's inner difficulties. More usually the social worker works with those areas of wellness that can be directed toward participation in the reality of everyday living and working. These two—the psychiatrist and the psychiatric social worker—are but a part of the total institutional process that is offered to the patient to be used according to his capacities.

As the psychiatric team members observe improvement, steps are taken toward modifying the treatment program. There may be presentation of the patient's progress at a staff meeting. It may be agreed that other forms of care should be explored—whether return to own family or foster care family. The social service department will be working not only with relatives around their resources and responsibilities but will be reviewing other possibilities. Here again the worker will face fears and anxieties on the part of patients and relatives; fears, this time, not about entering but about leaving the hospital.

Even when the patient leaves the hospital, there is help to be offered. It is necessary to observe how the patient is adapting to his new situation, how satisfactory the employment experience is, whether visits as an out-patient to the hospital (or to a near-by clinic) will be beneficial—in short how satisfactory, as well as satisfying, is the movement from illness to wellness. This is not to imply that all patients who enter a mental hospital will leave it, nor that all patients who leave manage to remain in the community. It does demonstrate, however, by the use of all the treatment services on behalf of the mentally ill person that fewer patients must stay in hospitals indefinitely and that more persons may be helped to return to family and community. Thus not only is the total financial cost of mental illness diminished but the creative energies of people are furthered toward constructive living. With the increased knowledge of various therapies and the more extensive use of social services in and out of the institution there should be fewer parties for patients who have been in residence in mental hospitals for fifty years! [11]

[11] See Crutcher, Hester, *Foster Home Care for Mental Patients.* New York, The Commonwealth Fund, 1944, p. 1.

Psychiatric Social Work in Psychiatric Clinics

The psychiatric clinic is a second area in which the psychiatrist and social caseworker are associated. The child guidance clinic, to be discussed in the section that follows, is a third area.

The clinics which shall be dealt with here bear such titles as: neurological clinic, neuropsychiatric clinic, mental hygiene clinic, and psychiatric clinic. Some of them are connected with general hospitals, some with mental hospitals, some with courts (criminal or juvenile), and some are community-sponsored in the sense that voluntary contributions are made to provide psychiatric services under the auspices of one social agency or on behalf of all agencies.

Regardless of the affiliation or the sponsorship the essential relationship of psychiatrist and psychiatric social worker is there. As in the case of the mental hospital, there is considerable variation in the nature of the service offered. In most clinics the intake interview is conducted by the psychiatric social worker. As with all initial contacts wherever sound casework is practiced, there exists the opportunity for engaging the client in a dynamic process. The application interview enables the troubled applicant and the social worker to explore what appears to be the difficulty, or difficulties, to examine the possible resources of the agency, and to come to a sense about the usefulness of the clinic. As treatment is undertaken, the psychiatrist carries medical and psychiatric responsibility. The psychiatric social worker keeps himself related to the reality problems of the client, concentrating upon the concrete aspects of day-by-day living, such as finances, living arrangements, family members, job, etc. Not infrequently the worker may be in contact with other members of the client's family or with resources within the community. However, as with the mental hospital, there is a complementary role of psychiatrist and psychiatric social worker, each focusing on his particular area and each coming into conference and collaboration the one with the other on behalf of the client who asks for help.

Child Guidance Clinics

Although it was not until 1922 that the first child guidance clinic was established, there had been anticipations of such development for several decades. As early as 1896 Lightner Witmer had begun a psychological clinic at the University of Pennsylvania, the primary interest of which was educational. In 1909 Dr. William Healy began his notable work with delinquents referred by the Juvenile Court of Chicago to the Juvenile Psychopathic Institute, of which he was the first director. Serving as physician-psychiatrist, he was assisted in his researches into criminal behavior by psychologists who made mental tests and by field workers who gathered information pertaining to the delinquents' background. The work of both Witmer and Healy produced overwhelming evidence of the vital importance of the relation between the child's emotional life and his maladjustments and delinquencies. This was entirely consistent with the earlier findings of American child psychologists and was being reaffirmed constantly by the contributions from the more dynamic field of psychoanalysis.

By the time World War I had ended, steps had already been taken toward the professional education of its personnel. Likewise, the war had made possible the expansion of our knowledge of mental abilities through the unprecedented opportunity to test millions of men who had been called to arms. The specialty of psychiatry had been going on apace, as well, and by 1918 had accumulated a valuable store of information not only about war neuroses and psychoses, but also about the adjustments which the human personality makes under stress. This was added to the already existing knowledge gained from psychiatrists in mental hospitals and others who had been working with children's disorders. All these developments and more besides were being incorporated into the mental hygiene movement and pointed the way, by the beginning of the third decade of the present century, to a new synthesis to be achieved by bringing these various specialties—psychiatry, psychology, social work—into a new combination.

The Commonwealth Fund

The new combination proved to be the child guidance clinic which took form in 1922 under the auspices of the National Committee for Mental Hygiene. The means by which this step was undertaken was the support given the National Committee by the Commonwealth Fund, a private foundation established in 1918. What stamped the child guidance clinic as unique was the fusing of these different specialties into a new whole with all of the attendant possibilities of developing a body of knowledge and skills in dealing with children who presented behavior or personality difficulties. It may be a matter of historical interest, in view of the changed emphases of the present-day clinics, to observe that the original purpose of the child guidance clinic was to reach the problems of juvenile delinquency by concentrating upon the child referred by the Juvenile Court. Evidence of this is reflected in the fact that it was through the Division of Delinquency that the National Committee for Mental Hygiene conducted the first demonstrations of child guidance clinics.

In accordance with the original purpose of the leaders of the movement, a five-year experimental program was adopted in November 1921 and initiated in the Spring of 1922. According to the 1922 annual report of the Commonwealth Fund the program was designed:

1. To develop the psychiatric study of difficult pre-delinquent and delinquent children in the schools and juvenile courts; and to develop sound methods of treatment based on such study.
2. To develop the work of the visiting teacher whereby the invaluable early contacts which our school systems make possible with every child may be utilized for the understanding and development of the child.
3. To provide courses of training along sound lines for those qualified and desiring to work in this field.
4. To extend by various educational efforts the knowledge and use of these methods.

A number of organizations already in existence were utilized to help carry into effect the first three of these purposes. The New York School of Social Work was placed in a position to offer additional courses for psychiatric social workers, to provide fellowships for training students in this new field, and to establish a psychiatric clinic for the study and treatment of children presenting special problems and for the field training of students. The National Committee for Mental Hygiene, through its newly formed Division on the Prevention of Delinquency, was to carry on the demonstration child guidance clinics; while the Public Education Association of New York, through its new organization known as the National Committee on Visiting Teachers, was to conduct demonstrations of visiting teacher work in different areas of the country. To attain the fourth objective the Fund set up its own agency, the Joint Committee on Methods of Preventing Delinquency, to act as a co-ordinating agency for the program as a whole and as an interpreter of the work through published articles or special studies.

Early in 1922 the first demonstration child guidance clinic was initiated in St. Louis with a staff consisting of one psychiatrist, one psychologist, and one psychiatric social worker. Children with behavior difficulties were referred by schools, institutions, private homes, and the juvenile court. Three-fourths of these were via the juvenile court, and it was soon realized that if a preventive service were to be offered, it would have to be done, in a great many instances, long before the child was brought to the juvenile court. If the purpose of the newly established clinics was to give meaning to the title of the committee on the Prevention of Delinquency, it—the clinic—was doomed to ineffectiveness because so much of the responsibility for preventing delinquency rested with other agencies than the clinic. Throughout the remainder of the demonstration period in the cities of Norfolk, Virginia, Dallas, Texas, Minneapolis and St. Paul, Los Angeles, Cleveland, and Philadelphia this fact became more and more self-evident. It was realized that the community services such as those of the school and of social agencies, particularly children's agencies, were valuable because they helped the child to achieve a constructive objective for himself and because they furnished a more natural medium for approaching the child. At the same time, it became apparent that more stress in the clinic setup would need to be placed upon social work, and accordingly the ratio of workers was changed to one psychiatrist, one psychologist, three social workers.

The Clinic in Operation

The study and treatment process in a child guidance clinic is initiated when referral is followed by application for service. In most instances the clinic prefers to have the parent come for the application interview without the child. During this interview the parents—it may be both together or either father or mother—present to the psychiatric social worker the nature of the difficulty which they are having with their child. At the same time the social worker gives the parents some idea of the clinic, the kind of service it offers, and the arrangements under which the clinic appointments are carried out. During this interview the parents are turning over in their own minds whether this is the place to bring their child for treatment, while the clinic person is also considering whether this is the kind of difficulty which is within the scope of the clinic's service. If a "meeting of the minds" results, each side agreeing this is a matter with which the clinic may help, then appointments for the child with the psychiatrist, and the parent with the psychiatric social worker, are discussed as well as the fee, which is adjusted according to the income of the applicant. If either a medical or psychological examination of the child is indicated, arrangements are made for such service either within or outside of the clinic. Since every child guidance clinic has a psychologist, the testing is usually done in the clinic, while in most cases the medical examination is either performed outside of the clinic or by a physician on the staff, but usually not by the psychiatrist who will see the child.

Once appointments have begun, the usual procedure is for the child to be seen weekly by the psychiatrist and the parent by the psychiatric social worker. Throughout the course of treatment there are frequent conferences between psychiatrist and social worker by means of which each is kept informed of the progress, or lack of progress, of the other. In those instances in which the referral has been made by another social agency or by a school it is customary to keep them apprised of developments in the treatment interviews and to bring them into a joint conference at the clinic. For the clinic it is important to know of changes taking place in the life of the parents and the child, while the social agency or school also needs to know what is happening in the clinic. The conferences with the psychologist are more likely to be held following application in order to clear the ground as to whether the child under consideration falls within the intelligence group with which the clinic can work most effectively. Experience has shown that the child of decidedly subnormal mentality cannot profit as much by clinic treatment, and it is customary not to accept such children. During treatment there may be occasion for other conferences with the psychologist in order to have an interpretation of the child's capacities as they are stacked up against his use of them in the clinic, in school, or at home. Another conference that is usually held, although not necessarily for every case, is the staff conference which brings together psychiatrists, psychologists, and psychiatric social workers. Such a meeting furnishes occasion for an exchange of point of view and an opportunity to bring out the varying differences between these specialties from which there may eventuate a new approach to the problems presented in the case. Such interprofessional group thinking is one of the valuable contributions which the child guidance clinic has been able to make in working in the field of personality and behavior.

In many instances clinics offer a diagnostic and consultative service to schools, social agencies, and parents pertaining to school problems, matters touching upon intelligence and special abilities or the lack thereof. The clinic may be able to indicate where some of the difficulties seem to lie and to suggest referrals to appropriate agencies or community facilities. The opportunity to consult with the clinic sometimes obviates the long treatment period. Clients often take help best through infrequent contacts with the clinic.

Function and Process in the Clinic. In the early days of the child guidance clinic the title was accurately descriptive of its approach. The assumption was made, quite naturally, that the parent came for advice about guiding his child's life, and that if only he were told what to do, he could then proceed to do it. At a later period the clinic concentrated upon the parent, seeing him as the focus of the problem, his own or his child's. What was simpler, then, than to remake the parent! No sooner, however, had the error of this way been perceived than there occurred a swing to the opposite extreme. The child became the object of direct treatment and the parent was relegated to a secondary role, to be considered, as the law would have it, as an accessory before the fact.

Time and experience demonstrated the limitation and ineffectiveness of all three of these approaches. Just as futile were the alternations of clinic philosophy which sought to eliminate undesirable behavior either through changing the child by means of moralizing, or with sweet reason, or by means of changing the environment. It was no wonder that many people, including the clinic workers themselves, began to question the value of the clinic. So long as the clinic undertook to wave a magic wand that superficially changed the child, just so long could parents evade facing their own problems that bore some causal relation to the behavior of the child. It was not until fuller account was taken of the role of emotional factors in the development of personality and behavior that any perceptible progress was made. Basic to all of this was the belief that there could be no change in behavior without a change in those elements that had produced the behavior.

The more recent emphasis takes into account the interrelatedness of the child and parents in their life outside of the clinic as well as during treatments in the clinic. While the clinic still retains the title of "child guidance" it realizes that its help is offered to both child and parent. Indeed, the clinic has learned by now that if the help that is offered is to have any meaning for either child or parent, it must be directed to both parties as integral parts of the clinic function. Consistent with this newer orientation, the primary function of the child guidance clinic is conceived to be the helping of a child in his emotional development so that he can realize more the capacities which he has for attaining an adequate adjustment within himself and to his environment. All this applies to the parent as well, with the added qualification that the help is directed toward his relationship with the child. Adjustment is usually a matter of definition and of standard, but the clinic continues to insist that the criterion of adjustment is the use which the individual makes of his abilities in his relations to other people and within himself. Most children are normal mentally and physically and manage to adapt themselves to the ordinary demands of life with little apparent difficulty. It is, however, in the realm of their emotional relationships with other people—parents, brothers, sisters, playmates, schoolfellows, teachers—when demands are made upon them, or they are faced with prescribed limitations, that many of their difficulties become evident. When this situation becomes serious enough to be threatening to the parent or is impeding the emotional development of the child, the clinic stands ready to help. The clinic, as a community agency, is willing to have its services used by parent and child, but it leaves the responsibility for coming to the clinic entirely to them, and also the decision as to whether this is the kind of help they need and want.

The Child, the Parent, and the Clinic. This interrelated movement of child and parent in a clinic is basic to the clinic process. Two people such as a child and a parent—mother or father—come to a clinic because something has gone askew in their relationships or because of some blocking in the growth or experience of either or both. If the clinic is to be of any service, it must take them as they are, and offer to each the help which they need and are able to use. The clinic can in no wise take away the individual's responsibility for living his own life. The capacity of the client to work on his own problem must be respected. This helping process goes on between psychiatrist and child, and between social worker and parent. Change, if it takes place at all, generally comes slowly and is related to what is happening with the other person. For example, despite the mother's initial insistence that the clinic make over her child, no real change takes place in the child until the mother herself realizes she is a part of the situation and undergoes change too. The necessity for this mutual modification of behavior responses is made all the clearer if a hypothetical situation is illustrated. Suppose the clinic by some magic could alter the child's behavior and leave the mother untouched. It is extremely doubtful whether the child's difficulties would remain cleared up for any length of time for the very important reason that his mother (family, etc.) is a part of the living world to which he reacts. It was from this situation that he was brought to the clinic, and it is this situation to which he returns; and if all the other factors remain the same, the chances are excellent that he will revert to his original use of self, since personality seldom changes in a vacuum. Much of this would be just as true if it were the mother and not the child who changed by reason of the clinic experience. Nor is this a matter of allocating blame. The clinic is concerned not so much with who is at fault as it is with helping where there is need. It recognizes that children and parents are different, that children come into the world with certain potentialities, that children build on these potentialities a personality that is considerably affected by the persons in the environment. It also realizes that parents have developed their personality patterns over a period of years and continue to do so in their adjustments to the developing personalities of their children and of the world about them. This dynamic concept of human personality affords the clinic a working premise in its services to children and parents.

At no point is it the purpose of a child guidance clinic to order the life of a parent. The clinic recognizes the uniqueness of the human personality and the differences which distinguish individuals. From such a belief there follows logically the proposition that a life plan can only be set up by the individual himself and not by an outside agency. The individual comes to the agency, in this instance the clinic, not to be turned upside down, inside out, and made over into another person, but rather for help in living with the kind of self that he is. A mother asks for help in one or two little areas, and will resist, almost to the death, any effort to remake her. She comes to the clinic of her own accord, takes what help she can use, and leaves when she feels her needs have been met. Even though she may, ostensibly, ask for advice either for herself or for a child, actually that is the last thing that she wants or needs. The clinic has long since learned that advice is entirely gratuitous unless it is related to the movement that is taking place in the client. There are at least two definite reasons for this. One is that the giving of advice seldom, if ever, rests upon a knowledge of cause. Before either a person can change or a situation be changed, it is necessary to know the causal elements that have produced the end result. To offer advice, too frequently, is merely equivalent to short circuiting cause and result. Secondly, to undertake to give advice to another person robs that other person of the right of self-determination. What the adviser is doing, in effect, is saying, "If I were you, this is what I would do." Actually, nothing could be more false. How can one person ever predict what he would do if he were someone else and in another situation? Furthermore, whose life is it?

It is necessary to dwell a moment longer on what it is that brings a parent to a child guidance clinic as well as to make clear the role of the clinic. The parent in coming with some problem with a child is giving expression to a vital impulse that arises from what seems an impassible and impossible situation with a child. This impulse, and those subsequent impulses which find expression in the treatment situation in the clinic, carry more of the fears, hopes, dreads, loves, and hates of the parent within herself and in relation to the child. In coming to the clinic she has admitted the need to take these feelings outside of her normal sphere, to take them to a neutral, understanding person. In many instances she must do this in order to be able to face them and to resolve some of her ambivalence about herself, her child, and his need for help. The worker recognizes and meets the mother's feelings and works with her in furthering her capacity to take help and eventually to leave the clinic more secure in her ability to deal with her own problems and her child's difficulties. The agency realizes that this is not done all in a day. It requires time for the parent to take on the clinic experience as a growth experience, to be able to accept help and yet not to be overcome with the fear of losing her own identity in the process, and at the same time to get a sense of her own capacity for living.

This idealized description of the child guidance clinic does not overlook its many shortcomings. The clinic, with all its specialized knowledge of human behavior and personality made possible by the combination of psychiatrist-psychologist-social worker, does not have all the answers to the riddle of personality. Nor has it developed sufficient skills to be of help in every situation with which it is faced. In the light of our present knowledge and skills there are many children and parents who present difficulties that the clinic simply does not reach. Because of the highly individualized character of the helping process there are no two clients to whom the same specific therapeutic skill can be applied. At the present time there are many people whom the clinic is unable to help. There are cases in which the clinic cannot assist because a parent or child has resolutely set itself against accepting any help from the clinic, or from anyone. In other instances the power to help is limited by the training and experience of the clinic staff. During its three decades of existence the child guidance clinic has demonstrated its usefulness, and at the same time has acknowledged its limitations. It has performed what at times seemed like miracles and at other times has failed abysmally. It has made significant contributions to the understanding of behavior and personality, yet stands today upon the threshold of a still greater knowledge that waits to be born.

The Experience of Two World Wars

While World War I did not initiate psychiatric social work, nevertheless we have noted in another section of this chapter the tremendous impetus which it furnished. Yet despite the developments in the mental hygiene field in the quarter century between wars, the nation was shocked with what Selective Service rejections showed about the mental health of our people. The record was still sorrier when we realized the volume of discharge from the armed forces for mental and personality disorders. One cannot but wonder whether all of the mental hygiene efforts in the period between these two wars had been of any avail. On the other hand, one cannot but speculate what our situation might have been without those years of psychiatric advance.

By 1941 World War II was upon us. What did psychiatry and what did psychiatric social work have to contribute to the successful prosecution of the war? Psychiatrists were used in many places, such as induction centers, general and station hospitals in this country, and in general, station, and evacuation hospitals overseas. They were placed in specialized neuropsychiatric hospitals here and abroad; in outpatient units, called mental hygiene consultation service; in basic training camps where they aided recruits in their adjustment to army life and advised the command on matters relative to morale and mental health. They were assigned to all large transports and hospital ships which carried psychiatric patients. They were stationed in disciplinary barracks and in the centers for the rehabilitation of military prisoners. Psychiatrists served in combat divisions. They were a part of the examining team in distribution centers and separation centers. They served as consultants to theaters of war, service commands, armies, and air forces.[12]

Military Psychiatric Social Work

For the first time in American military history the army psychiatric social worker was granted an occupational classification—SSN 263, Social Worker, and MOS 263, Psychiatric Social Worker. As Elizabeth Ross pointedly states it, a military psychiatric social worker "is a soldier with social work duties, assigned to a psychiatric unit, under the administrative and professional direction of a psychiatrist." [13] What was the job of this worker? Again, the answer is simple and direct: to help win the war by increasing fighting manpower. To quote Mrs. Ross again:

[12] Menninger, William C., "Psychiatric Experience in the War, 1941–1946." *American Journal of Psychiatry*, CIII, March 1947, pp. 577–586. The confirming experience of the Navy is reviewed by Braceland, F. J., "Psychiatric Lessons from World War II." *American Journal of Psychiatry*, CIII, March 1947, pp. 587–593. The Air Force experience is presented by Murray, J. M., "Accomplishments of Psychiatry in the Army Air Forces." *American Journal of Psychiatry*, CIII, March 1947, pp. 594–599. See also Menninger, William C., "Psychiatry and the War," in *Modern Attitudes in Psychiatry*. New York, Columbia University Press, 1946, pp. 90–115.

[13] Ross, Elizabeth H., "What's So Different About Army Psychiatric Social Work?" *The Family*, XXVII, April 1946, p 70.

Army administered social services are provided to help produce first-class fighting troops to vanquish the enemy. They exist to serve the army group purpose, as does army medicine and psychiatry . . . in principle, the army is deeply concerned with the growth and development of each person . . . as a soldier. It is to speed up and to maintain effective soldier development that the military has provided, more in this war than in any other, services for the individual.[14]

In concert with the psychiatrist the psychiatric social worker shared the aim of helping to restore to active service soldiers who were experiencing mental and behavior difficulties. For those individuals who could not be returned to duty the maximum benefit was to be provided before return to civilian life.[15] Generally speaking, army psychiatric social workers worked wherever army psychiatrists worked, except for special assignments of surveys, administration, and research. In the period since the end of World War II an extensive bibliography of army psychiatric social work services has appeared. This is material prepared very largely by the workers themselves as they were in the midst of their war assignments, or since as they evaluate what the experience has meant to them, to psychiatric social work, or to the profession of social work as a whole.[16]

Psychiatric social work service was available following induction and on through training, classification, reclassification, replacement, rehabilitation, discharge. This statement does not imply that it was everywhere available, and at any time, or always with adequately trained staffs. It does mean that by the time we entered World War II there was a quarter century of psychiatric social work skill that could be used to

[14] *Ibid.,* p. 64.

[15] Menninger, William C., "Psychiatric Social Work in the Army and Its Implications for Civilian Social Work." *Proceedings of the National Conference of Social Work,* 1945, p. 78.

[16] No attempt is here made to present the mass of published material on psychiatric social work in World War II. However, the reader who is interested in any or all phases of such work is referred to a number of useful bibliographies that have so far appeared. Several of the more useful references are: Field, Minna, *Bibliography of the Development and Practice of Military Psychiatric Social Work,* July 1945, made available by the Josiah Macy, Jr., Foundation, New York; Crow, Dorothy L., *Selected Bibliography on Psychiatric Social Work,* May 1945, American Association of Psychiatric Social Workers. The bibliographical references of Saul Hofstein are worth noting: Hofstein, Saul, "Differences in Military Psychiatric Case Work Practice." *Journal of Psychiatric Social Work,* XVI, Winter 1946–1947, pp. 74–83. The substance of the experience of psychiatric social work as adapted to the military setting is recorded in Maas, Henry S. (editor), *Adventure in Mental Health,* New York, Columbia University Press, 1951.

further the end for which our armies existed—i.e., to win the war. Despite the difficulties encountered in having psychiatric social work recognized as a useful specialty in the army organization there is now no doubt about its valid place alongside an infinite number of other services in contributing to the successful prosecution of the war.

As in civilian life, the psychiatric social worker focused his service around the reality situation in which the soldier (the client) found himself. In an army of over 11 million there were certain to be a number of individuals who experienced difficulties in adjusting to new and different situations. This statement applies as well to the man (or woman) who volunteered as well as the person who was called by Selective Service. Army life is not civilian life. Wives, children, parents, homes, the usual job, are not a part of it. Yet these are the things in civilian life to which he may have made a satisfying adjustment. What does the army offer in the place of these? Training for the purpose of defeating the enemy. This training is carried on in huge cantonments where as many as a hundred thousand men may live and work together for weeks and months on end. Then comes shipment overseas, fighting on beaches, in jungles, deserts, and mountains. Hunger, exhaustion, injury, and death are all part of the soldier's lot.

Is it any wonder that at any step along the way or at any moment of the day or night some human beings may need help in accommodating themselves to these demands? From the thousands or even hundreds upon hundreds of thousands who somehow find themselves in that huge mass and unit called an army, there comes no cry of distress. These, like most people in civilian life, somehow effect an adjustment and manage to achieve some satisfaction in what they are doing. It is the person who experiences great difficulty or difficulties in fitting into this kind of life who comes to the attention of the sergeant, the company commander, the station hospital, or the disciplinary barracks. These are the persons for whom help is offered by the psychiatric team.

The problems these persons bring are limitless in their variety. They may be problems of moving from civilian life where one has satisfactions of job, home, family, friends, to army life where one is lost in the multitude of human beings most of whom are also encountering confusion, bewilderment, frustration, desperation. The individual who has somehow managed to keep himself on even keel through the protective devices of civilian life may find himself completely overwhelmed by the lack of substitutive props in his early army days. He may respond by retreat into illness, or running away, or by aggression against the authority which the army represents.

Some individuals who survive the shock of induction and the early postinduction camp life may experience difficulty in the training program. They may be unable to assimilate the training the army demands or to find expression for their particular talents in the army's specialized occupational program. Despite sufficient intelligence and adequate occupational experience they just do not seem to be able to gear in with the military situation.

Others may not develop their difficulties until later in the training program, frequently as the end of training approaches and the possibility of overseas assignment takes on the aspect of certainty. Others may hold out until actually faced with combat before giving way under their fears and anxieties. Still others experience their greatest stresses when they are injured, or face prolonged hospitalization, or are about to be returned to combat duty after recovery from injury.

Other problems that beset the soldier may come quite late in his military career, indeed may climax it as he faces permanent disablement, or even discharge as a neuropsychiatric casualty. With still others the problems of return to civilian life may assume staggering proportions.

Let it be said here, and said emphatically, that the foregoing instances are descriptive of a relatively small percentage of our soldier population. All persons who move from civilian to soldier, through camp life to combat, and through to discharge, experience difficulties. It is the individual whose response to those difficulties is such as to lessen materially the fighting strength and power of the army who is being referred to. It needs to be repeated here that the driving and unopposable goal of the army is to defeat the enemy. Whatever contributes to that end is utilized. Whatever hinders is discarded, or if possible salvaged and converted to usefulness. It was to serve this latter purpose that the psychiatry and psychiatric social work services were instituted and used increasingly by the armed services.[17]

[17] The contribution of the American Red Cross to the development of psychiatric social work during World War II calls for special mention. Not only did the American Red

Having successfully contributed to the war, does psychiatric social work have a valid place in this postwar world through which we are all struggling so desperately? Yes, perhaps with nothing quite as spectacular as followed the last war, but nevertheless tremendous potential contributions in helping individuals (and even nations) to achieve a more satisfying use of their capacities for creative living. The need for these services and contributions is recognized in the widespread demand for trained psychiatric personnel. In an effort to provide the services and the workers a national program supported by tax funds has been started. The United States Public Health Service has been charged by the Congress with responsibility for furthering and developing a nation-wide mental health program. According to the terms of the National Mental Health Act its purpose

. . . is the improvement of the mental health of the people of the United States through the conducting of researches, investigations, experiments, and demonstrations relating to the cause, diagnosis, and treatment of psychiatric disorders; assisting and fostering such research activities by public and private agencies, and promoting the coordination of all such researches and activities and the useful application of their results; training personnel in matters relating to mental health; and developing and assisting States in the use of the most effective methods of prevention, diagnosis, and treatment of psychiatric disorders.[18]

The stimulation and substantial support furnished through the United States Public Health Service, according to the intent of the National Mental Health Act, has given tremendous impetus toward the encouragement, initiation, extension, and enrichment of programs throughout the country. These programs include not only the training of personnel in psychiatry, clinical psychology, psychiatric social work, and psychiatric nursing, but also research projects and the development of mental hygiene services in states and local communities.

Nor did the use of psychiatric knowledge or personnel within the military organization cease with the end of the war. The lessons learned

---

Cross make available to the military establishments hundreds of highly qualified social caseworkers, but the standards of performance required of and executed by that personnel did much to contribute to the well-being of our military men. See Young, Imogene S., "American Red Cross Psychiatric Social Work," in Maas, *op. cit.,* pp. 228–238.

[18] Public Law 487—79th Congress, Chapter 538—2nd Session. HR4512, signed by the President July 3, 1946. Page 1, Section 2.

through the use of psychiatric knowledge in the stressful situations of war were just as essential in the maintenance of a peacetime military establishment that might be called upon again to defend the liberties of the American people. Provision has been made for the training of officer personnel and for the use of officer and noncommissioned officer personnel throughout the armed services.

There are a number of specific and concrete evidences of the values placed by the Army on military psychiatric social work. With a standing peacetime army provision already has been made for the officer position classification of psychiatric social worker. A regular Army officer has been appointed as Chief of Branch, in the Neuropsychiatric Consultant's Division, Surgeon General's Office, Department of the Army. Furthermore, psychiatric social workers in the Army are included in the Medical Services Corps, and programs are under way for the training of enlisted personnel to assist the officer psychiatric social workers.[19]

The Veterans Administration program has also developed psychiatric services to an extraordinary extent. Such services are available not only in general hospitals and regional offices but are the core services provided in the neuropsychiatric hospitals distributed throughout the country. The tie-in between the Veterans Administration hospitals and adjacent medical schools through the device of a Dean's Committee helps to insure a consistently responsible quality throughout the Veterans Administration facilities.

Individual Therapy and Group Therapy

Practically all of the foregoing discussion was based upon the one to one relationship which exists between the client and the psychiatrist or the client and the psychiatric social worker. Increasingly, however, it is becoming clear that help can also be offered through a relationship involving the psychiatrist or psychiatric social worker and a group of clients or patients. This is not to be confused with the usual range of activities carried on with groups by workers in group work agencies. Rather it is a recognition that the lives of most of us are lived in groups, and that what is termed socialization of the individual takes

[19] Camp, Elwood W., "Psychiatric Social Work in the Army Today," in Maas, Henry S., *op. cit.,* pp. 202–220; also *Military Psychiatric Social Work.* Technical Manual, 8–241, Department of the Army, March 1950.

place essentially through group activity. Likewise when difficulties within any one of us become serious enough as to require outside help there is a substantial resource through group participation and the services of psychiatrically specialized personnel.

Group therapy, or group psychotherapy, is a relatively recent development, having been pioneered by S. R. Slavson of the Jewish Board of Guardians in 1934. By World War II enough had been learned out of the experience with disturbed children and parents to adapt the essentials to the military experience. It must be recognized here that in addition to the basic values inherent in group therapy the additional virtue so far as the military forces was concerned was the opportunity it provided to reach a large number of soldiers who needed and could use such a service. Group therapy was provided in practically every military hospital where psychiatric patients were treated in large numbers. It was also offered to military prisoners in various rehabilitation centers, in mental hygiene clinics operated at various camps, at clearing stations near the front, as well as in "exhaustion centers" and convalescent hospitals further to the rear of the fighting lines. Since the end of the war and with an expanded Veterans Administration program, group therapy is an integral part of the hospital—in-patient and out-patient—care offered to veterans.

In addition to its use in the military setting, there is an increasing application in state mental hospitals, child guidance clinics, prisons, and occasionally in residential treatment centers for emotionally disturbed children. It must be made clear that group therapy is not used as a substitute for or a replacement of individual therapy. Rather it is serving a useful purpose in its own right and for the values inherent in it. At the same time it becomes evident that there is an interrelationship between the two, for a number of agencies and institutions use them complementarily, i.e., persons in the group therapy sessions also have access to the psychiatrist for individual service as well. The relation of the psychiatric social worker to the psychiatrist is maintained as in all the services that were previously described in these pages with the ultimate medical and psychiatric responsibility residing on the psychiatrist.

Conclusion

Psychiatric social work as described in this chapter has dealt with the use of social casework in the clinical team of psychiatrist, clinical psychologist, and psychiatric social worker. By the very nature of its origins in relation to the fruitful developments in psychiatry, psychoanalysis, and psychology there has been a tendency to worship psychiatric social work as the alpha and omega of social casework. No competent caseworker indulges in this erroneous presumption; yet there is enough loose thinking abroad to require these few words of explanation. Social casework existed before there was a specialization known as psychiatric social work. As psychiatric social work developed, it borrowed from and added to social casework. Today wherever and under whatever auspices social casework is practiced, it utilizes the richnesses that have come from psychiatric orientations. What realistic caseworkers have come to recognize is the validity of the various emphases and settings in which social casework is practiced. They also realize that there is a helpful interchange between areas of practice. The family caseworker draws from the psychiatric caseworker and vice versa. The probation officer utilizes some of the contributions from psychiatric casework just as the psychiatric caseworker utilizes some of the contributions made by caseworkers with the convicted offender.

In addition to the foregoing, it is important to recognize that contributions from mental hygiene have reached almost every area in which human beings undertake to be of help to others. Where these services tend to get well defined and to be offered to individuals by social work agencies they are called casework services. Where, however, they remain under non-social work auspices, they nevertheless have very real value and constitute important services within our culture. Thus the pastoral and counseling services of the ministry are a case in point; or the consultative services to parents around problems of child rearing and family life; or the services with individual children in nursery schools.

These are all valuable services, but they should not be confused with the essential elements of social casework practice in conjunction with psychiatric services. Psychiatric social work, too, has its important part to play in helping people with their difficulties. It should be recognized as one of the services which people need, and accepted as such rather than having all the mystic and occult powers attributed to it.

BIBLIOGRAPHY

Books and Pamphlets

Alexander, Franz, and Ross, Helen (editors), *Dynamic Psychiatry*. Chicago, University of Chicago Press, 1952.

Allen, Frederick H., *Psychotherapy With Children*. New York, W. W. Norton & Company, 1942.

Beers, Clifford W., *A Mind That Found Itself*. New York, Longmans Green & Company, 1908.

Berkman, Tessie D., *Practice of Social Workers in Psychiatric Hospitals and Clinics*. New York, American Association of Psychiatric Social Workers, 1953.

Clifton, Eleanor, and Hollis, Florence, *Child Therapy: A Casework Symposium*. New York, Family Service Association of America, 1948.

Crutcher, Hester B., *Foster Home Care for Mental Patients*. New York, Commonwealth Fund, 1944.

Deutsch, Albert, *The Mentally Ill in America*. rev. ed., New York, Columbia University Press, 1949.

———, *The Shame of the States*. New York, Harcourt, Brace & Company, 1948.

Dollard, John, and Miller, Neal E., *Personality and Psychotherapy*. New York, McGraw-Hill Book Company, 1940.

———, Auld, Frank, Jr., and White, Alice M., *Steps in Psychotherapy*. New York, The Macmillan Company, 1953.

Education for Social Work: Proceedings of the Dartmouth Conference. New York, American Association of Psychiatric Social Workers, 1950.

English, O. Spurgeon, and Pearson, Gerald H. J., *Emotional Problems of Living*. New York, W. W. Norton & Company, 1945.

Freeman, Lucy, *Fight Against Fears: a Very Personal Account of a Woman's Psychoanalysis*. New York, King's Crown Press, 1951.

———, *Hope for the Troubled*. New York, King's Crown Press, 1953.

Gardner, George E., *Case Studies in Childhood Emotional Disabilities*. New York, American Orthopsychiatric Association, 1954.

Greenberg, Harold A., Pathman, Julian H., Sutton, Helen A., Browne, Marjorie M., *Child Psychiatry in the Community*. New York, G. P. Putnam Sons, 1950.

Hamilton, Gordon, *Psychotherapy in Child Guidance*. New York, Columbia University Press, 1947.

Horney, Karen, *Neurosis and Human Growth*. New York, W. W. Norton & Company, 1950.

Lowrey, Lawson G., *Psychiatry for Social Workers*. rev. ed., New York, Columbia University Press, 1950.

Maas, Henry P. (editor), *Adventure in Mental Health: Psychiatric Social Work With the Armed Forces in World War II*. New York, Columbia University Press, 1951.

Pearson, Gerald H. J., *Emotional Disorders of Children*. New York, W. W. Norton & Company, 1949.

Rennie, Thomas A. C., and Woodward, Luther E., *Mental Health in Modern Society*. New York, Commonwealth Fund, 1948.

————, Burling, Temple, and Woodward, Luther E., *Vocational Rehabilitation of Psychiatric Patients*. New York, Commonwealth Fund, 1950.

Slavson, S. R., *Analytic Group Psychotherapy with Children, Adolescents, and Adults*. New York, Columbia University Press, 1950.

Sullivan, Harry Stack, *The Interpersonal Theory of Personality*. New York, W. W. Norton & Company, 1954.

Witmer, Helen L., *Psychiatric Interviews with Children*. New York, Commonwealth Fund, 1946.

Significant Articles

Alt, Herschel, "The Role of the Psychiatric Social Worker in the Residential Treatment of Children." *Social Casework*, XXXII, November 1951, pp. 363–369.

Berkman, Tessie D., "The Contribution of Psychiatric Social Work to the Field of Social Work." *Journal of Psychiatric Social Work*, XXII, June 1953, pp. 200–205.

Bosserman, Eleanor V., "Trends in Casework Treatment in In-Patient Service in Hospital Settings." *Journal of Psychiatric Social Work*, XXII, January 1953, pp. 61–64.

DeWitt, Henrietta B., "Family Care as the Focus for Social Case-Work in a State Mental Hospital." *Mental Hygiene*, XXVIII, October 1944, pp. 602–631.

Hofstein, Saul, "Interrelated Process in Parent-Child Counseling." *Jewish Social Service Quarterly*, XXVI, December 1949, pp. 286–299.

Knee, Ruth, "The Open Question: Is There Anything Unique About Psychiatric Social Work." *Journal of Psychiatric Social Work*, XXIII, October 1953, pp. 42–48.

"Psychiatric Social Work in the Psychiatric Clinic." Report No. 16. Topeka, Kans., Group for the Advancement of Psychiatry, September 1950.

"The Psychiatric Social Worker in the Psychiatric Hospital." Report No. 2. Topeka, Kans., Group for the Advancement of Psychiatry, January 1948.

Rosenthal, Leslie, "Group Psychotherapy in a Child Guidance Clinic." *Social Casework,* XXXII, October 1951, pp. 337–342.

Rooney, William S., Ryan, Francis J., Cross, Grace A., "Psychiatric Casework in an Army Setting." *Social Casework,* XXXII, January 1951, pp. 31–37.

Sylvester, Lorna, "Family Relationships in Child Guidance." *Jewish Social Service Quarterly,* XXVII, December 1950, pp. 180–186.

Tennant, Marion A., "Psychiatric Social Work in a Private Mental Hospital." *Journal of Psychiatric Social Work,* XXIII, June 1954, pp. 234–241.

Wood, Velma, "Casework Practice in Mental Health Clinics." *Journal of Psychiatric Social Work,* XXII, January 1953, pp. 64–66.

Psychiatric Social Work in the Rehabilitation of State Hospital Patients

ELSE JOCKEL, D. S. W.,
Director of Psychiatric Social Work
Springfield State Hospital
Sykesville, Maryland

The objectives of the psychiatric social work program of Springfield State Hospital are social recovery of the patient and his eventual return to life in his home community. To accomplish these objectives, social services are rendered at those phases of hospitalization where social problems most frequently block the hospitalized mentally ill from moving forward constructively.

Original recognition of need for social work in total hospital service stemmed from the fact that many recovered patients had not been able to leave the institution because they had no families who would take them home. Springfield was the first of the five state hospitals in Maryland to enlist the services of a social worker who initiated a Foster Care Service for patients who were without a suitable home to which to return. These beginnings, though small, form the hub of experience out of which emerged in this hospital the concepts of today on the purpose and function of social casework in this kind of hospitalization.

The following material will illustrate today's social services in action. The case of Lillian Thomas will describe the social worker at the admission desk, helping the patient enter his hospital experience constructively. Elizabeth Rogers will picture the admission caseworker helping the relative prepare for the patient's return when he gives the social history. The case of Dorothy Williams portrays the part the social caseworker plays in initiating and sustaining the gradual process of social recovery in the patient in Pre-Parole Service, Foster Care, and Clinic Service.

Admission Service

Admission care in this institution is based on the belief that rehabilitation begins as the patient enters the hospital. Accordingly, the three major rehabilitating services—treatment, care, and social service—are represented in the admission process to give the patient the opportunity to test out from the beginning what the hospital is like. As hospitalization usually enters the patient's life at a critical time—at a point of impasse between himself and society—the social worker who has special resources with which to assist individuals in times of social crisis is the first person of the hospital staff to meet the new patient and his family. He can enlist the participation of the troubled individuals and engage them in a process, wherein they can begin to experience the hospital as a source of help.

The caseworker secures face-sheet information, encouraging, as much as possible, the patient's and his relatives' participation. The caseworker lets them feel out the institution, explains its routines, and introduces the patient to the admitting physician. It is again the caseworker who stays by the relative during the ordeal of waiting for the admission examination and who helps the patient and his family through the experience of having to part from one another.

Though the patient's admission to a Maryland state mental institution must be properly authorized through medical certification, quite often the family's plans for state care have been made in secrecy. Upon arrival at the hospital, therefore, the patient feels tricked, and the relative guilty and ashamed.

In this hospital it has become the responsibility of the social worker to face these issues frankly with patient and relative, in the belief that both can, with help, restore their relationship, and do this on a healthier and more realistic basis.

Lillian Thomas

Mrs. Lillian Thomas, a frail, blonde young woman, was lying still on her ambulance stretcher when I introduced myself as her social worker who was here to help her come into this hospital. She responded to me with only a faint signal. Mr. Thomas, on the other hand, showed obvious relief.

Stepping forward to tell me that he was the patient's husband, he responded eagerly to my request of the ambulance drivers that they assist Mrs. Thomas in coming into the admission office. He helped by wheeling the stretcher inside.

After we were settled, I noticed that the patient's wrists were still strapped to the stretcher and, turning to the patient, I asked if she did not think that we could get along without these restraints. Looking anxiously at me, but later becoming more animated, Mrs. Thomas said with satisfaction that she believed she could take off the straps herself. She actually proceeded to do so, and after this, settled herself quite comfortably on her bed.

I spoke to both about my being here to help them with some of the things which had to be done about Mrs. Thomas' coming here today. Could we begin by talking a little of this coming? Did Mrs. Thomas know, for example, what kind of a place this was?

The patient, shaking her head as if to say that she did not belong here, spoke then of this being the "coo-coo house," "an insane asylum, wasn't it"? With rising feeling, she joked that she was "not coo-coo, just a little diddle-de-dum," and then, fighting back her tears, she continued that she would not have thought that "he" would do something like this to her.

I acknowledged first that this was a mental hospital—a place where people could come when they were ill as she was—and then recognized that, no matter how much one might need this hospital, coming to it could still be a very hard thing to undertake. I added that it could be especially hard since I gathered that the two had not been together on the idea, and wondered if we should not talk about this first to see if I could help them make a new start. Turning to the commitment papers, I suggested that we begin with something which we all knew at this moment—the fact that Mr. Thomas had consulted two doctors who had felt that Mrs. Thomas should have hospital care. I wanted them to know that this kind of care was available here for Mrs. Thomas, and that I hoped that I could help them find out a little later what the hospital was like.

With some recognition and support from me, Mr. Thomas could admit that it had been too hard to tell his wife that she needed to come here. Sadly, he spoke of her fear of him, of her running away when frightened, and of his own apprehension lest something be done. The patient returned his tender glance with a shiver, and then, as if she had need to brush aside her own more positive feelings, she giggled slightly, and explained in an off-hand manner that she was just "diddle-de-dum." Yet, when she thought I was not looking, I noticed that she glanced at him in considerable warmth.

It is obvious that Mrs. Thomas had been committed without her knowledge. There remains little doubt that she found her worst fears confirmed when, strapped to a stretcher of a police ambulance, she was brought into the admission office. Her self-esteem was at the lowest ebb. As can be noted, Mrs. Thomas responded quite positively to the recognition she received. Though she must call the hospital in defiance by a slang name, she can give evidence that inwardly she feels that she is not coming to a penal institution, but to a place of help.

One notes the caseworker's use of relationship and special emphasis on encouraging patient and relative to participate from the very beginning in some activity. Through this emphasis, the couple becomes engaged:

I left them a little time for silent interplay, and then spoke of the first step in our admission procedure here. I hoped that Mrs. Thomas could help us with the personal information for our record, for I knew that there were many questions only she could really answer correctly. Did she want to try? The patient sat up on her stretcher, listened attentively and, with obvious satisfaction, gave me most of the pertinent facts about her life. As we continued with the face sheet data, I could note that it reassured her to be able to demonstrate her ability to remember details about her circumstances. I commented finally upon my observations, adding that I was glad to see her so willing to begin to help herself.

Mr. Thomas filled in the circumstances which precipitated commitment. According to him, the patient runs away from home. Recently, she was gone all day, and was found finally half frozen and frightened in one of her father's trucks. Mrs. Thomas brought out her fear of her husband, saying that she had to run away from him. He looked hurt by her comment, and sat sadly shaking his head. I tried to encourage them to speak of their feelings while they completed with me the statistical information.

When we had finished this task, I spoke of the doctor's coming, and asked the patient if I could help her in any way to get ready for this. She nodded, and asked what was to happen next. I told her that after the examination, a nurse would be coming and take her to the ward. Recognizing her apprehension, I explained about the beginning ward. The doors would be locked. There would be many other patients. She asked anxiously how long she would be in such a ward. I told her of how patients move from ward to ward with increasing freedom and more privileges, depending upon their ability to get along. I could not tell her how long she would be there, since it really did depend a great deal on her. Could she see herself begin, even if what I could say right now would not give her much relief? Tomorrow morning when I would come to see her on the ward, she could tell me how it had gone during the first night. She nodded a little tearfully, but was satisfied to leave it that way and waited for the doctor to come. We spoke together about the hospital rules and routines, the visiting days, etc. Mrs. Thomas asked about church on Sunday, expressing her fear that her husband would miss church if he came to see her. Mr. Thomas comforted her and told her that he would find a way to get to church and see her too. I referred to her question about church services for herself— a Christian Scientist.

I regretted that there were no Christian Scientist services here at the hospital. All we had on Sundays were general devotional services. I knew that this might not be enough for her. Yet, did she think she might be able to get some comfort from such services and pray in her own faith? She nodded, sobbing softly, while Mr. Thomas and I waited for her.

We were just completing this discussion when the doctor came for admission examination. After I had introduced Mr. and Mrs. Thomas, Mr. Thomas and I went to the reception room to wait for the patient. In the beginning, Mr. Thomas could think of nothing but to get away before his wife had to leave for the ward. He asked hastily for forms so that he could fill them out at home. I gave him the forms and told him that he was free to leave if he had to, yet hoped that he could stay by to see his wife to the ward. I said that I wanted to help him with the problem all of this was to him. Mr. Thomas' face quivered. Then he said that it was just too much; he has been worrying so much for such a long time. His wife has two sisters who have also had some mental trouble. He just doesn't know whether it is going to go with her the same way. I could understand how this could worry him. Perhaps he had some feeling, too, about my having brought it out in the open that he had made arrangements about Mrs. Thomas' commitment without her knowledge. At first he denied feeling, but later he was able to share that he had had uncomfortable moments in the admission office. I said that this could not help but be uncomfortable for him, yet it seemed to me that he was doing something new today. He had brought his wife to a hospital to see whether she could be helped. This hospital was here for this. Could he do just one more thing today about helping her come in? He decided to stay, and spontaneously asked if he could write to me during the week before his history appointment next week. I said that he surely could.

The patient was now ready for the ward, and Mr. Thomas and I joined the nurses who had been summoned, and all of us participated in the farewell. Mrs. Thomas got up from the stretcher, stood with her husband silently for a moment, and then walked stoutly to the ward.

Elizabeth Rogers

Mrs. Elizabeth Rogers had been brought into the hospital by her husband and 15-year-old daughter, Florence, who had watched her mother's admission to the hospital in silent agony. When father and daughter had left the admission office, Florence said tearfully, but with a warm gleam in her eyes, that she thought she would try to help with the homemaking while her mother was away. In the first ward interview the morning after admission, Mrs. Rogers had expressed great worry about the fact that her child had witnessed her coming to this hospital. In the second ward interview with Mrs. Rogers the worker had seen the patient again, and had encouraged her to leave a message to her husband about her daughter's care and about the management of the home while she was away.

The *history interview* with Mr. Rogers centered primarily in the relative's need, focused on giving the husband a part in the patient's hospital experience:

Mr. Rogers came promptly for his history appointment, and was unusually well prepared. In addition to having filled out the questionnaire (having gathered most pertinent information from several of his wife's relatives), he had prepared a long written statement on the progress of his wife's illness, and on the circumstances which precipitated her commitment. His preparedness was in sharp contrast to the apprehensive attitude with which he approached the interview. Yet, as soon as I reminded him of my having said last week that I would be ready to help *him* today, he was able to tell me of how pressed he had felt, and of the feeling he had about having to bring his wife to this hospital.

He commented on how different this was from "the old days," when they took people to a place like this, and thought that they were putting them away. Somehow, it did not seem to be like this, though he had to confess that it was not easy.

After giving recognition of the fine job he had done on the history, I agreed with him that today we looked to the state hospital for treatment. I added that this meant a new kind of hope, but also new problems for families. Could he tell me whether he had found it hard to carry out the things we were asking of him as the husband of a patient here? He denied any problem, saying that nothing could be quite as hard as the trying times during the onset of Mrs. Rogers' illness. He spoke of her several desertions, of how he had kept up the home, and of the strain in keeping up both caring for family and home and keeping a job.

Finally, after speaking of his own burdens, he asked in poorly disguised discomfort how she was and whether she was worried about anything at home. I told him of my visit to Mrs. Rogers this morning, commenting that she had spoken to me twice of her general worry about home, about her concern over Florence and about finances. I mentioned that she was out of bed and was occupying herself a little in the ward kitchen.

I suggested that before he left, he might wish to speak further with his wife's physician about this. I could talk with him of what he might want to do. I gave warm recognition to his work on the history, saying such work was the kind of thing which could help now, and asked if he had found anything of value to himself in bringing all of this material together for our interview today. While he seemed proud of his work on the history, he continued to look pressed. In an effort to engage him, I mentioned how much people in the hospital waited for mail, wondering whether he could bring himself to write to his wife. He looked a little guilty, but then, feeling my understanding, he could admit that it was hard to do more for Mrs. Rogers when he could barely forgive her for causing him so much trouble. He could say then that it was good to talk with me about this. There was another side to all these things. For example, there was the trouble about finances. She was always worrying about finances because she resented it that he was supporting his own aged mother. Rather defiantly he added that he feels right about giving to his mother, since he makes a good enough salary to support his family. His wife knew before they were married that he would look out for his mother. He resented the question about the hospital bill. He had been informed by the county that he will have to pay $50 per month for her. Why she bothered about a thing like this at such a time, he could not see.

I acknowledged his anger, not only toward the patient, but also toward me, for talking about these private matters. Would he rather not go into this with me? While he denied this, he said again that hospitalization was very different from "the old days." I agreed, adding that this change in the way he thought of hospitalization did mean change also for everyone who became involved with us. It was precisely because of this, that I was available to him today instead of simply letting him give the history information. I thought that the very idea of his wife's coming home again some day, could be a problem, and I believed that he might doubt her readiness to do this.

Mr. Rogers was then able to tell me that he was concerned about what all of this was doing to Florence, who was not growing up in anything like a normal home atmosphere. He wanted me to know that the child was fine. She cooks his meals, makes the beds, and has returned to school. When I encouraged him to tell me more of how they were managing, he said that though he was glad the youngster was finding her place in the household chores, he was not sure that it was right for her to carry so much. We talked of his questions, his fears that Florence might be asked by her friends where her mother was. With further help from me, he was able to share his apprehension. Looking helplessly at me, he inquired whether I thought it had been wrong for him to bring Florence along for her mother's admission. We talked together of the fact that there didn't seem to be any real "right" or "wrong" in such a matter. It seemed to me, however, that Florence would have needed to be here last week—hard as it was—and did he think Florence needed to have a share in helping her mother get care?

I said that for him and for Florence, last week they had to bring a wife and mother to a state mental hospital. This was a serious thing for both. Mr. Rogers nodded, and then, with his face quivering, he got up and said that he had better leave before he started to bawl. When he moved slowly to the door I said that there are things that are worth crying about. Mr. Rogers sat down again, and I waited until he was ready to speak. He dried his eyes a little, but not bothering to wipe the tears from his face, he spoke of his love for his child, his conflicting feelings toward his wife, and his anxiety about what was to become of them all. In this was mingled his fear that if he broke down, there would be nobody to hold things together. I asked gently if for fear that it might break up, he might hesitate to undertake something new. Sometimes people needed a bit of help in the community for problems such as his. We worked on this a little, particularly after I had told him that admission service was a brief service, available only until the patient was in the hospital. To his anxious questions I said that she would have the doctors, the whole hospital in fact, at her disposal. Later, after she begins to think of moving on she can have a social worker again, if there are problems which stand in her way. I added that I could see him once more though, since it seemed to me that there was something still unfinished for him.

Mr. Rogers came for a second interview about three weeks after the history interview. At this time his attitude and behavior displayed how much he had used his previous experience with the social worker. His hostility toward the patient had greatly diminished. Instead, he had followed her gradual improvement, step by step, and at each visit twice a week, had taken on the hospital more as a place which would help her return to him and to their daughter—not one which would shut her away and relieve him of the responsibility of looking out for her general welfare.

Mrs. Rogers had responded well to treatment and the protective hospital environment and, in the opinion of her doctor, was ready for a trial visit in the community. However, the doctor, aware through the history of the complex social situation, recommended that Mr. Rogers give further thought to resolving the problem of getting the home ready for a convalescent. It was out of the doctor's concern for his patient, therefore, that Mr. Rogers found his way back to the social worker.

After reporting proudly on his wife's progress and, a little more shyly, on the progress he had made toward a new beginning with his wife and their child, he could affirm his belief that as long as it had become necessary for Mrs. Rogers to be hospitalized, not only she but he too, needed help in making a change, if things were not to end in another breakdown in their relationship. He asked for suggestions of community resources that could give the family additional support during the first difficult months of readjustment.

Mr. Rogers was helped in making a connection with the hospital's Out-Patient Clinic and, with the worker's assistance, the couple found their way to the clinic social worker who arranged for follow-up psychiatric services, and directed them to a family counseling agency for service until the patient could be discharged from the hospital.

Pre-parole Service

When the mental patient begins to rouse from his self-absorption in the hospital and starts to look toward his future, he is faced with a new crisis. Behind him lies the experience of failure in his home community which terminated in his commitment and admission to the mental hospital. Also behind him lies the slow, hard process of finding in hospital living a means for regaining social adequacy. As he considers whereto these changes will lead him, he realizes that going means that he must face the world where he has failed before, and that he must live down stigma and prejudice and people's memories of his previous unacceptable behavior. To help him with this problem, he may be referred by his doctor to the Social Service Department for Pre-Parole Service. This casework service is available to all patients, but it is most frequently used by those who must face the problems of leaving the hospital without the help of their families.

Through this service the patient is assisted in tackling the social problems arising out of his illness and are in his way of readjustment to community living. He is asked to demonstrate his readiness for outside living, while still in the hospital, by activities which show promise of his increasing self-responsibility. He is helped to find ways to participate in the occupational, recreational, and industrial therapies in the hospital and to explore the services open to him in the community.

Dorothy Williams

Mrs. Williams, a widow in her early seventies, was too bewildered and depressed at the time of her admission, two years ago, to make more than little use of her admission social worker. Accordingly, the many social problems in her family situation had remained unsettled until she started thinking about her future. At the time of her admission, she was diagnosed as suffering from involutional melancholia. While resting in the hospital, she had let her worries fade away. But as soon as she felt better, her unresolved problems became alive again. The patient had been committed to the hospital following an attempted suicide. For most of her life she had been able to manage without psychiatric care, despite her melancholy disposition. However, when the marriage of her 50-year-old bachelor son precipitated a sudden change in family setup, Mrs. Williams began to feel unwanted and in the way, and eventually decided to end her life.

The patient was offered Pre-Parole help following referral by her physician. This meant an opportunity to explore and discover her ability to return to the community without the aid of her family. Gradually, she found satisfaction in the chance to plan for herself. She learned to assume increasing responsibility for the choices and decisions she needed to make along the way.

Mrs. Williams used Pre-Parole Service as preparation for Foster Care. Eventually, because of this experience, her son accepted parole responsibility for her, providing a separate home for her in the community. The patient could be discharged from the hospital at the end of the parole year, approximately three months after the son accepted parole.

Beginnings in the hospital were slow. The patient could not bear that her son would not have her in his home, and had to deny her need for any outside help with her problems, although her cautious inquiries about Social Service bore witness to the apprehension and conflict underneath her stoic appearance. The pre-parole record opens as follows:

I found Mrs. Williams sitting rather forlorn among other patients in a closed ward, when I came to tell her of her doctor's referral to us. When her nurse introduced me to her, the patient's expression seemed to say "This is it."

I remained within the purpose of this first interview, offering her merely an appointment to talk with me since it was my understanding that it was necessary for her to make new plans for her future. With Victorian courtesy, she thanked me, declining my offer, since she was sure that her son would be taking her home. Nevertheless, she accepted the earlier of the two appointment dates I had suggested, and agreed to come to my office for this.

Though Mrs. Williams pronounced stoutly that she had no idea why I had come to see her on the ward the other day, she arrived promptly for this first planned appointment, assisted by her nurse, who awaited to take her back after the interview. Throughout the interview, she revealed that she was well aware of her unsettled circumstances. She kept on inquiring about social services, particularly Foster Care, arguing about requirements which I had not even mentioned. At the same time, she stated flatly that there was no need for any change. As previously, she clung to the assertion that she would go to her son, referring to the fifty years during which she and her son had lived closely together. Still, she allowed questions to come into this unrealistic surety. For example, while she did not admit to the existence of her daughter-in-law, she spoke of her son's mentioning a housekeeper, reminiscing that she used to take care of her son and their home. She even risked the unfinished sentence, "If I am not wanted . . . ," having to deny the thought in the same breath. I allowed her maximum freedom of expression, before giving the interview much direction. By acknowledging how uncertain she really appeared to me, I was finally able to engage her in the problem of how I could help her gain more clarity about the situation. It seemed to me that before the patient could accept that she had to make some decisions about her life, she needed to be clear about her standing with her family. We terminated the interview with the understanding that she and I would both write to her son, and we would see next week where we would be.

Mrs. Williams was a little further along in admitting her need for help in planning. She asked some more questions about Foster Care, hinted that she might not be wanted in her son's home, and asked for assurance that we would stand by her. However, her expressions of need were still too vague for me to discuss with her the choices open to patients who want to leave the hospital.[1]

After some more stalling, Mrs. Williams took me up on my question of what she was doing here to prepare herself for leaving the hospital. I had to

[1] Practically speaking, patients have a number of choices for leaving the hospital. While they are committed to the institution through medical certification, they retain their legal right for recourse through habeaus corpus proceedings. They may be paroled to their families, or be discharged. They may apply for Foster Care, or may even decide to leave the hospital without permission. (In this latter event, the hospital retains custodial responsibility and a search is made.) A final choice is for the patient to remain in the hospital.

let her know that I had begun to wonder about this, since in the final analysis, it would be she who would be doing the leaving from here, whether she would go to live with her son, or would make some other living plan. I could not quite see how she could tell me that she would take care of a home, shop and manage, when here a nurse still had to bring her to my office each time, and when she still needed the protection of a closed ward.[2]

In the following interview, we find the turning point in process:

Today Mrs. Williams appeared quite changed when she came for her appointment. She had hardly seated herself when she told me that she had obtained ground parole during the week. (Ground parole is the privilege of moving on hospital grounds unaided by hospital personnel.) She hastened to add, almost as if it was too much to concede any credit to me, that she had asked for ground parole for her *friend's* sake. This friend had been granted ground parole and would be alone without her. She went on to say that she asked the nurses how she could help with ward work, and described with quite a bit of satisfaction her job of wiping dishes and of dusting furniture.

I showed my appreciation of all she had been doing during the week, acknowledging the change that I had noted in her. The feeling of achievement seemed to give her new courage to venture forward. For the first time Mrs. Williams took the initiative of asking what I had heard from her son. Formerly, it was always she who told me how sure she was of him. Today, in this very asking, she seemed to be giving up some of her denial that things were not all well.

I told her of my interview with him yesterday, wondering whether the fact that he was not planning to take her home could really be news to her. She could sob, and could express her hurt, later her anger, and her feelings of abandonment. Grabbing my hand in a moment of despair, she cried out her question of whether there was any justice left. I accepted that she must feel this way, and stayed by her. Then I asked gently if it had to remain this bad. For a time she could not understand that her own child could do this to her. How different, when she was in her son's position! Not only had she taken care of her own parents, and would have never thought that it could be otherwise, but she also took care of her parents-in-law, when they were helpless! She wrestled with the pain she had suffered while she had been in the hospital, and which she had until now denied to me. Her son used

[2] Until it is known how well a patient can get along without hurting himself or others, he lives on a closed ward where he has maximum protection. It is an established practice of this institution to move patients from the closed reception ward to semi-open living quarters and open wards as soon as they show signs of being able to maintain themselves socially, and are able to perform their share of the housekeeping responsibilities of the institution maintenance.

to give her two dollars on each visit. Then he gave her one. And on his last visit he did not give her anything. Forty-five cents was all she had left.

After a brief pause, her sobs were no longer desperate. Weeping quietly, she said that this was the hardest thing she ever had to do, harder than childbirth. Then she straightened, as if she had discovered something, and said that she will not wait for her son's indecision, "Don't you think I may go ahead and plan with you?" Indeed she could. Restating that this was precisely what I was here for, I gave recognition to her courage to try to plan for herself.

With surprising resourcefulness, Mrs. Williams went into action. She questioned me in detail about how she can qualify for Foster Care, and what such service would be like. She wanted to set a date for the staff meeting where she could formally apply for Foster Care.

We talked about her preparation for this Staff, and this gave me the opportunity to let her experience that not everything could or needed to be done today. We set a time, and recognized that this would leave us two more interviews before Staff. It seemed to relieve her to know that there were some things to do, but that there would also be time to do them.

The patient began to move out of the hospital psychologically: by a new kind of separation from her past life, and by taking on the family and the hospital in a new way. This was very evident in an interview some weeks hence after she had established a working relationship with her children.

The patient came dressed in her best clothes, saying that she was "quite ready to leave the hospital." She spoke of the long wait from one interview to the other. As if she wanted to make quite sure that I would not misunderstand, she told me of the changes in her son's apartment, and of the fact that it would no longer be *her* home anyway, even if she were to go to her son's.

She seemed to have taken back her family in a new way. She spoke with warmth of the things they were doing for her now. While formerly, they just visited, and anything was good enough for her, now they had taken her out for a ride and to dinner. Her daughter had offered to take her on a shopping trip to select new clothes. Formerly, this same daughter had sent her whatever she had chosen to buy.

We rejoiced together over the new, satisfying relationship to her children, and then she had to tell me more of the fun she was getting out of doing new things here. She had gone to the hospital Post Office for her own stamps. She had changed money in the Office.

Her fitness for new steps reminded me that she would not be needing me much longer, and of the fact that after our next interview was Social

Planning Staff. Sensing her apprehension, I suggested that I show her the staff room. She found out where she would sit, and was comforted to know that her own doctor and I would be there.

The patient came to Social Planning Staff on the following week, and her application for Foster Care was accepted without question. Social Planning Staff determines the responsibility the hospital can take for the patient in the community. It is presided over by the Clinical Director. Present are all administrative psychiatrists and the whole Social Service Department, psychologists, and recreational therapists. The patient's physician and his social worker present their recommendations for placement to this Staff, but in reality, it is the patient who, in presenting himself, demonstrates his own readiness for leaving.

In the final interview with the pre-parole worker prior to the Staff meeting the patient could bear to separate from the hospital and from her worker:

The patient told me, upon entering my office, that her friends had already left the hospital, so that she is truly in a hurry to go. She will take the first home suggested, if necessary. She would even go under a tent—just to go.

There was a farewell atmosphere about Mrs. Williams. She seemed to want to say good-bye, even to me. She was wearing her best dress again, and told me that she remembered that I had said I liked it. My response to her warmth encouraged her to tell me of a disappointment she had had during the week. Her son and daughter-in-law had not visited last Sunday. They had sent her some cup cakes, though, because her son remembered that she liked them. There was also something good about their not having come. Her daughter-in-law wrote to her, and asked her if she could call her "Mamma." Mrs. Williams was touched and "honored."

As we went over the final arrangements for Staff, Mrs. Williams prepared to end her brief association with me. She spoke of my having been her "foundation," and asked if it would "be in line to thank in Staff for the courtesy," and if it was all right with me to tell the Staff about me, and of how much I had helped her. I assured her that the Staff would appreciate what she had to say. I gave warm recognition to all *she* had done, and we reminisced for a moment about the long way she had come.

When I asked her if she would not miss us here, she could say that she would. She would miss the nurses, and of course, she would miss me. Yet, she wanted to leave, just the same. She inquired about my first name and address, so that she could write to me.

For Mrs. Williams, the Staff meeting was an important experience:

. . . With old-fashioned politeness, Mrs. Williams seated herself next to Dr. B., and spoke quite freely and simply of her desire to leave the hospital. She could admit that she had been quite ill when she came, and that she had needed the five months of hospitalization to get on her feet. At first it had seemed that there was nothing more to live for, but then she found that she would like to try again. She did not make any special requests for the kind of home she wanted. Instead, she expressed her confidence in the hospital staff for helping her find a family with whom she could live. She already knew that she would have a new social worker after this meeting, and so took the occasion to tell the staff of the help she had received from me.

I helped her to the door, and assured her that I would stop in to see her later to tell her of the staff's decision and of her new worker.

Foster Care

Foster care is a psychiatric casework program which offers patients, who no longer need the protected environment of the hospital, the opportunity to live out their social recovery in the home of a family in the community.

Following Social Planning Staff, patients begin to explore the resources in the community. During this early exploratory period—the pre-placement period—the social worker takes the patient on trips to look for a home and, if employable, a job. When a home has been selected which meets the patient's choice within the permitted regulations and final evaluation by the patient's physician, the patient moves into "Foster Care."

Following her acceptance at Social Planning Staff, Mrs. Williams came into Pre-Placement:

I found Mrs. Williams eager to begin with me, and anxious to leave the hospital. Though my talking with her about moving into a home of a family to whom she was not related brought to her mind again that her son was not willing to take her into his home, she remained determined for a try in the community. The fact that, according to regulations, she could not leave for two weeks following Staff disappointed her at first, but did not discourage her. She even took in her stride the possibility that she might have to share a room with someone until a more permanent arrangement could be made.

Prior to my next appointment with Mrs. Williams I had a discussion about finances with her son. In view of the fact that the family is financially able to support Mrs. Williams, I had to take up with Mr. Williams that we looked to him for support of his mother. He verified his willingness to accept responsibility for her board, clothing, and medical expenses.

．　．　．

Mrs. Williams came a few minutes early for her appointment. She was ready for the trip to see Mrs. Farmer, who had recently completed her care-holder application and expected our visit today. Mrs. Williams and Mrs. Farmer were quite interested in trying out a boarding arrangement. Both were aware of the fact that this was their first try and the patient's first attempt to live again in the community, and they seemed prepared for the possibility that it might not work out right away.

On our way to Mrs. Farmer, Mrs. Williams and I had discussed the advantages and disadvantages of the Farmer home. I had recognized that nothing could be like her old home, and also pointed out that the Farmers lived a good distance from her son, which would make visiting a little difficult. Mrs. Williams had surprised me with her response: "That doesn't make any difference. After all, I am the one who will live there, and if I like it, that's the important thing. My son and his wife have their life to live, and so do I."

As we returned to the hospital "to sleep over the new venture," Mrs. Williams said: "Mrs. B., I am so happy I could cry"—and she did.

Ten days later, I helped Mrs. Williams move into Foster Care placement in Mrs. Farmer's home. Before final arrangements were made, we talked through the plans with her physician, Dr. G., who approved of placement. Mr. and Mrs. Farmer are nice people, though perhaps a little too much "for their own family" to be able to absorb a stranger. Mr. Farmer, especially, seemed hesitant about the idea. He was, however, willing to try.

Though this placement will be a rather severe test for the patient, in view of Mr. Farmer's doubts, it does have the makings of a good first experience for Mrs. Williams. The patient had a real part in selecting this home, and is deriving satisfaction from this. She does not allow her doubts to come out into the open. Mr. Farmer's hesitance should provide a realistic balance for this and give the patient the opportunity to test her desire to remain outside, even against odds.

The home, though carefully selected and supervised, is not to adjust to the patient. It is to be a real home of an average family, who have a need for another person in their midst in order to give the patient the experience of being needed and useful.

Throughout the parole year in Foster Care the social worker gives supervision and casework help to the patient as he faces problems that inevitably come with meeting the requirements of community living, and assists the person with whom the patient is living—the careholder—in meeting the problems created by the patient's living in her home. The worker keeps in very close relationship with the patient's doctor at the hospital, and also with community agencies available to the patient for his rehabilitation. To the extent to which the patient uses these facilities he is preparing himself for discharge from the hospital by showing that he can manage for himself.

The goal is for the patient to achieve discharge from the hospital at the end of his parole year. In order to do this he needs to find himself anew in the community in a way that is satisfying to himself and to the community. This usually means a new sense of self-dependence and, if there is a family, some measure of reconciliation with them. Adjustment is expected to be gradual:

Mrs. Williams' first month of placement went well. Careholder and patient seemed happy together. Mr. Williams visited his mother regularly, took her on shopping trips, and invited her to his home for weekends.

However, in time Mrs. Williams became rather lonely in the Farmer home. While Mrs. Farmer was cordial, her husband continued to have a problem about a stranger in their family circle. When Mrs. Farmer shared her concerns with me, mentioning also her fear of hurting Mrs. Williams' feelings, I helped her to see that Mrs. Williams needed to know about this and encouraged her to talk it over frankly.

Mrs. Williams was deeply discouraged at first when she learned that the Farmers did not want her to remain in their home. In her despair she prevailed upon her son to take her back, and he, in turn, asked for my support in sustaining his decision not to take her until she had found that she could make her own way.

The patient needed a great deal of help during this period. When she brought to me her feeling of not being wanted anywhere, I asked her if she felt that it was too much to try again. At first, she could not see any way out of her situation, and seemed to think of herself as totally abandoned. I encouraged her, asking her why she had to feel such total failure, when only a few weeks ago we had recognized that she might need to try out several situations before she could get settled.

Though struggling with the idea about assuming responsibility for his mother again, the patient's son became more and more interested in having the hospital step out of his family's life. He showed the foster care worker in several interviews held at his request that he had found in himself an increasing new willingness for including his mother. Though he did not think it wise to have her live in his own home, he did want to provide a home and care for her. In time, he could present a very responsible plan for her care in a protected boarding situation and, by demonstrating his willingness to use the Clinic, he gained for his mother a transfer from foster care to supervised parole.

Following my last interview with Robert Williams, I conferred with the patient's physician about the possible transfer of the case from Foster Care to parole to the family, and then arranged to see Mrs. Williams and her son to discuss the meaning of this transfer, and also tell them of the kind of service still available to them through us. I spoke to them about our Out-Patient Clinic and, though I do not believe that they will need intensive help from the Clinic, I feel that both of them were much relieved to find that they would not be totally without help from the hospital as yet.

In their presence, I called the Clinic worker. Mr. Williams signed the parole forms for his mother and the patient expressed her happy feeling over this. She reviewed with me her experience in Foster Care, thanking me briefly but warmly for the assistance.

Clinic Service

Springfield Hospital's Out-Patient Clinic offers psychiatric and social services to patients on leave from the hospital and to their families. While a part of total hospital service, the Clinic is more of a community resource for rehabilitation, than a follow-up service. Its focus is on helping former patients in their community readjustment to prevent social breakdown and return to the hospital. The social worker provides casework service designed to assist patients in re-establishing fresh connections in the community and to sever gradually their dependency upon the hospital.

Usually, as patients are paroled to their families, the Clinic social worker writes to the patient, welcoming him into the community and, recognizing that the new beginning is hard, offers help to him and to his people from the Clinic. If assistance from health or social agencies is needed, the resources of the community are called upon, in the belief that only as his community can go out to the patient, can he really begin to take root in his home again.

The problems which patients who have left the hospital, and their relatives, most frequently bring to the Clinic are centered in two areas —the parole and discharge areas.

While the patient is in the hospital, the family relinquishes a great deal of the responsibility for his welfare to the institution. As soon as parole is granted, the family is expected to assume a greater portion of responsibility again, and frequently, both patient and family feel apprehensive about this because of the social implications of psychiatric hospitalization.

When the discharge date approaches, problems often become again accentuated. Though there are many compensations for the patient in discharge, there is also, inevitably, fear about getting along without the familiar protection.

The Clinic service to Mrs. Williams and her son was very brief, serving mainly the purpose of a stable structure in terms of which they could end their experience with the institution. Both came in response to the regular discharge letter sent to them about a month prior to the patient's discharge. The worker recognized in this letter that they might be feeling apprehensive at this time of change, and offered to see them again in order to bring their case to a conclusion. The Clinic social worker made the following entry on this interview into the patient's record:

Mrs. Williams came to Clinic today, together with her son, in accordance with their appointment. They were to see Dr. S. about the patient's discharge which is to become effective next month. I recognized that before they would take official action on the discharge, they might wish to talk with me briefly about their readiness for this step, and I encouraged them to review with me their experience with this hospital.

In the beginning, both spoke only of the immediate past—Mrs. Williams' foster care experience and her son's wavering back and forth between wanting to care for his mother and being relieved of this responsibility. At one time Mr. Williams said that he might as well have had all the responsibility, for he always did pay for his mother's board in the careholder's home, and saw to it that she had diversions and proper incidentals. Yet, when I accepted his feelings that we had always expected a good deal of him, he affirmed his belief that he would not have had it otherwise. Slowly, they went back further and further into the past, until they reached the time when it had become necessary to have Mrs. Williams committed. Mrs. Williams said that she knew now how difficult she had been to live with. At the time she had thought that it was the "outsider," her new daughter-in-law, who was making all the trouble. Now she knows that it was she who was afraid, and in her fear she could not tolerate anyone who would enter her son's life. When they took her to the hospital, she thought her end of the road had come. When I inquired whether she had found it really this way, she smiled and said that, in a way, it was like starting all over again. At first, this seemed impossible, but as time went on, she found that it was like a new chance to do something over and better.

I commented on how well she looked today. Proudly she spoke of how she is taking care of herself, and how son and daughter-in-law let her help them in the household, when she visits them on weekends. Mr. Williams added to this that letting his mother help them was not entirely an unselfish thing. They needed mother's interest in homemaking when it came time on weekends to put loose ends together again. Both he and his wife are working during the week, and must rush through the things which make for a comfortable home. Both mother and son beamed as they told me of how they were learning to find where mother's place left off and the younger woman's place began.

I wondered then about the rest of the week when, as I understood them to say, they were not living together. Both told me that the patient was looking up her old friends, becoming acquainted with them all over again. One can surely know who is one's friend when one has been in a mental hospital! I remarked about the courage it took to see people who knew that she had been in our hospital. With a bit of sadness in her voice, Mrs. Williams said that not all of her old friends were still on her list. Yet, she feels that they did not abandon her. When she found them fearful or suspicious, she decided that they just did not know about such things. Perhaps, they couldn't believe, as "we" do at the hospital, that one can get well again and be different from before. Mrs. Williams finds that she has more than enough to do with those who come to see her. Two ladies suggested the other day that they investigate one of the Golden Age Clubs in the city. She does not know whether she will have time, but maybe she will at least go around to see once.

I said that I could hardly keep step with her—she was leaving us so fast. With this remark, both chimed in together to tell me that, after all, the hospital was getting ready to discharge Mrs. Williams. I agreed that this was right. Did it feel as if we were "putting her out"? Their response was a wavering between need for freedom and need for dependency. I guessed that discharge would always have a little feeling of "closed doors" mixed in with the pleasure. I didn't expect them to be altogether sure about this new thing just yet. Was it worth a try? After all, the hospital was staying right here, ready to help again, if the need arose.

Mr. Williams rose and, while putting one hand on his mother's shoulder, shook hands with me. The patient followed his example and asked for directions to the doctor's office. I accompanied them to Dr. S's door. About thirty minutes later I saw them leave the building, engaged in conversation.

The patient's record was returned to the file as "discharged."

chapter 10

Medical Social Work

Formal Beginnings in 1905

In the foregoing chapters the development of social casework has been presented together with applications to specific kinds of needs and within specific agency settings. Thus social casework is seen as the basic skill and method of the caseworker while the differentiated application according to needs and settings marks the child welfare worker, the psychiatric social worker, the public assistance worker, etc. Now we come to the use of social casework in relation to other needs and, correspondingly, in another setting. The needs are illness and medical care, the setting the medical institution with its wards, laboratories, and clinics.

In her informative volume *Social Work in Hospitals* Miss Ida M. Cannon traces in considerable detail the forerunners of medical social work: (1) services provided for the after-care of the insane in Germany, France, England, and America; (2) services furnished by lady almoners in London hospitals; (3) nursing, especially visiting nursing service begun by Lillian Wald and Mary Brewster in New York City; (4) and the field work training of medical students at Johns Hopkins Medical School and Hospital.[1]

These developments furnish the background for the more formal beginnings in 1905 when two Boston medical institutions introduced social workers on two successive days in October 1905. From one point of view this may have seemed mere "happenstance." From another point of view, i.e., analysis of the cultural antecedents, there was a

[1] Cannon, Ida M., *Social Work in Hospitals*. New York, Russell Sage Foundation, 1923.

kind of inevitability that medical social work would develop at about this time. This does not rule out the importance of the men and women who shared in these beginnings, but it does give some much needed corrective to the too commonly held opinion that a particular individual is solely responsible for a new development. Miss Mabel Barkley at the Berkeley Infirmary and Miss Garnet Pelton at the Massachusetts General Hospital in October 1905 were instrumentalities through whom medical social work came into being. According to a former member of the Board of Managers of the Berkeley Infirmary, the idea of establishing the Infirmary and the social work accompanying it were the outcome of Dr. Samuel Breck's experience in his office practice and his contacts with women and children in the Floating Hospital, of which he was one of the founders. He felt the need for wider follow-up work. Dr. Richard C. Cabot wanted to know more about the patient in order to help him use to the full all available medical care. It was he, a member of the staff of the Massachusetts General Hospital and associated for years with the work of the Boston Children's Aid Society, who envisioned the need to bring to the hospital an additional service from another field to enable the sick person to utilize more effectively what the physician and the hospital had to offer. What Dr. Cabot effected was not a numerical adding together of after-care, visiting nursing, hospital admittance, and the supplemental training of medical students. This is not medical social work any more than the numerical addition of wheel, internal combustion engine, differential gears, and brake is the automobile. The automobile is a product in which the wheel, the engine, the gear, the brake and other parts are integrated into a new creation which is something more than the sum of its parts. Likewise with medical social work. It was a combination of after-care, nursing, admission, training medical students, and social casework integrated into a new service for the sick person.

So much for relating medical social work to its cultural setting. It will be well at this point to recall Dr. Cabot's experience. A 10-month-old baby suffering with stomach trouble was brought to the Massachusetts General Hospital. Five weeks of care restored the child to its mother, without any instructions as to diet or care. Within a few weeks the baby was back in the hospital as sick as ever. Again, thirty dollars' worth of care was expended on the baby and again it was turned over to its mother "cured" and without instructions. Once more the trouble occurred and to Dr. Cabot the performance promised to approximate perpetual motion: "Baby goes out, baby gets sick, baby comes back, baby goes out and so on forever." Dr. Cabot's answer to this was to place on the staff of the hospital a social worker to study the conditions under which patients lived and to assist the patient to carry out the treatment recommended by the medical staff. From such early steps medical social work expanded, slowly at first and then with increasing acceleration, until at the present time there are probably few, if any, first-rate hospitals that do not have a medical social service department.[2]

The Institutional Setting of Medical Social Work

Several significant developments have occurred during the present century with respect to medical care for the American people. One of these is the greatly increased availability and use of hospital care. This is reflected in the statistics published annually in the *Journal of the American Medical Association*. The report of May 15, 1954, showed 4,359 hospitals in 1909 with a bed capacity of 421,065 beds, and in 1953 a total of 6,840 hospitals with 1,573,014 beds. As this is compared with population change over the same period of time, it becomes clear to what extent hospital care has developed. The population increased from 90,000,000 in 1909 to 161,000,000 in 1953—an increase of 78 percent; hospital beds over the same period increased from 421,065 to 1,573,014— an increase of 273 percent.[3]

Likewise within the present century the hospital that is being increasingly patronized is also becoming increasingly compartmentalized.

---

[2] In previous editions of this work the writer drew heavily upon Ida M. Cannon's invaluable record *Social Work in Hospitals*. The debt to Miss Cannon is increased further by virtue of the usefulness of her later (1952) book *On the Social Frontier of Medicine*. The latter work traces in revealing detail not only the early struggles to have medical social work introduced into hospitals, but also the sure growth of this service as an essential part in the total operation of the modern hospital. The thoughtful, daring, and pioneering work of Dr. Richard C. Cabot is frankly appraised and appreciated. In his foreword to Miss Cannon's volume Dr. James Howard Means refers to Dr. Cabot as the man who "had the genius to introduce social workers to the Massachusetts General Hospital for the purpose of improving the over-all medical care of patients. Social work already existed at that time, but not in hospitals. It was in its extension to medical care that Dr. Cabot's great contribution lay."

[3] Arestad, F. H., and McGovern, Mary A., "Hospital Service in the United States." *Journal of the American Medical Association,* CLV, May 15, 1954, p. 255.

Dr. G. Canby Robinson in his volume, *The Patient as a Person,* mentions the experience of Dr. Dochez

> . . . who contrasted the records of two patients with heart disease, one admitted to the hospital about twenty-five years ago and another to the same hospital in 1938. The first patient was cared for by a visiting physician, an intern, and one specialist, the pathologist-bacteriologist, and the completed record covered two and a half pages. The second patient had been observed and described by three visiting physicians, two residents, three interns, ten specialists, and fourteen technicians, a total of thirty-two individuals, and the uncompleted record of the case covered twenty-nine pages.[4]

Today there are departments of medicine, surgery, neurology, psychiatry, obstetrics, gynecology, orthopedics, cardiology, pediatrics, otolaryngology, ophthalmology, x-ray. These reflect and formalize the increasing specialization in medicine. The result has been, as frequently pointed out, that as medical science learns more and more about disease the practitioner knows less and less about the patient. In an earlier day when the sick avoided hospitals as a place where people died, the problem of knowledge concerning the person was not what might be called acute. Likewise, when the general practice of medicine was the prevailing mode, there was little question of the physician's knowledge of his patient and surroundings. He treated not a case of pneumonia or diabetes or malaria, but rather a sick person. Nothing stood between him and his patient; he required no one to interpret the patient to him nor to interpret his findings to the patient. His recommendations for treatment took in the patient as a person.

Institutionalization and specialization in medicine have changed much of this. When a hospital becomes highly departmentalized, when it adds clinic to clinic, multiplying specialist by specialist, and ends up with elaborate equipment and an endless line of patients, the point is reached where the sick person is in danger of being lost in the maze.[5]

---

[4] Robinson, G. Canby, *The Patient as a Person.* New York, Commonwealth Fund, 1939, pp. 7–8.

[5] Dr. Henry B. Richardson lightly but tellingly deplores this tendency to think of the patient as a structural defect in some vital organ by such references as "the metral stenosis in the second bed on the left," "the gastric ulcer in the fourth bed on the right." See Richardson, Henry B., *Patients Have Families.* New York, Commonwealth Fund, 1945, XIV, 209; see also, Simmons, Leo W., and Wolff, Harold G., *Social Science in Medicine.* New York, Russell Sage Foundation, 1954.

The best equipment in the world seldom proves an adequate substitute for the all-around knowledge of the patient which the physician needs. It is into this institutionalized, specialized, depersonalized mass situation that the medical social worker comes primarily to aid the patient, secondarily the physician.

The original reasons for the introduction of medical social work in 1905 still obtain to some degree. For Dr. Cabot medical social work served to assist the physician in diagnosis and treatment through study of the patient in his social situation and by interpreting the patient and his environment to the physician. In addition, the medical social worker was to assist by organizing resources in the hospital as well as in the patient's family and the community at large for making medical treatment effective. For Dr. Adolph Meyer of Johns Hopkins Hospital casework in the hospital was for the purpose of securing facts about the patient while he was in the hospital, insuring healthy conditions in the home in preparation for the patient's return, and maintaining such conditions after the patient's return home. Throughout all of this the social worker was to be in constant contact with the physician.

For Dr. Henry B. Richardson, a more recent student of the role of social and emotional factors in sickness, medical social service has as its immediate objective the relief of inner and outer pressures, whether these arise from external realities and illness or more from personal attitudes and feelings. "The ultimate objective is to enable sick people to draw on their own capacities in seeking or using medical care, in preventing illness or maintaining health." [6]

Another physician, Dr. H. M. Margolis, late in 1946 in speaking of the medical social worker as an integral member of the medical community of effort, observed:

In order to insure integrated help for the patient, the physician shares professional thinking and planning with the worker. We depend on her largely for an objective picture of the patient's social setting, his relationship with the family group, its socio-economic as well as its emotional resources. . . . We see her as having capacity for helping the patient to participate more fully and comfortably in the doctor-patient relationship and in the processes of medical diagnosis and treatment. From her must come the specialized knowledge of community resources for vocational job

[6] *Ibid.*, p. 212.

placement and for meeting the other social needs of the patient related to his illness.[7]

Most medical social workers will bear witness to the distinction in function that Drs. Richardson, Margolis, and a host of other physicians have emphasized in recent years. In the Memorial Lecture at Johns Hopkins Hospital in honor of Margaret Brogden (one of the pioneer medical social workers) Miss Cockerill recognized that the physician has primary concern and responsibility for symptomatology and treatment. To her the focus of the medical social worker was upon "the social factors which have helped to make the patient ill, the social problems which his illness creates for him, and the obstacles which may limit his capacity to make use of what medicine has to offer." In another part of her address she emphasized the point that the primary objective of the medical social worker's services is "to enhance the usefulness of medical care to the patient and to help the hospital to achieve its purpose in medical treatment."[8] Another medical social worker, Minna Field, moves one step beyond this—actually beyond the hospital—as she draws upon her experience in dealing with patients with prolonged illness. She emphasizes social service as part of total medical care and insists upon relating the ill person to his family and his community:

In this process of helping, the social worker, as part of the medical team, utilizes the same basic skills which characterize casework in general, namely, an understanding of human behavior and an ability to apply this understanding constructively to help in difficult situations. As in all casework, and particularly in dealing with those whose illness and incapacity tend to undermine their feelings of worth and status, the primary prerequisite is an appreciation of the dignity of the individual and a respect for his rights as a human being, regardless of the stage of his illness or the degree of his impairment.

. . .

Since we recognize the significance of the close emotional ties which bind members of a family group, and the importance of satisfactory family relationships for the welfare of the patient, the social worker must of necessity

[7] Margolis, H. M., "The Psychosomatic Approach to Medical Diagnosis and Treatment." Journal of Social Casework, XXVII, December 1946, pp. 298–299. For a specific instance of this "medical community of effort," see Schless, Bessie, "Achieving Maximum Adjustment in Chronic Illness." Journal of Social Casework, XXVII, December 1946, pp. 320–325.

[8] Cockerill, Eleanor, "The Use of the Psychosomatic Concept in Social Case Work." Bulletin of the Johns Hopkins Hospital, LXXX, January 1947, pp. 86–97.

be ready to render whatever help may be needed by family members. They may need assistance in meeting the problems which the patient's illness creates for them, or help to see the person behind the illness, to have regard for his intrinsic worth, to gear their demands to the limitations imposed by his illness, to utilize imaginatively his remaining potentialities, and to draw him into active participation in family living.[9]

Medical Social Work in Operation

The average lay person has a rather definite idea about hospitals. It is a place to which sick people go. The hospital's job is to get the person well. Even though the number and variety of departments may seem rather confusing at first glance, nevertheless the lay person can understand without too much difficulty what the doctors in the various departments do. Pediatrics? That means care of children. Obstetrics? That means delivering babies. Eye, ear, nose and throat? One doesn't even need a dictionary for that. General surgery? That's clear, too. X-ray? That's simple. Gynecology? That must have something to do with women's diseases. Urology? That's about urine tests and maybe the urinary system. Orthopedics? That's about bones. General medicine? Maybe that's what these others are not. But social service? What can social service have to do with a hospital? How is one to explain what a social service department of a hospital does? It prescribes no medicine, sets no bones, makes no tests. What does it do? What does it bring to the hospital that isn't already there, and how does it help to get a person well?

The answer to these very natural queries reaches to the very heart of medical social work. Illness is the central problem of medical social work just as it is of the hospital. When a sick person enters the hospital, the entire machinery is set in motion to help him get well. All that medical science knows and all the skill it has is directed toward repairing and restoring him. Blood is tested and corpuscles counted, lungs are x-rayed, heart is tested, skin is tested, urine is tested, reflexes are tested, digestion is checked, to mention but a few of the more usual and less strenuous goings-over. All of this is for the purpose of finding out what is wrong with the patient as a basis for treatment. What, however, sometimes happens is that the hunt for the disease becomes so intense that the person is

[9] Field, Minna, *Patients are People*. New York, Columbia University Press, 1953, pp. 229, 230.

overlooked. Once the discovery is made, i.e., the diagnosis, then the disease gets treated. Elaborate treatment plans are laid down according to the precepts outlined by the best textbooks. And once again it is the disease and not the patient that is treated.

Clearly, these are overstatements. They do not apply to all hospitals nor to all physicians. If they did, there would be no social work in hospitals today because the very origin and continued existence of social work rested and rests upon those physicians who are convinced that it is the person and the disease that must be treated. The statements are, however, descriptive of enough hospitals and physicians to make necessary the supplementary service of a social caseworker in a hospital setting. Nor are these observations made without appreciation of the indispensable role of the physician on the hospital staff. They are made in recognition of the fact that medical training is primarily concerned with knowledge about disease, and that the tendency in a modern hospital, with its elaborate equipment, its corps of technicians, its technically conditioned staff together with an unending stream of patients, is to stress increasingly the medical aspects of disease. On the other hand, it frequently happens that the physician in training and on the hospital staff is the type of individual who understands that the sick are first of all people to whom he applies his knowledge of disease.

The Social Worker in the Hospital

The social worker is invariably drawn into a co-operative relationship with a professional person in another department. Suppose, for instance, a patient is found in the surgical service to require an operation for a stomach ulcer. Conceivably the surgeon might decide to operate without any questions asked, or, very likely, he will want to know a good deal about the patient's background (more than just a medical history), his work, family responsibilities, attitude toward and readiness for his job possibilities after the operation, etc. Few surgeons on a hospital staff have sufficient time or the necessary special skill to make a thorough inquiry. The social service department exists to work with the patient to help him use hospital treatment and also to work with the surgeon so that his time may be conserved and his particular skill made accessible to the patient in a manner most beneficial to him. This service to the patient involves a relationship with the physician that rests upon the recognition of the primary medical service of the hospital, but which also recognizes that that service is destined for human beings. That is the basis of the teamwork of physician and social worker which should be mutually understood. This relationship is an integral part of the total medical institution.

The medical social worker's approach is upon the basis of the patient's needs. Part of those needs will relate to medical care such as a brace, a bed in a hospital, pneumothorax treatment, a brain tumor operation. Another part will relate to the individual's emotional reactions to illness and to the steps toward recovery. It is the physician's job to provide medical care, it is the social worker's to help the patient to utilize medical care so that health will be achieved. To do the latter job the social worker must first know and understand the patient, how and why he feels as he does, what his capacities are for assuming his share of the responsibility of getting well. He, the worker, will need to know where the patient is blocked and why and what can be done to help the patient move on from there. He will want to learn what meaning this illness has for the patient and how it affects his feelings about himself and also how it affects or is affected by his social relationships. In short, the worker will be dealing with the medical problem without being the physician; he will be dealing with the emotional elements without being the psychiatrist. But he will be dealing with both of these in relation to the social situation and the social relationships of which the patient is a part. It is this strictly defined function of medical social work that cannot be emphasized too often if medical social workers and hospital staff are going to continue to work harmoniously.

The Patient as a Person

Throughout this chapter the expression "the patient as a person" has been used. It is not an original statement. Yet it is perhaps the most succinct and arresting of those many expressions that have gained currency within recent years, emphasizing the essential "individualness" characteristic of each human being. The stress upon the individual in the field of education and in all forms of social casework are other instances of the same trend. Educators speak of the student who is first of all a person who learns. The probation or parole officer or the social worker in a correctional institution conceives of an offender who first of all is a person who commits a crime. The medical social worker sees the patient first of all as a person who is sick. The consistent principle that runs all through these is that the human being who needs help, whether he be a student, a probationer, a parolee, a prisoner, or a patient, has as his core his own unique personality. This personality distinguishes him from every other human being.

All of this is pertinent with respect to the person who is sick. What he will do about his illness, about getting himself to a doctor or a hospital, how he will be able to face the diagnosis and all that it may mean to him, how he will carry out recommended steps in treatment and make the necessary adjustments in his life are decisions which every sick person must face. No two persons will react the same way, not even to the same disease, if for no other reason than that a disease never means the same to any two people. The crucial point involved here is: What is the meaning of this disease to this person at this time?

Not only must the hospital staff, including medical social workers, consider the patient together with all of his attitudes about disease and about himself, but that same staff, especially the medical social worker this time, must see him as part of a configuration of social relationships. This configuration would include especially his family and job. No individual manages to live unto himself, and what a particular person may mean to his family and what his family may mean to him are entirely relevant whenever anything goes wrong, whether it be in the field of behavior such as delinquency and crime or in the field of health such as tuberculosis or syphilis. Much the same may be said for the job. For most people "the job" means not only status that comes from being able to provide for oneself and one's family, but also the personal satisfaction of accomplishing something. In addition the job makes possible a stability that becomes a factor for strength in the development and expression of the individual. What the loss or surrender of that job because of illness may mean to the individual is essential not only to diagnosis but also to treatment.[10]

---

[10] A number of excellent treatises have emphasized the points mentioned in this and other sections of the chapter. The student who wishes to explore further these concepts and to find substantiation through a variety of illustrations is referred to the following: Field, Minna, *Patients are People.* New York, Columbia University Press, 1953; Richardson, Henry B., *Patients Have Families.* New York, Commonwealth Fund, 1945; Robinson, G. Canby, *The Patient as a Person.* New York, Commonwealth Fund, 1939.

The Psychosomatic Approach

Within the past two decades considerable attention has been given to what is rather arrestingly referred to as the psychosomatic approach. Essentially this expression means a taking into account of the emotional as well as the physical factors in disease. Actually this is not a new concept, for it goes to the very basis of diagnosis and treatment and has had to be reckoned with ever since there was an art of healing. However, as Dr. H. M. Margolis points out, the phenomenal discoveries of modern medicine tended to obscure the interrelatedness of mind and body.

Medical discoveries in bacteriology, pathology, surgery, biochemistry, and biophysics, with their potentiality for help to the sick, came as an overwhelming avalanche of medical progress. These advances were stirring; they had a mathematical precision that was unknown before; they literally swept away the existence of certain infectious diseases and created specific cures, hitherto undreamed of. All of them focused on the physical constitution of man and his ills and emphasized the accomplishments that could be achieved by physical means. Actually, medical literature dropped the word "man" and began to speak of the human organism, which was being studied so precisely and which could be manipulated so mechanically. In time, medical students and physicians came to regard this human organism as a biological unit not different from the amoeba or the turnip. They forgot that the individual was more than a turnip; he was a biologic unit, it is true, but endowed with a highly sensitive nervous system that held in delicate balance a highly complex emotional apparatus with a storehouse of memories, loves, hates, fears, feelings of security and anxiety.[11]

It is because these loves, hates, fears, feelings of security and anxiety are related to the precipitation of illness, the duration of illness, and the recovery from illness that the practitioner needs to be aware of both the emotional and the physical factors. There is an increasing literature being made available to the practitioner that emphasizes the emotional components in what used to be thought of as only physical ailments. The impressive 2,300-item bibliography in Dr. H. Flanders Dunbar's volume *Emotions and Bodily Changes* (1935, 1938, 1946) constitutes substantial evidence of the increased interest in the psychical and physical factors of illness. Dr. Dunbar's presentation of the gist of these studies

[11] Margolis, H. M., *op. cit.*, p. 291.

in her more recent publication intended for the layman *Mind and Body*: *Psychosomatic Medicine* contains many illustrations of the interplay of the *psyche* and the *soma*. Case histories are given of the emotional elements of such ailments as: appendicitis, arthritis, asthma, cancer, colitis, diabetes, eczema, hay fever, heart diseases, migraine, pneumonia, rheumatic heart, skin diseases, tuberculosis, and ulcers. The further work of Drs. Weiss and English in their text on psychosomatic medicine, of Drs. Alexander and French in their published studies in psychosomatic medicine, and the recent volume of case histories by Miles, Cobb, and Shands bear further testimony to those developments. To all of this must be added the quarterly journal *Psychosomatic Medicine* which has been appearing for over a decade.

A balanced judgment is necessary here lest the assumption too readily be made that psychosomatic medicine is a new and radical departure in medical practice. Dr. Weiss, whose textbook has been mentioned, denies the validity of the either/or concept; i.e., that an illness is either functional or organic. Instead it is necessary to deal with the interrelatedness of the two. He then observes that as psychiatry is established on a firm scientific basis and is integrated into general medicine "we will no longer need the term psychosomatic because good medicine will be psychosomatic." [12]

In much the same vein with the emphasis upon the wholeness of the person Dr. Robinson observes: "Man is a unity of mind and body and medicine must consider this unity. Physiology, chemistry, and biology cannot alone or together explain all the intricacies of illness. The disturbances of mind and body cannot be dealt with separately; they form two phases of a single problem." [13]

The Patient's Reaction to Illness

It is necessary to realize what a threat illness can be to the personality of the patient and how it may affect the whole manner of living or way of life. Illness sets one off, accentuates one's differences or establishes

---

[12] Weiss, Edward, "Psychotherapy in Everyday Practice," in *Modern Attitudes in Psychiatry*. New York, Columbia University Press, 1946, p. 117; see also Alexander, Franz, "Present Trends in Psychiatry and the Future Outlook," in *Modern Attitudes in Psychiatry*, pp. 83–84.

[13] Robinson, G. Canby, *op. cit.*, p. 10; see also Hinsie, Leland E., *The Person in the Body*. New York, W. W. Norton & Company, 1945.

other differences which may be hard to bear, especially in the face of illness. It may accentuate or establish an inferiority, an inferiority that perhaps one could get along with while well, but which is too overwhelming during illness when one is robbed of the usual devices of defense. Other individuals may cling to illness because of what it gives them. With illness they amount to something, they get attention; without illness they are mediocrities who somehow get along without much notice. All of these possible reactions must be borne in mind by the medical social worker when he offers help to the sick person. No two of them will act alike. One patient will go so far as to deny illness and by this denial manage to spend the energy which otherwise would go into getting well, in keeping sick. Not admitting illness, of course, means taking no responsibility about getting well. Another person may acknowledge he is sick and not care to do anything about recovering. Actually such a person may get more satisfaction from being sick than in being well, the person we all know who enjoys ill health. Still a third person may positively admit his illness and by accepting what limitations inhere in his illness is able to release his energies toward getting well. Others may react differently at various stages of their illness or recovery. Some who start by affirming their illness may find the going too tough, may relapse and not have the will to go on. Others who began by denying illness may suffer such reverses as to be willing to face death or permanent incapacitation before they can come to grips with themselves and admit their need for help. Still others can take help so long as another stands by but are utterly incapable, seemingly, of carrying their own load. With all of these patients the medical social worker deals and must adapt his skills accordingly.

Most medical social workers learn early in their careers that, medical science notwithstanding, the patient has a good deal to do with whether or not he gets well. Some workers have gone so far as to say that no one can "cure" the patient but himself; that no matter how strongly the physician may want to cure, the real desire must come from the patient, not primarily from the physician or the social worker.[14] The realization

[14] Dr. Flanders Dunbar very dramatically illustrates this in the following passages:
"Two men lay side by side in the hospital ward, both advanced stages of cardiovascular disease. The seriousness of their condition is typical of hospital cases, since these victims generally do not arrive for anything they or their physicians regard as trivial. They wait until they require major treatment of some kind, and congratulate them-

of this truth early in his career spares the medical social worker many fruitless hours of trying to get over to the patient someone else's plan. This realization may be a bit discouraging, but its sobering effect does much to keep the patient-worker relationship centered around the problem of illness, its relation to the patient's social and social-psychological needs, and finally to the capacity of the individual to take help.

Probably the first step in this casework process of offering help is an understanding of the patient, of the disease and what it means to him, and of his ability to cope with the situation in which he finds himself. If the medical social worker is to be a part of the hospital and yet differentiated from it, if he is to bring something new into the hospital setting, it is this very difference that approaches the patient upon an individual basis, that understands him in relation to his disease, that expresses its concern with return to health, but which at the same time leaves the decision with the patient. To come upon this offer of help, to realize one is free to accept or to reject it, to know that there is someone to "go along with" him in the steps toward recovery may give the patient some understanding of what a social casework service is.

That the patient has come to the hospital and to the social worker upon referral by the physician or nurse means that he has moved in the direction of doing something about whatever is bothering him. He may not have as clear a notion of what he wants to do or of what the hospital will do to him as, say, the parent who takes a child to a child guidance clinic. Yet the very step of coming to the hospital—as the mother's steps to the child guidance clinic—indicates the possibility of movement. All that

---

selves upon their fortitude in holding out so long. They might have been cured easily at an earlier stage, but would not have showed so much courage. The two lying side by side were rather extreme examples. Each was pathetically eager to get well. Each watched the physician breathlessly during his examination. Each spoke his uppermost thought at the end.

" 'It's up to you now, Doc,' said one.

" 'I've got to do something to get well,' said the other.

"These patients were on opposite horns of a common dilemma. They were not quite sure of what their own role should be in working out their restoration to health. They had similar past histories and similar symptoms, which probably resulted in the acquisition of essentially the same disease. The personality of the first, however, was not so well integrated as that of the second. The result was that the response of the first to treatment was to leave it all to the doctor. The response of the other was: What can I do to get well? The first died, the second recovered, although laboratory tests and clinical examinations failed to show any real difference."—Dunbar, H. Flanders, *Mind and Body: Psychosomatic Medicine*. New York, Random House, 1947, pp. 65–66.

can be asked at this point of the medical social worker is that he understand the patient's feeling about his disease, acknowledge the steps he has already taken, and indicate his willingness to work along with him on the things that lie ahead. He must meet the patient where he is, not where he thinks the patient ought to be; take him for what he is, not what he ought to be; and start moving with him at his pace and in his direction rather than at the worker's own speed toward a preconceived goal. This does not mean the worker adds nothing to this relationship; he does, but he adds what the patient needs, not what he, the worker, needs.

The Patient's Use of Help

Before people can use help they must want help. This may sound commonplace enough, but certainly social caseworkers have had sufficient experience with the helping process to appreciate the fact that individuals, no matter how badly off they are, still have their own wants, wishes, wills, and need to work out their lives accordingly. To those who are well it must seem absurd to speak of sick people without the will to get well, just as absurd as it must seem to speak of sick people not accepting the fact that they are sick. Yet such is the case, and it is frequently at this point and for this reason that the medical social worker is called upon. A person may be diagnosed by the doctor as having heart trouble, a kidney disease, tuberculosis, syphilis, or cancer. The mere diagnosis does not make the person want to get well; it may actually arouse so many fears that he is unable to act. Even repeating the words of the diagnosis is not tantamount to accepting the fact of the disease. There is such a thing as intellectual acceptance of the disease, which is an entirely different acceptance than an emotional one. Emotional acceptance means admitting the disease is a part of oneself, then expressing a will to do something about the disease, and finally beginning to do something about it. Here is an area in which the medical social worker functions. The patient may need to be helped to understand the disease, what its course is likely to be, what it may do to the patient, the adjustments it will necessitate, temporarily or permanently, in the life of the patient, the kinds of limitations it will set and how these can be handled. The patient knows he is taking help when he comes to grips with his illness, when he feels freer to work and live within its limitations than to spend his energies fighting it. The very acceptance of the disease and the necessity of adjusting to it may actually prove to be a growth experience never before known to the patient.

These are more than theoretical speculations, they are borne out in the daily lives of countless people. Take, for example, the young man of thirty, single, successful in business, who comes down with tuberculosis. At first it is inconceivable that he has tuberculosis. It is only a cough that has hung on and besides he's been working too hard lately. Then come the fears. "Maybe it is tuberculosis. What'll it do to me, what about my job, my friends? No, I can't rest for six months or go to a sanatorium. I haven't saved any money. No, I can't have an operation. I couldn't walk around a cripple; I'd rather die and get it over with." [15]

These are not uncommon reactions with which the social worker comes in contact among rich and poor. Social service helps the person take himself for what he is, the disease, its implications, and limitations. The patient learns little by little how to accept the situation. He rests for six months only to find it must be for another half-year. When the year is up, he is placed on a restricted schedule, he must continue treatments, he must resume the job gradually, he must be moderate in his habits, hours, and recreations. What he could not face a year ago he gladly accommodates himself to now. In one sense, a year has dropped out of his life. In another sense he has learned to restrict himself, something which never seemed possible before. A year's invalidism has sobered his reckless disregard of health, his tremendous drive for success in business, his ideal of being a jolly good fellow. Two years later he is back in business with regular hours, his recreation and leisure-time program is tempered, he is married, and life seems to have a purpose. Perhaps any number of other traumatic experiences might have done these things for him, but the inescapable fact is that there is some relation between his acceptance of his illness and his working within its restrictions; some relation between accepting limitations in one small area of living— illness—and being able subsequently to use that as a creative experience

---

[15] For a recent analysis of the difficulty of patients facing tuberculosis see Brooke, Mary S., "Psychology of the Tuberculosis Patient." *Journal of Social Casework*, XXIX, February 1948, pp. 57–60. In this article Osler's famous dictum is repeated that "The cure of tuberculosis depends more on what the patient has in his head than on what he has in his chest"; see also Hartz, Jerome, "Human Relationship in Tuberculosis," *Public Health Reports*, LXV, October 6, 1950, pp. 1292–1305.

in a larger area of living. Instead of death, there is life with constructive meaning.

The Responsibility the Patient Carries

Feelings, emotions, and ideas eventually get expressed, in one way or another, in action—action being another word for behavior. The behavior with which the patient and the medical social worker are concerned is directed toward adjustment to illness and handicaps, or toward restoration to health. Not all sickness turns toward absolute health, yet an individual may need help in adjustment to a more or less permanent incapacitation or at least handicap, as well as to the happier movement toward recovery. The services of the medical social worker which consist of interviewing and counseling with patients are directed toward action on the part of the patient in making the accommodation to the limitations of illness or the step toward health. For either the doctor or the social worker to take over the patient's responsibility would be to rob him of the opportunity to take hold of his own problem. For them to allow him to carry his share of responsibility means that he is freer to move into action on his own behalf. It leaves him free to do something about himself. The social worker, by enabling him to express his fears, by taking him for what he is, by instilling confidence in him, by thinking out some of his difficulties with him, by being there to help him work out plans further if need be, provides releases that enable him to take his own next steps. Perhaps he cannot see far enough ahead to work out the whole problem alone, very few of us can, but he can relate himself to one small part of it and as he gains a feeling of sureness there, he can go on to larger areas. This step toward action very often is the answer to fear; for if a patient can only make a decision to act and then act, many of the fears that have beset him are dissolved away. Certainly the feeling of helplessness is not so great. There is no freer medium in which to express feelings without condemnation, to face fears, to feel accepted and understood than the relationship with the patient which the medical social worker is enabled to set up. Out of this relationship should come a freer use of the patient's self, his creative energies, his capacities to take on responsibility for his own life.

A sick person is part of the web of social relationships and a member of a social group in a community situation. He is a member of a family, he affects and is affected by the other family members, he has job responsibilities and community contacts of various kinds. His illness may remove him for the time being from that family and that community, but eventually he must return there. The adjustments he must make, the limitations he must bear are in relation to his social setting. This the medical social worker must constantly bear in mind. Sick people, like others, make their adjustment to a reality situation, not to a ready-made or ideal one. No matter what the skill of the medical social worker is nor how profound the personality needs of the patient, the central job is to relate the patient and the medical plan to the social situation. The ultimate test is whether, in the light of the capacities of the individual, the nature of his disability, and the demands of the social situation, the medical social worker has helped to effect such an adjustment of the patient to the community as will most satisfactorily meet his own needs and at the same time the requirements of the community.

Medical Social Work Outside of the Hospital Setting

Medical social work has operated traditionally within a hospital setting. Within recent years there have been developments which have used the medical social work approach to deal with problems outside the hospital. The components of these problems are essentially those with which medical social work has always dealt: people, illness, a social situation. The more spectacular of these newer medical social work services has been in the crippled children's program and in vocational rehabilitation.

Under the provisions of the Social Security Act of 1935 and subsequent amendments funds are made available by the federal government for crippled children's services throughout the states, territories, and insular possessions. States, territories, and insular possessions submit an acceptable plan to insure service to the crippled children which must provide among other things financial participation by the states, administration by a state agency, and co-operation with medical, health, nursing, and welfare groups in the state.

Pediatricians and orthopedists have welcomed the services of the trained medical social workers in the carrying out of a crippled children's program. Thus far the demand for service has been so great, despite the many years of excellent service which a score of private groups have rendered, that the physicians have been swamped and able to look into only the medical aspects of treatment. The necessity of seeing the patient as a person is as marked here as in the more conventional areas just described. If anything, the requirement is all the more urgent because of the disfiguring, disabling, and handicapping effects under which crippled children have suffered or do suffer. Here certainly is a place where the medical social worker must understand what illness and defect mean to the child, the accent on difference from other children, the loss of status in the home and in school, the feeling of not being wanted, of feeling oneself a burden, of feeling inferior to whole children. Here, too, even though the patient is a child, he must be helped to accept his crippled condition, to make decisions for himself, to work within limitations, and if cured to leave behind many of those compensations which inevitably accompanied his defect. Here, too, the child must be helped to share in community life. In short, the ordeal of crippling and the restoration from crippling may afford as excellent an opportunity as life will ever again allow to know what a real growth experience is. To be in a position to enable a child to realize his potentialities is one of the enviable opportunities few others can know.

Another service in which medical social work has been utilized increasingly is vocational rehabilitation. This service has been available on a federal-state basis since the Vocational Rehabilitation Act of 1920, but it remained for the Social Security Act of 1935 and the Vocational Rehabilitation Act of 1943 (Barden-LaFollette) as amended through 1954 to provide it with its greatest impetus for usefulness. In the preceding pages emphasis has been placed upon illness and adjustment in relation to it. Everything said on that score would be just as applicable to the handicap which disease or accident produces. Indeed, the vocational and emotional adjustment to handicap may be, and usually is, a lifelong one. Effective vocational rehabilitation requires not only medical diagnosis and treatment, but physical and occupational therapy, vocational training and retraining, financial assistance, job placement, and casework services. Here are at least three professions involved: medical, educational, social service.[16]

---

[16] It is also pertinent to mention several recent volumes bearing on medical social services in relation to rehabilitation and prolonged illness. For the former see Elledge,

Whether the services are supported by taxes as the federal-state-local programs or by voluntary contributions as with many of the national agency programs like tuberculosis, cancer, poliomyelitis, etc., there is increasing provision for medical social workers to be utilized in consultant and administrative staff positions. This has meant, increasingly, relating the medical social worker to public health departments both in the counties, particularly the larger ones, and in the state office. It has resulted, likewise, in the utilization of medical social work knowledge and skills in public welfare departments, especially in the state offices where medico-social problems are thrashed out and programs formulated. The addition to the public assistance programs, in 1950, of aid to the permanently and totally disabled has called for the equipment of the medical social worker to be increasingly available to public welfare programs. The growing problem of medical care for persons receiving public assistance as well as for persons not receiving public assistance but referred to as the "medically indigent" obliges state public welfare and health departments to draw upon medical social work as never before. In like measure organizations such as the American Red Cross, the state and national tuberculosis societies (as well as public and private sanatoria), the Veterans Administration, the United States Public Health Service, the United States Children's Bureau conceive of medical social work as an integral part of their services. While the medical social worker in those positions actually may not minister directly to ill persons, nevertheless his skill and knowledge are used indirectly, through policies and organization, to the end that a more effective service is ultimately available to more patients in more places. In all instances the core of his work is the discovery, development, and integration of medical and social resources for patients or clients.[17]

Caroline H., *The Rehabilitation of the Patient*. Philadelphia, J. B. Lippincott Company, 1948; and for the latter see Field, Minna, *Patients are People*. New York, Columbia University Press, 1953.

[17] In a useful pamphlet "Medical Social Services for Children" prepared by the medical social work staff of the United States Children's Bureau emphasis is given not only to the core of casework services in the maternal and child health and crippled children's programs, but also auxiliary services as essential to the medical social work function in these areas. Such auxiliary services were suggested to be: program planning, policy making, standard setting, community planning, educational activities, planning and participating in medical studies and research. See "Medical Social Services for Children." Washington, D. C., Children's Bureau, United States Department of Health, Education, and Welfare, 1953, pp. 10–31; see also Rice, Elizabeth P., "Medical Social Work,"

Conclusion

Medical social work, like other specializations within the casework field, has been responsive to the fundamental changes in philosophy and practice within the present century. The early emphasis was upon changing the environment so that there would be as ideal a situation as possible in which the patient was to live. Gradually this gave way to an approach that recognized the emotional factors involved in illness, and the necessity to explore the psychological needs of the patient and to reorient him to his illness in the light of his inner needs. More recently the focus has been upon the helping function to the ill person in relation to his social situation. This newer trend recognizes the important role of environment, but includes within it the much larger area of social relationships. With the followers and disciples of the psychoanalysts of the second period, it sees the part which the emotions, past experiences, etc., play in individual behavior, but it also sees those as related to other factors and to present situations. The medical social work of today is not to be regarded as a compromise of the first and second eras. Rather it is to be considered as a progressive movement which has retained their contributions but has fused them into a richer service, a service stressing the essential dynamics of the patient-physician-worker relationship and the greater possibilities of realizing the patient's potentialities within his particular social situation.

BIBLIOGRAPHY

Books and Pamphlets

Alexander, Franz, *Psychosomatic Medicine: Its Principles and Applications.* New York, W. W. Norton & Company, 1950.

Cabot, Richard C., *Social Service and the Art of Healing.* rev. ed., New York, Dodd, Mead and Co., 1928.

Cannon, Ida M., *On the Social Frontier of Medicine.* Cambridge, Harvard University Press, 1952.

Cockerill, Eleanor (editor), *Social Work Practice in the Field of Tuberculosis.* Pittsburgh, University of Pittsburgh, 1954.

in *Social Work Year Book.* New York, American Association of Social Workers, 1954, pp. 339–346.

Cooley, Carol H., *Social Aspects of Illness*. Philadelphia, W. B. Saunders Company, 1951.

Cressman, Edith W. (editor), *Functional Case Work in a Medical Setting*. Philadelphia, Pennsylvania School of Social Work, 1944.

Dunbar, H. Flanders, *Mind and Body: Psychosomatic Medicine*. rev. ed., New York, Random House, 1955.

Elledge, Caroline H., *The Rehabilitation of the Patient*. Philadelphia, J. B. Lippincott Company, 1948.

Field, Minna, *Patients are People*. New York, Columbia University Press, 1953.

Garrett, James F., *Psychological Aspects of Physical Disability*. Washington, D. C., Office of Vocational Rehabilitation, Department of Health, Education, and Welfare, U. S. Government Printing Office, 1953.

Goldstine, Dora, *Readings in the Theory and Practice of Medical Social Work*. Chicago, University of Chicago Press, 1954.

Hinsie, Leland E., *The Person in the Body*. New York, W. W. Norton & Company, 1945.

Miles, Henry H. W., Cobb, Stanley, Shands, Harley C., *Case Histories in Psychosomatic Medicine*. New York, W. W. Norton & Company, 1952.

Miller, Pauline, *Medical Social Service in a Tuberculosis Sanitarium*. Washington, D. C., U. S. Public Health Service, Federal Security Agency, U. S. Government Printing Office, 1951.

Richardson, Henry B., *Patients Have Families*. New York, Commonwealth Fund, 1945.

Robinson, G. Canby, *The Patient as a Person*. New York, Commonwealth Fund, 1939.

Simmons, Leo W., and Wolff, Harold G., *Social Science in Medicine*. New York, Russell Sage Foundation, 1954.

Thornton, Janet, *The Social Component in Medical Care*. New York, Columbia University Press, 1937.

Upham, Frances, *A Dynamic Approach to Illness: A Social Work Guide*. New York, Family Service Association of America, 1949.

Significant Articles

Abrams, Ruth D., "Social Casework with Cancer Patients." *Social Casework*, XXXII, December 1951, pp. 425–432.

Bartlett, Harriett M., "Perspectives in Public Health Social Work." *Children*, I, January-February 1954, pp. 21–25.

Cockerill, Eleanor, "New Emphasis on an Old Concept in Medicine." *Journal of Social Casework*, XXX, January 1949, pp. 10–15.

Dunkel, Mary L., "Case Work Help for Neurodermatitis Patients." *Journal of Social Casework*, XXX, March 1949, pp. 97–103.

Elledge, Caroline H., "The Meaning of Illness." *Medical Social Work,* II, April 1953, pp. 49–65.

Field, Minna, "Medical Social Work for the Aged." *Bulletin of the American Association of Medical Social Workers,* XXII, February 1949, pp. 4–16.

———, "The Role of the Social Worker in a Modern Hospital." *Social Casework,* XXXIV, November 1953, pp. 398–402.

Gordon, Eckka, "Treatment of Problems of Dependency Related to Illness." *The Family,* XXIII, October 1942, pp. 210–218.

Moffett, Margaret, "Casework with a Patient Having Cardiac Surgery." *Medical Social Work,* III, January 1954, pp. 21–31.

Rice, Elizabeth P., "Generic and Specific in Medical Social Work." *Journal of Social Casework,* XXX, April 1949, pp. 131–136.

Schless, Bessie G., "Social Case Work with the Arthritic Patient." *The Family,* XXV, January 1945, pp. 331–337.

White, Grace, "The Distinguishing Characteristics of Medical Social Work." *Medical Social Work,* I, September 1951, pp. 31–39.

Medical Social Work in a Veterans Administration Hospital

ARTHUR L. LEADER, Chief Social Worker
and
MRS. MABEL J. REMMERS, Case Supervisor
Winter Veterans Administration Hospital
Topeka, Kansas

The Veterans Administration (VA) operates a comprehensive medical program for all eligible veterans. It attempts to insure the highest possible level of medical practice through the utilization of modern facilities, the employment of competent personnel, and the participation in university training programs.

A veteran requiring hospitalization may apply directly to the VA hospital or Regional Office nearest his home. A physician of his own choice, either his own private doctor or a physician at the VA Regional Office, must sign and submit the application form to the hospital. The patient whose application is processed through the Regional Office is notified by the appropriate hospital of the scheduled date for admission. The date of hospitalization depends upon such factors as the need and wish of the applicant, the kind and severity of illness, the extent of the waiting list for his type of illness, and VA eligibility requirements.

In view of the variation in practices in VA hospitals, the following comments apply to the Winter Veterans Administration Hospital in Topeka, Kansas. Every applicant for hospitalization is examined by the admitting physician. If declared eligible for and requiring hospitalization, he is sent at once to the ward best suited to study and treat his illness. Comprehensive medicine now regards the sick person as a total person with physiological and emotional interrelationships. Regardless of any specialization of the hospital, the modern medical center treats the whole person whether his condition be primarily psychiatric or medical.

In the Topeka hospital the emotionally disturbed patient requiring a closed ward is sent to the appropriate closed ward following his examination by the admitting physician. There he is studied and treated by a team of experts consisting of the psychiatrist, psychologist, nurse, social worker, aide, and a number of rehabilitation therapists. The patient admitted to the hospital for an acute medical condition or an illness that appears to have no major psychological involvement is sent directly by the admitting officer to the appropriate medical or surgical ward. All other patients, including those presenting diagnostic problems, are processed through a special Diagnostic and Appraisal Unit and, after comprehensive study, are either discharged or transferred to an active treatment ward. The evaluation involves contacts with a psychiatrist, internist, social worker, psychologist, and other ward personnel. Together they make co-ordinated recommendations for further treatment.

Open-ward patients with medical illnesses are hospitalized in a designated section of the hospital. In acknowledgment of the psychosomatic importance in every illness, both internists and psychiatrists serve on these wards to treat collaboratively the total person. Such treatment, involving two kinds of doctors, requires careful co-ordination and communication with each other and with the rest of the ward personnel. In order to facilitate the centralization of medical authority in one person, one doctor, either the internist or the psychiatrist, is designated as the doctor in charge of a specific ward and the other doctor serves as the consultant. The medical staff through the co-operation and implementation of the other specialists plans an individualized treatment program for each patient. The doctor's understanding of each patient reinforced by the knowledge of each discipline and the response of the patient determines who will be doing what at what time. Hospital treatment, therefore, may involve a regime varying from bed rest without medication to intensive psychotherapy without medication to physiotherapy and occupational therapy to social services for some specific purpose or any combination of such treatments.

The social workers function as a regular part of the treatment team. In order to contribute maximum service to the patient in their area of competency, administrative arrangements have been made for them to attend all clinical, teaching, and administrative conferences, to participate on medical ward rounds, and to hold regular weekly conferences with each doctor (in addition to indicated daily contacts). Because of the structure and philosophy of this section, there is no distinction between medical and psychiatric social work. The condition of each patient determines the type of treatment, degree of collaboration, and need for social service activity.

A caseworker becomes active with a medical patient through a variety of ways. A plan involving the use of social work might have originated as a recommendation of the Diagnostic and Appraisal Unit. In this situation the patient himself may seek out the social worker assigned to his new treatment ward or the social worker may initiate contact with the patient on the basis of the recommendation. Discussions in clinical staff conferences often lead to appropriate referrals to social service either upon recommendation of the staff physician or as result of a proposal by the social worker. The participation of social service on ward rounds provides another source of referrals to the worker. Individual conferences with doctors, both scheduled and irregular, perhaps provide the greatest source of referrals. Communications from agencies in the community, often pointing up problems or concerns at home, serve at times as a source of entrée for the hospital social worker. Any member of the hospital staff may bring the social problem of the patient or his family to the attention of the social worker. In addition, the patient himself may seek out the service of the worker on his own initiative.

Regardless of the source of activity, it is the social worker's consistent responsibility to clear his plans and activity with the doctor and to relate his service to the over-all medical plan since in a medical setting he operates always under the authority of the doctor and in line with medical recommendations. The medical social worker in this type of setting at times has an added responsibility in relating to two different medical authorities. He must be skillful not only in clarifying consistently his current and potential area of service but also in communicating clearly and comfortably. He must at all times be clear about his own role, and he and the psychiatrist especially have to have a co-ordinated understanding and acceptance of the appropriateness of each other's service. Each should feel free to suggest to the other issues for further consideration. In addition to the necessity for active triangular collaboration between the two doctors and social worker, it is important for each team member to be in contact, as indicated, with a number of other hospital therapists. No one team member can treat the patient alone for his maximum benefit. For example, in helping a medical patient make plans to leave the hospital, the social worker has to consult regularly with the doctor regarding the current medical condition and anticipated date of discharge. Social work contacts with the patient and/or relatives may contribute toward a revision of the doctor's thinking in regard to either social plans or discharge date. If the psychiatrist has not been active with the patient, the social worker and internist want to agree whether psychiatric consultation or treatment might be indicated. If he has been active, the two physicians and social worker must jointly plan appropriately timed terminal contacts. In the same situation, the social worker may want to discuss the patient's hospital activities, for example, with the vocational advisor, occupational therapist, or musical therapist in terms of facilitating a post-hospital adjustment in occupational and recreational areas. The hospital is rich in rehabilitation resources, and it is the social worker's responsibility, along with others, to help the patient use these resources to expand the creative use of his personal and social capacities.

The following case material illustrates the medical planning for one patient and the role of the medical social worker.

During the weekly ward conference attended by the internist, psychiatrist, social worker, nurse, and aide, the ward nurse pointed out that the patient was concerned about a financial problem. He was having difficulty in meeting even his incidental hospital expenses, was restless, and had been found crying several times. The social worker learned that the patient, a 35-year-old, single Negro, suffered from an obscure glandular condition, as yet not clearly diagnosed. This was characterized by a number of nodules or lumps under the surface of his skin in the area around his neck and shoulders. The swelling in this area was painful and interfered with the patient's comfort in swallowing. At times it was almost impossible for him to eat, and he was chronically fatigued. He had had repeated hospitalizations here and at other hospitals for the same illness. Several weeks previously he had departed from this hospital against medical advice in the midst of his diagnostic work-up. It was agreed that the worker might help the patient with financial need and any other social problems. The internist would introduce this possibility to him during ward rounds.

The patient began the initial interview in a rather defensive but timid way:

He stated that he had come because he had been told I was the right person to come to. When I told him I guessed it was a little hard to come to talk with a strange person, he relaxed in admitting that it was. He didn't like to ask anyone for anything—was used to taking care of himself. I asked him gently why he couldn't do so now. When he spoke of his illness, I thought this was a pretty good reason and that he had done the right thing in coming to talk with me even though it took courage. He explained his financial need realistically.

I told him that in recognizing his need I could grant him a small amount of money from a special fund only if this were part of some plan that would be of real benefit to him. (This fund is available through a special arrangement with the local chapter of the American Red Cross for the personal expenses of hospitalized veterans for therapeutic purposes.) He went on to say that he hoped that this time he might use the money to prevent his precipitous departure from the hospital. He had to admit that there was a lot more than money involved in his previous flights, but he felt that he had to stay this time, once and for all, to find out what was wrong, what could be done medically, and then make better plans for making a living in the future. I said that this sounded like a big order in view of his previous pattern of leaving the hospital; if, however, he was interested in working with me toward better plans, I could see that he got the money. He was pleased in a boyish way.

I referred back to his statement that there was a lot more involved than money. With a rush of words, he explained that he had become upset in the face of not knowing what was wrong with him. It was even more frightening to feel that the doctors still did not seem to know anything about his illness. On top of this, he had really been extremely afraid of the methods of examination, particularly the needles used for biopsies. I recognized the difficulty for him and the physical and emotional pain involved in his staying this time, too. With a laugh he said that maybe this time he couldn't take it either. I said this could be and the decision would be his. Although in a sense it might be easier to run away, I felt that in staying he might be contributing toward his own better health. Though he was still doubtful about recovering, I said that I would be glad to see him again to help him tide over the period of indecision and waiting, and to make future plans if he were interested. He seemed eager for another appointment.

After the interview the worker reviewed with the internist her contacts with the patient, emphasizing the patient's anxiety about the unknown nature of the illness and his fears of some of the medical procedures. The doctor was particularly interested in learning that the attitudes of the patient might have contributed to hasty discharges in the past. The doctor himself indicated that although at this time he could not establish a definite diagnosis, he planned to talk with the patient in a paternal manner about the advisability of remaining in the hospital. Together they considered that the patient had a right to be frightened by the inexplicable appearance of nodules on the body and of the blotchy whitening of the skin. They both thought that casework service was indicated for the purpose of facilitating his remaining in the hospital and of making future plans.

This patient, like others, had no funds for even daily personal needs. Since financial resources are limited and can never meet the total need, social workers are able to grant money to patients in need only if they show some interest in improving their present situation. Although the worker could not be sure that the patient would use the money for this purpose, she felt, from the patient's frankness and honesty in expressing his feelings and his sincere yet teasing manner, that financial assistance coupled with the expressed interest of the social worker and doctor might this time help him remain for full treatment and for planning a more satisfying life following discharge.

Medical social work aims to help the patient to live more comfortably with his illness or to make whatever changes he can toward regaining his health. The worker during the first contact was able to help the patient bring out anxieties and fears that he had not expressed at all during any of his numerous hospitalizations. She recognized that these expressions were only the first step in a casework relationship that would be directed toward helping the patient assume as much responsibility as possible for improving his medical-social problems.

In the second interview the patient continued to express concern about his unknown condition. Lumps were occurring over many parts of his body, other people referred to his "turning white," and he was anxiously speculating on many possible sources and reasons for his illness. Some of his ideas were tinged with guilt as he seemed to be saying that he tried to live a "clean honest" life but perhaps despite all the self-imposed restrictions and consequent loneliness he still was somehow responsible. At the same time, he referred to his long-standing sense of responsibility in contributing financial assistance to relatives and his sadness in not being able to sustain this now. The worker could not give the patient any reassurance about his condition or his future. She could not even go so far as to encourage him to stay in hopes that hospitalization could result in definitive treatment, or even slight improvement. But as the following end of the interview shows, she did try to share with him as much as she could the feelings that were present in him and her respect for him:

I said that now he was doing something which took even more courage than supporting his relatives. I thought, though, that it would be pretty hard to believe that anyone else could understand what courage it took— waiting to find out whether the doctor could tell him what was the matter and whether he could be helped. He said nobody knew what he went through just waiting but somehow he felt a little better just talking about it. I told him that we in the hospital could feel in part with him and we were concerned about his welfare so long as he was. He said he believed this was true, and he has made up his mind to stay here and face whatever it is he had to find out. He wanted to know whether he could talk with me again, and I told him I should like to see him regularly once a week.

The patient has already made some important decisions—to remain in the hospital and to use casework services. This is no small gain in view of the patient's previous pattern. These decisions not only reflect the strength of the patient but demonstrate, as social workers experience daily, that people in trouble, when given an opportunity for expressing their feelings and using professional help purposefully, often are able to do something different about their problems. The worker knew, too, that in helping the patient to continue to "face" his situation and make whatever future plans were indicated, it was important to see him on a regular and continuous basis. Contacts once a week would offer him a regular opportunity to feel the genuine interest of the worker and to help him control any residuals from his old patterns of impulsivity.

In the next team conference as the worker described the patient's fear of "turning white," his reaction to the biopsies, his pattern of evading responsibility for his own health, and an undertone of depression, it was agreed that the ward psychiatrist would see the patient for an evaluation of his emotional status and the possibility of concurrent psychiatric treatment. The psychiatrist later concluded that although the patient was somewhat depressed, quite immature, and conflicted in regard to how much responsibility he wanted to take, he would not be considered a candidate for psychotherapy since his anxiety seemed more related to the realities of his physical condition and the situational problems stemming from it in terms of economic need, family relationships, and future plans. Thus it was recommended that the social worker continue to assume responsibility for help in these areas as medical treatment progressed.

Shortly afterwards, the patient's condition was diagnosed as sarcoidosis of the cervical lymphatic glands and tumor of the pituitary gland. The group of skin lesions is benign in nature and prognosis is generally guarded. Experimental treatment, involving the administration of cortisone, was begun. The patient's condition improved dramatically, and he was to continue on this drug.

The patient's improvement presented a dilemma for him. Not long after he had made a decision to stay, his movement toward health was in part directing his thinking again toward leaving. Despite the medical recommendation for continued hospitalization, it was his feeling at times, aggravated by a sense of guilt for remaining in the hospital while feeling vastly better, that he should seek immediate employment. In this way he explained he could continue to contribute to the support of family members and to pay back bills. In an effort to determine the basis of the patient's tendency once again to flee from the hospital and to help him carry out the medical recommendation, the worker consciously refrained from challenging his expressed reasons, for the spoken word at times serves only to mask the deeper feelings as those become too painful to face. It is sometimes easier to face these when there are opportunities for experiencing them bit by bit, within the framework of a warm, accepting professional relationship.

The worker did ask him to talk further about his financial responsibilities, and it became quite clear, first to the worker and then to the patient, that there was no urgent need for him to make any payments. He then felt free to reveal his deeper feelings. His fear that his improvement might not last tended to arouse excessive anxiety and to lead to an evasion of responsibility. At the same time, he expressed the feeling that the doctor might discharge him at any time. Since his feeling was in reality curiously inconsistent with the doctor's recommendation, the worker here too tried to reach the basis of the patient's feeling. When she pointed out that the doctor in fact had recommended continued hospitalization rather than discharge, the patient indicated that perhaps the doctor would not permit him to stay in view of his improvement. The patient was then able to recognize that he really wanted to remain and that he was receiving gratification not only from his medical treatment but from the interest of the worker and the doctor. He was able to admit, too, that in expressing the fear that the doctor might discharge him, he was seeking for active confirmation of his need to stay from the medical authority. In this way, too, he was able to find gratification of his dependency needs.

In a sense, all of us have these needs—to depend on others—in some degree. We all have our own ways of working these out. Some have to deny these needs and as a result may operate in an overly independent manner. These people are sometimes lonesome and do not get close to others. This patient had been essentially on his own since adolescence. He had had a struggle in making ends meet. His employment history had been sporadic, and he had very few friends. He consistently had to deny basic dependency needs.

In this hospitalization he was able through the help of the social worker and doctor to become dependent upon them and to tolerate within himself his conflicting feelings in regard to his dependency needs. He could even admit that he wanted to be in the hospital and needed the interest of the worker and physician. Thus, the medical social worker, recognizing the emotional and personal problems that illness and hospitalization created for him, helped him carry out the medical recommendation. In a similar way, the acceptance of financial assistance from the worker not only helped him meet a real need but also contributed to his tolerance of himself in a dependent role. And so in this hospitalization he was able to use the help of others as he had not done before.

Since the medical social worker is especially concerned with the social factors in illness, it was her hope that perhaps from this point on she could help the patient not only carry out medical recommendations but work out a life that could afford greater satisfactions within the limits of his medical condition.

In the same interview the patient went on to talk about his erratic work history. He attributed this, not to his illness, but to the superior attitudes of others and their complaints about his slowness. He himself volunteered that he was inclined to daydream and take little interest in his work. He hoped that when he left the hospital this time, it might be different for him. The following material is taken from the case record:

I asked him in what way he wanted it to be different, and he replied that he wanted a regular job which he could stick to for some time, and at the same time come home to a place he could call home. He was sick and tired of having no family close to him. Recognizing this as a real problem to him, I wondered how he planned to go about achieving these goals. He said that now for the first time in years his physical condition was improved, and he was regaining his strength. In addition, he somehow felt more settled and did not have to run away so much from himself. He had a lot of time to think about himself the past few weeks, and he has begun to realize he has been kind of floating in life without an anchor.

Then, as though this were almost too much of a break with his past and as a possible indication for further need for parental-like controls outside himself, he stated that the best thing for him to do was to apply for a job loading milk cans on a truck despite medical recommendations so that he could increase his earnings. I asked him what would happen, and he guessed that he might end up in the hospital soon. I said I suspected that it was not going to be easy outside the hospital, and in fact it might even be difficult to think of leaving.

With tears, he stated this was true. Ever since he had left the previous rooming house for his present one, things had not been right. His former landlady had really been a mother to him, and just when he thought he finally had a home, he moved away when she took in other tenants. He did not like the idea of sharing her attention with others. I asked him how he felt, and he said, "Angry"; and he admitted this was why he left. I supposed that being part of a family had its difficulties, especially when you had to share "mother" with others. He said that after he left he had become ashamed of his anger, and he hasn't been back there at all, though this was the best home he had known. She too really hated to see him leave. I wondered how she would feel, not hearing from him. He thought maybe she felt kind of bad because down deep there was a bond of affection between them. I explained that his feelings were natural, but I did not see why these had to keep them apart. I thought he'd be foolish not to see what could be done about returning there, if that's what he really wanted. He guessed he had been pretty impulsive; he thought he would get in touch with her.

Sometimes it is easier, though not so productive, to fight what one wants the most. This patient tended to fight the common human need of being cared for. Although he had sought out this care on many occasions, as evidenced by his repeated hospitalization, he consistently found it necessary to fight this need through flight from the hospital. In the same way, at the point when he found a "mother" and a substitute family, he had to run away. But with the help of the medical social worker he was able to diminish his "flight" and instead to admit to himself the existence of this need. This recognition contributed to his comfort and relaxation.

We are able to see that the patient's old pattern of denial and impulsivity, which had seriously interfered with his health, has begun to change. In the thinking of the social worker, it was important in behalf of the physical and emotional health of the patient that he take as much responsibility as possible for any indicated change in pattern. If he could participate in improving his personal and social relationships, there were better opportunities for sustaining his health and total adjustment in the community.

In a subsequent conference with the doctor, the worker learned that the patient would require hospitalization for several more weeks and would need to continue on cortisone indefinitely. The doctor planned to inform him of these recommendations, at the same time indicating that the patient would have sufficient time to work through his plans with the social worker. It was anticipated that, should the patient maintain his improvement, he would be able to undertake employment which did not require undue exertion. The doctor also recommended employment near the hospital, if possible, as this would facilitate close observation and stabilization of his condition through proper control of medication.

The patient could not wait until his next scheduled interview to tell the worker with considerable enthusiasm that he had talked with his former landlady and arrangements were worked out for his return to her home. He also said he had given up the idea of loading milk cans as a form of employment. He referred to past employment in the hospital as a kitchen helper, which he had not mentioned before. There were other positions in the hospital that interested him, and despite some initial reluctance he stated that he would contact the personnel office.

In the next interview the patient spoke haltingly about his contacts with the personnel officer. When the worker assumed the initiative, indicating she sensed that things had not gone well, he felt freer to state that employment in the VA seemed doubtful in view of his discharge from his previous VA job because of unsatisfactory performance. It had hurt to be accused of laziness. He attributed his poor work performance to illness, though unaware of it at the time, and to preoccupation with inability to contribute adequate financial support to a sick brother. Since the doctor had told the worker that the illness of the patient had been of long duration and could easily have been responsible for work inefficiency, the worker, particularly because of the patient's guilt and defensiveness in this area, assured the patient, as did the doctor, that there was every reason medically to attribute his poor performance to his illness.

The patient went through a difficult waiting period before he learned definitely that his application for employment was not accepted but that he could appeal this decision. The regular contacts with the worker seemed to help him weather this period. During this period he reviewed many of his past hardships including references to racial prejudice, growing up in poverty, and the loss of both parents when he was a child.

When he learned of his rejection for employment, he requested a special appointment, which in summary went as follows:

He was in tears as he said he was sure that the personnel officer felt he was "no good." He was going to prove to this man that he could be a good worker! When I raised the question as to whom he wanted to prove this, he said he really wanted to prove it to himself. He was not really certain what part of his former inefficiency had been due to illness, and now that he was quite well he was uncertain and fearful about his ability to sustain a steady level of productivity. I commented that it was natural to be somewhat apprehensive about operating differently in the future. He went on to say that essentially for that reason he was also somewhat afraid of leaving the hospital. I indicated that this too was natural and was pleased he could tell me his feelings. It might be difficult in the beginning on a new job. He wondered what would happen if he became ill again, and I smilingly asked him why he would continue to have a problem in using the services of the hospital to get well. He stated that he would just hate to return. He'd have to experience all over again the pain, the leaving of work, the uncertainty, etc. He also felt that the doctor and I might be gone and all would be changed. I pointed out that this might be possible but emphasized his courage in the past in coming here even before he knew either the physician or me. He wondered whether people really liked him —maybe the doctor was interested in him only because it was part of his job. I said that he did have likeable qualities, and then wondered why he did follow the recommendations of the doctor. He said, "You know, I really love that doctor, but I guess the real reason is that I want to get well!" I pointed out that even though the attitudes of hospital personnel were important to him, his own attitudes about himself and his desire to get well were the most important. In a sense he answered his own question in then referring to how well he was getting along both with other patients and ward personnel.

The patient then again referred to his concern in regard to his rejection for employment. I said that since this continued to bother him he might want to consider making an appeal, especially if he felt he now did have the qualifications. He also knew definitely, as I did, that the doctor had reason to believe it was his illness that could be responsible for his slowness. We talked further about the appeal, and I pointed out that if he went through with it, he would of course take the risk of a double rejection. He then said with real determination that he had been used to evading responsibility. He could see that so much more clearly after talking with me; now, however, he did not want to "back off" any more and he felt he owed it to himself to follow through on the appeal because it would mean he would have the satisfaction of doing all he could himself. I complimented him on his taking this kind of responsibility for himself.

The patient then talked about the responsibilities he had assumed for years for his relatives. He began to question why he had looked out for them. It seemed that he was so loaded up with their obligations and concerns, he had no real future for himself. He spoke of how he was the only fairly responsible member of a "shiftless" family, and he did not even get to enjoy the fruits of his own labor. He thought it was time to take care of himself. He did not anticipate much of a problem, particularly, because his brother was receiving care in another hospital, and his sister, who was contemplating marriage anyway, had been able to get along without his help. I recognized that despite what he had said, it might have had some meaning for him to have some connection with his own family. He nodded silently.

The over-all objective of social work is to help people in trouble to assume maximum responsibility for their own feelings and actions. The medical social worker has the same goal in mind with particular reference to the patient's illness. In connection with illness, patients at times are handicapped by their social problems or they experience feelings that may interfere with the restoration or maintenance of health. The medical social worker, aware of the importance of the social factors in illness, attempted to help this patient sustain his health through planning toward a more stable social life and increasing his feeling of confidence in himself. Without these important social and personal anchors there is greater likelihood of a return to old patterns of impulsivity, flights from medical care, work inefficiency, and gnawing feelings of guilt, ending in physical and emotional deterioration.

Therefore, instead of impulsively trying to "prove" his inadequacy to someone else, it was important for the worker to help him localize the problem where it belonged—inside himself. Helping him bring out anxiety and doubts that he himself had did free him to consider objectively the choices he had, including the possibility of an appeal. Otherwise, there was the possibility of attempts at righteous justification that could prove unproductive. There is often considerable difference in the selection of a course of action, depending on whether one has to deny or can admit feelings of doubt and insecurity about the future.

In the same way, when the patient raised question in regard to whether people liked him, the worker, instead of becoming involved in a lengthy search for an answer, helped him to focus on, understand, and take responsibility for his own motivation and strength in getting well. When the patient again brought out his concern about his rejection for employment, the worker again, instead of encouraging the patient to bog down in his deep sense of guilt, helped him to take responsibility for constructive action. As a result, the patient ended up far from needing to prove his adequacy to others but on the keynote of maximum responsibility for himself regardless of outcome. It was hoped that this further evidence of a change in pattern would contribute to a more adequate adjustment in his personal, social, and occupational spheres.

Following the interview, the patient presented and won his appeal. He became much more active and energetic. He was able to find a future job as a kitchen helper in a restaurant near the hospital, at a salary higher than the hospital would pay him. It seemed to be important for him, psychologically as well as medically, to remain close to the hospital. He mentioned to the worker that his new confidence in himself was as important as his medication. He made a weekend visit to his landlady and cemented plans for living with her. He expressed some reluctance in leaving the hospital because in a sense, even for so short a period, the ward seemed like a home to him.

As the patient's confidence increased, he began to explore spontaneously the meaning of his relationship to siblings and his own place in relation to them. The worker recognized that in this he wanted to take more responsibility for his own welfare and yet indicated realistically that there might have been reasons (perhaps unknown to either at this point) for him to have some liaison with his family.

During the last week of the patient's hospitalization, he indicated that he wished to talk further about his family. He had been thinking of why they all seemed so "shiftless." Perhaps there were reasons for their behavior, just as he had learned there were reasons for his. Besides, they were really not doing so bad now. The patient was able to recognize that his relatives, like himself, at times did feel like quitting. They had recently invited him for a visit, and he was able to plan for this trip, feeling that they no longer did regard him as "lazy" since he himself was now more accepting of his own illness.

Returning from a trip to his family, the patient described his experience with eagerness and satisfaction. He found himself on much better terms with them than he had imagined. As he explained his illness to them, they were understanding and sympathetic, and he felt it was important to keep up some connection with them as they were "my family." They worked out without conflict an equitable arrangement to share expenses for the moving of the family graves.

In a team meeting the nurse and aide reported that the patient was increasing his social activities and participation in recreational events. He had been accompanying several patients to the canteen and had taken a special helpful interest in another wheelchair patient who had been depressed and lonely.

As the patient's condition was considered stabilized sufficiently for discharge, the physician indicated that his condition would remain chronic and would require medication indefinitely. The doctor planned to tell him either to return periodically to the hospital or to make arrangements for private out-patient care for observation of response to and control of medication. The patient was to avoid strenuous activity and adhere to a moderate living regime.

In the final interview, the patient was eager to leave. He indicated that he was feeling well for the first time in years. Together the patient and worker discussed specific plans for expanding his social activities by joining a service organization and participating in church social affairs.

Since the patient's discharge over a year ago, the worker has seen him occasionally at the restaurant where he has continued to work steadily. He was enjoying his work, and it was obvious that he was well respected by his employer. From time to time he made arrangements with the doctor for appropriate brief periods of hospitalization. These were essentially unproblematic and required no service from the social worker. He has told the worker that he had several enjoyable "reunions" with his family. His condition has remained good with continued medication. He managed to have a friend of his move into the same home with him, and both of them were quite active in the church. In addition, they had purchased an old car together and were spending leisure time fixing some of the parts. He was even beginning to do a little dancing for the first time. And he was active in a service organization.

According to a statement in a Veterans Administration publication, "the objective of any sound present-day hospital program is to promote the health of its patients through treatment of illness, prevention of its recurrence, rehabilitation and restoration to the optimum state of physical, emotional, and social health. This approach presupposes an understanding, by all the professional staff, of the patient as an individual functioning in his own particular environment. . . ." [1] The medical social worker in addition to basic knowledge regarding the functioning of human beings must have comprehensive understanding of medical problems and their relationship to personal and social factors. It is the

[1] Cohen, Ethel, "The Social Caseworker's Responsibilities in a Medical Residency Training Program." *Veterans Administration Technical Bulletin* TB10–505, Washington, D. C., Veterans Administration, November 2, 1950.

function of the medical social worker to focus on the modification of personal and social problems that predispose toward illness or interfere with maximum utilization of medical care. In carrying out this function it is important in collaboration with the physician to establish a purposeful relationship with the patient and to give additional service when indicated to relatives or other key figures in the life of the patient. It is also important for the worker to mobilize appropriate resources in the environment for use of the patient.

In the case illustration used here an initial major concern of both the patient and the hospital personnel was the uncertainty of diagnosis and treatment. In order effectively to treat the patient's condition, it was important first of all that he remain for continued hospitalization. Since personal problems related both to illness and emotional conflict interfered with effective use of medical care, the social worker attempted to modify these problems. With her understanding of the basic needs of the patient and his tendency toward avoidance and denial, she was able to help him recognize rather than repress his feelings in regard to his illness and hospitalization. The illness had revived deeper feelings of inadequacy and conflict in regard to expression of dependency needs. Continuous supportive contacts with the worker, focused toward helping the patient assume responsibility for his actions and plans for the future, contributed toward a permissible gratification of his dependency needs and an increase in his self-confidence.

Despite the sudden improvement of the patient's condition, additional anxieties and fears converged to plant new seeds of self-doubt. As the patient was helped further to recognize the validity of his dependency needs with increasing comfort, he then was able to think more realistically about social plans for the future.

In order to "anchor" the life of the patient and to facilitate his carrying out the major medical recommendations of limited employment and regular and careful administration of medication, it was essential that he maintain a satisfying personal and social life. The social worker, therefore, helped him see that, instead of fighting the need to be cared for, it was to his physical and emotional advantage to make arrangements for his future care. He was then able to spend his energies in working out a favorable social situation which had in part been intolerable to him previously. At the same time the resultant increase in confidence permitted him to follow through with his appeal on employment, not so much to obtain work but as a symbolic indication of his newly found ability to act responsibly in his own behalf.

Having settled some major personal problems within himself, the patient was not only able to make satisfactory living arrangements for himself but was able to work out a new relationship to his own family. After years of isolation from and negative feelings toward his family, he was able to see them in a new light. At the same time, both while in the hospital and after discharge, he was able to expand his social and recreational activities. Although the continuing medical problem of the patient imposed limitations on the patient, he was able to live comfortably with these limitations. His life now had more stability, purpose, and richness in relation to others, and these important social assets have helped sustain his physical and emotional health.

chapter 11

The Correctional Services

Individualization and the Court

Criminal courts existed before institutionalized social services. Long before the time of the Elizabethan Poor Laws English courts had been dealing with the offender. By the time social work had begun to be a profession in this country the courts already had established a fixed pattern of administering criminal justice. If the charity organization movement of the last quarter of the nineteenth century is taken as the starting point of professionalized social work, it at once becomes clear how late, comparatively speaking, it appeared on the scene.

It is important to recognize this late appearance of social work in order to understand the slow headway it made in its approach to the court. The criminal court is essentially, and perhaps necessarily, a conservative, slow-changing social structure. It is little wonder then with over a thousand years of precedent and practice behind it that the court resisted the introduction of any new ideas or new ways from a profession just beginning to emerge. Furthermore, the very eagerness of the newer workers to insist upon the welfare of the individual as well as society as a whole must not have sounded very convincing to judges and lawyers who felt the court had always done that very thing. It may be said, by way of explanation, that in this early period social work had crystallized neither its philosophy nor its practice. Fervid convictions and enthusiasms, coupled with an evangelical zeal to help, were hardly tangible or impressive enough to be of much use to the court that had heretofore managed to get along alone. It is not surprising, therefore, in view of the lack of concrete contributions by social workers and the tendency of the court to hold to an ancient groove that very little resulted from this early contact.

An approach which proved more fruitful following this early period was the one which directed the energies of the sensitively minded lay person and the professionally interested social worker toward the establishment of a specialized service for the juvenile delinquent. When these two groups joined with court and administrative officials who were seeking a way to avoid the rigors of the conventional criminal court, the way was opened to a new departure in dealing with the offender. This did not happen suddenly. For the better part of a century the handling of younger offenders had been undergoing change. The establishment of houses of reform for juveniles was an early instance, as was also the modification of penalties for acts committed by minors. Later provision was made for separate hearings for juveniles, and later still the use of probation.

The Juvenile Court

Illinois enacted the first juvenile court law in July 1899. As early as 1891 a juvenile court bill had been introduced into the Illinois legislature, but it required eight years of effective education and support before the final measures drafted by Judge Harvey B. Hurd emerged as the world's first juvenile court law. The new law which provided for separate detention, separate and private hearings, and probation brought under one jurisdiction all cases involving delinquent, neglected, and dependent children. This was not the first time that the child had received special consideration. For years there had been a variety of services available for those children who were so readily grouped into the categories of the dependent, the neglected, or the destitute. The Courts of Chancery in England long had stood, whenever necessity demanded, in the place of the parent to safeguard the interests of the growing child and the future citizen. However, the child over 7 years of age who was delinquent or criminal did not share this protection. Let him commit a criminal offense, and the law quickly seized him and dealt with him as with any other offender.

All of this was true until the establishment of the first juvenile court in America in 1899. Under the common law of England children under 7 years of age were deemed incapable of entertaining the requisite criminal intent, between 7 and 14 years of age this presumption could be rebutted, i.e., established by the prosecution that the child was capable of entertaining a criminal intent, and over 14 years of age the child stood trial as an adult offender. These rules of law applied in the American colonies and later in the states as they were formed, either as part of the common law or of the statute law which was based upon the common law. However, with the creation of the juvenile court the chancery or equity principles (as they are more commonly called) were applied not only to the dependent, the neglected, or the destitute child, but also to the delinquent child under 16 years.

A socialized court, of which the juvenile court was the earliest example, concerns itself with the individual. It wants to know before court hearing by objective examination what kind of person the offender is. This becomes an essential part of the court process in arriving at a full understanding of the individual, the offense, and the present situation in order to determine what is the best plan to follow. This end is referred to as treatment rather than punishment and is a service which the individual can use in effecting his own adjustments within himself and in relation to other people and the community in which he lives.

The juvenile court has not been without its effect on other courts— the family court, and even the criminal court. Within recent years there has been an increasing recognition of the interrelatedness of persons within the family grouping and especially the problems that beset them. Family courts have been instituted in which a more individualized consideration can be given to family members and their problems by the judge and his probation staff. Much more emphasis can thus be placed upon understanding the difficulties within the family and of the skills needed to help. At the same time none of the conventional safeguards bearing on the legal rights of persons is in any wise sacrificed or jeopardized. These legal rights have been fought for during a thousand years and should not be abandoned or seriously modified through well-intentioned efforts to help. Individuals (and that means juveniles as well) need to have assured to them all of the rights to which they are entitled and at the same time have available to them services which will strengthen their wills and capacities to do something about the troubles that brought them to court. Likewise is this true insofar as the court for the trial of the adult criminal is concerned. No matter how well intentioned the court staff may be in wanting to help the offender, it is fundamental that all his legal rights be assured to him. All of this must be borne in mind in the discussion that follows concerning social services within the correctional framework.

Probation

Although the use of probation has been associated most closely with the juvenile court, actually it antedated the court by many years. As early as 1841 a Boston shoemaker, John Augustus, had begun as a sort of volunteer probation officer when he served as surety for a confirmed drunkard. In 1878, twenty-one years before the first juvenile court, adult probation was undertaken officially in Boston, and within two years the authorization was statewide. From that time until the present each of the 48 states has authorized adult probation, and since the initiation of the juvenile court in 1899, every state has made provision for juvenile probation. The federal probation service, begun in 1925, has developed into a national service for adults and juveniles involved in federal offenses.

The basic elements in the probation process are pre-sentence investigation and supervision. These in turn are based upon an adequate understanding of and insight into human personality and behavior. Indeed, the indispensable equipment of the probation officer, as of all social workers, is this knowledge and awareness of the human being as he is, with all of his feelings, attitudes, ideas, motivations, strengths, and weaknesses.

What is the worker's understanding of delinquent or criminal behavior? How purposive is the behavior of the offender? What are the individual's basic needs and what satisfactions is he seeking? To what extent is his behavior symptomatic, and symptomatic of what? Does the worker realize the necessity for understanding the uniqueness of each individual personality and of the attempts of each individual to make his adjustment in line with his own capacities and the environment in which he happens to be? By whose standards does the worker judge the offender? Is there an arbitrary, fixed standard applicable to all? Does the standard of the worker as it has developed under different circumstances and in a different personality become the standard which must be imposed upon other people? Can the worker differentiate himself sufficiently from the group of which he has always been a part and proceed to function in a helping relationship with individuals who have broken with the mores of that group? These are real questions to the worker in the probation, parole, or the correctional institution field. The attitude toward such questions and the working answers made to them determine to a large extent the approach of the probation officer to people and his effectiveness in working with them.

There is another aspect to this matter of understanding criminal behavior that may be overlooked too easily in our desire to reach deep into the personality of the offender. After all, the individual does not live in a vacuum; he has his relations with other people, he lives in a certain neighborhood and house, he has a job or he hasn't a job, but nevertheless he lives in a workaday world, he has leisure time interests, clubs, hangouts. All of these may be spoken of as influences outside of or external to the individual, but which nevertheless may have their effect upon him. The lack of a job, particularly over a long enough period of time, may have a good deal to do with whether a man suffers enough deterioration to turn to other ways of securing satisfactions or what he considers his rightful share of the world's goods. The prevalence of boys' predatory gangs in a neighborhood may not be without relation to the inclination of a given youngster to follow the crowd to gain some satisfaction otherwise denied to him. Living in a slum neighborhood in what is blithely referred to as substandard housing may have nothing to do with the formation of attitudes toward criminal behavior; on the other hand, it may. What must be obvious from these remarks is the interrelatedness of both the personality and the environmental factors. Individuals develop personality characteristics on the basis of their innate physiological equipment, the experiences which beset them from birth on and the relationships which they establish with other human beings and social institutions that surround them. After all it is an individual, not a house or a neighborhood that commits an offense, and to understand the offender one needs to comprehend the individual in his social setting.

The "How" of the Pre-Sentence Investigation. What is the purpose of a pre-sentence investigation? How does a probation officer go about making it, what does he look for, and what does he do with what he has obtained? These may seem simple enough questions, but it is only when the probation officer is clear about his function that he can act responsibly in this very important and critical stage in the probation relationship. It must be recognized, for instance, that probation can prove most helpful when it is conceived of and executed as a casework service. If this is understood, then it follows that the first interviews with the offender are vitally important and may do much toward setting the tone and quality of the subsequent worker-client relationship. The process of probation begins with the first interview of the pre-sentence investigation and continues until final discharge from probation.

Granting that this becomes a working conviction, importance attaches to *how* the investigation is conducted. A pre-sentence investigation might otherwise be an inquisition, a cross-examination, an extension, or a refinement of the prosecuting attorney's tactics. What it can be is an exploration together of the situation in which the individual finds himself. What are his personality needs, what relation do they bear to the trouble he got himself into, what potentialities does he have within himself to go to work on his difficulties or to avail himself of what probation has to offer? What are the factors in his environmental setting that may have had something to do with the delinquency or crime, what of his marital and family relationships, the kind of neighborhood he lives in, his employment experience, his associates, his connections with church, club or other activities? What does clearance with the social service exchange show of this individual or of his family?

After data concerning the individual and his situation has been gathered, it must be evaluated. At this juncture the probation officer is face to face with the question: Is this man probation material? The answer is not to be undertaken lightly. It is not a matter of whether there is an ailing wife or baby at home, or of a job hanging on the outcome, or of repeated pledges to sin no more. There may be sickness at home, a job may be waiting, conscience may have struck the man sore; but unless the probation officer can convince himself that, in the light of the potentialities of the individual and of the situation, the offender can utilize what probation has to offer, he is in no wise justified in recommending probation. For the probation officer to act otherwise would be to do a disservice to the offender, to be unfair to the court, to betray his profession, and be untrue to himself. So much of this depends in turn upon what it is that probation has to offer. For a probation officer to recommend probation must mean a faith in his own skills and in the essential helpfulness of his profession. In short, he must have a conviction of probation as a casework service, and security within his own competence as a social caseworker.

If the probation officer recommends probation he should do so if he feels the man can profit more by supervision in a free society than by imprisonment. The probation officer should also feel that the man has begun to come to grips with himself and with the world of people and things around him, and that the man is willing and able to do something about his difficulties with the help of the probation officer. The officer must recognize that some individuals are not able or ready to do this, and that for them there may be no alternative but imprisonment. Some offenders may only be able to profit during a prison experience or afterward. Imprisonment need not of itself be an unmitigated evil.

After the investigation is made and the probation officer's reports are in, the judge exercises his judgment in deciding whether to grant probation. If a juvenile court hearing has been held, the judge probably gets a fairly well-rounded picture of the child and of the situation, but this is unlikely if there has been a trial of an adult offender. The prosecuting attorney has presented the facts with a view to conviction; the defense, to acquittal. The judge is thus left in the anomalous position of supposedly knowing all about the offender when really he has nothing but contradictions with which to work. The probation investigation preserves what must otherwise be an arbitrary, no matter how well-intentioned, judgment. The better the probation officer has done his job the more enlightened a decision the judge can come to consistent with the needs of the individual. The probation officer owes this service as much to the court as to the offender, because it is only through the court, at this point, that the individual is reached.

Authority in Relation to Probation. The worker who knows what he is doing, recognizes that authority has real value in a casework relationship with the offender, and that it is a necessary part of the judicial and probation function. He will really need to have more than an intellectual acceptance of this; he will need to "feel it in his bones" and have it be a part of the way he works with probationers. How otherwise could he reconcile for himself or the probationer the modern concept of individualized treatment with the age-long traditional attitude of vindictiveness against the offender? Without it how could the probation officer explain in language that made sense the imposition of requirements by the court?

From the very outset the competent probation officer will realize that authority defines the area within which he and the probationer will work. There are certain requirements set up by the court that the probationer will have to live up to,[1] and if there is too great a deviation from these rules, the court may use other more drastic means of control. The probation officer sees himself as an agent of the court. The probationer sees him as the delegated authority of the court. It is here that the worker will want to be clear on his own role. Is he the court? Is he indistinguishable from the court? Does he embody the total authority of the court? Is he so caught in the web of authority that he is helpless to aid the probationer? The answer to these questions reaches to the very core of the probation function.

The Use of Limits. To simplify the analysis it will be well to examine the situation presented by a 15-year-old boy who has committed an offense. The very act of delinquency has reference to this matter of limits, for it may well be an expression of the inability of the boy to accept any kind of limits. Or it may indicate the need of some limits in order to achieve a working balance between the impulses within him and the demands which the community makes upon him. The overt delinquent act may signify the child's need for help with those limits. The child comes to the attention of the juvenile court and the probation officer. How can the court with all of its power, authority, and awesomeness for the child help with the problem which the child is presenting? If we are perfectly honest with ourselves and with all due respect to the court, we are obliged to doubt whether the court can be very useful were it to impose its total authority upon the child and compel him to be good. The child already has known the total authority of the community and has not been able to make his adjustment, nor will the imposition of the total authority of the court accomplish what the com-

---

[1] These rules may require regular reports from the probationer, regular work, regular hours, no operation of an automobile without permission of the probation officer, no marriage without permission, staying within the district or state unless granted permission to leave, etc.

munity has failed to do so far. This is not to deny the utility of the court but merely recognize its limitations without the right arm of probation. Basically the child cannot make use of the total authority of the court because the court seeks to impose too total a restraint upon the child for the responsibility for his act. The court in effect says: "You have broken the law of this community; the community has charged this court with the duty of dealing with you; we therefore command you to be good." The child's answer to this is to slough off any responsibility for improving himself and to defy the court to change him.

When, however, the court breaks up this totality and places a part with an agency and an agency which it has created for the purpose, a situation is produced whereby the child can begin to take help. Here is where the probation officer comes forward. The probation department is part of the court structure, it has certain duties to perform, it operates within certain statutory and functional limits. If probation is to serve the child helpfully, it must break up this totalness and separate itself from it and yet be a part of that authority. This is more than a mere playing with words. When probation has achieved that separateness, it can let the child know that the court has referred him to the probation officer for help which the child is free to accept or not. This places the decision squarely where it belongs—upon the child. The child may reject the offer of help and defy the probation officer to make him good. The probation officer may exercise all of his skill, but the decision whether to take help or not is still the child's. The child can so act as to have his probation revoked, and be committed to an institution for more restrictive treatment. If, on the other hand, the effect of the worker's definition of help has been to enable the boy to make the choice to accept responsibility for his conduct, then the two of them together have started work on the boy's difficulties. The delinquent act is a putting outside of the self of the child the responsibility for himself. Refusing the offer of help still keeps it outside. Accepting the probation officer's challenge may for the first time in the boy's life mean admitting his own share in what he is, and what he does, and why. Once the decision is made, the worker's task consists not in making the boy good, but in helping the boy to face and work through his share of the problem. Having really faced authority and accepted what it means, the delinquent is freer to work within it constructively rather than to be blindly fighting it all the time.

This extended discussion has aimed to develop the thesis that probation functions within a definite framework of authority; that authority is positively and creatively useful as it provides an occasion for and a way of dealing with limits; that genuine change comes from within when the individual is ready to take responsibility for himself. Basic to all of this is the quality of service the probation officer offers, which is functionally related to his conviction that many individuals in trouble can be helped to achieve an adjustment within themselves and to the demands of the community in which they live. This implies a belief on the part of the probation officer in the capacity of individuals to assume some responsibility for their own lives.

All that has been written here, while illustrative of the probation procedures of working with a juvenile delinquent, is just as applicable to the adult offender. The chief difference may be that the process seems more difficult with the older offender because he is more set in his ways and less amenable to suggestions. He seldom has the frankness and directness of the child or his uninhibited responses. The process may be much slower with the adult and there may be fewer dramatic transformations, but once the adult takes hold of himself, it is likely to be more lasting because of his greater stability and the reality of the everyday demands put upon him.

The Worker's Awareness of Himself and of His Service. The probation officer who possesses an awareness of the needs of the probationer and of the process by which those needs are met will already be familiar with the importance of the early probation interviews. This he will have demonstrated in his pre-sentence work. However, the very fact that probation has been granted, introduces an element of difference into the situation. The authority that probation expresses has defined and set a limit to the relationship. The probationer will need to know the nature of that relationship and what are its bounds. This the probation officer gets over not so much by what he says as by what he does and how he does it. The worker, for example, who approaches the offender with a punishing or vindictive attitude can put into words all the things probation should be, and yet by his very acts undo everything he has said. This is related very definitely to the worker's understanding of himself, of his emotional responses, his philosophy of casework, and the standards he has set for himself. Nowhere does this come out more clearly than in his authoritative relations to others. The worker who in his own developmental experience has not made his peace with authority can be of only limited help to the individual whose struggle is so largely with authority.

Likewise, the worker, let us say, whose own childhood suffered because of a father's desertion, may find it difficult, unless he has undergone the discipline of training, to deal understandably with a probationer who has deserted or is on the point of deserting his family. Another worker, who has never achieved the security of his own personality because he has never been able to make the emotional break from his family, may not be of much help to the individual who has already established his emotional independence. By contrast, the worker who is still going through the process of emancipation may identify himself so closely with his probationer who is undergoing the same experience that for all practical purposes the two of them are engaged in the same struggle. The one who is supposed to be exercising a helping function has become as helpless as the one he was to help. Instead of there being a worker and a client, there are now two clients and no worker. The individual who has never struggled through to a comfortable affectional relationship with another person may transfer his self-torture to the probationer who has not achieved any more balance in that struggle. All of this is a bit on the heavy analytical side, but it is pertinent to a casework relationship because so much of the worker's effectiveness depends upon the degree to which he has attained satisfaction in working out his own difficulties, personal and professional.

The Person and the Environment. It is necessary to emphasize the need for a balanced service to the probationer. Not every individual who commits a crime is engaged in an acute personality conflict within himself. Social workers will do well to acquaint themselves with the important role which cultural factors, material and nonmaterial, play in our everyday lives. Sociologists and anthropologists for years have been studying the interrelationships of personality and culture, and have accumulated a tremendous wealth of knowledge that has real pertinence for workers whose jobs bring them into touch with people's lives under every situation. Sociologists have long since established a case for the relativity of standards and values. They have shown over and over again that what the mores dictate to be "moral" or "right" in one place may not obtain elsewhere. Students of human culture have made a clear distinction between folkways and mores that would be helpful to some social workers who are only too willing to set up moral standards for other people or for other communities.

Some probation service may be directed toward help for the individual offender with his personality difficulties, and some may be directed toward environmental factors. A probation officer may learn early in his interviews that the probationer needs psychiatric treatment and will make a referral to the proper agency, if such exists. If no psychiatrist is available, the worker will nevertheless need to stay within his own probation function, giving such services as he can and that fall within the function of the court. In many instances the probation officer will deal with tangible services—jobs, for instance. Most workers know that obtaining a job for which the probationer is qualified means much in helping him to get on his feet. It often gives him a sense of belonging, of accomplishing something that furnishes the stability to carry on. The worker may need to keep in touch with the employer from time to time, or he may decide that it is better to keep out of the way. Most probation officers and probationers find it best to make clear to the employer the status of the employee rather than to let him carry around the weight of possible disclosure at any time. There may be other services to render, such as helping with living arrangements in a suitable neighborhood, or helping to establish leisure-time or recreational outlets, or with church, school, or vocational training contacts. Very frequently there may be occasion for referral to other social agencies, such as a family society, a child guidance clinic, the social service department of a hospital. The worker may also need to bring to the attention of the probationer or his family the services of governmental agencies such as departments of public welfare. These services are offered not because the probation officer must always be doing things *for* people, but because he, rather than the probationer, is the one who should be acquainted with all of the facilities of the community. The final decision to avail himself of these services is the probationer's not the worker's.

Interviews and Interviewing. Every probation officer, whether he has a small or a large case load, must develop his own way of conducting interviews. Much of the effectiveness of the interviews depends upon the worker's approach. A not uncommon practice of untrained probation officers is to direct the lives of their probationers. What seems to give sanction to such a practice is the obvious fact that the individual by his very act of transgressing the law has shown his inability to manage his own life, and hence what is more natural than to tell him what to do, to make the decisions for him which will oblige him to conform? Furthermore, the very injunction of the court to report any serious violation of probation seems to make it all the more imperative to keep the offender good. Despite the plausibility of this position, there is a fundamental contradiction inherent in it. The one unmistakable conclusion about the offender is that he needs help in accepting responsibility for his behavior. For someone else to direct his life means that the worker has robbed the client of the decision for his own life. This might be very well if probation officers supervised the offenders throughout their lifetime, but the real fact is that all probationers finish with probation at some time either successfully and by discharge or by failure and commitment. Some day the individual will need to make his own decisions, and the surest way to prepare him for that day is to help him while he is under supervision. Another aspect of this question pertains to what is happening to the individual when another person makes his decisions for him. Instead of the probationer carrying the responsibility for his decisions, he can always shift it over on the probation officer who made them. Thus the very opposite of the probation objective is accomplished; instead of helping the individual to do more for himself the probation officer makes it possible for him to do less.

Although there are general principles of helping the individual effect adjustments within himself and to the community in which he lives, there exists no formula for probation interviews. What goes on in the interview is governed by the help which the probationer needs and can use and the capacity of the worker to meet those needs. No doubt there are many instances in which the client will avoid his share of the interview by keeping it at a superficial level. According to him, everything is all right, the job is fine, affairs at home are fine, etc. All of which may be true, and the probation officer does not search for mountains where there are not even traces of mole hills. On the other hand, everything may not be all right, and the statement that all is well may be simply a refusal to face his difficulties. At this point the probationer will need more help.

Interviews may be held either in the probation office or in the home of the probationer. There are certain advantages to an office interview; it affords privacy, it places the interview in a professional setting, and it calls for a certain amount of initiative and exertion on the part of the probationer as something which he puts into the occasion. A home interview enables the supervisor to get a view of the man in his home setting and may make possible a more comfortable relationship for the client. This latter, the comfortableness of an interview, is not always determined by the setting. No matter how hard a supervisor may try there are probationers who can never be made comfortable; the capacity must be within the person. Continued home visits may relieve the probationer of some of the responsibility which attaches to probation. Probation is not simply a *doing to* someone else, it is a *doing with,* and a probationer may feel that all he needs to do is to wait for the worker's visit in order to be told what to do or what not to do. Most probation officers find a combination of home and office visits to be desirable, possibly alternately.

A third kind of reporting besides office and home interviews is common to probation supervision: monthly reports by mail. If the worker sometimes has reservations about his knowledge of what is happening with the probationer whom he sees in the office or in the home, how much more must he be skeptical of monthly reports that consistently affirm that all goes well? What probationer who has only a one-way contact with his worker is ever going to report anything else? This comment does not overlook the regulations, local, state, and federal, that require such a system of reporting, but it does look to the matter of its effectiveness. Suppose the individual were in difficulty, how would he get help from the supervisor? The offender who needs help seldom can communicate it by mail. A long-continued practice of mail reporting hardly encourages or justifies an appeal for help. If a probation department holds to its rule of mail reporting, let it not delude itself, the workers, or the probationers. It is never a satisfactory substitute for a personal interview.

Revocation of Probation. Not all probation is successful. Sometimes the probationer does not make the grade. At least two people are involved, the worker and the probationer, and whether success attends their efforts depends upon many factors, some within and some outside of their control. In the first place, there is the probationer himself and his suitability for probation as revealed in the pre-sentence investigation. Assuming for the moment that probation has been granted with a reasonably hopeful prognosis, there may still be other items that are essential to helping the offender. Without question the most vital of these is the quality of casework service which the probation officer can render. The resources within the community, the job opportunities, the presence or absence of recreational, cultural or social outlets, the attitude of relatives, friends, employers, and the community may have a good deal to do with whether the probationer can get hold of, and keep hold of, himself. The individual's adjustments do not happen of their own accord. They are earned within a reasonably helpful community setting with the combined efforts of the worker and client. Sometimes there is not enough help from the community, sometimes not enough from the probation officer, or sometimes there is not quite enough material to work with, especially in view of how little we know about human behavior.

Unquestionably, the probation officer must face several questions such as: What help have I been able to give the probationer? What help has he been able to take? What help does probation still have to offer this individual? In short, has he made sufficient progress on probation so that even in the face of a defection, he could still profit by the probation experience? So much of the answer to this question depends upon the faith which the worker has in probation. If probation is merely a prelude to imprisonment and a kind of club to be held over the head of the probationer, then the worker can force a certain degree of conformity without reaching to the problem at all. If, therefore, the probationer violates probation, the obvious step to take is to revoke. It may too easily be overlooked that the very failure of the probation may be not so much the probationer's as the worker's. Or, it may be that the individual has not been able to use what the probation officer has to offer and the decision to revoke will have to be made on that basis. The important point which must be borne in mind is that the probation officer must understand the basis of the decision to revoke; whether it is his own lack of professional skill or the inability of the probationer to benefit by probation, or the lack of community facilities which may militate against successful probation.

Community Attitude Toward Violation. A very real situation which every probation officer encounters at one time or another is the attitude of the community toward the violation, or more particularly, the violator of probation. There may be instances in which the nature of the violation may be especially reprehensible to the community, and yet in the opinion of the probation officer not of such a kind as to preclude a successful outcome. Specifically, a juvenile delinquent may have been placed on probation following some rather spectacular escapades which were shocking to the community. He is having a hard time on probation, but in the opinion of the supervisor he is beginning to take hold. However, sometimes the struggle becomes too hard and during one of those spells he backslides and commits another offense. The probation officer still feels the boy can profit by probation, but the public is demanding swift retribution. Shall the probation officer yield, or does he really have a conviction the boy can still take some help? Indeed, the worker may see the relapse as rather naturally related to the growth process that is taking place in the individual's struggle with probation. In such a situation the worker may be willing to stand by his professional guns, admitting that his primary consideration is the welfare of the probationer, which means protecting the progress he has already made. At this point the probation officer should submit an objective report, evaluating the recent criminal offense in the light of the probation experience as a preliminary consideration for the court.

One might just as well be realistic at this point and admit that a probation officer who differed with the court constantly would advance neither the cause of probation nor himself. The same dilemma springs up here as it does in every phase of social casework. The caseworker has developed by training and experience a certain competence in the field of human relationships as well as certain convictions about the values of social casework for the individual in need. Occasionally there is the making of a conflict between that point of view and a lay or community point of view as reflected, let us say, in the agent of the community, in this instance the court. The worker may choose to surrender all principle and run, or he may see his job as holding to his convictions, using his skill in trying to make clear his position, and then accepting with good grace the final verdict if it goes against him. No one can ask more of him, and professionally he has permitted the decision to be made where it belongs. If trained workers do not stand by professional principles, who will? Or who will bother to advance them? In few areas is this truer or more clearly illustrated than in probation, parole, and in correctional institutions where the worker is already dealing with society's scapegoat.

Casework in a Correctional Institution

It is recognized that the present state of knowledge of human behavior does not permit the abandonment of any of the three most common correctional institutions: the reform (or training) school, the reformatory or industrial school, and the prison. Despite the many enthusiasms for the ideal of probation, neither community opinion nor professional practice has yet succeeded in outmoding institutional care and treatment of the offender. Social workers, realizing that the institution will be here for a long time and convinced that casework has real utility wherever there is a human and social need, have pressed for the use of casework in an institution setup. Instead of being willing to relegate the offender to the dump heap, they have contended that offenders who have not been granted probation or those whose probation has been revoked have perhaps greater need than ever for an individualized help. Without any illusions about the institution furnishing an ideal setting for casework the social worker recognizes that there is still a valuable service to render within the limits of a correctional framework. Limits are recognized as a part of the reality situations facing both worker and client, and yet those very limits within an institution can be used constructively as a part of the casework process.[2]

Provision has been made for casework services within some state re-

2 For a penetrating analysis of the use of limits and of the larger area of the use of social casework in correctional services see: Pray, Kenneth L. M., "The Place of Social Case Work in the Treatment of Delinquency." *Social Service Review*, XIX, June 1945, pp. 235–244; Pray, Kenneth L. M., "The Principles of Social Case Work as Applied to Probation and Parole." *Federal Probation*, IX, April–June 1945, pp. 14–18; Pray, Kenneth L. M., "Social Work in the Prison Program." *Federal Probation*, VII, October–December 1943, pp. 3–7; see also Rappaport, Mazie F., "The Possibility of Help for the Child Returning from a State Training School." *Journal of Social Work Process*, V, 1954, pp. 21–46.

formatories and prisons and in most of the federal reformatories and prisons. In these institutions the usual plan calls for a social service department or at least a social caseworker whose work is co-ordinated with that of the other departments. The services of these departments, medical, psychological, educational and vocational, religious, parole, and social service, are in many instances considered vital to the functioning of the institutional organization. Wardens and superintendents have learned, as judges have with probation officers, that the social caseworker instead of being a necessary nuisance may actually have something useful to contribute.

By the time the offender has come to the institution he has had his brush with the law, i.e., the police, jail, and the court. He is not exactly anxious to hear the final clamp of the gates behind him signalizing his separation from family, home, friends, neighborhood, and possibly job. He comes very often with feelings of hatred that may either lie smoldering during his incarceration only to flare up vindictively upon his release, or which may burst out uncontrollably once imprisonment is a fact. It is early in his institutional career that he meets the social worker, possibly during his thirty-day quarantine period and as a prelude to the first classification clinic. He may carry bitterness and antagonism into his early interviews, much of it directed at the social worker and indicating inability to face the authority that crowds all around him and with which he never managed to make his peace when he was free. Or he may bury his feelings, distrusting any member of the prison staff, and refuse to let the worker gain any entrée into his real self.

The competent social caseworker realizes that he cannot force the inmate to get out his feelings, that it may take time for the individual to realize that the social worker is there to help him with his difficulties. In the initial interview the caseworker may be able to help the prisoner to express some of his feelings that have been pent up within him—to permit even the hostile explosiveness against all forms of authority. It may not be until he has faced some of his own projections that the prisoner can begin to make some constructive use of the time he has ahead of him. The reassurance that social casework is a helping service may need to be more than verbal. The person who has gotten as far as prison is rather distrustful of people who are supposed to help.

He mistrusts everyone connected with authority. On the other hand, for the first time in his life the individual, in view of what seems his hopeless plight, may actually face his need for help. Part of the worker's job will be to determine how much help the inmate needs, how much he can take, and, just as importantly, how much the worker and the institution can offer. Not infrequently the worker may misjudge any or all of these and so overwhelm the inmate with the offer of help as to make it impossible for him to take anything.

Perhaps the essential role which the social worker exercises has never been put as clearly or as arrestingly as by Richard Farrow when he wrote: "The most important discovery I have made about my job as a private agency social worker operating in prison is that if I am to be of help to prisoners, the main focus of my job will be not in getting them out of, but rather helping them get *into* prison." [3] The facing of the fact that he is in prison, and why, and then moving on to using that time and experience constructively are the areas in which the prisoner needs help. It is here that the social worker can be of real usefulness.

In many instances the inmate is likely to express his needs about concrete situations such as the way he left things at home, or the job he left behind, or some detail of institutional life such as change of work assignments, or living quarters, or a suspected discrimination against him in privileges. The basis of these complaints may be real and may furnish a specific issue upon which the caseworker and the inmate can work together. After this is cleared up, there may still remain the basic need which brought him to the worker. This may be some difficulty he may be having within himself, as evidenced by his inability to get along with his fellows, or with the guards, or to accept the authority of the institution. Or it may be related to his difficulties at home, of his struggle for independence which becomes all the clearer as he sees in retrospect a connection between the trouble he got into and the conflict that has been going on at home between him and his parents. It may require an experience in a reformatory or prison to bring close to him what is really happening.

The caseworker can rarely indulge in the energetic manipulation so often possible to the worker in outside agencies, who manages, as

---

[3] Farrow, Richard G., "The Basic Problem of Penal Administration." *Prison Journal,* XXII, April 1942, p. 202.

Gordon Hamilton puts it, to confuse effort with effectiveness. Instead he works with such intangibles as the inmate's attitudes and feelings toward his crime, his sentence, his presence here in the prison. The worker directs himself to a clarifying of the problem to the point where the individual is able to do something about it, and to cease putting the blame for his difficulties on to other people. What holds the worker to bed rock is the conviction that his function is to help the client with his problem without taking it from him.

The classification clinic, where such exists, affords an opportunity for the caseworker to be of help to the inmate. In the steps from arrest, to detention, to trial, to imprisonment the offender seldom meets with any individual consideration. All along he is one of a mass of criminals. Perhaps for the first time he comes to learn inside the institution that a worker exists who can help him with some of his difficulties. The individual interview which the caseworker has with each new inmate for the purpose of learning what program may best be worked out with him may open the possibility of further interviews. At least it indicates that there is available a worker to whom he may go. This is especially important in relation to the inmate's adaptation to the institution. The classification system sets as its object the fitting of the individual into the institutional scheme, and, so far as is practicable, the adaptation of the institution to the individual. It is an attempt at individualization in a mass situation, to offer proper job placement, educational training, housing and recreational facilities, and contacts with home. As such it must take into account the equipment of the inmate as well as his personality needs, and it is in this area of assisting the inmate in making the institutional adjustment that the social worker functions.[4]

Preparation for Release. Not the least important of the social services of a correctional institution is helping the prisoner to move toward release. In view of the variations in commitment and release practices there is considerable leeway as to the uses which the institution may make of the indeterminate sentence. It may use it destructively as a threat, compelling the inmate to submit to the institutional regime, or it may use it constructively as a means whereby the individual works on his own problem and prepares himself for release. Destructively used,

[4] See Pray, Kenneth L. M., "Parole in Relation to Classification and Case Work in Prison." *Yearbook of the National Probation Association,* 1944, pp. 182–195.

the institution undoubtedly will get conformity, perhaps only after the individual has rebelled, been quelled, and then has decided to play the waiting game. The inmate can conform, he can deny his part in making use of the institution, he can throw the responsibility for any change in him upon others, in short he can put everything outside of himself and refuse to get anything out of the experience. Nor is this reaction to the reformatory or prison regime surprising because it is only too common for such institutions to produce good prisoners but not well-integrated personalities. This may show up in the overwillingness with which an inmate "accepts" plans made for him as part of the classification and reclassification scheme or as a prelude to parole but which leaves the bases of his difficulties untouched.

Constructively used, the experience permits the individual to be faced with his share in the difficulty which brought him to the institution and to take some part in assuming responsibility for his own change or self-improvement. This unquestionably is a much harder job than conformity, for it may need to be done in spite of the institutional regime. It may also be done in the face of the distrust and disapproval of fellow prisoners to whom taking help may be interpreted as a "squealing" or a "selling out," a "breaking of the code." It requires extraordinary courage to be willing, within one's self, to change when those all around want to help in effecting that change; it calls for much more when such willingness to change is not supported and is even aggressively challenged by persons in the environment which is as closely lived as in prison. A competent social worker will recognize that although the decision as to how long he will stay is to a large degree the inmate's, nevertheless it is a decision that carries a degree of responsibility with which the individual may need help. Some inmates who have looked toward freedom from the day they entered prison actually when faced with freedom within a short time may feel unable to bring themselves to it without assistance. To the average citizen this must sound like sheer nonsense, but to the individual who has fitted too easily into the comfortable and relatively effortless regimentation of the institution it may be a rather threatening prospect to contemplate the insecurity of the outside world with all of its demands upon initiative, decisions, and responsibility.

Not only may the social worker help the inmate with his decisions but he may enable the offender to use in a positive way the experience of imprisonment and of leaving. There is a certain amount of pain that goes with such an experience that no one can take away from the individual, nor would. There is also a certain amount of frustration that comes of the blocking of normal impulses in an abnormal environment. This, too, no social worker can take away from the individual. But there is also a certain strength which may have been gained through the experience, and it is the realization of this that enables the individual to go on, to face the realities of life outside the institution, to endure the inevitable pains of readjustment and growth.

Despite the setting—indeed accepting the reality of it—the far more important factor is the quality of the relationship set up between the worker and the prisoner. William Nagel expresses the essence of this and its relevance to preparation for parole as follows: "Those of us who work in a treatment relationship with the men who are sent to our institution, try to provide him with an emotional experience in which he can grow. We let him struggle with us, hate us, love us, test us, reject us, and as he does he works out some of the conflicts which have been so destructive to him. Some knots in his emotional being begin to get untangled, and after a while he begins to react more maturely to situations which previously he would have met in ways which were unacceptable to the community. He seems to have changed. Indeed in a very real way he has changed, and we consider him ready for parole." [5]

Parole

It has been said frequently that preparation for parole begins before an offender ever gets to a correctional institution. The treatment he gets at the hands of police, jailers, prosecuting attorneys and judges leaves its impression with him and may have a good deal to do with his attitude when he leaves prison toward such officials and the agencies they represent. A more specific preparation for parole begins when he enters the institution, for despite all the strictures we pass upon reformatories and prisons they are designed to discharge offenders, presumably improved. This preparation commences with quarantine, pro-

[5] Nagel, William G., "Some New Areas for Casework Activity in a Correctional Institution for Young Men." *Journal of Social Work Process*, IV, May 1953, p. 40.

ceeds first to classification, then to reclassification and to the program which is worked out with the individual.

How ready the individual is for parole may depend in large measure upon how carefully these details have been shared with the individual. Who wants parole, the inmate or his people, wife, mother, etc.? Whose initiative is it, the inmate's, his family's or the social worker's? Who arranges for the sponsor? What part does the inmate have in locating a job; if someone else makes the contact, does the inmate have any choice in the matter? Trivial as these questions may seem as a person stands on the threshold of freedom, they may bear some relation to this subsequent adjustment. The eagerness of other people to get an individual out of prison may so deprive him of decisions and responsibilities that are his that he may be crippled in more ways than one when he is actually freed.

The man who is being considered for probation usually has not been robbed for years of his opportunities for decisions, nor has his life been interrupted as is the case with the parolee. But in practically every instance the individual who has been imprisoned has a more difficult readjustment to make. For one, he may be the more serious offender or one whose difficulties were so deeply rooted that the court thought probation inadvisable. In addition, he has lived in an unnatural environment and has lost many of the normal human contacts that most people find essential. Finally he may come out of prison, even the best prison, with feelings and attitudes which he has held inside of himself but which he now must get outside: bitterness, hatred, resentment. He also comes out with fears about his job, fear of failure, feelings of being rejected or persecuted, putting the blame for his mistakes on to other people, feeling dependent and yet fiercely resenting the need to be helped as well as the help offered. This is the person the parole officer is likely to meet no matter how fortunate the parolee's institutional experience has been.

The parole officer's job is not so different from the probation officer's, except that it is likely to be more difficult. Assuming that ideally parole is a continuation of the treatment begun in the institution or earlier, the parole officer is endowed with authority which remains a part of his relationship with the parolee. While parole is not voluntarily undertaken by the offender, the parole officer recognizes this as part of the situation, but nevertheless offers a helping service which the parolee is free to accept or reject. Much of what has been written in the forepart of this chapter about casework in probation applies as well to parole. The parolee may be able to use what the parole officer has to offer, or he may not. That in no wise affects the quality of the casework service offered. The worker needs to be aware of what the client is trying to express and to offer such help as the client wants and is able to use. Part of the answer to this latter question depends upon the worker's ability to determine how much responsibility the client can carry.

The parallel with probation proceeds throughout, for both probation and parole involve essentially casework relationships. Help may be needed with external and environmental factors or with internal and personality needs. This may be accomplished by help given the parolee by the parole officer or by referral to appropriate social agencies, public and private. The use of community resources may be just as important in work with the parolee as with the probationer. The matter of parole violation and revocation also will have to be reckoned with. Just as with the probation officer, the parole worker will have to weigh the seriousness of the infraction, the character of the offender, the capacity which the individual has already demonstrated to use the parole service, as well as an estimate of his potentialities if continued on parole or if imprisoned. If these are serious questions for the probationer, they must seem doubly so when affecting the life of the parolee. Many workers feel the parolee needs more help than the probationer, and there certainly is much to support such a conviction. When it comes to the point of discharge from parole, the worker will want to assure himself that the individual is ready to go on his own without help. If the institutional experience has been a constructive one and parole supervision has managed to help the parolee accept his share of responsibility for his own feelings and behavior, then the parole officer may feel fairly comfortable about the individual proceeding under his own steam. Both probation and parole must recognize the inherent ability of the individual to meet life according to his capacity.

Application to the Military Setting

Many of the lessons which were being learned slowly in peacetime were quickened by the impact of war and the resulting necessity to conserve manpower. In World War II the Army and the Navy with the assistance of leaders in the correctional field developed programs for dealing constructively with military offenders. There was never the slightest suspicion that the Army or the Navy were in the social work business; nevertheless, the military organization had to contend with thousands of offenders within the ranks. Rehabilitative programs were developed which incorporated some of the fundamental principles of dealing with offenders of all kinds. Both Richard Chappell of the Navy's corrective services and Austin MacCormick of the Army's described the programs as designed to treat offenders in such a manner that they would be restored to duty benefited, rather than damaged, by the period of confinement.[6]

Conclusion

Frequently it has been asked whether the principles of modern social casework are applicable to probation, prison work, or parole. Without going into an exhaustive analysis of the pro's and con's it can be said here that when the essential nature of social casework as well as the purpose of probation, prison work, and parole are understood, the answer is decidedly in the affirmative. Perhaps the most pointed presentation yet made has been the one by Kenneth Pray. This analysis examines the apparent contradiction between the authoritative character of correctional work and the customarily voluntary nature of social casework. Does an individual on probation, in prison, or on parole have a choice as to whether he will accept the worker's services and skill? The

[6] For additional references to services to offenders in the armed forces, see: Brodsky, Irving, "Disciplinary Barracks," in Maas, Henry S., *Adventure in Mental Health.* New York, Columbia University Press, 1951, pp. 99–117; Chappell, Richard A., "Naval Offenders and Their Treatment." *Federal Probation,* IX, April–June 1945, pp. 3–7; Chappell, Richard A., "What Did the War Services Develop in Correction Technique?" *Proceedings of the National Conference of Social Work,* 1947, pp. 361–368; Chappell, Richard A., and Logee, F. Emerson, "Training Wayward Sailor Men for Return to Duty." *Yearbook of the National Probation Association,* 1945, pp. 20–29; Fraser, Albert G., "Out of the Travail of War." *Prison Journal,* XXVI, January 1946, pp. 149–156; MacCormick, Austin H., "Some Basic Considerations in the Treatment of Military Prisoners." *Federal Probation,* IX, January–March 1945, pp. 7–11; MacCormick, Austin H., and Evjen, Victor H., "The Army's Rehabilitation Program for Military Prisoners." *Yearbook of the National Probation Association,* 1945, pp. 1–19; Menninger, William C., "Psychiatry and the Military Offender." *Federal Probation,* IX, April–June 1945, pp. 8–12; Wagley, Perry V., "The Army Rehabilitates Military Offenders." *Federal Probation,* VIII, January–March 1944, pp. 14–19.

answer is "Yes." True, it is a qualified "Yes," because the choice is related to the factors which have necessitated probation, imprisonment, or parole. Within the real and legal limits imposed by probation, imprisonment, or parole the offender—the client—has the freedom to accept or reject the help of the worker, just as any other client has. If he does not or cannot use the helping skill of the worker, he—the client—will have to carry the responsibility and the consequences, just as any other client.

Does the imposition of limits militate against the use of casework in probation, imprisonment, or parole? The answer is "No." There is no area of casework service that is without limits. There are limits in the situations in which family casework is offered, child placement, medical casework, etc. The differential is the nature of the limits. So, too, with the correctional casework services. Indeed, one is more aware of the limits in probation, prison services, and parole, but one also realizes the very necessity for them. When Mr. Pray asks about these limitations, he answers his own question by saying, "Not only is there room for such limitations upon individual freedom; again, there is positive, unavoidable need for such limits. They constitute the framework within which alone real freedom, real movement, and change is possible." [7]

Does the offender require the limitations which the authority of the court or the prison impose upon him? This question can be answered positively, with very little hesitation. In the article just quoted, Mr. Pray comes to grips with this, and says of the offender in relation to authority: [8]

It is particularly true of the delinquent that social readjustment must be founded upon the recognition and acceptance of the inherent, rightful, and essential authority that underlies social living. He has rejected or violated that authority in the past. He has to learn anew, through painful experience, that those limits, like his own capacities, are inviolable, and that his real satisfactions are to be found only within them.

Both Albert Fraser and Kenneth Pray apply the same principles to casework within the prison. There is no denying the reality of limitations which the prison imposes upon the offender. Nevertheless, if the prison experience is to be a useful one and the worker's service a genuine

[7] Pray, Kenneth L. M., "The Principles of Social Case Work as Applied to Probation and Parole." *Federal Probation,* IX, April–June 1945, p. 16.

[8] *Ibid.,* p. 17.

helping, these limitations must be frankly faced and dealt with. The offender must know he is in prison, accept it even though he does not like it, and work with himself and the situation as it is. Contradictory though it may seem, the caseworker's skill is to help the prisoner to get *into* prison (as Farrow expresses it), to face why he is there, and to handle himself in relation to it. Fraser well states it when he writes: "He needs to understand that not until he is ready to accept the commitment, to bring *all* of himself into the prison, can he begin to prepare himself for leaving it." [9]

These principles, based upon an understanding of the dynamics of the helping process, hold great promise for useful employment in probation, prison work, and parole.

BIBLIOGRAPHY

Books and Pamphlets

Applegate, Melbourne S., *Helping Boys In Trouble*. New York, Association Press, 1950.

Bates, Sanford, *Prisons and Beyond*. New York, The Macmillan Company, 1936.

Bowen, Croswell, *They Went Wrong*. New York, McGraw-Hill Book Co., 1954.

Bromberg, Walter, *Crime and the Mind*. Philadelphia, J. B. Lippincott Company, 1948.

Cohen, Frank J., *Children in Trouble*. New York, W. W. Norton & Company, 1951.

Davidoff, Eugene, and Noetzel, Elinor S., *A Child Guidance Approach to Juvenile Delinquency*. New York, Child Care Publications, 1951.

Dressler, David, *Probation and Parole*. New York, Columbia University Press, 1951.

Eisler, K. R., *Searchlights on Delinquency*. New York, International Universities Press, 1949.

Ellingston, John R., *Protecting Our Children from Criminal Careers*. New York, Prentice-Hall, Inc., 1948.

Friedlander, Kate, *The Psycho-Analytical Approach to Juvenile Delinquency*. New York, International Universities Press, 1947.

Glueck, Sheldon and Eleanor, *Delinquents in the Making: Paths to Prevention*. New York, Harper and Brothers, 1952.

[9] Fraser, Albert G., "The Function and Program of a Prisoners' Aid Society." *Federal Probation*, VIII, July–September 1944, p. 26.

————, *Unraveling Juvenile Delinquency.* New York, Commonwealth Fund, 1950.

Goldberg, Harriet L., *Child Offenders: A Study in Diagnosis and Treatment.* New York, Grune and Stratton, 1948.

Kahn, Alfred J., *A Court for Children: A Study of the New York City Children's Court.* New York, Columbia University Press, 1953.

Keve, Paul W., *Prison, Probation, or Parole.* Minneapolis, University of Minnesota Press, 1954.

Merrill, Maud A., *Problems of Child Delinquency.* Boston, Houghton Mifflin Company, 1947.

Peck, Harris B., and Bellsmith, Virginia, *Treatment of the Delinquent Adolescent.* New York, Family Service Association of America, 1954.

Powers, Edwin, and Witmer, Helen, *An Experiment in the Prevention of Delinquency: The Cambridge-Somerville Youth Study.* New York, Columbia University Press, 1951.

Wessel, Rosa (editor), *A Case Work Approach to Sex Delinquents.* Philadelphia, Pennsylvania School of Social Work, 1947.

Significant Articles

Anderson, C. Wilson, "Social Case Work in the Juvenile Court." *Prison Journal,* XXX, July 1950, pp. 46–53.

Farrow, Richard G., "The Basic Problem of Penal Administration." *Prison Journal,* XXII, April 1942, pp. 202–209.

————, "Prison and the Man." *Prison Journal,* XXII, July 1942, pp. 218–221; also reprinted in *Prison Journal,* XXVIII, October 1948, pp. 450–453.

————, "What the Parole Officer Has a Right to Expect From the Institution." *Federal Probation,* XII, September 1948, pp. 30–35.

Fink, Arthur E., "Parole Supervision: A Case Analysis." *Federal Probation,* XV, September 1951, pp. 39–45.

Nagel, William G., "Some New Areas for Casework Activity in a Correctional Institution for Young Men." *Journal of Social Work Process,* IV, May 1953, pp. 29–45.

Pray, Kenneth L. M., "Case Work Paves the Way in Preparation for Freedom." *Prison Journal,* XXVI, April 1946, pp. 166–171.

————, "Parole in Relation to Classification and Case Work in Prison." *Yearbook of the National Probation Association,* 1944, pp. 182–195.

————, "The Place of Social Case Work in the Treatment of Delinquency." *The Social Service Review,* XIX, June 1945, pp. 235–244.

————, "The Principles of Social Case Work as Applied to Probation and Parole." *Federal Probation,* IX, April–June 1945, pp. 14–18.

Rikelman, Herman, "Case Work in Prisons." *Jewish Social Service Quarterly,* XXIII, December 1946, pp. 149–156.

Studt, Elliot, "An Outline for Study of Social Authority Factors in Casework." *Social Casework,* XXXV, June 1954, pp. 231–238.

Wilson, Everett E., "The Nature of Probation." *The Social Service Review,* XX, September 1946, pp. 396–402.

Casework in a Correctional Institution

WILLIAM G. NAGEL,
Assistant to the Superintendent
New Jersey Reformatory
Bordentown, New Jersey

Bordentown is one of New Jersey's two reformatories for young male adults. With few exceptions, the age range spreads from 18 to 30 years. Most of the young men received there have had previous records of confinement in either juvenile institutions or other reformatories. The offenses for which they have been sentenced include most all the felonies.

Approximately 80 percent of the commitments are on indeterminate sentences with no minimum sentence and a maximum usually set at five years. The paroling authority is the Board of Managers of the institution, a lay group of men who are responsible, through channels, to the governor for the operation of the institution. The Board of Managers grants paroles on the recommendation of the institution's Classification Committee. This committee is composed of the various department heads of the institution including the superintendent, the deputy keeper (the chief custodial officer), the assistant to the superintendent (a social worker at present), the chief psychologist, the director of education, the industrial supervisor, and the institutional parole officer (an employee of the state Bureau of Parole). Within the institution the decisions as to the inmate's program, and in the case of the man serving an indeterminate sentence—his time, are made by this committee.

For the man sentenced to Bordentown on an indeterminate sentence certain procedures are prescribed between the date of arrival and his parole. On his arrival he will be registered, fingerprinted, and photographed, and certain case material will be obtained from him. He will then be issued clothing and taken to the reception unit where he will be housed for thirty days. During the first ten days of this period he will be confined in medical quarantine to his room. Ordinarily he will be seen only by the social worker assigned to the reception tier. The talks with this staff member will center around tangible problems which are usually present. Typical might be a request for approval of certain persons for mail and visiting privileges, the man's feelings and fears about being institutionalized, and his concern about his family.

At the end of these ten days he will be released from quarantine and will join with other new admissions in a twenty-day program of orientation conducted by a social worker. During this time he will be examined by the physician, dentist, psychologist, and psychiatrist, and interviewed by the institutional parole officer, the director of education, the Protestant or Catholic chaplain, the industrial supervisor, and the assistant to the superintendent. Each examiner prepares a summary of findings for the Classification Committee. During the same period a representative of the parole department will visit the man's home, talk to his parents or wife, inquire into his work and school record, and check with the sentencing court as to the specifics of his present offense. If the man has been on parole, a summary of his parole adjustment will be forwarded with this other material to the institution. All the data will then be transcribed into a case record by the classification secretary and his staff, and copies will be prepared for each member of the Classification Committee.

The new man will at that point, thirty days after admission, appear in person before the entire Classification Committee for assignment to a program which embodies four elements: the housing unit, the work assignment, the treatment program, and a custody classification.

Bordentown contains eleven housing units, and assignment to each is based upon careful evaluation of the new inmate. There is a unit for those men who appear nondelinquent in their thinking, another for those who appear exploitable, another for those who might exploit other men, another for the serious escape risks, and so forth.

The work program encompasses eight shops, porter work, commissary assignments, several clerical positions, and farm work including the operation of a large dairy, piggery, truck farm, and general farm. The assignments to these different types of work are made with consideration both for the inmate's skill and desires and for the institution's needs.

The treatment program includes possible assignment to grammar or high school, special groups for the retarded, classes in social education, individual or group psychotherapy conducted by psychologists and/or the psychiatrist, and social casework. Assignment to any of these phases of the treatment program is made by the Classification Committee only after careful consideration of the inmate's needs as determined by the committee. Often such assignments are met with resistance by the men who frequently don't recognize the fact that they have problems and that the particular assignment is designed to aid them with their problems.

Custody classifications are made exclusively on the basis of the committee's studied appraisal of the degree of supervision needed for each man to prevent his escape. Four general classifications are used: maximum, medium, minimum, and full minimum. Generally, but not always, the new man begins his stay at Bordentown under maximum supervision which is lessened as he approaches his parole.

Needless to say, the new man's appearance before the committee for his first classification is often of critical importance to him. The interaction between himself and the committee can have much influence on the use he will make of the institution during the intervening months between admission classification and his next appearance five months later.

While he is in the program which has been assigned to him, he is closely observed, and these observations are recorded and added to the case record. The housing officer reports on his attitudes in the housing unit, his associates, his spare-time activities, his cleanliness, his response to orders, and other factors. His work instructor reports on his progress in the shop, his skills, his ability to get along, his initiative, and the like. The teacher writes a comprehensive report describing the use he has made of his school opportunities. The chaplains describe his response to the religious activities of the institution. The psychologist summarizes any basic attitudinal changes which might have occurred since admission. The caseworker reports on his activity, if any, with the men. The recreation director records his participation in sports and other allied activities.

At the end of five months these reports are once again transcribed into the official record, and copies are circulated to each member of the Classification Committee. These are then studied independently by the individual members who make recommendations, at this time, as to how long the man should be institutionalized at Bordentown. The various recommendations are discussed by the committee in open session, and differences are resolved by a majority vote. The inmate then appears before the committee and is told how long he will remain at Bordentown if his present rate of progress continues. At the same time his entire program will be reviewed with him and necessary modifications made.

Usually this "time" classification has even greater emotional significance to the man than did his admission classification. At regular intervals until he is paroled, the man will appear for reclassification. If unusual progress has been made, the time classification may be reduced. Program changes may also be made whenever indicated.

Finally, when the inmate is within two months of the expiration of his time "goal," he is once more brought before the committee. New up-to-date reports have been incorporated in the case record, and if the man's progress has continued as expected, he is then told specifically what his release date will be.

The man then begins actively with the institutional parole officer to prepare the specifics of his parole plan. The parole officer in the community, who will carry supervision of the man visits the home and becomes familiar with potential parole problems. The institutional parole officer discusses these with the man. In addition, he conducts classes for all the prospective paroled men. These classes are designed to inform the inmates of parole regulations and general parole problems.

In the meantime the Board of Managers acts upon the recommendations for parole made by the Classification Committee and on the date set for the man to be released to the community under parole supervision.

Casework Services

One caseworker at Bordentown carries the title of "Assistant to the Superintendent," and in addition to his casework activities, he has administrative and supervisory responsibility for many aspects of the entire institutional program. He is a permanent member of the Classification Committee and of the Adjustment Committee. The latter is a three-man group which handles disciplinary infractions within the institution. He also supervises the other full-time caseworkers.

One full-time caseworker is concerned with the orientation of new men. He is assigned permanently to the reception unit where he has his office. His function is to help orient the new man to the institution. This is not an easy function. Most new admissions want to blot out the fact that they are imprisoned, and dream about the day of their release. They want to ignore their own responsibility for their present plight and consider it nothing but "one of those things." They often project onto the institution and its officials much of their deep-rooted hostility toward authority. They perpetuate their own maladjustment by focusing their hatred on the institution, rather than internalizing the struggle within themselves where the roots of their trouble usually lie.

It is the function of the case worker in the reception unit to begin a process designed to deal with these various symptoms of the new man's refusal to be truly and profoundly institutionalized. It has been said that it is impossible to prepare a man for parole until he is, psychologically, "in" the institution. To aid in this is the role of the caseworker at intake.

Another full-time worker and the two students from schools of social work function with the inmates during the "middle phase" of institutionalization. To them the Classification Committee assigns individuals with problems which appear amenable to casework skills. These may include a man with a marital problem, or one whose fight against the institution promises to be destructive to him unless it can be personalized in the one-to-one relationship with a trained and sensitive person. Students have been assigned to troublesome housing units, and they engage the men housed there in a helping relationship designed to enable these men to use their wills constructively rather than destructively.

The fourth worker is the institutional parole officer. His function is to help the men prepare, physically and emotionally, to leave Bordentown. It might be thought that men after two, three, or more years of imprisonment would be ready and eager to leave. On the surface they usually are eager enough, but beneath the skin are many fears. On the "street" they have been a failure in the past. Will they be again? On the "street" are family responsibilities. They have run from them before. Will they again? In the institution they have made friends and found acceptance. Will they now find rejection? All these and many more feelings frighten them. It is thought by many informed people that the failure of some parolees can be traced to their inability to separate themselves from the sheltered existence they lived in prison. The function of the institutional parole officer is to make this separation as dynamically helpful and complete as possible.

Chuck Morgan

In October Chuck Morgan was sentenced to Bordentown for an indeterminate sentence on a charge of robbery. He had been arrested on a motor vehicle violation charge and fined heavily. Unable to pay the fine and therefore faced with three months in the county jail, he held up a service station at gun point. With the proceeds he paid off the fine, but was soon apprehended on the robbery charge.

He spent October and most of November in the reception tier where the intake social worker had several contacts with him. It was almost immediately apparent that this man was finding the confinement difficult. He worried continuously about his wife and child. At night he paced his cell until early morning. The officer reported that he spent hours looking at a photograph of his wife and child and staring out through the bars toward his home sixty miles away. As the inmates say, "He was pulling a hard bit."

At the end of his orientation period he was assigned to work in the carpenter shop and was placed in one of the classes in social re-education. It was hoped by the Classification Committee that as he moved into the program of the institution he would "snap out of it," lose his intense homesickness, and make an adjustment to his new situation.

In January, two months after his assignment, the mail censor forwarded to the assistant to the superintendent a letter Chuck had written to his wife. It indicated that he was still depressed, and though he was doing his best to "keep his chin up," he felt he was fighting a losing battle.

The letter was referred to a social worker, as are most letters which reflect serious problems in adjustment. Chuck was immediately called for an interview.

1/26. I sent a pass for Chuck. Previous to this I had some contact with him in regard to his request to have an uncle placed on his mail list. Though this had been an extremely short contact, he carried from it the feeling that I was trying to help him. As a result, he seemed able today to move right into relationship with me.

I wondered about the letter he had written and showed him that I had it. He responded that his daughter was having a birthday, and he wanted more than anything to celebrate it with her. He added that he was "down in the mouth" primarily because he belonged out there with his wife and child who were not managing too well. I encouraged him to talk about this.

He said his wife was living in a rooming house with her mother. Neither were working. There were no cooking facilities. The only income was an aid to dependent children grant of $84 per month. He belonged out there with them. I inferred that his being there was not the immediate solution because it could not be.

He replied that he had been thinking a great deal about escaping. He had about reached the conclusion that it would be worth all the risk and consequences. I asked why he thought so. He said he belonged with his wife and child.

I reminded him that should he be successful in escaping the first action the institution would take would be to place a couple of officers on his wife's doorstep to wait for him. He would be apprehended, returned, and given an additional sentence. I wondered how that would help his wife's situation. His reply, "If I ever escape, they'll have to shoot me to bring me back." He seemed inflexible and certain that this was the only solution.

I asked him to consider with me other possible ways of dealing with this very real problem. He seemed unable to think of any. I suggested as a start that if he couldn't get out to see his wife and child, perhaps they could visit him. Her tight budget prevented this. I proposed that perhaps community agencies might help and suggested the parole office in his community as a beginning point. He blocked on this, recalling some unhappy experiences he had when he was on parole as a juvenile. I then suggested that we discuss the matter with the parole representative here at Bordentown. He insisted this would not help because Mr. M (the parole representative) did not like him. We spent quite some time on this, and he finally decided to talk to Mr. M, though "It won't do any good." Together we went over to the parole representative's desk, and after I had told Mr. M of the reason for the referral, I left them alone.

When Chuck finished his talk with Mr. M he returned to my desk. I wondered how he felt now and he replied, "Better." He now knew Mr. M better and felt he would try to help his family.

I wondered if escape now seemed the only solution. He still thought that it was "a solution." Suicide seemed another. I wondered aloud if escape was not in itself a kind of suicide. He did not respond to this.

By this time I was beginning to consider if it might not be necessary to move Chuck from his medium custody housing unit to B-1, which is maximum security. I discussed this with him, and he objected to it. I left him with the thought that such a transfer might be necessary. I told him that I would see him again tomorrow.

In a correctional institution such as Bordentown the referral to the social service department may come from many sources. Often it is the Classification Committee which recognizes that the existence of a problem requires the expert attention of the social worker. Frequently the custodial staff in their dealings with the inmates see the need for the individual skills of the social worker. Sometimes the Adjustment Committee, which handles discipline, refers the inmate whose disciplinary problems reflect the need for help. Many times the inmate, himself, seeks out the social worker. In this case it was the censor who spotted the problem.

The following morning the social worker again sent for Chuck, who expressed appreciation for the interest being given him. He said he now felt that for his own protection he should be placed in the maximum custody housing unit, and a transfer was effected. Three days later he was seen again, and though he said he felt better, he still talked excessively about ways and means to escape. He still could not see any solution to his problems.

It was now apparent that Chuck Morgan required an extended period of individual attention. The worker who had been assigned the case on an emergency basis after the censor's referral made plans for Chuck's transfer to a continuing worker, who would have the time for the prolonged casework service that was now indicated. After discussing this thoroughly with Chuck, the case was transferred on February 3 to a student worker who scheduled an interview for February 8.

2/8. The interview began with the social worker's greeting and acknowledgement of the possible problems which might be involved for Chuck in beginning with a new worker. The inmate said the transfer was okay with him and that Mr. A (the previous worker) had gone over the matter of transfer with him. The worker then summarized the reasons for the contacts as he had been told them by Mr. A. Chuck saw the problem in simple terms. He just wanted to be out of the place. He talked of his wish to be with his wife and daughter and of his particular desire to be with them in April for his wedding anniversary and his daughter's first birthday. The worker pointed out the reality that this could not be, and Chuck brought up a new problem. His wife had not written for over two weeks. This, he said, was most unusual, and he was worried. He had concluded that she must be ill. He wanted to know if the report from the parole office had yet been received. It had not.

He conversed about many things and then came back to his desire for "one day's freedom." The worker attempted to engage him on a reality basis. He reminded Chuck that if his concern was his wife and child "one day" was not the answer. Chuck was silent, and the worker discussed the suggestions which had been introduced two weeks earlier by the previous worker, but the inmate did not participate. The worker ended the interview with: "I told him I would be seeing him weekly now. Did that seem all right to him. Okay, he said. An appointment was made for February 15 at 8:15 A.M., which Chuck said was fine with him."

The following Monday found Chuck in a better mood. He was almost jubilant. His wife and child had visited on Sunday, and the visit had been wonderful. The child had been so friendly. He had held her and played with her almost an hour. He had been given his "one day," and all the escape talk seemed silly.

There was still a problem, however. His wife had been told that either she or her mother would have to go to work. The Department of Public Welfare had decreed that it could not continue its grant after March 1 since there were two able-bodied women in the home and only one child. As the worker discussed this new development, Chuck accepted the welfare department's position, but was still worried about it. His wife lived in a resort town, and employment was scarce through the winter months. He had no doubts but that she could find employment in May. But what could she do from March until May?

The worker helped him toward the consideration of many possible solutions, and what was even more helpful, he dealt with Chuck's ever present guilt caused by his not being outside to help. An appointment was set for February 23.

2/23. Chuck was looking much more depressed when I saw him today. He was able to flash a grin when I greeted him, and when I asked how everything was going with him he said, "O. K." I said, "I don't suppose you had a visitor this weekend?" He said he had not. I wondered about mail: Had his wife written him? He said he has received two letters from her since he talked with me last, and he is expecting another one today.

He wondered what, if anything, I had been able to find out about "state aid" for his wife and child. He said he has been worrying about this a good deal. I told him he would probably be disappointed with what little I would be able to relate to him. I told him something about the funds for this program, how they are set up for use by mothers who are unable to work because there are small children in the home who rely exclusively on their mother for care. I told him the people who administer this program must feel that his wife may be able to engage in some sort of employment outside of the home while her mother watches the child. Chuck spoke again of how terribly difficult it is to find any work at all at this time. He said his wife is capable; she has a high school diploma; she can get a good job when the "season" begins. He does not know what in the world she will do until then, though. I told him there might also be a possibility that if his wife really was unable to find employment, they might reconsider her case and extend this "aid" for another month. I cautioned him against planning on this because the matter would be left entirely up to the D. P. W., and they may not see their way clear to do this at all.

I asked how he was feeling now about being here and about wanting to be out on the "street." Was he still thinking about escaping? He did not look at me; instead he stared at his hands, looking very dejected. He said he still thinks about it; he cannot help but think about it. Every night he thinks about his family and how much he feels his place is with them. The agonizing slowness of time makes him want to scream sometimes at night. He would feel better if he could do this, but he is afraid they will send him to the state hospital if he does. He feels his life is being wasted in here. His rightful place is with his wife and child. He thinks about getting out a lot. I told him I knew that getting out was important to him, and I wanted to see him get out, but not by means of escape. I wondered if he knew what escaping would mean to his wife. What would she think about it? He said he has never really asked her directly, but he knows she would disapprove. He told me he thinks he is going to try to be with her for their anniversary.

I wondered if he were successful in getting out, how long did he think he could stay out. He knows what he would face when he came back, then how about the next anniversary, and the next one, and the next one, and the ones after that. How long could he expect his wife to wait for him if he received additional time?

He looked at me with damp eyes and told me his marriage day was the happiest of his life. Getting married and having a baby were the best things that ever happened to him. He then fell silent. I said, "I can appreciate what it means to you, and you still have all this. It is still waiting for you. What you do from now on, though, is largely going to determine whether or not you keep it." I stated that I knew how much he wanted to be out and how much his wife wanted him to be out, but I was sure she would not want it if it were achieved by escape. I said maybe he was being a little selfish in thinking only of his momentary desires. His wife is looking forward to a lifetime of happiness with him; his child will need him; does he want to deprive them of this by attempting to make a break that would only mean a few hours' freedom? (If indeed that much.) He replied he thinks it would be worth it. I asked to whom.

There was another long silence. I finally asked how long he felt he would be here; to which he replied 24 or 30 months. I asked if he thought it too much to endure, knowing what he has to look forward to when he is released. He answered affirmatively, adding that he fears he will "crack up," go insane, and be confined to the state hospital if he has to spend that long in this place. He said he is even afraid to meet with the Classification Committee when he comes up for his time. This is something else he thinks about a lot.

For the hour that I had been conversing with Chuck he seldom looked at me, and if he smiled at all, it was a forced, cynical grin. He really appeared to be emotionally "under the weather"—an almost complete reversal from his jubilant state of last week after his wife's visit. He remained silent, as though he was waiting for me to begin. I reminded him that we had been talking about his meeting with the Classification Committee. He nodded, saying nothing. I said "Chuck, I wonder if part of your desire to run in April stems from the fact that you will also be meeting with the Classification Committee during this month, and you are afraid to face this." He denied that this was true, saying it was all because he wanted to be with his wife and daughter.

He repeated to me the ironic circumstances that brought him here; his desire to remain with his family and out of jail; his robbery to obtain money to pay off a traffic ticket; his apprehension and sentence to Bordentown. He talked about his former behavior on parole, how he ran from it when his grandmother gave the parole officer a gun he had hidden in the house. I told him these were all instances in which he ran from something. Where did they get him? Why does he feel he can run from it again and come out on top? He remained silent for a while, then told me about meeting the Classification Committee for the first time a few months back, and about their pegging him as a "rough customer." He said somebody made the remark "I see from your record you like guns." He feels it was just coincidental that both times he was in trouble involved the use of firearms. He said that between those two times, all of the time he was married (1½ years), he stayed "clean," did not "monkey with" guns, and stayed out of trouble. He feels the only thing the Classification Committee has to base their judgment on is his past record, and he thinks that is biased unfavorably. What about the times in between? I told him I thought his present record would enter into their decision too. How he is accepting his incarceration would mean something. He averred that as much as he knows this might count, he cannot fight this strong desire to be out with his family, and he is willing to sacrifice almost anything to have this desire fulfilled.

Another long silence followed and then he remarked that if he were man enough, or had courage enough, he would take his own life. I inquired if he really felt it took a man to do that. He nodded. I said that if he really wanted to solve all of *his* troubles, that would be the easy way to go about it. It did not take courage.

He said "I know I owe it to my wife and child to stay here, do my time, and come out right, and I know I would feel better if I knew I was *forced* to remain here, but as long as I know there is a way out, I will think about it." I told him he not only owed it to his wife and child, he also owed it to himself. He has to show himself that he is capable of doing this, and perhaps come out a much more adequate person than when he came in. I said, "You say you want us to keep you in here—to *make* you stay. What do you suggest we do? You know we don't want you to leave—for your own good." He was silent. I asked how he was so sure there was a way out; it could not be guaranteed. He could always be picked up or killed in the attempt. To which he answered, "I know a way out of here now. I could go tonight if I wanted to." When I inquired why he didn't try it then, he stated that he wants to go and he doesn't want to go. He doesn't want it just to be out on the "street." When he goes, he wants it to mean something to him, to be for a purpose. That's why he is going to wait until April to run, if he runs at all. "If you had the door open and had your back turned, I wouldn't go now because it wouldn't have any meaning. I wouldn't have anything to gain." I asked him to think seriously about what he had to gain even by going in April. I came back to the question I had asked before which still remained unanswered, "If you would feel better knowing there was no way for you to leave, knowing you *must* stay here, what would you suggest we do?" I waited. He appeared tense, determined. He was looking straight at me, wanting to say something but not knowing how, or if he should. I said "Chuck, I want you to know that whatever you tell me isn't spread all over the institution." He blurted it out then, seeming to get a great deal of relief from the mere release of it: "I've got a hack saw hidden away." I was surprised by this, but I remained motionless, almost expressionless, watching him. He was not smiling, yet I could tell that the tension within him had subsided. He went on, more slowly now, "I can use it any time I want to, but I'm afraid to do it. I want to stick it out as long as I can, then if I can't take any more, I'll have to leave." He added that just knowing it is there helps him a lot because he knows there is always a way out. He hastened to tell me that it was hidden, that nobody knew where it was, although he suggested that somebody on the tier knew of his plans to escape.

I asked if anybody else was in on it with him. He said there were five others, beside himself, who were planning to leave together. I questioned how they knew he had the saw, if they did not know where it was. He said he showed it to some of them once, just to convince them. I asked if they were all in B-1. He said yes, they were.

Why was he telling me all this—about the saw and the other guys? He said he just thought he would feel much better knowing that I knew. I asked if he did feel better now. He said he did. I asked if he wanted to tell me where the saw was. He said no; he feels better knowing he can get his hands on it if he needs it. I countered with, "Maybe you would feel a lot better if you knew it was not there for you to use." I told him I felt that the saw was the source of a conflict within him: he wants to use it, but he knows what the consequences will be if he does. I thought he would feel more at ease with himself if he gave it up and resigned himself to remaining here. He agreed that he might feel better about it. I asked again if he wanted me to know where it was. His response was in the negative. Even if he does not "run" in April, he wants to keep it until he gets his time. If then he feels his time is too much for him to take, he will use it. He is not certain now how it's going to go with the Classification Committee. If he got too much time, he feels sure he would "bug out" before time to get back "on the streets." He's afraid of this. I informed him I could not bargain with him around this matter. I could not promise him less time if he turned in the saw. However, I did ask just how much time he felt he could take. He said 24 months, maybe 30, but 30 seems like a lot. He said he knew I couldn't bargain; he didn't want that; he just wanted me to know.

He then told me why he took five others in on it with him. He felt he would have a better chance making the break as a member of a gang. If there was shooting, the probability of his getting hit would be reduced. In this sense, he is "using" the other men. He is just "stringing them along," for as soon as they got outside, he's going to "ditch" them. He pictured them as "all pretty desperate men," in for a long time. I offered to bet that they did not have as much to lose as he did. I spoke of his family, and inquired if the other men had families. He said they did not. I asked if his wife knew he had this saw. He said no, and she probably would not like it if she did. I talked with him longer about how using it would affect her and his child. They would not be able to travel with him, and he would not be able to stay home with them. After considering this for a moment, he decided that he wants to talk with his wife about this and how much his being home on her anniversary means to her. Then, depending on what she says, he might tell me where it is. He would not give it to me because then it would have his name on it. If anything, he will just tell me where to get it. He thinks some sort of punishment might result in his turning it in. He made it a point to tell me that a search would not find it, and neither would putting him in lock-up bring it out.

I told him I respected him very much for telling me all of this. Then I talked more about the effect I thought knowing that he possessed a saw was having upon him. I said I thought he would be better off all the way around if he gave it up. He was silent again. After a while, he indicated that he would like to think about it and talk with his wife about it. Then maybe he can tell me. We were both silent. He said, "I'll think about it then, I really will, and we'll talk more about it later." We then arranged to meet on March 1.

In this interview the problem being shared with the student worker became so complex and critical that it would have confounded the most experienced caseworker. In the confidence of a one-to-one relationship between inmate and worker a problem involving the security of the entire institution was being uncovered. What should the worker do about it?

Many questions flashed through his head. Was this a hoax presented by a sophisticated offender, designed to test the confidentiality of the casework relationship? If so, would it not be possible that the relationship, and all that it offered in future helpfulness for the inmate, would be terminated if the worker shared this information with the institution's administration?

If it was not a hoax, but reality, would there not be disciplinary action taken against his client for this information which he had shared in confidence with the worker? Would Chuck Morgan or any other inmate ever share with him again? Would he not, in the parlance of the inmates, be a "rat" or "informer"?

It is perhaps seldom that a student social worker so early in his professional education has to face so dramatically one of the basic concepts that differentiates the profession of social casework from the other helping disciplines. That is the concept of the *social agency* as a factor in the helping process. Kenneth Pray in "A Restatement of the Generic Principles of Social Casework Practice" presented at the National Conference of Social Work in April 1947, enunciated that concept as follows:

The functional conception of the role and meaning of social casework as a serving and helping process, used by the client, rather than a treatment process, controlled by the worker, finds expression in another decisive and characteristic concept. The relationship within which this process results is not simply and strictly a person-to-person relationship, like that which the client has known in all his other experiences. A difference has been introduced which carries with it a new dynamic—a difference with which the individual must come to terms, must accept and take into himself, if he is to find and use help. That difference is the agency which the worker represents, a fixed and stable structure, governing both the worker and the client in this relationship, presenting limits within which the worker operates and with and against which the client can measure and define his own need, his own will, and his own powers. The worker is not just another person, ready and willing and able to yield himself to any need and purpose that may emerge from the labyrinthine maze of confusing and conflicting interests and impulses of this other person, nor is he the arbitrary, though beneficent, arbiter among those impulses or censor of them, capable of imposing his own personal conditions upon the nature and extent of his service, in relation to the client's problem and need.

He is the representative of an agency, which is itself a part of the fixed social reality within which the client must find his own satisfying solution and ultimate adjustment. . . . The individual worker may go or stay, the agency continues, with the same basic function and policy.

This the student worker knew, and though the test of this concept was now brought to him in an almost overwhelming manner, he recognized that he could not work in the reformatory if he considered himself an individual apart from his agency. He immediately requested a special conference with his supervisor and shared the entire matter with him.

The supervisor took the information to the assistant to the superintendent. On this level it was decided that the student worker would have to discuss with Chuck the full implications of the fact that he claimed to have a hack-saw blade. It was further decided that the institution wanted the blade. If he would give it to the worker, it would end there. If not, the custodial force would have to institute a search and take the necessary disciplinary action. In a correctional institution a hack-saw blade is a most forbidden item of contraband.

2/25. Since it was felt by my supervisor that the matter was too urgent to leave until March, I sent for Chuck by pass this morning. He met me in the halls, early for the appointment. He seemed willing, if not eager to talk with me again so soon. I asked him if he had any idea why I wanted to talk with him today. He smiled, saying he did. I told him I had been thinking about him and about what he told me a great deal since Tuesday. I felt a great sense of responsibility for what he shared with me, and I felt it important to talk with him again about it. He seemed to understand what I was saying. I wondered if he had given it much thought. He said he had, particularly last night. I asked him if he regretted the fact that he had told me what he did. He said no, he wanted to tell me, and he feels better now that he has.

I asked him where he had obtained the hack saw and was it a complete hack saw or just the blade. He replied it was just the blade; he got it inside of the institution. I asked if it was one that belonged here. He thought so, but he was not sure because he took it from another fellow—by force. I wondered why the other person had not "ratted" on him for taking it, or for having it in his possession. He said, "Simply because it's a blade. He wouldn't tell because it would be his neck too. We're both prisoners. It would be his word against mine, anyway." I asked if he was one of the men who planned to make the break with him. He nodded yes. I asked if he still wanted to keep it. After a moment's silence, he said he thinks he does. It means a way out for him, and even if he does not use it, just knowing it is there means a lot to him. I told him again that I felt a heavy responsibility for him and for the information he had given me. I wondered if he thought I had told anybody about it. He said he isn't in lock-up; they haven't "pulled" a search on the tier; so he knows I haven't.

I went on to say that I felt the saw was the source of a great deal of anxiety within him because he knows it will lead to nothing good. In fact, everything it holds for him will be bad. I asked why it was so important for him not to relinquish it. He answered he knows it is something he can count on, some way he has of beating this thing if it proves to be too much for him. If he finds himself in trouble, or about to get in trouble, he can always resort to it. I asked him if he felt it was a sort of security for him. He replied, "That's it." I told him that although it seemed to be a form of security, it was a false security. What could it get for him in the long run? It is similar to a gun a man keeps in his hand as a form of security against trouble. Then he discovers that the gun later actually brings on the trouble. It is not even a good crutch on which to lean because it is not reliable— not even a little bit. I reminded him that he had told me the day he was married and the day his baby was born were the two most important days in his life. I stated this might be the third most important day in his life because if he gave up the saw, he will no longer be running—he will realize that he is man enough to face up to this thing and stick it out.

He was silent for a long time. His jaw was set, twitching occasionally as he looked down at his hands. He shook his head no, very slightly several times, as if talking to himself. I remained silent. Finally he looked at me and said, "It's hard." I agreed with him, saying it was probably the hardest decision he has ever had to make, but I thought it would also be the most important. He said, "I want to—I really want to, but somehow I can't, not just now."

He contended he wanted to walk out right now and go up and get the blade for me, but he just could not. I asked what was keeping him from doing it. Why did it mean so much to him? Why couldn't he begin right now to work these things out by himself? It might be hard at first, but I thought he would find it rewarding later in the personal satisfaction he would gain from knowing he is man enough to do this.

I told him if he relinquished the blade, I would stick with him closely in trying to work out his problem. Maybe I was not being of too much help to him now because this "thing" is blocking us. If he is willing to give up the one thing that is preventing him from accepting the fact that he is here and must stay, we can go on from there. If he can meet this problem realistically, we can work through the others. There was no response to this. I suggested that actually this blade was a problem to him. He was worrying about it a lot. If he did not think I could offer him some help with this problem, he would never have brought it up to me. "But," I said, "frankly I am stumped at this point. What can we do together until the decks are cleared of the thing that is *really* bothering you?" He replied he just could not bring himself to do it, not at this moment.

I wondered if he knew what I ought to do with the information he had given me. He looked up and nodded yes. I said, "Now tell me what you think I should do in relation to you." He was still looking at me. His eyes were almost pleading. He wondered if he could have another couple of days. I asked about tomorrow morning. "OK," was his answer. Did he think he could bring it to me then? He said he was really going to try, but he has to think about it some more. I said maybe he would change his mind during the night and try to use it. He contended he would not; he does not want out now. Would he mind if I had a watch placed on him overnight as an escape risk? This was agreeable to him. I asked how he would react if I placed a watch on him as a suicide risk. He did not want that, for then he would probably be referred to the psychiatrist and maybe be sent to the state hospital. They might think he was going insane. I assured him I would only have an escape watch placed on him tonight. Then I would see him again the first thing in the morning. He promised to meet me, and he would try to bring the blade with him.

This was a difficult interview for the worker. To begin with, he could not bring himself to define clearly that he was part of the institution. He talked about what he "ought to do" with the information when in fact he had already done it. He stumbled through until suddenly it became clear to him that the hack-saw blade was actually blocking the client and the worker from establishing a relationship that might be helpful and he had the good sense to say it: "Maybe I wasn't being of too much help to you because this thing is blocking us."

This was the key point. Something happened. Chuck once again saw his worker as a helping person and not as a detective pursuing a hack-saw blade. Chuck's problem was not the blade; it was much more. Part of it was his refusal to accept the fact that he was in jail, and part of it was his concern for his wife and her financial problems. The blade was blocking his use of an available service on those problems. The worker brought things back into focus.

That night the custodial force was alerted to the possibility that there was a hack-saw blade on the maximum security housing unit. Chuck Morgan was kept under close observation.

The following morning another interview was scheduled.

2/26. Chuck didn't look particularly happy or pleased to see me when he walked in this morning. I sensed a certain resentment in his attitude, and I felt that this was present either because he (1) regretted telling me about the saw and decided to keep it, or, (2) regretted he told me, but decided to give it up, resenting me because I talked him into it.

He sat down quietly. I greeted him, asking how he was feeling today. He was silent for a moment, then said in a nervous voice, almost rapidly, "I gave the saw up last night." I was surprised, since I had not heard of this. I inquired what had happened. He related that his wing officer came into his room last night and told him he knew he had one. Chuck said he had the saw in his room at the time and knew it would be found if they searched, so he gave it up.

After a brief pause, I asked him if this was where the saw had been hidden all the time. He said no; he had just a half hour earlier taken it from a more secure hiding place on the tier and brought it to his room. I wondered why he had done this. He said he had done a great deal of thinking about our talk and had made up his mind to bring it in this morning. I said that maybe during the night he would have changed his mind and decided to use it, figuring it was now or never. He denied this strenuously, stating he had really made the decision, that he would not dare try anything like that anyway because he knew I had put a close watch on him. I told him that he must consider me pretty much of a "rat." I wondered if he felt sorry now that he had told me. He replied in the negative. I pointed out to him that I had to share my information with the administration because I felt so tremendously responsible for his safety. I wanted to see him stay and work this thing through so that it would mean the most to him when he was able to leave. When he had left me yesterday, I felt that he was going to bring the saw in voluntarily this morning. He said he was. "But," I added, "you had already made the decision, and even though you did give it to the guard, it was a voluntary act on your part."

There was a large silence at this point. Chuck still looked dejected, maybe less resentful. I asked how he felt about it all now—now the blade was gone and he did not have this "crutch" to lean on. He hesitated for a moment before saying that he really did not want to get out by resorting to such means. That was why he spoke to me about it in the first place.

He lapsed into silence again. Throughout the interview he was less talkative than he had been at other meetings. I tried to sound him out. I told him that I knew that what he did had a lot of meaning for him. Would he like to talk about it with me now, or would he rather be alone with it for a while? He stated he had not slept. Instead he had spent the night thinking about what had happened.

He said the saw scared him. Even the way he got it scared him. I asked what he meant by that. He said he was frightened by the meaning it had for him. It was important and yet he did not want to use it. Could I understand that? I replied affirmatively. He said when he first saw this blade one of the men on the tier was looking at it in his room. He knew then that he just had to have it. He told one of his friends that he was going into that room, and that he should shut the door behind him. He described how he ran in, oblivious to what might happen. There were three men in the room at that time. He literally took it away from them. When he thought about it afterward he was terrified at his actions in obtaining the blade. He knew that if he was that desperate to get it, he would be even more desperate to stay out once he made it. He did not think he would ever be brought back alive, and the thought of this made him shudder. He knew he had to give it up when he began talking to me. He just could not keep it because more than anything else in the world he wants to be with his wife and daughter. It would not work that way.

I inquired if he knew where the saw came from in the first place. He said he didn't. I then asked if the three men in the room when he got the blade were planning on making the break with him. He said yes. Could he tell me who they were? He said he didn't think so.

He was silent again. We both sat without speaking, he with his eyes on his hands. Finally he said, "I've told you this much, I might as well go all the way."

He then went on to tell the worker that there were rumors that guns were to be brought into the institution by the same method as had been the blades. It was obvious that Chuck was not "in the know" as to what the method was, but it did involve outside contacts and a window, and it did frighten him.

The interview continued.

He said now he's got it all off his chest. I wondered if he felt better about it. He said kind of, but now they would really think he was a foul ball and throw the book at him when he came up for his time. I told him I wasn't sure, but the circumstances under which this came out might mean a lot. After all, he was man enough to give this up voluntarily, realizing that it was the only thing to do. I said "I don't think you're a 'foul ball' for having done what you have. I'm certainly willing to go to bat for you." I told him it meant a lot for him to remain here; he knows that. He accepted B-1 because he knew it was in his best interests. He told me about the saw for the same reason. Whether he realizes it or not, he is making an adjustment—a big one. I felt that would be taken into consideration.

I asked if he was afraid of immediate punishment as a result of this. He said not. The guard had told him he would not go on report. I told him I thought if he did have fears in this area, I could assure him there would be no punishment.

Neither of us spoke for a long moment. I told him I knew he must be pretty shaken up by all of this. Did he want to talk further now, or would he rather be alone to think about what it all means to him? He replied that he did not feel much like talking more now. I told him I would like to see him again Monday morning. He said that would be fine.

When he got up to leave, he turned around and said, "I'm not repeating what I told you to *anybody*. I'm not going to say it again." I asked if he was thinking of staff or inmates when he said that. He said staff. He would not talk to any other member of the staff about it. Then I asked if he meant about the saw or about the guns—or both. He said both; he doesn't want to talk with anybody else about anything.

He also said he would not like it to get back to the tier because that would only lead to fights, and he thinks they would be senseless. I assured him none of the inmates would hear about it. When they realized he no longer had it, he could tell them it was found during a shakedown. He left then, agreeing to see me again Monday.

Later. Saw Chuck in the hall by the center. He did not look at me or show signs of recognition.

As a result of this information, the administration made an exhaustive investigation and learned that three—not one—hack-saw blades had been smuggled into the institution by a relative of one of the men on the B-1 housing unit. As for the guns, nothing could be learned except that they had not been smuggled in yet. One principal in the plot was sent to the State Prison, and the other was placed in segregation and deprived of future visits. The other two blades were located. Chuck had not known about them.

During the next week three interviews were scheduled with Chuck. Both worker and client remained preoccupied with the matter of the blades and guns. It was hard to leave something that had so emotionally involved the two of them.

This spell was broken by the reality of the institution's time structure. Men on indeterminate sentences to Bordentown receive their "time" exactly six months after the date of admission. On that date the Classification Committee reviews all the known factors in the man's background, his offense, his adjustment, his attitudes, and his use of the facilities of the institution for change in his personality and then decides on a goal in terms of time toward which a man can plan for his release. It was now March, and Chuck's scheduled appearance was set for April. This sent him into a near panic.

On March 3 he requested a transfer to the prison. The interview was recorded in this manner.

3/3. He asked me what his chances would be of getting transferred to the prison. I wondered why he inquired. He said he understands that ordinarily a man serves less time if he does it at the prison because the time is supposed to be rougher there. I asked where he had learned that. He said some guys here told him that a person with 30–36 months at the prison usually did only 8–12 months of it. I said I thought that if he went to the prison on a reformatory sentence he would do the same time there that he would have done here—only it might seem like *longer* instead of shorter. He said he thought maybe he could be sent up there before the Classification Committee meets to give him his time. Then he would get his time from the Classification Committee at the prison, and although he might draw more, he feels he would actually be serving less. He grinned and said, "Then too, I wouldn't have to meet with the Classification Committee here." I wondered what was the difference. Did he feel it would be easier to meet the prison Classification Committee? He said maybe not, but at least he would be postponing it for a while. Then maybe he could put it off further by getting transferred to Rahway. When he finally did come up for his time, he would probably have already served 15 months. The rest of the time would not be too hard to take.

He wondered about how much time he would actually have to serve if he drew 30 months. He thought maybe 26 with time off. He then asked me if I thought he could apply for a reduction in time during his last few months, and what his chances would be of having this granted. I said that would depend largely upon what he does with himself while he was here and also upon the number and nature of any disciplinary reports he might receive. He thinks he can stay out of trouble because it means an awful lot to him to be out.

This is what correction people mean when they say "It's necessary to get a man into the institution before he can be released." Men fight being institutionalized in many ways. Some deny their guilt and defy the institution's effort to change them. "I did nothing to come here so why should I change?" For them, being incarcerated is just so many months in a deep freeze. The more aggressive fight the institution as they have fought society prior to their arrests. They are the trouble-makers who deny any vested power the right to authority over them. Some withdraw almost into a catatonic state and merely go through the motions of living. They vegetate, making no use of the treatment facilities available, and finally are released with this will blighted by a kind of emotional dystrophy.

Chuck's response was typical of still others. He became paralyzed with fear at the thought of "facing the music." He wanted to delay the evil day of reckoning even if it meant being transferred to the prison. He was scared of the Classification Committee and of the power it held over him. During March several interviews were scheduled, and in all of them Chuck seemed unable to concentrate on anything except the Classification Committee and his time. The worker discussed these fears at great length, but the inmate seemed unable to make any adjustment to the reality that was closing in on him.

A new emergency then occurred.

3/19. I met the assistant to the superintendent on the way to my desk this morning. He gave me a letter Chuck had written to his wife the night before and said it indicated that he was feeling pretty low in spirits. He said, "We've got some news for Chuck that will make him feel lower still." He told me about a letter that had been forwarded to him from the front house telling of an accident in which Susan, his wife's best friend, had been killed.

I read the letter Chuck had written. It was sensitively written and well composed. He talked of his disappointment over not seeing his wife the past Sunday. He urged her to write, telling him about herself and the baby. He talked about the break, and his fears that he would be "buried with time" when he came before the Board. He said he needed her help. Would she help him? He's afraid, lonely. Then I read the letter from his wife that had arrived the day before. She told of going out with Susan and of picking up a couple of men to go out dancing with. Driving home late that night the car had overturned. They all emerged unhurt. She and Susan walked up to the highway, where an oncoming car hit them both. Susan was killed instantly. She, Chuck's wife, was hospitalized with minor injuries, including a cut under the left eye which required three stitches. She said she will never look the same—nor will she ever be the same inside. She feels that Chuck will have every right to blame and reject her, but hopes he won't do this. She ended the letter: "Oh yes, Carol (the baby) is *very* sick with a cold." It seemed to me this was enough to send Chuck's feelings plunging to even lower levels.

I sent a pass for Chuck and then met him in the corridor near Center. I asked how he was and told him I would like to talk with him. I told him I was sorry I had not been able to talk with him on the day before, as we had planned, but I went home early with a rather severe case of laryngitis. He said he had been told. I asked how he was feeling. He said, "Pretty good." I told him I did not believe him. I didn't think he was feeling "pretty good." He said I was right; he feels "like the dickens." His mood is really low today. I asked if he thought it could get any lower. He said no, "This is it!" He is thinking about the break the other night, and what the Superintendent might do about it in relation to his time. He thinks he has really had it now. He remained silent after this. I did not follow this up. Instead I told him I called him in this morning because I had some bad news for him. He practically leaped across the table, saying, "Oh my God, what happened?" He seemed to sense that something was wrong at home. I hesitated. His eyes were bright, intently focused on me, anxious, waiting. I wondered who Susan was. He said, very rapidly, "Tell me, tell me, what has happened?" I told him his wife and Susan had been in an accident. Susan was dead. He became hysterical almost immediately. He threw up his hands saying, "My God!", then he braced his elbows on his knees with his head between his hands. Tears were falling to the floor. I hastened to add that his wife was in the hospital, but not seriously injured. He sobbed uncontrollably. He managed to ask me about the baby. I said she is fine. She has a cold, but she was not in the accident. He asked how I knew about this. I said we had a letter. "From who?" he sobbed. I told him it was from his wife. He wanted to read it, he demanded to read it. I handed it to him. He clasped it to his chest, still crying; then he opened it. He read the first page, sobbing all the while. He crushed the letter in his hands and threw it on the desk, saying, "I can't read it now, I can't read it now." His head went back in his hands—he cried hard. He tapped his foot on the floor, trying to control himself. Unsuccessful at this, he got up from his chair and walked across the room, still moaning and sobbing.

He was going through a lot. I felt embarrassingly conscious of my presence in the room. I wanted to say something, do something, but I restrained myself for a long while. Finally, I lit a cigarette, walked over, and shoved it in his hand. He thanked me. I told him to "Go ahead and get it out." Then I walked back to the desk. He remained standing there for minutes, with his back to me. Finally he returned to the desk and sat down. His eyes were wet, red. He picked up the letter again, saying he could not believe it was true.

He held the tears back while he read the first page. When he reached the second page, where she gave the details of the accident, he pointed to it, saying, "She shouldn't have gone further than this." He began to cry again, rocking back in his chair. I said it must be pretty hard for him. He came back to the letter, reading slowly. When he finished reading, he put the letter aside and asked if he could leave Bordentown. I said I didn't think so. His wife's condition didn't seem to be that serious. I got the impression that she would not be in the hospital too much longer. He was quietly sobbing again. I waited with him. After a while, I asked him what he wanted to do. He said his wife needs help; the hospital can stop her from bleeding, but they cannot give her the other help she needs. He has to tell her that everything is all right, that she shouldn't worry. I wondered if he could not do this without actually being at her side. How about a letter? Eyes still moist, but choking back the tears, he said, "A letter! You can't put anything in a letter!" After a few moments he said he might send a telegram. I asked what he thought he might say in a telegram. He said he did not know, except that he was sorry it happened and that he hoped everything will be all right, that she will be well soon. He turned away, quiet now. I felt he had gotten a hold on himself.

I said maybe she can visit him at Bordentown before too long. He broke down again, sobbing. He said, with much emotion, "God, she can't, she's in the hospital." I let him cry it out again. It was perhaps five full minutes before he said, with a great deal of feeling, "Only yesterday I wrote her a letter. Everything in it was depressing. I know it will make her feel bad." He started to cloud up again. I removed the letter from my inside coat pocket and handed it to him without speaking. He took it and said thanks, then tore it in half, all the while sobbing heavily. His head went down again in his hands. After a few moments I asked him if he wanted me to bring the letter back to him. He nodded yes. I said I thought he might want it; that was why I took the liberty to do it. I waited again before asking him how he felt about me bringing the news to him. He replied he couldn't have taken it alone —he just couldn't have.

He was trying hard to control himself. I asked if he needed help. He said no. I wondered what he thought he could do for his wife now—here at Bordentown. He said, "Nothing here." Then he broke down again and sobbed. "Not a thing here." He cried freely, unashamedly, like a baby. A man crying like a baby in the presence of another man is a difficult situation. I felt a need to say something, to do something that would check his tears. I remained still, thinking he would feel better later if he got it all out of his system now. There were times during the interview when neither of us talked for ten to fifteen minutes. His grief was overwhelming. He would weep until one would think no more tears could possibly come; then he would cry more, shed more tears.

He quieted down again. I asked him how well he knew Susan. He said she was like a sister to him and his wife. His wife had practically been raised with her. He said it just couldn't happen—not to Susan. He fingered the letter, reading bits of it and choking back his sobs. I wondered if he thought this was too much for him to take. No answer. Did he think he might like to run away? He said that's no good—that would accomplish nothing. Only make matters worse.

We were both silent for a long while. He was crying very softly now. It was approaching time for the 11:15 count. I asked him if he thought he could make it back for this. He said he can—he wants to be alone now. He picked up the letter from his wife, saying, "I want to go now." I asked when he wanted to see me again. He said, "Tomorrow; this afternoon." I said I would send for him again this afternoon. On the way out he asked if I could find out whether or not he could see his wife. I said I would try, but I didn't think there was much hope.

This was time for sensitivity and warmth. The two major currents in this man's life were pushing in opposite directions. One was the institution and the caseworker who were demanding that this man accept his incarceration and prepare himself for the time that he would soon receive and have to serve. Now there was this new and powerful force demanding that he go home. It was not the shock of Susan's death alone that caused this intense grief nor was it his wife's injury. There was the still unspoken reality that his marriage might not survive a prolonged separation. Already, after only four months, his wife was going to dances, dating with other men.

During the next several weeks a big part of the caseworker's job was to keep Chuck thinking about the time he was soon to receive, to neutralize the effect of his desire for parole, and to accept the reality of his continuing incarceration. This he apparently did, and on April 7 Chuck appeared before the Classification Committee and received 24 months.

This ended the beginning of the casework effort with Chuck. Much time had been spent with him, but the result was rewarding. For one thing, Bordentown was not just a jail—it was a place where men with problems receive help. Chuck confirmed this himself immediately after his appearance before the Committee in his interview with the caseworker.

4/7. "I have a great deal of respect and admiration for the staff."
"Why?"
"I feel they know what they are doing and they are really trying to help."

"Do you feel I'm giving you a cheap psycho job?"

"No, you're not. I know you pretty well. I actually want to talk to you. This is a good place if a man has to be locked up."

This from a man who has just been told by the officials of that institution that they would keep him behind bars, away from his wife and child, for two more years.

It will be recalled that Chuck Morgan was originally referred to the social service department of the institution because it had been noted early that he was finding it difficult to accept confinement. The separation from his wife and child, together with his own feeling of failure and guilt, caused him great depression. At the moment of re ferral he was "fighting a losing battle" and seriously contemplating escape. It took many hours of understanding casework effort to help him safely over the threshold of institutionalization. By the date of his receiving his "time" this had been accomplished.

He then was more ready to use the institution in a manner that reflected his acceptance of it as a source of help and not just as a place of confinement. Reports from the other agencies of help within the institution reflected this change. The teacher of his social adjustment class wrote in his report to the classification committee:

"Chuck, at the onset, showed signs of instability and pressures from institutional life with which he was unable to cope. Because of those problems he was not, at the beginning, able to participate in the Social Adjustment Program constructively. However, in the last few weeks, he has been doing his share in group discussions and shows increasing alertness in the classes—especially those portions dealing with children and family life. He is making satisfactory progress in an environment that was once difficult for him."

His work supervisor made similar observations remarking that "Chuck's cooperation is now excellent and his dependability good. I sincerely believe that this man should be transferred from his present housing location (the maximum security wing)."

For several weeks after Chuck received his time he and the caseworker continued to work together. The theme of the talks centered on the inmate's attitudes toward his wife. This was an important problem area for the man, but he never allowed himself to become involved. He was too dependent upon her to risk any real probing into the various aspects of marriage that went beyond the superficial. He continued to insist to the end that any and all marital problems would be cured by his return home.

The caseworker moved toward an ending. The timing was real. The worker was soon to leave the agency. In the interview of May 17 the worker brought into the discussion the reality of the ending.

5/17. I reminded him that I was leaving in two weeks and that I would be seeing him twice more—next Monday and probably the following Tuesday (since the following Monday is a holiday). He said the time is rushing; he is going to hate to see me go. I wondered if he could tell me why. He said because of the close friendship we have built up. He can talk to me. Something he isn't sure he could do with another staff member. He asked if I would be back. I said not. He would like to have me here, he said, until he gets ready to leave. I wondered if he thought I was really that important to him. He became silent. I said I thought he could do the rest of it without me. He said then that he could—that he wouldn't need to talk with anyone else after I leave. I said he might feel differently later.

It appeared that Chuck was going to end with his present worker. He was affirming that he wanted no other worker. He had shared as much as he could, and he did not want anyone else. No doubt he feared a new person. The reason for his original referral had been centered on his getting into the institution, and this was now complete. He wanted to end before the discussion possibly moved into more threatening areas of his problem.

In the recorded case material the student has not yet developed many of the skills of the mature experienced worker, but he has offered Chuck relationship in abundance. In a reformatory this is a great deal. The greatest single lack of many men committed to correctional institutions appears to be their dearth of experience with wholesome people. In providing relationships which meet that primal need a reformatory becomes more than brick and bars—it becomes a living growth experience.

chapter 12

School Social Work

A Social Invention

In his provocative volume, published some years ago, Professor Og-burn [1] produced a list of inventions and discoveries made independently by two or more persons at approximately the same time. He showed that while mental ability is an important factor in invention, the state of the culture is also an indispensable element. The accumulation of cultural antecedents makes possible—even inevitable—next steps toward an integration which is an invention. The automobile is a classic example of this: wheels, gears, internal combustion engine, clutch, drive shaft, carriage body, gasoline, brought into combination.

But there are also social inventions which are as intimately related to and arise out of the social milieu as do mechanical inventions. The juvenile court, for example, may be termed a social invention, having been developed at a time when not only the need was present (it had been present for centuries) but when the antecedent conditions of our culture had prepared the way for such a step. Workmen's compensation, social insurance, the civil service system, the city manager plan are other instances. School social work is another.[2]

In 1906–1907 the beginnings of school social work were developed independently in three different cities—New York, Boston, and Hart-

---

[1] Ogburn, W. F., *Social Change*. New York, Viking Press, 1922.

[2] At the time of the first edition of this volume (1942) the terms "visiting teacher" and "visiting teacher work" were the accepted expressions, but since then they have come to be replaced—increasingly—by "school social work" and "school social worker." Wherever possible in this revised chapter the newer terms will be used. However, there will be instances, for historical reasons, that the earlier terms will be used.

ford, Connecticut. In New York the immediate impetus came from two social settlements that had assigned visitors to school districts in order that the settlement house and staff might keep in closer touch with the teachers of the children who lived in the settlement neighborhood. The initiating group in Boston was the Woman's Education Association that established a home and school visitor in one of the city schools for the purpose of insuring a closer tie between the home and the school. In Hartford the suggestion came from the director of the Psychological Clinic. At first the worker was known as a "special teacher" who assisted the psychologist by gathering case histories and later by carrying out the recommendations.

The simultaneous development of this social invention indicated a common culture base which these cities shared. It also indicated that there were definite fundamental conditions as well as changes which had taken place or were taking place that pointed up certain needs. The response to these needs in these three cities resulted in the development of school social work.

The School Child Individualized

What were some of these conditions and changes? A fundamental condition was a school population. Not only was this school population enlarging because of a rising total population, but also because of an increasing measure of compulsory school attendance. These changes necessitated shifts in educational philosophy and practice. Before the days of compulsory school attendance there was no great concern expressed for the child who did not keep up in his class work or who raised too great a rumpus in class. The easy thing to do was to drop him out of school. School was for those who could use it as it was. If there was any changing to be done, that was not the province of the school. However, with the advent of compulsory school attendance (which, interestingly enough, placed the compulsory requirement upon the state to furnish instruction) there arose the problem of large-sized classes and the tendency toward regimentation upon a mass basis. The individual child stood a good chance of being swamped in the school system. The situation was still further complicated by the interpretation of compulsory attendance as meaning attendance up to a prescribed age. No longer could the nonconformist be bounced out of school merely because he was troublesome. No longer could even the dolt be denied entry into the public school.

Teachers, and teachers of teachers, were not uninfluenced by thinking in other fields. From the realm of psychology there emerged concepts of individual differences, of the varying equipments with which individuals came into the world (confirmed by research in biology), and of their capacity to adapt to the changing demands made upon them. Sociologists were concerning themselves with the nature of the social order as well as the modifiability of the human personality. Social workers, too, in their day-by-day casework practice, were learning something about the capacity of the individual to make the adaptation to his environment together with a fuller understanding of how that environment in turn might be altered to meet the individual's needs.

During the first decade of the twentieth century the contributions of these various specialities were focused upon the child in school. Because of large classes and concomitant regimentation with stress upon teaching of subject matter and the compulsion upon the child to fit himself into the mold of the school, a counter tendency developed which emphasized the needs of the individual child. The shift meant greater attention to the capacity of each child to make the adaptation to the school; it signalized a departure from the traditional role of preoccupation of the school with the intellectual life of the child to a concern for some of the emotional factors that are related to learning. It veered away from the criteria of successful teaching as the inculcation of a quantity of knowledge to the idea that a teacher's success might be more rightly measured by the growth of the child. The newer approach was finding its ultimate expression in the increasing efforts of educators to adapt the school program to the actual needs of a growing child.

The change was accomplished not by theorizing alone but by implementing changing philosophies so that practice exemplified theory. Attendance departments, medical inspections, special classes, psychological departments, and special service divisions were instrumentalities by and through which these changes were effected. School social work brought to the school setting an emphasis upon the individual child and with it a technique that augmented the skill of the teacher in dealing with a classroom teaching situation. Let it not be supposed from these sketchy remarks that social casework came as a fully matured professional skill in the years of the first decade of the century; rather it developed hand in hand with that of teaching in the joint effort to meet the needs of individual children.

Commonwealth Fund Support [3]

The subsequent development of school social work in this country gave substance to much of the early promise. Following the pioneering efforts of private agencies, a number of public school authorities introduced visiting teacher projects into the publicly supported school systems. Rochester, New York, may be cited as an early, if not the earliest, instance of such a development. There, in 1913, school social services were supported and controlled by the board of education. The greatest impetus, however, came from the program inaugurated by the Commonwealth Fund with its fourfold approach to the prevention of delinquency. One part of that program was committed to the National Committee on Visiting Teachers, affiliated with the Public Education Association, composed of leaders in the fields of education and social work. Thirty approved centers located in 23 states served as bases for visiting teacher demonstration projects. In each instance the community was selected after application (only 30 out of 270 applications were accepted) with the proviso that there would be local sharing (usually one third) in the payment of the worker's salary and an understanding that if the project demonstrated its worth, it would be taken over by the local community. For the first five years of the period beginning in 1921 the Commonwealth Fund conducted these 30 demonstrations, while for another three years it concentrated its attention upon training teachers for such work, increasing the understanding of behavior problems on the part of teachers in training, improving the standards of the work by field visits and conferences, and advising school systems that were interested in establishing visiting teacher service. After having thus contributed for eight years to a demonstration of the possibilities of this form of social service the Fund withdrew from the field in June 1930. As of that date, 21 of the 30 demonstration communities continued the work as a permanent part of the school system. The contribution of the Fund, however, went far be-

[3] For historical reasons the term "visiting teacher" is retained in this section on the Commonwealth Fund. See footnote 2, page 394.

yond the boundaries of these 21 communities. Within the next decade and a half, as the conviction mounted that what was needed was more, not less, social services in the schools, an increasing number of school systems inaugurated such services. Substantiation of this statement is found in the fact that there are now over 500 centers in which this type of work is being done. Although, inevitably, visiting teacher work spread throughout the larger cities, nevertheless many small towns and even some definitely rural areas demanded and were willing to pay the price for this service which was rapidly proving its value. Indeed, some of the best work has been done in these smaller communities, an effect not unintended by the Commonwealth Fund.

The Child Meets the Worker

Throughout the twentieth century there has been not only an expansion of the school population, but an expansion of auxiliary services to the school population as well. No longer was the sole objective of the educational system to stuff a certain amount of knowledge and information into the student. Increasingly educators came to believe that the school experience was more than just preparation for life, it was life itself. The implications of this concept made clear the importance of understanding the child's emotional life and of meeting those needs. Success in school thus became more than attainment of an arbitrary intellectual standard. It consisted more largely in the adjustment of the child in and to the life experience he was undergoing. The child who made a fairly adequate adjustment in the school setting was likely to make a fairly adequate adult adjustment later. This did not necessarily mean he would be richer or more famous, but it did mean he stood a fairer chance of getting sufficient satisfaction out of life to keep an even keel.

The acceptance of this point of view meant that greater attention had to be paid to the growth needs of children in school. The developments of social casework in other fields coincident with this evolving educational practice led, quite naturally, to the use of social casework in the schools. Thus the school social worker became a worker in a school setting, a person whose job it was to give help to a child, a parent or a teacher with a problem that centered in the school experience and the child's adaptation or lack of adaptation to it. As a social worker in the school, he may be called a school counselor, a visiting social counselor, a home and school visitor, a visiting teacher, or a school social worker. Administratively, the service may be placed in a department of pupil personnel and counseling, in a division of special services, in a guidance bureau, in a division of child welfare, in the office of the superintendent of schools, or in a separate department of school social services. In most instances the supervisory personnel will be trained social workers. In all instances, regardless of the title of the worker or the organizational location of the service the ultimate administrative responsibility lodges in the superintendent of schools.

There are advantages as well as disadvantages to such close affiliation with the school. It permits a rather natural approach to the worker by the child and the teacher. It can be as casual or as intensive as they are willing to make it. Frequently the child comes to accept the worker as a staff member long before he may have occasion to visit or be referred to him. Being on hand when things happen or during emergencies (or what seem at the moment to be emergencies) has its strong points when the worker is there to help. Then, too, the association between the school and the home is a natural situation that very often affords an easy entry into the home, or a comfortable visit by the parent to the office of the school social worker.

On the other hand, there is the likelihood that some of the value of the worker may be sacrificed by too close an identification with the teacher and with the school system. Not infrequently the school social worker will be associated with the authority of the school and the authority of the teacher. The worker must realize that most, if not all, school children are still trying to find themselves in relation to authority—authority in any form: parental, societal, legal, educational. If what the worker offers is indistinguishable from other manifestations of authority, the child may not be able to use school social services. On the other hand, the worker as an integral part of the school system is inevitably and properly related to its authority. Hence, the worker must feel comfortable with the school's authority in order to use it constructively on behalf of the child. There is a fine balance to be maintained here for the worker to be of maximum use to the child, a balance based on the worker's clarity about relation to the authority of the school and on clarity about the worker's professional difference and attendant skills. His usefulness lies in his likeness to the school as well as in his difference in ways of working. As a member of the school staff, he shares certain educational objectives with the rest of the staff, but at the same time brings a different professional skill.

Children come to the attention of the worker through referral by teachers, principals, social agencies, occasionally by parents, once in a great while by other children who know the visiting teacher, or by self-referral. The difficulties may be those centering around the child's personality and behavior, or around school adjustments, or detrimental home conditions that have their effects upon the child in school. The service may be rendered to the teacher, the parent, or the child. The quality of the service is the same as that demanded in any other social work agency, i.e., according to the best practice in the field of social casework.

All of these points need elaboration. Experience has shown that principals and teachers make most of the referrals. This is understandable, since it is to the teacher that the child presents a problem or is troublesome. The teacher may either attempt to deal with the situation herself or take the matter up with the principal or the school social worker. Should the matter be placed before the principal by the teacher, then it is the principal who makes the referral to the worker. Parents are next most likely to make referrals, followed by social agencies. The attendance department, the medical department, and the psychological testing department are also sources of referrals.

Children are referred for various reasons. The problem which the child presents may not be his fundamental difficulty, it may merely mask it, i.e., be a manifestation of some feeling within himself that is expressed in certain kinds of behavior. Scholarship troubles may indicate either lack of mental equipment (which a psychometric test will help to reveal), or they may refer to still more fundamental difficulties not reached by tests and measurements. A child may be failing because he is expected to perform at a level beyond his capacity, or he may actually be working far below his ability because he is emotionally blocked, frustrated, or so torn with inner conflicts as to be unable to organize himself. The boy of 14 years with an I. Q. of 119 may be failing his first year in high school in large part because of his struggles at home with a tyrannical father and an overindulgent mother. Besides those cases of children failing because of lack of ability or failing although possessed of above average ability, there are other children of ordinary ability who are failing, or doing very spotty work, or children persistently failing in one subject, or other children with profound lack of interest.

Other children are referred because of health or physical defects. A child, for example, may have been referred for years to the medical service for diseased tonsils and defective hearing. For years the school nurse may have gotten nowhere with the parents and have finally thrown up her hands in dismay and discouragement. In a new school this child may come to the attention of the school social worker because of low grades, inattentiveness and general mischievousness. The worker may immediately discern some connection between deafness, inattention, low grades, new school situations and later find back of them all a father who has stubbornly refused medical care for his child's growing deafness and who, at the same time, has set an enormous premium on high grades. Many cases of this type may first turn up with the school nurse and eventually find their way to the school social worker.

Personality or behavior troubles may also bring a school child to the worker. A discerning teacher may be quick to spot the child continually obsessed with fears and phobias, or the child who is always friendless and unable to mix with his fellows. More usually she may be aware of the child who is continually fighting, or stealing, or truanting. Parents may come to the school and to the worker asking for help for their child who resists staying in school or for the child who has developed habits or practices with which the parents feel powerless to deal, such as enuresis, masturbation, or stuttering.[4]

---

[4] An unusually useful analysis of referrals, especially by school principals, was made by Mildred Sikkema in a study under the joint auspices of the National Association of School Social Workers and the American Association of Social Workers. Principals, in the twelve communities in which school social work practice was examined, made referrals as follows:

1. Children whose behavior becomes progressively more difficult, or whose behavior has become chronic.
2. Children who differ considerably from the group over any length of time, who are isolated, won't talk, won't come to school, are unhappy, can't get along with others.
3. Children who are not making normal progress within their capacities.
4. Children showing sudden change which can't be readily understood and is something more "sensed" than seen.

What the Worker Does

While the worker may follow the general procedures of any case-work agency, she necessarily adapts them to the school situation. Even though the child has not asked directly for help and may begin as an unwilling client, nevertheless the worker may sometimes want to have an interview or interviews with him. Seeing the child may not necessarily be the first step. Very often children, particularly those in the lower grades, are better helped by working through the adults who are already around them as a natural part of their environment. To have another adult, the school social worker, come into the picture would in many instances be too confusing for the child. On those occasions when the worker does see him, he will want to learn from the child something of what he sees of his difficulty, if he sees it at all and of how or where he feels he needs help and how and where the worker can give it. If the teacher or principal has mentioned the child to the worker, he will want to hear a clear story of the situation as the principal or teacher sees it. Should the parent do the referring, the worker will want to talk with him in order to help to define the problem and to explore with the parent where help is needed. As in any caseworking agency, the application interviews are for the purpose, as Gordon Hamilton puts it, of creating a condition of mutual confidence, of permitting a tentative exploration and diagnosis of the area of difficulty, and of furnishing a preliminary estimate of the applicant's and the agency's capacity to deal with it. As part of the beginning steps the worker may want to examine school reports, medical records, psychological tests, but he will always understand that these are supplemental to and not substitutes for personal interviews. If he is to work with the child, he will want to have it clearly understood at the outset whether the

5. Children who, having trouble in school, come from a home situation known to be complicated.
6. Children who need special class placement.
7. Children with attendance problems which are chronic—after teacher and principal have first tried to solve them.
8. Children found by the nurse to need help she cannot give.

Emphasis is given to the importance of distinguishing between the symptom for which the child is referred and the problem back of the symptom. See Sikkema, Mildred, *Report of a Study of School Social Work Practice in Twelve Communities*. New York, American Association of Social Workers, 1953, pp. 16–17, 21–22, 23.

interviews are to be regular or occasional. He will also want to clear with the teacher and the principal the distinction between interviews with the child or his parents or with the school people. He will probably need to arrange for appointments of various kinds for examinations, medical and psychological.

Early in his contacts the worker will determine the basis upon which service will be rendered. In one instance he may decide that the child requires some intensive treatment which a child guidance clinic is in a better position to offer. This infrequently may involve help for extreme behavior disturbances owing to a physical cause, postencephalitis, or glandular dysfunction, or more likely it may call for protracted therapy with a child whose difficulties are deeply seated within the personality. The school social worker will continue with the case, but will carry it co-operatively with the clinic, or he will probably arrange for parent and child together to go to the clinic. With another child or in another situation the worker may leave the responsibility of the child's problem with the teacher, and reach the child indirectly by reason of the help which he gives to the teacher. A still further possibility is for help to be offered upon a short service basis for those needs which can be met through the medium of the school services, such as special coaching. Much of the effectiveness of such help depends upon the capacity of the individual child, parent, or teacher to change. The essential of the short service contact is an awareness of need, a willingness to change, and a capacity to accept responsibility for the growth which takes place.

Relation to Teachers

There has been a distinct reorientation of the school social worker-teacher relationship since the early days when the worker was in reality a "visiting teacher," i.e., a person who visited children's homes and brought such information to the classroom teacher as she had managed to uncover. After passing through various stages of trying to educate and then "casework" the teacher, present-day workers have arrived at a working philosophy that regards school social workers and teachers as two different professional people who are working together on a common interest—the child in a school situation—each sharing a mutual goal which is the development of the child through the medium of the school experience. The worker is of service by helping the child to get more out of the classroom experience or by helping the teacher so that she feels more capable of handling the situations with the child in it. There is a complementary professional relationship involved. The teacher with a class of 30 to 40 or 50 children cannot always sacrifice the movement of the group because of a small number of nonconformists. Her primary concern is with the group as a group. On the other hand, the school social worker is dealing with individuals with their own unique needs. If the classroom situation resolves itself into a stalemate between teacher, class, and nonconforming child (or children), then some dynamic will need to be introduced, i.e., change either in the child, the teacher, or the situation. This is a legitimate area within which the worker functions. But it must be recognized that change does not come to people unless they are willing to have it. This applies as well to teachers, who are just as much individuals as the children in their classrooms.

Teachers may ask for help of various kinds and for various reasons. They may want help for a child who needs to get over a tough spot in his own development. Even though teachers in training today are getting a great deal more knowledge of mental hygiene than formerly, they still find there are areas in which a more specialized skill needs to be summoned. This recognition of inability to handle certain involved emotional difficulties is as much a part of the teacher's job as is her handling of the subject matter that sets a bound to her teaching field. In most instances of this kind of referral the teacher and the caseworker will need to work together closely, with the focus being kept constantly on the child's adjustment to the school situation.[5]

Working Creatively with the Teacher

Throughout all of this discussion of the use of the caseworker in the school system there has been an implicit assumption that the two roles

[5] In this connection the study of children's behavior and teacher's attitudes by Wickman is revealing. What to the teacher is a serious behavior problem may be rated entirely differently by the mental hygienist. To the teacher defiance of authority, truancy, untruthfulness, and disobedience are serious offenses. To the mental hygienist there are other offenses which rank far higher on the scale, such as shyness, sensitiveness, unsociableness, fearfulness, and dreaminess. The shy and fearful child may never give the classroom teacher any trouble but he may be on the way to some serious difficulties later on. The disobedient and impertinent child may be an awful pest to the teacher, but he may be making a far more natural adjustment to the school situation than the dreamy or unsociable child.

of teacher and school counselor are different. No school superintendent and no teacher wants a caseworker to come into a school system and show him how to teach. School officials, teachers, and school social workers realize that what is helpful for the school is a caseworker who will not undertake to usurp the teaching function, but will work with teachers to help them handle their own classroom problems more effectively and at the same time will render a service to the children who compose the school.

Much of the caseworker's effectiveness depends upon the way he works with teachers. In the first place, the caseworker recognizes the teacher's feeling about the problem she is bringing. This is especially important since very often some of the problem may be with the teacher, and help can begin only after the teacher has been assisted to an understanding of her part in the situation. The teacher, however, remains the teacher and in no sense becomes the client. Teachers may have a suspicion and fear of a person from another profession on the staff merely because the worker is there. To handle the teacher without the insight and understanding that is expected in any professional relationship is to invite resistance and open antagonism. The reality with which they both work is the problem as the teacher sees it and her feeling about it.

Some teachers are very reluctant to bring notice of classroom difficulties to another person, whether it be principal or caseworker. To do so seems to the teacher a reflection upon her own professional capacity and a confession of failure. Nothing that the caseworker can say will relieve these feelings or invite the teacher to come. Only as the worker carries on his day-by-day job, unthreateningly, and as he comes to be accepted by the rest of the staff, can teachers feel comfortable about bringing their troubles. The caseworker who recognizes that a teacher may not want to come, by that very attitude may leave the teacher freer to work with the difficulty alone or eventually to come for help.

In contrast to this situation are those occasions in which the caseworker, through his way of working with the child and the teacher, has made it possible for the teacher to use the experience creatively. Many teachers can take such help, whether they ask for it only casually or deliberately seek it, and use it for their own professional development. In this sense they add not to the teaching content of their courses, but rather to their own capacity to understand more of themselves, their relation to children in the classroom, and their capacity to function more effectively. The objective toward which the worker is striving with the school staff is to assist in such a way that the teacher herself is better able to go on from that point in helping the child. This may consist of helping the teacher to see another side of the child, or to see him as he is, or to accept him as he is. If the teacher can feel that someone else has an interest in her concern with the child, it may release her enough actually to bear some of the heretofore impossible behavior. A child who at one time presented such behavior as to outrage the teacher, may become to that same teacher a person whom she can endure and even work with. Likewise, the child, who carries the brunt of the teacher's feelings because of what the teacher cannot endure within herself, may actually seem to change into a person acceptable to the teacher. On the other hand, the help the worker gives the teacher may be simply to provide the teacher with enough self-confidence and stimulus to work out her program in relation to her students and the classroom situations. Strange as it may seem, the worker's purpose is to be of such help to child and teacher that they can proceed on their own ways alone and under their own power. The worker does not do it for or to them, he does it with them and then withdraws to let them realize their own growth potentials.

Relation to Parents

From time to time children evidence in school some of the difficulties in their homes which hinder them in making normal adjustments. These come to the attention of the school social worker because they have a bearing on the use which the child is making of what the school has to offer. Practically speaking, what happens in the home is almost bound to carry its effects over into the school, if for no other reason than that the child spends so much of his time and his life in the modern school. Within recent years so many of the functions traditionally belonging to the family have been taken over by other institutions such as the school, that the school bears a much heavier responsibility for the development of the child than it did in those days when its sole task was to inculcate a certain amount of rote learning. In token of this, many parents turn more and more to the school for help with the children. When this happens, the school social worker is in an excellent position to help because the client—here the parent—comes willing to put something of herself into the experience. The worker is also fortunately placed because of his very association with the school because he comes to stand for, in the words of Miss Edith Everett, "an expression of the school's interest in, and concern for the happiness and success of the child who seems at the time not to be fitting into the school regime."

There may be occasions when the parent either does not understand what is going on in school or is indifferent to what is happening to her child by reason of her treatment of him at home. Reference here is not to those flagrant cases of cruel or vicious treatment of the child, which are matters that very often come to the attention of other community agencies, but to the more subtle, and in many instances, unconscious practices which interfere with a child's growth. The parent who shields a child from all responsibility for his school work or for his conduct may be crippling him just as much if not more so than if she were indulging in the grosser and more readily condemned cruelties. A child who neither knows nor accepts responsibility for himself is definitely limiting what he can get out of the developmental years of school life. Such a child may be helped by the worker if he can work with the child, his teacher, and his parents. He must be allowed to plan part of his program, his teachers must assist in those efforts, and his parents must be helped to realize their share in permitting the normal opportunities for the child's growth. No child can grow to responsible adulthood if other people always make his decisions. Sometimes even well-meaning parents fail to comprehend that.

The Burden the Child Carries

Another child may be compelled to carry too heavy a load. Some parents may feel that this generation is entirely too soft, and that what was good enough for them when they were 10 or 12 years old is still good medicine for their children today. Such parents may not always appreciate what this is doing to the child in making him timid and fearful of accepting any responsibility for fear of failure. The heavy load may be the expectations which a brilliant father has built up for his average-ability child, whose brothers and sisters by the roll of the dice of heredity are as brilliant as the father. This child may be haunted by the fear of failure until he actually experiences the marvelous relief that comes of failure under such circumstances. Still another load that is rather heavy for youngsters to carry derives from the instability of a family in which parents are incompatible but still preserving the outward forms of the family, or from a situation in which a child has lost one home and not yet gained foothold in another. Much of the insecurity that stems from such experiences will be reflected in the child's adjustment or lack of it in school. Few children can compartmentalize these two areas of their living.

Still another instance in which the worker functions in the school-home area is to be observed when questions concerned with the child's health are raised. The child, previously mentioned, who was hard of hearing had presented a problem of diseased tonsils and adenoids and running ears to the school nurse for a number of years. Despite the unquestioned fact that the child's condition was actually getting worse, the school had been able to get nowhere with the parents. While the mother was willing to try something, the father was adamant, declaring that no doctor was going to poke around his daughter's ears. To make his case still stronger the father had convinced himself that the body needed every organ that was there, otherwise why did the good Lord put them there? As for his daughter's ears, he was certain that when they stopped running her hearing would be better, but you could not keep them from running as long as there was something there to run.

The handling of a situation of this kind sheds some light on the contribution which a caseworker has to make in the school. After the school nurse and the teachers had given the child and her parents up as hopeless, the worker was called in. A visit to the home revealed that these parents set a tremendous store on high grades. Unfortunately, or fortunately, their child was failing in school. Her increasing deafness made it difficult for her to follow her teachers, and she had been getting more and more inattentive and mischievous. The fact that the next report card would show her deficient in most subjects was more than the parents, particularly the father, could stand. He was not yet ready, however, to do anything about those ears until he had some assurance from the caseworker that the head doctor at the clinic would examine his daughter's ears—"no student was to fool with them." By clearing with the hospital the worker was able to give them this reassurance. At no point, however, did the worker force them in their decision. He recognized that the child was still theirs, that all the force of the school and of the school nurse had come up against a stone wall. The more that pressure was brought against them, the more determinedly they resisted it, until after a while even the daughter was lost in the struggle. It was not until the worker could interpret the matter in the light of what meant most to them—their child's school record—and could do it not so much by words as by his feeling that this was ultimately their decision, that they could really take the step toward getting help for her. Again and again this same principle of social casework comes out: people still have a right to make their own decisions. What a caseworker does is to assist in the clarification of the question and then help the individuals come to the decision they really want to make.

Relation to the Child

The child is the person for whom school social work exists. He may not come to the worker for help as an adult does, and he may not be willing to put as much into taking on help as an adult might. Yet the very fact that he is a child, that he is getting into difficulties, that he would not, voluntarily, come asking for help (even if he knew a social worker when he saw one or understood casework, which he does not), creates a responsibility for adults to make help available to him. The one thing a child has an inalienable right to ask of adults is the right to grow. A necessary corollary to this is the right to be helped when he is having difficulty in growing.

When a question comes up in school about a child's developmental difficulties, it is imperative to keep the service centered in the school. Outside agencies, such as a child guidance clinic, a boys' club or a settlement house, may be used, but the core of the job is still with the child in the school setting. Hardly is this said than one realizes how important the teacher is in such a concept and in its execution.

A caseworker quickly recognizes the differences between children. One aspect of this matter of difference is the response of various children to the referral by another person and an offer of help. Some exhibit fear in diverse forms. This experience faces the child with a new situation and summons up the fear expressions that most of us employ when we are brought near to the unknown. It may also arouse his fears over loss of control of a situation by appearing to pass under the will of another person. Or he may evidence all kinds of resentment and hostility which are an attempt to keep another person out. A still further reaction may be to deny the difficulty all together, which serves to limit the entry of a person who wishes to help, while the opposite to this is for the child to admit fully his involvement in the difficulty, which becomes an open invitation for the worker to take over the problem.

There are many occasions in which the social worker is dealing with concrete matters pertaining to the child. Service may call for changing a child's class either because he is too far behind or too far ahead in relation to the age and school rank of children around him. A child may need to be transferred to another school or to a special school, depending upon his needs and the availability of other facilities. Perhaps another child requires special tutoring, or a psychological examination, or medical or dental care. Sometimes conditions may be so damaging at home that either home conditions will need to be changed or other arrangements will have to be made. Once in a while the services of other agencies will be called upon, either caseworking or group-working agencies, i.e., family society, a child welfare society, a social settlement, Boy Scouts, etc. Within recent years school social workers have become alive to the services of public agencies for children as well as, incidentally, for other members of the child's family. Such public welfare services come to mind as aid to dependent children, aid to the aged, child welfare services, unemployment insurance, and old-age and survivors insurance.

Despite all these services—and one should never underestimate what they mean in the lives of those in need—the fundamental fact remains that the worker is dealing with a human personality. That personality is contained in, in fact is, a child, with all his hopes, his fears, his likes, his dislikes, his "cussedness" and his likableness. The caseworker can help to change a child's environment and still leave the child in as much trouble as before he appeared on the scene. If any change is to come, it will be because the child (and the teacher and the parent) is willing to have it come, and furthermore, is willing to put something of himself into the changing. A starting point in this process is to be found in the attitude of the child: his attitude toward himself, his home, his school, his difficulties. That in many cases is the most tangible factor the caseworker has to work with. Once attitudes change, other developments follow. It is often said that human nature does not change. Perhaps we are not in agreement upon what human nature is, but this much is certain, that attitudes change. The school social worker is content to work in that area of change, and the change in behavior that follows.

Trends

One very pronounced trend in school social work has been the vertical and horizontal extension of the service. Formerly, the work was restricted to the lower grades and has since been extended upward through the high school. Formerly, only the older and more difficult cases were brought to the school social worker, while today efforts are directed more and more to getting help for those youngsters who are just beginning to show signs of trouble. Formerly, the worker was located in schools in the underprivileged parts of the city, today increasingly school social services are being made available to the total population in a given city or area. Formerly, the worker was used on an emergency basis—after all other agencies had failed with the child he was brought to the worker for the purpose of holding off commitment to an institution. Today, the worker's skills are used earlier and more and more as a preventive service.

Consistent with this shifted emphasis has been the change in the school's attitude toward "problem" children and toward the school social worker. No longer does the referral of a child imply failure, no longer is it a negative reflection upon the quality of teaching. Rather is it a recognition that there are certain difficulties in the classroom which the teacher knows to be more within the province of a specialist, and a realization that good teaching requires a yielding of the problem to another rather than a jealous guarding of it. Furthermore, the teacher remains active by sharing with the caseworker the helping service for the child. More and more teachers are developing a responsibility to the child that goes beyond his intellectual needs. Under such conditions the child (a hundred or a thousand of them) is actually better equipped to utilize what the school has to offer and a higher level of performance is inevitable. For the child there is no longer the stigma attached to referral to the school social worker, particularly since all children at one time or another evidence difficulties in school which they are having around growing up. Referral may mean that this is the first specific offer of help that has come to him.

One token of the increased acceptance and usefulness of the service is the demand for consultative service by principals, teachers and parents. Principals desire consultation not only about children's behavior problems, but also about some of the perplexities of dealing with a school staff. Frequently the worker will be used in staff conferences to help in staff development projects. Teachers, themselves, very often will bring to the caseworker some of their problems. These may be beyond the ken of the worker and he will suggest the proper agency, or, if it pertains to the school situation, the worker may give what help he can. Parents, too, have come to talk over a child's difficulties or their difficulties with a child, just as they would consult as freely and as easily another social agency.

Group work and community relationships have received an increasing share of attention within recent years. School social workers have met with groups of teachers or groups of parents in order to help with problems centered in the school. Active participation in parent-teacher associations have, in many cases, been considered a part of the role which the school social worker plays in the community. By reason of his strategic position as a social worker and as a school person he frequently has occasion to interpret each field to the other. In many communities he is the one person upon whom the responsibility falls for making known the unmet needs of children and for furnishing the stimulus to meet those needs. Thus he not only interprets the school, its philosophy and its practice to the community but brings firsthand notice of what is lacking in the community in order that the schools may be enabled to do a still better job.

School social work traditionally has been rather closely associated, if not in practice at least in thought, with truancy and attendance work. Some of its early connections with the school were through the attendance department. In other places school social workers resisted being tagged along with "hooky cops" and maintained that theirs was a social casework, not a legal or compulsive service. Nevertheless, the school social worker as a part of a school system that has compulsory attendance laws is obliged not only legally but by his very profession to accept the realities and the limitations which attach to his job. He is a part of the authoritative setup of the school. The child who is truanting, for example, needs help. That help is offered by facing up with the child the rules under which they both operate. The youngster needs just that sureness, that definiteness, from a person who is in a helping role.

Within the last decade or so there has been a trend toward coordinating these and other school services, including the medical, psychological, and guidance. Some school systems have no provisions for caseworkers but have for attendance officers. The tendency has been to employ caseworkers wherever vacancies occur in order to strengthen the service of the school. In such a co-ordinated scheme the school social worker has insisted upon a clear definition of casework function that sought to give help to the individual whether truant or not. The worker is interested in truancy not for the sake of instituting court action, but because truancy may so often be but a symptom of an underlying maladjustment either within the child or in his home or school environment.[6]

Another trend is in the direction of setting up the service on a state-wide basis. Heretofore, school social services were associated with particular cities—Rochester, Minneapolis, Philadelphia, Pittsburgh, San Diego, Cleveland, Los Angeles, Portland, being a few of the several

---

[6] Martha Perry very pertinently observes: ". . . Compulsory education laws, and attendance departments to enforce them, were an early reflection of a need for protection of neglected and exploited children. With the growth of the mental hygiene movement, visiting teachers with social work background became increasingly valued by the schools, but they deliberately divorced themselves from attendance departments because of their connotations of authority and compulsion. As child guidance clinics developed in the schools, with a dual responsibility to help the individual child and to further the schools' understanding of all children, a changing concept of attendance work has also occurred in some places. But a recognition that handling truant children is a case work job requiring a diagnostic rather than a legal approach has lagged sadly behind a recognition of the symptomatic nature of other types of behavior problems. As a paradoxical result, the child whose personal or home difficulties lead him to truancy is treated as a violator of the law; but if his difficulties lead him to other kinds of atypical behavior, he is treated as a clinical problem requiring expert professional diagnosis and treatment." (Martha Perry, "Truancy Is Not a Crime." *Better Times*, XXVII, December 7, 1946, pp. 1, 14.)

For a valuable exposition of the integration of school social work and attendance services in four communities—Indianapolis, Minneapolis, San Diego, Pittsburgh—see the entire March 1951 issue of *The Bulletin of the National Association of School Social Workers*.

hundred. However, within the past few years Virginia, Louisiana, Michigan, and Georgia have instituted provisions for such services throughout all school districts. The programs that have been legislated in these four states differ according to definition, method of state-wide coverage, integration into school systems, qualifications of workers, and basis of payment. Despite these understandable and inevitable variations the significance lies in the movement toward a casework service to reach all children during their critical school years.

A glance at the forepart of this chapter will reveal the impetus that was given to visiting teacher work by the Commonwealth Fund. The early emphasis, it will be recalled, was upon the prevention of delinquency. Two decades later the primary emphasis is to provide a constructive treatment for all children. It has turned from a negative to a positive role. Undoubtedly it can truly be said that its possibilities are unlimited once that objective is implemented in practice. Perhaps this is nowhere better stated than in an article by Miss Edith Everett entitled "The Dynamic of Case Work in School Counseling." Using the terms school counselor and school counseling for visiting teacher and her work she wrote:

For the child himself, the counselor offers the opportunity to experience for a time a school relationship which is different from that with the group. He finds in it respect for him as a person, a new awareness of himself as an individual and the beginning at least of an ability to accept the requirements of the school as just and right for himself and others. For the majority of children this comes naturally, as part of their growing up. But in the classroom as in society as a whole there are always some who are unfortunately caught at some point in their development and are "flying blind." Help for them at the right moment to clear some of the fog and get a straight course set, is as much the business of the schools as is their attention to the educational process set up for the entire group.[7]

BIBLIOGRAPHY

Books and Pamphlets

Benedict, Agnes, *Children at the Crossroads*. New York, Commonwealth Fund, 1930.

[7] Everett, Edith M., "The Dynamic of Case Work in School Counseling," in Taft, Jessie (editor), *Social Case Work With Children*. Philadelphia, Pennsylvania School of Social Work, 1940, p. 184.

Culbert, Jane F., *The Visiting Teacher at Work*. New York, Commonwealth Fund, 1929.

Oppenheimer, J. J., *The Visiting Teacher Movement*. New York, Public Education Association, 1924.

Ryan, W. Carson, *Mental Health Through Education*. New York, Commonwealth Fund, 1938.

Sikkema, Mildred, *Report of a Study of School Social Work Practice in Twelve Communities*. New York, American Association of Social Workers, 1953.

Significant Articles

Alderson, John J., "The Specific Content of School Social Work." *Bulletin of the National Association of School Social Workers*, XXVII, June 1952, pp. 3–13.

Coleman, Jules V., "Meeting the Mental Health Needs of Children in School Today: Psychiatric Implications for the Practice of School Social Work." *Bulletin of the National Association of School Social Workers*, XXVII, September 1951, pp. 3–13.

Everett, Edith, "The Importance of Social Work in a School Program." *The Family*, XIX, March 1938, pp. 3–8.

———, "Social Work in the School: Value to the Child of Casework Services." *Bulletin of the National Association of School Social Workers*, XVI, December 1940, pp. 1–12.

Molyneaux, Mary L., "The Principal—Liaison Between Faculty and the School Social Worker." *Understanding the Child*, XIX, January 1950, pp. 26–28.

Palmeter, Helen, "The Child in School and the Helping Team." *Bulletin of the National Association of School Social Workers*, XXIV, June 1949, pp. 3–18.

Poole, Florence, and Sikkema, Mildred, "An Analysis of the Structure and Practice of School Social Work Today." *The Social Service Review*, XXIII, December 1949, pp. 447–459.

Talbot, Mira, and Hinson, Isabelle, "Pupils Psychologically Absent from School." *American Journal of Orthopsychiatry*, XXIV, April 1954, pp. 381–390.

Wille, Jane, "The Relation of the School to Protective Service for Children." *Bulletin of the National Association of School Social Workers*, XXIV, June 1949, pp. 19–26.

Archie Prince

JANE WILLE, Consultant,
Visiting Counselor Program
Bloom Township High School
Chicago Heights, Illinois

School social workers offer services to children who are having diffi-culty in making constructive use of their school experience. Teachers recognize that many children have ability, but seem to be troubled by problems which prevent their doing adequate work and may interfere in their relationships with other children. These problems may reflect unmet needs of the child, and may become increasingly difficult to modify when the child continues this pattern over a period of time.

School personnel are becoming increasingly aware of the meaning of difficult behavior and are turning to the school social worker for help in understanding this behavior as well as for direct service to the child. Referrals to the school social workers are made by any member of the school staff and sometimes by the child himself, or his parent. These referrals are usually cleared with the principal who has over-all administrative responsibility for the service in the school.

In the Bingham School the service of the school social worker was well known to all of the teachers. The referral of children to the worker was by means of a flexible procedure in which either Miss Bailey, the principal, or the teachers might discuss the problem of a child with the school social worker to consider the appropriateness of the use of school social service. Usually the teacher had talked with Miss Bailey about a child's problem prior to her conference with the worker.

Archie Prince, age 10 years 5 months, grade 5A, came to the school social worker's attention in the following manner: At a recent Parents' Night at school Mrs. Prince told Miss Bailey that she was quite wor-ried about Archie's babyishness. Mrs. Prince said he will not take re-sponsibility although she has been making him do things over and over. He wants to play all the time and is never serious about anything. His teacher told her that he behaves similarly in school, wasting time and never settling down to work. Miss Bailey had not had an opportunity to discuss this further with Mrs. Harris, Archie's teacher, since the meeting, but earlier this semester, Mrs. Harris had talked with her about Archie's difficulty in participating in class work. Miss Bailey believed that Mrs. Harris might like the assistance of the school social worker since she had mentioned this as her next step if Archie did not improve.

Miss Bailey said that she had been aware of several instances of Archie's behaving in an immature manner in his relations with his classmates. She recalled one recent incident in which Archie seemed unusually distressed by some teasing of other children. This had led to a fight of a minor nature. Archie reported this fight in some detail to Miss Bailey. He seemed to feel that he was blameless. Miss Bailey discussed this pattern of behavior with Mrs. Prince and suggested that the school social worker might be of some help to her and Archie. Mrs. Prince was interested in getting help and would be glad to have the school social worker talk with Archie and then discuss his problems with her.

In Miss Bailey's analysis of what might be causing Archie's difficulties, she stated that she believed that Mrs. Prince's insistence that Archie not be told anything about his real father was a factor which might cause him some concern, and might account for some of his problem in school. Archie was legally adopted by his step-father three years ago. At that time, Mrs. Prince came to the school and requested a change in the school record. She had stressed that his former father should not be mentioned to Archie.

Prior to conferences with Archie's teacher, the school social worker examined the cumulative school record to note any facts which might assist in understanding the problem which Archie was showing. Group intelligence tests were in the high normal range although recent achievement tests were middle fourth grade level. A notation on the school record showed change of name at the time of the legal adoption.

The school social worker's planning started with a conference with his teacher, Mrs. Harris. Since usually the teacher is the most meaningful person to the child in the school setting, it is important that the school social worker see her work as supplementing that of the teacher and that she work in close co-operation with her. Although Mrs. Harris had not requested help at this particular time, she had been aware of Archie's problems and had been considering the use of school social work service. The record gives an account of the initial interview with Mrs. Harris.

Conference with Mrs. H, Teacher. I talked with Mrs. H about the concern which Archie's mother had expressed to Miss Bailey, at the recent Parents' Night meeting. I wondered how Mrs. H felt he was getting along in the class. Mrs. H described Archie as a boy who "shows off" by making faces and seeking attention in other ways. He talks "babyish," cannot stay put, and hurries to finish work which is usually poorly done. Sometimes, he works ahead of his assignments in his work book. I said that I could understand that this behavior was difficult and realized that the persistence of such behavior was an indication that Archie was not developing responsibility for himself. Mrs. H said that she had tried to get some cooperation from his parents, but she thought that they were trying to shield him by making excuses for him. She gained the impression that Archie was "spoiled and petted" at home. At different times Mrs. Prince has written notes complaining of the small happenings on the way to and from school. She said that she has been concerned about Archie's lack of progress because she knows that he has ability. Mrs. H commented that I have helped her with other children, and that perhaps this would be a good time to refer Archie. I told her that Miss Bailey and Archie's mother also had been considering this together, but that Miss Bailey wanted to know how she felt about it. Mrs. H said that she was becoming more certain that Archie needs individual help. She suggested that she would explain to him why she thought I could help him. It was agreed that I should stop at the classroom the following day to help Archie find my office. I told Mrs. H that I would be planning to talk with her after my interviews with Archie. We agreed that it would be important that we work together closely since she would be helping Archie to participate more responsibly in the group, and I would be helping him individually with concerns which he might be revealing. We recognized that some of Archie's difficult behavior might be lessened if his mother could also use some help.

In considering tentatively some of the factors entering into Archie's school difficulty, the school social worker recognized the influence of the overprotective attitude of his mother toward him. She was also aware that, as is often the case in working with school children who have pronounced behavior problems, she might have to help Mrs. H with her feelings about Archie and Archie's feelings about his parents. The school social worker is aware that the teacher's major responsibility is to the total group of children, and that a teacher could not be expected to give the kind of individual help which a child like Archie seemed to need.

One of the principles in helping people is that if there is to be change, it is the person himself who must change. In the school setting parents, teacher, and the school social worker can all help the child in different ways, but, in the final analysis, the change must be within the child himself if it is to be effective. For this reason the school social worker always works with the child unless there seems to be some problem which could be considered specifically a parent responsibility, such as inadequate clothing, malnutrition, etc. The purpose of the school social worker's work with the child is to help him to understand his difficulty as the school sees it, to learn some of his feelings about the problem, and through a relationship with the worker to work on the parts of the problem for which he can take responsibility.

First Interview with Archie. I went to Archie's room for him at the time agreed upon. When he came to the door, I said that I was the school social worker. Archie seemed to expect me and came willingly to my office. I discussed with Archie some of the reasons why boys and girls come to talk with me. Archie said that he knew another boy who was seeing me and remarked that this boy gets into much more trouble than he does. I commented that he did not seem to be getting into so much trouble, but Mrs. H, his teacher, and Miss Bailey thought that perhaps he is not getting along as well as he could. What did he think about this? In reply to this question, Archie said that he thought that he was getting along all right. I talked with Archie about how for some reason, he was not making the progress which Mrs. H thought he could. Archie said Mrs. H had told him this, but he could not think why this was so. He said that he had trouble with some of the kids in school. He described an incident when four kids "jumped him" and gave him a black eye. Rather emphatically, he said that he does not like fights and does not start them, but if someone "jumps him," he tries to defend himself. I agreed that it was important that he defend himself. I wondered what he thought caused the fights. He could not say, but said there were mean kids in the school. I wondered if there were any other things that worried him. He could not recall any.

In reply to my question about how he likes school, Archie said that he likes school very much. I thought that it was fine that he likes school and said that perhaps it seems a bit hard for him to understand why Mrs. H and Miss Bailey think he needs some help. He has, however, told me about some problems he has in school, about fighting and not liking to fight, and I wondered if he would like to come again to talk to me about this to see if it would help him to get along better with other boys in school. Archie said that he would like to come and he felt O.K. about talking to me.

I said that perhaps he would tell me what kind of things he likes to do. He then told of activities with his father, such as building boats and model airplanes, and occasionally going hunting. He also described their workshop in the basement. As Archie talked, he referred often to "my father" and to all of the things he does for him such as helping him save money for his college education. He repeated several times that his father was very good to him.

Following Archie's reference to college, I inquired if he had thought where he might go to college and what profession he might choose. He was not sure, but he had thought of the university, and he would be a doctor or a lawyer. He gave the impression of having no real interest in college, but wanting to please his parents and me. I asked if his mother especially wants him to go to college. He said that she does, and added that he will do everything for her. I wondered if he is really interested in going to college, too. "Oh, yes," he replied. "I want to get a good education." His mother had asked him whether he wants to be a doctor or a lawyer and he told her "either one, whatever you want." I guessed he must think a lot of his mother to want to do everything to please her. He said he surely did, and added, "and my father too."

I suggested that Archie come in next week at the same time when we could talk more about the problem he had brought up about his fighting. He suggested that he would come to my office himself and left with a "Good-bye."

In this first interview with Archie, the school social worker attempted to determine how much recognition Archie had of his difficulty as seen by Miss Bailey and his teacher. It was apparent that Archie had considerable need to maintain that everything about school was all right and to minimize any indication to the contrary. Archie pictured himself as a boy who understands what is expected of him and who makes every effort to please adults. His ready compliance with the teacher's request that he see the school social worker was typical of his pattern of doing the expected thing. His behavior in Mrs. Harris' classes, where he did things which attracted attention, was something he could not accept responsibility for at this time. It seemed as if Archie had so much need to have approval that he denied the reality of anything which he felt might threaten this. Archie had pictured an ideal family relationship and seemed not to want anything which would conflict with his parents' wishes. The school social worker recognized that gradually Archie might be helped to assert some of his own wishes and needs. To help him attain some measure of self-assertion, the combined efforts of his teacher and principal, the help of his parents, and awakening his own interest in change would be necessary. Although Archie did not acknowledge the problem as seen by the school, he recognized, as most children do, that he did have some difficulty that was worrying him which he expressed in his fear of fighting.

Second Interview. For the first part of this interview, Archie talked easily and with some enthusiasm about his activities in Boys' Club and in the Cub Scouts, which had been of interest to him in the past week. Archie then described some boxing matches that he had watched at the Boys' Club. Although he takes part in the boxing there, he said that this seems like a game and he likes it. I wondered if he had been in any more fights on the way to and from school. He replied emphatically, "No, not yet!" I asked what he meant by "not yet" and he said that he hoped he would not be. He expressed himself very freely, saying that he does not like fighting and does not think anyone ought to fight ever.

I said that some boys do not like to fight because they are afraid that they might get hurt, and I wondered if this might be true of him. In a low tone, he said, "I guess that's it. I am afraid." Archie seemed to sense my understanding of his fear, and gave his own interpretation to explain it. According to Archie, when he first moved into his present neighborhood, a big boy fought him. He was so afraid of that boy that he has always been afraid to fight. I helped Archie to recognize his fear as a natural one. I reminded him that he had told me last week that he wanted to be able to learn to defend himself. I said that I thought it was important for him to be able to do this and that by learning to box well at Boys' Club, he might be able to take care of himself when other children threatened him.

The problem, as Archie presents it in this interview, is closely related to the problem as seen by his teacher and principal (babyishness, crying, and telling tales). These feelings of fear could be interfering with his ability to do academic work because it is evident that Archie is not comfortable with other children in school and is not free to use his abilities.

In his next interview Archie seemed secure enough in his relationship with the school social worker to begin to explore further his fears which he said that he had never discussed with anyone before. In this interview, he again talked about fighting, commenting that he is so afraid that he trembles inside if he even thinks someone is going to fight him, and that he wouldn't even fight back if a first grader picked a fight with him. As Archie talked with the school social worker about these fears, she told him that she understood how hard it must be for him in school when he has these fears and, in both manner and words, let him know that it was all right to have them and that she was not critical of his inability to fight. This relationship with the school social worker was a new experience for Archie since he had previously been told that such fears were "babyish" and that he should be more grown up. As Archie realized that the school social worker had respect for him as he was, there was some beginning change. He looked directly at her and smiled as he said, in a relaxed manner, "I'm not as scared as I used to be."

After this, Archie described another fear. When his mother and dad go out at night, he is afraid that something will happen to his mother. In discussing this, Archie mentioned specific instances and commented about one of them, "That was when I had my first dad." The school social worker realized that Archie was bringing out some of his underlying fears and that her acceptance of them would be reassuring to him. With this reassurance he might be more secure in his feeling about himself and begin to discover his capacity to grow and change. The school social worker told Archie that she thought that it was good that he had been able to discuss these problems, that she helped other children with similar problems, and that she would keep this time for him each week.

It is important for children to feel that their parents are interested in them and want to help them. The school social worker had told Archie that she would be seeing his mother and he had expressed willingness. Archie had talked with his mother about his interviews and knew that she approved. He seemed glad to take home a note to his mother from the school social worker which said it would be helpful to talk with Mrs. Prince, and suggested a time. (Often the child takes a part in making appointments with parents since this helps him know that he is participating in what is happening to him.)

Interview with Mrs. Prince. Mrs. Prince came exactly on time for her interview. She was a small, attractive, well-dressed young woman. Her manner was very friendly. She knew that Archie had been seeing me and said she was glad to have him do this. She said that she did not fully understand the service offered by the school to help children with problems like Archie's, although Miss Bailey had explained it to her. She said that she thought it was good for the school to help children with problems, but would I explain this further to her. I said that I knew she had discussed some of her worries about Archie with Miss Bailey, and that his teacher also recognized that he was having some difficulty. I explained that I help children and parents with such problems as Archie's because often they do interfere with school achievement and we recognize the importance of clearing them as quickly as possible. I described the interviews with a child as giving him an opportunity to express his feelings about matters which may worry him or may be causing concern to his teacher. Through understanding his feelings and helping him to work on his problems, we can help him to participate more responsibly in school. I said that Mrs. Prince's assent to Archie's coming had been quite helpful since this permits him to talk more freely to me. I suggested that together we work toward a better understanding of Archie and ways to help him in school. Following this interpretation, Mrs. Prince said that she felt that she should tell me about Archie.

She then began to describe her difficulties with Archie's father, which started soon after her marriage. Mrs. Prince spoke bitterly of the treatment she had received from Archie's father. Because he would not support her and Archie, she had to leave Archie with her mother until he was 5 years old. At that time, she married Mr. Prince.

Until Archie was adopted by Mr. Prince three years ago, his father came for him every Sunday. Mrs. Prince said that Archie did not like to go with his father and just stayed upset from one week to another. This continued until Archie's father gave up all rights to see Archie when he signed the adoption papers. A lady from the Court explained what his adoption would mean, and told him that he was not to see or know anything about his father from then on. I commented that this would probably be difficult for Archie, even though he had not seemed to enjoy his father's visits. Mrs. Prince replied that it did not seem to hurt Archie or his father; she, Mrs. Prince, was the only one who cried. From that time on, they have never talked about his father, and now she is wondering whether or not that was the right thing. She hesitates to mention it because she thinks that perhaps Archie has forgotten it or does not think about it any more. One time when someone knocked at the door, Archie said, "Maybe that's your ex-husband." Mrs. Prince said that she thought that was a slip of the tongue and ignored it. I wondered if that might not mean that he does think about his father but does not talk about it because it is a forbidden subject. Mrs. Prince said that she is beginning to feel that it might be better to talk about Archie's father some. She could see that he might worry about this and that it might help if she could answer any question he might raise.

Mrs. Prince then talked of her concern that Archie might grow up to be like his father. He has some of his characteristics, such as not taking responsibility and never being serious about anything. Mrs. Prince was particularly concerned because Archie has started lying to her. I thought it must be discouraging to her to have Archie seeming to be developing characteristics which she disliked in his father. I suggested that we talk together about these concerns particularly as they relate to Archie in school, and that through our discussion we might consider what may be possible to effect some change.

Mrs. Prince said that she was worried about Archie's most recent report card with failures in Reading and English and also an unsatisfactory rating in Citizenship. She has talked with his teacher, Mrs. H, who seems to consider him lazy and irresponsible. Mrs. Prince said that she is inclined to believe this is true but knows that something must be causing this behavior. After her conference with Mrs. H, Mrs. Prince felt that she would make every effort to bring about some change. She decided that the best way to do this would be to insist that Archie remain at home to study after school so she has forbidden his attendance at club groups. After his grades are improved, he can return to these groups. I said that it must be hard to hold to a decision to have Archie not take part in activities at the Boys' Club. Mrs. Prince agreed that it is hard, and she added that she and Mr. Prince did permit him to go to an initiation.

Mrs. Prince then expressed some of her uncertainty about what to do to help Archie become more responsible. She tended to blame herself to some extent since she had "babied him" when he was ill. She also realized that Archie did not really have a father until she started to go with Mr. Prince. Although she has petted Archie and "made him babyish," some people tell her she is too strict. I told Mrs. Prince that it will be important that she attain the kind of relationship with Archie in which she feels comfortable about her discipline of him.

Mrs. Prince said that she was glad to talk with me because Archie really is "a problem child." She had tried to get some help from different relatives, but was discouraged when both of Archie's grandmothers had said that Archie was just like his father and grandfather, and that there was nothing she could do. I said that Mrs. Prince's coming to school for help was an indication that she thought that there could be change. It seemed, from what we had discussed, that both she and the school saw Archie as needing help to grow up and assume responsibilities in keeping with his age and ability. I suggested that Mrs. Prince consider coming to see me regularly for a few weeks so that we could work together in trying to help Archie. Mrs. Prince seemed eager to make appointments, and we agreed on one for the following week.

In this first interview with Mrs. Prince the school social worker saw Mrs. Prince as a mother who recognized that she needed help with Archie. Since much of her concern centered about Archie's school difficulty, this seemed to be an area where Mrs. Prince might be helped to engage in a more constructive relationship with Archie. Mrs. Prince showed some capacity to modify her past attitudes as she questioned whether forbidding discussion of Archie's father was a good plan. The worker also noted indications of strength in Mrs. Prince's willingness to talk about ways of helping Archie become more responsible. She recognized that this was not going to be easy since Mrs. Prince also felt quite possessive toward Archie, but she noted the eagerness with which Mrs. Prince accepted appointments as a way of reaching out for continued help.

The following week Mrs. Prince was exactly on time again. She began telling me immediately that she had her enthusiasm somewhat subdued by the fact that Mr. Prince could not see why the school was "picking on" Archie. After her visit last week, she had been so enthusiastic that she could hardly wait until Mr. Prince came home to tell him about her interview with me. Mr. Prince responded by wanting to know why she had been asked to come to the school, and if Archie were so much worse than the other kids. When she tried to explain, Mr. Prince did not understand so she really began to wonder if she fully understood. I thought it was possible that not only Mrs. Prince felt disappointed that Mr. Prince had not understood the purpose of our interviews together, but that perhaps Mrs. Prince herself felt somewhat uncertain that she could get help in her problem with Archie through these interviews at school. Mrs. Prince was unable to acknowledge this, but she asked me to explain further. I recalled that when Mrs. Prince had talked with Miss Bailey of her concern about Archie, Miss Bailey suggested that I could help her with this. To do this, I started by seeing Archie since it was important for him to recognize the need for change and to take some part in it. Since Archie had been having difficulty in his school work and his relations with children for some time, it was important that we consider together what was causing that difficulty and together try to find a new way of helping him. This was of concern to both her and to us at school, since we believed that his school problems were a part of his total difficulty, which she knows is evident in other ways. It would be important to start with the school part of his problem if this was something she was concerned about and wanted to work on. Mrs. Prince listened intently. There was a short pause and then she said that she understood this better and thought that it would help her to continue talking with me. Although she has sometimes wondered if she makes too much of Archie's problems, she knows that this is not true and for the first time she feels better about being able to help Archie.

Mrs. Prince then said that since she had last seen the school social worker, Archie has had fewer complaints of getting into difficulties on his way to school. She believed that she has been able to be less concerned when he brings problems of name calling and similar small difficulties. She was particularly pleased that she had been able to let Archie take responsibility for making a trip alone which required going to the Boys' Club by street car.

I said I thought this sounded very good. I wondered if it were hard for her to let him go alone. It was, but then she remembered that when she was 10 years old she was riding street cars and going to town alone. She added, "And, after all, Archie is a *boy*." I said that I thought it was fine that she recognized that Archie was old enough to do this, but I knew that it would not be easy for her to let Archie do some things which he might also be able to do.

Mrs. Prince said that she knows that it is important to help Archie to develop more responsibility for taking care of himself, but added that it has been hard for her "to let him turn loose from my apron strings." I told Mrs. Prince that when we work with parents, we usually talk with both parents and that I thought it would be helpful for me to see Mr. Prince, particularly since he had some question about the service. Mrs. Prince said that she would talk to him about it, but that she was not sure that he would be able to get away from work.

The school social worker recognized that, although Mrs. Prince was concerned about Archie and had expressed an interest in helping him to change, it was also hard for her to do this. Her doubts about continued work with the school social worker were re-enforced by Mr. Prince's questions. The school social worker again explained the service to Mrs. Prince in such a way that Mrs. Prince realized that she will have a choice in the way in which she uses it. With this reassurance, Mrs. Prince was able to tell the school social worker that she was pleased with some of the change in Archie. As she described his trip to the Boys' Club, she showed some pride that she had been able to make a beginning in letting him move away from her.

Mrs. Prince's readiness to use the help of the school social worker constructively at this time was evidenced by the fact that, at her suggestion, Mr. Prince came in for an appointment. Mr. Prince's attitude toward the school social worker was so positive that it seemed that, out of her own doubts about the service, Mrs. Prince had overemphasized his questions.

Mr. Prince described Archie much as others had—"babyish, crying, etc." He attributed this to Mrs. Prince's overprotective attitude. He described her tucking him in bed at night, and not wanting him to participate in activities appropriate for a boy his age. Mr. Prince explained that, in his position as a step-father, he found it difficult to criticize in any way Mrs. Prince's relationship with Archie. He said that he had tried to be a good father through planning some recreation with Archie, taking him on hunting trips, and spending time with him in their workshop. When he and Archie are alone, they get along fine; Archie likes to work with him and takes his suggestions, but the minute his mother appears she means everything to him. He sees Archie as having passed the age when mother should be everything and being now where he needs a father's guidance. He frankly said he ". . . would not have Archie love his mother less, but in a less baby-ish way." Mr. Prince showed real warmth in his feelings for both Mrs. Prince and Archie. The school social worker gained the impression that he would be able to give a good deal of support to any change in Archie or in Mrs. Prince's attitude toward him. She told him she realized that he had tried to be a good father, and that Archie had spoken enthusiastically about their time together. She explained that she would be working with Archie, Mrs. Prince, and his teacher in help-ing him to become more mature. Mr. Prince said that he was "all for this service" and he was glad for Mrs. Prince to come. He said that he would continue to do everything he could to help. The school social worker suggested that if, at any time, Mr. Prince had any questions or would like to talk with her, she would be glad to have him come in, and that if she found other ways in which he could be helpful, she would call him.

As the school social worker works with the child and his parents, it is important that she talk regularly with his teacher. Through these conferences the teacher is able to acquire a better understanding of the child and his family. Through this understanding she is able to de-velop ways of helping to meet the needs of the child in the classroom. As the teacher and school social worker talk together about their progress in working with the child, both may develop better ways of helping. The teacher gains support as the school social worker accepts the validity of her feelings about the child. She often then is able to test out ways of helping the child and feels acceptance as she discusses these means with the school social worker. At times she recognizes that a feeling of irritation with the child existed because she only partially understood the meaning of the behavior to the child, and could not alone find a way to effect change. The school social worker's contribution to the teacher is not in making suggestions about classroom procedure, but is in freeing the teacher to use constructively her own creative ability. Although only a few interviews with Mrs. Harris are included, regular contacts were maintained. The teacher had recognized that Archie had needs which could not be met through the teacher-pupil relationship, but which were impeding his school progress. The school social worker helped her to understand some of the basis for Archie's problem. Through the understanding gained, Mrs. Harris was able to participate with the school social worker and the mother in helping Archie to develop more responsibility for himself. She also contributed understanding from her observations of Archie in the classroom which helped the school social worker. The following interview illustrates Mrs. Harris' ability to develop ways of helping Archie as she gains a better understanding of him.

Conference with Mrs. H. I talked with Mrs. H about Archie's mother and her attitude toward him; that in many ways she is overindulgent and overprotective, which may be responsible for his babyishness and irresponsibility; that, on the other hand, she is very ambitious for him and seems to be over strict in her demands to have him *good,* make good marks, and in everything be a model child. I described how severely she had dealt with him about the three U's on his report card by taking away privileges.

I commented that Archie is pretty anxious about the next report card. Mrs. H checked her grade book to see what Archie had done since the last report. She found that he was doing better than she thought. She believed he would receive an "A" in English next time.

I said that I had found, from talking with Archie, that he always thinks about things in terms of what someone else wants (mostly his mother) and that I have felt one thing he needs is to want to do things because of his own feelings or for his own satisfaction.

Mrs. H then made a suggestion to help Archie. She hoped I could help the mother to relieve him of all pressure at home about school work after the next report cards. She will talk with Archie about what his school work means to him and about how whatever he does with it is for himself, not for her (although she is interested and concerned) or for someone else.

We then talked about the possibility that the pressure and anxiety he felt might have been getting in the way of his progress. If these can be lessened, we shall both be interested in seeing what happens.

Casework service with Archie and his mother continued until the end of the school year, and regular conferences were held with his teacher. Following the interview with Mrs. Prince in which she described his trip alone to the Boys' Club, the school social worker commented to him that his mother had mentioned something that he did on Saturday and she thought he might like to tell her about it. Archie gleefully told about his trip to the Boys' Club, the street car ride alone, and the shopping. I wondered how all this made him feel, to which he replied, "It makes me feel like I'm grown up." This statement characterized the tone of further work with Archie. He brought many problems to the worker, at times seemed discouraged, but there was always a willingness to test out his strength in working toward a solution. With each accomplishment he seemed to grow in stature in his own eyes. Social workers know that progress is slow and that there are many periods when difficulties arise. They know too that with a child such as Archie who has been willing to participate in working toward change and has gained satisfaction as evidenced in such remarks as "I'm not so scared as I used to be," and happily says "It makes me feel like I'm grown up," that with skillful assistance, he will find ways to realize his potential for growth. Archie learned that he could count on the school social worker to be with him in his successes and failures. This was demonstrated to him when she recognized how pleased he was when he proudly brought in his report card with all "Satisfactory" grades and one "A." It was also apparent to him in her understanding of his feelings when he received an "Unsatisfactory" mark in Citizenship. Through her manner and actions, Archie learned that he could be sure of her consistent interest in him and her recognition of him as a person "in his own right."

Excerpts from interviews with Archie illustrate a growing recognition of himself as a boy secure enough that he no longer needed to maintain that "everything is all right," but could reveal both his positive and negative feelings. This was an important step toward becoming more mature.

There was a commotion in the hall and Archie said, "Miss V is always bossing people around. If anybody doesn't walk up the steps just like everybody else, they have to go all the way down and come up again." He went on to say that "Some people are born so they walk differently but they have to go back to walk just like the ones who do it on purpose." I wondered if he had to go back and walk up again. He replied emphatically, "No, not me!" and drew his shoulders up as though he'd never let it happen to him. Then he said, "Sometimes, I get so mad when someone bosses kids around." I wondered if he meant when other children were "bossed around." He said, "Yeah, and me, too."

In another interview he began to express a growing realization of his ability.

He made several drawings, changing from one theme to another. He drew a horse, paused, looked at it and said, "Look at that, I didn't know I could draw one so well." He drew several things, saying as he did about the horse—that he didn't know that he could do so well. I said that it was "nice to find out that we can do things well, isn't it?" He agreed and said that it was "funny, the things you find out you can do."

Although Archie was never directly critical about his mother, in an indirect way he began to reveal that he did not always consider her entirely right.

Archie said his parents will be at school tonight, and he surely wants his mother to go in his Arithmetic classroom because he has a paper with an "A" on it. He also wants her to see that they have only three numbers in the dividends of the problems they are working and not long numbers like she has been making him do. I wondered if he had not told her this and he said, "Heck, yeah, I told her, but it would be a lot better for me if she found out at school."

One of the high spots in Archie's taking initiative for something he very much wanted to do came in the following way:

Archie said, "Remember, I told you I couldn't ride a bike." I remembered, and he said that he had learned how to ride one on Saturday. When the other boys went in the house, he got on the bike and went flying down the hill. He was scared, but he rode. When they came out, they said, "Where is the bike?" There he was riding. He had been telling everybody he could not ride and now they all saw him riding. I said, "Sometimes we find we can do lots of things we thought that we couldn't do." We recalled how he had said about other things that it was funny the things you found out you could do. He then described how he was planning to sell his scooter, wagon, and three-wheel bike to get money to buy a two-wheel bike. "Of course," he said, "that might not be enough, but I'll see."

By the end of the year Archie's school work had improved markedly. Mrs. Harris reported that he was taking responsibility for himself. As one would expect, there were occasional lapses, but these were of brief duration and much less frequent. His relationships with other children in the class were greatly improved. When Archie experienced an accepting relationship, he could discuss his fears and bring out some of his problem with his school work. It was not necessary or desirable for Archie to understand the basic causes for his problem. Continued interviews with the school social worker helped him to express more of his real feeling and to recognize that it was safe to express some of his angry feelings. With this freedom came an ability on his part to develop more independence. This was enhanced by the change in his mother, but it was important that Archie also experience a relationship in which he could test out his own strength.

Mrs. Prince kept her appointments with the school social worker regularly. Although she understood that at times Archie's behavior would be difficult, particularly when he began to assert himself more, these periods were especially trying to her. Even as she complained to the school social worker about how annoying his behavior was to her, her interest in his becoming a happy child seemed paramount, as she assumed responsibility for her own change. Recognition of her own part in Archie's difficulties and evidences of real change are illustrated in the following interview:

Mrs. Prince seemed to have gained a bit of understanding of Archie and his problems. She said that after I discussed the plan concerning his homework with him he seemed to have the idea that he could do just as he pleased and that she was not to tell him anything to do. For the *first time* in his life he has been openly rebellious with her. Since the plan was discussed with her from the beginning, she knew what he had been told and that this was just his way of trying to become more independent. She let him know that there were some things, like his chores around the house, that he must do, but sometimes it had been a struggle. She said she expected this kind of behavior because of the things we had talked about, but if she had not been coming in to see me and finding out about these things, she wondered what she would have done.

I thought it was very good that she did understand and could let him bring out some resentment toward her while, at the same time, she set up some limitations for him. We talked about how he will want to be both independent and dependent. She could see this because when he was sick, he cried when he wanted more attention from her.

I told her what Mrs. H had said about his work. She knew that he had a "bad" paper from Mrs. H because he carried it home for her to see. She knew from the way he threw it on the table it was not good and when she said she was afraid to look, he said, "Go ahead, it won't bite." At first, he resented her even mentioning homework, but several times now he has asked for some help.

Mrs. Prince was able to bring out a good many of her feelings in the interview. During the holidays she noticed that whenever they had company or were visiting, Archie stayed with his dad and the other men and "didn't hang around me at all." I wondered how she felt about his turning to his father in this way. She said, "Oh, I think it's good for him, but I realize now I wasn't willing to let him do it before I started coming to see you." She wanted to tell me that when she first started coming in she thought everybody was trying to take Archie away from her. His dad was always saying she "babied" him too much. She thought he was just jealous. At school we were saying he needed to be on his own more and even the Boys' Club wanted to take him away for a summer camp. Now she sees all this as part of his growing up and she plans to let him go to camp no matter how much it hurts her. He always seems glad to go. I wondered if this might be because he wanted to be free from so many restrictions although he had not been openly rebellious. She said she had been thinking of that.

In the school social worker's contacts with Mrs. Prince, although many of the details of her relationship with him indicated some continuing concern about minor incidents, the degree of satisfaction with Archie increased as she recognized the normalcy of his behavior and as she received acceptance as a parent capable of improving her relationship with her child.

Toward the end of the school year she seemed comfortable in letting Archie participate in activities appropriate for his age. She mentioned his desire to have a two-wheel bicycle and said that they were planning to help him buy one. She recognized that his school work had improved since he was taking more responsibility for this himself. She and the school social worker agreed that unless more problems developed, continued interviews would not be necessary. Mrs. Prince seemed to confirm the ending by going to the principal to tell her about the help she had received from the school social worker.

Conference with Miss Bailey, Principal. Miss Bailey wanted to tell me what Mrs. Prince had said to her at a P.T.A. meeting. She thought Mrs. Prince was glad she had referred Archie for help. Mrs. Prince had said, "Miss Bailey, you have no idea what a difference it has made in our home since we know we can talk about Archie's real father." She continued to say that they did not talk about him often, but it was such a relief to know the barrier was down.

I discussed with Miss Bailey Archie's progress as I saw it and told her of the plan we had worked out concerning his school work. She was pleased with the way Mrs. Prince has accepted this service and the interest and enthusiasm she has shown in asking for and using help.

Archie's mother has continued to talk to Miss Bailey, from time to time, about his progress and her appreciation for the help she received from the school social worker when he was in fifth grade. Throughout the remainder of his elementary school years, through junior high school, and in his beginning years in high school, he has continued to show successful academic achievement and has participated in student activities.

The case of Archie Prince is representative of many of the cases referred to the school social worker. Although Archie was not presenting problems so serious that he could do no school work, there were evidences of difficulty which an alert teacher had recognized—his problem with other children and the fact that he was not working up to capacity as well as his mother's concern about his behavior at home. These problems, if not corrected, would mean, at the least, unhappiness for Archie in the present and might well indicate the possibility of much more serious difficulty later.

Work with Archie was begun in October, early in the school year, and ended in May. During this period the school social worker had weekly interviews with Archie and interviews with Mrs. Prince twice a month.

In evaluating Archie's problem it seemed that he was unusually dependent on his mother's approval. Her fear of his growing up to be like his father was so intense that it seemed almost as if she must keep him a baby. With Mrs. Prince's sensing the respect of the school social worker as she made efforts to help Archie, she became more secure in testing out ways which permitted him to develop responsibility. During this process she recognized that some of her fears were groundless. This seemed to give her courage to let Archie be himself, and the outcome increased her satisfaction as a mother. The essence of the school social worker's help was in providing through a casework relationship a new experience for Mrs. Prince, different from that which she had experienced with other people who had criticized her—one in which there was respect for her efforts and an opportunity to discuss freely her anxieties and fears as well as her satisfactions over what might have seemed minor accomplishments.

Early recognition on the part of the school social worker of the fact that Archie's only security seemed to be in trying to please his mother and the degree of his fear of possibly losing her indicated to the school social worker two facts—first, that it would be important that Archie's mother participate in and approve of any help which was given him and second, that he would need a great deal of help in gaining respect for himself as a person in his own right. Archie recognized that he had a problem in his relationships with other boys which he expressed in his fear of fighting. When the school social worker seemed willing to help him with this, he brought out other fears. His apparent pleasure when he was able to accomplish what he considered "grown-up" activities indicated his satisfaction in developing "on his own." He never missed appointments and participated actively in every interview. The school social worker's encouragement of his independent activity afforded him a relationship in which he was free to discover his strengths and to become less fearful of new undertakings.

chapter 13

Social Services for the Aged

Emerging Interest in the Aged

The United States of America, which is often referred to as a young country, only within recent times has come to a realization that it is growing older. From our colonial beginnings up to the first decade of the twentieth century and the eve of World War I, ours had been a "youngish" people. An almost unrestricted immigration, chiefly of persons in the childbearing age group, had served to keep our population weighted with the young rather than with the old. Related to this was the high birth rate that, despite a high infant and childhood mortality rate, tended to increase the total population at the same time that it increased the percentage of younger persons in the population. It was not, perhaps, until we began to be conscious of the plight of the aged following the ending of World War I and through the frenzied 1920s that we began to look at the proportion of various age groups in our population structure. Not until then did we, as a nation, begin to face some of the problems with which we had to deal. Only slowly did we note some connection between an almost standstill immigration, a shift from rural to urban concentrations, a decreasing birth rate, and improved mortality and morbidity (sickness) rate, a fiercely competitive, highly organized, industrial system, an aging population, and the problems that seemed to beset from all sides the older persons in our midst. It is the purpose of this chapter to present something of our population changes, to examine the financial dependence or independence of the aged, to analyze some (not all) of their needs, and to

435

discuss the range, variety, and helpfulness of the social services that are available or are being developed by, for, and with the aged.[1]

Age Groups in the Population

In the preceding section reference was made to our late recognition of population changes. Other nations—in existence longer than ours—have, before us, been conscious of the increasing proportion of their aged. Great Britain, for example, at least a generation earlier than we presented not only a demographic pattern such as now characterizes us, but also undertook considerable research and planning in relation thereto. The Report of the Royal Commission on Population (1947) showed that the age group 65 years and over had increased between 1891 and 1947 from 4.8 percent to 10.4 percent. During this period the total population of Great Britain had increased 45 percent. The estimate was made that by 1977 those over 65 years of age would constitute 16 percent of the British population.[2]

It is significant to compare these figures to the population structure in the United States, and estimates. According to the United States Bureau of the Census, the age group 65 years and over increased between 1900 and 1950 from 4.1 percent to 8.1 percent of the total population. The actual increase of the 65 year and over group was 298 percent. During this period the total United States population increased by approximately 98 percent. The estimate was made that by 1975 those over 65 years of age would constitute approximately 11 percent of the American population.[3]

---

[1] The recency of our concern for the aged, remarked upon by many writers, is reflected in the many beginnings of programs and confirmed by the analysis of social work literature. For over seventy-five years there have been annual conferences of social work, but it was not until the 1930's that any serious discussion pertaining to the aged was recorded in the published proceedings. See Bruno, Frank, *Trends in Social Work as Reflected in the Proceedings of the National Conference of Social Work,* 1874–1946. New York, Columbia University Press, 1948. Ewan Clague also remarked upon the interest in the aged as being expressed during the first half of the present century—first with the attacks upon the condition in poorhouses and almshouses, then proposals for pension aid assistance, and finally for social insurance and supplementary programs. See chapter on "Aging and Employability" in Tibbitts, Clark (editor), *Living Through the Older Years.* Ann Arbor, University of Michigan Press, 1949, pp. 141–153.

[2] Amulree, Lord, *Adding Life to Years.* London, National Conference of Social Service, 1951, pp. 18–19.

[3] Whelpton, P. K., *Forecasts of the Population of the United States, 1945–1975.* Washington, D. C., Bureau of the Census, 1947, pp. 39–51.

Not only is it important to understand the composition of our population, but it is additionally useful to have some sense as to how much longer we are living. In 1900, at birth, an individual had a statistical possibility of living until the age of 49 years. If, in 1900, he attained the age of 45 years, he had a statistical possibility of living an additional 24 years; if he attained 65 during 1900, he had a statistical chance of living 12 more years. However, if he were born in 1949, he would have a statistical possibility of 67 years of life; if he were to attain his 45th birthday in 1949, he had before him 28 more years; if he lived to be 65 in 1949 he could count, statistically at least, on 13 more years of life.[4]

Another salient point in this consideration of our aging population is the numerical disproportion of women over men after 65 years of age. According to the 1950 census, for every 89 men there were 100 women. As is to be expected, as contained in these census statistics confirmed by ordinary observation, a far larger number of women over 65 years of age are widowed than is true of men over 65 years. In the age group 65 to 74 years, 17.7 percent of the men were widowed, while 47.1 percent of the women were widowed.[5]

Still another pertinent fact concerns the living and household relationship of persons 65 years of age and over. According to studies made by the Social Security Administration in 1950, there were 69 percent, men and women, living in their own households. This living may have been with spouse, or with relatives, or with nonrelatives, or alone. Another 26 percent were living in households not their own—such as in the household of relatives or in the household of nonrelatives. A comparatively small percentage—the remainder—were in institutions, hotels, camps, schools, vessels, etc.[6]

What Is Age? Who Are the Aged? Why 65?

Is age a chronological fact readily ascertained by calculating the years since birth? Are all persons who are born in the same year of the

---

[4] *Fact Book on Aging.* Washington, D. C., Committee on Aging and Geriatrics, Federal Security Agency, 1952, p. 57.

[5] *Ibid.,* pp. 47–48.

[6] *Ibid.,* p. 48. The reader is referred to this very valuable pamphlet for additional statistical material pertaining to the aged, obtainable from the Federal Security Agency (since April 1953, the Department of Health, Education, and Welfare), Washington, D. C. Since 1947 the New York State Joint Legislative Committee on Problems of the Aging has published annually legislative documents which have contained useful material.

same age? Are the aged to be considered as a group, a category? Do individuals of identical chronological age behave alike, think alike, feel alike, work alike, play alike, have needs alike? It must be obvious from these questions that older persons, in common with all persons of all years, are still individuals, each with his or her own biological history, family influences from birth on, educational and work experiences, and emotional life. All these constitute a uniqueness that differentiates one from all others. It is a trite but nevertheless accurate observation that one person is old at 50, while another is young at 70—recalling, perhaps, the remark attributed to the late Justice Holmes in his ninety-second year, "Oh, to be young and 70 again." Likewise two persons of 70 may vary tremendously. What then is the measure of "oldness" or age? For whom are the programs that are being developed on all sides intended? Why is 65 years seized upon so automatically?

Whether one is old at 65 years of age does not seem to be so important as the unthinking and "unthoughtout" prescription that workers should retire at 65, that eligibility for old-age assistance begins at 65, and that old-age benefits under our federal social insurance program may be obtainable at 65 years. In this connection it may be pertinent to recall the pressures during the depression of the 1930's for older workers to make room in the labor market for younger workers. Nor was it accidental that as the Social Security Act was being written during that same decade (signed August 14, 1935) the number 65 came to be fixed as the standard for old-age assistance and old-age insurance. One cannot but wonder, if the Social Security Act were being written today (1954), whether the age might have been fixed at 70 rather than 65 years. The practice for many years of insurance companies stressing endowment policies to mature at 65 years also helped to fix that age as the time for retirement. For the purpose of this chapter and this volume, and without further discussion of its merits, the commonly accepted age of 65 years will be used—with, however, a reservation about its validity as a sufficient criterion for old age.[7]

[7] Before leaving this section it may be well to see in historical perspective the changed position of the aged person. In an earlier age and in a patriarchal state the aged person was considered the embodiment of wisdom and authority. This status continued, without fundamental modification, through the feudal and medieval years, as well as through agricultural and early industrial economies. With the impact of modern industrialization the individual was less able to provide for his late-life needs, has been increasingly

Income Maintenance

Since one of the very real difficulties facing any older person is his capacity or lack of capacity to manage financially, it is important for our purposes to see the situation as it affects all older persons. In order to provide a comparison, testimony will be drawn from a period before the Social Security Act was passed and from a period some time afterward.

During the 1920's a number of studies of the aged were undertaken. Some of these were by public bodies such as those in states like Massachusetts and New York, and others were by nonpublic bodies such as the National Civic Federation. Despite structural and procedural variations between the studies such as methods of sampling, measures of need, etc., there is considerable agreement that in the relatively prosperous decade of the 1920's, a substantial number of aged persons were disadvantaged in their efforts to attain or maintain independence. For the sake of simplicity and clarity, some of the evidence of the National Civic Federation is presented:

1. Some 25 percent of the men and 34 percent of the women over 65 years of age owned no property.
2. Some 40 percent had no income from work or business, and some 17 percent had neither property nor income.
3. Over 25 percent were totally unable to work, and 30 percent could do light work.
4. About 40 percent were assisted primarily by children and to some extent by other relatives and friends.
5. More than 60 percent had been forced to retire because of accident, blindness, deafness, paralysis, chronic illness, mental disease, etc.[8]

---

dependent, and his position within the family as well as within the larger social group is affected accordingly. No longer is he the patriarch and final arbiter. Quite likely he is tolerated, sometimes respected, and not infrequently pitied. See Simmons, Leo W., *The Role of the Aged in Primitive Societies*. New Haven, Yale University Press, 1945. Abraham Epstein, in commenting upon the changed status of the aged, goes so far as to declare that "The progress of a nation may be marked by the care which it provides for its aged." See Epstein, Abraham, *Facing Old Age*. New York, Knopf, 1922, p. 2.

[8] National Civic Federation, Industrial Welfare Department, *Extent of Old Age Dependency*. New York City, 1928; Massachusetts Commission on Pensions, *Report on Old-Age Pensions*. Boston, 1925; New York State Commission on Old Age Security, *Old Age Security*. Albany, 1930; Epstein, Abraham, *Insecurity, A Challenge to America*, 3d. ed. New York, Random House, 1936, pp. 491–506; Rubinow, Isaac, *The Quest for Security*. New York, Henry Holt and Company, 1934, pp. 244–252.

During the decade just referred to and the first half of the succeeding one numerous states had enacted old-age pension (assistance) laws. The first of a number of state laws to remain on the statute books was that passed in 1923 by Montana. The earlier Arizona law of 1914 and the 1923 laws of Pennsylvania and Nevada had been invalid, and subsequently legislation was required to rectify the unconstitutional points involved. By 1934 old-age assistance was in existence in 34 states. In the next year the Congress had passed the Social Security Act, which included federal-state provision for old-age assistance, thus bringing to successful fruition efforts as early as Congressman Wilson's (Pennsylvania) bill which was introduced in 1909.

To what extent had the enactment of a federal-state program, within a few years on a nation-wide basis, affected the dependency status of aged persons? In 1946 when the Social Security Act was under consideration for revision, data were presented to the Congress to show how the aged were faring. It must be borne in mind that this country had emerged from a depression, had gone into a period of prewar production, then war production and actual war, through a victorious war, and was embarking upon a period of sustained postwar industrial productivity. As of June 30, 1945, there were about 4 million persons over 65 years of age, constituting 40 percent of the population 65 years and over, who were receiving some form of assistance. Somewhat over half of this assistance was from governmental sources, chiefly old age assistance; while something under a half was from friends and relatives.[9]

Another study a few years later found that aged persons were still in an unfavorable position despite more than a decade of federal old-age insurance and federal-state old-age assistance programs. Only a fourth of all persons aged 65 and over were currently employed. Of the 11 million aged, about 8 million had some income which was distributed as follows:

2,500,000 with under $500 for the year
2,300,000 with $500 to $999
1,600,000 with $1,000 to $1,999
750,000 with $2,000 to $2,999

[9] *Issues in Social Security.* A Report to the Committee on Ways and Means of the House of Representatives, 79th Congress, 1st Session, Washington, Government Printing Office, 1946, pp. 270–271.

500,000 with $3,000 to $4,999
200,000 with $5,000 to $9,999
100,000 with $10,000 or more

These figures must be understood in relation to a budget computed by the Bureau of Labor Statistics of from $1,600 to $1,900 (depending upon geographic location) to maintain a "modest but adequate" level of living. According to the available statistics, the average benefit for retired workers was about $42 per month and for a retired worker and his wife, 65 years and over, the benefit was $68 per month. In many instances the old-age insurance benefit had to be—or was—supplemented by old-age assistance.[10]

Additional information about the aged—specifically those who are receiving old-age and survivors insurance benefits as of 1952—shows that the insurance program has not provided even the minimum of security that was envisioned by its proponents in the 1930's. An analysis of those receiving benefits shows that three out of every five are partially dependent on relatives or upon public or private assistance. About one out of every six beneficiaries received cash payments from public assistance in the course of the year. A number of other beneficiaries were living below the standard set as the public assistance level— $63 a month for single persons and $100 a month for couples. This and other studies have verified what is generally believed—namely, that insurance and assistance programs have lessened, to a limited though encouraging degree, some of the morale destroying dependencies that have so characterized the aged within modern industrial times. In the words of the author of the last article to which reference has just been made: "This study of the resources of old-age and survivors insurance beneficiaries shows, as have all the earlier ones the Bureau (Old-Age and Survivors Insurance) has made, that insurance benefits have been an essential source of income for most beneficiaries. In only a few cases, possibly one out of 20 in the study, would the beneficiaries have been fairly comfortably situated without benefits. For many, benefits spell the difference between independence and dependence on relatives or public assistance. When they need financial help, their benefits decrease the amount of support children or other relatives or public assistance

---

[10] Cohen, Wilbur J., "Income Maintenance for the Aged." *Annals*, CCLXXIX, January 1952, pp. 154–163; see also *Fact Book on Aging, op. cit.*, p. 49.

have to assume. For these men and women benefits often constitute the one element of economic dependence they have left." [11]

Employment and the Aged

Just as income, or lack of income, is related to the aged person's independence or dependence, so too is employment related in a marked degree to income received. To what extent are persons 65 years of age and older gainfully employed? As of March 1952, there were 41 percent of men and 8 percent of women, 65 years and over, who were still in the labor force. To some this may seem a rather high proportion, and it is necessary to relate several other facts to it for fuller understanding. The first of these is that this 41 percent is a distinct drop from the 87 percent of men and 28 percent of women who were in the labor force between 45 and 64 years of age. The second item to be taken into account is that about 60 percent are wage and salary workers, while 40 percent are self-employed. Of the self-employed, one half are in agriculture, the other half engaged in their own businesses, many of them small. Not an inconsiderable number are part-time employed, whether working for themselves or for others. The third point of importance is that the proportion of older persons employed has been decreasing throughout this century (the period of war production was an exception) from 68.2 percent of men 65 years and over in 1890 to 45 percent in 1950. [12]

Looking realistically at the employment situation affecting the older worker, it is essential to examine some of the difficulties that confront him in an economy that is dominantly industrial and urban-centered. What stands in the way of utilizing the labor and skill of the worker who is moving on in years? Is there a supportable case for automatic retirement at a designated age? Does the older worker have a useful place in the modern industrial system? Can or will industry make an adaptation to the reality of an aging working population?

The barriers which the older worker faces may be those imposed by industry—that might be termed external—and those which he, the

[11] Wentworth, Edna C., "How Old-Age and Survivors Insurance Beneficiaries Get Along." *Public Welfare*, XI, April 1953, p. 42; see Wentworth, "Economic Situation of Aged Insurance Beneficiaries: An Evaluation." *Social Security Bulletin*, XVII, April 1954, pp. 13–22, 26.

[12] *Fact Book on Aging, op. cit.*, pp. 54–55.

worker, places upon himself, that might be termed internal. Foremost among the former are those that derive from the unmistakable fact of the dominance of the machine in modern industry. In a simpler economy, agriculture, the individual was to a far larger degree in control of production and his part in it. Not so with increasing mechanization. Now the machine seems to determine the pace of production, and increasing reliance is placed upon it. Indeed the processes of production are geared to the speed of the machine, and it is the human being that must fit into this scheme of things. The younger worker is in greater demand because of his supposed adaptability to the speed as well as the uninterruptedness of the machine. The greater emphasis upon piecework as it relates to the time factor and the greater capacity of the younger person to work under pressure tends to favor the employment of the younger rather than the older worker.

Another aspect of this dominance of the machine is the belief on the part of the managers of industry that the skills of the older worker tend to become obsolete with newer changes in machine production. According to this assumption the machine is modified or replaced by a newly invented one, but the older worker does not make as rapid an adaptation to the change as the younger man. He—the older worker—is less likely to be considered as productive as the younger one.

Other beliefs or assumptions affect the employability of the older worker. He is thought to have higher accident and sickness rates. Since he is not as nimble as a younger man and since the machine does not slow up to account for human fallibilities, the older worker is regarded as the victim of the machine to a disproportionate extent. Likewise, because he is growing older and because it is commonly assumed that older men are more sickness prone, the conclusion is unthinkingly come by that the older worker is a far greater sickness risk than the younger worker.

A still further barrier to the employability of the older person is related to the practice of many firms of providing pension plans and the disinclination of those firms to weight the working force with too large a proportion of older workers because of the effect upon premium rates. In many instances these pension plans antedated the Social Security Act, and in some they have been instituted because of the very shortcomings of the federal old-age and survivors insurance program.

In either case the individual firms have wanted to hold their premium payments as low as possible, and this has emphasized the advantages of a younger working force.

A concluding consideration (the foregoing are but a fraction of the total) has been the decision on the part of many employers—particularly the larger companies—for a compulsory retirement age for all employees. Usually, but not always, the age has been set arbitrarily at 65 years regardless of individual factors of good health, alertness, productiveness, etc.

The greatest and usually most defeating self-barrier has been the attitude and feeling of the worker himself: he has often lacked the conviction about his own usefulness. Affected by general opinion for a number of years and then overwhelmed by the actual realization of his 65 years (to use the commonly accepted figure), he has not had the confidence to "sell" himself. Failing that, he too readily may accept commonly held stereotypes and in time may actually evidence many of the ailments and disabilities attributed to people of his years.

What Are the Facts?

Many of the traditionally held beliefs as stated in the preceding section have had a deterring effect upon the hiring as well as upon the retention (except when insisted upon by labor union policies) of the older worker. Very little effort has been made until quite recently to test many of these assumptions. Surprisingly enough few of the assumptions are sustained by investigation. For example, absenteeism is less among the older workers than among the younger. There are fewer accidents among older workers than among younger (although the older injured worker requires a longer period for recovery). The older worker is characterized by a greater reliability and dependability. His performance may not be as speedy; yet in most operations involving judgment and stability, he is a more efficient worker than the younger man and usually a more productive one. Perhaps the clearest comment concerning our admitted incomplete knowledge in this area was made by Ewan Clague, of the United States Bureau of Labor Statistics, when he pointed to the following conclusions: "(1) Many older people retain their full faculties and vigor to an advanced age and can successfully hold a job or practice an occupation far beyond the arbitrary time of retirement; (2) Many other old people experience some accident, disability, debility, or simple decline in powers which lessens their capacity for their previous jobs but which does not make them at all unemployable; (3) Some old people (an actual minority) become permanently ill or disabled (not at any fixed age but at varying ages) so that they cannot or should not be required to earn their own living.[13]

Arbitrary Retirement?

Within recent years there has been lively discussion of the relative merits of withdrawing workers from the labor market at a fixed age— usually 65 years. Many of the larger industries maintain that a fixed retirement age is the fairest and most democratic. It is contended that where the retirement policy is settled and known to all employees, it has the effect of treating all employees alike and without discrimination. Such a policy also enables employee and employer to do the necessary planning for retirement. It permits the retired worker a number of active years during which he may devote to useful community activities as well as pursuing his own hobbies and interests. The clinching argument is usually the one that retirement at a definite age makes way for and furnishes incentive to the younger worker. One retirement at or near the top of a large organization may mean promotions affecting 10 to 20 persons in the various subsidiary echelons of the company, with attendant improvement in morale.

The opposing contention is that the readiness for retirement is so highly individualized as not to lend itself to an arbitrary policy applicable to all. Some individuals should retire at 50 years, some at 55 years, others at 60 years, while others are still useful to themselves and to industry at 70 or even 75 years.

Many factors, such as health, variations in job requirements, family situations, etc., need to be taken into consideration rather than reliance being placed upon age alone. Employers, whether in industry

[13] Clague, Ewan, "Aging and Employability," in Tibbitts, Clark (editor), *Living Through the Older Years*. Ann Arbor, University of Michigan Press, 1949, pp. 149–150; see also Abrams, Albert J., "Barriers to the Employment of Older Workers." *Annals*, CCLXXIX, January 1952, pp. 62–71; Abrams, Albert J., "Industry Views Its Elderly Workers." *Birthdays Don't Count*. New York State Joint Legislative Committee on Problems of the Aging. Albany, 1948, pp. 141–162; also Williard, Joseph W., "Employment Problems of Older Workers." *Proceedings of the National Conference of Social Work*, 1948, pp. 395–402.

or government, who act on these premises insist that "functional" age furnishes a more valid basis for decisions about employability than does "chronological" age (indeed, most students of aging insist upon the usefulness of the concept of "functional" age in all matters affecting older persons). Policies based on functional criteria do not require compulsory retirement at a fixed age; workers may be assigned lighter or less demanding work (with or without a change in compensation rates); there may be a tapering off of a full working load through lessened hours or fewer days per week or with longer vacation periods; workers may be permitted to work beyond the usual (but not compulsory) retirement age and thus accumulate larger credits toward their eventual pensions. Many thoughtful employers favor a pre-retirement counseling program so that the worker may be more ready for retirement when it actually comes and able to retire usefully, and, hence, satisfyingly.

In not a few instances, resources are available for the retired worker through what is known as a sheltered workshop where the work program is geared to the worker's limitations of health as well as age. In some communities, philanthropic and nonprofit employment agencies have stimulated the interest, as well as the initiative, of some employers in the potentialities of the older worker. Many older workers can still carry on usefully part-time employment as a means of supplementing rather limited social security benefits. (Beneficiaries of old-age and survivors insurance may earn up to $75 per month in "covered" employment without jeopardizing their monthly benefits. Incidentally, this figure was raised from $15 to $50 and then to $75 since the Social Security Act was passed in 1935. In 1954 the amount was placed at $1200 per year. When the insured person is over 75 years of age, there is no limitation on his earnings.)

One fundamental consideration persists throughout this entire question. The gross national product of goods and services is distributed each year among the total number of persons who compose our population. In view of the increasing proportions of our older age groups in the total population together with the decreasing proportion of older workers in the labor force, it appears that a smaller percentage of the working population is being called upon to produce the goods and services for the total population which includes a larger percentage of older persons who are nonproductive. If persons are not contributing to the total product of goods and services by reason of being out of the labor force, and yet are sharing in the consumption of the product, there will be a heavier load placed upon the producers or there will be a smaller total product to be distributed. This observation is especially pertinent when it is realized that many of the workers arbitrarily pushed out of the labor market still have considerable productivity for years to come either as full-time or as part-time workers—nor should these statements be interpreted as arbitrarily holding in the labor force any older workers who choose for their individual reasons to leave it. The essential issue involved here is a plea for decisions and policies to be based upon the realities of the situation affecting our total economy as well as the welfare of the individuals who compose our society.[14]

Age and Health

In a previous section of this chapter, reference has been made to changes in our population structure—i.e., an aging population—by reason of an almost unlimited immigration up to World War I and its practical cessation thereafter. It is now appropriate to list several other factors responsible for an aging population. These are a declining birth rate and an increasingly effective control over certain diseases. The latter—control of disease—is particularly pertinent in this section not only for what has been done, but also for what still remains to be done.

Despite a declining birth rate in this country, there is considerable evidence that a larger proportion of conceptions eventuate into births than was formerly the case. Likewise, the chances of survival are greater than ever before. Babies who attain one year of life have increasingly better chances of attaining the second, the third, the fifth, the tenth year, etc., than ever before. The conquest of childhood diseases —especially the communicable diseases—has increased the statistical chances of children surviving into adulthood. By the same token

[14] Barkin, Solomon, "Organized Labor Says No." *Annals,* CCLXXIX, January 1952, pp. 77–80; Cochrane, Craig P., "Some Managements Prefer Flexibility." *Ibid.,* pp. 74–77; Hope, Stanley C., "Should There Be a Fixed Retirement Age? Some Managements Say Yes." *Ibid.,* pp. 72–77; Mathiasen, Geneva (editor), *Criteria for Retirement.* New York, G. P. Putnam's Sons, 1953; *Company Practices Regarding Older Workers and Retirement.* Edwin Shields Hewitt and Associates. Libertyville, Illinois, 1952.

the attendant elimination of many of the previous *sequelae,* or consequences of these diseases, the impaired heart or kidney, etc., have enabled more people to reach maturer years.

The practical effect of all this is that as people reach the years of the late forties, the fifties, and into the sixties they are likely to fall before the as yet unconquered ills—the degenerative diseases. An examination of the leading causes of death of persons 65 years and over during the year 1945 illustrates this point: heart disease (39.1 percent), cerebral hemorrhage (12.9 percent), cancer (12.8 percent), nephritis (8.1 percent), and pneumonia (4.0 percent) account for more than three fourths of deaths. This becomes clearer when one notes the shift in causes of death over the last half century. In 1944 heart disease ranked first among total population as cause of death, while in 1900 it ranked fourth; cancer was second in 1944 and eighth in 1900; cerebral hemorrhage was third in 1944 and seventh in 1900; diabetes was eighth in 1944, and twenty-seventh in 1900! arteriosclerosis was tenth in 1944 and thirty-fourth in 1900.[15]

In all likelihood the most useful data on illness and disability in the general population as well as among older persons were those obtained in the National Health Survey of 1935–1936, a house-to-house canvas conducted by the United States Public Health Service. Disabling illnesses lasting seven or more consecutive days occurred relatively more often in the group aged 65 and over than in the population as a whole. For all ages the rate was 171 per 1,000 persons; for the group 65 and over the rate was 279. With respect to chronic illness classified as temporary, the rate for all ages was 36 per 1,000 persons; for the group 65 and over the rate was 114. Chronic illness classified as permanent had a rate for all ages of 12 per 1,000; for the group 65 and over the rate was 63. A further measure is contained in the record of days of disablement per year. For all ages in the population the annual days disabled per person was 9.9; for the age groups 65 and over the number of days was 36.1.[16]

[15] Dublin, Louis I., "Significant Trends in the Health of the Aging," in *Birthdays Don't Count.* New York State Joint Legislative Committee on Problems of the Aging, Newburgh, New York, 1948, pp. 189–194.

[16] Perrott, G. St. J., Goldstein, Marcus S., Collins, Selwyn D., "Health Status and Health Requirements of an Aging Population," in *Illness and Health Services in an Aging Population.* Public Health Service Publication #170, Washington, D. C., Federal Security Agency, 1952.

The experience of public health officers, of physicians in general practice, as well as specialists including those in geriatrics confirms the foregoing data. These persons and all others whose interests take them into the larger area of the study of aging and the aged—known as gerontology—realize there is as great and as useful a task on behalf of the aged as was present a half century ago on behalf of the child. Persons who have had years of useful experience are still a considerable asset to society. The best that medical practice and medical research can make available should enable older persons to continue to be useful to themselves as well as to others. Medical science should be used not only to relieve or ease the pains of the aged, not only to treat the large numbers of the chronically ill, but to emphasize prevention. It should also promote a healthier old age, thus furthering the satisfactions that accrue with a lifetime of satisfying living. These premises can rest upon an humanitarian base, or a base of realistic common sense that keeps people productive and independent rather than nonproductive and dependent. In a very substantial sense society has an investment of education, training, and experience in every older person, and it should be able to count on a return on that investment through the older years.

The significance of this material descriptive of the health of older persons is related not only to the present situation, but also to the future as an increasing proportion of the population is distributed through the older age brackets. This is important so far as health services and facilities are concerned, and also with respect to employment, housing, recreation, and the community's social services.

Aging and the Personality

Throughout life all of us are called upon to make adjustments. The aged are no exception. Each period has its identifiable demands—in babyhood, childhood, adolescence, early adulthood, maturity, later maturity, early aging, old age. As human beings, we express in one way or another our basic needs for emotional security and a sense of adequacy. Perhaps in some period—say, during adolescence—the difficulties involved in assuring such satisfaction may seem overwhelming, but somehow most persons manage to survive the experience. While not intending to allege that old age is as complicated and baffling as adolescence, nevertheless one brings to it whatever resources living has made possible, and one is faced with the very finality of life itself. That very finality may endow the late years with satisfaction and happiness or with pain and despair.

What the person does with those last years or what those last years do with the person are related, basically, to how one's life has been organized in the preceding years. How has one met change, adversity, success, accident, ill health? What has been the nature of one's relationships to other persons—to one's family members, fellow workers, friends, even to one's enemies? Have one's responses been those of aggression or submission, dependence or self-sufficiency, rigidity or flexibility? With these remarks in mind it may be well to examine three areas in which changes take place—family, job, health.

Families come into being, children grow up, enter upon careers, marry, move away, lead their own lives. Each of these changes in the family constellation asks different things of the family members. For the parent or parents moving on in years it may be possible to permit the children to lead their own lives—their reconstituted lives— or control may be attempted through overt domination or through subtler forms of emotional absorption. For the children to go may be interpreted as rejection, at the very time that parents feel the need for acceptance all the more. Attempts may be made, directly or indirectly, to have the married children live near by, or to visit at regular intervals, or to consult on all matters requiring decision—major and minor. On the other hand, the parents may welcome the establishment of a separate life for their children and feel in the release an opportunity to undertake many tasks and activities heretofore denied them by the exacting demands of family rearing. Parents with creative capacities within them may be able to go into a differently satisfying mode of work and living.

Another change in the family situation—the loss of the spouse—may call for quite another adaptation. Assume for the moment it is the husband who dies first (statistics reveal that women outlive men). There will be serious decisions to be made about housing arrangements— should the widow stay on in the same house, should she have her married child live with her, shall she live with a married child, shall she board, or shall she go to an institution? Can she continue activities she and her husband shared, or can she resume earlier ones that were put aside while the children were growing up? Or doesn't she have any interests now? Will the loss of a spouse so overwhelm her that life no longer seems to have meaning? Can she begin a new life of her own or is it simply a matter of hoping for this one to expire? Many of these same questions obtain where the surviving spouse is the husband.

A third aspect of this matter of relationship must be mentioned, and that pertains to the loss of close personal friends. These friends may no longer be on hand, either because of having moved away or because of death. Here again it will make some difference if one is with or without spouse, but in either case there are difficulties in adapting to other persons as the years advance. Loneliness is little comfort, especially when the younger generations crowd the older.

Throughout this chapter there have been repeated references to the question of whether 65 years should be an arbitrarily imposed retirement age. It must be obvious that the conviction of the present writer is on the side of flexibility and individualization. This is based on more than sentiment. There are personal considerations involved as well as matters of broad public social and economic policy.

Work in modern society has fundamental meaning for the individual. Not only does it involve the use of time, but it provides an outlet for abilities, and furnishes an income for support of oneself and one's dependents. It gives status—the work as well as the income. When employment ceases at an age usually fixed by someone else, the person is confronted with a situation that demands considerable adaptability. People vary in their responses to such a situation. Some may fight retirement, trying to convince themselves and others they are not through. Others may fold up and completely give in, having no resources within themselves to see themselves through this difficult period of readjustment. For others it means the surrender of a previous commanding and respectable role. For some, particularly when income is drastically curtailed, it may signify helplessness and an accentuation of one's dependence on others. For not a few, certainly in the early years of the Social Security program, it means a slender financial benefit and, not infrequently, a supplement from public assistance. This is felt to be an ignoble end of a lifetime of struggle.

There are others, however, for whom the cessation of customary employment may not be a catastrophe. There may be sufficient income to permit one to hold up one's head. There may be a leisure, hoped for throughout previous decades, that permits the development or the furthering of hobbies and avocations. There may be both time and occasion to busy oneself with community activities. There may even be opportunity for creative pursuits to climax the few days vouchsafed to all of us upon this planet.

Throughout life most of us are aware of the importance of good health. Perhaps at no period are we more mindful of this than in the later years. By then the natural processes of the body have "caught up with us," as it were, and we find ourselves obliged to run (or walk, limp, or crawl) our course with whatever equipment we still possess. For some old age may mean chronic illness and disability, with life literally a burden. Others cannot accept the physical failing of the body and consume themselves with denials of the reality of old age. For others aging is a welcome time of slowing down, an acceptance of the inevitability of the human mechanism wearing out, and an adjustment of one's tempo and habits accordingly. As is true of so many of the adaptations required of the aged, the clue to them is usually within the individual's own life history of adjustments in the previous active decades.

Individualized Services for Older Persons

Too frequently, and unthinkingly, old age is referred to as a problem, or a social problem. It is questionable whether a process as natural as aging should be called a problem, any more than other natural processes such as birth, growing up, or dying should be called problems. This is not to deny that there are difficulties associated with these natural processes, but to make it clear that these difficulties derive from our ways of meeting—or not meeting—the needs that are inherent in the natural processes. It is upon these needs—and particularly our ways of meeting them—that our thinking and our services should be focused.

Do not the aged share with other people the need for security and the need for love? Do they not want to be needed, to be useful? Do they not require to be related to other people and to feel themselves an essential part of the on-going world around them? These questions could be extended indefinitely and to all of them an affirmative answer could be given. What would be more useful would be to consider some of the difficulties that develop or that are accentuated because of what happens to persons as they move on in years and as they are affected by what happens to those around them.

Adults marry, have children, raise families. During this period the wage earner is the main provider, and while children are in school and preparing for their careers there is a dependency relationship existing between the two generations. The children marry, raise their own families, and support themselves. The two generations have moved—usually and normally—to a basis of equality relations between them. In time the original parent has moved out of the labor market—voluntarily or involuntarily—and has found the range of human contacts considerably restricted. Increasingly the relationship between the two generations is that of dependency of the original parents—a reversal of the original pattern.

These changes—and many others—develop feelings in older people that need to be understood, not only by family members but especially by social workers. There is little question but that some of these shifts in role and status do produce a loss of self-esteem at the same time that they accentuate dependency feelings. Fears of all kinds, many of them vague and diffused but nevertheless threatening, are released. Feelings of isolation—not always a matter of distance—may be devastating in their effect.

What do older persons do with these feelings and with the situations in which they find themselves? What is the helping service of social work? In so many instances, and of course this is not characteristic of older people only, the adjustment and the efforts exerted toward such are definitely related to previous life experiences. Persons who have lived satisfying lives, who have both given and received love and security, who have made adaptations to people and to life situations, and who have developed a maturity with it all—these persons will be able to face the limitations placed upon them by aging with equanimity and without panic. They will not be without their difficulties, but on the other hand they will not be consumed by their frustrations and continually taking refuge in various defense mechanisms.

Social work's most important contribution to the older person is its recognition of him as an individual and its insistence that all programs shall embody this conviction in practice. This may seem an utterly obvious and nondisputable position, but an examination of much current thinking and practice evidences a too facile grouping of everyone over 65 years of age, and a too ready assumption that decisions and programs must be made for them. The nub of the controversy about arbitrary retirement, for example, is largely that of dealing with persons of 65 years (or 60 or 70 years) as all of one group, and as a group *for* whom the decision must be made. Likewise, if we are candid with ourselves, we, too often, are inclined to lump all of the retired—voluntarily or involuntarily retired—as a group and to prepare and carry out programs *for* them. We do this, of course, with the best of intentions, failing however to conceive of them as individuals and as persons capable of working *with* rather than *for*.

What are some of the basic convictions upon which social work strives to operate? First, is the belief in the worth of the individual. True, this is not original, nor peculiar, nor exclusive with social work—what may be unique are the methods or processes by which its convictions are translated into action and into actual services. Second, is a regard for the right of self-determination, for the individual to make his decisions concerning himself which seem to meet his basic needs. This is contrary to a widely held supposition that individuals cannot make wise decisions for themselves; instead decisions must be made *for* people. Third, is a consideration for the privacy and the feelings of the other person. This privacy and these feelings are not surrendered because an individual asks for help or as a price for receiving help. Fourth, is a respect for the individual's capacity for change, for with change can come growth and adjustment in relation to other persons as well as to situations.

Educational Services

Using the concept of education in a broad sense, it can be said, with considerable accuracy, that its purpose is directed not only to the present, but to the future as well. Thus in the early school experience education aims to educe native capacity, to develop it, and also to prepare for the next steps in growth. Likewise is this true for each stage that follows so that by the time later maturity or old age is reached there will have been adequate preparation for useful and satisfying living. When one realizes the importance of the kind of adjustments which the individual has been evolving throughout living and how they bear on the adjustments he makes in older age, the continuity of the learning and the living process becomes evident.

It seems necessary to evoke the foregoing remarks because of the too easy assumption that educational services to the aged begin when age 65 is reached. Actually education as we know it in this country has a life-span responsibility, with its greater contribution to the aged being placed upon the opportunities it affords for continuing exercise of the individual's capacities and for continuing as a participating member of society.

The degree to which education (or more properly educators) has expressed this responsibility has been related to the leadership that has been available in many areas. Sometimes this leadership has stimulated industry to help prepare the older worker for retirement (hopefully a flexible retirement system) or even for retraining for a larger period of usefulness. Sometimes the leadership has manifested itself through community agencies—churches, clubs, libraries, museums, welfare groups—with resulting vital programs. Not infrequently—but not frequently enough—educational institutions have taken literally their responsibilities to all age groups and have ventured their facilities and personnel for experimental and serviceable programs. Such institutions as Cleveland College, University of Chicago, Illinois, Michigan, and Syracuse are among the most enterprising in this field.

At the present time there is some difference of opinion as to whether the educational programs offered under university auspice should be restricted to the older age group. If account is taken of the wishes of older persons that they be not segregated but dealt with as a part of the total population, then the program offered by the University of Michigan commends itself to favorable consideration. At Michigan the offerings have been on a noncredit basis and have been open to any interested person. While the majority of the attendees have been older people, there has been an age range from the second to the eighth decade of life. Professional workers, members of families which have aged parents, as well as older persons have constituted the group. Professional workers have wanted to know more about aging in order to increase their usefulness. Family members have wanted help in understanding the needs of older persons who are living with them. The older enrollees have wanted knowledge, understanding, and direct help with some of the adjustments that are facing them. A glance at the course description will give some idea of its range and usefulness: "The broad fields of information covered in the course include the biological aspects of aging, maintenance of physical and mental health, psychological changes, living arrangements, religion, creative activities, social and economic security, legal problems as related to wills and inheritances, and responsibilities of the community in providing citizenship, recreational, and other types of suitable activities." [17]

The Role of the Church

Whether or not older persons have been consistent church goers, there is a substantial contribution that churches can make to their lives. This does not imply a deferred conversion or a specific preparation for a future life, but rather an acceptance of what people are and a willingness to help them realize more fully and satisfactorily their capabilities. This is not too different from that which can be asked of other community agencies, but it can be more specific because of the personnel and facilities which the churches have. Thus the fellowship of worship may have very real meaning not only for the persons who have always known it, but to others to whom it may be a rewarding experience as it comes later in life. This is especially true for those persons who are surviving their kin and accustomed friends and for whom loneliness is a present reality.

Pastoral counseling which is a normal part of the pastor's work may be a source of encouragement and satisfaction to the older person and a welcome supplement to the congregational meetings. Another recent development has been pastoral psychiatry which draws substantially upon many of the findings of modern psychiatry and makes them usable to the pastor in his service to his disturbed and troubled communicants. There has been an increasing number of institutes on pastoral psychiatry that hospitals have set up to help clergymen in their ministrations to the ill—among them older persons. Friendly visiting

[17] Donahue, Wilma, "Age With a Future," in *Social Work in the Current Scene.* National Conference of Social Work, 1950, p. 78; see also Donahue, Wilma, "Education's Role in Maintaining the Individual's Status." *Annals.* CCLXXIX, January 1952, pp. 115–125.

with older persons may also be developed as part of the church's program, with this taken on by other persons within the congregation and involving some of the older persons themselves as visitors.

The church's physical plant lends itself to many kinds of group activities. Increasingly, the meeting rooms of churches are being put to use throughout the greater part of each hour of the day and evening and of each day of the week. In some instances the church may have staff to assist with group activities, in other cases its rooms may be used with staff provided by other community agencies. Here, too, is an area in which many of the older persons themselves can exercise leadership and example in order to facilitate a larger and more effective participation.

Some, but not many, churches may be of such size and possess such resources as to have social service staffs of their own which may offer services directly to older people. In most communities, however, social services are available through the public welfare departments as well as voluntary social agencies, and churches will make referral to them rather than set up parallel or competing services.

One of the increasingly important services of the church has been the support of homes or institutions for older persons. This development has been not unlike that in the children's field of a century ago when so many institutions—particularly for orphaned children—were offered under denominational auspices. Within recent years children's institutions have had to take stock of their purposes and programs and have redefined their services in the light of newer understanding of children's needs and of changing conditions and times. Today, as we know and learn more of the needs of older persons as well as of the variety of services available, there is a more thoughtful approach to the place of the institution for older persons. Increasingly the admission policies are being carefully defined as we become surer of what the institution has to offer and of the value of noninstitutional services which are available throughout the community. There is a tendency in many quarters not to let the institution for older persons become a general depository, but rather to encourage public and voluntary (including church) agencies to develop appropriate services and programs outside the institution so that there is a range of services available each to meet appropriately the specialized needs of older persons. In this way the church exercises its role as one of the essential and co-operating agencies working on behalf of all people.[18]

Housing and the Aged

Among the many adjustments which older people frequently encounter is the one relating to housing. Even when an older couple own their home, possibly the one in which their children were born and reared, there may come a time for decision as to whether to remain, or to move to smaller quarters, or to live with the children. These questions are not always simple ones with an open or shut answer, but are complicated by many pertinent factors such as income available, state of health, accessibility of children and friends, and even climate. Another decision may involve possible institutional living and demands most careful consideration.

There seems to be a preference which older people express in many ways for remaining in their own and familiar surroundings as long as possible. Their abiding interest is in noninstitutional living. They wish to remain a part of the life they have known rather than to be shunted into an institution and separated from active age groups. It may be claimed that these are very broad statements, and example may be given of the increase in number of institutions and of the persons residing in them throughout the country. To this the answer must be given that even though some do exercise the choice to enter an institution, the overwhelming number prefer other arrangements.

Living alone is not without its difficulties: this is true if it is a couple that is living together or a surviving spouse. For the older couple who have raised a family and in the process have dissolved many of their differences, it may come as something of a shock to realize how irritating and even unbearable some of these differences are when only two people are involved. The unremitting daily association without the relief of children's troubles may so accentuate difficulties as to put substantial strain upon the living relationship. On the other hand, years of living together may have developed an understanding of and a tolerance for the other person. This, together with the joys and sorrows commonly shared in the rearing of children, may have resulted,

---

[18] Maves, Paul B., and Cedarleaf, J. Lennart, *Older People and the Church*. Nashville, Tenn., Abingdon-Cokesbury Press, 1949.

by later years, in the mutual affection and respect that surmounts most minor irritations. The sufficiency—or lack of it—of income is not without its effect as couples deal with the various aspects of living together.

Living with one's children may have its satisfactions, but it also has its problems if the arrangement is an involuntary one, i.e., of necessity. Many of the difficulties may be accentuated to the point of mutual exasperation or even destructiveness. Generations do not easily adapt to each other, especially when over a span of years the roles are reversed. Not infrequently, there are sufficient antagonisms carried from childhood to adulthood for the struggle and tension to be well nigh intolerable between former child once in dependent role and parent who is presently in dependent role. Likewise the relationship between mother-in-law and daughter or mother-in-law and son may be less than amicable in many, if not most, instances. Somehow the father person seems to come off somewhat easier in this process of adaptation of the generations to each other, although the mother may be a more useful person insofar as household tasks are concerned.

When a third generation arrives, many of the difficulties in the child rearing process may be reactivated as the (now) grandmother and mother relive many of the struggles which engaged them years before. It is not easy for a parent who has reared one generation to refrain from imposing the lessons learned therefrom upon the next two generations of child and grandchild. Nor is it always possible to escape the guilt or the expression of that guilt for what, as a parent, one did or did not do.

Despite considerable recent discussion (largely in national and state conferences on the aged) of alternative living arrangements, the institution remains as the third way of dealing with housing for the aged.[19] The institution may be a nursing home with primary focus on the medi-

[19] For two informed yet succinct presentations of housing developments here and abroad, the reader is referred to: Abrams, Charles, "Housing the Elderly Here and Abroad," in *Birthdays Don't Count*. New York State Joint Legislative Committee on Problems of the Aging. New York, 1948, pp. 247–252; Kraus, Hertha, "Housing Our Older Citizens." *Annals*. CCLXXIX, January 1952, pp. 126–138. In addition, the National Association of Housing Officials reports from time to time on developments in housing affecting older people. Recently, reports have mentioned the action by the Massachusetts Legislature (1953) of providing subsidies to keep rentals low on dwelling units for older persons; the setting aside in a federally aided, low-rent housing project in Memphis (Tennessee) of one and two bedroom units specifically for the aged; the plans by labor unions and some industrial establishments to provide entire communities for retired workers. Headquarters of the National Association of Housing Officials is in Chicago.

cal care and treatment of the aged person, or it may be the home for the aged in which admission turns on the age factor and in which the medical services are provided as a part of the operation of the institution—in the same sense in which medical services would be provided in a children's institution. The institution for the aged may range anywhere from the county poor farm or county old folks home, through fraternal, charitable, or denominational homes, to privately supported homes for which fees of varying amounts are paid. Obviously it is hazardous to characterize institutions of such variety, but aside from the medically specialized institution for the aged (for those persons who could not receive the service otherwise) there is considerable doubt about the wisdom of multiplying indefinitely the number of institutions for the aged under whatever auspice. There seems to be a far stronger case to be made for exploring alternative forms such as residence clubs, senior apartment hotels, modified dwelling units in housing projects, etc. A still further possibility will be elaborated upon in the sections on nonresident and on foster home provisions.

The questions raised about institutions for the aged might be dealt with upon the basis of the human personality factor or upon the financial aspect. As noted in some of the preceding pages, the preference of most aged persons is to be in familiar surroundings, with people whom they have known, and not to be segregated and treated as a group apart. Even though they are old—or possibly because they are old—they still want to be in the stream of life. Their movements may be slower, but they are more adapted to their physical and emotional needs. Even though older, they still want the contact with the young and the younger. The institution represents shelving, a getting put out of the way, an isolation, an accentuation on the end of life with death the immediate exit. No matter how comfortable the appointments may be, how palatable the food, how adaptable the visiting hours, how convenient the medical services, nevertheless one can never forget that one is in an institution for the aged, surrounded by the aged, and expected to act accordingly.

This is not to overlook the experience that some older persons may prefer institution living. Institution living may be less demanding, psychologically. It may be less threatening to the older person, since he can submerge himself in the group. It may seem to offer "security" as it provides to the end of life a habitation, food, and medical care. It may be the welcome release from a lifetime of unrewarding struggle.

The financial cost of institutions and institutional care must also be considered. This refers not only to the initial cost of construction but also to the continuing cost of operation. The per capita cost of all institutions—children's, educational, medical, correctional, etc.—is high. Institutions for the aged, because of the necessary amenities for the comfort as well as the safety of its clients, may run higher than usual, except perhaps prisons and hospitals. Buildings also tend to become obsolete and do not lend themselves too easily to changes in ideas or practices. There is some prospect that we may as overbuild for the aged in this century as we did for children in the nineteenth century. The very existence of children's institutions, in many instances, impeded newer and more effective programs of child care because of the unadaptability of the institution—or rather of the institution managers—to changed ideas and conditions.

The operating cost of institutions for the aged is considerable, and past experience indicates that operating costs always increase. They never seem to decrease. The better managed an institution is, the better qualified its staff, the more extensive its program, the higher per unit cost there will be. We have learned from two centuries experience with children's institutions that it is no economy, certainly in human terms, to run an institution at a low-quality level. It certainly would not be for the aged, who are a far more vocal group than children, especially where comfort is concerned.

The practical effect of this is: (a) an institution for the aged that holds itself out as low-cost operation is not able to meet the physical, medical, emotional, or social needs of aged persons, and hence, cannot justify its existence before the community; (b) an institution that has too high an admission fee or rates (weekly, monthly, annually) cannot meet the need of most of those who may require its services. Certainly if the figures on the income of older persons are studied (see mention earlier in this chapter), it is evident that few persons have sufficient resources to utilize institutions—even if institutions were the answer to their prayers —or the prayers of their children.

The foregoing paragraphs may appear not only harsh but even unfair.

That we may challenge the accuracy of these words reflects our sensitive concern with those institutions for the aged that have erred and records our determination that institutions for the aged can serve a constructive purpose in the lives of its patrons. At the same time it expresses our hope that we shall have learned from the two preceding centuries of institution building for children. Denominational and religious bodies, philanthropic and fraternal agencies, labor and industrial organizations faced with the contemporary imperative of wise stewardship, are in a position to develop institutions and institutional programs that will effectively and creatively serve the needs of older people. Such institutions and their programs are focusing more and more upon services for those requiring medical and custodial care. They are also keeping their policies flexible enough so that a "Home Care" service permits applicants to remain in their own homes as long as they are able to, with community agencies providing medical and housekeeping services, and with provision for institutional admission when it is no longer possible for the aged person to remain at home.[20]

Interest and Activity Programs

As an increasing number of older people have moved into retirement (voluntarily or involuntarily), programs have been developed to provide satisfying expression of interests and abilities. Many persons throughout an active working life may have neither the inclination nor the occasion to discover or express those capacities within themselves which are not job-connected. Some may have lived to a period of leisure literally not knowing what to do with themselves. For many persons to whom the job has been demanding, unceasing, and unremitting, a period of leisure—particularly if it is enforced—may accentuate their loneliness, their helplessness, and their lack of purpose. Community programs are designed to offer opportunities to convert much of this aimlessness into satisfying and possibly even useful pursuits.

In a number of instances existing facilities have been used to provide a setting for the various programs. This is especially true in the larger cities where settlement houses are located. True, most settlement houses

[20] *Standards of Care for Older People in Institutions.* New York, National Committee on the Aging of the National Social Welfare Assembly, 1953; *A Home in the Later Years.* New York State Association of Councils and Chests, 1953.

have always been available to all age groups within a neighborhood, but the emphasis has usually been upon youth programs. However, with older persons having time throughout the day, it has been possible to use the facilities morning, afternoon, and night. Since their beginnings in the late nineteenth century, settlement houses have evidenced remarkable adaptability in meeting the leisure-time needs of their surrounding populations. With few exceptions, they have acted with remarkable alacrity in opening their buildings and with exceptional resourcefulness in developing programs for older persons.

Other community agencies have made their facilities useful: churches, parks and playgrounds, some educational institutions, as well as libraries and museums. Perhaps the most encouraging development has been the day center, as exemplified in the William Hodson Center in New York City. In addition to these agencies, the sponsoring or stimulating agency may range from municipal recreation departments, councils of social agencies, to national organizations such as the National Council of Jewish Women.

A review of the programs will give some idea of the variety of interests and activities that are afforded expression. For those who find satisfaction in working with their hands and with materials, there are the arts and crafts, such as painting, sculpture, ceramics, woodwork, metal work, leather work, sewing. For others who prefer a different way of expressing themselves, there are opportunities for writing, editing the group's newspaper or magazine, acting, folk dancing, folk singing. Others may find satisfaction in group contacts such as afforded by social clubs of which the Golden Age clubs would be an example. Some few may engage in the physical activity of some of the less strenuous sports.

What must be apparent from the foregoing paragraph is that the activities of older persons are essentially the activities of people of all age groups—with the possible exception of the more active and competitive sports. What this also illustrates is the importance of providing the opportunity and permitting the choice to be made. Older persons prefer to express themselves in their own ways and, like all the rest of us, according to their own decisions. They resent, like most of the rest of us, an overorganization by someone else of leisure-time interests. It may even be that some older persons prefer not to indulge in any activity and may make a choice of traveling at their own pace and using up their energy without too much motion. If such persons prefer to sit quietly and unactively, it may be the better part of wisdom of the program planners to recognize that sitting quietly, apparently doing nothing, may have very real value and satisfaction for some people.

The Day Center

One of the most promisingly useful of the many developments is the day center. This is literally a center—a place and building—to which older persons come during the day to engage voluntarily in satisfying activities. There are a number of such centers throughout the nation, chiefly in larger cities. The William Hodson Center in New York City may be used to illustrate the diversified program and its satisfaction for the aged. It offers all of the activities mentioned in a previous paragraph—and more besides. Among its other group activities are monthly birthday parties, holiday celebrations, lectures, an annual bazaar, boat rides, summer camping, outings to park, and sound movies. Although there is a nucleus of a professional staff, the greater part of the organization is on a self-government basis with the following committees: executive, refreshment, clean-up, shopping, serving, sick-visiting, entertainment, house grievance, editorial, and library. Individual counseling services are also available with help asked for such matters as housing, medical and dental care, convalescent care, terminal care, employment, legal matters, social security and public assistance. Since the Center opened in 1943, there has been an increasing membership so that at the end of its first decade there were 1,000 members. Of this number about 300 are in daily attendance, with a year's attendance somewhere between 40,000 and 50,000. About one half of the operating budget is supplied by the New York City Department of Public Welfare (the Center, one of thirteen in New York City, is named after William Hodson, who before his tragic death in an airplane accident, had been director of the Department).

The annual review of the program shows not only participation in the opportunities for self-expression and individual recognition (with new activities added each year, camping being one of the latest examples) but certain collateral evidences of the value of the Center in the lives of its members. Many individuals who used to spend their time in frequent trips to medical clinics and were preoccupied with their ailments, real or fancied, have found the Center's activities so satisfying that they have shifted their interests from the medical clinics to an increasing participation in what the Center offers. Another noticeable change is the lowering of the age at which persons come to the Center. In the earlier days of the Center there was a pronounced interval between the older person's retirement and the time he could bring himself to trust the Center (or himself) sufficiently to use it. In many instances this signified the lack of adjustment to retirement, the years of loneliness, brooding, self-absorption, a sensitivity to mixing with other people. That interval is now less, and persons are participating earlier in the Center's program. Another identifiable value of the Center is reflected in the low rate of admissions to homes for the aged from the membership. At the end of the first five years of operation, it was reported that ten persons, of about 500 membership, sought admission to a home for the aged. Three of these later decided they preferred to live in furnished rooms in the community and have returned to the Center. Further confirmation of its value is reflected in the fact that during the same period there has not been a single admission to a mental hospital from among the membership. Incidentally, this is corroborated by centers in both Minneapolis and Philadelphia, two other cities that have developed forward-looking programs for older persons. It is otherwise well known that admissions of aged persons to mental hospitals is decidedly on the increase.[21]

Other Group Work Programs

While there are a number of effective programs in various other cities —Chicago, Cleveland, Detroit, Milwaukee, Philadelphia, San Francisco, Washington—it is important to mention here the diversified program in Minneapolis and its utilization of group work knowledge and skills. The County Welfare Board several years ago created the position of group work consultant to help stimulate a community-wide program for older citizens. Through the consultant's services it has been pos-

[21] See *Five Years' Achievement,* being the Fifth Annual Report issued by the Board of Directors of the William Hodson Center, 1943–1948, New York City, and subsequent Annual Reports to date; also Levine, Harry A., "Community Programs for the Elderly." *Annals.* CCLXXIX, January 1952, pp. 164–170; see also Kubie, Susan H., and Landau, Gertrude, *Group Work with the Aged.* New York, International Universities Press, 1953.

sible to encourage a number of organizations such as churches, schools, libraries, industries, and settlement houses to sponsor group activity for older persons; to co-ordinate the activities of these organizations into an over-all community program; and to establish new services for the older age group as they are needed.

Because the program in Minneapoils is community-wide, it is possible to offer a tremendous range of activities to all groups of older persons according to their many and varied needs. Emphasis is placed upon the helpfulness of group work skills in working with groups of older persons. The role of volunteers is recognized as important. Services in institutions as well as boarding homes are a valid part of the total community program.[22]

While few, if any, homes for the aged can carry on as varied and as extensive a program as the aforementioned William Hodson Center, nevertheless there are signs, here and there, of such institutions increasingly adapting their resources to the fuller needs of the aged. One evidence of this is the shift from a purely sedentarily centered institution to one that lends itself to use by the community. In some instances the facilities of the institution have been opened on a day basis so that activity programs can be developed not only for the residents of the home but for older persons who will come from their own living arrangements and share in the opportunities so provided. This serves not only to vitalize the home's program but to extend its usefulness to a larger segment of the community.

Thus, whether the programs are in institutions for the aged, in settlement houses, in churches, community, or day centers, there is convincing evidence that they are meeting, increasingly, the needs of older people as they undertake to make their own adjustments to retirement and still maintain satisfying and useful lives. Again, whether we call such programs recreation or interest or activity programs, it becomes clear that they make possible what the late Eduard Lindeman said about recreation—that it is an opportunity for a continuing educational process, a development of skills, a participation in esthetic experience, and an engagement in the affairs of the community. All of these have meaning for the older person.

[22] Kaplan, Jerome, *A Social Program for Older People.* Minneapolis, The University of Minnesota Press, 1953; Woods, James H., *Helping Older People Enjoy Life.* New York, Harper and Brothers, 1953.

A Resident Program (Institution)

A number of references have been made in this chapter to children's institutions. Within the present century they have been subjected to vigorous examination, and casework services have come to be considered an integral part of their programs. Today, as institutions for older persons are being built under various auspices, they—or their managers and staffs—are increasingly aware of the importance of casework service as an essential part of the living program within the institution. As with children's institutions, the casework service in the institution for older persons begins before admission and continues throughout the institutional experience. Unlike children's institutions, far less of the casework service is around discharge, although there is still the possibility as the situation may require.

Helping the applicant and the applicant's family with questions of intake calls for casework skills. Two fundamental questions should be faced: (a) What are the needs of this applicant? and (b) Can the institution meet these needs? If there is a mutuality about the answers to these questions and the person becomes a resident, there remains a continuing casework service throughout the experience of institution living. The questions then resolve themselves to: What use is the person making of what the institution has to offer, and how is the institution's program adapting itself to what the individual needs? As with children's institutions, the family from which the person has come remains very much in existence, and the communication between resident and family offers a substantial area of helping to the alert caseworker. Even though there may be few discharges from institutions for older persons, it is nevertheless important to face that as a possibility and to offer the maximum quality of service when a given situation demands it.

An Out-Resident and Nonresident Program

The experience of some institutions (or homes) for older persons reveals that the usefulness of the service may be extended through the provision of residence in a private room with a family near the institution. By such an arrangement the person is entitled to all the rights of any other resident who is in the congregate building of the institution, as well as participating in all of its activities. The Montefiore Home in Cleveland, which offers such an out-resident program, has worked out arrangements whereby the older person may have a private room in a residence and takes meals in the institution or has kitchen privileges in the private home and may prepare one, two, or all of his daily meals. The family accepts the older person as a welcome resident in their house, not merely as a roomer. The family also agrees to notify the Montefiore Home of any emergency situation—medical or otherwise—affecting the resident person. The rent agreed upon is paid monthly in advance by Montefiore Home. The services of the caseworker are as available as they are to all other clients of the Montefiore Home.[23]

Peabody Home in New York City has approached the matter from a somewhat different angle based rather largely upon analysis of applications over a period of time. This analysis showed that 80 percent of the applicants did not need the protective care of an institution. "These were anxious, lonely, bewildered women, discouraged or broken in spirit, bitter and resentful against a world that seemed to have no place for them. At the time of application, some were potential suicides, others had become hypochondriacs and adherents of strange cults or food fads in their confused search for security, and still others expressed their frustration in difficult behavior, much to the exasperation of their relatives, friends, and neighbors. They were women who needed help and guidance, but not necessarily institutional care."[24] Accordingly, provision was made for a limited number to be accepted as nonresidents and to live where and how they chose. Some live in their own apartments or share them with others; some live in furnished rooms with or without cooking facilities; some who neither like to cook nor eat out live in boarding homes; some live with friends or relatives. Casework services are available to the nonresidents, and provision has been made for group activities in connection with a centrally located social service office. Nonresidents are considered members of the Peabody Home Family and are invited to all major social events at the Home. Each nonresident has assurance of eventual admission to Peabody Home, an assurance that tends to relieve fears of the future, reduces pressure for immediate admission, and makes possible a feeling of security.

[23] Weill, Helen K., "An Outresident Program in a Home for the Aged." *Jewish Social Service Quarterly*. XXIX, Spring 1953, pp. 310–315.

[24] Laverty, Ruth, "Non-Resident Aid: A Community Program for the Aged." *State Government*. XXV, October 1952, p. 222.

Foster Care

The philosophy and the practice of foster home care have proven useful in a number of areas—with children, with mentally ill, with the offender. Within recent years it has been adapted to older people where it has been found to call for the same quality of casework service as with the groups just mentioned. The same fundamental questions are involved here as with the others, namely: What are the needs which the client (the applicant) is presenting, and can foster home care most effectively meet these needs? The foster home is but one of a range of possible services for older persons. Resources for independent living, which usually do not involve social services such as apartments, single units, housing developments, etc., have been mentioned in an earlier section of this chapter.

On the basis of their experience since 1948, the Jewish Community Services of Long Island has found that applicants for foster home care may be distinguished as follows:

1. The older person who is unable to fend for himself and wants to remain in the community as long as possible. This person does not wish to consider institutional placement under any circumstances, even if it is available;
2. The older person who is on the waiting list for a home for the aged and needs an interim period of care;
3. The older person in need of a temporary placement for a definitely stated period of time. The person, for instance, whose adult children with whom he lives go on a trip or are ill.[25]

The eligibility requirements are quite flexible. Since the agency is sponsored by a religious group, applicants must be members of that faith, and at least 60 years of age. It is important that the applicant make his own application. A medical examination by the agency physician is called for. Those who are bed-ridden or psychotic are not accepted, although the agency's experience over a number of years has included the successful placement of persons with a history of mental illness, as well as persons discharged directly from mental hospitals. A minimum payment of $90 per month is made by each client, this figure being arrived at by the agency because it is what the Department of Public Wel-

[25] Posner, William, *Foster Care of Aged in a Multiple Function Agency*. New York, Council of Jewish Federations and Welfare Funds, June 1952, p. 3.

fare grants to old-age assistance recipients living in boarding homes. The maximum payment is $145, so that based on ability to pay the rate may be anywhere from $90 to $145. An applicant unable to pay that much is referred to the Department of Public Welfare and if found ineligible for old-age assistance, the agency (Jewish Community Services of Long Island) is prepared to accept less, based upon the client's ability to pay. At every step the applicant is dealt with as the responsible client, consistent efforts being directed by the agency to help the older person to use himself effectively within his limited situation. Throughout the worker's service—whether in pre-placement, placement, or end of placement—there is the consistent exercise of sound casework skills. This is far beyond a "housing" service, for it carries with it a fundamental conviction and premise of social work to the effect that persons, yes older persons, can change and grow and can be helped to handle responsibly their situations—particularly where it is a helping *with,* not a doing *for.*[26]

Visiting Housekeeper

A visiting housekeeper service has been found to have considerable usefulness for helping older persons to continue with their present living arrangements or to make such modification as to preclude change to a contemplated institutional setting. When such services have been offered—and it has usually been by privately supported family agencies—it has been an essential part of the casework function of the agency. It is generally for a limited period of time and may involve the full-time or the part-time service of the housekeeper. The housekeeper is on the staff of the agency, paid by the agency, but with fees—where circumstances permit—paid directly by the client to the agency.

Since its primary aim is to preserve family strengths, it has been used to help families through temporary difficult situations. There have been instances of its use in families, usually older couples, that have been managing satisfactorily until an acute illness or an accident tipped the scales against them. In other instances where the household consists of two or possibly three generations, and where circumstances have arisen

[26] Posner, William, "Casework Process in a Private Residence Program for Older Persons." *Journal of Social Work Process.* IV, May 1953, pp. 9–28; see also Wagner, Margaret W., "Foster Home Care for the Aged." *Journal of Social Casework,* XXVII, October 1946, pp. 238–242.

so that the burden is too heavy on the middle generation, the house-keeper service has been useful in helping the several generations through a crisis situation and eventually arriving at alternative living arrange-ments that proved more endurable and compatible for all concerned. Or there have been situations in which the households may have been separate but with a married daughter carrying not only the tasks of her own family but also those of a parent living elsewhere. Here, too, where the double burden threatens the stability of one or more families, the visiting housekeeper has furnished a temporary service so that other arrangements could be worked out. Along with the housekeeper serv-ice, there has been the opportunity to confer with the agency caseworker so that many of the unspoken difficulties between the generations—the guilt, the rejection, the unconscious hostility—may be seen for what they are. In this way they can be dealt with on a reality basis rather than as destructive projections on parents, spouse, or children. "In be-ing dutiful children to the aged, they become destructive parents to their own children." [27]

A variation—or perhaps adaptation—of the visiting housekeeper serv-ice consists of financial assistance to aged persons of low income to enable them to utilize household help for special tasks such as heavy cleaning once a week. The aged person is usually able to manage his own or her own for most of the household tasks and, thus, to remain in his own habitation without the aid of a visiting housekeeper. How-ever, there are times where the resources are so limited that a supple-ment is necessary (usually provided by a voluntary agency) so that the heavy work is done. It may mean the difference between staying in one's own home or going to an institution or some other form of care.

Public Welfare and Community Responsibility [28]

Other services to older persons are available through the local de-partments of public welfare. The specific programs are old-age assistance,

[27] Davis, Gertrude R., "Visiting Housekeeper Service for the Aged." *Journal of Social Casework.* XXIX, January 1948, p. 23.

[28] There are developments in other areas that have special relevance for the aged, even though the services are intended to cut across all age groups. The hospital home care program as offered by the Montefiore Hospital in New York City is an example, whereby chronically ill patients may leave the hospital when not in need of hospital care. The hospital provides complete medical services in the home, even hospital beds, social service, and housekeeping service. When hospital care is again required, the

aid to the permanently and totally disabled, general assistance, and, in those instances in which a parent (or parents) has children of 16 or 18 years (if in school), aid to dependent children. Since these services are dealt with in the chapter on public welfare, it suffices here to emphasize the quality of the casework which the worker offers. With large case-loads in the public welfare department and with an increasing number of older persons in the population, there is the hazard that the services to older persons may become of a perfunctory nature. Especially is this true when county welfare boards are niggardly in their financial policies or when workers do not have sufficient conviction about the impor-tance of casework services with the aged. Even though many of the newer developments in casework services for older persons are being pioneered by voluntarily supported agencies, there is nevertheless a sub-stantial responsibility on the part of the public welfare agency to afford the highest quality of service to its older clients. At the same time, it may not be unthinkable—or even without precedent—for the public agency to do some pioneering on its own account. The plight of the chronically ill, for example, offers such an opportunity.

Another example of the usefulness of public welfare services is in those agencies that have exercised initiative and resourcefulness in the development of boarding home care for older persons. Considerable

---

patient is readmitted (see pamphlet entitled *Home Care,* issued by Montefiore Hospital, New York City, 1949).

Services for the chronically ill is another instance of where needs of the aged are being met to some degree as programs related to chronic illness are stimulated through-out the country. Much the same could be said for rehabilitation services, as they are being offered with increasing effectiveness to the total population (see especially the work of the Commission on Chronic Illness, Baltimore, Maryland, and the work of Dr. Howard A. Rusk and others in the Institute of Physical Medicine and Rehabilitation, New York University, Bellevue Medical Center).

Interest and concern about the aged are being expressed at a time when we are in-creasingly conscious of the dependence of programs and services upon research. This is quite unlike that which prevailed when many of our welfare programs were being developed over the past century. Today, however, research on aging is going on in many areas—physiological, biochemical, psychological, sociological; and under many auspices involving the use of tax as well as nontax funds. The interested reader is referred to the numerous items on research recorded in *Related References on Aging, An Annotated Bibliography,* compiled by the Committee on Aging and Geriatrics of the Federal Se-curity Agency, 1952 (now Department of Health, Welfare, and Education), and available through the U. S. Government Printing Office, Washington, D. C.; and Shock, Nathan W., *A Classified Bibliography of Gerontology and Geriatrics.* Stanford, Stanford Univer-sity Press, 1951.

casework skill is required in order that such a service may adequately meet the needs of older clients.[29]

Questions have arisen, inevitably for a program that has developed so recently and with so many ramifications, as to where the social services should be placed, who should carry responsibility for co-ordination, stimulation, and leadership. To date the services have grown up under various auspices. The casework services have been developed, principally, by private and voluntary agencies—usually sectarian. This is particularly true with respect to foster care and institutional casework services, whereas the public welfare department has carried the bulk of the long-time financial needs, such as old-age assistance and boarding home care. Public agency caseloads have not permitted an intensive casework service, useful and justifiable as that might be. Many of the group work agencies have exercised considerable initiative in adapting their facilities and services to the older groups. Councils of social agencies have been quite resourceful in stimulating new services through the use of committees or existing organizations. As yet, there is not a clear definition nor acceptance of the respective places of the various agencies —public and private, casework, group work, community organization. This is quite understandable and is certainly the tradition of how most of the social services and their organizations in America have developed. While a number of communities have developed extensive service programs, it is generally recognized that there is still room for considerable experimentation. While we may look for the voluntary agency to continue its historical role of beginning new projects on a limited and experimental basis, we may be more insistent that the public welfare agency shall exercise greater leadership than heretofore. It has been within the past three decades that this country has become increasingly aware of its population changes and the necessity for providing appropriate services in relation to those changes. It has been within the last two of those three decades that public welfare has developed to the stage where it is the predominant force in the total field of social welfare. This—a program of services for the aged—is the greatest challenge as well as opportunity that has come to public welfare since it has been

[29] Prussin, Dorothy V., "Helping Older Persons Remain in the Community." *Public Welfare*. XI, July 1953, 103–105.

endowed by legislation and by common expectation with such powers and resources.[30]

Let it not be concluded from these latter remarks that social work is to carry the total load. Far from it! There is much to do in the expanding area of welfare service, but the social services for the aged are but a fraction of the total of services and programs. A review of much of the factual presentation in this chapter shows how many factors need to be taken into consideration and how many of them need to be related to each other. In this chapter we have touched on, without proposing programs, such matters as income maintenance, employment, health, vocational rehabilitation, housing, commercial recreation, research. These are all of concern to the field of social welfare because welfare feels the impact of people when their needs are not adequately met. Programs need to be worked out to deal with those larger items. As they are worked out and as the social services assume their appropriate place, then we can gain some of the satisfaction that comes from facing difficulties, understanding them, and of dealing effectively with them. The aged in this century present this opportunity.

BIBLIOGRAPHY

Books and Pamphlets

Bond, Floyd A., *et al., Our Needy Aged: A California Study of a National Problem.* New York, Henry Holt and Company, 1954.

Burgess, Ernest W. (editor), *Aging and Retirement.* Entire issue of *The American Journal of Sociology,* January 1954.

Breckinridge, Elizabeth, *Effective Use of Older Workers.* Chicago, Wilcox & Follett Co., 1953.

Derber, Milton (editor), *The Aged and Society: A Symposium on the Problems of an Aging Population.* Champaign, Ill., Industrial Relations Research Association, 1950.

[30] Hilliard, Raymond M., "Planning Services for the Aged: (1) By the State Welfare Department." *Proceedings of the National Conference of Social Work.* 1947, pp. 402–410; Kaplan, Jerome, *A Social Program for Older People.* Minneapolis, University of Minnesota Press, 1953; Levine, Harry A., "Community Programs for the Elderly." *Annals.* CCLXXIX, January 1952, pp. 164–170; Welfare Council of Metropolitan Chicago, *Community Services for Older People.* Chicago, 1952. Wickenden, Elizabeth, *The Needs of Older People and Public Welfare Services to Meet Them.* Chicago, American Public Welfare Association, 1954.

Donahue, Wilma, and Tibbitts, Clark (editors), *Growing in the Older Years*. Ann Arbor, University of Michigan Press, 1951.

——, *Planning the Older Years*. Ann Arbor, University of Michigan Press, 1950.

——, Ray, James, Jr., and Berry, Roger B. (editors), *Rehabilitation of the Older Worker*. Ann Arbor, University of Michigan Press, 1953.

Epstein, Abraham, *The Challenge of the Aged*. New York, The Vanguard Press, 1928.

Fact Book on Aging. Washington, D. C., Federal Security Agency, Committee on Aging and Geriatrics, U. S. Government Printing Office, 1952.

Kubie, Susan H., and Landau, Gertrude, *Group Work with the Aged*. New York, International Universities Press, 1953.

Kaplan, Jerome, *A Social Program for Older People*. Minneapolis, University of Minnesota Press, 1953.

Man and His Years. An account of the First National Conference on Aging, sponsored by the Federal Security Agency. Raleigh, N. C., Health Publications Institute, 1951.

Mathiasen, Geneva (editor), *Criteria for Retirement*. New York, G. P. Putnam's Sons, 1953.

Maves, Paul B., and Cedarleaf, J. Lennart, *Older People and the Church*. Nashville, Tenn., Abingdon-Cokesbury Press, 1949.

Monroe, Robert T., *Diseases in Old Age*. Cambridge, Harvard University Press, 1951.

New York State Joint Legislative Committee on Problems of the Aging, Newburgh, New York. *Birthdays Don't Count*, 1948; *Never Too Old*, 1949; *Young at Any Age*, 1950; *No Time to Grow Old*, 1951; *Age Is No Barrier*, 1952; *Enriching the Years*, 1953; *Growing with the Years*, 1954.

Selected Papers on the Aging. National Conference of Social Work, Columbus, Ohio, 1952.

Shock, Nathan W., *A Classified Bibliography of Gerontology and Geriatrics*. Stanford, Stanford University Press, 1951.

—— (editor), *Problems of Aging*. New York, Josiah Macy, Jr. Foundation, Inc., 1952.

——, *Trends in Gerontology*. Stanford, Stanford University Press, 1951.

Simmons, Leo W., *The Role of the Aged in Primitive Society*. New Haven, Yale University Press, 1945.

Smith, T. Lynn (editor), *Living in the Later Years*. Gainesville, University of Florida Press, 1952.

——, *Problems of America's Aging Population*. Gainesville, University of Florida Press, 1951.

Stern, Edith, and Ross, Mabel, *You and Your Aging Parents*. New York, A. A. Wyn, Inc., 1952.

Stieglitz, Edward J., *The Second Forty Years*. Philadelphia, J. B. Lippincott Company, 1946.

Tibbitts, Clark (editor), *Living Through the Older Years*. Ann Arbor, University of Michigan Press, 1949.

—— (editor), *Social Contribution by the Aging*. Philadelphia, *Annals of the American Academy of Political and Social Science,* January 1952.

Welfare Council for Metropolitan Chicago, *Community Services for Older People: The Chicago Plan*. Chicago, Wilcox & Follett Co., 1952.

Wickenden, Elizabeth, *The Needs of Older People and Public Welfare Services to Meet Them*. Chicago, American Public Welfare Association, 1954.

Williams, Arthur, *Recreation for the Aging*. New York, Association Press, 1953.

Woods, James H., *Helping Older People Enjoy Life*. New York, Harper and Brothers, 1953.

Significant Articles

Davis, Gertrude R., "Visiting Housekeeper for the Aged." *Journal of Social Casework,* XXIX, January 1948, pp. 22–27.

Galpern, Marie, Turner, Helen, and Goldfarb, Alvin, "Psychiatric Evaluation of Applicants for a Home for the Aged." *Social Casework,* XXXIII, April 1952, pp. 152–160.

Hill, Ruth, "Focusing Attention on Older People's needs." *Journal of Social Casework,* XXX, December 1949, pp. 405–411.

Lemkau, Paul V., "The Mental Hygiene of Aging." *Public Health Reports,* LXVII, March 1952, pp. 237–241.

Mountin, Joseph W., "Community Health Services for an Aging Population." *Public Health Reports,* LXVII, October 1952, pp. 949–953.

Posner, William, "Casework Process in a Private Residence Program for Older Persons." *Journal of Social Work Process,* IV, May 1953, pp. 9–28.

Rapp, Sarah S., "Boarding Care for the Aged Sick." *The Family,* XXVII, June 1946, pp. 192–196.

Reynolds, Rosemary, Powell, Amy S., and Zelditch, Morris, "Casework and the Aging Population." *Journal of Social Casework,* XXX, February 1949, pp. 58–65.

Savitsky, Elias, "Psychological Factors in Nutrition of the Aged." *Social Casework,* XXXIV, December 1953, pp. 435–440.

Wagner, Margaret W., "Foster Home Care for the Aged." *Journal of Social Casework,* XXVII, October 1946, pp. 238–242.

——, "Mental Hazards in Old Age." *The Family,* XXV, June 1944, pp. 132–137.

Mrs. Benson

WILLIAM POSNER, Assistant Director, and
ARTHUR S. FARBER, Associate Supervisor
Jewish Community Services of Long Island

Introduction

Foster Home placement (or Private Residence care as we prefer to call it) of the aged is a relatively new departure in the over-all programs available in communities for the care of older persons who are unable to live in their own homes or with relatives. Reference has been made earlier (See Chapter 6) to the emerging interest in this type of service by family agencies, particularly, and although still in its early stages, a body of knowledge and practice has been developed. In the ensuing pages the services of the Jewish Community Services of Long Island and the place of the Private Residence program within its framework will be examined.

The Jewish Community Services is a multiple Service Family Agency subdivided into three divisions of service—Children's and Youth, Family Services, and Services for Aged. Within this framework each division provides a variety of services related to its special focus. Among the services provided are counseling, psychiatric treatment by a panel of psychiatrists, financial assistance (exclusive of maintenance help) of various types, homemaker service, group counseling, referral to other agencies, etc.

The private residence program for older persons is a special service that is made available in the division on Services for Aged. There is another community agency that places children in foster homes. Thus, insofar as placement is concerned, the agency is involved exclusively with older persons.

The Older Client

Eligibility for this service is limited to Jewish persons in the Greater New York area, aged 60 and over. Occasionally the service is made available to persons under the age of 60 where for casework reasons this appears indicated. The second basic eligibility requirement is the inability of the older person to live either with his adult children or by himself as the result of emotional or physical difficulties or both. The physical or medical requirements are very flexible. Only those persons who are completely bedridden are considered ineligible. All other persons, even those partially ambulatory and in need of special care, are considered physically eligible. Similarly eligible are persons with a background of mental illness. Actually then, from a physical or medical standpoint, the program excludes only those requiring custodial care. More important, as far as the agency is concerned, is the emotional readiness by the older client to become involved in a casework process with the agency around his request for placement and the acceptance of the various requirements of the placement process.

Another requirement is to undergo a complete medical examination by the agency physician prior to placement. The purpose of this is less to determine eligibility for placement than to ascertain correctly the state of the client's current condition in order to know precisely the type of care to be required once in placement. In all instances it is the worker and the agency who determine final eligibility for placement.

A final requirement is a financial one—the ability to reimburse the agency a minimum sum of $90 per month. This amount was chosen because it is the equivalent of what the department of welfare pays to old-age assistance clients living in boarding homes. The thought of the agency was that any older person unable to pay this minimum sum might be eligible for old-age assistance. Exceptions to this rule are made where clients unable to pay this amount are found by the department of welfare to be ineligible for assistance. In these instances lower payments are mutually arrived at. Where, on the basis of our fee scale, larger payments can be made, this is worked out in detail. The maximum payment is $145 per month, which is the sum paid to residence owners for each client.

In accepting the client for placement the agency commits itself to

permanent care. In the event the client is unable to continue in placement, help is given in leading him to other facilities. In placement the
agency provides medical care by its own physicians, clothing and other
budgetary needs where necessary, as well as referrals to employment
and recreation facilities.

Although reasons for placement are varied, the one common element
that assumes great importance in foster care is the older person's desire for this type of care. Such a person usually does not wish to consider institutional placement under any circumstances. His desire is
to remain in the community for as long as he possibly can rather than
to have to adjust to the group living of an institution. This person frequently views institutional living as synonomous with complete loss of
independence and hence prefers an arrangement which allows him as
much freedom as possible. There are many older people, of course, who
would prefer the over-all "protection" of an institution but apply for
foster care placement because they are either ineligible for home for
aged admission or have to wait years for admission. These persons, however, are few.

Most of the older persons are referred for placement by such community agencies as hospitals, homes for aged, and by the Central Bureau
for the Jewish Aged, which is a referral and co-ordinating agency in
the community. A surprisingly large number of older persons are referred by members of the agency's board of directors and by other lay
persons in the community.

The Private Residence

Persons interested in having their homes used as private residences
or foster homes apply directly to the agency for this type of service. Occasionally they come to the JCS through newspaper advertising. The
residence owners are largely middle-aged persons with grown children or whose children have already left the home. There are many
young families, however, that show an interest in this work, too, and are
eager to have a "grandfather" or "grandmother" in the house. Similarly,
more and more older families have been used by the agency as private
residence owners. Caring for less fortunate older persons has given
these families a real sense of usefulness.

The private residence families are paid a rate of $145 per month per client, which includes room, board, incidentals and a small amount for service. Other requirements are the following:

1. The family must be Jewish.
2. The family must have an income of its own in addition to the board payment.
3. There must be readiness to be interviewed at the agency's office and to file an application.
4. Readiness to permit the agency to visit the residence during the applicacation process as well as to interview members of the immediate household is required.
5. Medical verification by the applicant's own physician of physical ability to undertake the care of another person is essential.
6. A private room must be offered.
7. There must be readiness to observe dietary needs of residents as well as to prepare special diets.
8. Readiness to care for older person during periods of illness is essential.
9. Extension of socially accepted hospitality toward client's family and friends is expected.
10. Readiness to supply basic necessities such as soap, linens, use of telephone is required.
11. Readiness to work with the agency and to accept agency supervision and help is a basic requirement.

One further requirement is necessary where the older person to be placed is receiving public assistance. In such cases the home and family must also be approved by the department of welfare prior to the placement.

Once placement has been effected, the agency maintains regular and consistent supervision of both client and residence owner.

Mrs. Benson Requests Placement [1]

Mrs. Benson, a widow, aged 85 and enjoying good health, was referred to the JCS for placement by the Central Bureau for the Jewish Aged. Mrs. Benson has been living with her daughter, Mrs. Glick, for several years since her arrival from Germany, but in recent months considerable emotional difficulties and clashes have arisen between Mrs. Benson, her daughter, son-in-law and granddaughter. Mrs. Benson is described as a "prima-donna" who expects everyone to wait upon her.

[1] Mrs. Ruth Goldan was the caseworker throughout this service.

The first telephone call between the worker and Mrs. Glick brings forth a repetition of the above material. In addition, she says angrily her mother has been telling the neighbors that her daughter refuses to feed her and mistreats her in other ways. The worker also learns that Mrs. Glick has not talked with her mother about placement and expects that the agency will arrange for placement without Mrs. Benson's participation. It also becomes clear that this situation will require financial assistance by the department of welfare. Mrs. Glick, after considerable discussion, agrees to discuss placement with her mother as well as to explore financial assistance with the public agency. It is decided that as soon as she takes some action in these two matters, an appointment will be arranged. The worker also emphasizes the value of having Mrs. Benson herself call for an appointment.

Several days later Mrs. Benson telephoned the worker requesting an appointment. Mrs. Glick spoke to the worker at the same time and agreed to come to the agency office with her mother. Even over the telephone one could sense the deep hostility between the two.

It is important to point up several elements in this beginning phase of the application process. One element, of course, is the involvement of the older client herself in the process. Agencies engaged in the placement of older persons find that in most instances it is the adult child who makes the initial request for a parent's placement. In this situation the matter was not even discussed with Mrs. Benson by her daughter. Yet it is the older person who will have to be placed and involved in it directly. Adult children, of course, have considerable guilt in approaching the parent's separation and hence naturally find it difficult, in spite of the situation, to face the parent directly with the fact. But, unless they can take this responsibility, very little can be done by the agency. Frequently, they need help in being able to take this responsibility and the agency is ready to offer this help. Frequently, too, adult children tend to infantilize their parents on the assumption that they are too old to make decisions for themselves.

The agency thus has the obligation, even in the initial phase, to convey the idea that the older person does count; that the adult child must assume the initial responsibility of discussing her feelings with the parents and even further than that, points to the value of having the parent take responsibility to make the appointment. This more than many other factors makes concrete to all concerned the older person's direct involvement in the application for placement.

7/31. Mrs. B and her daughter Mrs. G were prompt for an early morning appointment. I saw Mrs. B alone first although Mrs. G wanted to accompany her mother to the interview. I began by commenting on how alert and active a woman she seemed to be in spite of her age. She remarked she had gone through a great deal and spoke a bit of her experiences in a concentration camp in Germany. She has learned to be strong. I said it appeared she was now faced with another change. Mrs. B started by telling me how anxious she was that we find her a home in private placement. Mrs. B went into a good bit of detail about the mistreatment she says she is getting in her daughter's home. Much of the story sounded quite disorganized and from some of the things that Mrs. G told me later, it was difficult for me to judge how much of Mrs. B's complaints were projection of her own feeling toward her daughter. What does seem clear is that both mother and daughter seem to be fairly controlling persons, and there is a constant clash. At least one of Mrs. B's complaints of disinterest and hostility on the part of her children (there is another daughter living in Massachusetts) seems based on fact. This daughter has not once come to see her mother since she arrived from Germany. Although there were times when she visited New York in the past, she has made no secret of the fact that she does not want to see her mother. Apparently the children felt that their mother was always a difficult and controlling person and after their father died, she made many demands upon them. When I spoke to Mrs. G later she told me that because of her great sense of guilt that her mother had had to suffer in a concentration camp, she permitted herself to forget how difficult living with her had been and against her sister's advice brought her mother to this country three years ago. Mrs. G feels, however, that although Mrs. B is so very difficult in her relationship with her children, she gets along fine with members who are not in the family.

Although Mrs. B had insisted that she could not understand anything other than German, after she felt herself more comfortable in my office, and had aired her feelings of persecution, she told me that if I found it difficult to talk German, she could understand Yiddish. But when her daughter was back in the office and the two of them were here together, she insisted that she did not know any Yiddish. Mrs. B had also told me how important it was that she be in a Kosher home. In the latter half of the interview when Mrs. G was present, she said that she did not think it would matter to her mother if she did not have a Kosher home, and then Mrs. B said she would prefer that kind of a home. Her daughter countered by saying she would have to compromise on many things now. They seemed headed for a clash and I finally pointed out that the choice of a home is something we will consider at another point. Mrs. B's primary interest, however, is in having a home where she can talk her language, German. She clings to that difference and is not anxious to try to learn anything else.

I was able to tell Mrs. B that if she proved eligible for our placement program I would certainly try to find her a place with German-speaking persons.

Although Mrs. B seemed anxious to leave her daughter's home and find a boarding arrangement elsewhere, she is just as interested it seemed to me, in punishing her daughter. She seemed very disturbed at the thought that her daughter would not be making financial contributions toward her placement. I explained that that would depend upon the department of welfare, and if they found her eligible for assistance from them, it would hardly seem likely that her daughter could afford to pay anything. I think too, that Mrs. B was a little disturbed when I said that I knew of no German-speaking foster family in Brooklyn at the present time. This, in spite of the fact that she had told me that she wants to get as far away from her daughter as possible. She really is finding the separation quite difficult.

This first interview, although exploratory in nature reveals some of the basic concepts that assume importance in working with older persons. One such element is to emphasize again in concrete terms that the older person is our primary client. Seeing Mrs. Benson alone and first gave emphasis to this fact. Although she is hardly an inhibited person, being able to talk with the worker alone gave her a sense of freedom she could not otherwise have. She can air her complaints about her children and come to a decision herself about the service she requests.

For the agency the importance of this lies too in knowing that the request for placement is not merely the daughter's but the parent's as well.

In addition, this first interview makes clear that in considering placement and in continuing to plan toward it, the adult child has an important role—a different one from the parent's role but a significant one nonetheless. The adult child too needs help in resolving her guilt around the placement of a parent. Mrs. Glick feels guilty for having actually mentioned her mother's behavior in the very first telephone call.

8/1. Mrs. G telephoned. She was quite disturbed because the department of welfare worker said she was going to close her case unless we could make placement immediately. I called the worker and after a long discussion she took the matter up with her supervisor and agreed to send me the statement at once.

8/14. Mrs. G telephoned. She said that it was at her mother's suggestion that she had called. They are both becoming quite concerned. Mrs. G had recently been operated on for an ulcerated condition of the stomach and in the last few days she has again begun bleeding and there is fear that she will have to possibly return to the hospital. This is making her mother all the more anxious that plans for her placement go ahead as rapidly as possible. I told Mrs. G that it would be necessary that I see her mother again, but in view of Mrs. G's own physical condition and inasmuch as it is quite impossible for her mother of 85 to make the trip herself to the office, I agreed that I would visit at the home. I was planning to be in Brooklyn this afternoon and Thursday afternoon—if I could possibly make it I would get there today— if not, I would come on Thursday.

I had not yet received any communication from the department of welfare, and I suggested to Mrs. G that it might expedite matters if she would get in touch with the department of welfare worker, if they are still planning to refer the situation to us.

8/16. I visited Mrs. B in her daughter's home. The family occupies a walk-up apartment on the fourth floor. Only Mrs. B was at home. She was very hesitant to open the door until she heard my name and then acted very surprised but exceedingly grateful that I was there. She took me to her room which was spotless, and judging from Mrs. B's appearance, I feel fairly certain that she cleans her room herself. Although she did talk a great deal about her complaints against her daughter, Mrs. B. was able to focus with me on plans for her placement, and what it would mean to her. She knows that she will be with strangers but she feels that here it is worse than with strangers, and Mrs. B took me to her daughter's bedroom to show me how untidy it is in contrast to her own room. Although I feel that Mrs. B may be using this to some extent to rationalize for her hostility, it is undoubtedly emotionally very upsetting to her. Without directly saying so, she also implied that her daughter is not married to the man with whom she is living and that for her is a bitter pill to swallow. Despite this Mrs. B was able to tell me that Mr. G has until very recently been quite decent to her—at any rate he has not made her feel as unwanted as her own daughter and granddaughter have. She feels that it is Mrs. G herself who eggs everyone on. She has made Mrs. B feel guilty for the very food she eats. I could understand that to Mrs. B the very modern and expensive new electrical equipment that her daughter has in this apartment would be indication that they certainly could afford to keep Mrs. B. Despite the fact that placement in one of our private residences would mean that both the department of welfare and our agency was paying for her care, Mrs. B feels that she would not feel nearly as unentitled to things as she does here in her daughter's home. The daughter from Massachusetts has been sending $10 a month to her mother (the impression I had gotten at my first interview was that this daughter in Massachusetts had had no contact whatsoever with her mother since she has been in this country). This money Mrs. B will have to take care of her personal needs.

Judging from the appearances of her own room and her person, Mrs. B can well take care of herself in placement. However, when we discussed the things that she might have to wash, she did say that it would be very difficult for her to wash her dresses or winter underthings and perhaps if we were able to place her in Brooklyn, her daughter would do these things for her. However, she agreed that the first consideration is not where the placement shall be, but that it be with German-speaking people so that she would at least have someone with whom to talk. She is so utterly lonesome here. Although I still feel that Mrs. B may exaggerate a good deal, there is much basis for her hostility, and I feel better about placing her without having a psychiatric diagnosis. I explained to her the next step in the process, and she realizes that she will have to come to the office when I am ready to introduce her to a prospective private residence owner.

Mrs. B seemed so very grateful for my visit. When I was leaving, she took hold of my hand and I thought she was going to kiss it, but she had enough pride not to do that.

In this interview the worker gets a more rounded picture of Mrs. Benson as one who is a rather independent person, knows what she wants, and is able to take responsibility for her decision. Since the first interview Mrs. Benson seems to have become confirmed in her desire for separation from her daughter. There is the feeling that placement may be akin to the beginning of a new life for her. Perhaps her acceptance of the as yet unknown is too total an acceptance—her feeling that strangers would be better than her daughter. There is recognition by the worker that there must be emotional upset here and will have to be handled as she moves closer to placement.

On the other hand, experience with older persons who live with children has demonstrated that surprisingly enough separation from children is often looked upon as a way of re-establishing long lost independence and security. For in living with their children they had experienced a striking reversal of roles. It was their children who took care of them, who supplied them with daily necessities, who supplied them with money and clothing and food. They had lost their traditional parental role to their children. The inability any longer to live with their children is in many instances thus a result of this struggle for reassertion of role and for independence.

Another factor that appears in this interview is Mrs. Benson's ability to consider change for herself. This comes out in the discussion of where the private residence should be. She agrees that place of home can be a secondary consideration over language of the home, which rightfully must take priority.

In essence, then, we have a picture of an alert, independent woman responding normally, so to speak, to a distressing situation.

8/17. Mrs. G telephoned. Her mother had told her that I was proceeding with plans for placement but apparently she wanted to reassure herself on that basis. Then almost as if she felt quite guilty for pushing the thing, she told me that she would not be so anxious for her mother to leave had she not "done so very much to upset our home life." Although Mrs. G felt it would not matter what part of the city we were able to make placement, she would keep in constant touch with her mother, she said. I was able to tell Mrs. G that I had gotten the letter from the department of welfare. I also mentioned the fact that some arrangement would have to be made in the budget for her mother to have some kind of spending money to take care of little personal needs. Mrs. G did not say that she would do anything about it, but felt that her sister in Massachusetts should be responsible for it. I could judge from her voice that there is apparently a good bit of hostile feeling against her sister. When I asked her, she told me that this sister has been sending $10 a month to Mrs. B and that she was urging her mother to write to the sister to ask that this be continued after placement.

The guilt felt by Mrs. Glick comes through so clearly in this telephone discussion as she realizes that placement is coming closer.

9/11. Before leaving on a short vacation I had spoken with Mrs. Laura Goldman, a prospective residence owner and she seemed interested in meeting Mrs. B with the possibility of having her come to live in her home. Mrs. Goldman was in the process of being approved by the department of welfare, and I had hoped this could be completed while I was away. However they would not send an investigator in until such time as we were certain that Mrs B would be moving into this home, and I could not arrange a meeting between the two of them before my return. I had sent a letter to Mrs. B explaining my absence and telling her I could see her in my office in Far Rockaway on the morning of 9/11. I suggested that she confirm the appointment with the office. Mrs. G had not called to confirm the appointment, but by 10:00 in the morning she and her mother were in the office after a long trip from Brooklyn. I saw Mrs. B alone, and she told me how much her daughter had grumbled about the time it was taking her to come and the expense of making the trip. I could gather that what she was telling me was real, after having seen Mrs. G's face in the waiting room. She looked at her mother with the greatest annoyance, and so far does not seem to have felt comfortable enough to transfer some of that hostility to me or the agency. Mrs. B was very disappointed that she was not to meet Mrs. Goldman today. It was hard to hold her to even thinking of some of the negative in placement. She had wanted Brooklyn, and I was offering her Manhattan, but she felt that life in her daughter's home was becoming so unbearable that anything would be better. She expressed some guilt too because she knew that her daughter's condition of high blood pressure was brought on by excitement, and although she felt that Mrs. G had no right to be excited over her presence in the home, the fact was that she did. Mrs. B kept repeating that she does not know what has happened to this daughter of hers, with whom she used to get along so well, and who now cannot stand the sight of her mother. She could agree that Mrs. G was cooperating and despite the apparent difficulty because of her physical condition did manage to bring Mrs. B on this long trip. When I told Mrs. B that she would have to make another trip to the office in order to meet Mrs. Goldman, she was terrified, not because of the physical strain on herself (and I had tried to get her to talk about that a little bit) but because of the gaff she would have to take from her daughter about the effort and expense and time that it would be costing her.

During the entire interview Mrs. B seemed to forget my name and kept calling me Mrs. Angel. I discussed this with her and let her know the agency is involved in trying to help her, department of welfare included, but to Mrs. B I was concrete evidence of her "deliverance from evil." When I later spoke with Mrs. G alone, I tried to get her to talk about how angry she might be with me for making it necessary for her to make still another trip with her mother to meet the home owner. She denied having any hostile feelings toward either me or our agency but leveled a lot of hostile feeling toward the department of welfare. This came out particularly when I had to put in the tentativeness of it even after her mother and Mrs. Goldman would meet.

I indicated that both she and her mother were doing something concrete toward bringing about change in the living arrangements. Could she not be just a little patient and not let herself get so wrought up? She will apparently aggravate her ulcer condition as well as her high blood pressure. Mrs. G at first tried to project the feeling for haste on her mother and said, "You don't know how miserable she makes life for me because she wants so much to leave," but then could admit that it was she who wanted her mother gone. "She has done so much against us." This "so much" apparently was talking to a neighbor about the friction between herself and her daughter, and to Mrs. G they were all untrue. I wondered if she could not see that although it might be untrue that she had struck her mother, that the way she feels about her mother could feel to Mrs. B as bad as being struck. Mrs. G felt that she has done everything possible to make life comfortable for her mother, but she was not well and she could not be expected to spend all her time with Mrs. B, and now her husband, who she repeatedly said has been so good to her, is getting impatient and wants her mother gone. I have a feeling that Mrs. G has a lot of trouble in her relationship even with her daughter and possibly her husband. There certainly seems to be a good bit of guilt toward her marriage. She denies this, but she speaks about it a great deal. However, I did not feel it my function to be working with her on that and so I could recognize with her what a difficult position she was in, but now that she and her mother were really taking concrete steps to bring change, perhaps she could be a little more patient about it.

The meeting with Mrs. Goldman was to be in another office. Mrs. G seemed somewhat concerned about that, but when I pointed out that it would cost much less to get there, it did help. She let me know of the many changes she would have to make and how hard it would be for her mother, etc., but it was very clear that she certainly would be there.

In this interview both mother and daughter are able to come closer to the implications of placement. For the first time some veiled hostility is expressed toward the agency in connection with travel to the office and the other requirements such as coming in once more to meet the residence owner and the tentativeness of arrangements thus far.

There is recognition here, however, that although there is some basis for these troubles the real problems—particularly Mrs. Glick's—stem from the emotional meaning separation from her mother has. She is unhappy about her own marital situation, also her own illness which in turn transfers itself to her negative feeling toward her mother. One gets a sense here too of some understanding on Mrs. Benson's part of her daughter's troubles and her own feeling for her daughter's condition.

What is most important in this interview is that the agency's requirements and the use of them play a great part in bringing to the fore the inner stresses and problems of the clients. As difficult as they may be for clients, it is only through these concrete steps that the meaning of placement and separation can take hold.

9/13. Mrs. B and Mrs. Goldman met with one another in the Jamaica office. I let them talk together for about 20 minutes, and for the first time after that interview with Mrs. Goldman I saw Mrs. B smile. She told me how good it felt to have someone to talk German with and she seemed to like Mrs. Goldman herself. She seemed to be very concerned about how her daughter would feel about making this added trip, but for herself she would like to go to see Mrs. Goldman's room right now.

I spoke to Mrs. Goldman alone, and she too seemed to have taken to Mrs. Benson. She said that to her it seemed the old lady is just starved for a little affection, and she is so lonesome for the sound of the language she knew. From what Mrs. B told her, it seems to her that Mrs. G would like to have her mother become Americanized too quickly. Mrs. Goldman's own mother who is 82, finds it so hard to give up her old ways and the old language, and Mrs. Goldman has a real feeling of understanding for this client. Mrs. Goldman was quite ready to have them come with her today to see the apartment.

A meeting between the prospective residence owner and the client in the agency office is one of the steps in the placement process. It is a crucial point for the client. On the day of the meeting both persons are seen first by the worker and then introduced to each other. They are given an opportunity to talk with each other alone, and both can discuss what they can give each other, the arrangements, etc. After this meeting both clients are again seen briefly by the worker for their initial reactions.

Again, both are left free to decide whether they really want each other. If both come to a positive decision, an appointment is arranged for the client to visit the residence. This gives him the opportunity to see the place for himself—the room, the home, the neighborhood. If this is satisfactory, a date is decided upon for the client's placement.

In this brief interview one obtains a real sense of the meaning of this meeting to both, the sensitivity to each other, and their understanding of each other's needs.

A word about the residence owner, Mrs. Goldman, may be in order. Mrs. Goldman is a widow, aged 50. She has two sons, aged 17 and 14, and her mother, aged 82. She is a well-organized person, and although she has an income from an estate, she has occasionally taken boarders into her house. She was referred to our agency originally by a hospital social worker to whom she had talked. Mrs. Goldman has a large seven-room apartment and has already had two older persons in placement from the agency. During her work with these clients Mrs. Goldman showed real ability to work with the agency. Having older persons in her home is not only of value to her but also to her own mother who finds companionship with them. Mrs. Goldman is considered by the agency to be a rare person accepting older persons' behavior and their families. The children in the home are similarly well disposed to older clients and consider them as grandparent persons.

It was not surprising, then, for both Mrs. Benson and Mrs. Goldman to "hit it off" well together.

10/17. I notified the department of welfare immediately about Mrs. Goldman's acceptance of Mrs. B. The home-finding investigator had gone out

within 24 hours and approved the home. I called both Mrs. B and Mrs. Goldman and explained that they could arrange the moving date whenever they
found it convenient to each other. It was agreeable that Mrs. B come in on
the 1st. Mrs. G let me know that she would move her mother on Sunday,
and then she would come the following day also to get her room straight. I
wondered if she could permit Mrs. Goldman to help instead of making the
two trips, since traveling, she has said, has always been so hard for her. She
declined this and insisted that only she knew how to fix all the little things
to make her mother comfortable.

Here placement is finally arranged after more struggle. What comes
out more clearly is Mrs. Glick's guilt. She will fix up her mother's room
in spite of the travel. It is so hard for her to take placement. Coming in
and taking over is her way of coming to terms with her own inability
to care for her mother.

10/23. I visited Mrs. B in her new home. The change in this old lady was
truly remarkable. She was sitting in the living room with Mrs. Goldman's
mother and sister, and just chattering away. She had a lovely apron on, and
looked as if she felt herself completely at home. She greeted me with joy, and
then excused herself of the company and took me back to her room. Mrs. B
has a very attractive room in the front of the house. In her extreme gratitude
for having a home where she can again feel like "a human being," Mrs. B
quickly leaned over and kissed my hand. I did not withdraw it but told her
she need not feel this was my doing. I brought in the part that both our
agency and the department of welfare played. I also wondered if she did not
realize that she too had something to do with it, that despite her advanced
years she came to the office as often as I had required, and that as she had a
part in bringing herself here, so she had a great part in staying here. Mrs. B
muttered something under her breath about my modesty, but she was able to
settle down to a real discussion of what it felt like to be in a new place. There
was no regret apparently about leaving her daughter's home, but when I
asked for it, she was able to bring out some negative, namely that the bath-
room was not as nice a one as she had had in her daughter's home, that she
had been having a little difficulty with sleeping because so much light comes
in, but that Mrs. Goldman was going to put darker curtains on to shut out
the light. She was able to agree that in every living situation there are some
things which are not as good as one would like them. I find this woman of
85 unusually well able to relate to the present situation. I discussed with her
her department of welfare check and some of the financial calculations, such
as what she would owe Mrs. Goldman out of this present check, etc. It was
quite involved, but she could follow it very well. When I left her she understood that I was going to be talking with Mrs. Goldman alone, and I do not
think this carried any threat to her at all.

When I spoke with Mrs. Goldman she could foresee only one problem that she might have with Mrs. B, namely that Mrs. B is so sensitive that Mrs. Goldman is afraid she might hurt her feelings inadvertently. I let her know that if this was to become a real living situation, Mrs. Goldman would just have to let herself be herself, and we together would be meeting any problems that arise. Mrs. Goldman said she was convinced that the problem had been Mrs. B's daughter. Apparently the day after Mrs. B moved in Mrs. G came with some stiffly starched doilies, and removed all of those which Mrs. Goldman had put in the room, despite the fact that they were clean. She commented that her mother was very fussy. Mrs. B too had spoken about this act of her daughter's, and as far as she was concerned, she was critical of it.

In this first visit, which always takes place within a few days after placement, we note Mrs. Benson's beginning adjustment. Having wanted this so much it could be expected that Mrs. Benson would find it very difficult to express negative reactions to the home, or to separation from her daughter. The worker, however, encourages her in this and Mrs. Benson expresses some complaint. Similarly, Mrs. Goldman is free to express her reactions.

The worker, however, is faced with Mrs. Glick's feelings. She learns that the daughter came to the home and in a sense "took over," much to everyone's distress. This was expected, but it will not have to be handled directly.

10/30. Mrs. G came a half hour early for an early morning appointment. She had accepted this appointment without any demurring although it meant she would have to leave her home before eight.

There was something about Mrs. G that looked different today. She appeared more matronly. Every time she had come with her mother she looked the part of the child—a truculent one. She had even worn a ribbon in her hair. The subsequent discussion brought out the fact that that was the major bone of contention between her mother and herself. She put it all on her mother with the contention that Mrs. B would not recognize that her daughter was a grown woman. Mrs. G does not see her part in this, and I did not try to engage her in a discussion of it because I felt she could use a period of counseling on it and would have to get it in Brooklyn where she is a resident.

Today Mrs. G let herself give voice to the hostility to me which was growing, I am sure, as she thought of me as becoming more identified with her mother. Her guilt at wanting her mother out of the house was obvious even to herself, and I was instrumental in helping her to fulfil that want. She tested me out by passing some comment about not knowing whether workers —ostensibly the department of welfare—expected the truth from her. I brought it back to myself, and she could agree at first coyly, and then with real hostility, that it felt to her as if it were expected of her that she think only of her mother and not of herself. I tried to get her to realize that I had felt that placement was valid to protect her sense of self as well as her mother's. I wondered if just the separation in itself was enough. I had discussed with her the responsibility she felt for straightening her mother's room in the new home, etc. and wondered if she could not permit her mother to assume responsibility for either making any changes she wanted or for asking the homeowner for them. When Mrs. G asked whether I thought a visit once a week was too much, I replied that was something she had to decide for herself, but I reminded her of how she had complained of the strain on her when she came with her mother once a month to my office. She smiled and said "My mother was with me then!" Mrs. G felt enough acceptance of herself to tell me of all the decorating changes that are being made in the apartment now that her mother has left. She was aware of feeling much guilt and put all the activity on her daughter who she said is paying for it.

I told Mrs. G that it seemed to me that she was very much aware that her problem is deeper than just the friction that was created by her mother's presence. She agreed and told me that she had even approached her doctor with the suggestion that she might need psychiatric care. I informed her of the services of the Jewish Family Service, and she was interested in knowing that I would be glad to refer her if she wants it. Our contact would concern the problems that her mother's placement may present.

There is a new found freedom here for Mrs. Glick which permits her not only to feel differently toward her mother but to begin to think of herself, unencumbered by her mother. There is recognition too that she may have to work on her own problems.

11/7. When I visited today, I spoke with Mrs. Goldman first. She—and her sister who was present during part of the interview—find Mrs. B a very lovable old lady. She is considerate and "so smart." The last two days Mrs. Goldman has not felt well and Mrs. B has tried to be helpful to the best of her physical strength. Mrs. Goldman's son brings her books from the library, and they are all amazed to realize how alert she is. As if expecting that I was asking her to look for fault, Mrs. Goldman said she cannot help but like Mrs. B. She needs warmth and affection and she is ready to give it to her. I let Mrs. Goldman know that I was pleased to hear of such a good adjustment and I know that she will feel free to talk about little things that do not seem right to her as they come up. Then Mrs. Goldman was able to tell me that Mrs. B has no hesitation to ask for more food—like fruit and cookies at times other than for dessert. Here her hostility was leveled at the daughter saying that Mrs. G had insisted that her mother had a right to these things.

After she aired her feelings about it though, Mrs. Goldman felt that if this helped Mrs. B to feel at home it was not too much for her to give.

Mrs. Goldman told me that when Mrs. G visited immediately after she had been to my office she seemed so different. But this past week Mrs. Goldman was in the room when mother and daughter were talking on the phone. She was aware that Mrs. G told her mother of all the changes that she was making at home, but when Mrs. B spoke of how happy she was here and mentioned things that were done for her, Mrs. G cut her short with anger, and Mrs. B has been grieving much over it. Mrs. Goldman is troubled by the fact that Mrs. B dwells so much on her grievances against her daughter. I did not feel that I should be discussing with Mrs. Goldman the problems between Mrs. B and her daughter, but I did comment that with all her feelings about how considerate Mrs. B is, the relationship between mother and daughter were of necessity on a different level. Mrs. Goldman could see that there may have been difficulty in Mrs. B wanting to have an accounting every time her daughter went out. Mrs. B has tried to find out where Mrs. Goldman goes although she is discreet about it. Mrs. Goldman does not feel that she must share this with Mrs. B and does not. I feel she is very realistic about Mrs. B.

I went in to visit Mrs. B in her room. She keeps her door shut because she keeps her window open despite the low temperature outside. She was so glad to see me and again tried to kiss my hand in gratitude for having found her this place that feels more like home to her than she has known in years.

Mrs. B, of course, is most enthusiastic about Mrs. Goldman. She takes a motherly attitude toward her and is concerned about the fact that Mrs. Goldman was not feeling well. However, in talking about how hard Mrs. Goldman works, Mrs. B was able to agree with me that this was Mrs. Goldman's responsibility. Mrs. B told me of how it gives her pleasure to be cleaning her own room not only because it helps Mrs. Goldman but because she feels she is still able to do for herself. This brought her to discuss the treatment she received from her daughter. I let her know I realized how painful this had been to her, but her placement would not serve its best purpose if she lived only in the past or even gets too upset about what her daughter is doing now. She agreed, but asked if I could bear with her until she worked some of it out of her system, and with a gesture of putting her hand under the breastbone, she said she had had to suppress it for so long. I thought I could have patience as long as I felt she could look to the present and the future, and since she had mentioned her age several times, I told her I certainly did not feel her age was any obstacle to her making a good adjustment.

In this interview it is obvious how Mrs. Benson and the private residence family began to relate to each other in a more meaningful way. The young son of the family brings library books for Mrs. Benson; the latter asserts herself with regard to food. We begin to see more clearly, too, Mrs. Glick's hostility to the placement of her mother. As Mrs. Benson talks about this, we get the feeling that she, too, is reacting to the difference which placement has for her. She continues to talk about her daughter's treatment of her. There is yet the tie to the past. The worker points this up for Mrs. Benson in such a way as to give her the right to enjoy the present with its satisfactions and pleasantness. It is almost as if Mrs. Benson cannot quite believe it and to feel it would possibly imply a rejection of her daughter with whom things were so different and negative. To accept the change quickly is not simple, and it will take time for her to make the adjustment to her own new feeling.

Throughout this period and for the following weeks it became clear that Mrs. Glick, the daughter, would have to be helped to clarification of her own new role. To be of such help to adult children is accepted by the agency as part of the casework process in placement. In following through on this objective a series of interviews was arranged with Mrs. Glick. The following two interviews are illustrative of the casework activity with her.

2/29. Mrs G came for her appointment looking angry. I took this up with her almost as soon as she came in. She could admit her anger because of her need to make this trip. Although she could accept responsibility for requesting the appointment, she felt she had no other choice since it seemed that despite the mother's placement, she still was being held responsible for her physical and emotional well-being. She noted that she herself is not physically well enough to make the frequent trips from Brooklyn to upper Manhattan. I tried to give Mrs. G recognition for how taxing her frequent trips to her mother were, but she insisted, in so many words, that her own physical condition did not matter, that she had come here to talk about her mother's needs. I could agree that she was not here to do anything about her own physical needs, but in so far as they infringed upon her feelings about what she was doing for her mother's well-being, perhaps we would have to discuss them. Again I wondered why she felt obligated to be visiting her mother a minimum of once a week no matter how sick she felt. From the discussion came Mrs. G's admission of guilt for having brought her mother to this country and then not having made a home for her. Although at first she projected on her mother by saying, "You don't know my mother. She makes me feel this way." She could take it back on herself by saying, "This is the way I am," and that as sick as she feels nothing gives her greater gratification than to hear her mother praise her for the things she was doing for her. I also was able to point out that in the early part of the placement I must have felt to Mrs. G like the "good daughter" while she was the bad daughter. Smilingly she was able to admit it, but now that she recognizes that the agency is not taking over as another child, she is again beginning to resent the responsibility that she feels is hers, and mostly because of the fear that should her mother become entirely incapacitated, it would again be hers to carry the full responsibility. With much feeling, she told how she had approached her mother on the subject of an application to a home for aged where everything could be done for her, and although, according to Mrs. G, Mrs. B had been making complaints about things in Mrs. Goldman's home, just as soon as the home for aged was mentioned, Mrs. B retreated and said she would not even think about it. I wondered what Mrs. G felt she wanted to do about it. I brought up again that we were not a home for the aged and she was right in feeling that perhaps more responsibility did still remain with the family for those persons who were in residence placement with us. However, we could neither ask nor expect that she take more responsibility for her mother than she feels able to. It is for this reason that I suggested this appointment so that we could discuss what the agency might be helping with financially since I know that this is a problem for Mrs. G. As long as she feels that she must and wants to visit her mother frequently, it seems right that perhaps it should be she who would be taking her mother to a doctor.

After Mrs. G had been able to get out all her feeling about the fear about what her future responsibility might be, and although I could not take it all away from her, I could at least give her assurance that the agency would be there to help in any planning. Mrs. G was then able to discuss with me just what could be done for obtaining dental work for her mother in a shorter time than at the department of welfare's clinic. I explained that although we had no dentist connected with the agency, if she could get an estimate from a dentist as to what it would cost to have this dental work done, we would see if it were possible to supplement it. It was then that Mrs. G herself was able to suggest that she would find out from Mrs. Goldman about a dentist in the neighborhood so that she would not have to bring her mother to Brooklyn, and that she would then submit the estimate to us. At the end of the interview when I commented that this had not been an easy time today for either of us, Mrs. G herself was able to state that she feels that here she can say what she feels. I think it is a good thing that Mrs. G no longer is as obsequious as she seemed in the beginning, so full of gratitude for everything. I complimented her for doing what she could for making her mother comfortable. I commented that maybe it has been a little difficult to understand just what was expected of her since in the beginning of her mother's placement I was cautioning her to stay out more, and here I am asking her for involvement again. Mrs. G seemed to feel thoroughly comfortable about the situation now.

This interview points up clearly the ambivalent feelings of Mrs. Glick toward her mother, the agency, and even herself. This shows itself particularly in reference to the assumption of responsibility after placement. Part of the philosophy of foster care for the aged is the continued responsibility of adult children for certain aspects of care such as taking the parent to the doctor or dentist. Although Mrs. Glick made great effort—actually taxing herself—to visit her mother, she had resented the agency requirement of taking her mother to the dentist. It became clear in this interview that part of the reason for this was in her feeling about the agency and worker which through placement of her mother gave the latter a happiness she herself could not give while her mother was with her. Although, therefore, she was ready to visit her mother to fulfill her own need, she demurred when it came to fulfilling an agency requirement and to do something her mother needed. As a good daughter she had to visit her mother but to participate in the medical and dental care of her mother while the latter was living in another home—for someone else to take the credit—was psychologically abhorrent to her. The recognition given to Mrs. Glick by the worker of her inherent strength and that by participating in planning for her mother she was really taking responsibility helped Mrs. Glick to change much of her attitude.

In essence what happened in this interview was that Mrs. Glick was able to see more clearly her rightful role; that although she could not care for her mother herself she could still be the daughter by helping her mother in another home and that this was the very thing which could resolve much of her guilt.

3/28. Mrs. G had telephoned me to ask for an appointment for today. Her voice was cheerful and confident, and she had no problem whatsoever in setting the hour for the interview. When she came for her appointment, unlike all the other times, she was not early although she was prompt. She looked quite relaxed in the waiting room and had taken off her coat, making herself at ease.

Mrs. G started the interview by asking whether it was really possible to feel a relationship. She went on to say that to get along with people one must keep oneself under control. I encouraged her by saying that we all need some place where we can express our true feelings; that maybe for some people that is impossible in their family relationships. She followed this up by telling me that her husband, who had always been a fairly calm individual, now gets irritated very easily since he has not been well, even more easily than she used to. I commented that she did seem more relaxed to me today than at any time I had known her, and she told me that she thinks she is learning that nothing serious will happen if all the work she lays out for herself at a given date does not get done. Perhaps it's more important for her husband's sake that she not wear herself out so physically. Mrs. G then with a smile said some people just have to fight and rebel at everything—even when they know what is being suggested to them is right. I thought maybe it was not so bad to rebel if one thought suggestions were like an order. Mrs. G came back and said it felt so good to her that she had called up and asked for an appointment and commented on how she had rebelled at her last visit to the office, even though in her heart, she knew that she had not been ordered to come. She laughingly said I should have chastised her like a mother does a bad child. I could understand that there might be moments when it felt to her that I was her mother. I certainly did not want her to do anything she did not want to do. Maybe with the way she was feeling about the responsibility she felt for her mother, it might have seemed that my suggestion that she come in did feel like an order and she certainly had a right to express her feeling about it. I was very pleased if she could feel differently about it now. We then talked about just how placement in a residence home could be different from institutional placement. Since we are a family agency, it seemed right to me that we should be interested in working together and maintaining some connection between her and her mother; but we are interested in making that connection a comfortable one. With what felt like a lot of sincerity to me, Mrs. G could say that that was really what she wanted for herself, some spot where she would feel right about the things she could not do for her mother and at the same time she would feel very unhappy if there were not things she could do for her. There was a great deal of tenderness about her when she spoke of what an embrace from her mother meant; but this time, it was not so much that she wanted approbation as the "feel of those old bones."

With all of this good feeling on her part, I thought maybe she might begin to feel a little more comfortable with herself and with others in regard to her mother. Then she described all the lovely things Mrs. Goldman had done for her mother at birthday time. I had felt that with all her appreciation of what the residence owner had done, she might be feeling that it made her mother compare the two of them to her discredit. Although she again denied it, when I suggested that there are always two sides to our feeling, Mrs. G could say that she guesses she always will try to not look at the unpleasant side of her feelings. Perhaps it is so that she has been very upset by this seemingly unfavorable comparison. She could recognize, however, when I injected the thought into our conversation that no matter how kind Mrs. Goldman might be, she could never take the place of Mrs. B's daughter; that is she could never take the place of Mrs. G to her mother. Mrs. G then told me of instances where she was very much aware of this.

Later. Later in the day I had occasion to call Mrs. Goldman around some other situation and she told me that Mrs. G had been there and there was such a change in the relationship. She was so pleasant with the residence owner as well as with her mother and discussed with Mrs. Goldman the part she could play in getting her mother to the dentist. So that although Mrs. Goldman will be taking Mrs. B one day this week, Mrs. G will take her the other days.

In this interview we see a continuation of Mrs. Glick's real change both in herself and with respect to the other relationships in placement. She recognizes her previous feelings as representing her need to rebel, to fight. She had to do this because she lacked a sense of self, a sense of her own worth as a person. She was insecure in relation to her mother, to the agency, and to the residence owner and thought she could gain security by fighting everybody. The caseworker helped her to recognize that all of this represented her own insecurity, her own inability to feel.

In venting her hostility and her mixed feelings and in getting assurance from the worker, Mrs. Glick is able to accept her role—herself—so much better. She is able to feel, and there is a tenderness about her. Doing for her mother is now less complicated by feelings of guilt. These feelings have been replaced by a sense of responsibility. There is room for compromise, for reaching out to her mother and to Mrs. Goldman. In her new found security she can actually feel happy in doing for her mother and for herself.

Conclusion

Casework with the aged whether in foster home placement or in another setting requires first of all what might be called a special sensitivity on the part of the caseworker. Old age has a distinct cultural and psychological meaning in our society. People view old age with fear and dread. They see it as a time of utter uselessness and dependence, of loss of work and income. They regard it, too, as a time of loneliness, as a period in life when friendships and relatives are lost through death and illness. As for the older person himself, he has in many instances internalized these external attitudes so that he, too, in spite of his difference from others in the same age group has become emotionally insecure in his own living, by accepting as valid for himself these very same attitudes.

Many social workers have these very same attitudes toward old age and are thus unable to identify with the older client coming for help. They may see no challenge in working with older persons both because of their attitudes and their own psychological fears of aging.

Positive attitudes then and a basic identification with the older person is a basic requirement to helping in this field. To assist the aged person we must see him as an individual in his own right, as a living organism, as one who possesses emotional strengths, and who, though limited in many ways, can still respond to changing aspects of his living.

In working with older people we cannot always expect dramatic changes to occur. We must content ourselves with limited goals, with small changes and small reactions. Perhaps these small changes are also dramatic when one thinks of life-long patterns and attitudes which older people give up to accept change.

A final factor is that in working with older people we must also work with their adult children. It must be seen as a totality with all parts receiving equal concern. In placement, the residence owner is similarly part of this totality. The case presented here points this up rather dramatically. All of the parts impinged upon each other with equal force.

Separation—which placement entails—is as traumatic an experience as one can find in life. Although the placement of an aged parent may be more culturally acceptable than, for example, the placement of a child, it nevertheless generates all of the feelings of guilt and ambivalence that is true for child placement. Because the social agency has this awareness, it considers its task to be that of helping not only the older parent but the adult child as well. The agency's goal in foster home placement is to create a new balance of relationship between parent and adult child. This can only be achieved through a recognition of its responsibility to all concerned in the relationship.

chapter 14

Social Group Work

Social work is made available through services to individuals, to groups, and to communities. While we are prone to take these services for granted today, the pace of their development has varied in both quality and quantity. Social casework as we know it, and as already discussed in an earlier chapter, has had the longest period of consistent study and evolution as a social work service. Group work as an integral part of social work is more recent, in part because phases of its development have been outside of or only partially associated with social work. Certain aspects of this growth will be traced following a brief consideration of the function of groups in our life today.

The Role of Groups in Contemporary Society

Although still not fully understood and appreciated, groups have always made an important contribution to individual development. Anyone whose social growth is not to be arrested at the infantile level of self-centeredness must develop the capacity for interpersonal relationship in a wide variety of groups. This means learning to accept other people as well as becoming acceptable to them, becoming a social rather than an asocial or antisocial being, developing altruism to balance selfishness. It means a growing social maturity.

The family group has long been recognized as a major factor in this social evolution. Out of family relationships are developed the tools for building wider social associations. The quality of these tools depends on whether confidence or fear, friendliness or antagonism, freedom or restriction, sympathy or callousness, inward control or revolt against authority are the materials out of which the tools are being forged.

meet them became more specific and specialized, social organizations began to circumscribe and restrict their services. Through the imagination and courage of common social leaders, these programs arose originally from the same social needs, moved through a period of separate and individual development, then again merged into a common profession more specialized and more adequately defined.

Out of the social milieu mentioned above, a variety of social organizations evolved in the leisure time and informal education field. The Jewish Center movement started in 1854, and it now covers every major Jewish community in America. Early adult education programs began to take shape at Lake Chautauqua about 1874. Settlements started in this country in 1886. One of the unique contributions of the settlement movement, patterned after the early English experiments, grew out of the fact that many of the staff workers went to live in the neighborhoods they were serving. They became "neighbors" with the focus of much of their work on the family, although in reality they worked with individuals, families, groups, and neighborhoods. By 1911 there was a sufficient number of settlements in cities throughout the country that a need was felt for channels of communication between these organizations which had a common core in philosophy and methods but had developed in accordance with the particular needs of the community each one served. The National Federation of Settlements was organized in 1911 to provide such a structure for the sharing of vital information and for joint planning that would increase the effectiveness of all affiliate organizations. Recently the Federation changed its name to the National Federation of Settlements and Neighborhood Centers, denoting a broadening area of interest, concern and service.

The first Y. M. C. A. was established in Boston in 1851, some seven years after the program had been initiated in England by George Williams. By 1866 this movement had developed to a point where a national organization was deemed necessary for the ordered growth of the organization. The first local Y. W. C. A. was founded in New York in 1858. For a time there were two Y. W. C. A. organizations—one in the East centered in New York and the other in Chicago. Since 1906, when the two combined, there has been one National Y. W. C. A. organization. Actually, both the Y. W. C. A. and the Y. M. C. A. are international organizations.

The New York Young Men's and Young Women's Hebrew Association in 1874 was one of the founders of the Young Men's and Young Women's Hebrew Associations. Out of World War I came the Jewish Welfare Board to co-ordinate the work of Jewish community centers and the Young Men's and Young Women's Hebrew Associations.

In 1896 the first Boys' Club was launched in Salem, Massachusetts. By 1906 the number of Boys' Clubs had increased to the point where they too formed a national organization for consultation and co-ordination.

The year 1910 saw the initiation of the Boy Scout program, followed two years later by both the Girl Scouts and the Camp Fire Girls.

The 4-H Club program was developed in 1907 under the auspices of the Department of Agriculture in Washington, D. C., and the various state agriculture colleges. Later government-sponsored programs included the Future Farmers of America, initiated in 1928 for agriculture majors in public high schools throughout the country. Supervision and sponsorship is the responsibility of the Office of Education of the Department of Health, Education, and Welfare.

The Catholic Youth Organization originated in Chicago in 1930. This program is found mainly in the larger cities but is spreading rapidly.

This listing is merely indicative of the types of programs that were introduced throughout the country and the relative periods of their development. Some were voluntary, while others were publicly sponsored; some were for boys and young men, while others were for girls and young women; some were family focused; some developed with strong central guidance that produced relative uniformity throughout the country (such as the Scout program), while others were more or less autonomous and free to build their own program emphasis in relation to local needs and interests (such as the settlements); some were rural, most were urban; some were secular, others had religious sponsorship. Through this variety of philosophy, structure, program, and methods there ran a common purpose—to help develop to the fullest extent possible the social capacities and potentialities of the members served.

It has been indicated that the identity or lack of identification of these services with social work had to be viewed through an historical perspective focused on the source and main currents of thought that influenced philosophy and methods. While most of the more familiar programs in the leisure-time field were established prior to World War I or about that time, there were major developments between World Wars I and II that vitally affected the philosophical as well as the scientific foundation of these programs. During this developmental period both philosophy and operating practices evolved from three major sources, namely (1) public recreation, (2) education, and (3) social work, primarily social casework.

Public Recreation

The place of recreation and leisure time activities in the building of morale was recognized during World War I when organizations such as the Y. M. C. A. and the Salvation Army were brought into military establishments to conduct activities. By World War II the value of such services was so well established that on military bases leisure-time programs were operated solely by military personnel. During the depression years in the nineteen thirties public recreation programs (such as playgrounds, parks, recreation centers and programs operated in public schools) were augmented by a rapidly developed work relief program which included the Works Progress Administration and the National Youth Administration. They supplied staff, and to some extent equipment and supplies, for the necessary enlargement of activities to meet depression needs. Developments in the national parks and forests, wildlife conservation, flood control programs that made available lakes, camping and fishing sites, the Federal Security Agency buildings and facilities in the vital war production and training centers during World War II are only a few of the activities that led to both the expansion of such programs and to the general acceptance of the philosophy that leisure-time services were a legitimate and necessary function of government—national, state and local—the same as health, education, or police protection are logical responsibilities of government. During this time development of recreational activity skills progressed rapidly as well as criteria for planning and construction of facilities, for the training of recreation leaders and the evaluation of programs. Social group work as we know it today drew heavily from these developments.

Education

From the field of education during the 1920's came developments that gave vital impetus to the leisure-time activities which were growing by leaps and bounds, but without the essential clarity of purpose and a scientific base. Social psychologists began to identify the interpersonal relations—the interplay that is the essential "social process" within a group but which is not present in a crowd. This emphasis on the "group" as distinguished from the crowd, the mob, or just people in close proximity provided a focus for further insight and research.

In the middle of the decade, primarily from progressive education, came the "project method" of providing a variety of learning opportunities through one activity participated in by a group of pupils. From this development evolved an interest and focus not only on *what* people did but also *how* they did it. The "process" became increasingly important, and with that, an attempt to find out what type of process was most effective in terms of the goals the program was set up to achieve.

Later in the period workers who were in the field of mental hygiene and guidance began to emphasize the impact of social experience on personalities, values, attitudes, ideas, and behavior of individuals. Out of this growing body of knowledge education was given an *individual focus*. Attention shifted from group focus only, to both the group as a unit and the individual in the group. From these contributions group work found resources to help build up its philosophical and scientific base.

Social Casework

In the early years of the 1930's contributions from social casework began to make their imprint. The contacts with social casework gave rise to a search for more refinement in purpose and procedure, a recognition of the need for more adequate recording, and improvement in referral practices which helped etch the close identity and the complementary nature of casework and group work services. Through this relationship a growing concern for standards of practice and professional training was evident. Both have been fundamentally affected by the insights and conceptual base of psychoanalysis.

Social Work Identification

Thus social group work as we know it drew heavily upon the fields of public recreation, education, and social work. For a period of time most workers in group work programs coming from a background in any one of these areas felt their closest identification with the field of their basic training and experience. As a result there was a genuine confusion and uncertainty as to which of the three major fields represented the logical base for the professional identification and professional education for social group work.

Another timely development bearing on this struggle for basic orientation was the formation of a Group Work Section of the National Conference of Social Work, which met for the first time as a separate body in 1935. This strengthened not only the recognition of developments in group work but also its identification with social work.

In the following year the American Association for the Study of Group Work was organized, with many of the same persons active in the formation of the National Conference section participating here also. This was in no way a professional association. It was open to anyone interested in the serious study necessary for defining social group work function, for determining the educational base essential to carry out such goals, and for developing the underlying philosophy and concepts. Membership was still drawn from the fields of public recreation, education, and social work, but those from social work were in a majority from the beginning. For a period of ten years the Association operated under this type of organization. During that period other related developments occurred. An association of workers in public recreation [4] was organized, and at the same time professional associations within the field of education [5] were becoming stronger both in membership coverage and in effectiveness of program. With these workers finding closer ties in their own field, membership in the

[4] Society of Recreation Workers of America—presently known as the American Recreation Society.

[5] Such as the National Education Association; American Association for Health, Physical Education and Recreation.

American Association for the Study of Group Work became even more social work based.

Following World War I when the Community Chest movement began to spread rapidly, most of the private agencies offering programs in the leisure-time field became members of the Community Chests and therefore became affiliated with Councils of Social Agencies, further strengthening their associations with social work. By 1946 this trend toward social work identification had reached the point where the American Association for the Study of Group Work membership voted to become a professional association with membership based primarily on educational qualifications. As this was defined, it still left the way open for those trained in social work, education, or recreation but the large majority came from the schools of social work. In 1952 the American Association of Group Workers, as the professional association was named, voted overwhelmingly to participate in the program to combine five social work professional associations [6] into one social work organization. This move was a final step in social work identification.

Definition of Group Work Function

This historical background is essential for understanding the growth and present stage of social group work development, for as there is no generally accepted definition of social work, there is no generally accepted definition of social group work. However, a generally accepted description of the social group worker's role does exist. This statement was developed by the American Association of Group Workers with members from across the country participating. A 1953 committee has been appointed to revise the statement first released in 1949. Because of its importance, it will be quoted in full.

The Group Worker enables various types of groups to function in such a way that both group interaction and program activities contribute to the growth of the individual, and the achievement of desirable social goals. The objectives of the group worker include provision for personal growth according to individual capacity and need, the adjustment of the individual to other persons, to groups and to society, and the motivation of the individual toward

[6] American Association of Social Workers, American Association of Psychiatric Social Workers, American Association of Medical Social Workers, American Association of Group Workers, National Association of School Social Workers.

the improvement of society; the recognition by the individual of his own rights, limitations and abilities as well as his acceptance of the rights, abilities and differences of others. Through his participation the group worker aims to affect the group process so that decisions come about as a result of knowledge and a sharing and integration of ideas, experiences, and knowledge rather than as result of domination from within or without the group. Through experience he aims to produce those relations with other groups and the wider community which contribute to responsible citizenship, mutual understanding between cultural, religious, economic and social groupings in the community and a participation in the constant improvement of our society toward democratic goals. The guiding purpose behind such leadership rests on the common assumptions of a democratic society; namely, the opportunity for each individual to fulfill his capacities in freedom, to respect and appreciate others and to assume his social responsibility in maintaining and constantly improving our democratic society. Underlying the practice of group work is a knowledge of individual and group behavior and of social conditions and community relations which is based on the modern social sciences. On the basis of this knowledge the group worker contributes to the group with which he works a skill in leadership which enables the members to use their capacities to the full and to create socially constructive group activities. He is aware of both program activities and of the interplay of personalities within the group and between the group and its surrounding community. According to the interests and needs of each, he assists them to get from the group experience the satisfactions provided by the program activities, the enjoyment and personal growth available through the social relations and the opportunity to participate as a responsible citizen.[7]

Educational Potential in Group Experience

In all social group work there is a consistent and concurrent dual concentration on meeting individual needs through the group on the one hand and the furthering of broad social goals on the other. Participation in group activities makes possible the achieving of status with one's contemporaries through making a contribution to the group and achieving recognition for that contribution based on what one does rather than who one is. Within this accepting yet demanding social climate the individual feels free to express himself in a creative manner, to learn out of this experience what types of behavior are socially acceptable and which ones are socially handicapping. It can help the shy individual gain confidence in social relationships on the

[7] "Definition of the Function of the Group Worker." *The Group*, XI, May 1949, pages 11–12.

one hand and hold the aggressive individual in check on the other. It provides the opportunity to test out both leadership capacities and the ability to follow. This all adds up to the ability to participate in a democratic relationship that requires both give and take, sharing as well as receiving, accepting responsibility, as well as expecting others to assume it.

Program activities are the channels through which these meaningful experiences become possible. It may be a discussion, a business meeting, arts and crafts, music, dramatics, athletics, games, camp, dancing, trips, parties, and other special events or any of an endless list of potentialities. The ability of the group worker to guide the spontaneous reactions to the activities in such a manner that the experience is enjoyable and at the same time meaningful and educational is a key skill. With a group of adolescent girls sitting around and talking about a movie where the relations between the mother and daughter were crucial, the group worker was able to help them express and examine some of their own feelings and problems in a manner that was new to them but very beneficial. The boy who came to the shop group after a frustrating school experience started out to bang with the hammer in a violent manner, but gradually was able to direct his energy to a more productive use as an understanding leader helped him handle his emotional frustrations in a socially acceptable manner. The shy youngster stood fascinated outside the craft room door for a long time until finally with the encouragement and support of the group worker the boy was able to come in and participate. He discovered a talent for craft work that gave him status and recognition such as he had never enjoyed from his peers. This resulted in a feeling of acceptance and security that made possible personal relationships in this group that were more and more free and spontaneous in contrast to the previous shy, nonparticipation reaction. The boy who failed to make the basketball team, turned out, with the understanding and guidance of the group worker, to be such a good business manager for the team that in this manner he gained the satisfaction and recognition which previously he had attempted to gain through an athletic skill he did not possess. He not only gained status and recognition, but he also had the satisfaction of making a genuine contribution to the team in a manner he had previously been unable to do. The boy who gained needed recognition by swearing every other word found with the help of an accepting and understanding worker a much more satisfying and socially acceptable form of recognition by developing a newly discovered athletic skill. And so it goes. Examples could be given endlessly illustrating how the atmosphere created and the understanding skill of the group worker makes it possible for the everyday experiences of group participation to become socially satisfying and socially maturing.

In order to provide a social climate that will offer such growth potentialities, attention must be paid to the development of the group as a whole. It is important to recognize that while the possibilities mentioned above may be realized through group experience, they are neither inherent nor inevitable, but must be planned for through skilled leadership. A group experience can be as damaging to an individual as it can be beneficial if the social climate conducive to positive growth is not achieved. Thus the social group worker must help a group be clear about its reasons for existence and what it is trying to accomplish. He must help create a social climate that can make possible the desired goals. Groups, like individuals, have a personality and a characteristic mode of operation. Some always do what they are supposed to do; some always have a chip on their shoulder; some are restless and continually active, while others are slow and lethargic; some are outgoing and welcome new members and new experiences, while others become ingrown and restrictive; and some show a steady growth and maturity, while others remain infantile. Maturity in groups, as with individuals, is a matter of progressive and continual growth as long as the group is in existence. It is not something that can be achieved and then maintained with little further effort. Groups mature or regress; they are never static.

The Role of the Group Worker

Any social agency which offers group work services must assume the responsibility for making them as educationally sound as possible in the light of present-day knowledge. This means supplying professional leadership. Not too many years ago, leadership meant someone who "took over," who held the limelight, and it was not uncommon to hear one of these leaders say with pride that his had been a good group with a fine program "But it fell apart when I left." Today the basis of evaluation is how well the group has been helped to develop independence, a growing maturity and self-sufficiency appropriate to the members' age, social, intellectual, and emotional maturity and previous experience as a group. Any good leader must also be a good follower. No one is always in the position of leadership. With the very young, the mentally ill, the mentally retarded, or the inexperienced, the group worker must obviously play a more dominant role, but the emphasis is on the development of the potentialities of both the individual members and the group itself.[8]

The group worker must approach the group in much the same manner the caseworker approaches the individual. That is, in order to understand the group with which he is working, the worker must carefully identify pertinent information already known, see what gaps exist, and collect additional facts. This is a continual process of refining and evaluating the material available, but that does not mean the worker has to have complete information before he can act. The more he learns about a group, the more adequately he can work with it, but he must from the first contact apply all of his knowledge of individual and group behavior. To do this the group worker must, for one thing, look for pertinent information regarding the composition of the group. Is it homogeneous or heterogeneous in such factors as age, socio-economic background, mental ability, social maturity, previous group experience, interests, ability to make use of adult leadership, and other vital factors? Important also is information regarding the relationships between the members. Who are the most popular, and who are the least accepted? What is the basis of status and popularity in this particular group? Does the indigenous leadership shift, or is it relatively constant? Another factor is the unity of the group. Do members work toward a common goal as a unit, or is it split up into cliques and subgroups? Do subgroups change, or are they stable? What is the basis of the clique formations? Is the group *esprit de corps* high and steady, or is it unstable and changing? Are activities of interest to most of the members, or do subgroups follow their own individual

---

[8] To avoid confusing the social worker and the indigenous leader the term *worker* is frequently applied to the professional group worker and the term *leader* to the group member who assumes a leadership role.

interests? Is this a friendly or a hostile group? How is adult leadership accepted? Are they dependent on adult leadership? Do they reject it, or do they use it constructively as needed? Are they an important part of the agency where they meet, or is there little real identification? What kinds of situations bring on conflict? What is the nature of the conflicts? How are they settled: by adult authority or group action? Who determines the program? How is this done? What activities are most enthusiastically received? Which ones rejected? Why?

The group worker must also know about the individuals who compose the group. He looks for important clues to help in his understanding of the members. How well is the member accepted by the rest of the group? How well does he accept the other members? Does he accept the group worker in his social work role as a helping person on the agency staff or does he look on the worker as a parent or a teacher or some authority-wielding adult to be circumvented where possible? Does the member assume responsibility when appropriate? Can he follow as well as lead? Under what type of situation does friction occur, and when can he relate easily? What are his most important strengths and weaknesses? Is his behavior consistent or quickly changeable? What are his primary interests and aversions? Is he healthy? How does he relate to his peers, to adults, and to members of the opposite sex? What background information concerning his home, school, or neighborhood seems pertinent? These are only brief indications of the kind of information that bolster the understanding of the group and the individual members composing it.

The group worker to accomplish the social objectives of his profession must operate on the basis of deep convictions, common to all social work, regarding the capacity of individuals to grow, to develop, and to change; and a deep belief in the inherent worth of every individual regardless of race, creed or color.

The group worker draws upon his knowledge of individual growth and of the dynamics of group functioning as well as social, political, economic, and cultural forces operating in the community. To be able to make use of these factors the group worker must be skilled in using *himself* as an integral part of the group process. Development of the individual and the group is the central focus, and the group is the primary tool for fostering individual development. An awareness of community resources outside of the agency is also essential. His group work skills must be sufficiently varied to include different types of groups such as mass activities, large and small, formal and informal, coed and single sex, homogeneous and heterogeneous, and those meeting over extended periods of time or where contacts are limited.

The group worker helps the group experience to be meaningful to each member of the group. Members participate in leisure-time programs to have a good time, and unless they do, the other potential benefits will never materialize. The size, purpose, composition, mode of operation, and sponsorship of groups vary, but the essential ingredients—acceptance and rejection, decision making, conflicts and controls, diversity and unity—are always present.

One worker with a group of young adolescent boys was helping them learn to function as a group while at the same time making that learning experience enjoyable. This group wanted to be a well-organized unity, and to symbolize that unity for each of them they took the first letter of each boy's name and worked them into a club name—a name that sounded like nonsense to most of their friends but one that meant group spirit and sharing to them. The worker helped them to catch and feel the real significance of this. When election of officers was held, everyone wanting an important office could not get it. Feelings of jealousy, disappointment, satisfaction, and success were all present. The worker helped them handle these feelings. He assisted those who had achieved the success of their coveted office to accept their responsibility seriously and with fairness to all members. The elected secretary had wanted to be president and was not sure he could accept such a position, but the worker tactfully suggested that perhaps the responsibilities of secretary and treasurer could be one job. Everyone readily agreed, and a new status was given that responsibility. But equally significant, the boys recognized together that all jobs were important to the success of the club program. They continually needed skilled help. They wanted to learn how to get along with the opposite sex, but were uncertain how to start out. Many discussions, several meetings, and a crisis or two ensued. They learned how to dance, gave a coed party, and were learning the social graces all adolescents must learn. The group worker did not do it for them, but he helped them identify their real interests, helped them with suggestions of ways for meeting these interests, and gave them support in implementing these suggestions. As they discussed these matters together, bit by bit they shared more of their real selves, their convictions, their fears, their ambitions, their prejudices, and their faith. No one came out of that experience untouched. The skill of the worker is a major factor in determining whether that influence is beneficial or not. This is not a responsibility to be taken lightly. It requires more than good intent, it requires skill based on the knowledge of behavior, motivation, and group process, guided by a philosophy of deep respect for all persons.

Volunteers

Only a small percentage of groups, however, are actually led by professionally trained group workers. Two major reasons explain this. In the first place, the number of trained workers is so small in comparison to the demand that it would be a physical impossibility to staff all agencies with sufficient professionally educated personnel. Most of the group workers with this educational background are in supervisory and administrative positions.[9]

The second reason for the large number of volunteers is based on philosophy rather than necessity. Volunteers have been an important part of group work since the days long before the term group work was coined, when there were no professional workers and when all work was carried on by volunteers. They continue to be an important part of the programs today. This is one major difference between the development of casework and group work, for volunteers have practically ceased to exist in the actual giving of direct casework service to clients.

In group work settings volunteers lead groups of various kinds, assist full-time staff members, offer clerical services, assist in the trans-

[9] There is one area of group work service where this is not the case. It is in the comparatively new development of group work programs in psychiatric settings where there has been a slow but steady growth over the past six or seven years. Within these psychiatric settings, whether a hospital, a child guidance clinic, or some other special setting, the groups are led by professionally trained workers. The group worker in these settings becomes a member of the treatment team, along with the psychiatrist, the psychologist, the nurse, the social caseworker, and others. The group program, therefore, must be related to the treatment goals for each group member. In these settings the untrained worker is seldom used.

portation in special situations such as helping aged or the crippled to attend activities, and serve in administrative capacities on boards and committees. Our concern here will be on those working directly with various group activities.

One point from which much confusion and misunderstanding has resulted needs to be clarified. The term volunteer is used in contrast to the paid staff. The paid workers may be full- or part-time, but the volunteers are practically always part-time workers. The basic distinction of importance however is not so much whether the person is or is not paid but rather how well equipped he is through training and experience to do the job to which he has been assigned. A trained group worker who has left full-time active service because of marriage may volunteer a session or two at some social agency. This person's value to the program must be evaluated on the basis of competence, not whether paid or not. Similarly, a skilled cabinet maker may volunteer a session in the shop and be the most competent person in the agency within his own sphere of activity. Too many times volunteers because of their irregular hours, because of the attitude of the full-time staff, and for related reasons, never become an integral part of the total agency operation, and therefore never gain the satisfaction of seeing their own contribution within the context of the agency as a whole.

Only a limited number of volunteers are highly skilled. Many have not developed particular skills but are eager to contribute to the agency program in meeting individual, group, and community needs. The key factor in successful utilization of volunteer help is the amount and quality of responsible supervision and inservice training supplied by the agency. Jobs for volunteers should be as carefully defined as those for professional workers. Qualifications for those assignments should be as carefully evaluated. Not all persons desiring to volunteer are emotionally mature enough to lead a group. Each person must be placed in a position where his maximum contribution can be utilized and where growth and development are possible. When volunteer service is handled in this responsible manner, opportunity to serve the community becomes a significant part of the agency's service. One major role of the professionally trained group worker in present-day programs is the recruitment, selection, training, and supervision of volunteers.

Miss Sims has listed some of the following trends in agency use of volunteers.[10] More men are offering to volunteer; more young people individually and in groups are giving outstanding service; tasks appropriate for volunteers are being better described, thus making it possible to use a wider range of abilities and skills; state mental hospitals are turning more and more to established agencies for volunteers; new stress is being placed on volunteer training and there is a marked increase in the number serving in administrative capacities at area, regional, and national levels.

Casework-Group Work Co-ordination

While, professionally, group work is one of the younger members of the social work family, there are many areas where its contributions and those of social casework complement each other. Social work developed areas of specialization first, and only then began to identify the common base. In fact this step is still in progress, and as this occurs, the common base becomes wider and deeper. What happens to the individual, in the final analysis, is the basic criterion for the evaluation of all social work. The belief in the right and responsibility of the client, member, group, or community to self-determination is a common conviction. The philosophy that underpins all social work must be the same. The paths by which those goals are reached will vary. While casework deals primarily with individuals, and group work with groups, this generalization, though frequently used, is a dangerous oversimplification. When we look closely, the group worker must frequently deal with his group members as individuals and the caseworker must frequently deal with his clients in a group situation as in the family setting. However, the group worker becomes involved in individual problems *only* to the extent they relate to and affect the individual's ability to utilize group experiences.

Frequently one hears the distinction made that casework deals with the maladjusted and group work with the normal. This too is a very

---

[10] Sims, Norma J., "Volunteers in Social Work." *Social Work Yearbook*. New York, American Association of Social Workers, 1951, p. 541.

misleading generalization. Much more accurate is the statement that group work programs are set up to reach a cross section of the community it serves. Within any representative cross section of a community will be found a wide variation between the two extremes of the socially well-adjusted and the socially sick individual or *group*. If the group work program really does serve a cross section, individuals will be reached whose problems will be found to be too deep and outside the competence and service of the particular group work program. It then becomes the responsibility of the agency to help, where possible, the individual or family accept referral to an agency offering the needed service. It might be any of a variety of services, such as casework, health facilities, mental health, or guidance clinics. Over the years, experiences between representatives of many different agencies have been shared and discussed in attempts to refine referral procedures. At what stage in the referral process should the agency to which the referral is to be made be brought into the picture; how is the best way to help an individual or family see the need for and accept referral; what are the respective responsibilities of each agency when more than one is involved? These and many other questions have been given much time and consideration. In 1951, a group of representatives from the five professional social work organizations in Pittsburgh formed a committee to discuss these very problems among others.[11] The encouraging feature of this committee's approach was that the principles and procedures developed were related to referrals between social and health organizations—*all* such agencies. It was no longer necessary to consider separately referrals between casework and group work programs, group work and health agencies and so on, as though each required special procedures. This is another indication of the growing awareness of the common base of all social services. This committee's deliberations resulted in agreement on principles and procedures for intake, for continued service, and for termination of services.

Intake requires conferences identifying the nature of the new service needed; the use the client is making of the current service; the degree of the client's participation in the decision to request referral; and

---

[11] American Association of Social Workers, American Association of Group Workers, American Association of Medical Social Workers, American Association of Psychiatric Social Workers, National Association of School Social Workers.

agreement on each agency's responsibility. Following preliminary oral conferences, written confirmation of agreements is the next step. As soon as the new agency and the client make decisions regarding acceptance or rejection of the referral, the referring agency is formally notified. When both agencies remain active, joint planning and evaluation is of utmost importance, and pertinent information must be shared promptly.

When either or both of the agencies feel that termination of services is appropriate, joint decision is desirable. Reasons for termination of service might be because the desired service has been rendered; because of an indication that the client is unable to make use of services in two areas at the same time; because the agency is unable to offer further service; because the client is unable to make use of it or the client may withdraw on his own initiative.

While such procedures are an essential part of any referral process, many questions have to be answered before referral becomes appropriate. If a participant in a group work activity is unable to make use of the service, the question "why" becomes the first concern. Is it because of the nature of the program? Is it because this specific group is inappropriate for that particular individual? Has the method of dealing with the individual been suitable? Is the member rejected by the group because of his behavior, attitudes, or ability? Are race, religion, or similar factors involved? Does the member reject the group for some of the same reasons? Does the member's personal needs make this particular activity an inadequate or impossible place to meet them?

Great care must be exercised to ensure that conclusions are not assumed from one or two incidents or experiences in only one group. Identification of relatively consistent patterns of behavior in a variety of experiences should be the basis of such evaluation. Once the decision is made that referral is advisable on the basis of a careful evaluation of all available facts, a determination must be made of the appropriate agency for referral. Only then does the referral procedure outlined above become operative. Once the referral has been made, the casework agency determines the specific nature of the service needed. The same procedure holds for casework referrals to a group work program, for there the group worker determines the appropriate group activity for the member referred.

Both casework and group work have special contributions to make toward meeting the needs of individuals, but both also have their limitations which should be realistically recognized. Referrals either way should be made at a time when there is a maximum opportunity for benefit. Sometimes referrals are made too late because of a slow or inappropriate diagnosis or because of hesitancy to try a new service. Prompt and appropriate referral is recognized as an integral part of competent professional service.

A group worker may refer members to a casework agency for such reasons as the fact the individual's needs are too deep to permit him to participate with satisfaction in a group, the member may need more individual attention than can be given in a group situation, or the individual may be unable to participate at all in a group until his personal problems have been dealt with individually first.

The caseworker may refer for group work service as a supplement to diagnosis. It is not possible to get as complete a picture of the individual in a conference as it is in actual, living relationships with his peers. The group provides a real life experience. The group experience may provide an opportunity for the individual to develop security in relation to an understanding adult in a situation different from the home, the school, or the casework interview. The group may provide a milieu to work out feelings of rivalry with his brothers or sisters, for in the group the worker must be shared with others. These are merely examples of the kinds of problems and reasons behind referrals. The services are complementary. Either or both may be necessary at various stages of the individual's development.

New Demands for Group Work Skills

There has been continual development of the group worker's skill in meeting the needs of the members in the so-called traditional social agencies such as those described earlier. However in the last few years the scope of the demands for the skill of the professionally trained group worker has grown much faster than any ability of the schools of social work to provide education for such workers.

Among these new areas of development is the military. Recently the Army declared eligible for a commission a person holding a Masters Degree in Social Work. Most of the professionally educated group workers placed by the Army are assigned to military hospitals, with a concentration in the psychiatric settings. Use is also made in limited numbers in the special-services programs for the leisure-time and welfare activities. The Air Force is making increased use of social work skills. The Navy health and welfare program is one area of assignment and the disciplinary program is another, but the Navy has no special classification for the commissioning of persons with social work degrees.

Another area of rapid growth and interest throughout the country is programs for the aged. Under a variety of sponsorships throughout communities, leisure-time activity for this group is being organized. Many are sponsored by organizations offering group work services.[12]

Institutions are just beginning to be aware of the importance of group work in their organizations. In such a setting the group worker has a contribution to make not only in conducting groups but also through his knowledge of the dynamics of group functioning. Institutional living is *group* living. It consists of living groups, school groups, work groups, leisure-time groups, friendship groups, age groups, and a wide variety of other group associations. It is becoming increasingly recognized that any successful institution will be so in no small degree because of its skill in making constructive use of these group relationships which are an inherent part of the very structure of any institution. Some of those which have made some use of the group worker's skill include penal institutions for both youth and adults, institutions for the mentally deficient and handicapped, homes for the aged, institutions that are a preparation for foster home living or for those for whom no foster homes are available, and convalescent homes.

As the relation between physical illness and the state of the individual's emotional health becomes more clearly understood, the two become more and more closely intertwined. Group work programs make a contribution through providing opportunities for constructive use of free time, but the contribution of the group worker is in no way limited primarily to that. It includes the understanding of the group nature of institutional living mentioned above and also makes it possible for many of the institution residents to make a constructive

[12] See Chapter 13 on Social Services for the Aged.

use of the institution's services. By the very structure of an institutional setting, many if not most of the policy decisions, regulations, and programs must be determined and initiated by the administrative staff. This varies with the nature of the institution from a maximum amount of administrative authority in an institution for the mentally ill to a small home for children where much democratic participation is possible. Discussion groups led by group workers have demonstrated repeatedly that the residents of these various institutions have many fears, that they lack understanding of the over-all program and the reasons behind many of the procedures, and that they have many "gripes." Although the group worker is a full member of the institution staff, the nature of group program activities makes it possible for the group members to participate, to the extent of their ability, in the determination, planning, and execution of the programs. Thus the worker develops a different type of relationship with the residents than do most of the staff. This makes it possible for these discussion groups to create an atmosphere where these "gripes," fears, and unknown facts can be identified, clarified, and frequently worked upon constructively by the residents. If there is some misunderstanding about the medical procedure necessary, a doctor can be invited in and the matter cleared up; if it is about the meals (and it frequently is), the dietician can be consulted by the members or asked to meet with the group. Through this helping to create a frame of mind that is positive toward the total service of the institution, through creating an identification with the program, the members very often are helped to make a much more effective use of the services.

This applies to medical and psychiatric settings as well as convalescent or other types of institutions. The major difference is in the adaptation of group work skills and activities to the needs and abilities of the participants. In a medical setting the participants may be in various stages of physical ability to participate. Some may be bedridden, some in wheel chairs, some on crutches, some able to get about at will. The program must be adapted to the physically handicapped—whether the handicap be from the loss of use of arms or legs, a weak heart, epilepsy, or convalescence from an appendectomy. It also makes a difference in what stage of care the individual is. If the major treatment is still before him, his interests and concerns will be of one nature. If he is in the midst of medical treatment, his reactions to that will determine much of his interest. If he is in the convalescent stage with the return to home and community imminent, then the focus will be on helping that transition from the dependency of the institutional setting to the relative independency and interdependency of the home and community. In the psychiatric setting the focus, as mentioned earlier, is on the treatment needs of each individual in the group. The activity will be determined by the degree of mental illness involved and the patient's ability to relate on a reality level. Thus in the institutional field the nature of the group relationships is being more and more recognized as a factor of major importance in the effectiveness of the total program of services. To this understanding, group work has a contribution to make, a major contribution, but it is only one of many others needed for a well-balanced institution.[13]

In the field of camping, group work has been an important skill for many years. However, developments in camping have made many of the group work skills increasingly important. Not only have the regular types of camp programs been steadily improving in content and effectiveness, but the range has been greatly expanded. In some sections of the country camping has been made an integral part of the school year, and for certain grades all children spend a week or two in camp. Camps have been established for the blind. Family camps provide an experience for the whole family where possible and for the mother and children in the others. Crippled children are being provided with camp experience both by integrating a limited number into regular camps, and through camps set up especially for the crippled. The same procedures are being experimented with for the mentally retarded. A recent development is camping for the aged, usually for those 60 or 65 and over. As in institutional settings, the program must be adapted to the physical and emotional ability of the participants, but the underlying philosophy and the basic skills remain the same. Skill in adaptation is one of the major requirements for the group worker once he has learned the particular demands and requirements of the setting.

[13] For more detailed consideration see Konopka, Gisela, *Therapeutic Group Work with Children.* Minneapolis, University of Minnesota Press, 1949; Schulze, Susanne (editor), *Creative Group Living in a Children's Institution.* New York, Association Press, 1951.

A further trend is the growing recognition of the value of group work skill in church-sponsored and church-centered programs. Some churches are looking for program directors who not only have religious education training but social group work also. More and more church groups who train their own religious education workers are introducing group work courses into their curriculum. Not only is there a trend toward more group work in the training of religious education program staff, but there is a trend toward more co-operative relationships between social agencies and religious groups. This important trend is typified by developments in the Jewish Center field in Chicago where arrangements have been worked out between the Jewish community centers of Chicago and various synagogues. The synagogue sponsors the program, supplies the facilities and equipment, while the trained leadership is supplied by the Jewish community centers. Throughout the country other churches are offering more leisure-time programs, and many are now becoming interested in offering activities for the aged. Likewise there are increasingly better referral relationships between social agencies and religious groups.

While Germany was under the jurisdiction of the occupation forces many trained group workers were sent to help train youth leaders in the philosophy and methods of democratic leadership. At the same time, many German youth leaders were sent to this country for training periods lasting from three months to a year or in some instances longer. Such programs however were not limited to occupied countries, for through Fulbright scholarships and other exchange arrangements, social workers from this country are being asked to teach or conduct institutes in other countries of Europe and South America and to some extent in countries around the world, and vice versa. Slowly but surely social work is developing a world-wide co-ordination that should help us identify those parts of basic philosophy which are truly universal and those which are culturally determined locally. We have a tendency to overestimate the universality of our base and to underestimate our own cultural bias.[14]

With the developments in the Research Center for Group Dynamics

---

[14] Some of the cultural factors influencing group work practice have been discussed by Alan F. Klein in his book *Society, Democracy, and the Group.* New York, Whiteside, Inc., 1953.

located at the University of Michigan and at the Bethel, Maine, Laboratory for Group Development [15] more attention is being directed to the relationship between social group work and group dynamics research. At the 1950 National Conference of Social Work two important papers were given as a step toward a better basis of understanding.[16] As Miss Coyle pointed out at that time, the term group dynamics is sometimes erroneously used as a form of practice, that is "doing group dynamics" when in reality the term is based on the concept that "the group process is dynamic and that scientific study will reveal the nature of the process." [17] The research is geared, as Miss Coyle states, to "the production by scientific means of the basic knowledge of human behavior." [18] Group workers are concerned with the improvement of their own practice, and they draw upon the basic knowledge of human behavior regardless of the discipline which produces it. Researchers can select a particular segment of the group process and look at it in as isolated a form as possible, but the group work practitioner must deal with individuals within a total group process operating within interacting community forces. The training of the staff of the Research Center is primarily that of the social psychologist and the sociologist. The training of the social group worker is social work. Thus while there can be mutually beneficial co-operation, the programs have different goals, different techniques and must be evaluated with different sets of criteria.[19]

As with all social work, group workers are recognizing more and more the necessity of correlating research developments in sociology, psychology, social psychology, cultural anthropology, and many other disciplines, with social work content and methods. There is at the same time a growing awareness that this is a much more complicated task than superficial examination might indicate. Each discipline has

[15] Jointly sponsored with the National Education Association with many universities and organizations co-operating.

[16] Coyle, Grace L., "Group Dynamics and the Practice of Social Group Work." *Proceedings of the National Conference of Social Work.* 1950, pp. 266–276; Festinger, Leon, "Current Developments in Group Dynamics." *Proceedings of the National Conference of Social Work.* 1950, pp. 253–265.

[17] *Ibid.,* p. 267.

[18] *Ibid.,* p. 269.

[19] For a recent statement of developments in the Group Dynamics area, see Cartwright, Dorwin, and Zander, Alvin (editors), *Group Dynamics—Research and Theory.* Evanston, Ill., Row, Peterson and Company, 1953.

developed a language of its own for purposes of more scientific accuracy within the particular discipline, but this makes interchange of concepts and research findings more difficult. In this direction, however, may be the most fruitful developments in the next few years.

BIBLIOGRAPHY

Books and Pamphlets

Addams, Jane, *Forty Years at Hull House.* New York, The Macmillan Company, 1935.

Blumenthal, Louis H., *Administration of Group Work.* New York, Association Press, 1948.

Cartwright, Dorwin, and Zander, Alvin (editors), *Group Dynamics—Research and Theory,* Evanston, Ill., Row, Peterson & Company, 1953.

Coyle, Grace L., *Group Work With American Youth.* New York, Harper and Brothers, 1948.

——, *Studies in Group Behavior.* New York, Harper and Brothers, 1937.

Cunningham, Ruth, and Associates, *Understanding Group Behavior of Boys and Girls. New York,* Teachers College, Columbia University, 1951.

Dimock, Hedley S., *Rediscovering the Adolescent.* New York, Association Press, 1937.

Elliott, Harrison, *The Process of Group Thinking.* New York, Association Press, 1928.

Follett, Mary Parker, *Creative Experience,* New York, Longmans Green & Company, 1924.

Haiman, Franklyn S., *Group Leadership and Democratic Action.* Boston, Houghton Mifflin Company, 1950.

Hendry, Charles E. (editor), *A Decade of Group Work.* New York, Association Press, 1948.

Jennings, Helen Hall, *Leadership and Isolation,* rev. ed. New York, Longmans Green & Company, 1950.

Klein, Alan F., *Society, Democracy, and the Group.* New York, Whiteside, Inc., 1953.

Konopka, Gisela, *Therapeutic Group Work with Children.* Minneapolis, University of Minnesota Press, 1949.

Lindenberg, Sidney J., *Supervision in Social Group Work.* New York, Association Press, 1939.

Meyer, Harold D., and Brightbill, Charles K., *Community Recreation. Boston,* D. C. Heath & Company, 1948.

——, *State Recreation: Organization and Administration.* New York, A. S. Barnes & Co., 1950.

Pacey, Lorene M. (editor), *Readings in the Development of Settlement Work*. New York, Association Press, 1950.

Romney, G. Ott, *Off the Job Living—a Modern Concept of Recreation*. New York, A. S. Barnes & Co., 1945.

Schulze, Susanne, *Creative Group Living in a Children's Institution*. New York, Association Press, 1951.

Simkhovitch, Mary K., *Neighborhood: My Story of Greenwich House*. New York, W. W. Norton & Company, 1938.

Slavson, S. R., *An Introduction to Group Therapy*. New York, Commonwealth Fund, 1943.

——, *Recreation and the Total Personality*. New York, Association Press, 1946.

Sullivan, Dorothea F. (editor), *The Practice of Group Work*. New York, Association Press, 1941.

——, *Readings in Group Work*. New York, Association Press, 1952.

Taylor, Graham, *Chicago Commons Through Forty Years*. Chicago, Commons Association, 1936.

Trecker, Audrey and Harleigh B., *How to Work with Groups*. New York, The Woman's Press, 1952.

Trecker, Harleigh B., *Social Group Work—Principles and Practice*. New York, The Woman's Press, 1948.

Wald, Lillian D., *Windows on Henry Street*. Boston, Little, Brown & Company, 1930.

Wilson, Gertrude, *Group Work and Case Work*. New York, Family Welfare Association of America, 1941.

——, and Ryland, Gladys, *Social Group Work Practice*. Boston, Houghton Mifflin Company, 1949.

Wittenberg, Rudolph M., *The Art of Group Discipline*. New York, Association Press, 1951.

——, *So You Want to Help People*. New York, Association Press, 1947.

Woods, Robert A., and Kennedy, Albert J., *The Settlement Horizon*. New York, Russell Sage Foundation, 1922.

Significant Articles

American Association of Group Workers, "Definition of the Function of the Group Worker," *The Group*, XI, May 1949, pp. 11–12.

Bradford, Leland P. and French, John R. P., Jr., "The Dynamics of the Discussion Group," *Journal of Social Issues,* IV, Spring 1948, entire issue.

Coyle, Grace L., "Social Group Work," *Social Work Year Book*. New York, American Association of Social Workers, 1954, pp. 480–486.

Dyer, Donald B., "The Role and Responsibility of Public Agencies in Building a Total Community Program," *Selected Papers in Group*

Work and Community Organization. Raleigh, Health Publications Institute, 1952, pp. 25–27.

Hall, L. K., "Group Workers and Professional Ethics," *The Group,* XV, October 1952, pp. 3–8.

Kaiser, Clara A., "Group Work Education in the Last Decade," *The Group,* XV, June 1953, pp. 3–10, 27–29.

Klein, Alan F., "The Effect of Cultural Variables on Group Work Practice," *The Group,* XV, February 1953, pp. 13–14, 23–26.

Konopka, Gisela, "Resistance and Hostility in Group Members," *The Group,* XVI, October 1953, pp. 3–10.

Lippitt, Ronald, "Applying New Knowledge About Group Behavior," *Selected Papers in Group Work and Community Organization.* Raleigh, Health Publications Institute, 1951, pp. 7–17.

Martin, Alexander, R., M.D., "Utilizing New Knowledge About Individual Behavior in Work with Groups in the Leisure Time Setting," *Selected Papers in Group Work and Community Organization.* Raleigh, Health Publications Institute, 1951, pp. 18–31.

Pennock, Mary E., and Weyker, Grace, "Some Developments in the Integration of Case Work and Group Work in a Child Guidance Clinic," *The Group* XV, December 1952, pp. 2–10, 22.

Polansky, Norman A., "On the Dynamics of Behavioral Contagion," *The Group,* XIV, April 1952, pp. 3–8, 21, 25.

Reynolds, Rosemary, "Services to Individuals within a Group Work Setting," *Selected Papers in Group Work and Community Organization.* Raleigh, Health Publications Institute, 1951, pp. 32–42.

Vick, Hollis, "The Role and Responsibility of Voluntary Agencies in Building a Total Recreation Program," *Selected Papers in Group Work and Community Organization.* Raleigh, Health Publications Institute, 1952, pp. 28–32.

The Mid-Town Boys' Club [1]

BETTY HEPNER, Field Instructor
Young Men's & Women's Hebrew Association
Pittsburgh, Pennsylvania

It has been emphasized in the preceding chapter that our society is composed of many groups to which individuals belong both by choice and by circumstance. The family is the first introduction to group life. Contact is then broadened to include teachers and classmates. Early in school day experiences the need "to belong" becomes important, and informal classes, discussion groups, or social clubs start their reign over leisure time.

Because an individual is a member of some group from infancy it is difficult to realize that being able to work or play effectively with others does not come naturally. We learn through our many life experiences how to participate as a member of a group. And it is this ability which determines our effectiveness throughout life as a member of the directing groups in our society, whether they be religious, political, or social.

The following material is focused to illustrate this process of learning to become an effective group member. In addition, it gives a picture of the group worker as he affects this process in helping the individual members and the group to move toward social maturity. The excerpts below are from a group record kept by the worker to help him identify and relate pertinent information, so that he could plan on the basis of increasing knowledge and understanding.

The Y at which the Mid-Town Boys' Club met is located in the civic center of the city. In this area are the cultural activities which feed the outlying residential areas. As a result, the population of this section

[1] The record of the Mid-Town Boys' Club is used with the permission of the Young Men's and Women's Hebrew Association, Pittsburgh, Pennsylvania. All names have been changed and the interpretation is solely that of the author.

is mostly transient or seasonal. In addition, the central district has neighborhoods within it of permanent residents.

The Mid-Town Boys' Club began because of another club which met at the Y. Therefore, it is necessary that we start with a brief review of the older club, the Mid-Town Teens. In the fall of the year under discussion, the Mid-Town Teens met at the Y as it had for the preceding six years. These older adolescent boys began planning their activities as they had previously. However, they found that the motivation to be the outstanding club in the center was lacking. Most of the boys had entered college or were making a beginning in the working world. Their club advisor helped them see the effect of their "growing up" on their group life. The members decided that the solution to this situation was to secure younger boys who could eventually take their place in the Mid-Town Teens. This they did, but, with the worker's help, it did not take long for them to recognize further that their "outside" interests were demanding so much of their time that they could not even get a quorum for a meeting. With the worker's help, they called an emergency meeting and disbanded the club.

Of the several boys who were visiting the Mid-Town Teens when it disbanded, only the two youngest boys responded to the worker's inquiries about the formation of a new group. Steve and Ben brought five friends to the first meeting of the new club, and this was the membership of the Mid-Town Boys' Club for their first program year.

All of the boys were 13 or 14 years of age. Arnold, Jack, Saul, and Larry were in the eighth grade, while the others had already entered the local high school. Each boy except Ben had an active interest in athletics. Ben was a heavy-set, slow-moving fellow, who attempted, with little success, to look neat. He wore glasses and had little co-ordination. Steve was of average height and appearance. Arnold was tall, thin, and well-co-ordinated in his movements. He looked older than the others. Larry was very short, measuring just over five feet. Saul had well-cut features and gave a handsome appearance, while Jack was rather thin. Howard gave the impression of being round and seemed to dislike any unnecessary movement.

All seven boys lived in the neighborhood surrounding the center, as had their predecessors. However, they were not quite old enough to start a charter group of the National Teens Organization so they decided to keep the title, Mid-Town, but to call themselves a Boys' Club. One of their objectives, however, was to become a member group of the National Organization the following year, when they all reached the minimum age of fourteen years.

At their first meeting the boys displayed eagerness in setting up their own new group, but needed the help of the worker to begin:

11/19. I then suggested that the boys elect a temporary president to preside over this meeting. I assured them that I would help the new officer conduct the meeting and pointed out that it would give them some practice in running their own affairs. On a secret ballot, each of the boys cast a ballot for himself. Larry suggested that in order to make sure that this did not happen again, the members had better nominate candidates. . . . Arnold won the election by a 5-to-2 vote.

As this new club group got underway, the first matter of business, election of a chairman, gave evidence of their need to work together rather than as independent individuals. Then, as they explored the structure they wanted for their club, they found the need to make other decisions. Sometimes these were made by Steve, who had "experience" from watching the older club; sometimes by the group as a whole. Dues were decided upon; methods of voting in new members were set up; and then, because of the club's interest, the worker described a little of what happened at Mid-Town Teen Club meetings. The group decided to have an opening ceremony of Bible reading and a closing ceremony of "Good and Welfare."

These seven boys, all of whom lived in the same neighborhood and had contact with each other outside of the center, looked to this new group for satisfactions over and beyond their personal relationships. Through their group the boys hoped to "do things" together and make themselves known.

Throughout the first meeting the boys were eager to set up group structure, but at the same time they displayed their lack of organizational experience and their dependence upon the worker. They wanted to be like the old club, but being different, evolved a structure of their own.

At the following meeting, when the boys arrived, they indicated by casual conversation that they were already considering an activity for the club. After conversing with the boys, the worker was able to pick up on this at the meeting:

11/26 (Present: All members). After elections I mentioned to the group that they had discussed the possibility of a bowling party and a swimming party among themselves before the meeting and suggested that this might be a good time to discuss this. At this point, Ben brought up the question of money. He also brought up the matter of not having the party, regardless of the kind, on Friday or Saturday night. All of the boys except Howard seemed to realize that this was because of the Orthodox home from which Ben came, though no one made mention of the fact. Arnold said that it would be best for the group to have a swimming party. This met with the approval of the entire group. Ben kept mentioning that he did not know how to swim, but this objection to the swimming party was overridden as it was pointed out that he could stay in the shallow water. Arnold and Saul then brought up the question of having girls at the party. The rest of the boys were opposed to this and Ben once again mentioned that he could not swim. Arnold and Saul kept up their advocacy of the coed party, but the group refused to reconsider. . . . As the group left the room, Saul said that he and Arnold would bring seven girls to the party so that even if the rest could not bring girls, there would be enough for everyone.

At the following meeting, after a brief discussion of the swimming party, the worker and Arnold went to the pool to make arrangements for the party. However, since the Athletic Director was not there, the worker agreed to see him during the week. At the next meeting Arnold, who had thus been involved, raised a question about what had happened.

12/11 (Present: All members). Arnold then asked what had been done in connection with the swimming party. I reported that the group was to appoint one or two boys to work with the life guard on duty in making plans for the swim. Howard, who was previously assigned to work in planning the games, was appointed, and no one else in the group wanted to share the responsibility with him. At this point, Arnold again brought up the question of having girls at the party. Larry pointed out to him that the group had already settled the matter, but Arnold again went on. At this point, I interrupted and told the group that in order for the club to function, it would seem necessary that all of the members abide by the decisions of the group as a whole. . . . The conversation now took a turn to, "Do we want a swim party?" It seemed that no one was opposed to this, but the boys who had wanted to have girls at the party were not very enthusiastic. The boys continued to plan the party.

As can be seen here, the boys eagerly started planning for their first activity, but could not come to a group decision, which would be comfortable to all of the members. As a result, as the planning continued, each persisted in having the party his own way. When the worker helped them look at the need to abide by a majority decision rather than their own individual interests, the worker recorded that their enthusiasm waned.

As was pointed out earlier, it is not easy for a group of boys to come together and act as a club unit, even though they have had previous personal relationships. Arnold and Saul were ready for heterosexual relationships and could not see the need of the group to have a beginning activity of their own. To them, the club should do what they were interested in personally, regardless of the other members. At the other end of the developmental stage, Ben neither was interested in girls nor could he swim so that he maintained a pull in the opposite direction.

As the worker recorded this, he must have questioned how he might have helped the boys plan a party which would meet their interests. Later events will show that the swimming party no longer had any appeal as a group project. The decreasing interest in one activity seemed to spur the group on to their other choice, a bowling party.

12/11 (Continued). Arnold again brought up the question of the bowling party. The boys wanted to have the party on Friday evening, and Ben reminded them that he was unable to attend any Friday evening function. Howard still wanted the Friday date for the bowling party and did not seem to understand that Ben could not attend because of religious convictions. At this point, I again interrupted and explained that Ben came from an Orthodox home and that consequently he would never be able to attend any club function that took place on a religious holiday. I further went on to mention that as the group was modeling itself after a Jewish organization, it might be wise to observe some of the religious holidays in the planning of activities, though the Mid-Town Boys' Club was, after all, completely independent and could make any sort of decision on this matter that it might care to make. The factor of the group's being a Jewish organization seemed to carry far more weight than the fact that Ben could not attend, and the group merely decided to drop the consideration of the Friday date. It was decided that the bowling would go on in place of the next week's meeting. Saul said that he would take care of the arrangements for reserving the alleys, but that he did not know exactly what he was supposed to do. I assured him that I would give him the necessary instructions after the meeting was over.

Thus, the members of the club planned another affair, this time for the club members themselves. But at their stage of learning the boys still found it difficult to take others into consideration when it affected their preference. Although there was little or no consideration of the restrictions which Ben felt, the group members were affected by what the Mid-Town Teens might have done. They wanted to be like them and like the National Organization to which they had belonged.

Unfortunately, the bowling party was also a failure as a club event, since only three boys attended. The worker then felt the time had come to help the boys look at what had been happening, before helping them to plan a new venture.

1/8 (Present: Arnold, Jack, Saul, and Steve). Steve then proposed that the group plan an ice-skating party. At this point I interrupted to suggest that it would be a good idea if the group first go back over what had happened at the other two affairs that the group had planned: what could have been improved, and why the affairs were not as successful as they might have been. The boys nodded assent, but no one seemed to know how to begin. I then suggested that since Howard was not here (he had been the chairman of the swimming party) some one ought to review, in his place, what had happened that had called the affair off. Both Steve and Jack began telling the story, not talking at the same time, but each supplementing what the other had said. In essence, two of the boys had had colds, it was cold out, and through a series of phone calls between the members, the group decided not to go.

Steve then reviewed what had happened at the bowling party. I remarked that it had been Jack's birthday and asked who had gone to the movie with him on that evening. Saul said that he had, but no one else had done so. I then asked if it would not have been more fun if the club had given a party for Jack, instead of some of the members doing one thing and some another. Saul said that this would have been a good idea and he was sorry that no one had thought of it. I then pointed out that in planning activities, the group might keep in mind the sort of things that they could do as a group, but could not do as individuals. I then asked what were some of the things that might have been done to make the affairs more successful. Arnold then called on Steve, who suggested that perhaps the affairs might have been successful if all of the members had attended. The other boys agreed with this, and I asked how this might be accomplished. No one seemed to have the answer. I then suggested that each of us remember our responsibility to the group to attend its affairs and that the person in charge of each activity might be responsible for contacting all of the members to remind them to come.

The group having exhausted their ideas on the past affairs, Steve again suggested a skating party for the future, but none of the other boys liked the idea since they could not skate. Steve then suggested that the group have another bowling party. I pointed out to the group that bowling was a good activity which all of us enjoyed, but that it was something that the members could do as individuals and did not need a club to carry it out. Steve suggested that the boys form two teams from the club which could bowl against each other once a week. The rest of the group thought that this was a good plan, would increase their good time, and yet was the sort of thing they could not do unless all of the members co-operated. Steve then suggested that the group bowl after the meetings each week. Everyone turned to Arnold, whom they knew had a number of restrictions placed on his activities on school nights. Arnold said that if he knew that he would be home before 11 o'clock, he would be able to participate.

With the help of the worker, the boys were able to look at their past experiences not as failures, but as learning experiences which could help them in future planning. They then evolved a club program which would necessitate total group involvement. One could again question whether this was realistic planning on the part of the club, since it necessitated full co-operation for success, but it did show progress in not just requiring individual participation. The worker also helped the boys look at another way in which the club could better serve them, by suggesting the possibility of birthday (and other) celebrations.

The following week, several boys got involved in a basketball game prior to the meeting and came in late and tired. The meeting reflected this mood.

1/16 **(Present: All members).** Arnold again called for order and told the group that he was resigning as president. I said that I was sure that none of the members wanted him to resign, and I asked him if he would care to tell the group why he had decided to give up the office. Arnold replied that, "I don't feel that I have enough interest in the club to be its president." Saul asked, "You want to quit the club?" Arnold replied, "No, it isn't that. It's just that I don't feel that I am interested enough to be president." He went on, "Nominations are now open for president." Steve nominated Ben, and Larry nominated Steve. As soon as Steve and Ben left the room, Saul said, "I'm so glad that those two got the nomination; they're the worst members and I wanted to have the worst people as president." He said it in a joking manner, but seemed quite serious about his words. Steve won the election by a 3-to-2 vote, Saul casting the deciding ballot.

At this point in the club's life, it is interesting to look at the importance which the club members have placed on their group. Arnold resigned from the presidency, and in the elections, Ben, one of the least accepted members, was put up for office by Steve. Steve might have done this to promote his own chances of becoming president. But Saul's reaction left no doubt that club morale was low. Nothing of importance had been accomplished by the group.

It would have been interesting if the worker had stepped in at this point to help the boys see that their feelings about the club need not determine their elected leadership. The boys did not permit the group to fall apart, however, for although Steve might not have won a popularity poll in the club, he was sincere and interested in the job which he undertook, constantly thinking of the good of the club. His fellow clubmates must have been aware of some of these qualities.

Although morale was low at the last meeting, the boys decided to buy club T-shirts and went bowling after the meeting. However, the worker recorded that there was no real enthusiasm displayed. Recognizing the need for the boys to carry through some project successfully, the worker attempted to help the boys think ahead and do some planning at the next meeting. However, the boys "just talked" and came to no decision about plans. At the tenth group meeting, the boys had to change their bowling plans due to parental pressure. In this discussion, something new happened, in that the boys themselves were now saying, for the first time, that they should plan activities as a group, for the group.

1/23 (Present: Arnold, Jack, Howard, Larry, Saul, and Steve). Steve said that the members of the club had announced that the boys were staying out too late on meeting nights and that they would be unable to go bowling that night. I interceded at this point and showed the group that this was more or less related to the problem that I had pointed out the week before, namely that the group was trying to do too much in one evening. Steve then said that Mr. Smith, Arnold's father, had agreed to take the group bowling on the days that I could not accompany them. Then came the discussion of when the group could go bowling. Once again the time decided upon was Friday night, with Ben reminding the group that they could not expect him to go on that evening as his father would never permit him. Now Jack became angry. "It's always the same thing. You can't do anything."

Then Steve made a speech, "We expect the club to cut down on all of its activities because one member can't take part. The bowling league is one of the few activities that the group has, and it is a club function that we can't give up for one man." Ben agreed, but Larry did not. "You go bowling at least five times a week. We don't have to go bowling just because you want it." Then Jack reversed himself. "I want to go bowling, but it is no good to do anything that all of us can't take part in." Then Steve called for a vote on the matter. . . . Before the vote had been completed, Steve suggested that though I could not go with the group on Sunday, Arnold's father might take them then. Saul interrupted to say, "At least that's one time when we can go bowling without having to wait around all day for an alley." I asked the group if Mr. Smith would be willing to go with them every week. Arnold nodded his head yes. I then asked Jack and Larry if this was all right with them (they had not had the opportunity to vote), and they both agreed that the arrangement would be all right provided that the group did not start before 3 o'clock. This was the time agreed upon.

During this month of activity, the boys also got busy calling prospective new members to increase the size of their club. Although many of those boys attended one or two meetings, none of them joined the club. By the beginning of March, all of the new boys had dropped out, giving varied reasons. The Mid-Town Boys' Club had been meeting for almost four months before they started to plan their third major activity. Do not be under the misconception, however, that this time was then wasted. For, while the boys were meeting and "just talking," they were getting to know each other in a new and different way: learning to participate in group discussions, making decisions, etc. In other words, many things were happening to them as individuals and as club members. We cannot expect any group to be able to plan activities or carry out projects just because they are of a certain age. Each group learns differently and this group had to find its own way.

2/26 (Present: Arnold, Ben, Jack, Larry, Saul, Steve, and three visitors). Arnold then began to talk about the bake sale idea that had been rejected the previous week. He said that he was now in favor of the idea. Ben still wanted to have a carnival. Steve then pointed out that many of the boys who had voted in favor of the carnival at the meeting two weeks ago had decided not to join the group and therefore a new vote was in order. The other boys agreed. The majority of the group voted in favor of a bake sale. I told the group that I would find out if a sale would be all right for the following Sunday and let them know at the next meeting.

3/5 (Present: Arnold, Jack, Larry, Saul, and Steve). Arnold commented that attendance was very poor this week, to which Jack replied that the group of boys there was really the backbone of the club, and that maybe the group would get something done this week. The entire atmosphere of the meeting seemed much more relaxed than it had in weeks. Saul called for the dues, but for the first time did not bother to read the total of the club's treasury. I then announced to the group that as I had been requested to do, I had secured clearance for the bake sale for the coming Sunday. Steve quickly spoke up pointing out that less than half of the members were present and that it would be impossible for the group to go ahead with the plans. He asked if the affair could not be postponed for a week. The rest of the members were quiet, as Steve acted as spokesman. I replied that I would try to secure the new date, but in the meantime, I thought that it might be a good idea if the group were to make certain assignments in regard to the project so that the additional time that they had could be taken advantage of. This last statement met with unanimous blank stares. Then Arnold suggested that whatever duties there were to be assigned, should be done by lot. His statement met with no response—visibly. Steve asked what sort of things I meant, and I replied that someone would have to make posters to publicize the project. Steve quickly replied that Ben would do it. I went on to mention that there would have to be some sort of table decoration, perhaps a banner. Again, Steve replied that Ben would do it.

I cautioned Steve that the making of posters and the banner might involve quite a bit of work, and I wondered if it were quite fair to Ben, who was not present, to assign all of this work to him. Arnold picked up the cue. "Ben'll do this and Ben'll do that. Ben won't do nothin' and then where'll we be?" Steve ignored the remark and asked me to go on. The other boys just listened attentively to what was being said. I replied that the other duties were of the type that did not require as much advance preparation and might be assigned at the next meeting when every member of the club could have a chance to carry some share of the responsibility. Steve, however, said, "If we wait for them, we won't get anything done." I listed some minor responsibilities and asked if anyone else could think of anything that I had missed. No one did.

Now Jack renewed Arnold's suggestion of drawing the duties from a hat, and this time Steve supplied the hat as well as tearing up the paper and marking an x on one piece. Saul got the x on the first drawing and was responsible for bringing some sort of table covering. Arnold was to bring paper plates, and Larry twice got the marked paper which meant that he was to make price tags and bring something with which to cut the cake. Jack and Steve drew no duties. This, according to Larry was grossly unfair, especially since he had drawn a double responsibility. Steve replied that he could not help it if he were lucky. I again suggested that perhaps too much had been assigned to Ben, and that since some of the group had no duties, they might take over part of his assignment. Steve then said that he would help make the posters and Jack quietly added that he would help.

Saul now moved for adjournment and it carried. The boys were rather slow about gathering their clothes and though they were doing nothing purposive, it was almost five minutes after the adjournment, that the boys left the room. This is contrasted to the usual rush for the door, following the meeting.

At this meeting, although the boys did not know where to begin nor did they volunteer for responsibilities, there is still an indication that they were anxious to begin planning for their new project.

The next meeting was in sharp contrast to the enthusiasm and interest displayed here. The boys showed their determination to move ahead, but were also feeling let down by a small attendance. At the following meeting the worker again attempted to help the club look at what it had accomplished and worked with them to establish some direction.

3/19 (Present: Arnold, Ben, Jack, Larry, Saul, and Steve). As soon as he finished reading (the Bible), Steve began, "Before we do anything else, I want to say that I think if we're going to get anywhere, the group is going to have to be bigger; and the only way that this is going to happen is if we combine with the Kings. We can't do anything because we don't have enough members." For the moment the whole room buzzed, and it seemed that everyone was speaking in favor of the idea.

At this point I stepped into the conversation. I told the group that before taking any such step, there were many things to be considered and now was a good time to get at the root of the troubles bothering the club. I then asked why the club had been formed. What was its purpose? Steve replied that the club had been formed as a social and athletic group. I then asked what the club had accomplished. Arnold, then Steve, then Larry, replied, "Nothing!" Steve then said that the group hadn't done anything because it hadn't enough members. I then asked why the group hadn't enough members; why members weren't attending meetings. Arnold answered, "Because we don't do anything when they get here." Larry said, "Nobody is attending meetings or joining the group because the group has nothing to offer them." I then looked around the room at each of the boys, "Is that what you mean?" Arnold said yes. I then reviewed all of the things that the group had talked about and did nothing to attain. I mentioned that the group had ordered jerseys and had gone bowling together, and that was about the extent of the things they had done.

Steve once again began to talk of merger. He asked me if I could get in touch with the advisor of the Kings to talk the matter over. When he finished his question, Arnold talked up a little angrily. "You want to merge, so we merge. Let's vote on this thing before we do anything about it." Then Larry spoke up, "We made fun of those guys ever since they started their group. Now you want to go crawling to them on your hands and knees. I've got some pride, and I'll be damned if I'll join their group." Arnold spoke out, "You don't join their group anyway; you ask them to join our group."

I then reminded the group that they were forgetting some very important points. First of all, they did not know if the other group would care to merge with them. As they had pointed out themselves, they had done so little that they were having trouble attracting their own members to their meetings. What did they have to offer any other group? I then suggested that they get back to the basic point: Why weren't they doing anything? Whose fault was it? Steve replied, "Mine, I guess." I answered, after no one else had contradicted him, that it was not just his fault. Then Jack replied that, "It's your fault, your fault, etc. (Pointing to everyone in the room) and my fault." Everyone nodded in agreement. I then asked, "Well, what are you going to do about it?"

In answer, Jack and Larry began to talk of a dance, and the discussion once again fell into the pattern of other meetings. Then Larry suddenly spoke up, "Here we are talking about something again and we're going to end up doing nothing." I mentioned the fact that the group had postponed the bake sale twice, and asked if they were going to go ahead with it. Steve replied that they had done this because there had not been enough members to carry out the project. I then asked if it would not have been possible for those who were present to have carried out the project if they had wanted to. Jack immediately said that they could have done it easily. The discussion again went back to the idea of a dance, but none of the boys had anything definite in mind. I suggested that perhaps for the first project of the group, something simple like the bake sale might be valuable in teaching them how to work together so that they could undertake something more complex like a dance later; but added that the decision on what to do and how to do it was up to them. Steve was unaffected. He called for a vote on when a good time would be to hold a dance. Again Arnold called him down, demanding that the group first decide whether they would go ahead with the plans for the sale or would want a dance. Reluctantly Steve called for a vote. The bake sale was voted for unanimously.

I then said that if we are going to do something rather than just talk about it, now was the time to make definite assignments. When would the group hold the sale? The group decided that if Saturday, the 28th was unavailable, then the 29th would be the day. I promised to clear the date. Ben again reminded the group that he could not handle money on Saturday, and two of the boys mentioned that they had to work. Steve then asked Ben if he could help out, cut the cake and the like, if he did not have to handle money. He replied that he could and would. Larry suggested that the group paint posters at the next meeting so that the group would be sure that they got done. The suggestion was approved.

Steve then went around the room and each boy said what he would supply in the way of baked goods. The members decided that they would be at the Y at 12:30 to set up the tables and that the sale would go from 1:30 to 5:00. The boys would take time out during the long afternoon and go in turns.

Many important things happened at this meeting. The boys made definite decisions about what they wanted to do, and even caught themselves a few times when they lapsed back into the old pattern of "just talking." Arnold seemed particularly aware of this and kept reminding the rest. Steve, while not usually concerned with the other members' desires, responded when reminded, and called for the group to vote. He was even able to work out a way of including Ben, without the usual antagonism. In short, the members were so enthused with the desire for the club to move ahead, that the members pooled their efforts and made specific their plans.

This record illustrates graphically the effect of the previous meeting experiences. However, in the new area of considering another club, there is a need for additional work. The boys are beginning to know each other, but need help to move in this new direction.

The following meeting, as planned, was one devoted primarily to the making of posters and a banner. Enthusiasm ran high, and several of the members stayed overtime to finish. That weekend the bake sale was held. While the worker had other agency responsibilities that day, he prepared for the Mid-Town Boys' Club and visited them when he could during the afternoon.

4/2 (Present: All members). Steve then suggested that the next thing that the group should take up would be the matter of the bake sale. He went on to say that it had gone very well, but that if the group were to do it again, they now would do some of the things differently. I then asked why the group had made a success of it. Steve spoke up and said that it was because of the fact that all of them had taken a part in it; everyone had been present for at least part of the afternoon and everyone had contributed something to be sold. Then the boys began to talk about specifics that could have been improved. . . .

Jack then mentioned the fact that he thought the group ought to hold a dance. I said that it might be a good idea to decide what the purpose of the next affair would be before deciding what they would do. This met with blank stares. I went on to explain that if they were primarily interested in influencing new members to join the group, perhaps they would want to hold a stag for new members. If they wanted some sort of social activity, then they might plan a dance or a party to which they might invite dates or perhaps invite a group of girls. If they were still interested in forming some sort of affiliation with the Kings, then they might plan some sort of activity which the two groups could sponsor co-operatively and see how well they got along with each other. At my mention of the last item, Steve indicated that he was all in favor of the idea. Larry then objected that they did not want to merge with the Kings and this had been decided. Jack held out in favor of a dance. The suggestion to hold a dance was called to a vote and lost by a 4-to-3 margin.

Then Jack suggested that perhaps, since one of the objections to holding a dance had been that there were not enough people in the club to have a sufficient number of couples for a good time, perhaps the Mid-Town Boys' Club and the Kings could work together on a dance. He hastened to add, looking significantly at Larry, that this would not mean any sort of merger, but would just be working with the other group so that they might do something together which neither group could do alone. I then reminded the group that the members of the Kings would have something to say about this too, and if the group wanted to do this, they would have to notify them. Saul said that he saw the president of the other group every day in school and that he could talk to him about it. I asked if they were sure that they wanted to go ahead on the idea of a joint affair since there had been no actual vote on the matter. I received a wordless confirmation.

At this meeting the boys seemed like a new group in many ways. They started their own evaluation of the bake sale, and then plunged into a discussion of a new activity. The worker continually helped them to look at varied aspects of the dance so that their decisions could be based more firmly on what they really wanted to achieve.

4/9 (Present: Arnold, Jack, Larry, Saul, and Steve). Once again the group began to wander into private conversations, and Steve, as he sometimes does, found himself in the middle of one. I realized that part of the reason for the aimlessness of the meeting was because I had not seen Steve previous to the meeting time.

Steve then said that regardless of what the Kings decided to do on the matter, he felt that the group should go through with the dance. He and Arnold had evidently been discussing the matter between themselves before the meeting, and they exchanged knowing glances and laughed about how the matter had been decided already, though Arnold reminded Steve that the group still had to vote on it. Saul said that he had seen the president of the Kings in school and had jokingly mentioned something about the two groups working together and had been told that this could never happen, also in a joking manner. As far as Jack was concerned, this meant that the two groups could not work together. I reminded the group that no formal letter had been sent, and furthermore, that Billy, president of the Kings, only one member of the group, had been engaged in a joking session with Saul. I added that the matter had not been thoroughly discussed by the other club. I then asked if someone would take the responsibility for writing a letter to them. . . . Later in the meeting, Arnold read a letter, and all of the members listened and approved.

I then mentioned that it had seemed to me that the group had been and still was, quite interested in joining the National Teens Organization. I realized that they had run up against quite a few difficulties in getting enough members to do this and thought that perhaps they might write a letter to Mr. Cantor of the NTO explaining the difficulties, but making clear the fact that they were still interested. Steve then assured me that the reason that he was so interested in getting together with the Kings was because this would give them enough members to join this group. Jack seemed a bit bewildered by what this all meant, saying that they would all be old enough to join the group the following year and he could see no reason for any sort of incorporation. Larry then began to jeer at Jack, asking if he meant that they would all join a different chapter of NTO, already in existence. Jack said that this was his impression. Steve then took up the ball and practically shouted between his teeth that the idea had been for them to form their own chapter. This was why those who were old enough had not already joined existing ones. Jack clamped his mouth shut and said nothing. Steve went on to say that he felt that no letter should be written to NTO until the result of the letter to the Kings had been seen. I asked if this were the opinion of the group, realizing that Steve quite often expressed his views as being those of the other boys, without first consulting them. The other boys nodded in agreement.

4/16 (Present: Arnold, Ben, Jack, Howard, Saul, and Steve). While we had been waiting for the other boys, I had reminded Steve that several weeks before I had asked him to come early to the meeting so that I might talk over with him some of the things that might have to be discussed, but that since that time, both of us had forgotten about it. He replied that it was now before the meeting and what were we waiting for. I then spoke to him briefly, pointing out that since the boys seemed to be in a hurry, we might limit the discussion to the dance. . . .

Steve, after the Bible had been read, told the group that the first and most important order of business was the dance. Saul then reported that he had talked with Billy seriously about the affair, and Billy had indicated that he was interested and the rest of his club probably would be as well. I noted that perhaps the other group would want one of our representatives to speak to the entire group about what we had in mind, and that was why it was so important that we discuss the matter thoroughly before the meeting is held with the other group. This seemed to excite Saul who announced to the group that Billy had told him that he wanted him to come to one of their meetings and talk to the group.

I then suggested that we get down to some concrete planning for the dance so that we would really have something to offer. I also pointed out that if they declined to help us, the more that we got done in the meantime, the better chance we would have of success working on our own. The boys, however, did not know where to start, and I realized that though I had talked with Steve about what to discuss, I had not gone into enough detail with him. I then pointed out that one of the first things that would have to be decided was when the dance was to be held.

The worker then helped the boys see the importance of publicity, program, refreshments, and all of the other areas necessary to planning a dance. During the next few meetings the planning progressed with the Kings club. Of course, there were difficulties—restless meetings, not knowing what to do next, all of the problems that are inherent in working with another club group. The worker met with the planning committees that had been set up individually to help them carry out their responsibilities, and finally the dance was held. The worker helped prepare the boys for those aspects which might be disappointing, so that the boys were able to have a good time, in spite of little outside participation.

5/28 (Present: All members). I had prepared the boys in my group to have a good time at their own dance, but not to expect much of a turnout of outsiders. This proved to be what happened. Boys from both clubs came with their dates, Ben being the only member not to have a date. There were two outside couples and in addition, about five girls who came stag. The boys all had a good time and enjoyed the magician's act. There was some concern on the part of the club members about whether the dance would break even and several times during the evening one member or another approached me to ask about this. . . .

The preparation for the dance found all of the members of the group, except Ben, taking part. . . . Personal evaluation of the dance was that it went very well for a first affair and in light of the fact that it was held on a poor date. . . . The boys should be able to go ahead on a similar affair next year with much less fear.

At their final meeting of the season, the boys discussed club business only briefly. They were not interested in making any decisions for the group, because they really saw the dance as their final meeting and reconvened only for a last group celebration.

6/4 (Present: Arnold, Ben, Jack, Larry, Saul, and Steve). My bringing up the question of how they got along with the Kings brought a generally favorable comment as to the members who were there, with the exception of one. I made some interpretation here as to the fact that the group as a whole had to be considered and that in almost every group, there were one or two persons who might not get along as well as the rest. The boys agreed that they all had a good time, but were disappointed in the number that turned out. In a way though, they were glad for the small turnout, because it just seemed to be suited for the facilities as we had set them up. The boys did not seem to want to go on with the evaluation of the dance though, and attempts on my part to draw them out on this matter did not work. I got the feeling that they were well pleased and that next year they would have less trouble with the affair.

The Mid-Town Boys' Club which started the year as a new unorganized group, met at the end of the club season with a record of slow, hard-won progress.

All of their events can be seen as steps, built one at a time, for a firm foundation. If each activity can be seen, not as an end in itself, but as a means of helping the members and the club to learn about group living, then we can judge the year, not as failures and successes, but as having been this group's learning experience.

From this point of view we can see that many things happened to the individual members and to the club itself. Both gained confidence in their ability to accomplish. The members had worked out their own club design, and although it incorporated aspects of the Mid-Town Teen Club, it became their pattern of procedure. This group had a particularly difficult time making decisions, but in the course of the year they began to increase the ability to take more than their own personal preferences into consideration. The club ended the year with confidence in their club and a spirit or bond that was not present early in the year.

To be sure, progress was made faster by some members than by others; but in any area individual differences show themselves. Arnold was perhaps the quickest to use past group experiences in new situations. Not only did he check the whole club on its actions, but he also constantly checked Steve so that the group did not move on one member's opinion. Steve, on the other hand, had great difficulty in helping the others come to a decision on any matter to which he did not immediately agree, but he was able to begin considering the other boys without giving up his strong desire for the group to become known; in addition, he made considerable progress in becoming acquainted with other responsibilities with which a president must cope.

Saul, Larry, and Jack, all exhibited progressive ability to accept responsibility for the group. While little movement was recorded here for Howard, the worker reported at the end of the year, "Though I can point to nothing tangible, except Howard's increased regularity in attendance, I get the feeling that he is increasingly becoming more of an in-member of the group." Ben was able to participate least in this group, since the other boys moved too quickly for him. However, he joined in activities and discussions, which were new experiences for him.

Because of this year's experience, this group of boys have a foundation on which to build for future group participation. As they continue in this club or move out to other activities, they will make use of this, their beginning venture in organized group life.

In many of the situations it would have been a simple matter for the worker to take over and do things for the club; however, this would have defeated his goal of helping the group members learn from their experiences. He was available for giving direction to discussions, for helping the boys look at each situation as clearly as possible, and for acting as a resource person because of his broader experience. In addition, he used his understanding of individuals and groups to help him act appropriately in each situation to help this club progress.

chapter 15

Community Organization for Social Welfare

Casework, Group Work, and Community Organization

The specialized areas of social work operation—casework, group work, and community organization—vary in the degree to which they are identified and defined as basic social work processes. Casework is generally recognized as a social work process and historically has been practically an exclusive social work term. Social group work is becoming more and more recognized as the social work component of the broader leisure-time and recreation field. Community organization is a term that had broad usage a long time before it was identified as one of the basic social work processes. Community organization is a term applied to both social work programs and to many different types of community enterprise with no direct connection to social work or social welfare problems. This discussion will be limited to those phases that are the concern and primary responsibility of the social worker.

Community organization in its simplest sense is concerned with meeting the needs of the individuals and groups that compose the community. It is an organized attempt on the part of the community to identify and define the social, biological, and psychological needs of the individual members and the needs of the community groups. In fact, the community itself as a corporate group has certain basic needs that must be met just as surely as those of individuals who live in that community. Community organization is the attempt to bring existing resources to bear on the problems involved in meeting these needs, to modify resources if necessary for more effective functioning, to eliminate specific services if they have failed to keep pace with current needs, and to develop new resources when necessary.

The community organization worker, however, is concerned not only with the need for various health and welfare facilities being available—such as family and children's services, institutional and foster home facilities, mental hygiene clinics for youth and adults, proper courts for family and children's cases, leisure-time programs, and the multitude of similar services—but also with the relationships between the existing organizations. Mere multiplication of services is not enough. The most effective and efficient co-ordinating and co-operative relationship is of prime concern. No longer is it possible for any social agency to operate effectively except in co-operation with other public and private welfare resources. No agency any more than any individual is sufficient unto itself.

Historical Development

Historically, developments in community organization began about the same time and out of the same conditions that fostered casework and group work. However, this growth began only after there were a sufficient number and variety of organizations and groups operating social work programs to cause confusion. It was out of this situation along with recognized gaps in available service that the necessity arose of doing something about co-ordination and evaluation of existing facilities and the need to plan services for unmet needs. One of the first attempts at organization on a community-wide basis was that carried out by the Charity Organization Societies in the latter part of the nineteenth century. They had been organized to bring about order in the confusion of variety and quality of services and relationships between agencies as well as to provide direct service. It was out of this experience that one of the basic principles of community organization was formulated. It soon became apparent, through sad experience, that it was impossible for the same agency to give direct service and at the same time attempt to co-ordinate and pass judgment on the quality of service of the same kind (primarily casework) performed by other agencies. From this and similar experiences came separate organizations for fund raising, program co-ordination, and standard setting on the one hand and direct service on the other. The objectivity, the position of noncompetition, the broad community outlook as opposed to the one agency focus all made it necessary for the two types of service to be separate and distinct. This particular chapter will be limited to the co-ordinating, standard-setting, and fund-raising types of activity.

Fund Raising

Our present-day fund-raising groups commonly known as Community Chest, Community Fund, or United Fund drives, originated primarily out of the interests and concerns of the people who contributed a large share of the funds to support voluntary social agencies. As the complexity and number of social agencies grew, it became less possible for the large contributors to know personally both the staff and operation of the social agencies. It soon reached a stage where there was much honest searching for some kind of service that would help contributors know whether an agency soliciting funds was really offering not only a needed type of work, but also whether it was operating with a quality of service that would warrant financial support in comparison to others also seeking funds. The search for this type of help resulted in the Community Fund movement.

The biggest development came during and immediately after World War I, although there had been some preliminary work on this problem before that time. As early as 1889 Denver had grouped together some fifteen or sixteen agencies in a co-operative joint fund-raising venture, although at that time this group did not raise all of the funds for these agencies nor did it promise the community only one drive. About 1900 the Cleveland Chamber of Commerce, in attempting to meet this need for some type of accreditation, set up a Committee on Benevolent Institutions to investigate and approve or disapprove the validity of an agency's claim to community support.

The impetus for these developments came primarily from the lay group rather than from the professional social workers of that time. There were at least four reasons behind this development. Big contributors (1) felt that they were being asked to give more than their share, (2) believed that an educational program was necessary to encourage the wider public to assume a share of these community enterprises, (3) deplored the inefficiency and high cost of so many agencies conducting individual, separate fund-raising drives, (4) thought that there was more and more duplication of services but that they were not always competent to identify the most effective and indispensable.

The War Chests of World War I furnished the real proving grounds for the Chest movement. Soon after the Armistice these War Chests were converted into the peacetime Community Chests. From these early partial explorations evolved the present community-wide drives based on the philosophy that it is more efficient and administratively sound to have one good drive which reduces the heavy overhead necessary for ten, eighty, or a hundred separate drives; which releases the time of the agency professional staff for the service job; which provides machinery for investigation and approval of community programs thus protecting the public from fraud and incompetency; where the contributor is approached once rather than dozens of times. One of the problems created is that in a campaign covering so many programs and agencies it is difficult to "pin point" the appeal. The personal interest growing out of the intimate knowledge that a person had when he contributed directly to a specific agency is usually not carried over when many agencies are united in one drive.

New types of programs have continued to develop. Some have joined the central campaigns and some have not; therefore, the problem of multiple drives is again becoming a crucial problem (this will be discussed later in the chapter). In spite of the problems still involved, experience in general has been very encouraging, and the number of cities and organizations participating in such drives has grown steadily. The first 225 Chests reporting their 1953 campaign reported $71,720,075.00 or 97.6 percent of the goal set. Of this number, 208 had also reported for 1952 and the amount they raised for 1953 was 105.4 percent of the amount raised for 1952.[1]

Co-ordinating and Standard-Setting Programs

While the fund-raising drives were inaugurated primarily through the interest and initiative of the layman, the standard-setting and co-ordinating programs known today as Councils of Social Agencies,

[1] Moore, Esther, "How Did the Campaign Go?" *Community*, XXVIII, January 1953, p. 83.

Community Planning Councils, Welfare Federations and similar names, originated primarily through the interest and initiative of the social workers who carried the responsibility for service to clients and members. This program also reached its developmental stride in the years during and following World War I, although it too had its beginnings prior to the war in Pittsburgh, Rochester, Milwaukee, and Cleveland. These early experiences were attempts to co-ordinate the services of existing programs and to improve the quality of the services. Concentrated interest in the quality of the programs however was a later development. There was an exchange of ideas, plans, and programs leading to better co-ordination, co-operation, joint planning, and common agreement on the setting of standards. The central idea always was to improve the quality of service.

In the early days the name Council of Social Agencies or Federation of Social Agencies was commonly used. More recent changes in titles are indicative of a steady pattern of growth that has vastly broadened the scope and outlook and as a result, the effectiveness of such programs. From Councils of Social Agencies the names have been changing to Community Councils, Community Planning Councils, and Health and Welfare Federations. The vital progress reflected in these name changes has been the result of the inclusion of an increasing number of public agencies (whereas the earlier councils had been composed primarily of private organizations) and a much wider representation of lay membership including not only representatives of the boards of the member organizations but also representatives of various related fields as medicine, nursing, public health, education, religion, labor, business, and many others.

The federation or council commonly operates through a delegate body made up of two or more representatives from each member agency. Representation is both lay and professional, and frequently includes the president of the board and the executive. Where membership is large, the delegate group is too big to conduct much of the council's business so it restricts its administrative activities to such responsibilities as determining the constitution and by-laws and electing the board of directors, which is the policy-determining group. The board selects an executive director to whom the responsibility for professional staff and carrying out of policy and program is delegated.

Many of the councils, in the larger cities especially, have broken the over-all operation down into divisions, and in the smaller councils into committees whose interests are concentrated on particular phases of the work such as health, family, and children's services, or group work and recreation programs. There are also, depending on the size of the organization, research sections or committees, and special functions such as social service exchange, information service, public relations committees, and volunteer bureaus which centralize service for the recruitment and training of volunteers. The chairman of these various divisions or committees are practically always laymen, but the division secretary in the larger community is a professional social worker. The division also operates through officers and usually an executive committee and a delegate body made up of representatives from the various member agencies. Each division has representation on the board of directors so that there can be over-all co-ordination of the whole organization at the policy-making level.

A variety of methods is used to carry out the program, such as study committees composed of lay and professional members, various other types of division or over-all committees for discussion and planning, and research departments or committees. Consultation service by the professional staff and the use of experts from outside the local community are common practice. Co-operation with professional associations, such as the American Association of Social Workers or the American Association of Psychiatric Social Workers, and affiliation with national organizations, such as the Family Service Association of America, the Child Welfare League of America, or Community Chests and Councils, provides country-wide service and scope to the local operation.

Co-ordination between chests and councils is maintained through board members serving on both boards; through staff conferences, joint committees, joint services, such as information and public relations, and other means appropriate to the local scene.

There are several patterns of relationship between the fund-raising and the planning and co-ordinating organizations other than their operation as two autonomous groups. In some of the larger cities and many smaller ones, there is one organization housing both functions. In some there is a common board and executive, with the fund-raising and planning functions being set up under different divisions or committees. In some instances there is one executive, but each group, fund-raising and planning, have a separate board of directors although there is usually some overlapping in board membership. Some overlapping is usually the case even in the larger cities where each group operates independently.

There is one basic difference in the relationship between the council and its membership and the chest and its member agencies. Since the chest allocates funds, it has potentially a much greater degree of control over member agencies. All agreements between council members are arrived at after joint discussion, but the council neither has nor wants any power other than voluntary agreement to enforce such decisions. Only as the members are convinced of the soundness of the decisions and operate in a spirit of co-operation are the desired results likely to be achieved. Chests, on the other hand, having the responsibility of allocation or withholding of funds have a powerful source of sanction or control.

There can never be—nor should there be—a complete separation of the social-planning responsibilities from the fund-raising and allocation responsibility. There is the utmost necessity for planning, fund raising and allocation to be carefully integrated and co-ordinated. Funds can be effectively allocated only on the basis of a carefully devised procedure that takes into consideration total community needs, total community resources, both public and private, and the quality and quantity of services rendered. There are seldom sufficient funds to meet total requests, even after the most careful scrutiny and study by allocating groups. Budget committees are consistently faced with the question: Given a limited amount of money acknowledged to be insufficient, how can it be used in the best interests of the total community? The question of new services usually brings up this point. If there are not enough funds available to meet acknowledged needs of existing programs, why should new services be sanctioned? This points up the fact that social-planning and fund allocation is a process of continual evaluation, both of over-all needs and of existing resources. Are new needs more pressing than some for which facilities have existed for many years? The fact of long-time existence in and of itself is no reason for continuation. Quality and quantity of service is the only justification. In social welfare as in other areas of life, it is easier to start new services than it is to eliminate those no longer necessary or sufficiently effective. Both existing programs and those seeking public support should justify their support in terms of total community needs.

The Social Work Component of Community Organization

Over the years the National Conference of Social Work has played an important role in the efforts to develop a comprehensive definition of community organization and its social work component. In 1939 one of the Conference committees reported on a year's work focused on the study of the concept of community organization and its implications for the Conference. The report was based on the results of discussion groups in six different cities.[2] It was found that, even as today, the term was used to mean both a process and a field of work and frequently was used with these meanings confused; that some community organization was carried on within the field of social work and some outside; that in social work community organization was conducted in some agencies as a primary process and in others as a secondary or incidental phase of the program; and that community organization was carried on at a variety of levels from the local neighborhood to the national scene [3] (and today on an international level). Throughout succeeding years various meetings and papers attempted further refinement in the definitions, techniques, concepts, and philosophy.

A more recent series of meetings and papers, a milestone in this process of definition and study, occurred in 1947 when the National Conference of Social Work met in San Francisco. Papers by Kenneth Pray of the Pennsylvania School of Social Work, Wilbur I. Newstetter of the Pittsburgh School of Social Work, and Lester Granger of the National Urban League among others, made significant contributions toward the definition of that portion of community organization which is an integral part of social work and that which is outside the area of social work but nonetheless important to total community development.

---

[2] Boston, Buffalo, Detroit, New York, Pittsburgh, and Chicago.

[3] McMillen, Wayne, *Community Organization for Social Welfare*. Chicago, University of Chicago Press, 1945, pp. 36–39.

Mr. Pray's paper discussed "When Is Community Organization Social Work Practice?". Before delving too far into that topic, Mr. Pray had to answer, first, the question not *when* but *whether* community organization was social work. He concluded that it:

. . . is social work practice, that its practitioners can share in the development of a single profession of social work, on three conditions: (1) if and when their focal concerns and their primary objectives relate always to the development and guidance of the process by which people find satisfying and fruitful social relationships, and not to the attainment of specific, preconceived products or forms of relationship; (2) if and when these objectives are sought consistently through the realization of a democratic philosophy and faith which respects the right and the responsibility of communities, as of individuals, to create their own satisfying relationships, and to use those relationships to their own chosen ends; and (3) if and when the basic processes, methods, and skills that are demanded and employed in actual practice are those that inhere in the worker's capacity to initiate and sustain a helping, not a controlling, relationship with individuals and groups.[4]

Social Intergroup Work Process

Mr. Newstetter's paper was entitled "The Social Intergroup Work Process." The term social intergroup work introduced a new concept into the attempt to clarify the social work component of community organization. It in turn is based on a specific view point of the community itself. There are many different ways of looking at or defining a community. In some instances it is considered as a geographical area with man-made boundaries or with natural topographical boundaries; some define it in terms of psychological identification and so on. The idea of intergroup work is based on a definition of the community which is a paraphrase of Eubank's definition of a group, namely:

A group is two or more persons in a relationship of psychic interaction, whose relationship with one another may be abstracted and distinguished from their relationship with all others, so that they may be thought of as an entity.[5]

Mr. Newstetter's definition of community substitutes the word community for group and groups for persons.

[4] Pray, Kenneth, L. M., "When is Community Organization Social Work Practice?" *Proceedings of the National Conference of Social Work*, 1947, pp. 203–204.
[5] Eubank, Earle E., *The Concepts of Sociology*. Boston, D. C. Heath & Company, 1932, p. 163.

This definition is based on the concept that there must be genuine relationships, psychic interaction, between the groups before there is any feeling of community. Just being present with no relationship interactions is not sufficient. It is also based on the belief that the individual who has status and influence, who truly is in a position to exercise leadership within the community, is in that position primarily because of his association with certain groups and his ability to enlist the support or influence of those groups. It may be a family group, a religious group, a business association, a labor union, a professional organization, or any of a wide variety that could be identified. The individual, as such, has little meaning in contemporary community life separate from his group ties.

Effective community organization in this sense is thought of in terms of relationships between community groups which are involved in or are in a position to influence a particular program. Since it would obviously be impossible as well as impractical for numerous large or even small groups to sit down en masse, these relationships are fostered and facilitated through representatives. If a community organization project was aimed at better recreation facilities for the community, representatives from the city recreation department, from the school, from parent-teachers groups, citizen groups, from the Y. M. C. A. and the Y. W. C. A., settlements, boys' clubs, and many other leisure-time programs might get together and have a very congenial meeting and even agree on a plan for meeting the needs of their community. But this would avail nothing unless the groups they represent (the city government, the school board, the leisure-time organizations and the churches) actually get together and provide services and facilities.

Intergroup work then involves: (1) working with individuals who are representing groups, (2) working with the groups that are represented, and (3) working with the group of the representatives, the "intergroup."

The representatives can be of three different types. In some instances the representatives are "official" delegates from their group in the sense that they are both selected and instructed by their group. In the above example, the board of education might have a definite philosophy regarding the division of responsibility between public and private organizations plus a definite policy on what it would be able to do in terms of available funds, staff, and facilities at that particular time. The board might then select one of its staff to represent it with instructions to present and represent the board's position.

In other instances, the representatives might be official but not be instructed. A social settlement might send a staff or board member to represent it at this meeting and prior to the meeting, the staff and board, or both, might discuss the matter thoroughly. Its representative then would be guided by this thinking and these suggestions, but would not be committed to vote a particular way. If in the course of the discussion in the intergroup meeting some new points were presented or some new facts made available, the representatives would be free to vote in the best interests of the community and the settlement as he saw it.

A third type would be those who are merely "representative of" certain groups or groupings but are neither selected by them nor are they responsible to them. Mr. Y might be asked to represent the newspapers. He would not represent his own paper as such, but would merely be able to express in general the attitude of the press toward this particular problem. He would be able to speak neither for any one paper nor be responsible to report back to any of them. The first two types of representatives point up one of the basic necessities for the successful operation of an intergroup, namely, there must be the responsibility of the representatives to bring ideas from their own group to the intergroup and they must take back actions, ideas, and suggestions from the intergroup to their own group. The "two-way" relationship involved here is both the most important and the most difficult part of the whole procedure.

To ensure that this intergroup process is also a social work process, two foci are essential. In the chapter on group work we saw that both interpersonal relationships and individual needs and social or community needs were emphasized. In the intergroup work process there is also the dual responsibility of mutually satisfactory relations between the groups involved and the social goals that have been selected and toward which they are working. Here personal needs are dealt with only to the extent that they hinder the ability to function as an intergroup member. In this process, individual needs are subordinated to the group and community needs. Social goals must be an integral part of any program that is true social work. Both social goals and mutually satisfactory relations between the groups involved must be consistently and concurrently pursued.

This paper also indicated some of the times when Mr. Newstetter felt the intergroup, that is, the social work process,[6] was appropriate:

When the essential task in response to specific invitation, or accepted offer of service, is to enable groups through their own representatives to determine specific social goals, to enable groups to plan co-operatively for the achievement of these goals, and to obtain unity of responsible action and interaction in their achievement; when the quality of the relations between groups is just as important a consideration as the specific goals pursued; when the role of the social worker is primarily a disciplined enabling job in the area of intergroup relations; when the worker feels that his role, while doing all of this, is at the same time to give equal emphasis to community need by helping groups to identify the wider community interest in the social goal, and to enable the intergroup to include representatives from all groups who have a stake in the specific goal, then I suggest we need the application of social work methods which will produce the social intergroup work process.[7]

The Educational and Promotional Process

At the same time that he was defining intergroup work as the social work component of community organization, Mr. Newstetter identi-

---

[6] It is important to understand the use of the term "process" in this chapter since it is used in several different frames of reference.

   a. *Process* is "a systematic series of actions directed to some end." (*The American College Dictionary*. New York, Random House, 1947, p. 965.)

   b. *Social process* is a series of interactions between people; not just being at the same place at the same time, but interaction that involves mutual awareness, some sort of communication and some mutual influencing of subsequent actions.

   c. Social process becomes *social work process* when "(1) the objectives are social work objectives; (2) the process is being consciously effected by a person selected or accepted by the groups involved, whose professional capacity is primarily that of bringing the disciplines of social work knowledge and methods to bear on the problem." (Newstetter, Wilbur I., "The Social Intergroup Work Process." *Proceedings of the National Conference of Social Work*, 1947, p. 206).

   d. Social work process as a general term can be further classified into:
     1. Casework process.
     2. Group work process.
     3. Intergroup work process.

   e. Community organization process as a general term can be further classified into:
     1. Intergroup work process (social work).
     2. Administrative process.
     3. Educational and promotional process.

[7] Newstetter, Wilbur I., "The Social Intergroup Work Process." *Proceedings of the National Conference of Social Work*, 1947, p. 217.

fied two other processes in community organization which he felt were of primary importance, but were not considered to be social work processes. One of these was the educational and promotional or selling process. In this instance, the decision to carry out a particular program may be made by some central group with all major policies and program procedure determined by that group. The plan is then sold to a number of communities or groups who carry out essentially the program worked out on the central level whether it be local, state, regional, or national. The Polio, Cancer, or Heart drives are examples of this educational and promotional procedure.

The various steps in this process were outlined by Granger.[8] The first step necessary is education. It is necessary to develop an awareness on the part of the general community of the nature of the problem involved. Not only the nature of the problem but a spelling out of the special interest the general public has in it is essential. No doubt the reader is well aware of the dangers involved in tuberculosis, cancer, or heart disease. Over a period of years the public has been "educated" in the nature of these illnesses, the need for prompt care, and the possibility that they might strike any family. The second step, following awareness of the problem, is identification and elaboration of what *positive* steps can be taken. The positive aspects are essential if any continued interest is to be held. Such steps include both the general public's responsibility, such as providing funds, prompt co-operative action in reporting, and the like, and also the place of the community's specialized agencies such as the hospital, the clinic, and the research program. Once these two steps have been taken, developing awareness of the need for doing something and detailing what that something is, the next step is promotion. Not only is it necessary, for sound promotion, to have carefully and effectively carried out the first two steps, it is also necessary to know and understand community attitudes that may affect the program. This means both favorable and unfavorable aspects. Programs of this kind to be effective must enlist the assistance and interest of a cross section of the community, people from all walks of life.

[8] Granger, Lester B., "Educational and Promotional Process in Community Organization." *Proceedings of the National Conference of Social Work,* 1947, pp. 218–226.

The Administrative Process in Community Organization

The third process identified in community organization programs was the administrative. Again, this is not primarily a social work process in itself, but it is an essential part of all community organization. When the job to be done is primarily administrative, it becomes the central process. The Social Service Exchange (or Index as it is sometimes called) is a good example of this process. The Exchange is set up as a clearing house for social and health agencies, both public and private, in order to prevent duplication and overlapping.[9]

It should be clearly understood however, that the three processes identified—intergroup, educational and promotional, and administrative—never occur in a "pure" state, so to speak, to the complete exclusion of the other two. The three overlap in almost every instance. It is more accurate to say that the name applied to any one or the other is appropriate when that particular process is the major or primary focus. The administrative process is involved to some degree in each of the others. Even in the intergroup work process where there is the widest use of group discussion and mutual agreement democratically arrived at, once a program is decided upon there is of necessity an educational or promotional process necessary to ensure the fullest support. Obviously there must be an effective administrative process if the plan of action is to move beyond the discussion stage. One of the major responsibilities of the social worker in community organization is to know which is the appropriate process for a particular situation or program.

Thus the identification of these three processes represents an attempt to clarify the social work component of community organization. Further study and research may identify other processes, may demonstrate that these are inadequately identified, or may show that they are all components of one process, but for the present, they are useful tools in the attempt to refine the definition and concept of community organization.

[9] The Exchange will be described in more detail later in this chapter.

The Role of the Professional Worker in Community Organization

It can be seen from the discussion thus far that the social worker has a variety of responsibilities. In general, there are three broad areas within which any social worker must be responsible at any level of operation in community organization:

1. The social worker must help the representative group (by what-ever name—council, intergroup, delegate body, assembly) to deter-mine and create suitable organization, structure, and operating practices to achieve the social goals that the group has selected.

2. The social worker has the responsibility to help the participants function as adequately as possible in two major roles:
   a. As a *group member*.
   b. As a *representative*.

3. The social worker must help the groups represented work more effectively together in the most appropriate fashion for their par-ticular project. In other words he has to work with the *repre-sentative group,* with the *representatives,* and with the *groups represented.*

In relation to the first general responsibility, organization and oper-ating practices, many questions would be appropriate as a general basis for collecting information needed for evaluation. Probably the most basic is whether the group is clear about why it is in existence—what is its purpose. This may seem so obvious as to appear facetious, but the number of groups having only a vague idea of their real purpose is both surprising and disturbing. In many other groups different mem-bers of the organization will have widely varying interpretations of what the purpose is. Obviously few groups could get 100-percent agree-ment on this, but any group that is to be effective must have worked out a goal and a direction that makes unified and concerted action possible. It would be necessary to know when the organization was formed, why, and by whom it was first started. How does the program and operating practices implement the stated purpose? Who are mem-bers? How are new members selected? Is the operation democratic or is a small clique in control? Are meetings held regularly or only periodically? Who decides this, and how is the decision arrived at? What provision is there for the various representatives to report to their groups? Has there been real two-way representation and sharing or is it more a personal than a representative relationship? Is action taken on the basis of carefully collected and analyzed facts or on emotion and whim? Is the representation such that all groups which are affected or are in a position to affect the program are involved? If not, is it because they have refused to participate or because they were never given the opportunity to participate? Is the representation broad and inclusive, that is, does it include public and voluntary groups—welfare, health, civic, professional, labor, social, fraternal organizations? What social levels are represented? Are sex, age, religious, nationality, racial, geographical, and economic groups involved? These are only a few of the areas a worker might need to know and be aware of in his evaluation of the structure and operating practices.

In working with individual members, the social worker in community organization is professionally responsible for dealing with the personal problems of the representative only to the extent it affects the individual's ability to operate as an effective group member or representative. He would have, however, the responsibility of trying to help a member accept service from some appropriate source if needed. The role of the social worker in the community organization setting is not that of a caseworker. The individual is participating in a community project, and the role of the community organization worker is to help him do so. Where personal problems make participation impossible, referral to appropriate resources is indicated where possible.

To understand the relations and position of the member both in the representative group and in his own, it is important to know how that person was selected. Was it by general vote, as a real responsibility and honor; by appointment and if so with general approval or as the spokesman for an individual or clique; by default because no one else was interested; or as a reward for service rendered rather than any particular ability to do this particular job? Did the representative really want this responsibility or was it foisted upon him? What is the status of the group he represents in comparison to the other groups represented? How is the representative's status affected by that of his group? What is the individual's standing in the group in relation to such factors as previous experience, intellectual capacity, social ease, race, religion, social, or economic status and all of the other factors that go into determining status and influence? Not only must the social worker be aware of these factors and which ones are important in any particular setting and group, but he must also be consciously trying to help the individual become more effective both in the group and as a representative. How can the low status member be helped to gain status? How can the monopolizer be helped to share? How can the shy be helped to be more secure? How can the aggressive be socially controlled? How can a self-centered individual be helped to become more socially minded? How can the prejudiced be helped to look at the facts and not make predetermined emotional judgments? All of these and many more are faced with painful regularity. And yet each situation is different and unique and requires from the worker the utmost in the way of knowledge and skill in dealing with individual, group, and community behavior.

In the third general area are the problems of helping the groups represented work more effectively together. Here it is essential that the various groups be helped to identify their common social goals and aims so that a common base can make possible co-operative effort. As groups acquire experience in working together, there is the likelihood that that base will become wider (or break off completely), although it may be a very narrow interest that makes the first venture possible. There is much similarity between the problems faced here in the relationships between the groups and those between the individuals that represent them. For in intergroup relations there is also status, influenced by economic, racial, social, religious, political, and similar factors. There is the same struggle to gain, hold, and improve status in relations between groups that there is between individuals. Dealing with groups and intergroup relations requires the knowledge of group dynamics as well as the dynamics of individual behavior, of intergroup relations as well as group, and of community dynamics as well as intergroup.

Even this brief identification of some of the responsibilities and duties of the social worker in community organization opens up some of the wide problem areas involved, with an indication of the challenging nature of the demands made upon the social worker. The record at the end of this chapter gives a picture of a worker in a neighborhood council and illustrates some of the principles and procedures discussed.

Community Organization in Relation to Casework and Group Work

It is obvious by now that community organization has much in common with casework and group work, but also that some important differences exist. All three are built upon the same basic philosophy of respect for the individual, the same belief in the right and responsibility of the client to determine and work toward his own social goals within the framework of community cultural patterns whether that client be an individual, a group, or a community. All are based on a body of knowledge regarding the physical and social functioning of individuals, groups, and communities. All social workers need the understanding of community dynamics, but the community organization worker faces it more consistently at firsthand contact. The community is the client of the community organization worker rather than the individual or group (or probably more accurately, certain groups in the community). The goals are community-oriented rather than individual or group. The method of working with representative groups opens a new dimension not present in other social work practice. Interviews, meetings, discussions, conferences, minutes, records, and similar methods are used in varying degrees by all social workers, but the emphasis and immediate goals vary. The caseworker's emphasis in general would be the client's personal, individual needs; the group worker's on group needs or the member's personal needs as they affect his ability to function adequately as a group member; the community organization worker's on the needs of the intergroup, the community, or the individual to the extent they relate to his operation as an intergroup member.

Goals are identical in one aspect since every social worker is striving to help the client or member operate at the highest level of potential social functioning, and this applies equally to work with individuals, groups, or communities. The difference in emphasis as mentioned above makes it more a matter of degree than of kind.

Community Organization Process Within an Organization

In many agency settings representative groups are an integral part of the organization's program. Many settlement houses and similar organizations have what are called house councils, age-group councils, or similar organizations. The councils are usually made up of representatives of member club groups of either the total agency or of designated age or departmental groups. They are usually delegated certain specific responsibilities and authority in the realm of activities or policy. A two-way relationship is essential if these councils are at all effective. The clubs must know what the councils are doing and the council must act in the best interest of the total program. Age group councils operate on the same pattern except the representatives are limited to clubs or groups whose membership falls within a certain age range, such as junior, young adult, or teen age. The emphases must continually be on the representative nature of these groups and the two foci of group needs and social goals, or the council will become merely a group not an intergroup. When the latter occurs, the members start to use the representative group for meeting their own personal needs and the representative channel ceases to function.

Another type of council similar in some respects to those mentioned above are the interbureau committees of the federal government. These involve more than one bureau or government agency and are formed on a representative basis for joint planning and to carry out certain co-operative programs. There must be constant two-way relationships between the representatives and their bureaus. The members definitely represent their bureau with variation in their freedom to act, although no policy commitment can be made outside regular administrative channels. The persons selected to represent a bureau or agency are frequently those who are in administrative positions of sufficient rank to be able to help implement any agreed-upon program. An example of a government interbureau committee is the Interdepartmental Committee on Children and Youth, which was formed in 1948 by the Federal Security Administrator at the request of the President. Its purpose was to help strengthen the co-operative work of federal agencies so that each department's work would make more effective all of the others. The members included representatives of the Departments of Agriculture, Defense, Justice, Interior, Labor, the Administrative Office of the United States Courts, the Federal Security Agency, Housing and Home Finance Agency, and the Selective Service System. Representatives of bureaus or subdivisions of the departments and agencies which were involved in children and youth programs also served as associate members in appropriate roles.

The concern of the social worker at this level of operation is primarily agency wide in scope. He helps the delegates represent their groups. In many instances this is the member's first experience in this role, and he may therefore need considerable help in being a representative, in concentrating on the needs of his group and the agency rather than his own. The worker also helps the groups of representatives see beyond their own group to agency-wide responsibilities and opportunities. The groups represented usually need help in participating in this co-operative venture, for it may be a first venture for some of them too. An individual must be relatively secure within himself before he can operate effectively in a group. A group must be relatively secure in its own operation before being able to participate in a co-operative venture. The worker must help individuals and groups reach that level of social maturity.

Community Organization on the Local Level

Both community chests and community councils have been discussed earlier in relation to their historical backgrounds. They are good examples of organizations whose major function is community organization. The chests raise and allocate funds and the councils co-ordinate, plan, and help to raise the standards of the service of all programs, public and voluntary. Persons serving on most of the committees of a community chest do not specifically represent their agency or organization. For the most part they represent the chest itself or are "representative of" some group, such as business or labor, with no responsibility or channels for reporting back to a particular group. For example, the budget committee represents the chest board. The board is responsible to the community. The chests, however, usually cover a whole city and in increasing numbers are operating on a county basis, covering both the urban and rural areas within the confines of the county or other defined area covered. In such instances there is usually a definite attempt to have various geographical units represented.

The councils or federations frequently operate on a county basis also, but are more likely to be concentrated in the urban areas. Essentially such organizations are representative bodies with the representatives being designated by the member agencies. There are various roles carried by these assignments. At the division level the delegate is required to perform at least two roles. In some types of voting he is definitely expected to represent his agency. If a group work division was discussing the adoption of job descriptions and a salary scale, each agency represented would expect its own philosophy and point of view to be presented by its delegate. The two-way process would be necessary if the representatives were to be effective either from the point of view of the agency or the federation. At the time of a final vote on a program, however, the delegate would no longer be representing his agency but would be representing the federation and it would be his responsibility to vote for whichever plan seemed in his best judgment, most appropriate for improving agency programs in the interest of those served and the community at large. Frequently delegates operate at less than their full potential because they are confused about their proper role and try to represent their agency when they should represent the community.

Another type of community organization program on the local level operates in the small neighborhood. They go by various names. In many places they are called Co-ordinating Councils, in others, Community Councils, and in still others, Neighborhood Councils. By and large, however, organization and structure as well as operating practices are quite similar. The major focus is on the improvement of life in the neighborhood, and the range of activities is limited only by the scope of the members' interests and imagination. Many of the early councils were interested in juvenile delinquency primarily, with the emphasis on prevention and reduction of juvenile offenses. The councils soon found however that any group interested in delinquency had to be interested in a wide range of social factors for they were all related to delinquency. This included school programs, health programs, police protection, the caliber of movies and radio programs (and now television), the kind of literature available to youth, and many others.

In the last analysis, almost any influence affecting the life of the community comes within the scope of the councils. Some of the councils fell under the control of one particular individual or group trying to use it for selfish purposes. This situation led to almost inevitable downfall, for the strength of such a program rests in the fact that all groups —business, labor, professional, religious, racial, and all of the rest—are acting in the best interests of the total community and not for any one segment. Such councils might be described as the modern town hall, an attempt to return to the neighborhood or small community the opportunity for democratic, grass-roots participation that is fast disappearing in urban communities.

Another type of council that operates on the local community level is concentrated on one particular type of problem in contrast to the neighborhood council whose activities encompass a wide range of interests. An example of this more specialized program might be a Civic Unity Council or similar organization with major emphasis on intercultural, interracial, and interreligious relationships. Some of these organizations are official in that they are part of the city government while others may be purely voluntary groups. There is usually an attempt to have various religious, racial, labor, industry, and educational groups for example, represented in such councils. In some instances these representatives are chosen by and represent groups, while in other situations they are appointed as "representative of" these groups. In either case membership in and identification with such groups is the basis of selection. Here again is an example of the fact that the individual has little status or influence in the community separate from the groups with which he is associated.

The Social Service Exchange was mentioned earlier as an example of a community organization process, primarily administrative. Here on the local level, the Exchange serves only the member and co-operating social and health agencies and even then in a limited but most important manner. All member agencies register with the Exchange a client who is receiving service of any kind whether it be medical, casework, or group work. Not all group work agencies, however, make use of this type of service, but a growing number do. When a family applies for help to casework Agency A, it would clear with the Exchange to see whether the family was receiving help from a similar type of organization. If the family was receiving help from Agency B, Agency A would clear with Agency B, and between them they would decide whether the new request for help was legitimate or merely an attempt to get double service. The Social Service Exchange would tell *only* that some other agency was active. They neither have or give out any information about the nature or extent of the service. Any such information must come directly from the agency giving the service and then only to the extent necessary to meet the needs of the situation. Thus the Exchange is only a clearing house and as such is primarily a matter of administrative responsibility, but it can save a community untold dollars through eliminating duplication and in assisting in over-all planning. Here the service itself is not social work, but it makes possible more effective social work.

The focus of the social worker at this level of operation is primarily community wide in scope. While in the agency the groups involved are mostly clubs and informal groups, here the groups are community or neighborhood wide in scope: social, religious, labor, civic, business and others. The same general responsibility of the worker remains, but on the whole both the individual members and the groups have had wider experience and have attained a greater degree of social maturity and outlook.

Community Organization at the State Level

One example of state-wide operation is the State Conference of Social Work. These conferences are associations of both lay and professional membership. One of their primary methods is to provide an open forum as a means of exchanging information and stimulating discussion toward the development of sound public and private welfare services through the particular state. Usually an annual state-wide conference of two or three days' duration is held and sometimes smaller regional conferences throughout the state. Various committees are active throughout the year, both for the preparation of the state-wide and regional conferences and for ongoing year-round programs of study, research, and interpretation. Membership is usually both individual and agency. When an agency belongs, one or more members, depending on membership arrangements and the amount of dues paid, represent the agency when they attend.

Another type of state-wide association is interested in bringing about within the state the best welfare program possible through both public and private sources, but which turns particular attention to the legislative programs as they affect facilities and program services. These organizations are usually independent, nonprofit, voluntary, citizens associations. They operate through programs of research and information to create an informed public opinion and understanding leading to community action on problems of health and welfare needing state-wide attention. An example of such an association is the Pennsylvania Citizens Association, with offices at both Philadelphia and Pittsburgh. The type of organizational pattern such associations use has real meaning in terms of their effectiveness. Some concentrate their efforts primarily on individual membership. Such members are almost always key people in their community and as such are in a position to enlist the co-operation and interest of many groups throughout their communities. However, with the membership largely individual rather than delegate, there is not the direct tie into the activities of the groups whose support is needed. Whichever plan of organization is followed, one of the objectives is to get public support for or against proposed welfare or health legislation. For example, in Pennsylvania two different laws were proposed in the state legislature to meet serious gaps in existing adoption provisions. Citizens groups had to know the implication of each approach in order to arrive at a valid basis for backing one or the other. The Pennsylvania Citizens Association took leadership, along with others, in interpreting the similarities and differences between the two proposed acts, and issued a point of view regarding their stand. Such programs are primarily educational and promotional in nature.

Community programs are aimed at state-wide problems. Helping representative groups, the groups represented, and the representatives is still the worker's major role. The experiences of assuming increasingly wider responsibility should have contributed to a deepening and more mature social responsibility by the participants at this level of operation. But the problems of learning to operate on a state-wide basis, to see beyond their own organization or community are similar to those of the individual representing for the first time his club in an agency council. The social maturity of the participant, the goals, the focus, some of the specific skills and methods change somewhat, but the basic philosophy and social work principles still apply.

Programs on the National Level

One of the organizations operating at the national level in social welfare for many years is the National Conference of Social Work which has an unbroken existence since 1874. The 1874 meeting was held under the sponsorship of the American Social Science Association, and was attended by representatives from the State Board of Charities from the states of Massachusetts, Connecticut, New York, and Wisconsin. The first meeting was called the Conference of Boards of Public Charities. It has at various times been known as the Conference on Charities and Correction, the National Conference on Charities and Correction, and its present title the National Conference of Social Work. From a handful that attended the first meeting, the Conference has grown today to some 7,000 members. The purpose and activities of the Conference are: "To promote and share in discussion of the problems and methods identified with the field of social welfare and immediately related fields. The Conference is a forum for such discussion. It does not take an official position on controversial issues and adopts no resolutions except occasional resolutions of courtesy." [10] The Conference has both individual and agency memberships, but since it does not take a stand on issues, the program is primarily an educational rather than a social action program. Not only does the Conference bring together both lay and professional, public and private, local, state, national, and international groups in its general sessions and section meetings, but it also enables a large number of affiliate groups to hold sessions and exhibits in conjunction with the annual meeting, thus expanding the range of potential educational experience. This helps to make it possible for specialized groups to get together at this time. Such groups include professional associations, service organizations, probation and parole groups, and literally dozens of others. The Conference publishes proceedings consisting of selected papers from the annual meetings. In order to make the annual meetings accessible it meets in various cities over the country but about every

[10] *Social Work Year Book.* New York, American Association of Social Workers, 1954, p. 640.

other year it meets in the eastern section of the country since a high percentage of the membership lives in that area.

The National Social Welfare Assembly is another example of a co-ordinating group operating on a national level. Its purpose and functions as outlined in its 1952 *Annual Report* are:

1. To study and define social welfare problems and plan action to meet them.

2. To serve as an agency for consultation and conference on social welfare needs and problems.

3. To facilitate more effective operation of organized social welfare.

4. To provide leadership and facilities for affiliate organizations, associate groups, and individual members so they may plan and act together voluntarily in matters of common interest.

5. To encourage and strengthen voluntary joint action of all agencies and individuals in behalf of social welfare.

6. To act in behalf of social welfare where representation of its interests is desired.[11]

Membership as indicated in the above is both individual and agency. Membership for 1952 included 216 persons and 61 alternates. Part of these were nominated by affiliate organizations and associate groups and part were elected members-at-large, representative of local leadership throughout the country. Fifty three voluntary and fifteen government agencies were affiliated with the Assembly.

The Family Service Association of America is an example of an organization operating on a national scale within a more circumscribed scope, limiting its objectives to the promotion and development of family social welfare and wholesome family life. In reality this association operates on an international scale in that it includes Canadian members, but the term international agency will be reserved in this discussion for agencies operating on a wider scale than two countries. The Family Service Association offers several types of service. It provides consultation to both public and private family and related agencies. It offers an information service in the area of its interest and also assists in the development of qualified personnel in the family field. It carries on broad interpretation of family social service, hoping to increase the understanding and support the general public gives to such agencies. Membership is composed of individuals, lay and professional,

[11] *National Social Welfare Assembly Annual Report.* 1952, p. 2.

as well as agencies both public and private. Here again we see in operation all three of the community organization processes. The consultant seems to rely largely on the educational and promotional aspects; nevertheless, he works with many local groups which are operating on a representative basis, and so he is involved in the intergroup process also.

An excellent example of a government-sponsored activity in this country-wide organization procedure is the White House Conference, which has been held five times starting with the 1909 Conference called by Theodore Roosevelt under the name Conference on the Care of Dependent Children. Succeeding conferences were called in 1919, 1930, 1940, and 1950. The 1950 Conference was one of the most significant from the point of view of community organization process. Instead of being planned at the national level almost exclusively, there was a series of committee structures in each state on a state-wide basis, and these committees in turn encouraged the development of committees in the local communities throughout the state. In this manner there were channels from the local community to the national level through state and region. The purpose of this was both educational and administrative. Some of the topics chosen for discussion and some of the actual reports given at the conference came directly from the community where the problem was being faced, where gaps in service could be related first-hand to the problems encountered, and where present procedures could be evaluated. These preliminary meetings and conferences which gradually channeled the local material to the state and national levels took many months of organization and effort. Not only were public and private agency officials in the area of child welfare involved in the planning, along with lay board members, but parents and youth themselves were represented at various levels including the culmination of this tremendous planning process, for youth played an important part in the final Conference in Washington. Another equally important phase of this process occurred when many of the same groups that had taken part in the original study, investigations, research, and definition of problems were asked to take some responsibility for seeing that something concrete was done about the recommendations that were adopted by the Conference. This represented one of the greatest aggregations of individuals and organizations that have ever co-operated on such a national project. Bringing in the ultimate recipients, the youth themselves, provided a new pattern of co-operative approach to this nation-wide program. Again all three of the community organization processes discussed earlier were used. Most of the young people who attended the Washington meetings were sponsored by schools, various social agencies, and other similar groups, and as delegates or representatives they in many instances took the responsibility of reporting back not only to the group that sent them but a few even reported to other interested community groups. This was a responsible representative procedure.

The focus of the social worker is now national in scope as are most of the groups represented. Many of the participants still find difficulty in assuming a national viewpoint in place of state or regional identification. Some groups or individuals still try to use such organizations for their own purposes. Some groups are not mature enough to operate on that level. A few individuals and groups are willing to assume social responsibility, and many more are willing to let them. Again, the worker's role is basically the same, but the problems of dealing with such matters at the national level naturally involve new dimensions, new problems of relationships going all the way back to the local communities. Past experience and precedence is less adequate at this level.

Community Organization on the International Level

The International Conference of Social Work operates on an international level in much the same manner as the National Conference of Social Work operates on the national level. The officers come from a number of different countries and the conference meets in various sections of the world. The first International Conference was held in Paris in 1928 with delegates from some 42 countries, 32 governments, and 21 national committees.[12] When the conference met in Paris again in 1950, there were 47 countries represented with approximately 1,800 in attendance. Here the delegate system operates on an international basis, but with provision also for individual members who may

[12] Hoffer, Joe R., "Conferences of Social Work." *Social Work Year Book,* 1954. American Association of Social Workers, pp. 128–135.

not be official representatives of any group in their country. As many individual agencies are members of the National Conference and send delegates from their organization, so many agencies operating on an international basis also hold membership in the International Conference and send their representatives to the biennial meetings. Examples of such organizations operating on an international level are the Red Cross, the Young Men's Christian Association, the Young Women's Christian Association, the Cooperative for American Remittances to Europe (CARE), the Catholic International Union for Social Services, and the Salvation Army. The principles that apply to a local neighborhood regarding responsible delegation and representation are just as applicable in operation on the international scene.

Another example of an international organization operating on a representative and delegate basis is UNESCO (United Nations Educational, Scientific, and Cultural Organization). In this instance the program, policies, and budget are determined by the delegates of the member nations through a delegate body called the General Conference. As the title would indicate, the purpose is to make a contribution to the peace and security of the world through education, science, and culture. It is impossible for local neighborhood groups to work together effectively until some structure is available that provides a common goal around which all have a genuine conviction. This is even more true on an international basis. Even with the structure and the inclination, it takes skilled leadership and patience. All of the same problems of being able to look beyond one's own group to the larger unit are still present—in the local community ability to look beyond one's own group to the welfare of the total community, in UNESCO to see beyond the boundary of one's own country to the welfare of the world. As the scope broadens from neighborhood to international, people must be of an increasingly mature and statesmanship bent. The focus of the social worker becomes international. This is the most difficult level on which to operate, for we have less experience, less precedence, less understanding of how to deal with problems of relationship on this level. And yet at each level the responsibility of the worker becomes increasingly important for an increasing number of people are involved and affected by the outcome.

Trends in Community Organization

When community chests were discussed, it was pointed out that one of the major selling points and one of the most important contributions of this method of financing was *one* drive which replaced numerous individual ones. In recent years this has again become a matter of concern, for there is an increasingly large number of organizations local and national which raise their funds outside the community chest drives. Since affiliation with community chests is voluntary, no agency can or should be made to participate, but major contributors are again asking why so many solicitations? If one of the big advantages is elimination of numerous expensive drives and provision of a channel through which money can be given with the assurance that the program has been reviewed and approved as a valid health or welfare service, why are so many outside? Even though such organizations as the American Red Cross, the March of Dimes, Heart or Cancer drives to mention a few, have never been questioned as necessary and essential programs, the multitude of campaigns did and does raise serious problems. In recent years there has been developing one method of meeting this. As a first step, within some of the large industries, the unions allowed their members to be solicited on the job only once. The union took up one fund and out of this contributed to the chest, Red Cross, and any others they might decide on. In Detroit, Michigan, a new type of campaign was tried. It was called the Torch Fund and was aimed at uniting *all* independent drives including the Detroit Community Chest as one of many. In other words, this was a "super" drive that would include all others. While no city using this method gets 100-percent co-operation, there has been a very high percentage of participation. Among some of the major objectors are the national health drives, such as Tuberculosis, Polio, Cancer, and others who feel that any combined drive kills or seriously weakens the special appeal of any one agency and that they not only can raise more money on their own, and thus provide more extensive and better services, but they feel they can do a better job of interpretation and public education through their own single, one-emphasis drive. The over-all type of campaign, on the other hand, has the advantage of getting the whole community active at one time, and with this truly united effort it is possible to run a more efficient campaign. These drives are spreading in popularity and use, but there are many problems still to be worked out. One reason it is hard to make a decision on this question is the absolute sincerity on both sides and the fact they both have only one goal in mind, the best possible service that will meet the needs of the community. The variance is over methods more than goals, but methods also involve philosophy and goals.

State-Wide Drives

Another development is state-wide drives similar in nature to the local torch funds. The state drive organizes many rural areas and small towns that have never been organized, and appropriations are made on an allocation basis according to the needs of the particular community. The pioneer Michigan program is called the United Health and Welfare Fund and its central office is in the state capital. Some of the advantages attributed to this system are that it reduces the annoyance and confusion of many campaigns, it conserves manpower, reduces campaign expenses, by careful budget review it increases the public's confidence in member agencies, it eliminates competition between the various agencies which were running separate campaigns and makes possible a budget committee that can make allocations in view of the over-all needs of the community, eliminates competition and makes joint planning and co-operative efforts much more feasible. By uniting the whole community at one time, there is a greater benefit to all concerned. Michigan had its first state-wide drive in 1949 and the number of participants and the amount of money raised since then has shown steady growth.

Conclusion

Within this brief review, we have seen that community organization for social welfare is concerned with both needs and resources. Adequacy of resources to meet individual, group, and community needs is more than just a matter of quantity or quality. It is also a matter of relationships. Co-ordination and co-operation directly affect quality and the degree of coverage. We have looked at some of the efforts directed toward defining the social work component of the broad community organization field. There is general agreement that community organization is a process and one of the basic social work processes. Community organization as a social work process is part of many agencies' operation, in some as a primary service as in a Community Welfare Council, in others as a minor factor. We have looked at examples of such programs on various levels of operation from local neighborhoods to international.

Central to the whole program is the social worker. The caliber of the worker's skill in facilitating co-operative relationships between individuals and groups is the crucial aspect of the worker's professional role. This skill includes among other things the capacity to work with all kinds of people representing a wide variety of groups, to enable both individuals and groups to work together in meeting community needs, to help develop community leadership, to use appropriate research methods, to be able to deal with conflict situations, to be a good administrator, and to keep the focus on community rather than partisan or individual needs.

The quality of service a community or nation gets is based on how effectively all programs of health and welfare are co-ordinated and geared into a total program. Community organization is the process that will determine how effectively this co-ordination is or is not carried out. Thus as co-ordination becomes more and more necessary, the quality of health and welfare services at whatever level, will stand or fall on the effectiveness of the community organization process. This is a tremendous challenge and a responsibility that will require the best in courage and insight and an ability to see beyond one agency, or community, or even one nation.

BIBLIOGRAPHY

Books and Pamphlets

Alinsky, Saul D., *Reveille for Radicals*. Chicago, University of Chicago Press, 1946.

Buell, Bradley, and Associates, *Community Planning for Human Services*. New York, Columbia University Press, 1952.

Colcord, Joanna C., *Your Community: Its Provisions for Health, Education, Safety and Welfare*, rev. ed. New York, Russell Sage Foundation, 1947.

Community Chests and Councils of America, Inc., *Outline for Appraisal of a Community Welfare Council*. New York, 1949.

———, *Policy Statement on Community Planning for Social Welfare*. New York, 1950.

Dillick, Sidney, *Community Organization for Neighborhood Development: Past and Present*. New York, Whiteside, Inc., 1953.

Eubank, Earle E., *The Concepts of Sociology*. Boston, D. C. Health & Company, 1932.

Hayes, Wayland J., *The Small Community Looks Ahead*. New York, Harcourt Brace & Company, 1947.

Hillman, Arthur, *Community Organization and Planning*. New York, The Macmillan Company, 1950.

Howard, Donald S. (editor), *Community Organization—Its Nature and Setting*. New York, American Association of Social Workers, 1948.

Hunter, Floyd, *Community Power Structure*. Chapel Hill, University of North Carolina Press, 1953.

Johns, Ray, *The Cooperative Process Among National Social Agencies*. New York, Association Press, 1946.

———, and DeMarche, David F., *Community Organization and Agency Responsibility*. New York, Association Press, 1951.

Karpf, Maurice J., *Jewish Community Organization in the United States*. New York, Bloch Publishing Co., 1938.

King, Clarence, *Organizing for Community Action*. New York, Harper and Brothers, 1948.

McMillen, Wayne, *Community Organization for Social Welfare*. Chicago, University of Chicago Press, 1945.

National Social Welfare Assembly, *Shall We Make a Study?* New York, 1949.

Norton, William J., *The Cooperative Movement in Social Work*. New York, The Macmillan Company, 1927.

Ogden, Jean C., and Ogden, Jess, *Small Communities in Action*. New York, Harper and Brothers, 1946.

Pettit, Walter W., *Case Studies in Community Organization*. New York, Century Company, 1928.

Steiner, Jesse F., *Community Organization*. New York, Century Company, 1930.

Stidley, Leonard Albert, *Sectarian Welfare Federations among Protestants*. New York, Association Press, 1944.

Stroup, Herbert H., *Community Welfare Organization*. New York, Harper and Brothers, 1952.

United States Woman's Bureau, *The Outlook for Women in Community Organization in Social Work*. Washington, D. C., Government Printing Office, 1951.

Significant Articles

Andrews, Emerson F., "New Trends in Corporate Giving," *Social Work Journal*, XXXIII, October 1952, pp. 172–176.

Benjamin, Paul, "State-Wide Community Organization," *Proceedings of the National Conference of Social Work*, 1946, pp. 139–148.

Clark, William E., "A Project for Pilgrims—The United Fund as an Experiment in Democracy," *Community*, XXIX, September 1953, pp. 4–5.

"Code of the Chest and Council Movement," *Community*, XXVIII, April 1953, pp. 160–161.

Farra, Kathryn, "Neighborhood Councils," *Proceedings of the National Conference of Social Work*, 1940, pp. 445–455.

Granger, Lester B., "Educational and Promotional Process in Community Organization," *Proceedings of the National Conference of Social Work*, 1947, pp. 218–226.

Green, Helen D., "Sociometry and Social Intergroup Work," *Sociometry*, XIII, February 1950, pp. 22–28.

Lynde, Edward D., "The Role of the Community Organization Practitioner," *Selected Papers in Group Work and Community Organization*. Raleigh, Health Publications Institute, 1952, pp. 118–128.

———, "Two-Pronged Approach to Community Planning," *Selected Papers in Group Work and Community Organization*. Raleigh, Health Publications Institute, 1951, pp. 104–107.

Moore, Esther, "How Did the Campaign Go?" *Community*, XXVIII, January 1953, pp. 83–87.

Nelson, Amalie K., "The Council Led Off," *Community*, XXVIII, December 1952, pp. 69–71.

Newstetter, Wilbur I., "The Social Intergroup Work Process," *Proceedings of the National Conference of Social Work*, 1947, pp. 205–217.

Nicholson, James T., "Effective Development in International Social Welfare Programs to Improve Conditions of Living," *Selected Papers in Group Work and Community Organization*. Raleigh, Health Publications Institute, 1952, pp. 73–79.

Pray, Kenneth L. M., "When Is Community Organization Social Work Practice?" *Proceedings of the National Conference of Social Work*, 1947, pp. 194–204.

Van Valen, Donald, "Community Organization: Manipulation or Group Process?" *Proceedings of the National Conference of Social Work*, 1949, pp. 325–342.

"What Makes a Good Council?" *Community*, XXVIII, March 1953, pp. 126–127.

Oakhurst Community Council [1]

JEAN H. LEE, Acting Director
Bureau of Community Councils,
Health and Welfare Federation of Allegheny County
Pittsburgh, Pennsylvania

Background Information

I. Facts on the Community of Oakhurst
   A. This is an isolated part of a large industrial city, the place named covers roughly 15,000 people. These people live in an exceptionally hilly district, and about 5,000, including most of the Negro population, are cut off from the main community and are not considered by the others when the name is used. The community for all practical purposes is one of 10,000 people who have a network of about 25 organizations. These cover the usual categories of civic, religious, educational, social, and recreational. There are no buildings housing programs of any social or health agencies, all these services are utilized through the city offices of these agencies. There is no bank or library, two lacks keenly felt by the residents. Oakhurst is an old and well-established community of lower- and upper-middle class people, almost all are native born, the incomes slightly above the average for the city; the larger number of homes are owner occupied, occupationally white collar workers predominate. Educationally the average is better than high school. Religiously, the community is nearly fifty percent Catholic, forty-five percent Protestant and five percent Jewish. There is an active business center along the one street which is relatively level and which runs along the top of the largest hill. The street has the aspect of a small town, perhaps intensified by its isolation. Once people get up the hill, they tend to stay. The community has a clear sense of its own identity and of its relationship to the city, almost everyone works "downtown." The major conflict is between the two ends of the area, Moore and Oakhurst proper, which are respectively the oldest and middle-aged sections. The newest sec-

[1] This record is used with the permission of the Bureau and has been disguised to preserve the confidential nature of this staff record. Miss Lee is now secretary, Family and Children's Division, United Community Services, Omaha, Nebraska.

tion, Elmcrest, has been developed within the last five years and its people are just beginning to make themselves felt. They are above the average for Oakhurst in income, education, and type of job.

B. The community is noteworthy for the excellent programs which go on in a number of organizations but which receive little co-operation from others who should be interested. All community improvements tend to be the work of one organization at a time or of a few individuals at a time. The ministerial association is very weak, yet all the individual churches are strong. The district committees for Boy and Girl Scouts suffer from lack of leadership, yet troops flourish. There is consistent talk about the need for more recreation, yet dances, little league baseball, and athletic programs are well done by several organizations. The Catholic Church is well established but participates hardly at all in such community affairs as the Christmas Tree, the annual picnic, or the Hallowe'en parade. The Board of Trade has become a civic club for lack of support from the merchants, who are not organized in any way. The Italian organizations (there is a relatively large second- and third-generation Italian population) do not carry high status though their members are part of such high status groups as the American Legion, the Board of Trade, and the Catholic Church. The Negro population is not much in evidence. The leaders of Oakhurst individually refer to the Negroes as "old residents." During the health project, the Health Committee was in touch with two Negro churches and an interracial Parent-Teacher Association, but did not succeed in bringing these groups into this project. One Negro minister is a member of the Ministerial Association. Probably a factor in the social distance between the white and Negro population is the physical distance created by the Negroes living "down over the hill" where they have developed a subcommunity.

The Oakhurst Council has had the objective of helping all organizations to co-operate on projects which are of concern to the total community. The emphasis has been on co-ordinating efforts and on informing all organizations as to the work done by each. In this emphasis, considerable attention has been given to encouraging member organizations to take on tasks falling within their function. This has left the Council to pick up on projects which no other organization could do or projects which required the combined efforts of several organizations. Such a project is described in the following excerpts.

C. In Oakhurst there are no obvious social problems such as bad housing, poor health, lack of recreational facilities, economic insecurity, etc. The problems rather are in the area of establishing communication between all segments of the community and in the area of training qualified persons to become leaders in the total community.

II. Data on the Council

A. History of the Oakhurst Council shows that Oakhurst has had a continuing interest in this type of community organization for fifteen years but that the life of any one council is about four years at a time. Councils generally have been developed around a particular community concern such as Oakhurst's tremendous interest in victory gardens during the war and the need for a community swimming pool (the impetus for this council four years ago). The present council weathered a bad community conflict two years ago which arose out of a temporary misplacement of funds which had been raised by a council project in health. Illness of the former chairman who had been in charge of the funds, caused him to lose track of them for a year. Money is usually surrounded by feelings of all kinds and in this case they were feelings of guilt, tension, suspicion and anger, all projected on the chairman who was helpless for a year and could not be approached by anyone because of the serious nature of his heart condition.

In the first year of the conflict, the Department of Neighborhood Councils withdrew staff service because there was too much conflict at play in Oakhurst to overcome. At the end of the year the Department was informed by three residents of Oakhurst that "something" had to be done to help this community. This was the first expression of any readiness within the community to "pick up the pieces." Staff was assigned to Oakhurst on the basis of determining whether the leading organizations of this community were able once more to work together. From September to June contacts were made with each of the 25 organizations and their leaders and with some 20 individuals who were members in at least three organizations each and were regarded as community leaders. Out of these contacts came clear understanding of the nature of the conflict, the leaders of the opposing forces, and suggestions for solution. This was a public audit of the council's books for the past three years and a statement from the former chairman as to his disposition of the misplaced funds in the bank. The funds were located, the audit was made, the bank statement balanced, and the community reaction was one of relief. This was accomplished by February and by June, the Field Secretary had assisted the community in re-establishing the council with a revised constitution and a duly elected set of officers (none of them had ever held a council office before, and none had ever been a delegate to the council). The following September (where this record starts) is the beginning of the new regime. The Council membership list showed exactly the same organizations being the most active as had been active before the conflict.

B. Membership in the program year described in the record numbered 13 paid organizations and 3 nonpaid. (The latter were two schools and the Girl Scout Committee which by charter are not permitted to pay dues to organizations like community councils which only indirectly serve the interests of these organizations.) Attendance by this membership at the 8 meetings of the delegate body was an average of 10 organizations per meeting. The membership is as follows:

Officers: Chairman, Mr. Paul McHugh; Vice Chairman, Mr. Stephen Johnson; Recording Secretary, Mr. Gordon McCrae; Corresponding Secretary, Mrs. Jane Leeds; Treasurer, Mr. Alfred Maganini.

Ten individuals are elected as members-at-large for their wide interest in community activities. These people are the only individual members in the council, all other members are organizations, clubs, associations or groups. From the 10 individual members, the council elected its chairman and treasurer.

Organization members:

B'Nai Israel Congregation	Boy Scouts
Oakhurst P.T.A.	Board of Trade
Oakhurst School	American Legion
Christian Church	Church of Latter Day Saints
Girl Scouts	Italian Sons & Daughters
Moore P.T.A.	Methodist Church
Presbyterian Church	Senior Women's Club
Moore School	Moore Community Club

C. Program included one long-range project, under the Health Committee, and three short-range projects, one of which was the course on leadership training. The program year is from September through June.

III. Staff Work in Oakhurst

A. Staff service included work with the delegate body, the Executive Committee, and the committee to plan and put on the course on training leaders in organizations. The field secretary for Oakhurst also served two other councils and carried administrative responsibility for the Department of Neighborhood Councils.

B. The following excerpts from the staff process record deal with the Council's work on putting on the course in leadership training. This idea was introduced from a member group in November, the course was conducted for four evenings in April, and the proceedings were approved by the Council in September. The record traces the growth of the idea, the involvement of the delegate body, the work of the committee, and the analysis of the sessions and the role of the field secretary.

Oakhurst Community Council

The field secretary of a community council is responsible for assisting member groups in their use of the council for action on affairs which the members cannot handle by themselves. Often, therefore, the field secretary will agree to act as speaker for member groups which want a speech on some broad phase of community activity. Such an occasion arose when the field secretary for the Oakhurst Council spoke to the Moore Civic Club on activities of community councils in other sections of the city and county. In her speech, the field secretary points up specifically the purpose of community councils, including that of locating, developing and training neighborhood leadership. This point is used as follows by a member of the club. (Throughout the record the field secretary is designated as "I.")

11/10. After the meeting had broken up for refreshments, Mrs. Shields introduced herself as a past president of the club and said, "People regard me as a community leader, but actually I don't know what to do to get things organized. Yet I know more than some. Can't we do something about this for me and others through the Council?" She reminded me that I had quoted one purpose of community councils as that of locating, training and assisting citizen leaders to take their places in community affairs. I asked a few questions about Mrs. Shields' experience and found her a very intelligent person. I suggested that if she sees a need for training leaders of all kinds of organizations in the management of the organizations, she could bring this idea to the Council. The more we talked about it, the more natural a project for the Council I thought it would be.

I introduced her to the Council chairman, who had come in late, and he agreed that it might be something the Council could do. I purposely left them to talk about it and went to speak to the club president.

The field secretary identifies with Mrs. Shields' concern and realizes that training people in the management of organizations could be a common problem. She helps Mrs. Shields to bring her idea to the Council by introducing her to the Council chairman. She shows judgment by leaving these two to work together on plans for the Council meeting because as the field secretary she has no role to play in rehearsing with people the form the request should take. She respects the ability of both persons, the chairman and Mrs. Shields, to plan logically, and her confidence is justified when the chairman says he will do some exploratory work. He sees this as helpful to the discussion at the Council meeting.

The delegate meeting on 11/14 is attended by three of the five officers and delegates from eleven of the seventeen member organizations. The chairman moves easily through the minutes, treasurer's report, two committee reports (one on the Council's long-range project on health), a statement on the status of the community chest campaign, and a report on a workshop sponsored by the Association of Community Councils before coming to new business. Heading this list is Mrs. Shields from the Moore Civic Club.

. . . Mr. McHugh, Council chairman, called on Mrs. Shields of the Moore Civic Club to present an idea growing out of the club meeting on 11/10. She presented the idea very well, mentioning that many club officers in Oakhurst were inexperienced when they assumed office. She said this had been her own situation, and that although she is regarded as a community leader, she really knows very little about the techniques of leadership. There was immediate interest in what she had said, and it seemed evident that most of the people present had been in the same situation. She suggested that the Council consider gathering information on techniques of running groups and make this available to groups. I summarized the discussion after a while by saying that the interest expressed tonight would be sufficient to put on a course in leadership training. This course could be lead by experts on such subjects as discussion leading, parliamentary procedure, etc. The Council immediately decided this was what should be done, and there was discussion about how the course could be organized. At first this was in terms of the social side like the serving of refreshments, introduction of members, etc. Later on the discussion considered what the course should contain. Mr. McHugh finally cut off the discussion by saying that the Executive Committee would appoint a special committee to plan and put on the course. He turned to me to ask where leaders for the course would be found, and I said that the Group Work Division of the Community Welfare Council should be consulted on this point. I thought the committee could talk to the Division once it had outlined the subjects to be covered and the type of course discussed. The Council decided to have the committee report on the outline of the course as soon as possible although they recognized that the course itself probably could not be given until after Christmas. I suggested that the committee appointed be representative of the organizations who would be most interested in participating. Mr. McHugh immediately said the P.T.A.'s, the Moore Civic Club, and the Senior Women's Club would no doubt be the organizations to consider. The representatives of these four organizations agreed they would like to work on the committee, but Mr. McHugh urged them to discuss the idea with their organizations first. He suggested that all representatives present do the same thing and report any interest to him, and he would pass it on to the committee.

The field secretary helps the Council analyze the idea of putting on a course to train leaders of organizations. She summarizes the points made on content. This is important to do in a new and unfamiliar subject because it is through such summaries that next steps are seen. In this case, these were in terms of how the course could be organized and what it should include. The field secretary helps the chairman in his plan to form a committee by indicating that the committee might be composed of representatives from organizations who would be most interested in the course. This is unusual in council work because in general committees are not representative of organizations in the membership. This is due to the fact that generally committees are regarded as administratively responsible to the delegates and that delegates are serving on them to carry out the will of the council not the desires of member organizations. However, in this case it is appropriate because the committee in charge of the course will be responsible for its promotion and should, therefore, be in as close touch as possible with the organizations most concerned. The field secretary also carries her role as resource by saying that the committee can consult with the Group Work Division of the Community Welfare Council about obtaining speakers. Thus the county-wide planning organization is brought to the neighborhood level for use by this small neighborhood. The Council chairman shows a good sense of the need for involving member organizations in this new piece of council program by suggesting that all representatives present discuss the idea with their organizations and report any interest to the chairman who would pass it on to the committee. It is evident that this Council is used to handling new ideas, the chairman feels free to refer matters to the Executive Committee, to lead discussion, and to involve member groups; the delegates likewise discuss freely and charge a committee to report back on how it proposes to carry out the plan.

During December while the Field Secretary is on sick leave, she carries her responsibility in two ways; one, by writing a letter describing steps the committee might take in organizing a course and outlining some ideas as to content. This was done at the request of the chairman who wanted "some cues for the Executive Committee to look at in working with the committee to put on the course." Secondly, the Field Secretary arranged for another staff member to go to the December delegate meeting. In January a committee of five women is organized, representatives from the Moore Civic Club, the two P. T. A.'s, and the Senior Women's Club. It has been a long time since 11/14 when the idea was originally proposed but extenuating circumstances are in the holiday season and the field secretary's sick leave which extended through the first week of January. The delegate meeting of 1/16 and the Executive Committee of 1/30 were both informed by the chairman that the committee had been appointed but had not met. The field secretary in the first two weeks of February makes several attempts to find a good meeting time, having been asked by the chairman to call the meeting together. He has not appointed a committee chairman. It is not uncommon for field secretaries to make arrangements for meetings though this is to be avoided as often as possible because responsibility taken by council leadership heightens the participation by delegates and strengthens the council's ability to run its own affairs. Realistically, however, council leaders are also volunteers when it comes to community affairs and thus can be aided to do a better job if relieved now and then of mechanical detail. The committee to plan the course finally meets on 2/16.

2/16. Meeting of the leadership training course committee was attended by Mrs. Tate of the Moore Civic Club, Mrs. Johnson of the Moore P. T. A., Mrs. Peterson of the Oakhurst P. T. A., Mr. McHugh and myself. Mrs. Schmidt of the Senior Women's Club and Mrs. Stevens of the Moore P. T. A. could not attend. Mrs. Tate in the beginning made it plain that she was serving as an alternate for Mrs. Schroeder who is ill with an eye condition. (Mr. McHugh announced that the Council would now meet on Wednesday. He had arranged for the leadership training committee to meet in the Presbyterian Church since it had not been possible to work out a meeting at the home of

Mrs. Peterson as she had suggested in January.) Mr. McHugh was quite uncertain about how to proceed with this committee and made no effort at all to explain the purpose of the committee nor the fact that they had to elect their own chairman. In fact, he became very dependent upon me, and this is the first time that he has been unable to function. He seemed to regard himself as a member of the committee but was not able to share responsibility, a lot of which he assumed himself. This was a problem in getting the ladies to consider the organization of the committee and the end result was that we had no chairman.

Since Mr. McHugh refused to speak to the purpose of the meeting even though I asked him to, I reviewed this in order to get things started. I said that the responsibility of this committee now was to plan the course, decide whom it would be for, decide when and where it would be held and to make arrangements for getting in touch with organizations who could supply leaders for the sessions. I asked the group where it wanted to start on these questions, and Mrs. Peterson suggested we begin outlining the course. This was done by way of everyone suggesting subjects to be discussed with Mrs. Peterson proposing most of the ideas. The following topics were listed—qualities for leadership, qualifications for jobs, the right way and wrong way of parliamentary procedure, the duties of the chairman, discussion leading, the responsibility of the nominating committee, and pulling together as a community. The committee then discussed the type of course this might be and thought it should be open to officers of all organizations. However, Mrs. Tate objected saying that she thought it should be open to anyone who wished to come. The other women said this might be hard to manage because the subjects would have to be broader to interest people who are not officers. I wondered if this question could be decided by the Council membership or perhaps it would have to be decided by the size of the place in which the course might be held.

At this point Mr. McHugh assumed that he would make arrangements about the space and said that he was sure he could get the lecture room of the Presbyterian Church. He went off to consult Reverend Robertson, and the committee went on to discuss the number of sessions the course might cover. I asked how many sessions the women thought people would attend and at first they thought a six weeks' course would be good. I asked when they thought the course might best be given, and they realized that it could not be given before the first of April because of time needed to secure speakers and to promote attendance. They finally agreed that since April would be best, it ought not to be more than four weeks because May is the month of annual meetings and election of officers in many organizations. Mr. McHugh returned to announce that Mr. Robertson thought the course could be given at the church the first Monday of April and on succeeding Mondays. This happily fitted into the women's plan and they felt pleased at the progress they were making. They went off into a discussion of refreshments and decided that each organization represented on the committee could supply the refreshments. Mr. McHugh was sure that the women of the church would be able to supply coffee and then corrected himself to say that this would have to be paid for. Mrs. Johnson wondered why the Council couldn't pay for it, so Mr. McHugh said this should be included in the committee's report to the Council. He asked which of the women would make the report, and it appeared that it would have to be Mrs. Tate because the others were not going to attend. Mrs. Tate was very fearful of making a report and said that she had never done this. I said that I would draw up the outline of topics suggested and would also include the purpose, time, and place for the course if this would make it easier for her. Mrs. Peterson thought the outline ought to be mimeographed and distributed so that people could take it back to their organizations. I suggested if this were to be done we add a registration form so that we could begin to get some idea of how many people would be interested. It was agreed this should be done.

The committee apparently felt that their job was about over so I reminded them of the need to discuss the plan with the Group Work Division, and Mr. McHugh again assumed that this would be his business. The women were happy to let him do this and urged that he get "outstanding speakers for us." I asked when we should meet again in order to receive Mr. McHugh's report, and the ladies thought that a week from today would be fine. They wondered what else they would have to do, and I said that they probably would have to get in touch with the speakers suggested and would want to make arrangements for telling the speakers what was expected of them. They asked if I could not do this. I said no, it would be better for the official invitation to come from them. I wondered what arrangements would be needed for taking minutes which were necessary for two reasons: one, to inform each speaker of what had happened; and second, to serve as a basis for a booklet from the course if it was good enough to publish a report. Everyone was immediately interested in the possibility of a report which Mrs. Johnson thought could be sold.

There is no lack of interest in the course nor lack of ideas as to what it might cover, the committee members are obviously involved and aware of their responsibilities to produce an outline which can be discussed by the Oakhurst Council members. The field secretary has to assume too active a role because the Council chairman suddenly refuses to "function." This takes the field secretary by surprise, and she realizes suddenly that the chairman's inability to function is going to block any organization of this group as a committee. Instead of helping the committee to become organized as a committee, the field secretary goes on as though chairing the group. She should have pointed out that committee organization is important to handle such details as placing responsibility for calling committee meetings, making reports to the Council, and for co-ordinating progress on all the committee's work such as contacts with speakers, publicity, refreshments, registration for the course, etc. As a discussion leader, the field secretary does an able job because the discussion is free and open and of good quality. The ladies, however, do not have a free hand in carrying their share of responsibility for the arrangements for the course since the Council chairman takes this over as his job. He likewise assumes it is his business to get in touch with the Group Work Division. It is no wonder that the ladies ask, "What else can we have to do?" The field secretary indicates they are to invite the speakers which they resist as is to be expected with no more involvement than they have had in the actual work. However, with the possibility of exhibits and movies to get, the ladies have a little more sense of participation and agree to meet in a week. The central problem here is that the field secretary was diverted in her role by the unusual performance of the chairman. Had she concentrated either on getting him to chair the meeting or on getting the group to pick a chairman, the group would have become a committee. The field secretary's mistake was in identifying with the chairman as a person rather than with him in his role as chairman. In spite of this mistake in practice, the work was well enough outlined, responsibility was assigned for the report to the Council, and a date was set for the next meeting. The resources of the Community Welfare Council were opened up appropriately, and the job of the committee in relation to speakers, attendance, location, number of sessions, etc., is well advanced. The freedom of the chairman to use his church is of interest in identifying him further: he is an at-large member in the Council but definitely has an organization (his church) behind him.

Three officers and delegates from eleven organizations attended the delegate meeting. After a report on the Council's health project, the leadership training committee reports.

2/18. Mrs. Tate did a good job with the report of the leadership training committee and was helped considerably by being able to hang on to the outline. The outline was well received, and the following suggestions were made. The course should be broad enough so that a picture is given of the total organization in which can be seen the jobs of the various officers and the relation between each job. It will be important to describe the delegation of authority to committee chairmen and how the chairmen have responsibility for working with committees. The training of leaders by the organization is important, and there should be discussion of how this training can be done. This was connected to the problem of having enough people to do the job so that the same people do not continue. The question of how many committees an organization should have was mentioned. After these suggestions were listed, the problem of a date was discussed, and Mr. McHugh pulled from his notebook the calendar of organization meetings which had been prepared by the field secretary last spring. From this it appeared that Monday night was the best night so that the committee's suggestion of Monday was finally approved. The question of who should attend the course brought out the feeling that it should be open to everyone. In order to find out how much interest there would be, it was decided to send the outline prepared by the committee to all of the members of the Council. There was some thought that it should go to nonmembers as well, and it was finally agreed that it should go to the entire mailing list.

This meeting again shows freedom of the delegate body to instruct its committees and changes are made in the content of the course. Plans are laid to promote attendance by sending the outline to the full mailing list. The Council is aware that success of this project depends on no other meetings competing and so the chairman uses his calendar (prepared last year by staff) to clear dates of meetings of the leading organizations of Oakhurst.

2/20. By appointment Mr. McHugh came into the office to confer about his contact with the Group Work Division regarding their assistance on the leadership training course. (Mr. McHugh wanted particularly to know whether the Division would be able to supply the speakers and whether it would be able to provide exhibits. I said that all these questions could be answered by Mr. Elkind, Division secretary.) Mr. McHugh said there was increasing interest in the course and that he knew of some people from the Presbyterian Church who wanted to attend. He had also heard from Mrs. Stevens that some people had signed up even though she had not been at the committee meeting. I said this was excellent because as far as I knew it was the first time that a council had made it possible for organizations to get this sort of information. I thought, therefore, that the Group Work Division would be interested and willing to help if at all possible. At Mr. McHugh's request I put him in touch with Mr. Elkind and they arranged an appointment for 2/21. Mr. McHugh thought it wise if I came along, and when I asked why, he said, "You know more about this than I do." He went on to say that he thought I would probably be the person who would have to "keep things rolling" since the speakers would not be Oakhurst people, and some arrangement would have to be made for them to get to the sessions as well as for informing them as to what had happened at the previous sessions.

2/21. Conference with Mr. Elkind and Mr. McHugh. Mr. McHugh handled the conference ably and clearly explained the purpose of it. He gave Mr. Elkind the outline as prepared by the committee and said that the committee was prepared to work with the Division in any necessary way. Mr. Elkind was at once interested in the idea and said he was sure that the Division would co-operate. He made some tentative suggestions for speakers but said he would like to get other ideas from the Executive Committee of the Division. He asked Mr. McHugh to put the request in writing so that he would have a record of this for the Division to act on. Mr. Elkind thought that this was an unusual kind of project for a council and asked how much interest there was in it. Mr. McHugh said there was a lot and he thought we would end up with about 30 people in the course.

Following the conference, Mr. McHugh and I worked on the letter and he asked me if I thought it should be discussed with the committee. I thought not because the committee had authorized him to proceed with the Division and the letter was not out of line with that.

2/25. Letter to Group Work Division from the Council chairman.

2/27. Meeting of Executive Committee. Mr. McHugh reported progress on the leadership training course, describing very adequately his conference with Mr. Elkind. I gave him the copy of the letter sent and there was some good-natured joking about the fact that he probably did not write this letter. He took this in good faith and said that the ideas were his but that actually I had written the letter. He added with a laugh, "She's good, don't you think?" Mrs. Schmidt raised the question of money for refreshments, saying that she was sure cookies could be provided by members of the committee but she thought coffee or tea would be nice to have too. Mr. McHugh was all for allotting $10 to be spent but the other officers checked him and said this would have to be passed by the Council. He said that the serving of refreshments would be done by the women of the church.

3/5. The leadership training course committee met at the Presbyterian Church. Present were Mrs. Tate, Mrs. Schmidt, Mrs. Schroeder, Mrs. Johnson, and Mr. McHugh. Mr. McHugh made no effort to get the committee to appoint a chairman and assumed even more responsibility for directing the course of the meeting. The ladies were immediately excited by the letter from the Group Work Division and with some stimulation from me divided up the list of people to contact. The choice of speakers was made on the basis of the organizations they represented and their positions in them. Mrs. Johnson agreed to call Mr. Thomas Delft of Community House and

Mrs. Schmidt to call Mrs. Cameron and Mrs. Davidson. The fourth speaker, who actually will be the first one, is Mr. Elkind of the Division. He had agreed to serve as speaker in our conference and confirmed this in the letter. I suggested it might be well for a letter to follow the conversation by phone with each speaker and Mrs. Johnson said she would draft the letter. Mr. McHugh announced that the church had definitely agreed to donate the lecture room and that a committee of church women would serve the refreshments. The women were pleased at the thought of refreshments until I reminded them they would have to get authority from the Council for money. Mrs. Schroeder was given the job of making this request. The question of exhibits was not entirely settled although the women thought that Mrs. Peterson should work on this since she had contacts through the P. T. A. Council. I asked what they thought we could do about taking of minutes, and they all thought that this would be hard to work out unless I were to do it. The problem is finding someone who would take minutes quickly and easily and get them typed up in time to send to the next speaker. Recognizing this point, I agreed to act as reporter and said that I would get in touch with each of the speakers before the session to see that he or she had all the necessary information.

3/18. At the delegate meeting, Mrs. Schroeder made the report on the leadership training course which was well received. The Council voted to spend up to $10 for refreshments. There was general expression about the need for the course and many people said it would be helpful to all organizations. Mr. McHugh used this to urge representatives to promote attendance which he said was open to all people.

The chairman is more and more regarding the course as his special project and has to be checked in this by his fellow officers. He is showing need for individual work with the field secretary through which his proper role with the committee could be explained and through which he could gain enough perspective to let the committee do its job. At present his officers are holding him in check. In the delegate meetings he is well able to encourage participation. The field secretary assists in this at intervals by asking how many people are coming and what arrangements are to be made for details. The field secretary appropriately assumes the job of recording the sessions because of the timing involved in getting weekly minutes out to the next speaker. Ordinarily such a secretarial task should be done by members of the Council but under unusual circumstances it can be done by staff, especially when the people concerned recognize their inability to do the job and ask staff to do it. The members of the committee show that they can take responsibility for calling speakers, writing letters of confirmation, and getting out publicity. The group is really operating as a group in spite of not actually being a committee. At the meeting of the Council's Executive Committee, the following plans are made.

3/27. Mr. McHugh moved on quickly to the leadership training course in which by now he has invested a lot of himself. Mrs. Schmidt reported that Mrs. Cameron of the Girl Scouts and Mrs. Davidson have accepted the invitation to speak at the sessions of 4/20 and 4/27. I showed her the letter which Mrs. Johnson had sent to Mr. Delft confirming his engagement for the 13th and suggested she send it to the two women. She said she would have her daughter type it for her. She asked who was going to take minutes, and Mr. McHugh said that I had agreed to and would forward them to each speaker as preparation. I raised the question of stimulating attendance for the course. The group thought that two things should be done—one was newspaper publicity which should go in the issue of 4/10 (of the local *Oakhurst Gazette*) and the other was phone calls to organizations. Mr McHugh said he would be responsible for the phone calls if a member of the committee would do the publicity. I suggested using the flyer which had been sent out announcing the course and also said that the committee members could help with calls. The last remark was to help Mr. McHugh, if possible, to let this committee do its own job. I also wondered if the Council should not send out a second announcement of the course now that we had the speakers lined up. There was such resistance to this in terms of notices also going out for the open Council meeting on the health project that I did not push the suggestion.

Things are well in hand for the course with the field secretary recognizing more clearly that the chairman has been in the way of the committee's operation. However, more is needed than suggestions to him, a discussion of the importance of freeing committees to work and ways to do this should be a part of a conference between the chairman and field secretary. The field secretary is more and more able to let the committee keep its responsibilities and to focus on ways in which all organizations can be encouraged to attend. Personal contacts, publicity and a written announcement are all to be used and all come from the committee or from the Executive Committee; the field secretary's question as to ways to stimulate attendance is all that is needed to help in the formulation of these plans.

4/27. The leadership training course concluded this evening with an excellent session led by Mrs. Stanley Davidson, board member of the Community Welfare Council and of the Community Chest. The minutes of all sessions are on file in the correspondence folder. A statistical summary reveals that 12 organizations participated, sending 35 different people. Sessions had an average attendance of 22 each. Eleven persons came 4 times, 7 came 3 times, 6 came 2 times, and 11 came 1 time. Five organizations were represented 4 times, 4 were represented 3 times, 2 were represented 2 times and 1 was represented once. The committee had three newspaper articles; one before the course started, the other two during the course. At the final session Mr. McHugh asked the group whether it wanted to recommend that the proceedings of the course be published because so many people had asked if this could be done. The group immediately voted to have the Council publish the proceedings for sale to all organizations, but with participating organizations each receiving a free copy.

The spirit in each session was excellent. There was a great deal of informality, aided by the refreshments. Comments made at each session included some on the warmth and friendliness of each speaker who while obviously expert in his subject was also a human who had troubles too in his organization. In two sessions there was some cross discussion among the audience though the sessions had not been planned to engender this at all. In all sessions over half of the group asked questions or made comments. During the refreshment period very few people talked with speakers, and most of the audience returned to their seats to eat. This is quite typical of this community; the social polish is lacking but the feeling of friendliness is there and flourishes as introductions are made and people encouraged to speak to each other. This I prompted by talking to as many people as I could at each session and by suggesting they speak to the speaker.

In addition to this kind of role, I assumed full responsibility for arranging to take two speakers to Oakhurst and did get minutes to all speakers in advance as planned. Miss Field, another staff member, substituted on the 20th when I had to be at another meeting unexpectedly.

At the last session, Mr. McHugh tested his idea of calling a community-wide meeting of organization leaders to discuss recreation programs. This grew out of Mrs. Davidson's comments on councils' roles in community planning for recreation. The group was interested in his plan and urged that he call together members and nonmembers of the Council. He said he would, adding that this might be a good way to recruit new members. He invited everyone to the Council's Annual Meeting on 5/20 and to the Association's Annual Meeting on 5/23.

The leadership training course is one of the few clear examples I have seen of the "pure" operation of an intergroup—in this case the idea was brought from a member group, a committee was selected by the Council, composed of representatives of interested organizations, this committee reported regularly to the delegates, the course was put on and was a success, to the point where proceedings are being asked for. The only flaw in this sequence is the fact that the committee process was weak. The committee never actually operated as a group, due partly to Mr. McHugh's need to dominate it and my lack of time to work with him and the committee on details of organization.

This is an excellent and thoughtful analysis of the progress of the course with insight into the main problem. This type of recording is important in order that workers see mistakes made and also see service carried through to successful completion.

The chairman's Annual Report to the Council has this to say about the leadership training course. The fact that he wrote this report himself shows his excellent understanding of the purpose of a council.

5/20. I believe we have established this Council upon a firm foundation. The member groups think of the Council in terms of how can the Council help us? Actually that is the purpose of a council, not to domineer over any organization or group of organizations but to bring to the attention of all groups the problems of one group, thereby exposing the problem to all of the organizations, and in a delegate body of this size the know-how is usually forthcoming. We have seen in the past year the principle of a council in action; in the following report, note the co-ordination and co-operation of the member groups and individual delegates.

. . . 6. *Leadership Training Course.* The Moore Civic Club presented a request for some type of training for officers. Through the efforts of a committee consisting of five Council member groups and our field secretary, the program was presented with the co-operation of the Group Work Division, Community Welfare Council. It was held in the Presbyterian Church on April 6, 13, 20, 27. Twelve organizations sent thirty-five different people. Average attendance was twenty-one.

On 7/9 the field secretary concludes her responsibility for the course by sending the draft of the proceedings to the chairman with a memo requesting him to ask the committee to revise the draft to meet the desires of the Council. Also given are figures on costs of producing the proceedings so that the chairman has some basis for estimating the number of copies.

On 9/25 the Council's first delegate meeting of the new program year approves the publication of 120 copies of the proceedings to be sold at 15¢ each.

The field secretary throughout this program year used various devices to carry out her responsibility to the Council. She met with the Council's delegate body, with the committee, and with the chairman; she

talked with speakers and prepared minutes and the draft of the proceedings. She constantly strove to involve the delegates in planning and
in participating. She shows sensitivity to relationships by identifying relationships between the committee and the delegate body and between
the delegate body and the community as a whole. She serves as liaison
to the Community Welfare Council and as secretary to committee and
course; when not able to be present, she provided substitute staff service.

As noted, the weakest point was the omission of individual work
with the chairman of the Council by the field secretary. This is an essential part of the field secretary's role with a council because (as these
excerpts show) the chairman has a large job in administering the affairs of the council. Any chairman needs guidance in developing the
ability to form committees, to let them operate freely, and to help people take responsibility. Had the field secretary conferred with the chairman after the first meeting of the leadership training course committee,
she could have pointed out to him the way in which he blocked the committee process by taking too much responsibility. A second point where
an individual conference was indicated was after the March Executive
Committee meeting in which the other Council officers checked the
chairman in his plan to make a decision by himself rather than letting
the Council make it. In community organization the role of the field
secretary calls for relationships to individuals in their various roles with
the council so that these individuals see the need to work co-operatively
with others and do not feel that they have sole responsibility. Omission
of essential steps such as individual work with chairmen always create
blocks in the complete and successful use of the social intergroup work
process. In this instance, the committee members, the Executive Committee, and the delegate body were so well aware of the Oakhurst Council operation that they were able to compensate for the chairman's er-
rors.

‖‖‖

chapter 16

The Profession of Social Work

A Platform and an Association

Social work is a modern professional service whose principles and objectives arise from, and are closely identified with, the key beliefs and aspirations of a democratic society. Foremost among these are:

1. Firm faith in the dignity, worth and creative power of the individual.
2. Complete belief in his right to hold and express his own opinions and to act upon them, so long as by so doing he does not infringe upon the rights of others.
3. Unswerving conviction of the inherent, inalienable right of each human being to choose and achieve his own destiny in the framework of a progressive, yet stable, society.

The foregoing principles are the foundations of social work's essential objective to assist persons, individually or in groups, to attain satisfying relationships and standards of life in accordance with their particular wishes and capacities and in harmony with those of the community. The profession of social work seeks to create and give specialized services which aid individuals and groups to achieve these goals and, with the experience gained in providing these specialized services, to play its part in modifying or reshaping social and economic institutions which are inimical to the attainment of these broad democratic goals.[1]

With these opening words the members of the American Association of Social Workers adopted in 1951 a platform statement of *Standards for the Professional Practice of Social Work* which is binding upon its members. Perhaps this idealistic enunciation signifies the awareness of its members of recent steps toward professionalization after centuries of

---

[1] *Standards for the Professional Practice of Social Work.* New York, American Association of Social Workers, 1951.

social work practice. It may be recalled that social services have been provided under the auspices of the church for better than a thousand years, under the auspices of the state for over three hundred years, and under the auspices of voluntary agencies for something between two and three centuries. Yet it is only within the present century that these services have come to be looked upon as professional services or the persons providing them as professional people.

One measure of the recency of professionalization is the date of the organization of the over-all professional association, the American Association of Social Workers, in 1921. Membership is based upon training in a graduate school of social work and ranges from student membership through the temporary junior membership to the full membership available to those who have a two-year graduate degree in social work. As of mid-1954 there were about 13,000 members distributed through 133 chapters in 48 states and territories. The aim of the Association is to improve the quality of the social services under whatever auspices they are offered and to aid in the public understanding of the profession of social work. Its 13,000 membership is but a fraction of the total of 100,000 persons occupying social work positions, and while the Association is interested in the expansion of its membership, its basic concern is with the quality of the social services and the qualifications of the workers who offer them.

Perhaps nowhere is this concern more explicitly formulated than in the following code of ethics that was adopted as an integral part of *Standards for the Professional Practice of Social Work*. Because it is basic to all social work practice and should be binding upon every person practicing social work as a vocation, it is here reproduced in its entirety.

CODE OF ETHICS

The principles of ethical conduct which follow define the discipline necessary for carrying out the purposes of the profession, are binding upon members of the American Association of Social Workers and should be binding upon every person practicing social work as a vocation.

PRINCIPLES OF PROFESSIONAL CONDUCT

The social worker practices his profession in several areas of relationship with clientele, the employing agency, his colleagues, the community, and the profession itself.

A. RELATION TO CLIENTELE—whether individuals, groups or communities

The American Association of Social Workers believes that the social worker should:

1. Regard as his primary obligation the welfare of the persons served, consistent with the common welfare and as related to the agency function and/or defined by law.

2. Accept that in professional relationships his professional responsibility takes precedence over his personal aims and views.

3. Accept the right of persons served to make their own decisions and to act for themselves unless they freely give this authority to the agency or unless the agency must act in a protective role in order to safeguard the persons served or the community.

4. Accept the obligation to make available as objectively as possible all pertinent data needed to enable individuals and groups served to make decisions on an informed and responsible basis.

5. Respect and safeguard the right of persons served to privacy in their contacts with the agency, and to confidential and responsible use of the information they give.

6. Conduct all relations with and concerning the persons served with respect for individual differences and without discrimination either because of special interests or of personal identification with particular ideologies.

B. RELATION TO THE EMPLOYING AGENCY

The American Association of Social Workers believes that the social worker should:

1. As an applicant for a position, give accurately all information pertinent to determining his qualifications for the position.

2. As an applicant, and as an employee, inform himself concerning the agency's program, policies and personnel regulations.

3. Accept employment and continue to work only in an agency whose policies and procedures permit him to follow, substantially, the ethical principles in this code; or, if the agency does not have such standards, remain only if the agency makes a planned effort to revise its policies and procedures in accordance with these principles.

4. Observe an employment contract unless changed by mutual consent.

5. Take into full consideration his own limitations in accepting assignments. When employed as supervisor or administrator, the social worker should take into full consideration the worker's competence both in connection with employment and in making assignments.

6. Hold himself responsible for quality and quantity of performance in carrying out agency objective and policies according to established procedures; and work continuously through agency channels to improve its procedures, services and personnel practices.

7. Accept responsibility, when functioning in an administrative or supervisory capacity, to provide channels for staff participation in formulation of agency policies and procedures, and to encourage and facilitate use of these channels by the staff.

8. If agency policies and procedures violate professional standards, a) accept the obligation to make all due effort to effect change through appropriate agency and professional channels; b) refrain from irresponsible public criticism of agency's policies; c) appeal to the wider community on the basis of objective and substantial evidence only after agency and professional channels have been exhausted.*

9. Upon termination of employment with an agency for whatever reason, have a continuing obligation to act responsibly in accordance with professional ethics regarding disclosure of information obtained during employment.

C. RELATION TO COLLEAGUES

The American Association of Social Workers believes that the social worker should:

1. Treat respectfully the position and accomplishments of colleagues and express judgment on matters related to professional performance only through established channels.

2. Assume appropriate responsibility for sharing knowledge with colleagues.

3. Conduct himself in such a way as to support, rather than obstruct, his colleagues in fulfilling their responsibilities.

4. Treat respectfully differences of opinion between himself and his colleagues and, as far as possible, take positive steps to resolve such differences.

5. Treat all colleagues without discrimination.

6. If working in a setting where another profession or group has major responsibility, maintain identification with the social work profession and integrate it with the major function and purpose of the organization.

7. Give employment references in which: a) data are complete, factually correct and related to professional performance; b) a true appraisal of the worker is given; c) no information is given which has not been shared in substance with the subject when the writer has been professionally responsible for evaluating the subject; d) the writer clearly states his relationship with the subject.

8. Seek references in a responsible manner and hold in confidence the references he receives.

9. Employ, promote, demote, dismiss personnel, or recommend for employment, promotion, demotion or dismissal of personnel, on the basis of objective and relevant data obtained through appropriate channels.

* In some cases, the employee may choose to resign his position in order to free himself from obligations inherent in his employment with the agency.

D. RELATION TO THE COMMUNITY

The American Association of Social Workers believes that the social worker should:

1. Contribute his knowledge, skills and support to programs of community improvement.

2. Affirm and interpret the importance of professional education, training and experience as they relate to professional competence.

3. Affirm and interpret the rights of social workers to good personnel practices in agencies.

4. Accept responsibility to initiate and to share in the effort to protect the community against unethical practice on the part of individuals or organizations engaged in social welfare programs.

5. Render professional service in public emergencies.

6. Hold himself responsible to the public for quality and quantity of performance and for accounting of his stewardship.

7. In public statements or actions, make clear whether he is acting or speaking as an individual or as a delegated representative of a professional association or agency, and, at all times, be accurate, exercise proper restraint and show respect for the opinion of others.

E. RELATION TO THE PROFESSION OF SOCIAL WORK

The American Association of Social Workers believes that the social worker should:

1. Support and consistently work to improve the standards of the profession.

2. Sustain and enhance public confidence in the profession through maintaining integrity and self-discipline in personal behavior.

3. Defend the social work profession against unjust attack and misrepresentation.

4. Assume responsibility for determining objectively and for helping correct conditions which lead to justifiable criticism of the social work profession.

Professional Membership Organizations

In addition to the American Association of Social Workers there are six other professional membership associations within the field of social work. The oldest of these is the American Association of Medical Social Workers, organized in 1918 as the American Association of Hospital Social Workers; and the most recent, the Social Work Research Group organized in 1949. The National Association of School Social Workers was organized as the National Association of Visiting Teachers in 1919, the American Association of Psychiatric Social Workers came into being in 1926. The American Association of Group Workers was formed in 1946 out of the American Association for the Study of Group Work. There is also the Association for the Study of Community Organization.[2]

Since 1949 efforts have been directed toward an over-all professional organization. During 1953 and 1954 these organizations have drawn up plans which look to one organization within the near future. There are many problems to be worked out, many vested interests to be jealously guarded, many misgivings about possible loss of identity, and substantial concern about finances so that progress has been discouragingly slower than some had hoped and faster than some had feared! [3]

Agency Associations

Other associations in social work may be distinguished from the foregoing by reason of their emphasis upon agency membership based upon standards of competence. There are six of those associations: The National Federation of Settlements and Neighborhood Centers, 1911; the Family Service Association of America, 1911; the Community Chests and Councils of America, Inc., 1918; the Episcopal Service for Youth, 1919; the Child Welfare League of America, 1920; and the Council of Jewish Federations and Welfare Funds, 1932.

Other Social Work Organizations

In addition to the organizations just mentioned in which individual membership is based upon professional training and experience or upon agency membership based on standards, there are other organizations in which membership is based upon a concern and, usually, a participation in certain interests and activities. In the order of their founding these organizations are: National Conference of Social Work, 1873; National Conference of Jewish Communal Service, 1899; National Probation and Parole Association, 1907; National Conference of Catholic Charities, 1910; American Public Welfare Association, 1930; and the Christian Social Welfare Associates, 1930 (successor to Church

---

[2] Information about membership requirements, usually training in a graduate professional school of social work, may be secured from the Association whose purposes and addresses are carried in the 1954 *Social Work Year Book*.

[3] Glasser, Melvin A., "Target: A Single Professional Membership Organization in 1955." *Social Work Journal*, XXXV, April 1954, pp. 57–60.

Conference of Social Work and the Association of Church Social Workers).

Professional Training [4]

Professional training for social work practice, which is over fifty years old, marked the beginnings of a definite break from the heretofore apprenticeship system. This development was not unlike that in the field of legal education. Speaking before the National Conference of Charities and Corrections (later the National Conference of Social Work) in 1915, Mr. Felix Frankfurter, then of the Harvard Law School, reviewed the three periods of legal education: first, apprenticeship to a practicing lawyer; second, the establishment of the proprietary law school, of which Judge Reeves' school in Connecticut would be an example; third, recognition by universities of the obligation of training men fit to practice and administer law and the establishment of law schools as part of the university. The establishment of the Harvard Law School in 1817 is an instance. Social work education moved from apprenticeship, through proprietary school (the first school of social work in this country, the New York School of Philanthropy, was begun under the aegis of the New York Charity Organization Society), and finally, to association with the university (by action of the American Association of Schools of Social Work in 1939 all schools of social work must be a part of a college or university approved by the Association of American Universities).

Professional education for social work in this country stems from the first training courses held in the summer of 1898 by the New York Charity Organization Society.[5] In 1903 the training programs included a six months' winter session, and in the following year these training courses developed into the New York School of Philanthropy. Later this became the New York School of Social Work of Columbia University. The second school grew out of a series of courses

---

[4] The excellent studies of Esther Lucile Brown on professional education deserve special mention, especially: Brown, Esther Lucile, *Lawyers, Law Schools and the Public Service.* New York, Russell Sage Foundation, 1948; Brown, Esther Lucile, *Social Work as a Profession,* rev. ed., New York, Russell Sage Foundation, 1942; Brown, Esther Lucile, "Comparative Developments in Social Work, Medicine and Law." *The Family,* XXIV, November 1943, pp. 243–255.

[5] Meier, Elizabeth G., *A History of the New York School of Social Work.* New York, Columbia University Press, 1954.

under the Extension Department of the University of Chicago, then known as the Chicago Institute of Social Science. In 1908 this venture was incorporated as the Chicago School of Civics and Philanthropy, later to become the School of Social Service Administration of the University of Chicago. Other schools of social work have developed within this five-decade period until in 1954 there were 58 accredited schools located throughout the United States, Canada, Hawaii, and Puerto Rico.

In 1919 the universities, colleges, and independent schools concerned with standards in social work education formed themselves into the Association of Training Schools of Professional Social Work. This group, augmented by other schools that had developed training programs in 1933, took the name of the American Association of Schools of Social Work. In 1952 the Council on Social Work Education was established, bringing together into one organization graduate schools of social work, undergraduate departments, public (tax supported) agencies, voluntary agencies, professional membership associations, and delegates-at-large representing interested citizens and higher education. On July 1, 1954, the Council membership included 58 graduate schools of social work, 75 undergraduate departments offering pre-social work courses, 29 agencies, 7 membership associations, 27 co-operating groups, and 330 individuals as associate or contributing members.

Education for social work consists of at least two years of professional training leading to the master's degree. Admission calls for personal suitability and adaptability, as well as for the baccalaureate degree usually with a prerequisite major in the social sciences. The curriculum consists of class work and supervised field instruction in a welfare agency. Within recent years, particularly since the formation of the Council on Social Work Education, greater importance has been placed upon an integrated and generic two-year curriculum rather than, as formerly, on trade training or acquaintance with an array of courses or subjects. The curriculum policy statement of the Council emphasizes that "the curriculum is a cohesive whole, designed to impart a substantial body of professional knowledge and skill, to communicate an understanding and appreciation of the nature and methods of social work practice, and to ensure a beginning competence for the performance of social work functions. It should provide a framework of classroom and field courses and research within which the student may test and use theoretical knowledge, acquire professional skill, achieve a professional self-discipline, and develop a social philosophy rooted in an appreciation of the essential dignity of man." [6]

Class work and supervised field work may be conducted concurrently, i.e. during each week of the academic year, or a "block" system of field work placement may be used in which there may be a period of class work on the campus—usually a semester—followed by field work in an agency away from the campus for a semester, and then a period of class work to round out the first year's program. The same sequence is carried out in the second year, whether on a concurrent or a block system of field work. In the second year there is opportunity for concentration in various areas of practice such as public assistance, child welfare, school social services, psychiatric social work, medical social work, the correctional services, social group work, community organization, administration, and research. The placements in the appropriate agency according to the students' expressed interest and aptitude in the second year are arranged by the school, with the immediate supervision under the direction of the agency.

The agency supervisor is in close contact with the school of social work on all matters pertaining to the development of the student. Regular supervisory conferences are held between the agency supervisor and the director of the field instruction program on the staff of the school. Field instruction is closely integrated with class work, and class work is closely integrated with field instruction. Work which the student is doing is not only discussed between the student and supervisor, but an account of it is also brought into the classroom and is discussed by student, fellow students, and instructors. This applies not only to the field work placement in casework but also to placement in social group work, administration, and community organization. The field instruction is part and parcel of the total curriculum and joins in with the other courses in developing knowledge and skill in the student in training. The supervision of the student in the agency is essentially a helping-learning process, and while it has its differing aspects, it shares with other learning evoked through the classroom experience.

Upon the satisfactory completion of the two years' program, includ-

[6] Kendall, Katherine A., "Education for Social Work." *Social Work Year Book,* 1954, p. 174.

ing the thesis, a master's degree is awarded. The majority of the schools grant the professional social work degree—the Master of Social Work. Upon the satisfactory completion of the first year's program some schools award a certificate of proficiency. Twelve schools of social work have developed programs beyond the master's level leading to the doctorate—either the Doctor of Philosophy or the Doctor of Social Work.

As of November 1954, there were 3,925 full-time students enrolled in the schools of social work of the United States and Canada. Almost one half of the number in the preceding year received awards for the completion of the two-year program. There were 1,091 faculty persons engaged in social work education, either as teachers, field work supervisors, or a combination of these. A trifle more than one half such persons were in full-time employment in social work education.

Training in Administration

Many administrative positions in social work are held by persons who have had neither training nor experience in social work before assuming the post. Professionally trained social workers are aware of this and occasionally are shocked when such an appointment is made, especially to a top administrative position, for political reasons. A bit of reflection usually reveals that there has been very little training in administration in schools of social work. In answer to this situation a number of schools of social work have developed opportunities for training in administration to mature and experienced second-year students or to advanced students who have already achieved the master of social work degree and who have had successful working experience. This seems especially important in states with predominantly rural and sparsely populated counties because in so many instances workers are moved, prematurely, into the county superintendency of public welfare. Some schools have departed from the conventional academic courses on administration and have moved on to a more dynamically oriented program of instruction, supervision, and consultation with gratifying results.

Research

Reference was made in the chapter on social casework to the necessity for social casework to carry on research. This is just as true in the other areas—such as social group work, community welfare organization, and administration. Social work practice has developed largely out of providing services. For years the demands to meet people's and communities' needs have been so insistent that social work practitioners have not taken the time, have not been inclined, and may not have been qualified to do a careful research analysis. But increasingly within recent years social workers have had to face the embarrassing questions put by social scientists and even by laymen as to whether they—the workers—know what they are doing; why they are doing what they are doing; why they are doing it that particular way; whether that way is effective, and if so why and if not why it is not; and is there a more effective way. These and a myriad of other questions that scientists have asked themselves are now directed to social workers. Scientists have shown what research can do in opening up new ways and new worlds. Schools of social work are beginning to move beyond a polite and evasive response to a serious facing of these demands upon the profession. Some of the agencies—public as well as voluntary—are beginning to look beyond the obvious statistical reports that have passed heretofore as research. There will always be the necessity to provide social services to people—and expandingly so—but there will be a compelling necessity to accompany such service with a willingness to study, analyze, and even to create new worlds of knowledge and understanding.

The Responsibility of Schools of Social Work

Throughout the more than fifty years of education for social work the schools have been called upon to modify their programs in closer relation to the reality of demands made upon professional workers. Within the decade beginning with the passage of the Social Security Act in 1935 and the development of a federal-state-local public welfare program the whole field of practice has undergone a fundamental and revolutionary change. There are no indications that the changes are over. Indeed, every trend is in the direction of an increasing role which the tax-supported services will exercise in our economic and political life. At the same time that these changes are occurring in the public welfare field the important experimental, demonstration, and supporting role of the private and voluntarily financed welfare agencies is being emphasized. These developments, as never before, place upon the professional schools of social work an undeniable responsibility for keeping abreast, if not ahead, in their particular area of competence.

In answer to these requirements, social work education has pressed toward a strengthening and a broadening of an integrated and integrating social work curriculum of class and field instruction. This movement toward a more effective training program is based not only upon the need to supply workers for the immediate lower echelon positions in the welfare departments, but also to provide students with the basis and the substance for eventual progression to the higher administrative and policy-making positions.

To carry out the high demands of professional social work training the school of social work needs to be an integral part of a university. It needs to have staff soundly trained and thoroughly practiced in contemporary social work. It needs the counsel and contribution of other university departments. It needs freedom to develop curriculum according to what is fundamental to social work education and currently related to social work practice. Only with these prerequisites can it exercise its function as a responsible part of university education and rightly serve the people for whom it is established.

Preprofessional Preparation

The demand for workers to fill the social work positions, especially in the public welfare field, has been so great and the number of students leaving schools of social work after either one or two years of training so few (in relation to the demand) that many students have been taken into the field immediately upon graduation from college. Sometimes the student has a background in the social sciences, sometimes not. In order to meet this situation many colleges and universities throughout the country offer one or more courses to undergraduate students which will enable them to be somewhat better equipped than otherwise for the beginning positions, particularly those in the county welfare departments. If only one course is offered, it is usually called either *The Introduction to Social Work* or *The Field of Social Work* and is generally placed in the junior or senior year. If several courses are offered, they may include the introductory course and perhaps others on public welfare, child welfare problems, the history of philanthropy, community leadership, etc.

Despite the apparent case for instruction in social work methods or techniques to undergraduate students, the weight of experience and opinion is against it. Instruction in skills and techniques is definitely a part of professional training carried on at the postgraduate level. It calls for a matured and disciplined experience in training the graduate student under intensive and responsible supervision. Furthermore, many teachers and practitioners believe, and rightly so, that to take from the undergraduate the time to teach courses beyond his capacity is to do him not only that disservice but to be cheating him of those other broader cultural courses that more properly belong in his undergraduate program. Many welfare departments meet this problem by asking that their workers have a sound social science background, and then provide in-service training for the beginning workers. After this experience workers frequently find that social work is the work they want and can do, whereupon they proceed into a graduate professional school of social work for one or two years of training.

Jobs and Salaries in Social Work

As indicated in the preceding lines most students with a social science background can secure, upon graduation, a position with a county welfare department. These positions are variously classified as casework assistants, visitors, investigators, case aides, etc. Salaries vary according to states and regions, but a safe estimate would be about $2,400 to perhaps $2,800 per year.

For workers with one year of training there are positions available in county welfare departments, with some state welfare departments, with children's and correctional institutions, with some Red Cross chapters, and with some few family service agencies. Salaries range from $2,400 to $3,600 per year.

Graduates of schools of social work with a master's degree have an almost infinite array of positions confronting them: in county welfare departments, state welfare department field staffs, family service, child placing, medical social service, child guidance clinics, mental hygiene clinics, social service departments of mental hospitals, the correctional services, Red Cross, school social services, community chests, community planning councils, social settlements and group work agencies—in short, the whole field of social work is open. Salaries may begin, depending upon previous social work experience, anywhere from $3,600 to $4,000. Exceptional offers occasionally come from Veterans Administration services ranging from approximately $4,000 to $4,500 per year.

Advancement depends upon personal qualifications, performance, turn-over in agency, and opportunities offered by other agencies. Caseworkers may go on to supervisory positions; supervisors may go to administrative positions. Caseworkers, supervisors, administrators may move to consultant positions, with state organizations, national organizations or Federal regional or central office positions. While no social worker ever becomes rich on his salary, there is at least opportunity for salaries to range for top positions anywhere from $6,000 to $10,000 to $15,000. True, there are not many at this top figure, but there are enough around it to make it an objective for the ambitious who can combine satisfaction for the exacting demands of administrative practice with the exhausting demands of decision-making and the resolution of countless policy and personnel differences.

Publications in Social Work

As members of a young and self-conscious profession, social workers are given to a great deal of writing, speaking, and discussing of their professional thinking and practice. This is reflected in the multitude of journals, proceedings, pamphlets, reports, and books which are in constant appearance and circulation. As is so often true, the new departures in thinking and practice, the experiments, the demonstrations, are reflected in the periodicals and annual proceedings much more readily than in the book literature. To the beginning student or worker this may seem very confusing and yet it is perhaps the surest way for him to ascertain the vitality which is in social work.

The National Conference of Social Work publishes an annual volume of *Proceedings,* more recently named *The Social Welfare Forum,* which contains some of the featured addresses of the last annual Conference. In addition, there are supplementary publications in pamphlet form of collected papers in several areas such as casework, group work, community organization, social security, the aged that were given at the preceding annual meeting of the Conference. Other national conferences, such as Jewish Communal Service, Catholic Charities, National

Probation and Parole, the Church Conference of Social Work also publish papers and proceedings. Some state conferences of social work also publish proceedings.

The *Social Work Year Book* is published in alternate years by the American Association of Social Workers and contains valuable articles on the many aspects of social work practice.

There should also be mentioned the special studies, reports, and collected papers which a number of agencies produce from time to time —such agencies as the Child Welfare League of America, Community Chests and Councils, Family Service Association of America, American Public Welfare Association, the American Association of Social Workers, the Council on Social Work Education, the American Association of Psychiatric Social Workers, the United States Children's Bureau, and the Social Security Administration.

Periodicals and Reports

In addition to the published proceedings of annual conferences, and the studies and reports which agencies or associations publish occasionally, there are a number of periodicals in the social work field with which the student and worker should have familiarity.[7]

Many of the state departments of public welfare publish journals, usually monthly or quarterly, which contain up-to-the-minute accounts of developments in the public welfare field.

A number of publications and special reports issued by agencies of the federal government should be known to all students and workers in social work. The most important of these are products of the Department of Health, Education, and Welfare: *Aging* (Committee on Aging and Geriatrics); *Children* (Children's Bureau); *Public Health Reports* (Public Health Service); *Social Security Bulletin* (Social Security Administration).[8]

The annual report of the Secretary of Health, Education, and Welfare, containing, in turn, the annual reports of the Social Security Administration, the Children's Bureau, the Public Health Service, the Office of

[7] Information about these periodicals and their publisher, address, frequency of publication is to be found in the *Social Work Year Book,* 1954, pp. 675–679.

[8] Besides containing useful, authoritative articles and valuable social and economic data bearing on social security, the *Social Security Bulletin* carries each month current annotations on the new book, periodical, and pamphlet material.

Vocational Rehabilitation, is a source of information on accomplishments as well as tasks that lie ahead. The publication *Federal Probation,* issued by the Administrative Office of the United States Courts in co-operation with the Bureau of Prisons, contains valuable articles on probation, parole and the correctional services. Likewise the annual reports of the directors of these respective organizations are worth reading. For years the annual report of the United States Bureau of Prisons has been the clearest and most attractively presented report of any agency in the federal government. The use of legible type, illustrations, ample margins, and carefully prepared text have demonstrated that a government report can be readable as well as substantial.

Films

An extraordinary number and variety of films appear each year on subjects which are at the core of social work as well as some on the periphery. Many of these have usefulness for teaching and learning, and in many instances are more effective than the written or spoken word. Because so many films appear each year and quite a number become obsolete or obsolescent no attempt is made here to name any of them. It is sufficient to list a number of the sources for these films and to have interested persons make their own inquiry.[9]

[9] The following references are a selection. Frequently state departments of health have useful films, particularly bearing on children, and the aged.

Armed Forces Institute of Pathology, Chief, Medical Illustration Service, 7th Street and Independence Avenue, S. W., Washington, D. C.

Association Films, Inc., 347 Madison Avenue, New York 17, N. Y.

Athena Films, 165 W. 46th St., New York, N. Y.

British Ministry of Information, 30 Rockefeller Plaza, New York 20, N. Y.

Columbia University Educational Films, 431 W. 117th St., New York 27, N. Y.

Educators Guide to Free Films, Educators Progress League, Randolph, Wisconsin.

Educational Film Guide, H. W. Wilson Co., 950 University Avenue, New York 52, N. Y.

Encyclopedia Britannica Films, Inc., 20 N. Wacker Drive, Chicago 6, Illinois.

Film Documents, Inc., 208 E. 72nd St., New York 21, N. Y.

Film Publishers, Inc., 25 Broad St., New York 4, N. Y.

Filmstrip House, 25 Broad St., New York 4, N. Y.

"Guide to U. S. Government Motion Pictures," Library of Congress, Washington, D. C.

Ideal Films, 207 W. 37th St., New York 16, N. Y.

International Film Bureau, Inc., 57 E. Jackson Blvd., Chicago 4, Illinois.

McGraw-Hill Book Company, Text Film Department, 330 W. 42nd St., New York 18, N. Y.

Mental Health Film Board, 166 E. 38th St., New York 16, N. Y.

Biography and Autobiography

In the foregoing pages the emphasis has been largely upon historical development and process. Occasionally persons were named, but it was seldom the reader could get much sense of the effect of individuals upon the development of social work. This was perhaps inevitable in the kind of book which this is. However, the point must be made explicit here that practically every step that was taken in social work—particularly within the past two centuries in England and America—was by or in response to individuals. The fact that this volume was written on the basis of history and process is not to be taken as overlooking persons. Indeed, it may be claimed that it was implicit throughout that change came by and through persons—even the social work developments of the depression of the 1930's while they appeared to embody the force of events nevertheless it was individuals whose efforts were both moving and productive. Actually there could be a companion volume to this one that would be based almost solely on the traceable influence of individuals on the development and the processes of social work.

There is much of value in both biography and autobiography, whether in book or periodical form. In the bibliographies attached to a number of chapters there is reference to such volumes. The interested reader is urged to explore some of that biographical material—whether it be of Clement Atlee, Beatrice Webb, Jane Addams, Lillian Wald, Dorothea

---

"Mental Health Motion Pictures," National Institute of Mental Health, U. S. Government Printing Office, Washington 25, D. C.

"Motion Pictures on Child Life," U. S. Government Printing Office, Washington 25, D. C.

National Association for Mental Health, 1790 Broadway, New York 19, N. Y.

National Film Board of Canada, John & Sussex Sts., Ottawa, Canada; also 620 Fifth Avenue, New York 20, N. Y.

National Film Bureau, 6 N. Michigan Avenue, Chicago 2, Illinois.

National Mental Health Foundation, 1520 Race St., Philadelphia, Pa.

National Probation and Parole Association, 1790 Broadway, New York 19, N. Y.

Navy Department, Chief, Bureau of Medicine and Surgery, Potomac Annex, 23rd & E Sts., N. W., Washington 25, D. C.

New York University Film Library, Washington Square, New York 3, N. Y.

Pennsylvania State University, Audio-Visual Aids Library, State College, Pa.

Teaching Film Custodians, Inc., 25 W. 43rd St., New York 17, N. Y.

United World Films, Inc., 1445 Park Ave., New York 29, N. Y.

Veterans Administration, Chief, Psychiatry and Neurology Division, Department of Medicine and Surgery, Washington 25, D. C.

Dix, Clifford Beers, Franklin Roosevelt, Harry Hopkins, Edward Devine, or William Matthews.[10]

Social Work and the International Scene

Social work as we know it today in America derived from a Europe
that was emerging from feudalism. Social work as we know it today
in America stands at the opening of the atomic age. Social work as we
know it today is not the exclusive property of any one country, but the
property of all mankind.

In the foregoing pages considerable analysis has been given of the
helping role of social work with families, children, the sick, the handicapped, the offender; its helping role with groups; its helping role with
communities. Yet what has been written within the confines of our
own culture is just as applicable wherever peoples—one, a million, a half
billion—are struggling to live satisfying and productive lives.

Speaking of the revolutionary age ushered in by the ending of a
global war and the release of atomic energy, Kenneth Pray, in his 1946
presidential address before the National Conference of Social Work,
said:

> The goals of this revolution are our goals. The kind of world it is creating
> is the kind of world—the only kind of world—in which social work can feel
> truly at home. For only in such a world can social work achieve its one
> ancient, simple, all-inclusive objective of helping human beings to find the
> opportunity and the incentive to make the most of themselves and so to make
> the largest possible contributions to the progress and well-being of the whole
> society. Only in such a world can our profound faith in the inviolable integrity
> and the inherent creative capacity of the free human personality be finally
> tested and validated.[11]

These words are real wherever there are people. They inhere in all of
the efforts expended by American social workers and American social
work organizations in every part of the world. They apply whether our
services abroad are offered through our own governmental agencies,
through voluntary agencies like the American Red Cross, the Ameri-

---

[10] Herbert Stroup, of Brooklyn College, has in manuscript a useful monograph entitled "The Use of Biography in Preprofessional Social Work Education" and also a
selected list of biographies. These will be of especial interest to the beginning student
or worker.

[11] Pray, Kenneth L. M., "Social Work in a Revolutionary Age." *Proceedings of the
National Conference of Social Work,* 1946, pp. 6–7.

can Friends Service Committee, the National Social Welfare Assembly, or through international bodies such as the United Nations containing within it the World Health Organization (WHO), the United Nations Children's Fund (UNICEF), the United Nations Educational, Scientific and Cultural Organization (UNESCO), the International Labor Organization (ILO), or the Food and Agriculture Organization (FAO). They apply for whatever services are offered—relief of hunger, rebuilding of war-torn communities, resettling refugees, technical assistance to communities for self-help projects, educational seminars, and fellowships and scholarships for training.[12] Our services, if we are to continue to offer them abroad and if they are to be accepted, should be offered solely on the principle enunciated by Mr. Pray—to help people to find the opportunity and the incentive to make the most of themselves and so to make the largest contribution to the progress and well-being of the whole society. It is here that social work stands in the early years of the mid-twentieth century.

BIBLIOGRAPHY

Books and Pamphlets

Abbott, Edith, *Social Welfare and Professional Education.* rev. ed., Chicago, University of Chicago Press, 1942.

———, *Some American Pioneers in Social Welfare.* Chicago, University of Chicago Press, 1937.

Atlee, Clement, *As It Happened.* New York, Viking Press, 1954.

———, *The Social Worker.* London, G. Bell and Sons, Ltd., 1920.

Beveridge, Janet, *Beveridge and His Plan.* London, Hodder and Stoughton, 1954.

Bisno, Herbert, *The Philosophy of Social Work.* Washington, D. C., Public Affairs Press, 1952.

Brown, Esther Lucile, *Social Work as a Profession.* New York, Russell Sage Foundation, 1942.

Bruno, Frank J., *Trends in Social Work as Reflected in the Proceedings of the National Conference of Social Work, 1874–1946.* New York, Columbia University Press, 1948.

Cole, Margaret, *Beatrice Webb.* New York, Appleton-Century, 1940.

[12] An informative account of programs under way and of the opportunities in the area of international social work is to be found in the article "International Social Work." *Social Work Year Book,* 1954, pp. 266–285.

French, David G., *An Approach to Measuring Results in Social Work*. New York, Columbia University Press, 1952.

Goldmark, Josephine, *Impatient Crusader*. Urbana, Illinois, University of Illinois Press, 1953 (last chapter Florence Kelly)

Hollis, Ernest V., and Taylor, Alice L., *Social Work Education in the United States*. New York, Columbia University Press, 1951.

Hunt, J. McV., and Kogan, Leonard S., *Measuring Results in Social Casework*. New York, Family Service Association of America, 1950.

Kasius, Cora, *Nancy Clark, Social Worker*. New York, Dodd, Mead & Company, 1949.

—— (editor), *New Directions in Social Work*. New York, Harper and Brothers, 1954.

Lee, Porter R., *Social Work as Cause and Function*. New York, Columbia University Press, 1937.

Marshall, Helen E., *Dorothea Dix: Forgotten Samaritan*. Chapel Hill, University of North Carolina Press, 1937.

Meier, Elizabeth G., *A History of the New York School of Social Work*. New York, Columbia University Press, 1954.

The Outlook for Women in Social Work. General Summary. Social Work Series Bulletin, No. 235–8, Women's Bureau, U. S. Department of Labor, Washington, D. C., 1952; see in same series *The Outlook for Women in Social Case Work in a Medical Setting*, No. 235-1, 1950; *The Outlook for Women in Social Case Work in a Psychiatric Setting*, No. 235-2, 1950; *The Outlook for Women in Social Case Work with Children*, No. 235-3, 1951; *The Outlook for Women in Social Case Work with Families*, No. 235-4, 1951; *The Outlook for Women in Community Organization in Social Work*, No. 235-5, 1951; *The Outlook for Women in Social Work Administration, Teaching, and Research*, No. 235-6, 1951; *The Outlook for Women in Social Group Work*, No. 235-7, 1951.

Oxnam, G. Bromley, *Personalities in Social Reform*. Nashville, Tennessee, Abingdon-Cokesbury Press, 1950.

Pray, Kenneth L. M., *Social Work in a Revolutionary Age*. Philadelphia, University of Pennsylvania Press, 1949.

Public Social Welfare Personnel. United States Department of Health, Education, and Welfare, Washington, D. C., 1953.

Reynolds, Bertha C., *Learning and Teaching in the Practice of Social Work*. New York, Farrar and Rinehart, 1942.

——, *Social Work and Social Living*. New York, Citadel Press, 1951.

Sherwood, Robert E., *Roosevelt and Hopkins: An Intimate History*. New York, Harper and Brothers, 1948.

Simkhovitch, Mary Kingsbury, *Here Is God's Plenty*. New York, Harper and Brothers, 1949.

Social Work as Human Relations: Anniversary Papers of the New York

School of Social Work and the Community Service Society of New York.
New York, Columbia University Press, 1949.

*Social Workers in 1950: A Report on the Study of Salaries and Working
Conditions in Social Work—Spring 1950.* New York, American Association of Social Workers, 1950.

Webb, Beatrice, *My Apprenticeship.* London and New York, Longmans,
Green and Co., 1926.

Webb, Beatrice (edited by Drake, Barbara and Cole, Margaret), *Our Partnership.* New York, Longmans, Green and Co., 1948.

Witmer, Helen L., *Social Work, An Analysis of a Social Institution.* New
York, Farrar and Rinehart, 1942.

Significant Articles

Bowers, Swithun, O.M.I., "Social Work and the Social Worker in the Next
Half-Century." *Social Work Journal,* XXXIII, October 1952, pp. 167–171,
200.

Cockerill, Eleanor, "The Interdependence of the Professions in Helping People." *Social Casework,* XXXIV, November 1953, pp. 371–378.

Gordon, William E., "The Professional Base of Social Work Research—Some
Essential Elements." *Social Work Journal,* XXXIII, January 1952, pp.
17–22.

Howard, Donald S., "The Common Core of Social Work in Different Countries." *Social Work Journal,* XXXII, October 1951, pp. 163–171.

Stroup, Herbert H., "The Use of Biography in Preprofessional Social Work
Education." *Social Casework,* XXXIII, May 1952, pp. 179–186.

Tyler, Ralph W., "Distinctive Attributes of Education for the Professions."
Social Work Journal, XXXIII, April 1952, pp. 55–62, 94.

Index